WINSTON S. CHURCHILL

1874–1965

EARLIER VOLUMES OF THIS BIOGRAPHY

Volume I. Youth, 1874–1900 *by Randolph S. Churchill*
  Volume I. Companion (in two parts)
Volume II. Young Statesman, 1900–1914 *by Randolph S. Churchill*
  Volume II. Companion (in three parts)
Volume III. 1914–1916 *by Martin Gilbert*
  Volume III. Companion (in two parts)
Volume IV. 1917–1922 *by Martin Gilbert*

OTHER BOOKS BY MARTIN GILBERT

The Appeasers (*with Richard Gott*)
The European Powers, 1900–1945
The Roots of Appeasement
Recent History Atlas, 1860–1960
British History Atlas
American History Atlas
Jewish History Atlas
First World War Atlas
Russian Imperial History Atlas
Soviet History Atlas
The Arab–Israeli Conflict: Its History in Maps
Sir Horace Rumbold: Portrait of a Diplomat
Churchill: A Photographic Portrait
The Jews of Russia: Their History in Maps and Photographs
Jerusalem Illustrated History Atlas

Editions of documents

Britain and Germany Between the Wars
Plough My Own Furrow, the Life of Lord Allen of Hurtwood
Servant of India: Diaries of the Viceroy's Private Secretary, 1905–1910
Churchill (*Spectrum Books*)
Lloyd George (*Spectrum Books*)

For young readers

Winston Churchill (*Clarendon Biography*)
Winston Churchill (*Jackdaw*)
The Coming of War in 1939 (Jackdaw)
The Second World War

WINSTON S. CHURCHILL

by

MARTIN GILBERT

VOLUME IV

Companion

Part I

Documents

January 1917–June 1919

HEINEMANN : LONDON

William Heinemann Ltd
15 Queen St, Mayfair, London W1X 8BE
LONDON MELBOURNE TORONTO
JOHANNESBURG AUCKLAND

434 13013 3
First published 1977

Printed and bound in Great Britain by
Richard Clay (The Chaucer Press) Ltd
Bungay, Suffolk

Contents

List of Maps

Introduction

THIS VOLUME OF documents continues the publication of the Churchill papers began in 1967 by Mr Randolph Churchill. Like each of its three predecessors, it is designed to make available a comprehensive selection of these papers to those who need to consult them for historical research, or who enjoy reading primary historical sources.

The Churchill papers constitute the richest single private archive of twentieth century British history. Nevertheless, where there are gaps I have tried to fill them from other archival sources, both private and public, including those in which Churchill is the subject of comment by others. For the six years covered by this volume I have drawn material from more than sixty archives, some of which contain important letters written by Churchill himself, but of which he himself kept no copy.

Some of the documents in this volume were published, mostly in short extracts, in *Winston S. Churchill*, Volume Four, but the majority of them are published here for the first time, and cover every aspect of Churchill's political life as a member of Lloyd George's coalition. From July 1917 to October 1922 Churchill was successively Minister of Munitions, Secretary of State for War and Air, and Secretary of State for the Colonies; for him this period was dominated first by the need to defeat Germany, then by the post-war settlement and the Allied intervention against the Bolsheviks in Russia, then by the civil war in Ireland and by Britain's newly acquired responsibilities in the Middle East, and finally by the Chanak crisis during which the Government appeared on the verge of declaring war on Mustafa Kemal's Turkey. It was also a period when Churchill's personal life underwent many sadnesses, among them the death of friends in action, the death both of his mother and of his youngest daughter, and a growing awareness of the strong forces of disruption and chaos with which the twentieth century was being threatened. These feelings are reflected in the many private letters published here, which show the range of his moods and the extent of his fears.

This volume opens with twenty-one letters which were not available to me during the preparation of Volume Three. These include seventeen personal letters which Churchill sent to his friend Sir Archibald Sinclair during 1915 and 1916; letters which were believed by Sinclair's family to have been destroyed during the London blitz, but which had in fact survived among Sinclair's papers. These letters show the extent to which Churchill confided in Sinclair at a time when his political prospects seemed hopeless. I have also included in this first section three letters which Churchill sent from the Western Front to his cousin, the ninth Duke of Marlborough; these letters were earlier believed, by the tenth Duke, to have been lost, but are in fact now on permanent loan at the Library of Congress, in Washington. Three other documents included in this first section are a previously unpublished article by Lord Beaverbrook—then Sir Max Aitken—written when Churchill had been removed from the Admiralty in May 1915; a letter which Churchill sent from the Western Front to Josiah Wedgwood in December 1915, in which he sought recognition for his efforts while First Lord of the Admiralty; and a 2,500 word memorandum written by Churchill in November 1916, setting out his view of the many different potential uses of mechanical power in offensive warfare.

Following these extra documents from the 1914–1916 period is a section from January 1917 to July 1917, covering the first seven months of Lloyd George's premiership, during which time Churchill was without office. This section includes the full text of Churchill's defence of his action at the time of the Dardanelles campaign, written in a letter to Lord Justice Pickford on 1 May 1917; a selection of the strong Conservative protests during June 1917 against Churchill's inclusion in the Cabinet; and Churchill's previously unpublished memorandum urging an active naval war policy, written on 7 July 1917, less than two weeks before he entered the Government.

Churchill was Minister of Munitions from July 1917 until November 1918. Among the documents printed here for the first six months of this period are the wide-ranging queries and instructions which he issued to his subordinates during July and August 1917; his War Cabinet memoranda and interventions, including a memorandum of 5 October 1917 about the need for bomb shelters; his letters dealing with organization of French and Italian munitions supplies; and his letter of 29 December 1917 to Sir Archibald Sinclair, rejoicing that there were to be no further British offensives on the Western Front. From February to October 1918 Churchill went on a series of visits and missions to France, during many of which he sent his wife full and vivid accounts, beginning with a letter from the Western Front on 23 February 1918. I have also published Churchill's draft appeal to Lloyd George, written on 24 March 1918, following the German break-through, and the seven telegrams which he sent Lloyd George between 29 March and 1 April 1918, during his mission to France to ascertain whether the Allied line could hold. Among the documents printed for 23 March 1918 is an extract from the original diary of the Chief of the Imperial General Staff, Sir Henry Wilson. From January 1919 to January 1921, when Churchill was Secretary of State for War, Wilson saw Churchill almost every day, with the result that his diary entries form a major source for Churchill's policies and activities, as well as providing important information about many controversial episodes of the period A second diary on which I have drawn, and which gives many unusual personal glimpses of Churchill during Lloyd George's premiership, is that of his Liberal colleague, H A L Fisher, the Minister of Education.

Throughout these volumes Churchill's many letters to Lloyd George, most of them sent, but some held back, give a remarkable picture of Churchill's political hopes and beliefs, and of his complex relationship with the man of whom he had written so bitterly to Sinclair in June 1915 'tout est fini', but on whose patronage he was so dependent, and towards whom he turned repeatedly for advice, support and encouragement. Lloyd

George did not always answer Churchill's long appeals, but when he did, his replies are published here in full; some of them are highly critical of Churchill's views.

From May to November 1918 Churchill's work at the Ministry of Munitions spanned many aspects of war policy, including bombing raids on Germany (see his memorandum of 30 May 1918), the urgent need for more munitions workers (memorandum of 12 July 1918), opposition to a negotiated peace (draft letter to Sir George Ritchie of 3 August 1918), advocacy of reprisals against the Bolsheviks for the murder of a British officer in Petrograd (Cabinet memorandum of 4 September 1918), and plans for the massive production of special camouflaged Tanks (letter to General Seely of 4 October 1918). His letter to General Tudor of 4 November 1918 reveals how very closely he came to driving, by accident, into the German lines during the last month of the war; while his Cabinet memorandum of 19 November 1918 shows how, only eight days after the armistice, his mind was already focussed on the complex material and moral problems of the post-war world.

As 1919 progressed, it became dominated for Churchill by the British intervention against the Bolsheviks: all his principal Cabinet arguments and proposals about Russia are published here, as are the counter views of his colleagues. The demobilization of the armies was another topic which generated much controversy, while the future of the Royal Air Force was also an important feature of Churchill's correspondence (see his letter to Lord Birkenhead printed on pages 563–5, his correspondence with Sir Hugh Trenchard, his letter to Sir Henry Wilson of 12 May 1920, his letter to Austen Chamberlain of 11 March 1922, and his memorandum of the same date).

For Churchill's mission to the Paris Peace Conference in February 1919, to discuss the intervention against the Bolsheviks, I have published material from the archives of those who saw him in action there, as well as his own letter to A J Balfour of 16 February 1919, his two telegrams to Lloyd George of the same day, and Lloyd George's replies. Much can be learnt of Churchill's views, and of the evolution of Government policy towards Russia, from the minutes he exchanged with members of his Army Council, including Sir Henry Wilson, Sir Percy Radcliffe and Sir Charles Harington: I have tried to give as full a selection as possible of these exchanges, which show the day-to-day work in the War Office under Churchill's administration, and the evolution of policy under his guidance.

Throughout the four peacetime years of Lloyd George's premiership, I have drawn on substantial, and previously unpublished, extracts from the minutes of the War Cabinet and its Committees, and on the Ministerial correspondence which these meetings generated, including Churchill's frequent exchanges of letters with Lord Curzon and Austen Chamberlain. Among the diarists whose comments I have used are Sir Maurice Hankey, Thomas Jones, and Lloyd George's secretary, Frances Stevenson.

During 1920 Churchill wrote several documents in defence of his Russian policy, including a proposed press communiqué of January 22, a draft letter to Sir W R Nicholl of January 31, and three letters sent to the Leicester and District Trades Council on August 5 and 19, and September 1. His attitude towards the Russo-Polish war can be followed in his memorandum of 26 June 1920, his minutes of 20 July 1920, and his draft memorandum of 29 August 1920. His fierce dislike of trade with Soviet Russia was expressed in a Cabinet memorandum of 16 November 1920.

Among the many non-Russian topics with which Churchill was concerned in 1919 and 1920 were the post-war economic situation (see his Cabinet memoranda of 1 and 9 August 1919); the enquiry into the origins of the Tank (see his own recollections quoted on pages 886–93); the growing British conflict with Turkey (see his memoranda of 25 October 1919, 6 January 1920, and 23 November 1920); the problems of Britain's worldwide military expenditure (memorandum of 7 February 1920 and letter to Austen Chamberlain of 10 May 1920); and the decision to rule Mesopotamia by means of the Royal Air Force (letter to Trenchard of 4 March 1920 and Cabinet memorandum of 1 May 1920).

Among the more personal sets of letters are those which Churchill sent to his wife when they were apart, including those of March 1920, February 1921, and January, February, July,

August and November 1922. Churchill received many letters of sympathy after the death of his mother in July 1921, and after the death of his daughter Marigold in August 1921 (see pages 1618–23). Among the personal letters which Churchill wrote, but of which he kept no copy, are his letters of 25 September 1921 to Edwina Ashley on the death of Sir Ernest Cassel, and his letter to Lady Lytton of 12 September 1922. Churchill's letters to Lloyd George on policy and personalities continued throughout 1920, 1921 and 1922 at almost monthly intervals, and include the notes which he wrote for Lloyd George about Joseph Chamberlain (see page 1167). An unusual document is his 'Dissertation on Dining Room Chairs' (quoted on page 1935).

The problem of Ireland is present throughout the second and third parts of this volume. Churchill gave his views on reprisals in a minute of 18 September 1920; on the use of air power in Ireland in a letter to Trenchard six days later; and on negotiating with the Sinn Fein in a letter to Shane Leslie of 2 October 1920. I have also printed the full text of all Churchill's correspondence in 1922 both with Sir James Craig and with Michael Collins; his reports on the Irish situation to King George V; his letters to Sir John Anderson, General Macready, General Tudor, Alfred Cope and Lionel Curtis; and extracts from the minutes of several important Cabinet meetings and Conferences devoted to Ireland (eg 8 March 1922, 16 May 1922, 30 May 1922, 22 and 23 June 1922, 30 June 1922 and 2 August 1922). Also printed here are Churchill's memoranda on Ireland of 4 April 1922 and 11 April 1922, and Austen Chamberlain's reports to the King on Churchill's Parliamentary speeches during the passing of the Irish Treaty (eg 31 May, 1 June, and 27 June 1922).

During 1921 and 1922 Churchill was a persistent advocate of peace with Nationalist Turkey; his reasons and concern are shown in his letter to Lloyd George of 2 June 1921, Sir Charles Harington's letter of 14 June 1921, Churchill subsequent correspondence with Curzon and Lloyd George, and his Cabinet memorandum of 26 September 1921. Throughout 1922 Churchill was also a strong public supporter of the coalition, and of Lloyd George (see his draft press statement of 9 January 1922 and his telegram to Lloyd George of 12 January 1922). But his discontent with the coalition was also clear (see Sir Philip Sassoon's letter to Lloyd George of 13 February 1922, and Lord Beaverbrook's letters to Lloyd George of 13 and 15 March 1922). A serious breach with Lloyd George arose from Churchill's dislike of the Genoa policy of rapprochement with Soviet Russia (see pages 1757, 1814–6, 1818–21 and 1825–35).

During 1921 and 1922, as Secretary of State for the Colonies, Churchill was principally concerned with reducing British expenditure in Mesopotamia (see the Cabinet minutes of 31 December 1921, and the documents relating to Churchill's first six weeks at his new Ministry, pages 1288–98). At the Cairo Conference in March 1921 he laid down the basis of Britain's future involvement in the Middle East (see pages 1388–1416), and while in Jerusalem he gave his views of the growing Arab-Jewish conflict (see pages 1421–2). His sympathies with, and support for, Zionism were a notable feature of his remarks on three separate occasions to Palestinian Arab delegations (on 30 March 1921, 15 August 1921 and 22 August 1921). His letters to two British opponents of Zionism, Lord Islington and Lord Sydenham, are quoted on pages 1936–7, 1966–7 and 1970–2.

Churchill's Mesopotamian policy, and the reactions which it provoked, can be studied in his correspondence, much of it by telegram, with Sir Percy Cox and Sir Aylmer Haldane, as well as with his principal advisers, John Shuckburgh and Major Young. Both for his Mesopotamian and Palestinian policies I have also printed many of the departmental minutes, letters and telegrams which he exchanged with Colonel Meinertzhagen, T E Lawrence, General Congreve and Sir Herbert Samuel, as well as his own memoranda (eg of 4 August 1921) and his correspondence with Lloyd George of 1, 5 and 6 September 1922.

Among the other topics on which Churchill held strong opinions while at the Colonial Office were the future of Egypt (see his Cabinet memorandum of 22 March 1921, Lord Curzon's protest of 21 April 1921, and Churchill's draft reply of 2 May 1921); House of Lords Reform (memorandum of 6 May 1921); the status of Indians in Kenya (see his correspondence with Edwin Montagu); the Anglo-Japanese alliance (his memoranda of 4 July and 23 July 1921); and unemployment (his memorandum of 28 September 1921, Lloyd George's reply of 1 October 1921, and Churchill's further letter of 8 October 1921).

For the Chanak crisis of September 1922 I have printed long extracts from all the principal Cabinet, Conference of Ministers, and Committee of Ministers discussions from 7 to 29 September 1922, as well as the complete texts of Churchill's own daily telegrams to the Dominion Prime Ministers. Also included are the controversial press communiqué of 16 September 1922, Churchill's correspondence during the crisis with Lloyd George, Lord Curzon, General Harington and Sir Archibald Sinclair, and the full text of General Harington's telegram of 30 September 1922, in which the General explained why he had not yet delivered the British ultimatum to Mustafa Kemal.

For the purchase of Chartwell, which took place during the Chanak crisis, see Churchill's letter of 25 September 1922 to the owner of the house, and Viscount Esher's bitter comment of 2 October 1922.

Among several previously unpublished documents on the fall of Lloyd George's coalition, I have printed Churchill's letter to Balfour of 12 September 1922; extracts from H A L Fisher's diary for 4, 7, 17, and 19 October 1922; Sir George Younger's letter to Churchill of 14 October 1922; Churchill's letter of 27 October 1922 to his constituency chairman; and his exchange of letters with Sir Alfred Mond on 29 and 31 October 1922. For the election campaign of November 1922 there are several important notes written by Churchill while he was in a nursing home, and in bed at his own home, recovering from an operation for appendicitis. These notes include two fierce criticisms of the role of Lord Beaverbrook in British politics (pages 2100–2), a criticism of the part played by Bonar Law in 1922 (see pages 2102–5), and a denunciation of the conduct of the man who owned the two principal Dundee newspapers (pages 2108–10). Also printed here is Churchill's letter to Lloyd George of 2 November 1922 about election strategy; his protest of 3 November 1922 to C P Scott about the *Manchester Guardian*'s electoral policy; his telegram of 4 November 1922 to Sir Hamar Greenwood about Conservative hostility to the Irish Treaty;

and his two attacks, of 9 and 10 November 1922, on Lord Curzon's part in the Chanak crisis.

The volume ends with a selection of the letters which Churchill received following his defeat at the polls, one from T E Lawrence on 18 November 1922, another from his former headmaster, Bishop Welldon, dated 24 November 1922. I have also printed Churchill's own comments after his defeat, in letters which he sent to H A L Fisher, Louis Loucheur and Humbert Wolfe, to the latter of whom he wrote on 20 November 1922: 'When one thinks of the kind of lives the poorer people of Dundee have to live, one cannot be indignant at the way they voted'.

For every individual mentioned in the documents I have prepared a short biographical note, which appears on the first occasion he or she is mentioned in the text. I have also used footnotes to elaborate the historical background, and to provide relevant material not explicit in the documents themselves. Thirteen maps, covering the principal areas and incidents mentioned in the volume are printed in the volume.

As with my previous documentary volume, I should much welcome any corrections or additions on points of detail, and any new documentation, for inclusion in subsequent editions.

Martin Gilbert

Merton College
Oxford
2 December 1975

Acknowledgements

I AM EXTREMELY GRATEFUL to all those who, during the five years preparation of this volume, made available previously unpublished documents, or enabled me to consult their archives. I should like in particular to thank Her Majesty the Queen, who graciously gave permission for me to have access to the Royal Archives at Windsor. I am also indebted to the Controller of Her Majesty's Stationery Office, for permission to consult the archives of the Air Ministry, the Cabinet, the Colonial Office, the Foreign Office and the War Office; to the New York Public Library for permission to see the T E Lawrence papers in the Berg Collection; to the University Library, Birmingham for access to the Austen Chamberlain papers; to the Brown Library, Liverpool for the text of a letter from Churchill to Sir Robert Perks; to the editor of *The Times* and Mr J Gordon Phillipps, for material from the archives of *The Times*; to the David Satinoff Collection, for Churchill's letter to Lord Wimborne of 18 March 1918; to Christie's, auctioneers, for the text of Churchill's letter to Lord Midleton of 14 January 1919; and to the British Library Newspaper Library at Colindale for the text of Churchill's remarks of 30 March 1921 to the Palestinian Arab delegation, quoted in the *Egyptian Gazette*.

For access to the private papers in their possession, I should like to thank Churchill College, Cambridge; the Bodleian Library, Oxford; the Imperial War Museum, London; and the Central Zionist Archive, Jerusalem. I am also extremely grateful to the owners, executors, librarians and curators who made it possible for me to see, and to quote from the private papers of Lord Addison, Lord Altrincham, Leopold Amery, Major

Badcock, Earl Baldwin, Earl Balfour, Lord Beaverbrook, Andrew Bonar Law, Mary Borden, Sir Austen Chamberlain, Lady Randolph Churchill, Lord Cowdray, the Earl of Crewe, the Marquess Curzon, the 17th Earl of Derby, Viscount Esher, H A L Fisher, Viscount Haldane, Sir Ian Hamilton, Lady Hamilton, Lord Hankey, Colonel House, Dr Thomas Jones, T E Lawrence, Sir Shane Leslie, Earl Lloyd-George, Countess Lloyd-George, Louis Loucheur, the Countess of Lytton, the 9th Duke of Marlborough, Sir Edward Marsh, Countess Mountbatten of Burma, Countess Oxford and Asquith, Viscount Quickswood, Lord Rawlinson, Sir Horace Rumbold, the 4th Marquess of Salisbury, Viscount Samuel, Sir Philip Sassoon, C P Scott, Sir Leon Simon, Nahum Sokolow, Major-General Sir Edward Louis Spears, Baroness Spencer-Churchill, Sir Frederick Sykes, Viscount Thurso, Lord Trenchard, Lord Wedgwood, Dr Chaim Weizmann, and Field-Marshal Sir Henry Wilson. I am also grateful to all those who have given their permission to publish material in which they hold the copyright, and in particular to Her Majesty's Stationery Office, for permission to reproduce Crown copyright material.

In compiling the biographical and explanatory notes, I was helped, for material in addition to that already provided for main Volume Four, by Dr Robin Bidwell, Middle East Centre, University of Cambridge; D C E Burrell, Controller of Agencies, Lloyd's; David Butler; Mrs K F Campbell, Foreign and Commonwealth Office Library and Records Department; Sybil, Marchioness of Cholmondeley; W E Cook, Ministry of Defence (Navy); Patrick Devlin, Eton College; Carl Foreman; Miss Emma Jane Gammell, Regional Librarian, Embassy of the United States of America, London; Jean R Guild, Reference Librarian, Edinburgh University Library; Dr Derek Hopwood, Middle East Centre, St Antony's College, Oxford; A Jeffrey, Central Library, Stirling; His Excellency the Swedish Ambassador, Ole Jödahl; His Excellency the Danish Ambassador, Erling Kristiansen; Eric B Mackay, editor of *The Scotsman*; His Excellency the Turkish Ambassador, Turgut Menemencioglu; Mario Montuori, the Italian Institute, London; Kenneth Rose; Patrick Strong, Eton College; F M Sutherland, Librarian,

British Medical Association; Count Nikolai Tolstoy; Eileen Wood, and Miss E Wright, Embassy of Japan. I should also like to thank Stephen H King for his help in sorting many of the documents, and I am particularly grateful to Dr Christopher Dowling of the Imperial War Museum and to Miss Mary Tyerman for their help on some of the more difficult footnotes.

To my wife Susie, for her continued and invaluable contribution to the research in all its stages, no words of praise are enough; for more than four years she has been the sole research assistant on the Churchill biography, and has worked with unflagging zeal to help me complete the task ahead.

Prelude

1915–1916

Winston S. Churchill to Sir Archibald Sinclair[1]

(*Thurso papers*)

3 February 1915 The Admiralty

Archie my dear,

I was so sorry to miss you on my flying visit. But 'Plugstreet', Hill 63, Vermelles & Cuinchy all of wh I did thoroughly occupied every moment of daylight; & after dark I had much business to attend to.

Good luck to you in the trenches this spell. I wish I cd share it with you. My thoughts are often with the firing line and the gallant life they lead. Afterwards come over here and stay with us; & I will fix up a constituency for you. Write & let me know how you get on.

Next time I come I must try to see the cavalry section of the front.

Yours ever

W

[1] Archibald Henry Macdonald Sinclair, 1890–1970. Entered Army, 1910. 4th Baronet, 1912. ADC to Colonel Seely, 1915–16. Captain, 1915. 2nd in Command of the 6th Royal Scots Fusiliers, while Churchill was in command, January–May 1916. Squadron-Commander, 2nd Life Guards, 1916–18. Major, Guards Machine Gun Regiment, 1918. Private Secretary to Churchill, Ministry of Munitions, 1918–19. Churchill's personal Military Secretary, War Office, 1919–21. Churchill's Private Secretary, Colonial Office, 1921–2. Liberal MP, 1922–45. Secretary of State for Scotland, 1931–3. Leader of the Parliamentary Liberal Party, 1935–45. Secretary of State for Air in Churchill's wartime Coalition, 1940–5. Created Viscount Thurso, 1952.

Sir Max Aitken:[1] *draft article*[2]

(*Churchill papers 2/237*)

28 May 1915
Secret

'Exit Churchill'

Three weeks ago Mr Churchill was in supreme control of the greatest fighting service in the world. Today he is Ch of the Duchy of Lancaster[3] permitted while the greatest war in history rages, to concentrate his powers upon the magisterial perplexities of the County of Lancashire. This is far the most dramatic personal development in the recent changes. Mr Churchill has always interested his fellow countrymen. Today little more than forty years old he charged at Omdurman, he escaped from Pretoria, he has belonged to two parties & now he belongs to both. He has wielded vast powers in splendid offices. As Under Sec for the Colonies he was responsible more than anyone for the form which the South African Settlement ultimately took. And he has left in every office which he has filled the traces of a hungry industry and a masterful & fearless personality. Many Unionists, of whom I am one, have disliked much that Mr Churchill has said & done. But when the issue Peace & War sprang into life almost in a moment we all rejoiced that Churchill was in the Cabinet. For it is no longer indiscreet to state publicly what everyone knows, and its members have freely admitted, that the late Cabinet was sharply divided during the critical days which preceded the outbreak of War. One section to which Mr Lloyd George[4] & Sir John Simon[5]

[1] William Maxwell Aitken, 1879–1964. A Canadian financier. Conservative MP, 1910–16. Knighted, 1911. Canadian Eye-Witness in France, May–August 1915; Canadian Representative at the Front, September 1915–16. Newspaper proprietor: bought the *Daily Express*, his largest circulation newspaper, in December 1916. Created Baron Beaverbrook, 1917. Chancellor of the Duchy of Lancaster and Minister of Information, 1918. Minister for Aircraft Production, 1940–1. Minister of State, 1941. Minister of Supply, 1941–2. Lord Privy Seal, 1943–5. Known as 'Max'.

[2] This article was commissioned by Lord Northcliffe, who then refused to publish it. 'It represented a hell of a lot of labour at that time,' Beaverbrook wrote to Churchill on 14 September 1935, 'and a big disappointment when the Daily Mail would not print it.'

[3] On 26 May 1915 Churchill had left the Admiralty, to become Chancellor of the Duchy of Lancaster. Ten days later, on June 5 at Dundee, he defended his Admiralty policies since the outbreak of war, and his part in the Dardanelles Campaign, in a speech to his constituents. 'The times are harsh,' he told them, 'the need is dire, the agony of Europe is infinite, but the might of Britain hurled united into the conflict will be irresistible.'

[4] David Lloyd George, 1863–1945. Liberal MP, 1890–1931. Chancellor of the Exchequer, 1908–15. Minister of Munitions, May 1915–July 1916. Secretary of State for War, July–December 1916. Prime Minister, December 1916–October 1922. Independent Liberal MP, 1931–45. Created Earl Lloyd George of Dwyfor, 1945.

[5] John Allsebrook Simon, 1873–1954. Liberal MP, 1906–18; 1922–31. Solicitor-General, 1910–13. Knighted, 1910. Attorney-General, with a seat in the Cabinet, 1913–15. Home

—for reasons entirely honorable to them—adhered, would not fight unless Belgium were invaded. The other section, inspired & animated by Mr Churchill, vehemently contended that, whether Belgium was invaded or was uninvaded England could not without dishonor & disaster stand by & see France crushed. Mr Lloyd George's record in the War is so good that he can afford to have it said that had his view prevailed the victorious advance of Germany would today have submerged Calais Boulogne & Dunkirk. The Channel Ports today would have been as German as Antwerp. And the existence of England as a power independent of Germany would have been menaced by mortal peril. And our hold upon honour would have been considerably less than our hold upon existence. From these risks—& they were very real—Churchill contributed as much as any single man to protect England. And at a most critical point he saved precious time by mobilizing the fleet upon his own authority. The Navy was ready at once & there has been no shortage of shells or any other supplies in the Navy. Nor must it be forgotten that at the moment when the War broke out Mr Churchill's position was already impaired in his own party. A year ago Mr Lloyd George, with complete sincerity but with a tragic want of prescience, stated his view to a newspaper reporter that for twenty years a more favourable opportunity had not offered itself for a reduction in expenditure upon armaments. The whole Liberal party took the same view. Sir John Brunner[1] opened his Campaign. For weeks Mr Churchill contended for his estimates doggedly resolutely & almost alone, & he won. Today Mr Lloyd George is big enough to rejoice that Mr Churchill worsted him in the struggle which he challenged, & which he pressed with such persistency & spirit.

Since the War Mr Churchill's exertions have borne fruit. He has [been] much criticised in the press. But his record rests upon deeds & not upon ink. After nine months of War, under his direction The Navy which he fostered & for which he laboured is still the 'sure shield' of these realms. The High Seas are purged of Enemy Vessels save where the submarine does its furtive work. More than a million soldiers have been transported without casualty over nearly every sea in the World. The Nation meanwhile has been fed, ammunition has constantly flowed into our harbours & the great arteries of our commerce are open & intact.

Mistakes are made in every War. Every belligerent has made mistakes on

---

Secretary, May 1915–January 1916, when he resigned in opposition to conscription. Major, Royal Air Force, serving in France, 1917–18. Liberal National MP, 1931–40. Secretary of State for Foreign Affairs, 1931–5. Home Secretary, 1935–7. Chancellor of the Exchequer, 1937–40. Created Viscount, 1940. Lord Chancellor, 1940–5.

[1] John Tomlinson Brunner, 1842–1919. Liberal MP, 1885–1909. Created Baronet, 1895. Privy Councillor, 1906. Chairman of Brunner, Mond & Co, Alkali manufacturers.

land. The Admiralty has made mistakes. But in perspective these mistakes are trivial. When the War began no one could be absolutely sure of the Navy. It was untried as a combative force under modern conditions. It was tested & proved true & the whole Empire breathed more freely.

It seemed certain that Mr Churchill would hold the Admiralty in fee till the War ended, as surely as his illustrious predecessor Lord Barham[1] had done in an earlier crisis. But the Dardanelles campaign intervened. All members of the Cabinet of course were parties to the decision, Lord Fisher[2] was equally party to it, for he remained at his post & made himself responsible for the enterprise.

Then of a sudden, months afterwards—without the suggestion that a new fact had emerged, Lord Fisher resigned his position. A curious situation followed. If Lord Fisher was indispensible as an expert of course Mr Churchill had to go. And the country believed this to be the true position. It acquiesced in Churchill going (though doubtfully) because it believed that Lord Fisher was staying. But soon it appeared that an extraordinary position was developing. Lord Fisher was not to stay. Therefore he was not indispensible. But his quarrel with Mr Churchill (& therefore *ex hypothesi* with the Cabinet) was about the Dardanelles. The Cabinet therefore decided & quite logically that Lord Fisher who—according to the Press—had left his post against positive orders must go. But *why was* Mr Churchill to go? He disagreed with Lord Fisher's later view—so did the Cabinet.

Yet perhaps these questions are pointless. The changes have come upon us. The National Government must be made a success. It is all we have left, the Slender plank between the Empire & The Ocean. A brilliant, experienced & sagacious statesman[3] has taken Mr Churchill's place. Have the assets of Mr Churchill's four years unwearied industry been squandered? His successor has stepped into the vacant office (vacant no one knows why) with splendid public spirit, & for the same reasons that would take him into the trenches tomorrow if he could help England by going there. It is a paramount public duty to support & sustain Mr Balfour in every possible way.

Nor need Mr Churchill despair of his future. It will undoubtedly be high & even splendid, for he possesses many qualities which no other public man can

[1] Charles Middleton, 1st Baron Barham, 1726–1813. Became First Lord of the Admiralty in 1805, before the battle of Trafalgar, at the age of eighty.

[2] John Arbuthnot Fisher, 1841–1920. Known as 'Jackie' and, because of his somewhat oriental appearance, 'the old Malay'. Entered Navy, 1854. First Sea Lord, 1904–10. Admiral of the Fleet, 1905. Created Baron, 1909. Retired, 1911. Head of the Royal Commission on Fuel and Engines, 1912–14. Re-appointed First Sea Lord, October 1914; resigned, May 1915. Chairman of the Admiralty Inventions Board, 1915–16.

[3] Arthur James Balfour, 1848–1930. Conservative MP, 1874–85; 1885–1906; 1906–22. Prime Minister, 1902–5. First Lord of the Admiralty, 1915–16. Foreign Secretary, 1916–19. Lord President to the Council, 1919–22; 1925–9. Created Earl, 1922.

claim. If his future were as dark as I believe it to be bright he would I think encounter it with the same serene composure.

Winston S. Churchill to Sir Archibald Sinclair

(*Thurso papers*)

9 June 1915 Duchy of Lancaster Office
Very Private

My dear Archie,

It was vy nice to get yr letter. One must try to bear misfortune with a smile. You might look at a speech I made at Dundee—wh is the best that is in me. But the hour is bitter: & idleness—torture. Here I am in a fat sinecure vy well received & treated by the new Cabinet who have adopted my policy & taken all the steps that I was pressing for & more. From a political standpoint the situation is vy favourable. I thought it my duty to stand by the National Government at the outset, & especially until the grave decisions about the Dardanelles had been taken. But now all that is settled and I cannot endure sitting here to wait for a turn of the political wind. I do not want office, but only war direction: that perhaps never again. Everything else—not that. At least so I feel in my evil moments. Those who live by the sword——

Fisher is a mystery. Was it a nervous breakdown or a coup d'etat? or more likely than either both combined. And synchronising with this Lloyd George striking out for power in alliance with Northcliffe:[1] and Asquith[2] affectionate but weak & indolent & seeking self-preservation at all costs.

I am profoundly unsettled: & cannot use my gift. Of that last I have no doubts. I do not feel that my judgements have been falsified, or that the determined pursuance of my policy through all the necessary risks was wrong. I wd do it all again, if the circumstances were repeated. But I am faced with the problem of living through days of 24 hours each: & averting my mind from the intricate business I had in hand—wh was my life. I do not think I can go on here.

I am not yet decided what to do or wh way to turn. When I see clear again I will write to you.

[1] Alfred Charles William Harmsworth, 1865–1922. Newspaper proprietor. Bought the *Evening News* (1894), *Daily Mail* (1896), *Daily Mirror* (1903), *The Times* (1908). Created Baronet, 1903. Created Baron Northcliffe, 1905. Chairman, British War Mission to the United States, 1917. Director of Propaganda in Enemy Countries, 1918. Created Viscount, 1918.

[2] Herbert Henry Asquith, 1852–1928. Liberal MP, 1886–1918 and 1920–4. Home Secretary, 1892–1905. Chancellor of the Exchequer, 1905–8. Prime Minister, 1908–16. Created Earl of Oxford and Asquith, 1925. His eldest son was killed in action in 1916.

I have felt vy anxious about you and Jack[1] in the trenches & have watched the lists for casualties in the Canadian Mounted brigade. I am so glad you have done so well. He had a bad time to go through, but now at any rate he has a good clean-cut job.

Take care of yourself & don't let him run unnecessary risks. A wise & thrifty use of one's slender store of luck is one of the aptitudes of a modern Brigadier.

The political grouping and situation gives me now I think a clear run after a few years. But I do not feel at all attracted by our political prospect and am repelled by the political game. Between me & Ll G tout est fini.

I want a breath of fresh air. God bless you.

Yours always
W

PS. I was so glad you have been acting Bde Major. I hope you will be able to keep this work.

Winston S. Churchill to Sir Archibald Sinclair

(*Thurso papers*)

30 July 1915 — 21 Arlington Street[2]
Private

My dear Archie,

It was vy nice to get yr letter & I wish you wd write to me more often.

I have been watching over the fortunes of the D'lles enterprise wh we so seriously jeopardised by the late upset; & I have succeeded by hard & continual fighting in getting vy large forces & more abundant supplies directed upon that vital point. I now await results. The painful part of the situation is that it takes so long to get the necessary action taken & so many people have to be persuaded that the enemy has time to bring up reinforcements from all parts of his Empire so that what was originally sufficient for

[1] John Edward Bernard Seely, 1868–1947. Liberal MP, 1900–22; 1923–4. Under-Secretary of State for the Colonies, 1908–11. Secretary of State for War, 1912–14. Resigned in March 1914, following the Curragh incident. Commanded the Canadian Cavalry Brigade, 1915–18. Gassed, 1918, and retired from Army with rank of Major-General. Under-Secretary of State to Churchill, Ministry of Munitions and Deputy Minister of Munitions, 1918. Under-Secretary of State for Air, 1919. Created Baron Mottistone, 1933. His son Frank was killed leading his company at the battle of Arras, 1917.

[2] During June and July 1915, having had to leave Admiralty House, Churchill lived at 21 Arlington Street, off Piccadilly, the London home of his cousin, the 2nd Baron Wimborne. In August he moved with his wife and children to 41 Cromwell Road, opposite the Natural History Museum, Kensington, his brother John's house.

victory may now be insufficient. Still I am hopeful though anxious. Also I have now much time on my hands and can feel thoroughly every twinge. It is a horrible experience remaining here in the midst of things knowing everything, caring passionately, conscious of capacity for service, yet paralysed nearly always. It is like being in a cataleptic trance while all you value is being hazarded. But I have managed to bear it so far. It will comfort my soul to come out for a few months and serve with my regiment, & my mind turns more & more in its *malaise* to that. But till victory is won at the Dardanelles my post is plainly here.

This government of able men & opposed parties does not develop any of the qualities required for war. The personal & party elements neutralise each other: there are many opinions, much politeness, unlimited decorum but little action. The predisposition towards the negative is vy marked. Meanwhile there are restless movements, wh I watch attentively without joining. LG is necessary to the State. He has the war making quality. I do not intend to allow any personal feelings to prevent my working with him. But distrust based on experience is a terrible barrier.

It is strange to look back on a year ago and the tremendous exertions of that cataclysm. Now slaughter has become commonplace, & destruction the order of the day. My part in events is woefully shrunken. But I still think I shall have work to do—though not for many months. The war must be fought to the bitter end. Any half measured peace wd only be a truce. We must at all costs have a decisive result. We are not doing all we shd. Wd you believe it—I pass my days painting. It keeps ones mind at peace. These people here are mostly played out, & no new figures appear upon the scene.

You at least in honourable definite real though circumscribed activities may feel content. You have done so well. If you survive you will always look back upon these months[1] as the true and glorious period of your life, & I trust they may also prove to be in the history of the country.

I have a small farm house beautifully placed in Surrey.[2] Do come please—& let me know the earliest moment. Don't think of coming to England without warning me. Letters will find me here 21 Arlington Street.

Nellie[3] pursues her training in the hardest of schools, the London hospital, &

[1] Churchill originally wrote 'years', then altered it to 'months'. The war had still not lasted for a single year.

[2] Hoe Farm, near Godalming. A Tudor farmhouse which had been restored and extended by Edwin Lutyens fifteen years before the war. Churchill rented it for his family for the summers of 1915 and 1916. The house lay in a secluded, wooded valley. It was at Hoe Farm, in the middle of June 1915, that his sister-in-law, Lady Gwendeline Churchill, had persuaded him to take up painting as a relaxation, and it was to Hoe Farm that Lady Lavery came early in July and encouraged him to take up oil painting.

[3] Nellie Hozier, 1888–1957. Clementine Churchill's sister. While serving as a nurse in August 1914 she crossed over to Belgium, where she was captured by the Germans, but

is now on the verge of being made a regular military staff nurse duly paid £20 a year & board & lodging. Clemmie[1] is vy well & busy organising YMCA huts for munitions workers.

Do not let my letters fall into the hands of the Germans when they storm your trenches. The swine wd rejoice. You can always write through Freddie Guest[2] who takes this. It is better to burn letters:

Always your friend
W

Winston S. Churchill to Sir Archibald Sinclair

(*Thurso papers*)

28 September 1915 Duchy of Lancaster Office

My dear Archie,

I will speak to the PM & to Gulland[3] about Stirling Burghs.[4] It wd suit you admirably & I am all for it. You wd march with Dundee & I cd come & help you. During the war you wd get in without difficulty, if an opportunity arose. But the whole field of politics is obscured and no issues define themselves.

I am relieved to learn you are not in the forefront of this battle.[5] The tactical opening seems good & promising: but whether strategic alterations will be effected is not yet clear.

These events and the Bulgarian & Balkan situations make it vy difficult to see plainly. All the reactions are entangled. I never saw things so puzzling—& yet so cogent. In a few days it will be easier to decide—then—perhaps too

---

released almost immediately. In December 1915 she married Colonel Bertram Romilly (see p. 62, note 5), they had two children, Giles and Esmond.

[1] Clementine Ogilvy Hozier, 1885– . Daughter of Lady Blanche and Sir Henry Hozier. She married Churchill in 1908. Created Baroness Spencer-Churchill, 1965.

[2] Frederick Edward Guest, 1875–1937. The third son of 1st Baron Wimborne; Churchill's cousin. Served in the South African War as a Captain, Life Guards, 1899–1902. Private Secretary to Churchill, 1906. Treasurer, HM Household, 1912–15. ADC to Sir John French, 1914–16. On active service in East Africa, 1916–17. Patronage Secretary, Treasury, May 1917–April 1921. Secretary of State for Air, April 1921–October 1922. Liberal MP, 1923–9. Joined the Conservative Party, 1930. Conservative MP, 1931–7.

[3] John William Gulland, 1864–1920. Corn merchant. Director of the Edinburgh Chamber of Commerce. Liberal MP, 1906–18. Junior Lord of the Treasury and Scottish Whip, 1909–15. Government Chief Whip, May 1915–December 1916. Privy Councillor, 1916.

[4] A Scottish constituency with a large Liberal electorate. But Sinclair did not enter Parliament until 1922, when he was elected for Caithness and Sutherland. He retained the seat until his defeat there in 1945.

[5] The battle of Loos, which opened on 25 September 1915. By October 16, when the battle ended, more than 800 British officers and 15,000 men had been killed. The Germans lost less than 5,000 officers and men.

late. The course of events has drifted off the lines on wh I wd like to have seen them kept.

Naturally I have been thinking constantly of the possibility of escaping to simpler & more congenial tasks. But since we parted political events have laid hold of me, & I must abide their issue. Perhaps this new War Council of 8 of wh I am to be a member may be an improvement. I feel bound to serve as asked unless or until convinced that my presence is useless. But I am resolved to see that all necessary measures are taken if I am to bear a defined share of these formidable responsibilities.

We spent the Sunday at Maxine's:[1] & we thought much of you & hoped all was well. She has returned to her barge in Flanders. Diana[2] is much better & the Rontgen rays do not show any break.

I told Ben dor[3] myself. He is vy trustworthy. But all my plans are 'clouded with a doubt'. Presently we shall see clearly and then I shall know exactly what to do & where my duty leads me. I shall try vy hard to do what is right.

My heart is all with the army now fighting so well against such difficulties, and also with our poor friends in Dardanelles, so near & yet so far from results wh wd save months of slaughter.

Good fortune guard you. Love to Jack.

Yours always
W

Edward Marsh[4] *to Sir Archibald Sinclair*

(*Thurso papers*)

13 October 1915

W is much happier 'in himself' than he was, he is now on every Committee & has plenty to do. In these conditions, the worse things go, the braver &

[1] Jessie Dermot, 1868–1940. Born in Maine, USA. She adopted the name 'Maxine Elliot' for her stage career. In 1914 she organized a Belgian Relief Barge, from which in fifteen months, she fed and clothed some 350,000 refugees.

[2] Diana Churchill, 1909–63. Churchill's eldest child.

[3] Hugh Richard Arthur Grosvenor, 1879–1953. Known as 'Bendor'. 2nd Duke of Westminster, 1899. ADC to Lord Roberts, South Africa, 1900–2. Commanded an armoured car detachment, Royal Naval Division, 1914–15. Personal Assistant to the Controller, Mechanical Department, Ministry of Munitions, 1917. His uncle, Lord Hugh Grosvenor, a Captain in the Household Cavalry, was killed in action on 30 October 1914.

[4] Edward Howard Marsh, 1872–1953. Known as 'Eddie'. Entered Colonial Office as a 2nd Class Clerk, 1896. Private Secretary to Churchill, December 1905–November 1915. Assistant Private Secretary to Asquith, November 1915–December 1916. Private Secretary to Churchill, 1917–22 and 1924–9. Private Secretary to successive Secretaries of State for the Colonies, 1929–36. Knighted, 1937.

serener he gets—it was the feeling of being condemned to inactivity that was so terribly *depressing* to him.[1]

Winston S. Churchill to Josiah Wedgwood[2]

(*Wedgwood papers*)

9 December 1915 France

Private & Personal

My dear Jos—

It is foolish to be concerned with trifles but if you think well you might write in the following tenour to the Times about the enclosed paragraph.

'In your .... you state etc etc. Now at this time Mr Churchill was First Lord of the Admiralty & had these monitors proved wholly unsuited to their task or had they sunk by the way, as was always to be feared, the blame wd no doubt have been attributed to him, & he wd certainly have accepted the full responsibility. It wd therefore appear that in ordinary fairness he shd not be excluded from a share in the credit of this successful operation. As a matter of fact there is reason to believe that the then First Lord exercised a direct personal influence in the selection of these vessels. They were purchased by him on the eve of war, as is well known, on his own initiative. They were employed in the amphibious operations off the Belgian coast in Oct 1914 in wh he was certainly closely concerned. And it is freely stated in Admiralty circles that idea of sending these vessels to the Rufigi river to cut out the Konigsberg emanated directly from the First Lord & was not proposed by his principal naval advisers. Be this as it may, the practice of attributing all the blame of enemy loss to the personal action of the political head of the Admiralty Board, & the credit of every success to others is not easily reconciled with logic or justice.

It is reasonable to assume that if a Minister at the head of a fighting

[1] But on 11 November 1915 Asquith decided to exclude Churchill from the inner war Cabinet of which he had been a member since its formation in November 1914. Churchill decided to resign from the Cabinet altogether, writing to Asquith that same day: 'Knowing what I do about the present situation, and the instrument of executive power, I could not accept a position of general responsibility for war policy without an effective share in its guidance and control.' A week later, on 18 November 1915, as a Major in the Queen's Own Oxfordshire Hussars, Churchill crossed over to France to seek military employment at the front.

[2] Josiah Clement Wedgwood, 1872–1943. Liberal MP, 1906–19. Commanded armoured cars in France, Antwerp, Gallipoli and East Africa, 1914–17. Assistant Director, Trench Warfare Department, Ministry of Munitions, 1917. War Office Mission to Siberia, 1918. Granted the Labour Whip, May 1919. Labour MP, 1919–42. Vice-Chairman of the Labour Party, 1921–4. Chancellor of the Duchy of Lancaster, 1924. Created Baron, 1942.

department is seen to be exercising a great & possibly an undue influence in certain important episodes of wh details have been made public, he is not likely to have been a cipher in regard to others. It may be undesirable to discriminate between the responsibilities of various members of the Board of Admiralty for particular operations; but if this is to be done a uniform rule shd be followed in the apportionment both of praise & blame unless there is some well known reason to the contrary.'

If you have any difficulty about getting this published you might see Rothermere[1] about it. The facts are indisputable.

I am having great times out here in the open air with my soldier friends. The grenadiers are vy nice to me and I am thankful indeed to have obtained release from a cruel torment of responsible impotence. My battalion has been resting for 9 days after a 12 days spell in the line, & is now beginning another.

All good wishes—Write me what you decide to do.[2]

Yours ever
Winston S. Churchill

Winston S. Churchill to the Duke of Marlborough[3]

(*Marlborough papers*)

15 December 1915 GHQ
France

My dear Sunny,

I find yr welcome letter & inviting garment here on my return from the trenches for a few days. I have now been a month in the 2nd line with the Battalion of the Grenadier Guards, & have shared fully the experiences of a

[1] Harold Sidney Harmsworth, 1868–1940. Younger brother of Lord Northcliffe, with whom he had helped to establish the *Daily Mail* and *Evening News*. Created Baronet, 1912. Proprietor of the *Daily Mirror*, 1914. Created Baron Rothermere, 1914. Launched the *Sunday Pictorial*, 1915. Director-General of the Royal Army Clothing Factory, 1916. President of the Air Council, 1917–18. Created Viscount, 1919.

[2] Wedgwood sent the letter to *The Times* on December 11, and it was published three days later. Wedgwood followed the text as drafted by Churchill, but began with a sentence of his own which read: 'Your Naval correspondent, dealing with the good work of the monitors in destroying the Konigsberg and referring to the victory of the Falkland Islands, attributes all to Lord Fisher. Much was, no doubt, due to him, but the omission of any credit to Mr Churchill is unfair.'

[3] Charles Richard John Spencer-Churchill, 1871–1934. Churchill's cousin. Known as 'Sunny'. Succeeded his father as 9th Duke of Marlborough, 1892. Paymaster-General of the Forces, 1899–1902. Staff Captain and ADC to General Hamilton during the South African War, 1900. Under-Secretary of State for the Colonies, 1903–5. Lieutenant-Colonel, Queen's Own Oxfordshire Hussars, 1910. Employed at the War Office as a Special Messenger, 1914–15. Joint Parliamentary Secretary, Board of Agriculture and Fisheries, 1917–18.

company. I have made many friends & find everywhere much kindness & I believe respect. I have not so far encountered any danger or discomfort wh have ruffled the tranquillity of my mind. I feel myself impervious to any event that can happen to me in this sphere. Of course my heart is sick when I learn from home of the vacillation & infirmity of will wh marks every aspect of the Government's handiwork: & when I see the almost incredible foolishness of their policy. But the practical trifles of trench warfare & the caprice of shells occupy the mind, & enable one to view larger events with much detachment.

My feeling that my greatest work is still to do is strong in me, and the experience of adversity wh I am now going through will—if I survive give to my character qualities wh otherwise might never have been developed.

French,[1] on my arrival offered me a Brigade; but I asked first to go into the line as a regimental officer. A week ago he renewed his offer and specified a good Brigade in the 19th Division to wh he intended to appoint me. I suggested a battalion instead but he strongly advised me to take the appointment while it was in his power to make it: & I therefore accepted. Now all is in the melting pot again; & I expect that I shall be sent to a Battalion after all. I am determined to do any duty that may be assigned to me with a good heart.

Meanwhile I follow the sombre march of events & their consequences on the political situation. Asquith & Kitchener[2] are I think doomed & rightly so. It may be my duty at the proper time to appear again in Parliament; but I shd only do this if I were satisfied that my intervention wd be likely to produce lasting results. I keep in touch with generals & shd not act alone.

Letters are a gt pleasure out here & almost the only kind of reading one cares for. Do write & tell me all the news & all the gossip.

We have had a certain amount of fighting and I have really passed a vy happy month. I am vy sorry about French's departure, wh deprives me of a

[1] John Denton Pinkstone French, 1852–1925. Entered Navy, 1866. Transferred to Army, 1874. Lieutenant-General, commanding the Cavalry in South Africa, 1899–1902. Knighted, 1900. Chief of the Imperial General Staff, 1912–14. Field-Marshal, 1913. Commander-in-Chief of the British Expeditionary Force in France, August 1914–December 1915. Commander-in-Chief, Home Forces, 1915–18. Created Viscount, 1916. Lord Lieutenant of Ireland, 1918–21. Created Earl of Ypres, 1922.

[2] Horatio Herbert Kitchener, 1850–1916. Entered Army, 1868. 2nd Lieutenant, Royal Engineers, 1871. Attached to the Palestine Exploration Fund, 1874–8. Surveyed Cyprus, 1878–82; the Sinai Peninsula, 1883. Governor-General, Eastern Sudan, 1886–8. Commander-in-Chief of the Egyptian Army, 1892–8. Knighted, 1894. Defeated the Dervishes at Omdurman, 1898. Created Baron Kitchener of Khartoum, 1898. Commander-in-Chief, South Africa, 1900–2. Created Viscount, 1902. Commander-in-Chief, India, 1902–9. Field-Marshal, 1909. A Member of the Committee of Imperial Defence, 1910. British Agent and Consul-General in Egypt, 1911–14. Created Earl, 1914. Secretary of State for War, 5 August 1914 until drowned at sea 5 June 1916.

true friend and protector. I do not know at all how I shall stand with Haig[1]—we have always been on vy good terms. FE[2] is crossing over to see me on Saturday. I am looking forward to this.

With every good wish,
Yours always
W

Winston S. Churchill to the Duke of Marlborough

(*Marlborough papers*)

12 January 1916

6th Royal Scots Fusiliers
In the Field[3]

My dear Sunny,

Your letter was vy welcome & so also will be the food box when it arrives. I don't think it wd be impossible to arrange for you to pay me a visit in say 3 weeks time & to stay with us here for a few days—wh you wd find vy interesting & not uncomfortable. But everything must be settled on the right lines. Macready[4] begged me to apply to him if I wanted a visitor and assures me he wd gladly make things smooth. So if you really wd like to come let me know & I will approach these deities with the appropriate ritual & genuflexions, when I doubt not they will be favourably disposed.

Of course French's departure has been a most serious loss to me. Haig tho' friendly is not an acquaintance, & I don't expect that he will court any criticisms on my account. Why shd he?

The life of an Infantry Colonel in the line is not at all unpleasant. Creature comforts are not lacking, & everyone in the battalion is of course only

[1] Douglas Haig, 1861–1928. Entered the Army, 1885. Knighted, 1909. Lieutenant-General, 1910. Commander of the 1st Army Corps, 1914–15. His successful defence of Ypres, 19 October–22 November 1914, made him a national figure. Commanded the 1st Army at Loos, November 1915. Succeeded Sir John French as Commander-in-Chief, British Expeditionary Force, 19 December 1915. Field-Marshal, 1917. Created Earl, 1919.

[2] Frederick Edwin Smith, 1872–1930. Known as 'FE'. Conservative MP, 1906–19. Head of the Press Bureau, August 1914; resigned, October 1914. Lieutenant-Colonel, attached to the Indian Corps in France, 1914–15. Solicitor-General, May 1915. Knighted, 1915. Attorney General, November 1915–19. Created Baron Birkenhead, 1919. Lord Chancellor, 1920–2. Created Viscount, 1921. Created Earl, 1922. Secretary of State for India, 1924–8.

[3] On 4 January 1916 Churchill was appointed Lieutenant-Colonel commanding the 6th Royal Scots Fusiliers, and on the following day joined his Battalion in their reserve billets near the French town of Meteren. Three weeks later he and his Battalion took up their position in the front line, at Ploegsteert, in Belgium.

[4] Cecil Frederick Nevil Macready, 1862–1946. Entered Army, 1881. Major-General, 1910. Knighted, 1912. General Officer Commanding, Belfast, 1914. Adjutant-General, British Expeditionary Force, 1914–16. Member of the Army Council, 1916. Lieutenant-General, 1916. Adjutant-General to the Forces 1916–18. General, 1918. Commissioner of the Metropolitan Police, 1918–20. Commanded the Forces in Ireland, 1920–2. Created Baronet, 1923.

anxious to serve & please. There is a constant spice of danger. Daily shells, some vy near; & a certain amount of risk in moving about by day and night. I went to see an Artillery Strafe two days ago, with my friend of Bangalore days General Tudor[1] who commands the Artillery of this division. For one hour by the clock we were involved in a sharp cannonade and I suppose certainly a score of shells burst within 30 yards of us, covering us with dirt & debris. I have also had my tiny doghole where I sleep in the line smashed up by a shell which, had it detonated rapidly wd have been the end of my chequered fortunes. One becomes quite reconciled to the idea of annihilation, & death seems to be divested of any element of tragedy. The only thing to dread is some really life weakening wound wh left one a cripple, and invalid or an idiot. But that one must hope is not on the agenda of the fates.

I have meditated a good deal on the gt situation & have fairly clear views about it. Perhaps later in the year I shall come back to the House: but for the moment this is the course marked out for me. I see no reason to expect a Brigade for a long time & of course there can be no question of any military career. On the other hand I like soldiering for its own sake; & if I am killed at the head of any batallion it will be an honourable & dignified finale. Do you think I shd deserve the family motto—'Fiel pero desdichado'[2]? I am now passing through a stage in my journey quite beyond any that my father had to traverse. Your letters & affection are a gt pleasure to me. We must always try to keep together as the world grows grey.

Yours always
W

Winston S. Churchill to the Duke of Marlborough

(*Marlborough papers*)

22 January 1916

My dear Sunny,

Yr letter was vy welcome, & will I hope be repeated. I must write to old Morley.[3] He responds to attention: but he could not reasonably expect me to

[1] Henry Hugh Tudor, 1871–1965. 2nd Lieutenant, Royal Artillery, 1890. On active service in South Africa, 1899–1902. Brigadier-General commanding the Artillery of the 9th (Scottish) Division, 1916–18. Major-General commanding the 9th Division, 21 to 24 March 1918. Major-General commanding the Irregular Forces in Ireland (the 'Black and Tans') 1920–1, General Officer Commanding the special gendarmerie in Palestine (known as 'Tudor's lambs'), 1922, with the rank of Air Vice Marshal. Knighted, 1923. Retired, 1923, and lived in Newfoundland. In 1959 he published his first war diaries, entitled *The Fog of War*.

[2] 'Faithful, but unfortunate'.

[3] John Morley, 1838–1923. Liberal MP, 1883–95 and 1896–1908. Chief Secretary for Ireland, 1886 and 1892–5. Secretary of State for India, 1905–10. Created Viscount, 1908.

oppose the war or leave the Govt on its declaration. 'My propensities were all the other way.'

I have been commanding this battalion for the last three weeks, & now in a few days I shall take them into the line. I have paid a couple of visits to the trenches & they are among the best & most comfortable I have seen in what is now a large & varied examination of the front. They are dry, well supplied with dugouts, good communications, good wire & minor conveniences. Our battalion HQ will be in a farm about 500 yards from the front line. Few of the buildings in this area are much knocked about, but this farm has been hit a good many times & is a target. This is the blemish on an otherwise harmonious scheme. When we go into 'rest' we only retire about 1,500 yards, and so we shall dwell for the next few months continually within range of the enemy's artillery field as well as hearing. Things are, however, fairly quiet at present on this sector; tho' no doubt we shall stir them up a bit. We shall not be far away from that wood in wh you used to take an interest in the early days of the war. The battalion is one of the 9th (Scottish) divisions wh fought heroically at Loos, storming the German trenches with a loss of 6,000 men out of about 9,000 engaged. It is in consequence shattered & only 2 officers who were present in the battle are still at duty. I have no regular officer (except Archie Sinclair who I brought with me & made 2nd in Command) & hardly an officer over 25 years. The average must be about 23½. I have 19 2nd Lieuts. In these circumstances you will realise that my task is not an easy one: & that a vy great deal of labour & responsibility will fall on me when we are actually in contact with the enemy. The battalion has improved since I came & the utmost loyalty & wish to do right characterises everybody: & I am hopeful that we shall get in all right. But think what the professional soldiers wd have said 2 years ago of a battalion so comprised & officered.

I watch politics tho through a reversed field glass. LG seems after all his manoeuvres to be quite isolated & kept in control. He was foolish to throw me over for together we were a power. Asquith flourishes like the green bay tree, & everything looks like holding together for some time to come. Meanwhile so far as I understand it the policy continues to be unwise. We are locking up a large army at Salonika whose only role seems to be to make enemies of the Greeks & to prevent the Turks & Bulgars from falling out. We are locking up another large army in Egypt wh K & EG[1] have got on the

Lord President of the Council, 1910–14. Resigned from the Government on the outbreak of war; his *Memorandum on Resignation* was published posthumously in 1928.

[1] Edward Grey, 1862–1933. 3rd Baronet, 1882. Liberal MP, 1885–1916. Foreign Secretary, 1905–16. Created Viscount Grey of Fallodon, 1916. Ambassador on a special Mission to the USA, 1919. In 1906 his wife had died as a result of a carriage accident, and both his brothers were killed by wild animals in Africa, one in 1911 by a lion, the other in 1928 by a buffalo.

brain. The German game is a vy clear one. They shd continue to frighten us at both places with the expectation of an attack or do their utmost to push large Turkish forces to Mesopotamia & Persia & rouse the East against us. Meanwhile they shd invite us to break our teeth on their tremendous defensive lines in the West & in Russia. There is every reason to believe they will take this extremely disagreeable course, & that we shall continue to do at each stage exactly what they wish & need us to do. However I am not going to let myself be fretted by events I cannot control & of wh my view may at any moment be cut off.

With every good wish,
Your affectionate cousin
W

PS. Chelmsford[1] was an extraordinary choice [as Viceroy of India]. But I daresay he will do it vy well.

Winston S. Churchill to Sir Archibald Sinclair

(*Thurso papers*)

22 March 1916 6th Royal Scots Fusiliers

My dear Archie,

Bar a shrapnel wh saluted McDavid[2] & I at about 20 yards distance near left Coy HQrs no adventures. They shelled the town yesterday & the Norfolk Ave extension today. Last night the bomb boy[3] did no good. He is vy sticky. I took him out myself to about 20 yards beyond the outer listening post & descanted to him in the bed of the Warnave on the fascination of no

[1] Frederic John Napier Thesiger, 1868–1933. Elder son of 2nd Baron Chelmsford. Fellow of All Souls, Oxford, 1892. Barrister, 1893. He married Churchill's cousin Frances Guest, daughter of the 1st Baron Wimborne, 1894. Captain, Dorset Regiment, 1902–14. Succeeded his father as 3rd Baron, 1905. Governor of Queensland, 1905–9; of New South Wales, 1909–13. Viceroy of India, 1916–21. Created Viscount, 1921. First Lord of the Admiralty, 1924. Agent-General for New South Wales, 1926–8. Warden of All Souls, 1932–3.

[2] Jock McDavid, 1897– . Enlisted in the Royal Scots Fusiliers, October 1914. 2nd Lieutenant, April 1915. Acting Adjutant, 6th Royal Scots Fusiliers, November 1915. Promoted Lieutenant while serving as Adjutant, December 1915. Gassed, August 1918. Demobilized, October 1919. Area-Manager, Shell-Mex Ltd, 1919–28; Divisional Manager, 1928–34. Subsequently in the brewing and distilling industry.

[3] Edmund Hakewill Smith, 1896– . Born in South Africa. Served Cape Town Highlanders, August–September 1914. Royal Military College, Sandhurst, November 1914–June 1915. 2nd Lieutenant, Royal Scots Fusiliers, June 1915. On active service, 1915–18; twice wounded. Major-General, 1942. Director of Organization, War Office, 1942–3. Commanded 52nd Lowland Division, 1943–6. Governor, Military Knights of Windsor, 1951. Deputy Constable and Lieutenant-Governor, Windsor Castle, 1964. Knighted, 1967.

man's land: but in the end he only got about 30 yards further than I took him. Today a sergeant & a private from Vancouver have arrived from Lipsett.[1] They are first class men. I have taken them round & explained everything, & they go out tonight to hunt. I hope to get some real information out of them. Really I am surprised at the lack of enterprise & daring wh these young officers show. It is so unusual to have to press & spur officers. I have never come across it before. None of the younger ones are for it. They all want to live forever.

Furse[2] & Trotter[3] both came round this morning and I took them in charge. They were vy affable & appeared pleased with everything. Trotter is I think coming to dine tomorrow night to do our moonlight walk. I went over the ground last night vy pleasantly & easily. There was a little more shooting, & the bullets have taken to falling in our courtyard on the way to the minor establishments. We had one sergeant wounded in Lancs S Farm last night & a sentry in Burnt out F killed this morning. Otherwise no damage.

I can almost hear you and Clemmie arriving by the most noble of arguments at the conclusion that I must inevitably stay here till the day of Judgement:

NO NO—'That were some love, but little policy'.

I am not so lonely without you to grouse to as I had expected: Nevertheless come back ere long fattened, refreshed, & exhilarated.

You might I think sidle artistically into your discourse with the PM my natural reluctance to enter upon a course of political action wh must lead me into increasing friction with his Govt. Mind you write & tell me all about it. I am quite resolved what to do.

Yours ever
W

[1] Louis James Lipsett, 1874–1918. 2nd Lieutenant, Royal Irish Regiment, 1894. Major, attached to the Canadian Army, 1911–14. Brigadier-General, attached to the Canadian Expeditionary Force, 1914–16; commanded the 3rd Canadian Division, 1918. Churchill described him (in a letter to Sir Max Aitken on 28 March 1916) as 'a man of real merit & possibly even with genius as a commander. I believe both in big & in small affairs of war, this officer is altogether exceptional in his judgment & *flaire*'. (*Beaverbrook papers*)

[2] William Thomas Furse, 1865–1953. Son of an archdeacon of Westminster. Entered the Royal Artillery, 1884. ADC to Lord Roberts (then Commander-in-Chief, India), 1890–3. Assistant Adjutant General for Transport during the South African War, 1899–1900. Brigadier-General, 1914. Major-General Commanding the 9th (Scottish) Division, September 1915–December 1916. Master-General of Ordnance, War Office, December 1916–December 1919. Hon Member of the Munitions Council, 1917–19. Knighted, 1917. Lieutenant-General, 1919. Member of the Army Council, 1920. Director of the Imperial Institute, 1926.

[3] Algernon Richard Trotter, 1870–1945. Joined 2nd Life Guards as a 2nd Lieutenant, 1892. Captain, 1899. Served South African War, 1899–1900 (ADC to General Sir Redvers Buller, VC). Major, 1907. Lieutenant-Colonel, Reserve Regiment 2nd Life Guards, 1916. Colonel, Guards Machine Gun Regiment, 1918. Retired, 1923.

Winston S. Churchill to Sir Archibald Sinclair

(*Thurso papers*)

23 March 1916

6th Royal Scots Fusiliers
In the Field

My dear Archie,

They have just finished giving us 40 shells of the fizz-bang variety this morning—5 direct hits—only casualty Corporal Walls whose arm was broken in the new cookhouse. The traverse in the court-yard was hit directly & by many splinters. The orderly room, the store near it, the end of the barn, the men's latrine all got their dose. We tested the efficiency of our new defences by remaining at breakfast—all except the bomb boy who lurked in the Dug out. He thinks too much.

The Canadian scouts went out all last night & report

1. No listening posts & no enemy patrols.
2. Trenches no more strongly held than ours.
3. Sentries awake & looking out all night.
4. They fire back when we fire as a general rule.
5. Ground N of the river vy bare & unsuitable.

Canadians go out again S of river. The regimental scouting system must be thoroughly reorganised. These Canadians are a different breed of animal altogether.

The young artillery officer—Nicolls[1]—has been much tormented by me, & shows abyssmal ignorance under examination. He did not know what 'calibre' meant, or what weight of shell his guns fired, or what made shrapnel bullets travel forward after the burst. He thinks he will go into the flying corps. But I have deprecated the squandering of so much accumulated expert knowledge. Cigars have arrived.

Yours always
W

PS. The working parties on the new aid post & on the so called 'slits' were caught by 2 salvoes of crumps. Altogether 8 casualties today roundabouts—4 Fusiliers. This evening a beautiful pink coloured shrapnel arrived. He is the first of his kind.

[1] It has been impossible to ascertain, either from the records held at the War Office, or from the Imperial War Museum, to which Nicolls Churchill was referring.

Winston S. Churchill to Sir Archibald Sinclair

(*Thurso papers*)

24 March 1916 6 RSF

Archie,—

deep snow still falling & thawing: trench conditions damnable for the men: no shelling possible.

The Canadians made further scoutings last night. They say line is vy strongly held & many sentries are kept awake by order. The enemy are sure of themselves, do not require to go out in front, & that they court an attack. The line is weaker in front of us than in front of Lipsett, but the sentries much more numerous & the watch more thorough. The Canoots also declare that there are a number of slits diagonally cut all along the enemy's trenches on our front wh look like sally ports. They have never seen anything like this elsewhere. We are studying this attentively as you can imagine. Altogether the prospects of *our* doing any good here are vy small. The ground is most unpromising—the river line is the only possible approach & that a bad one. I will tell you the only sort of plan that wd have a chance when you come back. But the general outlook is strongly negative.

I have proposed to Bde the enclosed reorg-^{n} of the Scouting, Sniping & Int. services.

Dixon[1] arrived this morning to see our blessed McD and complained of 4 or 500 shells directed at the convent end of the town yesterday. Some vy big ones—he declares 12″—fired from far away to S fell vy erratically: 4 within 50 yards of our new home. He was himself blown back into his dugout by one wh burst only 30 yards off, while he was waiting to see it hit the town. This carelessness on the part of the Hun is most reprehensible.

Work is getting on pretty well.

Yours always
W

[1] The Medical Officer. In his book *With Winston Churchill at the Front* Captain Andrew Dewar Gibb later recalled: 'We had several MOs while Winston was with us, and he used to discuss them and compare and contrast their points as enthusiastically as though they have been specimens of some wild animals which he collected.'

Winston S. Churchill to Sir Archibald Sinclair

(*Thurso papers*)

25 March 1916

Archie,

If, as is probable, PB[1]s minor stunt comes off tonight, we are to remain an extra day in the line to get the benefit of any retaliation, & to avoid a relief at a disturbed moment.

Everything is quiet—tho the day is clear. No mail—nor newspapers. But tomorrow I shall hope to have news of you—& also possibly to receive other communications.

I do hope you are enjoying yourself & that the change & rest are doing you good.

Radcliffe[2] & Trotter are dining tonight.

I am greatly looking forward to your news. I remain here like the geni in the bottle in the Arabian nights—thinking a lot—but unable to say anything —What shall I do to the wight who removes the seal of Soldau by wh I am confined?

Yours always
W

Winston S. Churchill to Sir Archibald Sinclair

(*Thurso papers*)

26 March 1916

Archie,

PB's show failed last night. The armoured tubes worked well; but the trench when entered was full of wire. 5 off^rs & 2 men missing—4 killed—1 off^r & 7 men wounded—15 out of 36. No result. Enemy retaliated for our

[1] Henry Pelham Burn, 1882–1958. Entered Gordon Highlanders, 1901. Lieutenant, 1904. Captain, 1910. Major, 1916. Temporary Lieutenant-Colonel, 10th Battalion Argyll and Sutherland Highlanders, January 1916–April 1916. Temporary Brigadier-General commanding the 152nd Infantry Brigade, 1916–18. Brevet Lieutenant-Colonel, 1917. Lieutenant-Colonel, 1923. Colonel, 1927.

[2] Percy Pollexfen de Blaquiere Radcliffe, 1874–1934. Son of General Sir W Radcliffe. 2nd Lieutenant, Royal Artillery, 1893; Captain, 1900. On active service in South Africa, 1899–1900. Major, 1910. Brigadier-General, General Staff, 1915–17. Major-General, 1918. Director of Military Operations, War Office, 1918–22. Knighted, 1919. Mission to Poland, 1919, when he assisted General Weygand in the reorganization of the Polish Army. General Officer Commanding the 48th Division, 1923–6; the 23rd Division, 1926–7 and Scottish Command, 1030–3. Lieutenant-General, 1927; General, 1933. General Officer Commanding-in-Chief, Southern Command, 1933–4.

artillery barrages (wh were considerable) by about 60 shell on our btn. front line & communications—2 hit. We are remaining in the line to-day—& owing to change of plan are fireless—I am asking for 7 days out as compensation for our lost day, & then 2 spells of 5 to put it square.

Trotter & Radcliffe dined last night—dinner was quite good—sustained by one of yr salmon. Afterwards I took them up to the line *via* the shrine & across the fields. There was much more sniping than usual & I began to be quite anxious for our guests. However all was well & they were delighted with their jaunt.

I expect this is the last letter that will catch you before you return. I have received no news at all—but perhaps today's mail will bring me some. I do hope my dear you have a good time and are really benefited. You have had a vy long pull out here. I like to think that my incursions into yr affairs will have added a little variety to yr work, & given you a wider scope—if a more dangerous station. You have been a vy gt comfort to me & I shall always be on the *qui vive* where yr interests are concerned. I shall have a vy difficult task at home, & time & patience will be needed as well as other rarer qualities. But I do not feel unequal to the undertaking. The war goes ill: & I think the move agst Russia is now developing. We have no plan—no vision—no drive. But the allied nations are magnificent & their strength greatly superior.

I rather expect my affairs will be settled in about a week or ten days (Asquith going to Paris may be a cause of delay). Bring back plenty of good things with you. Always your affectionate friend

W

PS. They keep on shelling the artillery wire across from the wood here. But they seem to be vy accurate & careful, & we are not molested so far.

Winston S. Churchill to Sir Archibald Sinclair

(*Thurso papers*)

18 April 1916 41 Cromwell Road

Archie—

A big situation here is at full tension: & I am involved in it deeply. The outlook is hopeful. The debate is postponed through repeated Cabinet disagreements and may now run over to Monday or Tuesday. Very likely there will be a new conscription Bill—or else a smash, & either may detain me. I cannot tell. I am just off to dine with Carson[1] & Lloyd George, and have been able to unite various powerful wires wh were *criss cross.*

All my friends are vy cordial & confident.

Most tiresomely my haversack was left behind. Please take care of all the papers. I don't want any of them except the Grigg[2] letter. Post this home in another envelope addressed to Clemmie without delay.

I have read the enclosed message from you. It is cryptic & does not tell me what I want to know—viz: Can I on my own responsibility and at my own risk use this information in debate, without queering Furse's pitch. Please telegraph on this through the same channel. Be explicit & don't boggle at the necessary words.

Good luck to you my dear. I reproach myself with having been a tease & burden sometimes to you. If I come back I will be more considerate. If I stay here I trust I shall soon have the power to provide for yr fortunes in a satisfactory manner.

Yours affectionately
W

Winston S. Churchill to Sir Archibald Sinclair

(*Thurso papers*)

20 April 1916
Private

Archie dear,

I am expecting to hear from you exactly the position of the battalion: When is it going to be amalgamated; What is the process; what will happen to the officers. I presume I pass on to the unemployed list pending a new appointment: & I daresay it will be convenient to delay this till the com-

[1] Edward Henry Carson, 1854–1935. Conservative MP, 1892–1921. Knighted, 1900. Solicitor-General, 1900–6. Leader of the Ulster Unionists in the House of Commons, 1910–21. Attorney-General, May–October 1915. First Lord of the Admiralty, December 1916–July 1917. Minister without Portfolio in the War Cabinet, July 1917–January 1918. Created Baron, 1921.

[2] Edward William Macleay Grigg, 1879–1955. Editorial staff of *The Times*, 1903–5; 1908–13. Served in the Grenadier Guards, 1914–18. (Churchill shared his frontline dugout in November 1915.) Military Secretary to the Prince of Wales, 1919. Knighted, 1920. Private Secretary to Lloyd George, 1921–2. National Liberal MP, 1922–5. Governor of Kenya, 1925–31. National Conservative MP, 1933–45. Parliamentary Secretary, Ministry of Information, 1939–40. Financial Secretary, War Office, 1940. Joint Parliamentary Under-Secretary of State for War, 1940–4. Minister Resident in the Middle East, 1944–5. Created Baron Altrincham, 1945. Editor of the *National Review*, 1948–55.

pulsion crisis & the necessary legislation are settled. That is the view I am suggesting to Vesey.[1]

Our leave has been extended to cover the postponed debate ie Thursday next will be the day on wh I shd in the ordinary course return. Shall I find you then at the old place, or will the amalgamation actually have begun? You must answer these questions as far as you can.

The situation here is most obscure: but I believe the Government will against the conviction of the majority of them, be forced to propose general compulsion at the last possible minute & in the worst possible way. Then will follow a series of bills, in all of wh I shall be deeply concerned. I cannot look further than that.

I have seen the AG[2] about you. His view is that after 20 months of service at the front, you shd have a spell of staff employment at home; and you will I think be offered a Staff Captaincy under the War Office or in this country of an interesting & responsible character. I hope that unless something much better is in your reach you will be guided by me and accept this.

An election at no great distance is possible, & I want to have you home for this and other contingencies. Let me know.

I am now working in the closest accord with Carson: and indeed find myself as much in the centre of things as I have ever been.

The lack of faith & clear leading is pitiful to witness.

Will you show this letter to General Furse as it will explain to him how my affairs stand.

Yours affectionately
W

It is quite hopeless to stop the disbandment. All has been settled for weeks by WO & GHQ.

[1] Ivo Lucius Beresford Vesey, 1876–1974. 2nd Lieutenant, 1897. Major, War Office, 1914–15; GHQ France, 1915–16. Director of Recruiting and Organization, War Office, 1919–23. Knighted, 1923. Director of Organization and Staff Duties, Air Ministry, 1923–9. Major-General, 1928. Director of Staff Duties, War Office, 1931–4. General, 1937. Chief of General Staff, India, 1937–9.

[2] Sir Nevil Macready (see p. 13, note 4).

Winston S. Churchill to Sir Archibald Sinclair

(*Thurso papers*)

16 May 1916 41 Cromwell Road

My dear,

Come to see me as soon as you return. The WO were on the point of offering you a Staff Captaincy at home. I told them to hold on till you came South.

I am so glad you are enjoying yourself & having good sport. I am getting into the collar here: but now of course at times I look wistfully across the channel. What a fool I am! Well its lucky for me everyone has not seen my folly at as close quarters as you. This is the penalty & office of friendship.

Best love

W

Winston S. Churchill to Sir Archibald Sinclair

(*Thurso papers*)

23 August 1916 41 Cromwell Road

My dear Archie,

Where have you been? What have you seen?

I have been looking for some signs of activity on the part of the Daddy Long Legs: but not a whisker has stirred.

I had a line from Spiers[1] who is all right so far. I gather that the fighting has now settled down into the attack of small points after intense preparation. There is no harm in this: & I shd like to see it develop in more than one part of our front. I do not expect the Life Guards will have much charging to do—at any rate I hope not. I think the Germans have again got control of the situation in the East. Altogether it seems likely that no marked change will happen this side of the winter.

Here Parl[t] has finished for the time: & I am off to Blenheim for a week & then to Herstmonceaux.[2] I am busy with the D'lles commission, about wh I

[1] Edward Louis Spiers, 1886–1974. Joined Kildare Militia, 1905. Captain, 11th Hussars, 1914. Four times wounded, 1914–15. Liaison officer with French 10th Army, 1915–16. Head of the British Military Mission to Paris, 1917–20. In 1918 he changed the spelling of his name to Spears. National Liberal MP, 1922–4; Conservative MP, 1931–45. Churchill's Personal Representative with French Prime Minister and Minister of Defence, May–June 1940. Head of British Mission to General de Gaulle, 1940. Head of Spears Mission to Syria and the Lebanon, 1941. First Minister to Syria and the Lebanon, 1942–4.

[2] A castle in Kent, bought in 1913 and restored by the Conservative MP Colonel Claude Lowther, who had put one of his cottages at Churchill's disposal. In 1916 Churchill went

cannot but feel hopeful. I write & paint—& ponder. From my cottage at Herstmonceaux I can hear the guns better than at St Omer. They induce sombre reflections.

Do write to me and tell me all yr news.

LG is getting on well with Robertson.[1] I am to dine with them both next week.

The Admiralty dozes placidly.

Yours affectionately
W

Winston S. Churchill to Sir Archibald Sinclair

(*Thurso papers*)

15 September 1916 41 Cromwell Road

Archie,

I am glad to think you have not heard a shell since our pasting 'dud' at Le Gheer. Drilling is good for the young & inculcates humility & other virtues of that order.

You are right about Roumania. That is Hindenburg's's[2] proper *coup*, & I

---

there severa times to paint. Asquith's daughter, Violet, who was present on one such occasion, later recalled, in *Winston Churchill As I Knew Him*: 'The spell was only broken once that day by the dull distant thunder of the cannonade in France. He broke off then, laid down his brush and spoke with bitterness of his position; of the unfair attacks upon him for the failure in Gallipoli, of his desire for a public inquiry, in which he could have the chance of vindicating himself, of the Government's duty to lay the relevant papers before Parliament; of his sense of unjust exclusion from the great world struggle in which he knew that he could play an essential part, of all the ideas he could pour into it, now running to waste in the sand. "They don't want to listen to me, or use me. They only want to keep me out." '

[1] William Robert Robertson, 1860–1933. Entered Army as a Private, 1877. 2nd Lieutenant, 1888. Intelligence Department, War Office, 1900–7. Major-General, 1910. Commandant of the Staff College, 1910–13. Director of Military Training, War Office, 1913–14. Knighted, 1913. Quarter-Master-General, British Expeditionary Force, 1914–15. Chief of Staff, British Expeditionary Force, 1915. Chief of the Imperial General Staff, 1915–18. Commander-in-Chief, Home Forces, 1918–19. Commander-in-Chief, British Army of Occupation on the Rhine, 1919–20. Created Baronet, 1919. Field-Marshal, 1920. Known as 'Wully'.

[2] Paul von Benckendorff und Hindenburg, 1847–1934. 2nd Lieutenant, 1866. Fought in the Austro-Prussian and Franco-Prussian wars of 1866 and 1870–1. Retired from the Army with the rank of General, 1911. Recalled, 1914. Commander-in-Chief, 7th Army, 1914. In August 1914 he moved German troops rapidly by rail from Gumbinnen, where they had been defeated by the Russians, to Tannenburg, where they were victorious. Marshal and Commander-in-Chief of all German Forces in the East, 1915. Chief of the General Staff, 1916–18. President of the Reich, 1925–34.

believe a manageable one this year. I felt it the moment she came in. But of course all these things are vy speculative.[1] It wd be hard enough to forecast events if people acted wisely. But folly has no laws or processes.

The tanks are to be filled prematurely I fear. It wd have been worth waiting. I wonder whether they will be rightly used.

LG returned last night from his tour. He thinks a lot; but *so far* has done nothing.

I am occupying myself with the D'lles Commission wh is now about to begin. The case is an extraordinary one. I don't think anyone realises the full significance of the story wh is to be told. The Admiralty have simply put in the plans of Jackson[2] & Oliver.[3] These admirable papers on what is now the *highest* naval authority are the foundation of my case. They have behaved vy well in taking so much upon themselves. But of course I shall assume the fullest responsibility.

I am looking about to buy a country seat, & am just off to Sussex to examine one wh has been offered.[4] I wish to find a place to end my days amid trees & upon grass of my own! Freed from the penury of office these consolations become possible. Soon we shall correspond as between one landlord & another!

Poor Garvin[5] comes to see me sometimes to talk about his boy. This gallant lad on being mortally wounded, observed in a collected voice 'Tell Mr Porter to carry on with the company' & expired without a sigh. My heart is vy full of all these things—& I have much pain & mortification at my impotence enforced on energies of wh I feel the throb.

[1] Rumania had entered the war on the Allied side on 27 August 1916, by declaring war on Austria-Hungary. She was defeated, principally by German troops between 1 and 9 December 1916. In April 1918, her eastern province, Bessarabia, proclaimed its union with Russia.

[2] Henry Bradwardine Jackson, 1855–1929. Entered Navy, 1868. A pioneer of wireless telegraphy. Knighted, 1906. Chief of the Admiralty War Staff, 1912–14. Admiral, 1914. In August 1914 he was put in charge of planning the seizure of German colonies. First Sea Lord, May 1915–December 1916. President of the Royal Naval College, Greenwich, 1916–19. Admiral of the Fleet, 1919.

[3] Henry Francis Oliver, 1865–1965. Entered Navy, 1878. Naval Assistant to Sir John Fisher, 1908–10. Rear-Admiral, 1913. Director of the Intelligence Division at the Admiralty, 1913–14. Churchill's Naval Secretary, October 1914. Acting Vice-Admiral and Chief of the Admiralty War Staff, November 1914 to 1917. Knighted, 1916. Commanded 1st Battle Cruiser Squadron, 1918. Commanded the Home Fleet, 1919; the Reserve Fleet, 1919–20. Second Sea Lord, 1920–4. Admiral, 1923. Commander-in-Chief, Atlantic Fleet, 1924–7. Admiral of the Fleet, 1928.

[4] But not purchased. Early in 1917 Churchill did however buy a house in Kent (see page 45, note 2).

[5] James Louis Garvin, 1868–1947. Editor, *The Observer*, 1908–42. Editor, *Pall Mall Gazette*, 1912–15. Editor-in-Chief, *Encyclopaedia Britannica*, 1926–9. His only son was killed in action in 1916 on the western front.

Poor Harvey Butters.[1] Did you see I wrote a few lines about him in the Observer?

God bless you my dear Yr letters are a gt pleasure to me: so don't cut them off.

Yours always affectionately
W

PS. Last night I dined in the middle of the Government—Asquith, McKenna,[2] Curzon.[3] All vy caressing.

But you cannot make rivers run backwards.

Winston S. Churchill: memorandum[4]

(*Churchill papers: 8/104*)

MECHANICAL POWER IN THE OFFENSIVE

9 November 1916
Secret

Mr Montagu[5] having requested me to express my views on the question of the greater application of mechanical power to the prosecution of an offensive on land, I have prepared the following rough notes:—

[1] Henry Augustus Butters, 2nd Lieutenant, Royal Artillery, killed in action on 31 August 1916 at the age of 24. Born in South Africa, he had been educated in the United States and Canada, and in 1914 was living in San Francisco. Writing in the *Observer* on 10 September 1916 Churchill recalled: 'I met him quite by chance in his observation post near Ploegsteert and was charmed by his extraordinary fund of wit and gaiety. His conversation was delightful, full at once of fun and good sense. . . . He was a great "character" and had he lived to enjoy his bright worldly prospects he could not have failed to make his mark. . . . He did not come all the way from San Francisco only out of affection for the ancient home of his forbears or in a spirit of new adventure. He was in sentiment a thorough American . . . But he had a very firm and clear conception of the issues which are at stake in this struggle.'

[2] Reginald McKenna, 1863–1943. Liberal MP, 1895–1918. President of the Board of Education, 1907–8. First Lord of the Admiralty, 1908–11. Home Secretary, 1911–15. Chancellor of the Exchequer, May 1915–December 1916. Chairman, Midland Bank, 1919–43.

[3] George Nathaniel Curzon, 1859–1925. Conservative MP, 1886–98. Under-Secretary of State for India, 1891–2; for Foreign Affairs, 1895–8. Created Baron, 1898. Viceroy of India, 1898–1905. Created Earl, 1911. Lord Privy Seal, May 1915–December 1916. President of the Air Board, 1916. Lord President of the Council and Member of the War Cabinet, 1916–19. Secretary of State for Foreign Affairs, 1919–24. Created Marquess, 1921. Lord President of the Council, 1924–5.

[4] Although Churchill was not a member of the Cabinet, Edwin Montagu had his memorandum printed, and circulated, as a Cabinet paper.

[5] Edwin Montagu, 1879–1924. Liberal MP, 1906–22. Financial Secretary to the Treasury, February 1914–February 1915; May 1915–July 1916. Chancellor of the Duchy of Lancaster, February–May 1915; January–June 1916. Minister of Munitions, July–December 1916. Secretary of State for India, June 1917–March 1922. He married Clementine Churchill's cousin, Venetia Stanley, in July 1915.

1. The conditions of this war deny to the stronger power, whether on sea or land, its legitimate offensive scope. In all previous wars the stronger army was able to force matters to a final decision. The great developments of defensive power now prevent this.

2. We shall never have a superiority in numbers sufficient to triumph by itself. At present the fighting forces are much too evenly balanced. We have, perhaps, a superiority of five to four in fighting formations on all fronts, but the enemy's advantage of being on interior lines more than covers this. Even if we have a superiority of six to four, that will be insufficient, and we are not likely to see a greater superiority than this for a very long time.

3. Frontal attacks were abandoned forty years ago on account of the severity of fire. Now that the severity of fire has enormously increased and is constantly increasing, they are forced upon us in the absence of flanks.

4. Two methods of frontal attack have been tried. First, the unlimited, like at Loos and Champagne, where the troops were given a distant objective behind the enemy's lines and told to march on that; and second, the limited form as tried by the Germans at Verdun, and by ourselves and the French on the Somme. Neither produces decisive results. The unlimited simply leads to the troops being brought up against uncut wire and undamaged machine guns. The limited always enables the enemy to move his artillery away, and to sell a very little ground at a heavy price in life, gaining time all the while to construct new defences in the rear. It is true the limited attack has achieved a great deal in wearing down the enemy, but it is a disputed question whether the attacker does not wear himself down more, and certainly it was so in the case of the German attack on Verdun. Nothing in the great operations on the Somme affords any promise of finality or of a definite decision.

5. We must, therefore, either find another theatre or another method.

6. Leaving out the strategic question of other theatres and looking solely to method, it is clear that to achieve decisive results we must be able to make an advance in one bound of 7,000 or 8,000 yards, thus capturing the whole line of the enemy's guns. If this were done from two converging points on the well-known pincer principle, the enemy in front of our attack and in between both attacks would equally be destroyed, and an irreparable gap opened.

7. Therefore the problem is to advance a large army in one bound 7,000 or 8,000 yards. Is that problem insoluble? Let us see first of all exactly what it is that stops us.

8. An attack on two processes—

(*a*) Blasting power and
(*b*) Moving power;

blasting power is very well provided for in the constantly improving supplies of guns and shells, but moving power is in its infancy.

9. Two things stop the offensive movement of armies—

(*a*) Bullets and fragments of shell which destroy the motive power of men, and

(*b*) The confusion of the conflict.

10. Bullets would be much less well directed at night, but, on the other hand, confusion would be much greater.

11. If there were any means therefore by which confusion at night could be overcome, it would be a gigantic advantage. Under present conditions movement at night is almost impossible. The labyrinths of trenches, wire, craters, and natural accidents of ground impose insuperable obstacles to the movement of large forces. Everybody loses his way, and everything miscarries.

Yet it is at night that the offensive would have, if it could only act, all the advantages. It knows what it wants to do. The defensive has to wait on it and cannot move, even when it knows, until daylight comes. Therefore if there were an army able to develop the faculty of being able to carry out a sustained, concerted, continuous attack on the greatest scale, with the utmost precision and lack of confusion, throughout the dark hours, that army would have an inestimable advantage. It would move directly and surely to its goal; and morning would reveal an arrangement of forces arising wholly out of the pre-conceived decisions of the attackers.

12. If to this advantage you can add a comparative immunity from bullets and fragments, you are a long way on the road to decisive victory.

13. Here note that the object of fire is to scatter as many small missiles as possible. If steel protection against these small missiles can be afforded, the enemy is thrown back on the direct hit of a shell. By day it has been proved this is extremely rare on a moving target. By night it is practically impossible. A moderate multiplication of targets will baffle the direct hit. Darkness will prevent it except as a pure fluke.

14. If it should be found that the self-same methods which enable you to overcome the difficulties of confusion at night also impart this comparative immunity from missiles, we should be in presence of a military fact of the first order.

15. Such a method exists. It may be shortly described as 'the attack by armoured vehicles'. I cannot pretend to do more than outline it and suggest it. I am not an inventor or designer. I have no means of testing and elaborating these ideas. Evidently they require study, experiment, and at least six months preparation.

But now is the time in the winter to organise and perfect this method of attack. The 'Tanks' have shown the way. But they are only a beginning.

A hiatus exists between inventors who know what they could invent, if they only knew what was wanted, and the soldiers who know, or ought to know, what they want, and would ask for it if they only knew how much science could do for them. You have never really bridged that gap yet.

Parenthetically, let me point out the need of establishing without delay an Anti-Tank Committee to study the methods by which tanks can be defeated. This body should work in the closest harmony with those concerned in the production and design of tanks, each striving to defeat the other, exchanging information and perfecting their methods. It is not to be supposed that the Germans will not develop tanks in their turn. We have the enormous advantage of being able to experiment on ourselves with them, and to find out the best ways by which they may be defeated. We ought to have a complete anti-tank outfit by the spring. This is only what the Admiralty did before the war in keeping continually at work submarine and anti-submarine committees.

16. Subject to what I have said of the tentative and suggestive character of these observations, I will try to indicate the kind of attack I have in mind.

Broken ground, which forbids movements of bodies of troops by night, is passable to armoured vehicles.

If you look at the films lately exhibited you see that men moving over the broken or pock-marked ground, now rising on the crest of a crater, now descending into its trough, seem as much out of their element as a man overboard in a rough sea, while a tank forges along like a ship. You must master the physical difficulties of this broken terrain. You don't expect to accomplish your blasting process with human hands. You use several thousand guns and several million shells. Why should you suppose the moving process can be achieved simply through the agency of human legs? You must use the proper machinery in both cases.

Observe the obstacles remain a constant, but the size and power of the machine to overcome them is capable of considerable expansion.

17. The passage of suitable machines will roll paths or grooves, smooth and flat, across the terrain. Everyone will be able to follow them. In fact, by night they cannot do anything else. Instead of labyrinths of trenches and unknown terrain, you will have a pattern of smooth rectilineal tracks, cut more or less deeply into the surface and traversing trenches, &c. These tracks will supersede or super-impose themselves upon all other communications and accidents of ground during the night. The deeper they can be cut or squashed down the better. Along these smooth, unmistakeable tracks movement will be possible for the attackers.

Observe, incidentally, that the enemy's guns will be laid on the old communication trenches and regular night lines. They will not fire on these new tracks except by chance. Anyhow, it is proved artillery barrages alone will not stop good troops.

18. It will be possible to direct the movement of these track-making machines with accuracy and certitude. A good helmsman steering on a compass bearing will make the exact point required surely and punctually, and the assaulting infantry and all their appurtenances can follow, and *can only follow* where he has led.

(I omit details like shaded lights of various colours pointing backward along each path; every brigade its own particular series of coloured lights.)

19. Not only is the advance in a straight line possible; any portion of the attack can be turned to any fresh direction simply by the helmsman altering course according to chart and plan.

Therefore you can make your great plans with the utmost detail beforehand, and can be sure of having ten hours of darkness in which you will be able to unfold them stage by stage; while the enemy cannot make any important movement until morning, and can only fire his artillery on fixed points which you are mainly avoiding, and before dawn you will have been able with certainty to place your troops and their necessary supplies wherever you have designed.

This then is the foundation:—

The advance of a large number of track-making machines and the stamping through this agency of a pattern upon the ground which will guide and govern the development of the attack.

20. But there are a great number of details and accessories with which I am ill-equipped to deal. Please therefore take my numbers only as tokens.

Let us assume two converging pincer attacks, each on a 15,000 yard front with (say) an equal distance in between.

Assume ten divisions for each attack with five more in reserve.

Total assaulting divisions = 30.

Brigades attack on 500 yard frontages. Each brigade requires a track of its own.

10 by 3 = 30 tracks in each attack.

Two machines to each track (in case of accidents).

Total 60.

Two attacks = 120.

Add 30 for margin = 150 trackmakers.

(*Note.*—A trackmaker may also be a fighting-machine of a very powerful character.)

Minimum rate of advance—1 to 2 miles per hour.

21. Cover and clear the advance of the trackmakers by 300 fighting-tanks in each attack.

Total 600.

Two trackmakers and five tanks line ahead on each track, five tanks manœuvring in the intervals.

*On every alternative track one armoured trench-cutter for lateral communication and consolidation purposes.

*On every other track one tramway laying or duckboard laying mechanical unit. These last follow the assaulting infantry.

22. Formation of assaulting infantry.

First and second waves of assaulting infantry advance sheltered by the Tanks and trackmakers, and guided accurately by them, probably in platoon columns of fours, with shield carriers at the head and on the flanks.

Note.—Infantry should carry nothing but rifles, grenades, cartridges, food, water, and steel protection. They approach shielded but fight naked. The shield, which must be small and partial, leads you at once to the phalanx. A number of men, each partially protected by metal, will reciprocally protect each other.

All this must be ascertained by experiment and may break down under experiment.

Every infantry battalion will have *two caterpillar tenders*: Total, 240 in each attack; 480 in the whole.

These are lightly-protected motor lorries mounted on caterpillars. They follow along the tracks and carry everything the infantry requires—grenades, ammunition, smoke apparatus, food, &c.

23. Caterpillar batteries—

> Twenty-five 4-inch gun 18-pr. batteries in each attack; 200 vehicles total.
>
> Fifty heavy gun caterpillar trailers.

24. Total armoured vehicles:—

Trackmakers	150
Fighting tanks	600
Trench-cutters	50
Caterpillar tenders	480
Caterpillar artillery (light and heavy)	250
Total	1,530

25. The following must be taken as a mere sketch. The central conception is that a successful attack of this kind must be viewed as a whole, and all the different kinds of tools and tackle required made in concert like an outfit or a plant: everything should be foreseen and fitted into a general plan, like the large volume which contains a battleship design. It is not a case of merely building a lot of things on the chance that they will be useful, but of assembling the exact tools that you require for a particular, well-understood, mechanical job.

26. Don't familiarise the enemy by degrees with these methods of attack. Apply them when all is ready on the largest possible scale, and with the priceless advantage of surprise.

Winston S. Churchill to Sir Archibald Sinclair

(*Thurso papers*)

29 November 1916 41 Cromwell Road

Archie—Altho I owe you a letter, still I think you are a pig not to write more often. You will reply in the jargon of the day that in that case I am a super-pig. But I put off writing you from time to time on the chance that I may have good news to send—and something definite to say—& that chance lingers on the road. You on the other hand have no such excuse—tho' I do not doubt your ability to manufacture any number and express them at any length.

Well events are taking a sombre course & you may imagine the feelings with wh I watch the remoreseless unfolding of the terrible Balkan tragedy combined with the realisation of my forebodings in the west. The consequences of these latest episodes will be far-reaching. The internal condition of the Government is explosive, and its action paralytic. Northcliffe is its bitter foe, but continues to keep a side product of venom for me. The Generals have had sole direction of events; & now it is the 'politicians' who are to be blamed! The forces wh make for an inconclusive peace are gathering from every quarter and will I do not doubt when the hour is ripe receive encouragement from within the government itself.

I gather the Russians will make a sort of Chinese wall across Roumania from the mountains to the sea & try to hold the Germans there. Bucharest lies far outside their line. When the fronts are thus shortened, the enemy will either strike on with massed artillery into Russia (Odessa) or turn sharply back on to Sarrail.[1] I expect the latter as Constantine[2] no doubt has definite pledges. A fresh vista of misfortunes opens then.

These events will it seems certain entail changes in the Government: but I cannot tell their form or extent. The Admiralty is already reconstituted. You will know before you get this. But further alterations in the governing instrument are unavoidable, unless disaster is to end our efforts.

Everything I hear about the D'lles Commission encourages me. The interim report cannot now be long delayed and I have good hopes that it will be a fair judgment. I shd like to have it out as soon as possible. But the days slip away.

When will you be home again? I am going to Blenheim for Christmas & if you cd get away I am sure you wd be welcome there for a visit. FE will be there.

Let me know my dear—if you are in need of anything.

Spenser Grey[3] is rather offended at yr not answering one of his letters. Don't say I said so—but put it right.

I rejoiced to read of the glorious achievements of the RND. The heroic Freyberg[4] is here in hospital. They ought to make him a general.

Now write soon & often to your affectionate friend

W

[1] Maurice Paul Emmanuel Sarrail, 1856–1929. Entered the French Army, 1877. Director of Infantry at the War Office, 1907. Commanded the VIth Corps at the battle of the frontiers, 1914. Chief of the IIIrd Army in the Verdun Sector, 1915. Appointed Commander-in-Chief of the Allied Armies at Salonika at the end of 1915. His two principal offensives, in September and October 1916, were unsuccessful. A further offensive in May 1917 was likewise a failure, and Sarrail was recalled to France. In 1925, as High Commissioner in Syria during the Jebel Druse rebellion, he bombarded the native quarter of Damascus, as a result of which he was relieved of his post.

[2] Constantine, 1868–1923. Became King of Greece in 1913, when he was created a Field-Marshal in the German Army. Vetoed Greek co-operation at the Dardanelles, 1915. Refused to help the Allied Army at Salonika, 1916–17. Forced to leave Greece by the Allies, 1917. In exile, 1917–20. Returned as King, 1920. Abdicated after a military revolt, 1922. Known to the British as 'Tino'.

[3] Spenser Douglas Adair Grey, 1889–1937. Lieutenant, Royal Naval Air Service, 1913. One of Churchill's flying instructors, 1914. Lieutenant-Commander, August 1914. On active flying service, based at Antwerp, September 1914, when he took part in a bombing raid on the Cologne airship sheds. Sent on an Admiralty mission to the United States to purchase six flying boats, December 1914. Commander, flying boat experimental flying tests, Hendon, March 1915.

[4] Bernard Cyril Freyberg, 1890–1963. 2nd Lieutenant, Royal Naval Division, 1914. Temporary Lieutenant-Commander, 1915. Served at the Dardanelles, 1915–16, when he was awarded the DSO. Transferred to the Army, May 1916. In November 1916 he won the Victoria Cross when commanding the Hood battalion in an attack on a strongly fortified German position on the western front. During the attack he was wounded four times. Lieutenant-Colonel, Grenadier Guards, 1918. Major, 1927. Colonel, 1931. Major-General, War Office, 1934. General Officer Commanding the New Zealand Forces, 1939–45. Commander in Chief of the Allied Forces in Crete, 1941. Knighted, 1942. Governor General of New Zealand, 1946–52. Created Baron, 1951.

December 1916

Lord Curzon to Andrew Bonar Law:[1] *memorandum of a conversation*

(*Bonar Law papers*)

7 December 1916
Very Secret

(4) A prolonged discussion took place on the proposed constitution of the War Committee. . . .

(a) In reply to other questions, Mr Lloyd George stated that he had no intention of asking Mr W Churchill or Lord Northcliffe to join the Administration. . . .[2]

Winston S. Churchill to Sir Archibald Sinclair

(*Thurso papers*)

10 December 1916 — 41 Cromwell Road

Archie dear—

I am indeed yr debtor for a long & vividly interesting letter, & this is a moment when it is vy pleasant to receive the messages of a friend. The papers will have apprised you of the course of events, & you will have learned from them of the downfall of all my hopes and desires. These have not been unworthy, for I had an impulse & a gift to give to the war energies of the

[1] Andrew Bonar Law, 1858–1923. Born in Canada. Brought to Scotland at the age of twelve. Conservative MP, 1900–10 and 1911–23. Parliamentary Secretary at the Board of Trade, 1902–5. Leader of the Conservatives in the House of Commons, 1911. Secretary of State for the Colonies, May 1915–December 1916. Chancellor of the Exchequer, 1916–19. Lord Privy Seal, 1919–21. Prime Minister, 1922–3. Two of his three sons were killed during the First World War.

[2] This memorandum was sent to Bonar Law by Lord Curzon on 10 December 1916 with the covering note: 'My dear Bonar—Here is the Memo which Austen, W Long. Bob Cecil and I drew up of our conversation with Lloyd George on the 7th—Yours ever Curzon.' On 7 December the editor of the *National Review*, Leo Maxse, had written to Bonar Law: 'We are all terrified of having men like Max Aitken and F E Smith thrust upon us, or Winston Churchill. That way disaster lies as you start by chilling public confidence.' (*Bonar Law papers*)

country. But my treasure is rejected. If I cd reconcile the turn of events and of newspaper opinion with the true facts & the true values I shd be hopelessly downcast. But I am sure that these judgments are unjust and I have a good conscience & am confident of my record. Still you who know me so well will understand how unpleasant it is to me to be denied all scope in action at this time of all other times.

Of course I have every right to complain of LG who weakly & faithlessly bowed to Northcliffe's malevolent press. But this is not the hour when personal resentments however justified must influence conduct or colour opinion. I shall remain absolutely silent!

It was unlucky that the D'lles report shd have been delayed until after the crisis; for I am still hopeful that it will give a turn to public opinion. But everything has turned out ill for me since the war began. Perhaps we are now at the nadir.

It will be odd now on the Front Opposition Bench with all the furious ex-Ministers arriving. I expect they will soon be vy anxious to be civil to me. But I intend to sit in the corner seat in a kind of isolation.

The Liberal party will now gradually develop pacifist tendencies. Their resentment agst LG is fierce & concentrates upon his personal conduct & probity. The fact that no Liberal colleague wd serve with him is of course a serious testimony.

He may force an almost immediate dissolution with a view to securing a Parliament more in personal sympathy with him. If so I shall have to make a vy difficult decision wh it is not worth while anticipating. The new Government is a weak one,—so far as ability is concerned and largely inexperienced. Political considerations alone have ruled the formation of the War Council, & except LG not one of its members possessed any aptitude for war or knowledge of it. The exclusion of the Admiralty & War Office from the War Council shows an utter lack of comprehension of the interplay of forces. The difficulties before them are enormous, & only disasters lie ahead for many months. The position of Sarrail's army & the imbecile Salonika enterprise (of wh LG, Carson & BL are the principal initiators) is one of vy gt danger. No measures wh can be taken now can relieve that danger. Events will move rapidly there. One can only await developments.

If an election comes I shall *perhaps* be in a position to secure you a seat. But the future though imminent is obscure.

Yrs always

W

Sir Edward Carson to Andrew Bonar Law

(*Bonar Law papers*)

20 December 1916 Admiralty

Secret

My dear Bonar Law,

I fear this matter creates much difficulty. I do not yet know what the relations between the Admiralty & the Air Board are to be, but certainly it will require great tact & forbearance all round to get any new system into working order. I shd greatly fear friction if the appt is made. I much dislike having to seem opposed to the suggestion as my personal inclination is towards utilising Churchill's undoubted ability—especially so as he's so down in his luck at present but I hope some other, more suitable opportunity may be found.

Yours ever

E. Carson

Winston S. Churchill to Sir Archibald Sinclair

(*Thurso papers*)

20 December 1916 41 Cromwell Road

Archie,

Yrs of the 17th: & I am vy grateful for all the kindness you show me.

Secret 10 days ago LG sent G Riddell[1] to tell me he was keeping the Air Board for me at the first possible moment. Since then I hear this arrangement bruited in various secret & well informed quarters. I have not seen him however, tho' he threw a note across the floor last night asking me to come. I do not want to have a chatterbox talk. Unless I am *really* wanted I do not want to join them. However painful it is not to have work to do against the enemy, one must just wait. There is nothing to be gained by eagerness. The matter how hangs I suppose in the balance. I have seen nobody except FE since the crisis culminated—nor shall I seek to do so.

I hang heavy on his conscience & on his calculations.

But for the war nothing wd induce me to take office.

I look back a gt deal to our Plugstreet days, & wish I cd have cut myself

[1] George Allardice Riddell, 1865–1934. Began work in London as a boy clerk in a solicitor's office. Solicitor, 1888. Chairman of the *News of the World*, 1903. Knighted, 1909. Member of the Admiralty War Office and Press Committee, 1914. Liaison officer between the Government and the Press, 1914–18. Created Baronet, 1918. Created Baron, 1920. President of the Royal Free Hospital, 1925. Among his charitable bequests were £100,000 each to the Royal Free Hospital and the Eastman Dental Clinic.

more adrift from London & its whirlpools and been more content with the simple animal life / & death / wh the trenches offered. When I am *absolutely* sure there is no prospect of regaining control or part of it here, I shall turn again to that resort & refuge: & after all I have learned in disillusionment I think I cd do better. It is a mellow picture in retrospect. But I was always tormented by the idea that gt opportunities were slipping by at home.

And this is a fret. If I had stayed Chancellor of the Duchy and shut my mouth & drawn my salary, I shd today be one of the principal personages in direction of affairs. That was a costly excursion. Still I cannot regret it. Under a fair pretence of fine words, there is a gt *déconsideration* of all who wear uniform. They are discounted as persons 'under the law'. Not one of these gallant MPs who have fought through the Somme at the heads of their battalions, stands a chance agst less clever men who have stopped & chattered at home. This is to me the most curious phenomenon of all. It is quite inexplicable to me. Fancy putting Mond[1] & Cawley[2] in a War Government as representative Liberals, while excluding Jack Seely!

Young Blandford[3] has had a desperate operation for appendicitis, & till his fate settles itself (I hope for the best) our Blenheim plans hang in suspense. He is really charming—such a bright life. Assuming all is well, I shall go there on the 23rd & shall stay there over the New Year. You will be most welcome from the moment you arrive on the 30th. You have only to telegraph to me that you will come & I will arrange the rest. FE will be there & my little lot—whom you know. If *au contraire* Blandford's condition continues critical or the needle dips to the magnet, you will find us all here: & very welcome you will be. Telephone or telegraph on yr arrival (588 Kens)

Dardanelles report tho' mottled is I understand a document wh will

[1] Alfred Moritz Mond, 1868–1930. Son of a Jewish chemist who had come to England from Germany in 1862. Called to the Bar, 1894, and practised for a while as a barrister. Became a Director of Brunner, Mond & Co, 1895. By brilliant management and skilful amalgamation, he created, by 1926, the Imperial Chemical Industries (ICI), with a capital of £95,000,000. Liberal MP, 1906–10, 1910–23 and 1924–8. Created Baronet, 1910. First Commissioner of Works, 1916–21. Minister of Health, 1921–2. An enthusiastic Zionist, in 1921 he gave £100,000 to the Jewish Colonization Corporation for Palestine. Joined the Conservative Party, 1926. Created Baron Melchett, 1928.

[2] Frederick Cawley, 1850–1937. Liberal MP, 1895–1918. Created Baronet, 1906. Chairman, Liberal War Committee, 1916. Member of the Dardanelles Commission, 1916–17. Chancellor of the Duchy of Lancaster, December 1916–18. Created Baron, 1918. Of his four sons, three were killed in the war: Major J S Cawley in the retreat from Mons, August 1914; Captain Harold Thomas Cawley, MP, at Gallipoli, September 1915; and Captain Oswald Cawley, MP, in France, August 1918.

[3] John Albert Edward William Spencer-Churchill, Marquess of Blandford, 1897–1972. Eldest son of Churchill's cousin the 9th Duke of Marlborough. Captain, 1st Life Guards, 1916. Served in France and Belgium, 1916–18. Retired from the Army, 1927. Succeeded his father as 10th Duke, 1934. Mayor of Woodstock, 1937–42. Lieutenant-Colonel, liaison officer, US Forces, 1942–5.

greatly benefit me. Publication is imminent on the 'inception' phase: but poor old Cromer[1] is prostrated by his exertions & may never rally.

I have been enveloped in courtesies by the ex. Liberal Ministers: But I remain quite unattached.

Always yr affectionate friend
Winston

[1] Evelyn Baring, 1841–1917. British Agent and Consul General in Egypt, 1883–1907. Created Baron, 1892, Viscount, 1898, and Earl of Cromer, 1901. Chairman of the Dardanelles Commission of Enquiry, 1916–17. He died on 29 January 1917.

January 1917

Winston S. Churchill to Lord Curzon

(*Curzon papers*)

1 January 1917 Blenheim

I have been meaning to write to you for some time to offer you my heartfelt congratulations on yr approaching marriage.[1]

Some—probably most—people's lives maintain an ordinary daylight of fortune. But yours comes like sunshine on a cloudy day. When I first knew you, you were about to enter upon a brilliant period, & now after many years I earnestly hope you are about to enjoy another sun-blaze both in public & private life.

With all good wishes,
Believe me
Yours vy sincerely
Winston S. Churchill

Winston S. Churchill to Lord Fisher

(*Fisher papers*)

25 January 1917 41 Cromwell Road

My dear Fisher,

Many congratulations on yr birthday & on yr continued enjoyment of perennial youth & vigour. I was vy glad to get yr letter. I had heard from my mother of yr walk with her.

Like you I have seen no one political. One is quite powerless as far as the war is concerned. It is a pity, because a descent on the German coast, the bringing in of Denmark and the entry & domination of the Baltic wd secure

[1] To Grace Elvina Hinds, daughter of J Monroe Hinds (one time United States Minister to Brazil) and widow of Alfred Duggan of Buenos Aires. She married Curzon (as his second wife) in January 1917.

a decisive victory for the Allies, who otherwise will be forced to far less satisfactory alternatives after far greater sacrifices. Our common enemies are all powerful today & friendship counts for less than nothing.

I am simply existing.

Yours ever
W

PS. The *Manchester Guardian* has a vy nice article about you to-day, wh you shd read.[1]

[1] On 25 January 1917 the *Manchester Guardian* published an article to celebrate Lord Fisher's 76th birthday. During the course of the article they described him as the real Father of the modern British navy and added: 'To him is due not only the design of the Dreadnought, which was the material expression of a carefully-thought-out scheme of naval strategy and tactics, but also the change of front from south to east, quietly and skilfully carried out, which was necessitated by the growing threat of the German navy. . . .' The article ended: 'It is satisfactory to know that he is bearing seventy-six years very lightly indeed, keeping himself fit until his country calls for him.'

March 1917

Winston S. Churchill to David Lloyd George

(*Churchill papers: 2/97*)

10 March 1917

My dear Prime Minister,

The Government excisions in the Dardanelles Report are extremely injurious to me and incidentally to the late Government. They are so serious that they have altered the whole balance of the Report and decisively affected the impression produced upon the public. There are four excisions to which I draw attention.

First, the excision of my letter to General Callwell[1] of September [1].[2] In this letter at the earliest moment I proposed to take the exact course for which the Government is censured for not adopting, viz the examination of an amphibious surprise attack on the Gallipoli peninsula by representatives of the joint Staffs of the Admiralty and the War Office. There can be no genuine objection on military or diplomatic grounds to the publication of this letter for in its full text it contains the sentence, 'Turkey may make war upon us at any moment' thus showing that the project was only contingent upon Turkey declaring war and that there was no idea of attacking her before she declared war.

Secondly, the suppression of the terms of M Augagneur's[3] letter is unfair and alters the general balance of the Report. I agree however that it is for him and the French Government to decide on this point. It is all the more

[1] Charles Edward Callwell, 1859–1928. Entered Army, 1878. Intelligence Branch, War Office, 1887–92. Attached to the Greek Army during the Graeco-Turkish War, 1897. Colonel, 1904. Angered because several of his contemporaries were appointed to General Officer over his head, he retired from the Army in 1909. Satirized Army procedure and War Office routine in *Service Yarns and Memories*, published in 1912. Recalled to the active list, 1914. Acting Major-General, August 1914. Director of Military Operations and Intelligence at the War Office, 1914–16. Special Mission to Russia, 1916. Adviser on ammunition supply, Ministry of Munitions, 1916–18. Major-General, 1917. Knighted, 1917. Military historian.

[2] For the genesis of the Dardanelles campaign, Churchill's meeting with Callwell on 1 September 1914, and the subsequent correspondence, see the documents printed in Companion Volume III of this biography, page 75, pages 81–4 and 91–5. See also Churchill letter to Sir William Pickford, published on pages 50 to 59 of this volume.

[3] Victor Augagneur, 1855–1931. A distinguished French pathologist and colonial administrator. Minister of Marine, August 1914 to October 1915.

incumbent upon the Government to make sure that no other material facts are suppressed.

Thirdly, the complete suppression of the evidence of Captain Hall,[1] Director of the Intelligence Division of the Admiralty, as to what would have happened if the Naval attack had been resumed after the 18th is a vital point to me as well as to my colleagues. Captain Hall with the full knowledge of the Admiralty Intelligence Department stated on oath to the Commissioners that in his belief the Turkish forts were out of ammunition, that only one line of mines remained, that if the Fleet had pressed on they would have got through with the loss of one or two ships, and that the arrival of any portion of the Fleet before Constantinople would have produced revolution and put Turkey out of the war. I quite understand that references to Intelligence Reports must be stated in terms which do not reveal the identity of the agents relied upon. It is idle to pretend that the substantial facts adduced by the evidence cannot be stated in another way.

Fourthly, practically all reference to the effect produced upon the Foreign situation on the Balkan States by the Naval attack on the Dardanelles are suppressed without in my opinion any sufficient ground of public interest. The gap thus made in the integrity and balance both of the Report and of Roch's[2] Minute should be filled in some way or other so that the essential facts may be made known.

These remarks are based upon a comparison of the evidence marginally referred in the Report, to which evidence I am of course fully acquainted with, and not on a comparison of the unexpurgated and published forms of the Report. I wish now however to say that parties directly affected by the findings of the Commissioners ought in my opinion to see the Report in confidence not as a matter of courtesy but of right, and I would ask that this may be accorded to me.

Speaking generally I assert that quotations from the evidence included in the body of the Report do not in numerous cases represent the evidence given before the Commission and I shall certainly feel bound to press for a publication of all such evidence as is not directly barred during war time by public interests.

[1] William Reginald Hall, 1870–1943. Entered Navy, 1883; Captain, 1913. Commanded the *Queen Mary*, 1913–14. Forced to give up his sea command after three months of war because of uncertain health. Director of the Intelligence Division at the Admiralty, 1914–18. Rear-Admiral, 1917. Knighted, 1918. Vice-Admiral (retired), 1922; Admiral (retired), 1926. Conservative MP for the West Derby Division of Liverpool, 1919–23; and for Eastbourne, 1925–9. Conservative Party Principal Agent, 1924.

[2] Walter Francis Roch, 1880–1965. Liberal MP, 1908–18. A Member of the Dardanelles Commission, 1916–17. He published *Mr Lloyd George and the War* in 1920.

Winston S. Churchill to Lord Fisher

(*Fisher papers*)

12 March 1917
Midnight

41 Cromwell Road

My dear Fisher,

So many thanks for yr letter & enclosure. I have a strange recurrent feeling that you are going to have another chance. But we must have a talk. Above all don't get downhearted.

After all the Falklands and the Big Programme are lasting assets.

I looked in upon you this afternoon & found you out. I will try again.

Yours ever
W

Leo Maxse[1] *to Austen Chamberlain:*[2] *extract*

(*Austen Chamberlain papers*)

12 March 1917

I am sure you can have no idea of the indignation aroused at the Front by the perpetual Churchill–Smith intrigues against the Commander-in-Chief, which are known to be inspired by pure malevolence and the most unpatriotic motives. Simply because Churchill was not allowed to run the Army he is determined that no-one else shall. He ought to be told to go to the Devil, instead of which he is invited to become Chairman of a Committee at the War Office. Imagine the moral effect!

[1] Leopold James Maxse, 1864–1932. Journalist. His father bought the *National Review* for him in 1893, and he edited it from 1893 until his death. From 1899 he persistently warned his readers of 'the German danger' to Britain. After 1918 he opposed a *rapprochement* with Germany.

[2] Joseph Austen Chamberlain, 1863–1937. Conservative MP, 1892–1937. Chancellor of the Exchequer, 1903–5. Unsuccessful candidate for the leadership of the Conservative Party, 1911. Secretary of State for India, 1915–17. Minister without Portfolio, 1918–19. Chancellor of the Exchequer, 1919–21. Lord Privy Seal, 1921–2. Foreign Secretary, 1924–9. Knighted, 1925. First Lord of the Admiralty, 1931.

Winston S. Churchill to Sir Archibald Sinclair

(*Thurso papers*)

22 March 1917 33 Eccleston Square[1]
Private

Archie dear, I was delighted to get yr letter & to have news of you. The war weighs heavy on us all & amid such universal misfortune & with death so ubiquitous & life so harsh, I find a difficulty in setting pen to paper. I have liked to think you have been bored & not in danger, & I hope this condition will continue. I share it—so we are fellow sufferers. I remain inactive & useless on the edge of the whirlpool. I see a good deal of LG and hear how things are going. But otherwise I keep clear of the whole governing machine except FE. The Asquithians are all vy civil & friendly: but here again I keep a separate dwelling.

You will be glad to hear that the House of Commons is coming to hand again. The three speeches I have made this year have all been vy well received. The Dardanelles debate especially was vy successful to me personally. The grouping of forces in the House are proving increasingly favourable. The D'lles report has forced all who care about K's memory (and they are many) to join with all who adhere to orthodox Liberalism in defence of that operation: and I thus have strong bodies of public opinion between me & the malevolence of the Tory Press.

This is likely to govern my affairs. I fear that LG will seek to force an election altho there is no justification for it in the attitude of the House. But victory at the polls is easier than in the field. I am doing all I can to prevent such a disastrous event both by supporting the government in the prosecution of the war, & by protesting agst such a course. It wd grieve me to be drawn into such a struggle now. If it comes I shall I think be able to find you a good seat. Scotland is vy stable.

When is the next blow going to fall? There is the dominant question.

Please stay where you are with your sqn. It is much too late for you to go into the Flying corps.

Yours always W

PS. We are slowly getting in to Lullenden[2]

[1] In March 1909, shortly after their marriage, the Churchills took an eighteen-year lease (at £195 a year) on 33 Eccleston Square, near Victoria Station. In 1912 they moved to Admiralty House, and Sir Edward Grey took over the Eccleston Square lease. The Churchills returned in 1917, but after the war moved to 2 Sussex Square. In the 1920s 33 Eccleston Square was acquired by the Labour Party for their headquarters.

[2] A house in Kent, near East Grinstead, which Churchill bought early in 1917, and where he and his family lived until the purchase of Chartwell in 1922. The house cost Churchill £6,000. While Minister of Munitions, he tried to go there each weekend. On 29 July 1917 Lloyd George visited him there, and he showed the Prime Minister the potato field he had helped to plant.

Winston S. Churchill to Edward Grigg

(*Altrincham papers*)

26 March 1917 41 Cromwell Road

My dear Grigg,

I am very grieved to have missed you & beg you to forgive my apparent neglect. I was detained in Asquith's room & the messenger with yr card did not find me there. It is a gt disappointment to me not to see you before you return.

Please let this note convey to you my very warmest wishes for yr good fortune & safety amid so many dangers. I shall always remember as a vivid episode my sojourn with you & yr gallant Grenadiers & all yr welcome & kindness to me.

The year that has passed since then has been barren, and in contrast to its dreary stretches Rouge Croix, Laventie, the Red House & *even* Ebenezer Farm[1] present themselves in a pleasant light.

We are now entering upon the supreme climax: and I shd have liked very much to have yr views. Mine you know—they have never altered.

Once more the best of good wishes: & believe me always

Your sincere friend
Winston S. Churchill

[1] Ebenezer Farm was the front line headquarters of the 2nd Battalion Grenadier Guards in November 1915, when Churchill was attached to them for ten days. Rouge Croix was a hamlet a mile behind the line, and Laventie the nearest village. Edward Grigg was then in command of the Battalion's No 1 Company, in whose front line dugout Churchill slept on 21 November 1915. For Churchill's experiences with the Grenadier Guards, see Main volume III of this biography, pages 576-89.

April 1917

Winston S. Churchill to Sir Archibald Sinclair

(*Thurso papers*)

11 April 1917 — 33 Eccleston Square

My dear—

I am so sorry to hear of yr illness & I know how vexed you will be to be out of the fight. Never mind. Cavalry have no rôle on the Western front. There will be no galloping through, & even catastrophe will be prevented by the unfailing interposition of preliminary hard facts.

This battle[1] seems to have been well organised and the Artillery (fed by the abused LG & other 'politicians') has proved once again overwhelming on the limited area exposed to its attack. But the secondary stages are vy costly, and the forward movement must be gradual—ie step by step. Meanwhile there is much to cause anxiety. Russia! The Submarines!! The German reserve Army!!! (if it really exists). All these are factors of *fundamental* uncertainty.

It is vy joyous reading of this brilliant *episode.* 11,000 Huns glad to accept life at the hands of our small army. One likes to dwell on it, altho I fear the *tendencies* are no longer so favourable as they used to be. Still America—dear to your heart & mine, is please God a final makeweight.

Do not fret or chafe. Just do what is yr appointed task & May Heaven protect you till better days dawn & even after that—is the prayer of yr sincere friend

W

[1] On 9 April 1917, Easter Monday, Sir Douglas Haig launched a Spring offensive in the Arras sector of the western front. Within forty-eight hours the Germans had been driven back nearly four miles along a fourteen mile front. Among the British Generals who took part were General Sir Edmund Allenby (commanding the Third Army), Lieutenant-General Aylmer Haldane (VIth Corps), Brigadier-General Adrian Carton de Wiart (12th Brigade, wounded during the battle), and Churchill's friend Brigadier-General Hugh Tudor (commanding the artillery in support of the 4th Division). The total number of German prisoners taken was 7,587. The British lost over 200 officers and nearly 2,000 men killed, and a further 6,000 wounded.

Winston S. Churchill to Andrew Bonar Law

(*Bonar Law papers*)

[? 19] April 1917 House of Commons

My dear Bonar,

I am most deeply grieved to hear you have bad news.[1] There are still many chances. Do not assume the worst. Accept my deepest sympathy in your anxiety.

It is a fearful time.

Yours vy sincerely
W

Christopher Addison[2] to David Lloyd George: extract

(*Lloyd George papers*)

27 April 1917

Dear Prime Minister,

With reference to your suggestion that a Committee or Board might be formed over which Churchill could preside, to deal with mechanical aids to warfare, I have discussed this matter with him twice and have had a complete list of Stern's[3] staff and activities got out. I went over this list of staff with Churchill. On the whole, he was averse to taking any of the men

[1] The news that Bonar Law's son James (born 1894), a Captain in the Royal Flying Corps, had crashed in France when he tried to avoid a convoy of motor lorries which was crossing the airfield as he was taking off; he suffered severe concussion. He was killed in action on the western front on 21 September 1917. Another of Bonar Law's three sons had been killed five months earlier at the battle of Gaza, on 19 April 1917.

[2] Christopher Addison, 1869–1951. Hunterian Professor of Anatomy, 1901. Liberal MP, 1910–22. Parliamentary Secretary to the Board of Education, 1914–15. Parliamentary Secretary, Ministry of Munitions, 1915–16. Minister of Munitions, 1916–17. Minister in Charge of Reconstruction, 1917. President of the Local Government Board, 1919. Minister of Health, 1919–21. Minister without Portfolio, 1921. Labour MP, 1929–31; 1934–5. Minister of Agriculture and Fisheries, 1930–1. Created Baron, 1937; Viscount, 1945. Secretary of State for Commonwealth Relations, 1945–7. Paymaster-General, 1948–9. Lord Privy Seal, 1947–51. In 1934 he published his diaries in two volumes, entitled *Four and a Half Years.*

[3] Albert Gerald Stern, 1878–1966. Lieutenant, Royal Naval Volunteer Reserve (Armoured Car Division), 1914. Secretary to the Landship Committee, Admiralty, 1916. Major, Machine Gun Corps, Heavy Branch, 1916. Head of the Tank Supply Committee, Ministry of Munitions, 1916; Director-General, Mechanical Warfare Department (rank of Lieutenant-Colonel), 1917; Commissioner, Mechanical Warfare, Overseas and Allies, 1917. Knighted, 1918. He published *Tanks 1914–18: The Log Book of a Pioneer*, in 1919. Member of the London Committee of the Ottoman Bank, 1921–64. Director, the Midland Bank, 1933–58, and of the Clydesdale Bank, 1950–8. Chairman, Special Vehicle Development Committee, Ministry of Supply, 1929–43. Member of the Tank Board, 1941.

out of the Department and making a special group of persons to deal with Design and other kindred matters.

It appears to me that the most effective way of giving effect to your suggestion and making the fullest use of Mr Churchill's services, on the lines on which he feels free to assist, (viz:—without undue advertisement and without attaching to him special executive responsibilities) would be to form a small *ad hoc* Committee under his Chairmanship which should consider and discuss (1) the general question of the Tank programme, both as to numbers and types, and any other suggestions with regard to mechanical devices which may be worth considering. . . .

So far as the Ministry is concerned on the Supply and Design sides, we should be only too ready to give any facilities that might be required,—of course, consistent with living up to our War Office programme of Supplies. The military side of the case would have to be arranged with the Army Authorities and it would, I should think, fall to you to arrange it with Derby.[1]

I have not sent a copy of this letter to Churchill, as I thought perhaps you would wish to express your views on the subject to me first.

Yours sincerely,
C. Addison

[1] The 17th Earl of Derby, Secretary of State for War since December 1916 (see page 71, note 2).

May 1917

Winston S. Churchill to Sir William Pickford:[1] *extract*

(*Churchill papers: 2/102*)

1 May 1917
Confidential

Dear Lord Justice Pickford,

After studying the Interim Report of the Dardanelles Commission I feel entitled to draw your attention to certain aspects which are capable of giving a wrong impression to readers unacquainted with the evidence, and thus serving as a foundation for unfair and otherwise unfounded reflections.

Let me say at the outset that I appreciate most fully the immense difficulties laid upon the Commissioners and the singleness of their desire to do justice and establish the truth. The chief difficulties which I have in mind are, first, the impossibility of publishing the whole of the evidence in a complete form perhaps for many years; and secondly, the absence of any definite charge or charges against the persons whose conduct has been under review which they could specifically meet and endeavour to answer. On the first point, if the evidence as a whole could have been published, there would have been no occasion for me to address you. The public could then have formed their own opinion with full knowledge of all the circumstances. Again, if the Commissioners, in view of the fact that the evidence could not be published, had confined themselves to conclusions and to expressions of their own opinion I should have had little ground of complaint. But the Commissioners have seen fit to adopt another course, viz, to build up in detail the whole story of these transactions by means of brief extracts and quotations from documents and the evidence of witnesses. This method is in conflict with the sound principles so universally accepted that if any part of a document is quoted, the whole of the document should be quoted, and that the evidence of a witness must be judged as a whole and not on any isolated answer or expression. I can quite understand that having reached certain conclusions,

[1] William Pickford, 1848–1923. Judge of the High Court of Justice, 1907–14. Knighted, 1914. Lord Justice of Appeal, 1914–18. Member of the Dardanelles Commission, 1916–17; appointed Chairman on the death of Lord Cromer, 29 January 1917. Created Baron Sterndale, 1918. President of the Probate Division, Admiralty Court, 1918–19.

on which I should not presume in this letter to comment, the Commissioners thought it proper to support those conclusions by selections from the evidence. But in doing this they have, in my judgment, of course unintentionally, assembled a mass of extracts and quotations which though they tell the story, do not tell it fully or evenly, and which taken as a whole were likely to produce an erroneous effect in the public mind, and have in many cases done so. Documents of great importance are omitted altogether. A few sentences extracted from other documents, apart from the context, are built into the narrative in a manner which is in some cases actually misleading. The evidence of most important witnesses is represented by single phrases or sentences which do not give a true idea either of the evidence or of the fact. These partial quotations have in many cases attracted more attention from the public and in the newspapers than the conclusions which embody the matured and deliberate opinion of the Commissioners. There are also several inaccuracies and misstatements of fact which were no doubt inevitable having regard to the extent and complexity of the questions dealt with.

I will now proceed to give you some examples:—

An untrue impression is produced by the fact that the naval plans on which the Executive relied are altogether omitted. These lengthy technical documents, showing in clear detail the method of attack prepared by officers of the highest standing, for which they accept responsibility, were the foundation of my case. Instead, a few sentences are selected either from the documents or from the evidence of various witnesses, and these are presented as the sole expression of expert views. There is an essential difference between an expert 'assenting to' or 'acquiescing in' a particular operation, and in his showing in elaborate detail how it should be carried out. 'Assent,' which is implemented by exact and authoritative prescription of method is positive and active in its character, and differs fundamentally from mere expressions of opinion, cordial or half-hearted. It was on definite plans and not on expressions of opinion that the Government acted, and that I advised them. The plans speak for themselves. It is not to be supposed that officers of the standing of Admiral Carden,[1] Sir Henry Jackson, and Sir Henry Oliver would draw up plans which they thought were unsound, visionary, or impracticable, or that they could be induced to do so by pressure. I refer particularly to Admiral Carden's telegram of the 11th January, Sir Henry Jackson's memorandum of the 5th January, to his memorandum of the 15th January, to the Admiralty letter of the 5th February containing the War Orders, and to the Admiralty

[1] Sackville Hamilton Carden, 1857–1930. Entered Navy, 1870. Rear-Admiral, 1908. Admiral Superintendent, Malta Dockyard, 1912–13. Vice-Admiral in command of the Anglo-French Squadrons in the Eastern Mediterranean, and at the Dardanelles, 20 September 1914 to 16 March 1915, when ill-health forced him to retire. Knighted, 1916. Admiral, 1917.

letter of the 15th February containing Sir Henry Jackson's plans. The suppression of all but a few sentences of these important documents is deeply detrimental both to me and to the Government of that day. . . .[1]

I submit that it is impossible for anyone to appreciate the character of the expert advice apart from the detailed plans which the experts made, and which they were ready to carry out. Ability to make a practical plan and readiness to accept responsibility for it are the true and lasting tests to which professional opinion should be subjected.

A second serious difficulty which arises from the non-publication of the evidence is that the persons whose conduct is under review have no opportunity of placing the justification for or explanation of their actions before the public in a connected form. Where the matters dealt with are, as the Commissioners admit, largely matters of opinion on which dogmatic judgment is impossible, the disability is serious. The results of the decisions taken are obvious; the criticisms of any error of judgment or defects in temperament or procedure are also given the widest publicity; but the chain of argument and the numerous and convergent reasons which, while the event was yet unknown, led to the decisions being taken, have never been stated as they presented themselves to the persons responsible. A man has a right to defend his action in his own words and by his own method, and to present his case to public judgment as a connected whole. The Commissioners have a right and duty to state their opinion, and to lay emphasis on this or that set of facts; but the narrative so constructed, however impartial in its intention, can be no substitute for the above-mentioned elementary right of persons whose conduct is impugned to state their own case with as much publicity as is given to the judgment of the Tribunal.

My case, as the Commissioners are no doubt aware, rests not only on the plans of the naval experts, but on a considerable series of formal documents, Cabinet papers, Admiralty minutes, official letters and appreciations of the war situation extending from the beginning of these transactions down to the time of my leaving the Government. Rightly or wrongly, I hold that these documents will be decisive on the final judgment which will be formed on my share in these transactions; and that when the written opinions expressed before the event are compared with what actually happened, the coincidence will be regarded as remarkable. The Commissioners are able to judge how far this opinion of mine is well-founded; and I am sure they will understand why

[1] Each of these documents was published in *Winston S. Churchill, Companion Volume III, Part One*: Carden's telegram of 11 January 1915 on pages 405–6; Jackson's two memoranda on pages 376–7 and 419–21; the Admiralty letter of 5 February 1915 on pages 485–90 and Jackson's plans of 13 February 1915 on pages 506–12. In his memorandum of 1 May 1917 Churchill proceeded to give detailed illustrations of his complaint, covering seven printed foolscap papers. Only the final two pages are printed here.

I feel it a serious hardship that the whole of this series of documents should be withheld from the public, while almost every adverse fact is made public.

I recognise that national interests may require very considerable suppressions, both in regard to these documents and the naval plans during the continuance of the war, but if this is so it seems to me that the Commissioners might in their Report have endeavoured to compensate any persons thus injuriously affected by some reference in general terms to the existence and importance of the unpublished documents. I would ask that in any case an appendix to the Report should be prepared, including those very large portions of the vital documents which could without national detriment be published, and that this should appear at the same time as the final Report, subject to any deletions which the military censorship may require.

Another difficulty of which I have been acutely conscious has been the absence of any definite charge or criticism to which I could address myself. One after another I have endeavoured to deal with the serious charges which have been circulated broadcast through the land for the last two years; one after another they have been demolished to the satisfaction of the Commissioners, and I gladly recognise that such criticisms as are contained in the Report bear no relation whatever to these crude and untruthful allegations. But of the whole of this process of disproof and rebuttal no trace is apparent to the public; there is no statement in the body of the Report that this or that serious charge has been proved wholly unfounded. The positive criticisms of the Commissioners alone remain, and they are seized upon by important sections of the press as affording the fullest justification of the mendacious charges which have been disproved, but whose disproof is not declared.

It is from this point of view that I approach paragraph 92, which is the only part of the Report in which a definite reflection is cast upon me. It is far from my intention to suggest that I or anyone dealing with these formidable problems can in the light of after knowledge be held free from errors of judgment and defects of temperament which afford grounds for criticism. But the criticisms which would be just cannot be stated in the terms of paragraph 92, and had specific questions been put to me in regard to the statements of fact contained in this paragraph, I could have shown that, whatever criticisms are valid, they are not these which are here set forth. Take, for instance, the first sentence: 'There can be no doubt that at the two meetings of the 28th January Mr Churchill strongly advocated the adoption of the Dardanelles enterprise.' This statement is not correct. There was no necessity for me to add 'strong advocacy' to the general chorus of approval. Colonel Hankey's[1]

[1] Maurice Pascal Alers Hankey, 1877–1963. Entered Royal Marine Artillery, 1895. Captain, 1899. Retired, 1912. Secretary to the Committee of Imperial Defence, 1912–38. Lieutenant-Colonel, Royal Marines, October 1914. Secretary to the War Council, November

record of what took place shows in an abridged form practically every intervention in the discussion by any of the members present. Reference to this record will readily show the inaccuracy of the statement quoted above. The Dardanelles was only one of *ten* subjects dealt with at the morning meeting. At the evening meeting I confined myself to the bare announcement that 'the Admiralty had decided to push on with the project'. . . .

Secondly, it is not correct to state that I urged Lord Fisher 'to give a silent, but manifestly very reluctant, assent to the undertaking'. I urged him 'to undertake the operation'. The difference between the two statements is decisive. If I had urged the First Sea Lord to stand aside and 'acquiesce' in the operations, I should indeed have been culpable. He was the responsible officer who alone could direct them, and his agreement to do so was absolute and unreserved.

Thirdly, the Report states, 'It seems clear that he (Mr Churchill) was carried away by his sanguine temperament and in his firm belief in the success of the undertaking which he advocated.' Expressions of opinion about my 'temperament' lie wholly within the province of the Commissioners; but the phrase, 'firm belief in the success of the undertaking', is not only not founded upon any evidence of which I am aware, but is specifically contradicted by the following four pieces of evidence:—

(*a.*) My letter to Lord Kitchener of the 20th January beginning, 'As we cannot tell how things will go at the Dardanelles until the bombardment opens.'

(*b.*) My statement to the War Council on this very occasion, 28th January, submitted by me to the Commission, but omitted from the passages quoted by them in their report, to wit:

> 'Mr Churchill did not anticipate that we should sustain much loss in the actual bombardment, but in sweeping for mines some losses must be expected. The real difficulties would begin after the outer forts had been silenced and it became necessary to attack the Narrows.'

It is submitted that it would be difficult to have used language less misleading in fact than this, or more in harmony with the expert opinion. I do not understand why this important and significant observation should have been omitted from the record, which otherwise is quoted almost in its entirety.

1914–May 1915; to the Dardanelles Committee, May–November 1915; to the Cabinet War Committee, December 1915–December 1916. Knighted, February 1916. Secretary to the War Cabinet, 1916–18; to the Cabinet, 1919–38. Created Baron, 1939. Minister without Portfolio, September 1939–May 1940. Chancellor of the Duchy of Lancaster, 1940–1. Paymaster-General, 1941–2. His brother Hugh was killed in action in South Africa in March 1900. His brother Donald was killed in action on the western front in October 1916.

(*c.*) My note to the French Government of the 16th January (Appendix (C) 3), 'As the degree of the position to be met with cannot be anticipated, it is most undesirable to announce the full scope of the operations beforehand.'

(*d.*) My statement of the 27th February, ie, at the moment of our greatest success after the unexpectedly easy collapse of the outer forts. The War Council record states:

> 'Mr Churchill said he could not as yet offer any assurance of success. All that we could say at present was that the reduction of the outer defences gave a good augury of success. The real difficulty would arise when the Narrows at Chanak were attacked.'

It appears a reasonable ground of complaint that all this evidence is omitted, while a statement directly counter to it is published. I never on any occasion, privately or in Council, gave any assurance of success, or expressed any firm belief that success would be achieved. On the contrary, I presented the operation always as a hazard of war, but a risk which in my judgment it was worth while in the circumstances that then existed for us to run.

The Report having criticised me incorrectly on these three points in paragraph 92 proceeds to assign an excuse for my conduct which is also unfounded. I was not under any delusion about the opinions of the naval experts. I knew exactly what their views were, how they felt towards the operation, and why in the case of each man, and I take the fullest responsibility for the advice which, after mature consideration, I tendered to the War Council on behalf of the Admiralty.

Had I been questioned directly on the above points, I could, I conceive, have corrected, or at any rate modified, the impression which the Commissioners have recorded. I could also, I think, have assisted the Commissioners to appreciate more fully than they have done the character of these War Council meetings. They were not meetings where the technical details of operations were thrashed out, nor were they meetings where war policy was devised. All these matters were studied in the departments concerned, and repeatedly discussed by the heads of those departments, together and with the Prime Minister. Most of the action of the drama took place off the stage. The War Council meetings were chiefly for the purpose of registering decisions which had been in the main arrived at beforehand, and of obtaining the formal assent of the heads of departments and important military and naval personages concerned. But the war was carried on by the responsible heads of the fighting departments under the direct supervision of the Prime Minister, subject to the assent first of the Cabinet Ministers present at the War Council, and ultimately of the Cabinet as a whole.

I submit that, generally speaking, the quotations from the evidence of the naval witnesses are unfair to me and to the Government of that day. They do not represent the evidence of the witnesses nor the truth. They have in fact misled the public and produced an impression much more adverse than any that would be justified by the conclusions of the Commissioners. I submit that there is hardly any statement by the naval witnesses unfavourable from my point of view which has not been given the widest publicity, whereas on the other hand there is hardly any statement of the naval witnesses favourable from my point of view which has not been omitted. I invite a considered scrutiny of the evidence from this point of view. It was perhaps natural that the Commissioners should confine their quotations of evidence to such passages as would sustain the conclusions at which they had arrived, and that feeling it their duty to pass certain strictures on the conduct of public men, they should wish to fortify themselves by a rehearsal of those points in the evidence which they considered justified their conclusions. My complaint is that the materials so assembled are partial in their character and more damaging than the criticisms they were collected to support. . . .

Paragraph 109. The telegrams like others suffer very much from their paraphrasing. This is unavoidable. But the fact should surely have been brought out that these were Admiralty telegrams, the policy and exact wording of which were definitely agreed between the First Lord and the First Sea Lord. They bear the signatures both of the First Lord and the First Sea Lord. It was not a case of mere concurrence, but a complete agreement; and a complete agreement in a course of action which was a distinct advance upon the gradual method of attack which had been originally adopted. It is not fair to represent these telegrams merely as if they rested on the authority of the First Lord. Whatever Lord Fisher's misgivings at the outset of the operation, he and the Chief of the Staff and the First Lord were all in entire agreement in taking this very much more formidable step after the success at the outer forts had been achieved. This was the greatest naval decision which had to be taken, and it was taken by all the naval authorities at the Admiralty and on the spot in absolute agreement. Had the result been successful every one of the naval authorities would have been entitled to a direct share in one of the most memorable achievements of history. From the Report, however, it would appear that the First Lord was alone concerned, and that he was supported only by 'hesitating and half-hearted' expert advice. This impression would be quite untrue.

Paragraph 112 states:—

'In fact Admiral de Robeck[1] thought he had orders to force the passage

[1] John Michael de Robeck, 1862–1928. Entered Navy, 1875. Rear-Admiral, 1911. Commanded the 9th Cruiser Squadron, charged with protecting British merchant ships in the mid-Atlantic, 1914–15. Second in command of the Allied naval forces at the Dardanelles,

of the Dardanelles, and that it was his duty to do his best to carry out those orders.'

This statement is based on what Admiral de Robeck told the Commission a year and a half after the operation had failed. What he said before the attempt was made can only be judged in the actual words of the telegrams exchanged between the First Lord and him on the 17th March. The paraphrases of these telegrams give no true idea of the precise and definite nature of the questions put to the Admiral and of his equally precise replies. It is necessary for me to quote for your confidential consideration the actual words. 'I presume you are in full accord with Admiralty telegram 101 and Admiralty telegram 109 and Vice-Admiral Carden's answers thereto, and that you consider after separate and independent judgment that the immediate operations proposed are wise and practicable. If not, do not hesitate to say so. If so, execute them without delay and without further reference at the first favourable opportunity.' To which the Admiral replied, on the same day, 'I am in full agreement with the telegrams mentioned.' And, again, in another telegram, 'The second paragraph of Admiralty telegram number 109 expresses my intentions exactly.' It seems to me extraordinary in view of a question so categorical and an answer so precise given before the event, while the hopes of victory were strong and the chances open, that superior importance should apparently be attached to explanatory apologetics never uttered till long after the attempt had failed. Every consideration alike of private fair dealing and of public policy should hold military and naval officers, not less than Ministers, absolutely bound by a definit 'aye' or 'no' in regard to operations of war.

Paragraph 113, in the guise of 'summarising' the results of the bombardment of the 18th March, sets forth in meticulous detail every recognisable piece of damage caused to the *matériel*, down even to 'the "Albion's" foreturret' being 'put out of action for a few days'. It omits altogether to state that the loss of life in the operation, so far as the British were concerned, amounted only to sixty-one officers and men killed, wounded, and missing; and that the total losses in all the naval operations down to the time of their being finally discontinued did not exceed 1,000 men killed, wounded, and missing in both the British and French fleets. Considering the odium which is cast upon those responsible for the naval operations for the loss of life which was incurred and

---

February–March 1916. Vice-Admiral commanding the Allied naval forces at the Dardanelles, March 1915–January 1916. Knighted, 1916. Commanded the 2nd Battle Squadron in the North Sea 1916–18. Created Baronet, 1919. Commander-in-Chie of the Mediterranean Fleet, and High Commissioner at Constantinople, 1919–21. Admiral, 1920. Commander-in-Chief of the Atlantic Fleet, 1922–4. Admiral of the Fleet, 1925.

the widespread circulation of charges of 'murder' in regard to them, it may certainly be claimed that the actual losses of life should have been set forth with at any rate the same precision and prominence as is given to instances of slight and temporary damage to obsolete ships. I must recur to this point later on.

Paragraph 119. It was not possible for me to lay before the Commission all the evidence in my possession as to the situation in Constantinople and at the forts of the Dardanelles during and immediately after the naval attack. Of the evidence submitted to the Commission the most important pieces [ie, Mr Morgenthau's[1] statement and Captain Hall's 'evidence from a neutral source', that the forts were destitute of ammunition, and only one line of mines remained intact] were omitted from the Report. Thirdly, the Report of the Commission, already so attenuated in this respect, was further cut down by the Government censorship. The result is that this point, decisive from the point of view of historical judgment, is practically unrepresented in any versions which have reached the public.

I have already disclaimed any desire to comment on the conclusions of the Commissioners; but I do not understand why in an *interim* report of this character, terminating at the 23rd March, repeated reference should be made to 'the loss of valuable lives and treasure which was incurred'. The publication of an *interim* report relating only to the inception of the naval operations was bound in itself to create a false sense of proportion in the public mind. The naval operations were in reality only a very small part of the Dardanelles expedition, and, judged from the point of view of 'life and treasure involved', they were scarcely a 200th part of the Dardanelles expedition. The odium to which this enterprise has been subjected has arisen from the heavy losses and disasters of the military operations.

If the Commission had waited till the whole story could be told by them and an even and comprehensive judgment expressed in a final report, the true proportion of events would have been revealed. It would have been apparent after the naval operations had terminated that entirely new opportunities of success were open, that success was in fact very nearly achieved, and that had it been achieved it would have vindicated, or at any rate sustained all the previous stages, and the whole enterprise would have been invested with the highest credit. It was therefore invidious to select the naval operation for

[1] Henry Morgenthau, 1856–1946. Born in Germany. Emigrated to the United States, 1865. President, Central Realty Bond & Trust Company, 1899–1905. President, Henry Morgen thau Company, 1905–13. Chairman, Finance Committee of the Democratic National Committee, 1912 and 1916. United States Ambassador, Constantinople, 1913–16; where he was in charge of the interests of Britain, France, Russia, Belgium, Serbia and other belligerents, 1914–16. Honorary knighthood, 1920. Chairman, League of Nations Commission for the Settlement of Greek Refugees, 1923.

special treatment in an *interim* report. But if that were decided on, it might at least have been hoped that the report would be confined to the naval operation. Instead of this, further disadvantage is imposed on those responsible for the naval operation by the association with it of all the losses of valuable lives and treasure which were subsequently incurred without any account being given of the perfectly separate and avoidable operations which caused these losses.

There are in matters of justice certain well-understood and universally recognised processes of human thought from which I am confident you and your fellow Commissioners will not withdraw their allegiance. That these have not found full expression in the Interim Report is almost entirely due, first, to the non-publication or partial publication of the evidence; secondly, to the omission of the principal documents on which the Admiralty case rested; thirdly, to the absence of any definite charge against persons whose conduct was impugned which they could meet; and fourthly, the denial to them of an opportunity of laying their own case before the public in their own words. These serious disabilities can, it seems to me, only be removed by a fuller publication of the evidence on certain points to which attention has been drawn, and secondly by the publication as an appendix to the final Report, subject of course to military censorship, of the principal documents; not only those which relate to the second part of the Inquiry, but also to the first part to which this letter is especially directed.

I would also submit for your fair consideration that it is neither just nor reasonable that the final Report should in its conclusions be only sectional in its character and deal exclusively with what happened after the 23rd March. Now that the whole story from the beginning to the end has been laid before the Commission, it is right that a broad judgment should be formed of the whole episode and its chances, and that its different phases should be displayed in their true proportion.

Yours sincerely,
Winston S. Churchill

C. P. Scott:[1] *note of a conversation with Churchill*

(*Scott papers*)

3 May 1917

His tone was rather bitter in speaking of Lloyd George whom he had evidently come to consider as his destined antagonist. . . .

[1] Charles Prestwich Scott, 1846–1932. Editor of the *Manchester Guardian*, 1872–1929. Liberal MP, 1895–1906. A friend of Lloyd George, who often sought his advice.

There is a sort of hungry look about him in these days and he evidently feels his political isolation deeply.

Leopold Amery:[1] *diary*

(*Amery papers*)

10 May 1917

Down to the Secret Session, where Churchill opened with a very adroit but rather unsound speech, mainly in the direction of passive defence on the Western front till America can come in.[2] Lloyd George met his points very ably. . . .

Churchill had suggested modifying our proclaimed policy and LG, in replying to this, to my great surprise came out flatfooted and most emphatic against giving back the German Colonies or letting Turkey have Palestine or Mesopotamia.

Frederick Guest to David Lloyd George

(*Lloyd George papers*)

10 May 1917 House of Commons

Dear Prime Minister,

The impression in the House, lobby and smoking room is that you have made a great speech. It has been a good days work in more ways than one.

Winston's speech is also considered to be a fine statesmanlike effort.

Yours sincerely

Frederick Guest

[1] Leopold Charles Maurice Stennett Amery, 1873–1955. A contemporary of Churchill's at Harrow. Fellow of All Souls College, Oxford, 1897. *Manchester Guardian* correspondent in the Balkans and Turkey, 1897–9. Served on the editorial staff of *The Times*, 1899–1909. Conservative MP, 1911–45. Intelligence Officer in the Balkan and eastern Mediterranean, 1915–16. Assistant Secretary, War Cabinet Secretariat, 1917–18. Parliamentary Under-Secretary, Colonial Office, 1919–21. First Lord of the Admiralty, 1922–4. Colonial Secretary, 1924–9. Secretary of State for India and Burma, 1940–5.

[2] The United States had entered the war on 2 April 1917, but could not transfer substantial forces to France for at least nine months. At the Secret Session of the House of Commons on 10 May 1917 Churchill, who had himself suggested the session, made the principal opposition speech. In it he urged the Government not to embark on any further western front offensive 'before the American power begins to be felt on the battlefields', and he went on to warn: 'We have not the numerical superiority necessary for such a successful offensive. We have no marked artillery preponderance over the enemy. We have not got the number of tanks which we need. We have not established superiority in the air.' In his reply, Lloyd George had refused to commit the Government against a renewed offensive later that year.

David Lloyd George to Paul Painlevé[1]

(*Lloyd George papers*)

19 May 1917 10 Downing Street

My dear Monsieur Painlevé,

Mr Winston Churchill is very anxious to visit the French front. I ventured to say that I felt confident that you would give him every facility. I should esteem it a great act of personal kindness if you would permit Mr Churchill to call on you during his forthcoming visit to Paris and if you could give him the necessary permit to enable him to see something of the work of your great Army.

With kindest regards

Sir Douglas Haig to David Lloyd George: extract

(*Lloyd George papers*)

General Headquarters
24 May 1917 British Armies in France

My dear Prime Minister,

Your letter of 22nd reached me last night. I at once arranged to get into touch with Mr Churchill with a view to his visiting the British front. I cannot think why he should have troubled you in this matter, as it has never occurred to me to put any obstacle in his way of visiting the Army in France. Indeed his friend Repington[2] was told this by my Private Secy in reply to a question on the subject!

Winston S. Churchill to Clementine S. Churchill

(*Spencer-Churchill papers*)

29 May 1917 Hotel Ritz
Paris

My darling,

We had a vy pleasant trip. It was most carefully arranged & precisely carried out. We saw the devastated regions, the battlefield of Verdun & the

[1] Paul Painlevé, 1863–1933. Mathematician; Professor in the Faculty of Sciences at Lille, 1886; at the Sorbonne, 1891. Elected to the Chamber of Deputies, 1906, as an independent Socialist. Minister of Public Instruction and Inventions, October 1915–December 1916. Minister of War, March 1917–September 1917. Prime Minister, and Minister of War, 12 September–13 November 1917 (when he was succeeded as Prime Minister by Clemenceau). President of the Chamber, 1924. Prime Minister for the second time, April–November 1925. Minister of War, 1925–6. Minister of Air, 1930–1 and 1932–3.

[2] Charles à Court Repington, 1858–1925. Entered Army, 1878. Lieutenant-Colonel on Kitchener's staff at Omdurman, 1898. Forced to resign his commission because of a personal indiscretion involving another officer's wife. Military Correspondent of *The Times*, 1904–18. Military Correspondent of the *Daily Telegraph*, 1918–25.

Fille Morte sector in the Argonne on three successive days. There was no danger—& hardly the sound of a gun. The weather was beautiful & in the intervals of sightseeing we were banqueted by various generals commanding corps or armies. I found my old friend Fayolle.[1] He was delighted to see me & we had a long talk and afterwards luncheon. Whereas a year ago in Artois he commanded only one *corps d'armée*, the XXXIIIrd (who gave me my casque), now he commands a group of armies. Instead of 3 Divisions he commands 41! So he has gone up in the world. It was pleasant to find a complete agreement on all military questions. Indeed I think the French soldiers see vy clearly the truths of this front.

I dined with Pétain[2]—the *Général-en-chef*, but he did not enter into any serious subjects and I therefore made no attempt to do so. It was a pity: for I believe we are probably agreed on essentials. But as it turned out the only public matter we touched on was Salonika; & there we differed—though I did not press the argument! It appears he only got his appointment by some agreement with the late Ministry to go on with the expedition. So that he wd not be looking at the question from a military stand point. Such stuff I never heard.

I enclose you the programme which GHQ have drawn up for me. Evidently they wish to be vy considerate. It will be nice to be escorted by Neville Lytton[3] as bear leader. I shall try to get Jack[4] to come for a day also and to see Bertram[5] at some point on the road. I hope to bring Jack back with me on Sunday 3rd.

[1] Marie Emile Fayolle, 1852–1928. Entered the French Army, 1875. Professor, Ecole de Guerre, 1897–1907. General of Brigade, 1910. Commanded the 33rd Corps, 1915–16; the 6th Army, 1916–17; the Centre Group of Armies, 1917; the Group of Armies of Reserve, 1917–18; the French Occupation Forces on the Rhine, 1918–20. Marshal of France, 1921.

[2] Henry Philippe Benoni Omer Joseph Pétain, 1856–1951. Commanded an Infantry Regiment, August 1914; an Army Corps, October 1914; the 2nd Army, June 1915. In charge at the siege of Verdun, 1916. Chief of the General Staff, April 1917. Commander-in-Chief, May 1917–November 1918. Vice-President of the Supreme War Council, 1920–30. War Minister, 1934. Ambassador in Madrid, 1939–40. Prime Minister, 16 June 1940; he negotiated the armistice with Germany, 22 June 1940. Chief of State, 1940–4. Condemned to death after the liberation of France, 14 August 1945; the sentence was commuted to life imprisonment.

[3] Neville Stephen Lytton, 1879–1951. Son of the 1st Earl of Lytton. Painter. Amateur Tennis Champion, 1911 and 1913. Major, 11th Battalion, Royal Sussex Regiment, 1914–18. In 1915 he gave Churchill a series of notes on the technique of oil painting. Wounded, 1916; mentioned in despatches four times. Secretary, Société Nationale des Beaux Arts, Paris, 1936. Succeeded his elder brother as 3rd Earl of Lytton, 1947. In 1921 he published *The Press and the General Staff*, and in 1942 *The English Country Gentleman: Life in Unoccupied France*.

[4] John Strange Spencer Churchill, 1880–1947. Churchill's younger brother, known as Jack. A stockbroker. Major, Queen's Own Oxfordshire Hussars, 1914–18. Served at Dunkirk, 1914; on Sir John French's staff, 1914–15; on Sir Ian Hamilton's staff, 1915; on General Birdwood's staff, 1916–18.

[5] Bertram Henry Samuel Romilly, 1878–1940. 2nd Lieutenant, Scots Guards, 1898. On active service in South Africa, 1900–2 (DSO). Attached to the Egyptian Camel Corps,

You must make my excuses to the Asquiths: if that was the Wharf Sunday.

I have not had time to write or even to think about politics at home. We have been travelling vy long distances in motor cars and in continuous movement from daylight till night: & I expect this will continue. But I hope much to hear from you about things. You shd now write to GHQ: BEF.

I am to lunch this morning with Esher[1] & General Wilson[2] at the Café des Ambassadeurs: & tomorrow with Painlevé.

All are agreed here that Bertie[3] is utterly played out. It is high time we had a new representative.

I must tell you all about the French Army & how magnificent they are when I return.

It was nice of GHQ to think of the 6th Royal Scots Fusiliers in arranging my programme. Evidently all the claws of the military pussy cat are withdrawn into their sheaths and a soft purring sound is plainly audible.

What about my own equally fierce animal? Is she happy in her basket. Do her kittens thrive at Lullenden? What has happened to the goose the gander & the goslings. How are the Huns & the potatoes.[4]

My darling one, It has all been vy pleasant, but never for a moment does the thought of this carnage & ruin escape from my mind or my thoughts stray from the supreme problem. I am much stimulated by the change & movement, & new discussions with new people, & I am vy full of ideas.

Ivor[5] has stood the racket vy well and is much appreciated by everyone.

1903–14. On active service, 1915–17. Lieutenant-Colonel, March 1915. In December 1915 he married Clementine Churchill's sister Nellie. Military Governor, Province of Galilee, 1919–20. Commanded the 2nd Battalion, Scots Guards, 1920–4. Chief Instructor, Cairo Military School, 1925–8.

[1] Reginald Baliol Brett, 1852–1930. Liberal MP, 1880–5. Secretary to the Office of Works, 1895–1902. 2nd Viscount Esher, 1899. A permanent member of the Committee of Imperial Defence, 1905–18. In 1915 he was sent to Paris at the head of a British Mission, where he served as a Liaison Officer between the British and French War Offices.

[2] Henry Hughes Wilson, 1864–1922. Entered Army, 1884. Director of Military Operations, War Office, 1910–14. Lieutenant-General, 1914. Chief liaison officer with the French Army, January 1915. Knighted, 1915. Commanded the 4th Corps, 1916. Chief of the Imperial General Staff, 1918–22. Field Marshal, July 1919. Created Baronet, August 1919, when he received the thanks of Parliament and a grant of £10,000 for his contribution to the war. Ulster Unionist MP, 1922. Shot dead by two Sinn Feiners on the steps of his London house.

[3] Francis Leveson Bertie, 1844–1919. Second son of 6th Earl of Abingdon; uncle of Lady Gwendeline Churchill. Entered the Foreign Office, 1863. Knighted, 1902. British Ambassador, Rome, 1903–5; Paris, 1905–18. Created Baron Bertie of Thame, 1915. Created Viscount, 1918.

[4] For some months three German prisoners-of-war had been working at Lullenden, draining land and trenching a field for potatoes. Churchill paid them 25/- a week, and housed them. For their fate, see Churchill's letter to H E Cooke, of 15 March 1918.

[5] Lord Ivor Spencer-Churchill, 1898–1956. Younger son of the 9th Duke of Marlborough. Educated at Eton and Magdalen College, Oxford. Lieutenant, Royal Army Service Corps, 1917–18. Awarded the Légion d'Honneur, 1918.

He delights to see the aeroplanes shot at. You seem to have been having all the danger in England.

Tender & Fondest love my sweet Clemmie.

Your ever devoted & loving husband
W

Lord Esher to Sir Douglas Haig: extract

(*Sir Philip Sassoon papers*)

30 May 1917 Paris

My dear Douglas,

A true appreciation of Winston Churchill,—of his potential uses,—is a difficult matter.

The degree in which his clever but unbalanced mind will in future fulfil its responsibilities is very speculative.

He handles great subjects in rhythmical language, and becomes quickly enslaved by his own phrases.

He deceives himself into the belief that he takes broad views, when his mind is fixed upon one comparatively small aspect of the question.

At this moment he is captured by the picture of what *1918* may bring forth in the shape of accumulated reserves of men and material, poured out from England in one great and final effort; while, at the same time a million Americans sweep over Holland on to the German flank.

He fails to grasp the meaning to France, to England, to Europe, of a postponement of effort—through the long summer that was crammed full of artificial expectations—and a still longer winter. . . .

It seems not unlikely that L George will put Winston into the Government, or give him some showy position. There have been pourparlers between LG and the Tories on the subject: but Winston told me no details. He appeals to L George, because he can strike ideas into colour and imagery. But his ideas are 'Transpontine' that is to say too melodramatic; and nothing but steadiness and the very coolest appreciation of the factors in the problems of the war and its settlement can give us the position we ought to occupy at the War's end. . . .

The power of Winston for good and evil is, I should say, very considerable.

His temperament is of wax and quicksilver, and this strange toy amuses and fascinates L George, who likes and fears him.

You will find much that he has to say about the navy both interesting and valuable. All that he has to say about the army valueless. It may be worth your while to instruct him. Of this you will be the best judge.

To me he appears not as a statesman, but as a politician of keen intelligence lacking in those puissant qualities that are essential in a man who is to conduct the business of our country through the coming year. I hope therefore that he may remain outside the Government.

June 1917

Lord Rothermere to David Lloyd George

(*Lloyd George papers*)

[June 1917] Ritz Hotel
Confidential London

Dear Prime Minister,

Alick Murray[1] and I have been together this afternoon and curiously enough he is of the same opinion as myself, and you know I hold the view very strongly that if you saw your way to appoint Winston to the Air Board it would by reason of his driving power be popular particularly under yourself as you alone of all his friends can control him. Misfortune has chastened him. He really is very attached to you and it seems a calamity that his knowledge and energy should be lost to the nation at this crisis.

If you make this appointment you can rely upon me using all the influence I have to support it.

Alick sends his love and when you have time to turn round he is coming to see you.

Always yours faithfully
Rothermere

Frederick Guest to David Lloyd George: extract

(*Lloyd George papers*)

1 June 1917 10 Downing Street

Winston returns Sunday and I have therefore not written to him on the lines you indicated. I suggest that you let me see him on his arrival and tell him how matters stand before other influences have opportunity to operate.

[1] Alexander William Charles Oliphant Murray, 1870–1920. Liberal MP, 1900–5; 1906–10; 1910–12. Scottish Liberal Whip, 1906–9. Under-Secretary of State for India, 1909. Chief Liberal Whip, 1909–12. Created Baron Murray of Elibank, 1912. Director of Recruiting for Munition Works, 1915–16.

Lord Charles Beresford[1] *to Andrew Bonar Law*

(*Bonar Law papers*)

2 June 1917
Personal

My dear Bonar Law,

Please excuse dictation.

There is a rumour about, and a notice in the paper that Winston Churchill is to receive an appointment in the Government. I sincerely hope this is not true, and that the Unionist members will put their faces steadily against it.

I am writing to you, as head of the Unionist Party, to say that if Winston Churchill is appointed, I have a small Committee of well known and influential men, and we intend to hold meetings all over the country calling attention to Winston Churchill's career.

Personally, I have no animus against him at all, in fact when we meet we speak and laugh, but I have the most violent feeling with regard to his ever being in office again.

I need not enumerate to you the failure of Antwerp, Gallipoli, for which he is mainly responsible, the failure in administration of all his previous offices, the manner in which he turned the Navy upside-down by his autocratic methods, and, with Fisher, ruled it with favouritism and espionage.

I have papers and proofs which I shall make public, and we will stop at nothing for the sake of the country, if Winston Churchill again gets office.

You probably know his orders to the Fleet at the time of the Ulster Rebellion, when he got one Admiral, (Bayly[2]) to agree to them. The other Admirals and officers of the Fleet went to Bayly and told him that if he ordered them to fire on Belfast, they would refuse to obey his orders; in other words, he created a mutiny in the Fleet.

I am sorry to interrupt you in the middle of your work. I have seen several Editors of important papers, and they have promised to back us up in anything we do to avoid this scandal and danger to the State.

I have had letters from officers of the Army and Navy, and some of them have come to see me this morning. They are perfectly aghast at the idea of

[1] Charles William de la Poer Beresford, 1846–1919. Entered Navy, 1859. Conservative MP, 1874–80; 1885–9; 1897–1900; 1902; 1910–16. Knighted, 1903. Commanded the Mediterranean Fleet, 1905–7; the Channel Fleet, 1907–9. Retired from the Navy, 1911. Created Baron, 1916.

[2] Lewis Bayly, 1857–1938. Entered Navy, 1870. Vice-Admiral commanding the 3rd Battle Squadron, 1913–14. Knighted, 1914. Commanded the 1st Battle Squadron, 1914–15. Commander-in-Chief of the Western Approaches, 1915–19. Admiral, 1917.

Winston Churchill holding any kind of office at the present moment. These officers represent the feeling throughout both services.

Yours very sincerely,
Charles Beresford

Christopher Addison to David Lloyd George: extract

(*Lloyd George papers*)

4 June 1917 Ministry of Munitions

Air Board. I feel that we should get Winston in & the more it is talked about the more opportunity there is for opposition to gather. I should advise acting quickly in this so as to get the ice broken. . . . *Myself*. . . . Give me three weeks and I could get the estimates over & shape things here through my new Board of Directors so as to pave the way for Winston if you wished him to follow me.

Lord Curzon to Andrew Bonar Law

(*Bonar Law papers*)

4 June 1917 1 Carlton House Terrace

My dear Bonar,

Possibly there may be no truth in what we read in the papers as to Govt reconstruction e.g. Addison in the War Cabinet! Churchill at Air Board & so on. I just write a line to say that I hope none of these steps if contemplated will be done behind our backs.

As you know some of us myself included only joined Ll G on the distinct understanding that W Ch was not to be a member of the Govt—It is on record and to the pledge I and I think all my colleagues adhere.

Again if it is necessary to remove Addison from Munitions, as to which I know nothing, I can see no reason why he should be lifted up to War Cabinet to which he would add neither any views nor strength.

Yours ever
Curzon

Major-General J. E. B. Seely to Sir Archibald Sinclair

(Sinclair papers)

5 June 1917

Winston came to lunch and dinner the other day. He was very fit and much more cheerful than formerly.

General Smuts[1] *to David Lloyd George*

(Lloyd George papers)

6 June 1917 Savoy Hotel
Personal London

Dear Mr Lloyd George,

At the request of Capt Guest I saw Churchill last night and expressed to him my views that if Air was offered to him instead of Munitions (which you had previously mentioned to him) he should accept it. I pointed out that Munitions had become somewhat of a routine department while Air offered great scope to his constructive ability and initiative, and that with effective help from America our aerial effort might yet become of decisive importance not only in the anti-submarine campaign but also on the Western front in the next twelve months.

The result is that, although he prefers Munitions, he will accept an offer of Air on the assumption that real scope is given him and that he must control the higher patronage in the Air service.

In spite of the strong party opposition to this appointment, I think you will do the country a real service by appointing a man of his calibre to this department, the vital importance of which will more and more appear.

Yours sincerely
J. C. Smuts

[1] Jan Christian Smuts, 1870–1950. Born in Cape Colony. General, commanding Boer Commando Forces, Cape Colony, 1901. Colonial Secretary, Transvaal, 1907. Minister of Defence, Union of South Africa, 1910–20. Second-in-Command of the South African forces that defeated the Germans in South-West Africa, July 1915. Honorary Lieutenant-General commanding the imperial forces in East Africa, 1916–17. South African Representative at the Imperial War Cabinet, 1917 and 1918. Prime Minister of South Africa, 1919–24. Minister of Justice, 1933–9. Prime Minister, 1939–48. Field Marshal, 1941. OM, 1947.

Sir George Younger[1] *to David Lloyd George*

(*Lloyd George papers*)

8 June 1917

Dear Lloyd George

I do trust there is no foundation for the persistent rumour that Winston is to join the Government. I am seriously afraid that such an appointment would strain to breaking point the Unionist Party's loyalty to you. His unfortunate record, the utter futility of his criticisms of your War Policy at the last Secret Session, and his grave responsibility for two of the greatest disasters in the War have accentuated the distrust of him which has prevailed both in the House and outside of it for a long time past, and I feel certain that his inclusion in the Government would prove disastrous to its fortunes. I believe the Unionist Party in the House would unanimously back this opinion and I am certain that our great organisations in the country of which, as you know, I am Chairman would strongly assert it.

I have never in my life passed through a time of greater anxiety politically than during the last two or three months. I have been sitting on the safety valve all the time and up to now have succeeded in securing at least an official acceptance of the Government's Policy.

The last difficulty was created by the Franchise Bill and Bonar Law will be able to tell you by what a narrow squeak I managed to secure acceptance of the general principles of that Measure, with the result that no amendment of any kind against its main principles is being moved by the Unionist organisation.

To test their loyalty so soon again would certainly invite serious trouble, and I cannot be responsible for the result.

It would be an impertinence on my part to interfere in any way with your choice of Ministers, but it is my bounden duty to tell you, as I told Bonar Law last week, that I am satisfied from the present temper of the Unionists in the country that the greatest care is necessary not to put any further strain on their loyalty.

I write you direct as I do not care to trouble Bonar with letters just now.

Yours sincerely
Geo. Younger

[1] George Younger, 1851–1929. President of the National Union of Conservative Associations in Scotland, 1904. Conservative MP, 1906–22. Created Baronet, 1911. Chairman of the Conservative Party Organization, 1916–23. Treasurer of the Conservative Party, 1923–9. Created Viscount, 1923. Chairman, George Younger & Sons, Brewers, Ltd.

Lord Derby[1] *to David Lloyd George*

(*Derby papers*)

8 June 1917 Derby House
Confidential

Dear Prime Minister,

I much appreciated my talk with you this afternoon and I know you do not resent one saying exactly what one thinks. As to whether Winston Churchill will strengthen your Government or the reverse we must agree to differ as I do not think either could convince the other. I am really anxious to serve you and your Government and therefore feel you will forgive me if I put before you somewhat bluntly the position as it concerns me as head of the War Office.

If Winston Churchill is only to be a second Lord Cowdray[2] I do not mind if he will only do his work half as well. Lord Cowdray has done a real amount of good for the Air Service and has worked most cordially with the War Office without in any way attempting to interfere with the administration of that office.

While I regret Winston Churchill's inclusion in the Government—if he be included—as being a source of weakness I feel that it would not affect the War Office if it was clearly understood: (1) that he was not a member of the War Cabinet and did not attend any meetings unless specially summoned for business connected with the Board;
(2) that his duties as Chairman of the Board were the same as those of Lord Cowdray and that he had nothing to do with either personnel, tactics or the nomination of the War Office representatives on the Board; and
(3) that he received no War Office telegrams other than those which were in any way connected with his particular department.

I gathered from you this afternoon that the conditions I have named were certainly those on which you would understand that he should enter the

[1] Edward George Villiers Stanley, 1865–1948. Conservative MP, 1892–1906. Postmaster, General, 1903–5. 17th Earl of Derby, 1908. Director-General of Recruiting, October 1915. Under-Secretary of State at the War Office, July–December 1916. Secretary of State for War, December 1916–18. Ambassador to France, 1918–20. Secretary of State for War, 1922–4. Clementine Churchill wrote to her husband about Lord Derby, on 3 February 1922: 'People think he is bluff & independent & John Bullish but he is really a fat sneak.'

[2] Weetman Dickinson Pearson, 1856–1927. Head of the firm of S Pearson & Son Ltd, engineering contractors. Completed the Blackwall Tunnel under the Thames, 1894; and created Baronet at the opening ceremony. Liberal MP for Colchester, 1895–1910. Created Baron Cowdray, 1910. He had a controlling interest in the Mexican oilfields. Supervised the construction of the Gretna Green munitions factory, 1915–16. Created Viscount, 1917. President of the Air Board January–November 1917. His youngest son was killed in action on 6 September 1914. In 1905 his eldest son had married Churchill's cousin, Agnes, daughter of Lord Edward Spencer-Churchill.

Government and that being so as far as my own office is concerned I personally can offer no objection, though I am bound to say I think there is a big 'if' in the question that is *if* Winston Churchill will ever consent to occupy a comparatively minor position and do his own work without interfering with other people's. Perhaps you would let me know on Monday when I see you if I am right in my statement as to what your views on the position are.

You might let me know if you could give me a few minutes on Monday afternoon any time most convenient to yourself.

Yours sincerely
Derby

Lord Curzon to David Lloyd George

(*Lloyd George papers*)

8 June 1917 1 Carlton House Terrace

My dear Prime Minister,

May I again and for the last time urge you to think well before you make the appointment (W Ch) which we have more than once discussed? It will be an appointment intensely unpopular with many of your chief colleagues—in the opinions of some of whom it will lead to the disruption of the Govt at an early date—even if it does not lead as it may well do to resignations now.

Derby, who opened the subject to me of his own accord this evening & who has spoken to you, tells me that it will be intensely unpopular in the Army.

I have reason to believe the same of the Navy.

Is it worthwhile to incur all these risks and to override some of those who are your most faithful colleagues & allies merely in order to silence a possible tribune of the people whom in my judgment the people will absolutely decline to follow?

He is a potential danger in opposition. In the opinion of all of us he will as a member of the Govt be an active danger in our midst.

Yours sincerely
Curzon

Lord Derby to Sir Douglas Haig: extract

(Derby papers)

8 June 1917

There is rather bitter political controversy at the present moment in this country over the subject of the possible appointment of Winston Churchill to the Chairmanship of the Air Board. Personally I think his inclusion in any Government means its eventual downfall but the Prime Minister does not hold these views and personally I do not much mind his inclusion as long as he does not in any way interfere with the War and I hope that such conditions will be imposed upon him as will prevent that.

Winston S. Churchill to Andrew Bonar Law

(Bonar Law papers)

8 June 1917

33 Eccleston Square
S.W.1

My dear Bonar,

I am profoundly grieved to read in this morning's newspapers that yr hopes have been shattered & that your gallant son has paid a soldiers' debt. The uncertainty & the alternating feelings of relief & of despair must have added if it were possible to the pain & sorrow of your loss. Accept my heartfelt sympathy. I trust you will be able to find in gt responsibilities & constant work some means of occupying yr thoughts. Words are vain I know but I thought you wd not mind my writing to tell you how much I feel for you all in this solemn & heartbreaking hour.

Please don't answer.

Yours vy sincerely,
Winston S. Churchill

Lord Cowdray to David Lloyd George

(Lloyd George papers)

9 June 1917

Air Board

Private & Confidential

My dear Prime Minister,

I feel I ought to place the following facts and fears before you, viz:—

(a) The Air Board today is now turning out each week as many aircraft as were turned out in a month this time last year.

(b) By the end of the year it will be turning out fully ten times as many aircraft as it was during the summer months of 1916.
(c) The output of magnificent reliable aircraft, not only infinitely superior to the Germans, as regards quantity but also as to quality, will have undreamt of successes not only on the front but also (6 to 7 months hence) from long distance bombing.
(d) Winston will see that he, and he alone, gets all the credit from the very brilliant achievements of the Air Services which may have a very material effect on the duration & success of the war.
(e) Apart from every other consideration is it wise for you to have, as one of your Ministers, a dangerously ambitious man who will, I believe be able to point to achievements by the Air Services (provided he does not upset the programme now being worked to) that have largely revolutionised the war and being the means of bringing about the peace.
(f) The success would I fear, lead him to think that he was the most important man (in the eyes of the country) in the Government & therefore the proper man to make a bid for the Premiership.

Forgive this screed which please destroy. It is written to point out a possible and grave danger, both to the country & to yourself

Yours v. sincerely
Cowdray

Sir George Younger to David Lloyd George

(*Lloyd George papers*)

9 June 1917 17 Eaton Square

Dear Lloyd George,

I hadn't long to wait for conclusive proof of the correctness of the opinion expressed in my letter of yesterday morning.

In the afternoon there was a meeting of the National Unionist Council to consider the Executive's Report on the Franchise Bill. There are 300 delegates drawn from every constituency in England and Wales, and the Caxton Hall was crowded. Before the business began one of the delegates jumped up and asked the Chairman (Sir Harry Samuel[1]) whether it was true that Winston had joined the Government. He was stopped by Samuel and no

[1] Harry Simon Samuel, 1853–1934. Of Jewish descent. Partner in the firm of Montefiore Co until 1884. Conservative MP, 1895–1906 and 1910–22. Knighted, 1903. Privy Councillor, 1916. Chairman of the National Unionist Council of Constituency Associations.

reply was given. At the very end of the meeting—not too easy a meeting to guide as it was asked to accept and approve of the Executive's acceptance of the principles of the Franchise Bill—this man jumped up again and moved that it would be 'an insult to the Navy and Army if W were to join the Government'. It was cheered and at once seconded and Samuel put it to the meeting. This was quite irregular as no such resolution ought to have been put without proper notice, but it was carried amidst cheers and with only two hands held up in dissent.

I feel that you ought to know this.

Yours sincerely
Geo. Younger

Walter Long[1] to David Lloyd George

(Lloyd George papers)

10 June 1917 Colonial Office

. . . As regards W Churchill & the Gov I have made enquiries & from what E Talbot[2] tells me I am satisfied it would bring about a very grave situation in our Party & in these circumstances I am afraid I could not alter the view I expressed to you on Friday.

Lord Northcliffe to Winston S. Churchill: telegram

13 June 1917 Hotel Gotham
New York

Many congratulations on your appointment.[3]

[1] Walter Hume Long, 1854–1924. Conservative MP, 1880–1921. President of the Local Government Board, 1900–5. Chief Secretary, Ireland, 1905. Created the Union Defence League, the leading anti-Home Rule organization, 1907–14. President of the Local Government Board, May 1915–December 1916. Under-Secretary of State for the Colonies, 1916–19. First Lord of the Admiralty, 1919–21. Created Viscount, 1921.

[2] Lord Edmund Bernard Fitzalan Howard, 1855–1947. 3rd son of the 14th Duke of Norfolk. Assumed the name of Talbot, 1876. Adjutant, Middlesex Yeomanry, 1883–8; Lieutenant-Colonel, 11th Hussars, 1900. Conservative MP for Chichester, 1894–1921. A Junior Lord of the Treasury, 1905. Chief Unionist Whip, 1913–21. Parliamentary Under-Secretary, Treasury, 1915–21. Created Viscount Fitzalan of Derwent, 1921. Viceroy and Lord Lieutenant of Ireland, 1921–2.

[3] Lord Northcliffe's congratulations were premature. Churchill had not been appointed to the Air Board, and remained outside the Government.

Frederick Guest to David Lloyd George

(Lloyd George papers)

18 June 1917

Dear Prime Minister,

I made a tentative proposal to Winston on the grounds of the Chancellorship of the Duchy with elaborated uses & functions but without success.

He wished me to say that he regards the offer as completely friendly.

He feels however that he could neither serve *a national purpose* nor *your purpose* by being included in this manner.

He is prepared to forego & forget all political considerations in order to help to beat the 'Hun' in either of the following capacities.

1. To assist you in council in the War Cabinet, if necessary without salary.
2. To accept charge & responsibility for any War Department, as long as he has powers to actively assist in the defeat of the enemy.

I have used my utmost powers of persuasion but can do no more in this direction. My only comment on the situation is that your will & influence with your Tory colleagues is greater than you have credited yourself with and that sooner or later you will have to test it—why not now?

I have the strongest reasons to believe that the Tories mean to support your leadership even at the expense of their personal feelings.

Yours sincerely
Frederick Guest

Winston S. Churchill to Sir Archibald Sinclair

(Thurso papers)

21 June 1917 33 Eccleston Square

Archie dear—vy many thanks for yr letter & for the salmon. Its succulence revived memories of our banquet to 'Windy Bill'[1] at Lawrence Farm.

I am going on Thursday for a visit to the French & English fronts & expect to be away the best part of a fortnight. Thereafter we will meet (DV) in London town, & I will tell you a good many things wh are now too secret to put down even in a letter to you.

Yours always
W

[1] Major-General Furse (see p. 17, note 2).

July 1917

Winston S. Churchill: memorandum[1]

(*Churchill papers: 8/104*)

7 July 1917
Very Secret

NAVAL WAR POLICY, 1917

I.

The traditional war policy of the Admiralty grew up during the prolonged wars and antagonisms with France. It consisted in establishing immediately upon the outbreak of war a close blockade of the enemy's ports and naval bases by means of flotillas of strong small craft supported by cruisers with superior battle fleets in reserve. The experience of 200 years had led all naval strategists to agree on this fundamental principle, 'Our first line of defence is the enemy's ports.'

When the torpedo was invented, the French tried to frustrate this well-known British policy by building large numbers of torpedo-boats, and the Admiralty retorted at once by building torpedo-boat destroyers. These destroyers fulfilled two conditions, (*a*) they were large enough to keep the seas in most weathers and to operate across the Channel for sufficient periods, (*b*) their guns were heavy enough to destroy or dominate the French torpedo-boats. Thus, in spite of the advent of the torpedo, we preserved our power to maintain stronger flotillas in close proximity to the enemy's naval bases. Meanwhile, all along the South coast of England a series of fortified torpedo-proof harbours in the neighbourhood of our great naval establishments afforded safe, close, and convenient stations for our battle fleets and other supporting vessels when not actually at sea.

Early in the present century our enemy for the first time became not France, but Germany, and our naval strategic front shifted from the South to the East coast and from the Channel to the North Sea. But although the

[1] This memorandum was printed for the War Cabinet. Churchill himself entered the Cabinet (but not the War Cabinet) ten days after this memorandum was written. At that time the War Cabinet consisted of seven members, Lloyd George, Bonar Law, Lord Curzon, Arthur Henderson (until August 1917), Lord Milner, General Smuts and G N Barnes.

enemy, the front, and the theatre had changed, the sound principle of British naval strategy still held good. Our first line of defence was considered to be the enemy's ports. The Admiralty policy was still a close blockade of those ports by means of stronger flotillas properly supported by cruisers and ultimately by the battle fleets.

2. It was not to be expected that our arrangements on this new front could rapidly reach the same degree of perfection as the conflicts of so many generations had achieved in the Channel; and so far as our naval bases were concerned, we were still in the process of transition when the great war began. More serious, however, was the effect of the change on the utility of our destroyers. Instead of operating at distances of from 20 or 60 miles across the Channel with their supporting ships close at hand in safe harbours, they were now called upon to operate in the Heligoland Bight, across 240 miles of sea, and with no suitable bases for their supporting battle fleet nearer than the Thames or the Forth. Nevertheless, the Admiralty continued to adhere to their traditional strategic principle, and their war plans up till 1911 contemplated the close blockade of the enemy's ports immediately upon the declaration of war. Our destroyers were constructed with ever increasing sea-keeping qualities and with a great superiority of gun power. The Germans, on the other hand, adhered to the French conception of the torpedo boat as a means of attack upon our large ships. While we relied in our destroyer construction principally on gun power and sea-keeping qualities, they relied upon the torpedo and high speed in fair weather opportunities. But the much greater distances over which our destroyers had now to operate across the North Sea immensely reduced their effectiveness. Whereas across the Channel they could work in two reliefs, they required three across the North Sea. Therefore only one-third instead of one-half of our fighting flotillas could be available at any given moment. Against this third the enemy could at any moment bring his whole force. In order to carry out our old strategic policy from our Home bases we should have required flotillas at least three and probably four times as strong as those of Germany. This superiority we had not got and were not likely to get.

3. Therefore from shortly before 1905 when the French agreement was signed, down to the Agadir crisis in 1911, the Admiralty made plans to capture one or other of the German islands. On this it was intended to establish an oversea base at which from the beginning of the war our blockade flotillas could be replenished and could rest, and which as war progressed would have developed into a great advanced citadel of our sea power. In this way, therefore, the Admiralty would still have carried out their traditional war policy of beating the enemy's flotillas and light craft into his ports and maintaining a constant close blockade.

4. These considerations were not lost upon the Germans. They greatly increased the fortifications of Heligoland, and they proceeded to fortify one after another such of the Frisian Islands as were in any way suitable for our purposes. At the same time a new and vital factor appeared upon the scene—the submarine. The submarine not only rendered the capture and maintenance of an oversea base or bases far more difficult and, as some authorities hold, impossible, but it threatened with destruction our cruisers and battleships without whose constant support our flotillas would easily have been destroyed by the enemy's cruisers.

5. This was the situation in October 1911 when immediately after the Agadir crisis the Board of Admiralty was completely changed. Seeing that we had not for the time being the numerical force of destroyers able to master the enemy's destroyers in his home waters, nor the power to support our flotillas with heavy ships, and having regard also to the difficulty and hazard in all the circumstances of storming and capturing one of his fortified islands, the new Board revised altogether the War Plans and substituted, with the full concurrence of our principal commanders afloat, the policy of distant blockade set up in the Admiralty War Orders and so rigidly adhered to ever since.

6. The policy of distant blockade was not adopted from choice, but from necessity. It implied no repudiation on the part of the Admiralty of their fundamental principle of aggressive naval strategy, but only a temporary abandonment of it in the face of unsolved practical difficulties; and it was intended, both before and after the declaration of war, that every effort should be made to overcome those difficulties. It was rightly foreseen that by closing the exits from the North Sea into the Atlantic Ocean, German commerce would be almost completely cut off from the world. It was expected that the economic and financial pressure resulting from such a blockade would fatally injure the German power to carry on a war. It was hoped that this pressure would compel the German fleet to come out and fight, not in his own defended waters, but at a great numerical disadvantage in the open sea. It was believed that we could continue meanwhile to enjoy the full command of the seas without danger to our sea communications or to the movement of our armies, and that the British Isles could be kept safe from invasion. There was then no reason to suppose that these conditions would not continue indefinitely with undiminished advantage to ourselves and increasing pressure upon the enemy. So far as all surface vessels are concerned, most of these expectations have been confirmed by experience.

7. But a number of profoundly important changes have taken place in the naval situation since these plans were made. The submarine attack upon commerce ruptures the basis upon which the policy of 'distant blockade' and still more the policy of 'distant blockade and nothing else' stand. The sinkings

by submarines have already affected, and will continually affect, our power to carry on the war. They are perhaps at this moment the main cause of the prolongation of the struggle. It is absurd, for this and many other reasons, to speak of carrying on this war as if time might not be a decisive factor against us. It has also been proved that the economic pressure of our distant blockade upon Germany is not in itself sufficient to prevent the enemy from carrying on the war by land or to force him to come out and fight at sea. He rightly prefers to remain in his defended waters, enjoying the command of the Baltic, neutralising and containing Allied forces at least four times the strength of his own fleet, while ravaging all our sea communications with his submarines. On the other hand, we have been continually impressed with the obvious fact that we should only incur useless and possibly fatal losses by sending our present fast battle fleets naked into his defended waters, and we should thereby jeopardise all the solid advantages we now possess. We have, therefore, allowed ourselves to be driven by this new attack to purely defensive naval measures either of an active or passive character, such as eating less bread, ploughing up the land, cutting down the forests, dispersing thousands of guns on merchant ships, building more merchant ships for the submarines to sink, consuming hundreds of destroyers and thousands of small craft in escort and submarine hunting. These remedies may be good in themselves so far as they go: but the policy which dictates them is the negation of war.

8. In order to return to the old and definitely recognised policy of close and aggressive blockade, it is necessary to have ships which are comparatively immune from the torpedo, and which can therefore operate freely in the enemy's waters to support our flotillas and light craft. Protection against the torpedo, and to a large extent against the moored or floating mine, can be obtained by building bulges of a special construction round the sides of ships. This was done in the monitors and in certain older ships, notably the 'Edgars', at the beginning of the war, with the direct intention of aggressive action. These developments have not been proceeded with, but the experience gained since enables better bulge protection to be now devised than was then possible. And recently even with our first design of protection, the 'Grafton' (one of the Edgars) successfully withstood a direct hit amidships by a torpedo and proceeded on her course with practically undiminished speed.

9. The objection to applying these methods of protection to the more modern and more powerful ships of the Fleet has been the great reduction of speed which the increased breadth entails. Our superiority at the outset of the war was not sufficient to warrant any serious subtraction of first-class units from the Grand Fleet such as would be consequent upon their loss of speed if fitted with bulges. But as the war has progressed, the completion of many new

vessels of the greatest power, the concentration of all British Dreadnoughts in home waters, and, above all, the accession of the very powerful Navy of the United States—the third strongest Naval Power in the world—have vastly increased our margin of superiority.

10. Comparison of the Allied and enemy fleets shows that we now possess a preponderance in battleships and heavy cruisers of between 4 and 5 to 1. Moreover, our ships in every class are superior in size, gun power, and modernity. It is therefore possible to form *at least* two fleets, either of which could fight the German High Sea Fleet on favourable terms. One of these fleets should be a fast blue water fleet, like our present Grand Fleet, for maintaining the supremacy of the seas and oceans should the enemy emerge to challenge it; the other should be fitted with bulges and thus rendered comparatively torpedo proof, in order to discharge the functions of an Inshore Aggressive Fleet.

11. Specimen tables of both these fleets in comparison with the High Sea Fleet are appended. The best and fastest ships are taken to form the Blue Water Fleet, but their numbers are restricted to what is necessary for them to fight a battle in waters of their own choosing, and not close to the enemy's coasts. The Inshore Fleet is composed of second best ships with larger numbers of older vessels. Only the British, French, and American navies have been drawn upon, and any vessels obtained from Russia, Italy, or Japan would be additional.

12. It would be necessary, by a Naval Convention between all the Allies, to agree that whatever losses were incurred in the further stages of the war should be shared *pro rata,* so that if the losses fell unequally in particular navies, or if their ships were selected for the most dangerous duties, the relative strength of the various signatory Powers would not be affected at the close of the war.

13. The objects of inshore operations are to fight the enemy, to harass him constantly, to occupy and dominate his attention, to force him to recall many of his submarines for his own defence, to provoke him to engage in frequent action both with his flotillas and heavier vessels, and generally to beat him into port; and *thereafter* to mine him in closely with minefields so dense as to be a serious obstruction to submarines, and to keep him mined in by fighting and sinking any vessels he may send to sweep a channel. In short, to carry out, in spite of the submarine, and by means of special equipment, the old, well-recognised, true war policy of the Royal Navy.

14. It must here be observed that the policy lately adopted of scattering mines and sowing minefields a considerable distance out at sea, which are subsequently left unwatched and unguarded, is open to question. The enemy cannot be prevented from sweeping good broad channels through these mine-

fields which he charts carefully, and thereafter traverses with very little risk, either with submarines or surface vessels. We, on the other hand, are naturally shy of approaching our own minefields, and we do not know what channels he has swept through them. Our movements are therefore hampered, which is especially serious for the stronger fleet, while the enemy is not only not prevented from moving, but has his coast largely protected for him by our agency.

A minefield which is not watched and guarded is a barrier only to those who lay it.

15. Before describing in general terms the kind of inshore operations necessary to naval offensive, a new feature of naval warfare must be noted, viz, the submarine barrage. We rightly do not think it good enough to send 3,000,000*l.* vessels unprotected against torpedoes into submarine-infested areas. It is a fair conclusion that the enemy, with his fewer ships, shares our views. The display of submarines, therefore, acts as an effective deterrent on the movement of the best ships. Undetected, submarines are an ambuscade. Observed, they are a veto. (This was shown, on the 25th December, 1914, to some extent, when Commodore Tyrwhitt[1] remained for several hours in the Heligoland Bight during the raid on Cuxhaven, shielded only by a few submarines.) But now scores of submarines are available instead of eight or ten; and therefore it is possible, by interposing a 'barrage', or curtain of submarines, to isolate *pro tem* a particular area in which operations are to proceed, and to make it not worth while for the enemy's best ships to try to interfere with them.

The respective rôles of minefields and submarines, separately and in conjunction, require most careful co-ordination, and the difficulties are well known. But either or both may be made to serve the same purpose, viz, keeping the enemy's best ships at a distance whilst a particular job is being done.

It should be realised that the large numbers of submarines now available offer altogether new possibilities both to us and the enemy for holding off the main fleets while landing operations are in progress. Invasion problems as well as the taking of small islands are both affected.

16. To sum up, the situation which led to the policy of the distant blockade has now been modified in at least four fundamental conditions favourable or unfavourable. On the one hand—

[1] Reginald Yorke Tyrwhitt, 1870–1951. Entered Navy, 1883. Commodore commanding Destroyer Flotillas of the First Fleet, 1913–18. Knighted, 1917. Created Baronet, 1919. Commanded the Third Light Cruiser Squadron, Mediterranean, 1921–2. Commanding Officer, Coast of Scotland, 1923–5. Commander-in-Chief, China Station, 1927–9. Admiral, 1929. Commander-in-Chief, the Nore, 1930–3. Admiral of the Fleet, 1934.

(*a*) The pressure of the blockade has not caused the enemy either to make peace or to come out and fight at sea, and there is no evidence that he will do so.

(*b*) The submarine attack on our commerce imposes a time-limit on our power to continue the war.

On the other—

(*c*) Our naval force has so greatly increased that it is possible to provide a powerful fleet for inshore action without prejudice to the strength of the fleet needed to secure the general command of the seas.

(*d*) Our numerical superiority in destroyers (with the Americans) has now greatly increased, and further there is the 'submarine barrage' facilitating landings. It is therefore at once necessary and possible to resume the policy of close and aggressive blockade as an addition to and not as a substitute for our existing policy.

But in order that this may be done, it is indispensable to secure by one method or another a serviceable overseas base. Without this no naval offensive in any effective form is possible.

The relative weight of broadside from the primary guns alone of these three fleets is approximately as follows:—

Allied Bluewater Fleet.	German.	Allied Inshore Fleet.
430,000 lb.	160,000 lb.	220,000 lb.

II.

17. All attempts to unfold the method of a naval offensive must, at this stage, be tentative and general. It is to be observed that the problem is one the details of which must be solved by naval officers. Further, unless naval commanders of high repute can be found able and willing to devise, support, and execute such schemes *con amore*, no action against the enemy is possible. It is for the navy to provide the solution; and if they are finally convinced that no naval offensive is practicable, then the considerations as to the reduction of naval strength set forth in the concluding paragraph will apply. It is therefore only possible to give certain general indications of a suggestive character.

18. The object is to find a means of fighting and compelling the enemy to

fight and so to cow his naval forces, and then as the result of the fighting to establish a far greater control of all sea approaches to his harbours. This must be kept steadily in view. It is probable that the enemy would not tolerate the laying and maintenance of watched minefields in fairly close proximity to his debouches, and that therefore the attempt to do so would be strenuously resisted. This resistance would bring about continuous and severe action between the available forces, leading directly to a decision. But let us see what the enemy could do in this, the simplest case. The minefield would be laid overnight. If he sent out sweepers, our destroyers would sink them. If he sent out destroyer flotillas, our flotillas would engage them. This is what we want. If his fast light cruisers intervened, we should meet him with ours—far more numerous. If the waters were dangerous for one side, they could be made equally dangerous for the other.

If he brings up his heavy ships, he is in this dilemma: That the old will not be strong enough to face the watching squadrons of our Inshore Fleet, and that the new are too valuable to risk on our submarine barrage and minefields. Therefore, unless he has himself got ships strong enough to fight our Inshore Fleet, so protected by bulges as not to be afraid of operating in dangerous waters, he will be unable to support his flotillas, and, unsupported, they will certainly be beaten. And if his flotillas are beaten, he is beaten.

19. But since we seek to operate with flotillas at a distance of 250 miles from our home bases, while the enemy would be approximately 50 miles from his, we should, as already explained, be at a disadvantage, which would go far to diminish, though not by any means to remove, our large numerical superiority. The disadvantage would not prevent us from asserting our deadweight superiority for several weeks at a time. But it would impose an undue strain if such a position had to be indefinitely maintained. Decisive results in prolonged fighting are only to be obtained from the possession of an oversea base or bases, where our flotillas of destroyers, submarines, and small craft could refuel and rest without the need of returning across the North Sea to the Humber, Harwich, and the Thames. The capture or occupation of such oversea bases is, in itself, a supreme act of naval or amphibious aggression against the enemy. It doubles or trebles the obligation on him to prevent it; and if a base is taken and held, it opens up a whole series of advantageous possibilities, both military and aerial, additional to the naval advantages arising from this argument. These will be indicated later.

20. We have now to consider the possibilities of obtaining an oversea base or bases.

Holland and Denmark, if they entered the war on our side, or alternatively were violated by Germany, would afford without fighting a variety of bases, of which the best is probably the Texel. But this argument does not attempt to deal with such international possibilities or with the employment of large armies, and is confined to operations primarily naval in their character. No landing on the mainland of Germany or in Denmark is recommended, unless oversea bases have already been secured and the enemy's naval forces completely beaten and shut out from the North Sea by aggressive minefields. Therefore, Schleswig-Holstein and Oldenburg are also alike excluded in the first instance. There remain only the Frisian Islands and Heligoland. Of these islands, which, with Heligoland, number approximately 17, only three are suitable, viz, Sylt, Borkum, and Heligoland. Of these, Heligoland, though remote from all danger of land gunfire, is the most difficult to take and miserably small when taken. But both Sylt and Borkum present very high qualifications, ie,—

(*a*) They cannot be attacked from the mainland, except across several miles of sand intersected by channels, the whole flooded twice daily by the tide. This means that they cannot be attacked at all, except in boats and from the sea.

(*b*) They cannot be bombarded at any point by heavy howitzers or field guns.

(*c*) They contain deep water anchorages (6 to 8 fathoms), sheltered in all weathers, out of range of howitzers or field guns, and

(*d*) They are large enough to give ample elbow room for all our purposes once we have gained them.[1]

21. Some comparison between these islands may here be made (all distances are in sea miles—2,000 yards). Sylt, the northern island, is approximately 20 miles long, and varies from 2 miles to $\frac{1}{2}$ a mile in width. Borkum is approximately $5\frac{3}{4}$ miles in length by $3\frac{1}{2}$ in breadth. Sylt is less strongly fortified than Borkum, and its great length must be utterly disproportionate to any garrison which it contains. Therefore the capture of Sylt ought not to present insuperable difficulties. Borkum is more compact, more heavily fortified, and probably much more strongly garrisoned. On the other hand, the anchorage of Sylt for small draught vessels is on the landward side of the island and nearer to the mainland than the anchorage of Borkum.

Lister Deep, the heavy draught anchorage of Sylt is about 26,000 yards from the mainland, but is only an open roadstead. There is plenty of sheltered

[1] In advocating the capture of either Sylt or Borkum, Churchill was reviving one of the schemes prepared during his earlier wartime work at the Admiralty between August 1914 and May 1915. He had first explained it to the War Council on 1 December 1914. On 2 December 1914 he set out a detailed plan for the capture of Sylt in an Admiralty memorandum, and on 7 January 1915 he had informed Asquith that Borkum would be taken 'as soon as arrangements can be made'. But neither the attack on Sylt or on Borkum was ever put into effect, having both been eclipsed by the Dardanelles operation.

water north and north-east of the island 14,000 yards distant from the mainland. An air station in Sylt in the neighbourhood of Rote Kliff (about the middle of the island) would be 24,000 yards from the mainland, or the German island of Fohr. It would be an 85 miles' flight to Wilhelmshaven, 50 to Heligoland, and just under 60 to the mouth of the Elbe.

The anchorage of Borkum is 30,000 yards from the mainland of Germany; and an air station in the northern part of the island would be the same distance from German soil. It would be within 50 miles' flight of Wilhelmshaven, 55 from Heligoland, and 60 from the mouth of the Elbe.

The capture of Sylt would threaten Schleswig and react on Denmark; and the capture of Borkum would threaten Emden and Oldenburg and react on Holland. Borkum is about 240 miles and Sylt about 310 from Harwich.

Both islands are of the highest strategic value. On the whole Borkum is more worth having, though Sylt is the easier to get.

The storming and capture of any of these Frisian Islands constitutes a difficult feat of arms. But the operations are on a small scale compared to such immense enterprises as the capture of the Vimy or the Messines Ridges. The numbers of men involved are inconsiderable, and this argument proceeds on the basis that no naval unit necessary for our main supremacy at sea will, at any period, be endangered. On the other hand, failure would be clear-cut and glaring. The strength of the German garrisons maintained on their sea coast is, of course, largely a matter of conjecture. On this point the Intelligence Department must speak. But at this stage it is assumed that the permanent garrison of Sylt does not exceed from 3,000 to 5,000 men, and that of Borkum from 7,000 to 10,000 men, and these, in both cases, not field but fortress troops. It may be estimated, on this assumption, that one division would be sufficient to capture Sylt, and two divisions to capture Borkum.

It might well be found desirable to attack Sylt first, and then while we were establishing ourselves there and all the enemy's forces and attention were directed to that point, to launch a second attack at Borkum.

22. Both these specific operations, apart from the general policy, should, of course, be remitted to the joint study of the military and naval staffs. But, if desired, further preliminary details can be given, including estimates of the forces required, specification of the apparatus and equipment, selection of the points and method of attack, and of the chronological sequence of the various operations. Broadly speaking, however, the method of attack should be as follows:—

(*a*) The cutting off of the island and of the attacking forces from the intervention of the main German fleet by means of either minefields laid overnight between the islands and the enemy's naval harbours, or by submarine barrages similarly established, or, again, by the employment of both, one behind the other, at an interval of, say 10 miles.

(*b*) The bombardment of the forts and batteries by squadrons of the torpedo-proof fleet (including the monitors from shoal water), with good aerial observation maintained by aeroplanes and seaplanes rising from seaplane-carrying ships, themselves protected by bulges.

(*c*) The landing under cover of the guns of the Fleet, aided by gas and smoke, of the troops upon the island, from torpedo-proof transports by means of bullet-proof lighters. Approximately 100 should be provided for landing a division. In addition a number (say) 50, tank-landing lighters would be provided, each carrying a tank or tanks, fitted for wire-cutting in its bow, which, by means of a drawbridge or shelving bow, would land under its own power, to prevent the infantry from being held up by wire when attacking the gorges of the forts and batteries. This is a new feature, and removes one of the very great previous difficulties, namely, the rapid landing of field artillery to cut wire.

(*d*) The prompt establishment on the island of an aerial base sufficiently powerful to hold its own air and maintain artillery observation.

(*e*) The establishment of oilers and storeships in the anchorage, and the landing of the necessary stores, both for the troops and for the flotillas operating from the island.

23. It is necessary at this point to refer to the following argument: 'If we can capture a very strongly-fortified place 240 miles from home, why cannot the Germans retake it when it is only 60 miles from them, and the fortifications weakened or even destroyed in the process of capture?' The answer is three-fold. First, the initiative of attack and the choice of place rest with us. The enemy cannot tell which island or which part of his coast we are going for, or whether we are going at all, or whether any preparation we have made may not be a mere bluff designed to induce him to dissipate sorely-needed forces on coastal defence. Nor does he know when we shall come. We, on the other hand, having taken the island, know exactly what we have to hold, and the great need of the enemy to retake it. Secondly, it is not intended to take these islands merely for the pleasure of holding them, but only as an essential step in the development of a Naval and Aerial offensive, which must be accompanied by hard fighting at every step. Thirdly, we are superior to the enemy in all classes of vessels. He cannot attempt recapture from the sea until he has overcome our naval forces. That he should attempt to overcome these naval forces is exactly what we most earnestly desire; for then that series of flotilla, cruiser, and submarine actions will arise, with heavy losses on both sides, from which we hope to obtain a decision.

To take and hold islands in any quarter of the world is the prerogative of the stronger Naval Power alone.

24. The defence of the island or islands when captured rests on the following processes:—

(*a*) The superiority in all respects of our sea forces, having regard, *inter alia*, to the impracticability of the enemy bringing 3,000,000*l*. naked ships into areas infested by our submarines or by our minefields, which we will not allow him to sweep with small craft.

(*b*) The impossibility of a military attack across the tide-swept sands against our infantry forces holding the island: having regard to the impossibility of the attackers digging trenches at any point on the wide space to be crossed, or remaining there without being caught by the tide; and also having regard to the enemy's inability to bombard our infantry positions either by field guns or howitzers.

25. There remains (*c*) the power of the enemy to bring up long range naval guns on the mainland, and so harass and, if possible, render untenable our anchorages at the captured islands. On this it is to be observed:—

(i) That the nearest point where such guns could be mounted is at least 30,000 and probably, since they would not be placed on the actual beach, 33,000 or 34,000 yards distant from our anchorage at Borkum, and at least 14,000 plus 3,000 or 4,000 yards distant from our anchorage at Sylt.

(ii) Guns capable of throwing shells this distance cannot be easily or quickly brought into position. Either they are on railway mountings and can be located from the air, or regular emplacements must be built which is a matter of weeks and perhaps months.

(iii) With aerial supremacy conferring good aerial observation and with superior gun power from the outset, it should be possible to prevent these hostile guns from being brought into position or mounted, and to quell their fire should they be mounted. Six or seven monitors, mounting twelve or fourteen of the heaviest guns in the world, suitably disposed around either island sitting on the shoals at low water should, with good aerial observation, by concerted fire make it impossible for any serious attack by enemy long-range guns to be made or maintained.

(iv) Assuming that we maintain aerial supremacy, which is an essential condition even if it is limited to the air above the island, the enemy's long-range fire when or in so far as it was not quelled, would be extremely inaccurate. The use of smoke screens would veil the anchorage and any desired part of the island in mist and obscurity. (At the present time and for nearly two years past the Germans have had a heavy gun in position to shell Dunkirk and all our large naval establishments there at a less range than would be possible at Borkum, yet they have not found it expedient to continue the fire in view of reprisals, and the annoyance, such as it is, has not produced any military result. The two 14-inch monitors at the Dardanelles succeeded in dominating the Asiatic guns as soon as their observation was perfected.)

The fire of such distant guns, directed not at the vessels in the anchorage but at large upon the islands, would be wholly ineffective and not worth considering in its effects upon infantry scattered about in strong entrenchments among the sand dunes.

26. Finally, in this section of the argument, lies the question of communications. As we are superior at sea and would be seeking to demonstrate that fact by action on every possible occasion, it would not be possible for the enemy, unless he defeated our sea forces, to interfere with our communications by means of surface vessels of any kind. There remains the Submarine. Such submarines, be it observed, would necessarily be to a large extent withdrawn from their present attack upon our merchant shipping, giving us thereby the very relief we seek, and would be recalled for the far more difficult task of attacking escorted military vessels in the fighting zone. Every method of anti-submarine warfare which is now dispersed over such wide and various areas would be applied in a concentrated form for the maintenance of these communications. We are at the present moment, and have been for many months past, maintaining the continuous supply of very large armies across the channel to Boulogne, Calais, and Dunkirk, the last of which places is little more than half the distance from the enemy's nearest submarine and destroyer base than Borkum is from Wilhelmshaven. The naval and military forces that we should be maintaining on these islands would be incomparably smaller than those which are now supplied from Dunkirk. In fact, they might be almost entirely maintained by torpedo-proof supply vessels. At the worst, we should be fighting the same submarines that are now raiding our trade routes, but fighting them for a positive military object and in waters of our own choice. Every step in this naval offensive should result in forcing the enemy to concentrate his submarines in a definite area and in enabling us to concentrate our overwhelming but now scattered and dissipated resources against them.

27. The critical nature of this operation at its supreme moment, viz, the storming of the island must not be underrated. A check at this stage might entail disastrous results. We must not forget the power of the modern rifle and

machine gun in the hands of troops whose trenches and *moral* have not been completely shattered by prolonged artillery preparation. Although it should be possible to support the assaulting troops by the fire of 300 or 400 guns, many of the heaviest calibre, all firing from decisive ranges, this kind of artillery support could not be equal either in accuracy or duration to the artillery preparations now employed on the western front; nor could we expect a creeping barrage from floating platforms and naval artillerists. There is always the danger of the enemy getting wind of our intentions and reinforcing his garrisons with good troops beforehand, at any rate, so far as Borkum, about which he would always be very sensitive, is concerned. On the other hand, the landing could be effected under the shields of lighters, proof against machine-gun bullets, and too numerous to be seriously affected by heavy gun-fire; and the employment of Tanks in even larger numbers than are here suggested, especially the quick moving Tanks, and lighter varieties operating in an area where no preparations could have been made to receive them. These may be thought new and important favourable considerations.

From the moment the troops are landed until the capture is complete this part of the operation is mainly military in its character, and it remains to be seen whether a sound plan of attack can be devised by military authorities which would within a few days of the landing being effected, put an end to all resistance on the island. It is certain that the enemy has been continually strengthening his defensive arrangements along the whole coast ever since the outbreak of war, and although the means of attack have grown more rapidly in many respects than those of the defence, the hazard of the operation is obvious. If the assaulting troops were brought finally to a standstill on the island before we had the use of its anchorages as naval bases, the whole enterprise might miscarry, and a limited, though heavy price be paid both in men and ships. But what are we paying now and what shall we pay next year for a negative policy?

28. Reviewing all the foregoing considerations, which have been set out not so much to prescribe details as to illuminate the subject, it seems desirable to put forward, in the hope that it may receive simultaneous examination, a third alternative.

No naval offensive is practicable without an Oversea Base. If the capture and retention of this base are not to involve large armies, it must be on an island. If we cannot borrow an island from neutrals, and dare not take one from the enemy, the question arises, 'can we *make* an island'.

Only persevering study of this project should justify its dismissal. If it could be done without undue consumption of materials, the cost and trouble of it must be balanced against the hazards and heavier stakes of the oversea assault upon a fortified hostile position.

29. The sandbanks of the Horn Reef are, in fact, a barely submerged island. They may be found capable of being improved and developed into a torpedo-proof war anchorage, which could be used as an advanced Oversea Base both for replenishing and for refitting our destroyer flotillas, and possibly for sheltering medium vessels. The suitable areas of the Horn Reef lie about 20 miles west of the neutral Danish Coast, near the important landing place of Esbjerg, and more than 40 miles from the nearest German territory. It is therefore out of the furthest gun-shot from Germany. Any violation of Danish territory by Germany would give us a right to take protective measures by seizing one of the excellent Danish bases which are available. Therefore, we may assume that it would not be worth Germany's while to do this. The waters of Horn Reef vary in depth from 8 feet to 50 feet, and the reef itself gives good protection from the northerly gales. This area is about 90 miles from Heligoland. It is therefore not too distant for our destroyers to work from. It is also near enough for an aggressive air base.

30. One of the methods suggested for investigation is as follows: A sufficient number of flat-bottomed barges or caissons made, not of steel but of concrete, should be prepared in the Humber, at Harwich, and in the Wash, the Medway, and Thames. These structures would be adapted to the depths in which they were to be sunk according to a general plan. They would float when empty of water, and could thus be towed across to the site of the artificial island. On arrival at the buoys marking the island, sea cocks would be opened and they would settle down on the bottom. They could subsequently be gradually filled with sand as opportunity served with suction dredgers. These structures would range in size from, (say), 60′×40′×20′ to 120′×80′×40′. By this means a torpedo and weather-proof harbour, like an atoll, would be created in the open sea, with regular pens for the destroyers and submarines, and alighting platforms for aeroplanes.

This project, if feasible, is capable of great elaboration, and it might be applied in various places. Concrete vessels can perhaps be made to carry a complete heavy gun turret, and these, on the admission of water to their outer chambers would sit on the sea floor, like the Solent Forts, at the desired points. Other sinkable structures could be made to contain store-rooms, oil-tanks, or living chambers. It is not possible, without an expert inquiry, to do more here than indicate the possibilities which embrace nothing less than the creation, transportation in pieces, assemblement and posing of an artificial island and destroyer base.

31. Such a scheme, if found mechanically sound, avoids the need of employing troops and all the risks of storming a fortified island. It could be applied as a surprise, for although the construction of these concrete vessels would probably be known in Germany, the natural conclusion would be that

they were intended for an attempt to block up the river mouths, which indeed is an idea not to be excluded. Thus, until the island or system of breakwaters actually began to grow, the enemy would not penetrate the design.

A year's preparation would, however, be required.

32. No attempt is made here to describe the exact method of carrying out the general operation of seizing either Borkum or Sylt or establishing a base at the Horn Reef; but the sequence of the main phases may be stated:—

(*a*) On a given day, called Zero, all merchant traffic with these islands is suddenly greatly restricted and the ships held in port. That night begins the concentration of the flotillas of attack. These will be drawn in part from the escorting and convoying duties on the trade routes, in part from the Grand Fleet, and from Dover and Harwich. They will comprise a destroyer force twice as strong in numbers and four times as strong in gun power as the German flotillas. A similar concentration of British submarines and of small craft of all kinds, sloops, drifters, patrol vessels, &c., will take place.

(*b*) On the third night, or whenever sufficient force has been assembled, the isolation of the proposed base from Germany by an extensive process of laying mine-fields will be effected. These mine-fields will be guarded by the flotillas which come into action from the third day, with seven days' radius. The actual attack on the proposed base, or, in the case of the Horn Reef, its construction, will then begin. The Blue Water Fleet suspends refits, and the Inshore Fleet takes up its station to sustain the flotillas and cover and support the operations.

(*c*) Within five or six days after the attack oiling facilities must be available at the new base for the first relief of the flotillas.

Until flying stations can be established on the sands of the new base the aeroplane control and observation must be maintained from seaplane ships.

(*d*) It is probable that the German submarine forces are divided into three parts:—

(1) Those out hunting.
(2) Those in refitting.
(3) Those reserved for home defence.

During the first week we shall only have to deal with the third of these classes. The first will be still waiting on their beats for merchant traffic, and the second will be in dockyard hands. But from the tenth day onwards we must anticipate the recall of the commerce attacking submarines and the hurried re-equipment of those refitting. But by that time it is hoped that the main part of the work will be achieved, and a sheltered anchorage with re-fuelling facilities, the whole properly netted and surrounded by an extensive system of mines, will have been created, although not, of course, completed.

(*e*) If the above assumptions were correct, it is probable that about the tenth day we could afford—

(i) To make a further concentration in the area of anti-submarine vessels of all kinds; and
(ii) To resume our merchant traffic.

The phase of submarine fighting to prevent the occupation, construction, completion, and victualling of the new base would have begun, and until this phase had reached a decision one way or the other it is unlikely that the enemy would resume commerce raiding on any large scale. His energies would be concentrated on defending himself from a direct attack, the full scope and intention of which he could not possibly measure.

33. What can the enemy do to prevent the execution of such a plan? There is only one thing which he can do, and it is the one thing that we want him to do. He can fight. No doubt he will recall numbers of his submarines from our trade routes to attack our transports and supply vessels of all kinds. We shall meet this by the fullest use of all the means of counter attack which have been and are being developed. He will send out Zeppelins to drop bombs. These will be attacked by our aeroplanes, starting from seaplane ships. He might send out his destroyer flotillas to make night attacks. These, again, will be attacked by our stronger flotillas, and fierce, confused fighting will ensue, resulting, as we have a right to expect, on a survey of numbers and gun power, in his flotillas being worsted and driven off. In order to clear a way for his heavy ships through our minefields, he will send out mine-sweepers and other barrier-breaking craft, more or less strongly supported. We shall encounter all these with similar, but superior, forces. Further severe and continuous action will ensue. Do let us hold fast to the simple truth that the stronger Navy can assert its rights over the weaker, and that all it requires to demonstrate its rights is continued compulsion of the weaker to action. We can pursue a policy of ship for ship losses to any extent. He cannot pursue it except for a very limited time. We could even afford mathematically, to lose two ships for one, with the certainty that he would not be able to continue. With forces of approximately equal strength and quality, manœuvring gives the victory, but, with overwhelming superiority, mutually destructive fighting is the surest road.

34. But, it will be said, the enemy will at some point in these operations least convenient to you, send out his whole fleet, sweeping his way forward and protected by all his flotillas. His superior speed and manœuvring power will enable him certainly to bring our slow-moving Inshore Fleet to battle under conditions where all the manœuvring power which speed gives rests with him. In thinking this aspect out, we must first consider the strength of the Inshore Fleet. This fleet would contain many of the most heavily gunned Dreadnoughts or super-Dreadnoughts in the world, with as many older battleships as we think it right to employ. The destruction of such a force by gunfire cannot be achieved except at the cost of almost equal sacrifices and of many hours of battle. Though our Inshore Fleet would not steam more than 7 or 8 knots an hour, our under-water anxieties would be incomparably less than his. He would have to come into waters which we had systematically organised with our minefields, and expose his naked ships of the greatest value to the attacks of large numbers of our submarines, who would have full warning of the advance. His losses in the approach could not fail to be very serious, and might leave him equal or actually inferior by the time the main battle was joined. After the battle he would have to return, in all the disorder of the conflict, through the same dangerous waters, minefields and submarine barrages through which he had come. All the time our own fast Blue Water Fleet, showing an actual superiority in numbers alone of 3 to 2, would remain intact and, if it pleased, entirely outside the area of the conflict. Finally, the choice of the battle ground would, within certain limits, rest with us. We should know, by constant aerial observation, exactly when the German Main Fleet was leaving harbour. We should know that it could only be coming out at such great risk to fight our Inshore Fleet, or such squadrons of it as were at sea. Assuming that his fleet steam twice as fast as our Inshore Fleet, we could, if we wished before we were overtaken, add 50 per cent. to our distance from his base at the time of his advance. Assuming that the cruising station of this fleet were about 90 miles from Wilhelmshaven, we could force the enemy to fight, if we chose, approximately, 140 miles from port. If he steamed 15 knots from the time he left harbour, which is all he could do in company, nine hours would pass before battle could be joined. By that time our fast Blue Water Fleet, moving from the Forth, could, if it desired, be very near the scene. The conclusion of this argument is that the German High Sea Fleet would not be risked on such a hazardous enterprise. If it were we could ask for nothing better.

If, on the other hand, the High Sea Fleet is not employed, but only small craft supported by old battleships with or without bulges, then our superior Inshore Squadron and stronger flotillas will certainly break these up and defeat them, and the longer the matter is disputed the better for us.

35. Let us now endeavour to compute some of the advantages that would follow from the kind of operations described above, if they had been successfully executed.

From the moment when we attacked and invaded German soil, or established a naval base in close proximity to his coasts, and thus brought our great naval superiority into play, the operation, small though it be compared to the gigantic battles on the Western front, would demand and rivet the attention of the enemy and of the world in general, and particularly of the two small States, Denmark and Holland, which lie so near to the new theatre. Germany, at the very outset, would have to choose whether to risk and consume the whole of her sea forces in continuous action with our attacking fleet and flotillas, or whether to retire through the Canal while time remained with almost all her naval forces, and be content to retain the command of the Baltic. If she took the former course, that should be very agreeable to the Royal Navy, for then would follow a continuous struggle by submarines, by destroyers, by mining, by cruiser fighting, by aerial fighting, and by supporting ships, proceeding from crisis to crisis till a definite decision was reached. All the time our Blue Water Fleet, sufficient in itself to assure the supremacy of the ocean and the broad seas, would remain, safe and intact like the gold reserve in the Bank of England, as the ultimate guarantee. If, on the other hand, the Germans, after a certain amount of fighting, finding that their numerical inferiority did not allow them to sustain losses which they could not replace and which, unit for unit, must be more severe having regard to their relatively smaller numbers, should allow themselves to be driven back into their harbours and river mouths, an alternative situation of very great advantage would be created. We should proceed:—

(*a*) *By sea.*—To mine them in ever closer and closer, blocking particularly all those channels which are deep enough for submarines to come out and go in by. Great numbers of mines set at different depths, or strung together in necklaces, would be laid on a comparatively small arc before the enemy's debouches, but at a sufficient distance from his batteries; and these would be effectively watched and guarded. We should sweep and buoy channels through the existing fouled ground up to our blockading minefields, and thus we should be able to pass about this dangerous area, the dangers of which would soon become mysterious and prohibitive to the enemy. There is scarcely any limit to the mining policy which could then be pursued.

(*b*) *By air.*—This, in itself, almost a sufficient object. We should establish on the captured or improvised island aerial stations and bombing bases of a very powerful character, and from these, in easy striking distance of the most important military and naval places in Germany, we should levy a continued bombing attack. Essen, Wilhelmshaven, Cuxhaven, Kiel, the whole line of the Canal, all the dockyards, all the anchorages would be brought under continuous bombing by night and day from quite short distances. Aerial observation would reveal each morning the exact disposition of the German fleet, in each of its harbours or rivers, and at either side of the Canal. Every movement of the enemy would be known.

Until we have beaten the enemy's sea forces into port, and have mined them in there, and have established a serviceable oversea base from which to keep him mined in and blockaded, it is useless to think of invading Schleswig, or throwing an army into Jutland. Unless we can defend Denmark with an army we have no right to bring her in to her ruin. Until she comes in, it is unwise, if not impossible, to enter the Baltic.

But once the operations here suggested had been achieved, we should be in a position, *if we thought fit*, to invite both Holland and Denmark to join the coalition against Germany, and to support either or both of them by adequate armies either in Holland or Denmark, or conceivably we could ourselves invade Schleswig.

36. One more result that would follow from the success of these naval operations must be noted.

The effective mining in and close blockading of the debouches into the North Sea would remove the last possibility of invasion or serious raid on the British islands. It is absurd to suppose a military expedition could be despatched from Kiel through the Belts and the Skaw. Its interception would be certain. Therefore all the troops hitherto held in Great Britain for this already remote contingency would be released for offensive action. The garrisons of the captured island or islands could be found from home. It would not be necessary to weaken our army in France for this purpose.

Further, the whole of the Home forces would be available for invasionary action and come at once into play, and it would be easy to lead the enemy to suppose that a great operation was impending of which the capture of an overseas base was, as well it might be, only the first step. This would increase the inducement upon him to fight at sea and to divert troops from the main front. We must, moreover, assume that such a naval operation as has been indicated would be synchronised with the supreme offensive of the British, French, and American armies on the Western front. It might thus be made to take the form, apart from its own merits, of an immense diversion of the enemy's strength at the most critical moment. He might find himself forced, under the threat of invasion which might occur at so many points and on so wide a front, to withdraw forces utterly out of all proportion to those we should have to employ in the island operation, and this fact in itself might exercise an all-important influence on the great battles on the Western front, and consequently upon the fate of the war.

37. All the various schemes and arguments set out in this paper have only one object, namely, to discover for the Navy a method of offensive which will enable it to make the immense surplus force which it possesses tell effectively at the culminating moment in this war. A layman can only assemble arguments, point out the needs, and suggest expedients. No scheme has any chance of life or success that the Navy does not take up, elaborate, and champion itself. The difficulties of positive and creative action are enormous. Nothing is more easy in this matter than for experts to remain entrenched upon a negative policy, and receive every proposal with a fire of destructive criticism. But, if these ideas and other variants of them are rejected, if no alternative proposition is put forward by the Naval Service, and, if it is finally settled by the overwhelming consent of expert opinion that no means of a naval offensive exist or can be devised; that the war can only be won on land, and that the Allied navies, however great their superiority, can only 'keep the ring' and hunt submarines with small craft, then the following conclusion emerges with extreme plainness, viz, *that the large ships of all classes maintained in commission by the Allied navies ought not to exceed the minimum necessary to discharge this limited rôle*. We do not want upwards of 200 battleships continually maintained in full commission to 'keep the ring'. Every trained officer or man, every gun, every round of ammunition, every ton of stores, and every shilling of expense should be made to play some part of definite war utility. Keeping in full commission great numbers of vessels which are surplus, which are not needed for any definite war purpose at a time when men are being sent back after three wounds to the firing line, cannot be justified on any ground. Unless, therefore, some form of naval offensive, which utilises the surplus strength of the Allied navies effectively can be devised, the proportion of Allied resources in men, money, and material which should be assigned to the upkeep of the battle fleets clearly in need of the strictest scrutiny.

38. *Conclusions.*

(i) At the beginning of the war our margin of Dreadnought superiority in Home Waters was 7. It is now 22; to which may be added the 14 American Dreadnoughts, making in all a numerical superiority of 36.

But our superiority in quality and especially gun power far exceeds our superiority in numbers, the additions consisting chiefly of the most powerful vessels ever built.

The formation of two fleets for the separate purposes of bluewater and inshore fighting is now possible.

(ii) A method has been discovered whereby ships may, at a sacrifice in speed, obtain a high degree of immunity from torpedo attack.

(iii) The multiplication of our submarines enables barrages of submarines to be thrown between the enemy's heavy ships and any vessels we wish to use in any particular area. These barrages constitute adequate deterrents, if not absolute vetos, on the movement of heavy non-bulged ships.

(iv) Our superiority in destroyers and small craft is overwhelming, if it were not dissipated by a purely defensive strategy.

(v) We are therefore in a position to resort to the traditional war policy of the Royal Navy, viz, to beat the enemy's flotillas into port, and keep him closely mined and blockaded there by stronger flotillas properly supported by torpedo-proof heavy ships.

(vi) To carry out this policy effectively it is necessary to obtain an oversea base where our flotillas can refuel, &c., and whence aeroplane observation and attack can be constantly maintained upon the enemy's principal naval establishments.

(vii) The means of attack upon certain suitable islands have been greatly improved by various devices and mechanical improvements. On the other hand, the enemy's preparations for defence have probably also been improved.

(viii) The assumption of such a naval offensive will force the enemy to concentrate his submarines—or a large portion of them—upon his own defence and upon military objectives. We shall be able to concentrate a large proportion of our means of attack on submarines in definite and comparatively restricted war areas with consequent increase in the effectiveness of our attack and collateral relief to our trade routes.

(ix) The establishment of a close and aggressive blockade, supported by an oversea base or bases, will threaten the enemy with invasion either of Schleswig or Oldenburg, and will place it in our power to support either Denmark or Holland, or both, against him.

(x) All British troops maintained for Home Defence and other land forces in this country, numbering at least 1¼ millions, may thus, *without moving from Great Britain*, be made to acquire a war value as a potential invading army.

This will compel the enemy to make large diversions of strength from the main front in France, which will greatly assist our military offensive at its supreme moment.

(xi) An oversea base will enable an aerial offensive on the greatest scale to be constantly directed upon almost all the vital military objectives in Germany.

(xii) If the naval authorities decide that no aggressive naval action on a great scale is possible, and that the fleet can only 'keep the ring', it then follows that the battle fleets and cruiser forces maintained in commission should be strictly limited to what is necessary for that restricted rôle: and the surplus *matériel*, stores, and expert personnel should be released for other purposes. The guns and ammunition should go to the front. The officers and expert ratings should go to the Tanks or to the air, where they are greatly needed.

Viscount Grey of Fallodon to Winston S. Churchill

(*Churchill papers: 1/127*)

18 July 1917

Fallodon
Scotland

Dear Churchill,

According to the papers that get here you have gone into office again.[1] I don't know exactly what the position of a Minister is now, but I assume it means work & some responsibility & I send a line to wish you well.

Most of those, military, naval or civil, who occupied foremost places in the war have had some bad luck, but in some ways you had particularly bad luck; whether there is much opportunity for good luck where you are, I do not know, but when there is opportunity I hope you will get it.

I suppose you will now have to cease painting. I want to see your pictures but I don't see how I am to do that. I have passed through London once or twice, but have spent so short a time on each occasion that I have seen very few people. My spirits fall & I begin to become restless & wretched in London, so I don't stay there, whereas in the country I have great content, which amongst other pleasant things makes me feel goodwill to old colleagues.

Yours sincerely
Edward Grey

[1] On 17 July Churchill entered the Cabinet as Minister of Munitions; but he was not a member of the War Cabinet. In its leading article on 18 July 1917 *The Times* warned that the country 'is in no mood to tolerate even a forlorn attempt to resuscitate amateur strategy'. It also doubted whether Churchill had 'any qualifications at all' for dealing with Labour.

Robert Donald[1] *to Winston S. Churchill*

(*Churchill papers: 2/91*)

18 July 1917

The Daily Chronicle

Dear Churchill,

I am very glad to see you back in the Government & wish you every success. I was restrained from advocating your title to office some time ago by LG who did not think that it was in your interest or in his that I should do so, & I dare say he was right.

I am told that your policy for a time will be one of quiet activity but you really ought to be in The War Cabinet & I hope to see you there, while retaining your present office if necessary.

With all good wishes

Ys very truly
Robert Donald

Sir John Brabazon[2] *to Winston S. Churchill*

(*Churchill papers: 2/91*)

18 July 1917

Dearest Winston,

You will know how delighted I am. They—I mean the country—have treated you badly & kept you too long out in the cold, but now that you have got going again I feel confident you will prove to the world how prejudiced & narrow it has been in keeping so valuable an asset so long unemployed.

Best of luck to you, old comrade.

Ever yours
J. P. Brabazon

[1] Robert Donald, 1861–1933. Editor, *Daily Chronicle*, 1902–18. Chairman, Empire Press Union, 1915–26. A Director, Department of Information, 1917. A strong advocate of dropping leaflets over enemy territory. Knighted, 1924. A friend of the first Labour Prime Minister, Ramsay MacDonald, for whom he undertook publicity work.

[2] John Palmer Brabazon, 1843–1922. Entered the Army, 1862. Served in the Grenadier Guards and the 10th Hussars. On active service in the Ashanti war, 1873–4; the Afghan War, 1878–80, and the Sudan, 1884–5. Lieutenant-Colonel commanding the 4th Hussars, 1893. Commanded the 2nd Cavalry Brigade in South Africa, 1900. Retired with the rank of Colonel, 1901. Knighted, 1911. Major-General, 1911.

C. P. Scott to Winston S. Churchill

(*Churchill papers: 2/91*)

18 July 1917

My dear Churchill,

At last! I'm so glad, not so much for your sake—though one does like to see an injustice set right—as for the country's which I am quite sure you will well serve, brains not being too plentiful a commodity in this or any other Government. Now if you will bring back old Fisher we may get the better of the submarines.

Yours very sincerely
C P Scott[1]

Lady Cornelia Wimborne[2] to Winston S. Churchill

(*Churchill papers: 2/91*)

18 July 1917 Canford Manor

Dearest Winston,

My most hearty congratulations on the news I read this morning. I am so delighted. It is just the office for you & you are just the man for the place. I am also more than glad that you are identified with L George's Govt. Don't trouble to write, only my love

Cornelia Wimborne

My advice is stick to munitions & don't try & run the Govt!

Walter Long to David Lloyd George

(*Lloyd George papers*)

18 July 1917

My dear Prime Minister,

I hope you will pardon me if I say that I was greatly surprised to read some of the new appointments in today's Papers. Of course the selection of

[1] Churchill noted on Scott's letter: 'Thank you so much for yr letter. I have undertaken a vy formidable task & require all your powerful aid.' But Lord Fisher received no further appointment, either at the Admiralty, or in any other Government department.

[2] Lady Cornelia Henrietta Maria Spencer-Churchill, 1847–1927. Churchill's aunt; eldest daughter of the 7th Duke of Marlborough. She married in 1868, Ivor Bertie Guest (1835–1914), who was created 1st Baron Wimborne in 1880.

his Colleagues is a matter solely for the PM & one in which he is not expected to consult his subordinates & in ordinary conditions this rule works admirably & there are obvious remedies open to those who may find it difficult to co-operate with new colleagues. But these times are not ordinary, when you did me the honour to press me to join your Government you told me you did so because you considered that I represented the largest number of the Party to which I belong & you said they would be greatly guided by my actions.

Again when you contemplated making somewhat similar changes a short time ago you were good enough to send for me & ask my views. I made it clear that my objections were based on general & public grounds & you were also good enough to say you would see me again before making any appointment. I have however heard nothing more of the matter. I therefore find myself in a somewhat awkward position. I had, & have, no sort of objection to Churchill or Montagu[1] on personal grounds, I admire the great abilities of both, but I felt, & feel, that the inclusion of the former as M/M would weaken your Gov. would certainly make it extremely difficult for many of my friends to continue their support. As regards Montagu it seems to me, if I may say with great respect, that his recent speech on India is a very serious bar to his appt as S o S for India. All my friends ask me to tell them why I find these appointments satisfactory! I can only reply that I knew nothing of them.

I am sure we shall have great & increasing trouble, believe me the London Press does not represent independent opinion: & I can only repeat that I hope you will not consider I have taken undue advantage of your invariable kindness & courtesy to me by frankly & briefly expressing my views.

Very sincerely yours
Walter H. Long

Katharine Asquith[2] to Winston S. Churchill

(*Churchill papers: 2/91*)

18 July 1917

My dear Winston

I must add my word of congratulation to all the rest. I am truly glad of your return & was most delighted at this morning's announcement.

[1] Edwin Montagu, who had been Minister of Munitions during the last six months of Asquith's premiership, had received no office in December 1916. But in July 1917 he was appointed Secretary of State for India (a post which he held until March 1922).

[2] Katharine Frances Horner. Daughter of Sir John Horner of Mells, Somerset. In 1907 she married Asquith's eldest son Raymond, who was killed in action on the Somme in 1916. Her brother Edward was killed in action in 1917.

Its the first step which this Government has taken to give us any confidence & I can't believe that there is anyone in the country (except perhaps Mr Gwynne[1]) who does not feel the same. I do wish you all success.

Yrs
Katharine Asquith

Leopold Amery: diary
(*Amery papers*)

18 July 1917

. . . the bringing in of Churchill and Montagu into the Government have shaken its prestige and reputation seriously.

Bertram Romilly to Winston S. Churchill: extract
(*Churchill papers*)

19 July 1917

My dear Winston,

A very short line to tell you how delighted I am to read, in the newspapers just arrived, of your appointment. I have felt very much for you yourself, and also for the Country at being deprived of your services, during all these months of your official inactivity.

I read of your appointment in the *Morning Post*, & I can truthfully tell you that the hostile criticism of that newspaper does most emphatically not express the opinions of the men I see & talk with daily.

I hope so much to see you out here on a visit before very long. . . .

[1] Howell Arthur Gwynne, 1865–1950. Reuter's chief war correspondent in South Africa, 1899–1902. Editor of the *Standard*, 104–11. Editor of the *Morning Post*, 1911–37. One of Churchill's most outspoken public critics both at the time of the siege of Antwerp in October 1914, and in July 1917.

Clara Frewen[1] *to Winston S. Churchill*

(*Churchill papers: 2/91*)

20 July 1917

Ormonde House
Regents Park

Dearest Winston,

A thousand congratulations & many congratulation to our dear old England, to have got you back again.

With love & luck

Yours affectionately Aunt Clara

Major-General J. E. B. Seely to Winston S. Churchill

(*Churchill papers: 2/91*)

20 July 1917

Brooke House
Isle of Wight

My dear Winston,

All is well—I am so glad, not only for your sake who at last have an outlet for energies and talents, but even more for all of us who want so badly just what you can give. I am ever so glad, and need not tell you how earnestly I wish you all success.

If you and your wife can come here for a week-end it would be delightful —I shall be here about another ten days, then I must return to my Brigade.

Yours ever
Jack

I can walk without a stick and hope to be able to ride in a few days.[2]

[1] Clara Jerome, 1850–1935. Eldest daughter of Leonard Jerome and sister of Lady Randolph Churchill. In 1881 she married Moreton Frewen. Her daughter Clare, a noted sculptress, married Wilfred Sheridan, who was killed in action on the western front in September 1915.

[2] Three days after the death of his son Frank, in April 1917, at the battle of Arras, Seely had been wounded by a German shell, which threw his horse on top of him. While recuperating from his wound he married (as his second wife) the widow of his former Private Secretary, George Nicholson, who had been killed while on active service in the Royal Flying Corps in March 1916.

Sir Reginald Barnes[1] *to Winston S. Churchill*

(*Churchill papers: 2/91*)

20 July 1917 57th Division

My dear old Winston,

I was *so glad* to see about your appointment in the papers, my sincere congratulations.

Pile up the guns & shells & we will make the Hun sit up & beg, but we haven't got enough yet.

Au revoir & all luck.

In haste
Reggie Barnes

A satirical magazine article purporting to be a letter from Churchill to Haig, which was published in 'Town Topics' on 21 July 1917, entitled 'In a Month's Time'.[2]

Ministry of Munitions,
Whitehall

My dear Sir Douglas Haig,—I have not written to you before because I have been so busy readjusting and reorganising this department that I have scarcely had time to sleep.

I have made drastic alterations and have retired several chiefs of departments who refused to agree with me in my estimate of output; and now all is plain sailing.

Did I tell you that I had altered the shape of the shells? I did not care for the conventional style, which seemed to me somewhat lacking in novelty, but I have made arrangements for you to see the new variety before they are supplied to the artillery. They are a little larger than the old type, and instead of being circular they are square. In this way I hope to save a considerable amount of tonnage.

I am thinking also of having square guns to match them; let me know your

[1] Reginald Walter Ralph Barnes, 1871–1946. Entered Army, 1890. Lieutenant, 4th Hussars, 1894, and one of Churchill's close Army friends. Went with Churchill to Cuba, 1895. Captain, 1901. Lieutenant-Colonel commanding the 10th Hussars, 1911–15. Colonel, 1914. Brigadier-General, commanding the 116th Infantry Brigade, and the 14th Infantry Brigade, 1915–16. Commanded the 32nd Division, 1916–17 and the 57th Division, 1917–19. Major-General, 1918. Knighted, 1919.

[2] Churchill's first letter to Sir Douglas Haig from the Ministry of Munitions was in fact sent on 26 July (see page 112). Haig replied on 29 July (see page 116).

views on this subject. I have also invented a new type of aeroplane which I rather fancy will amuse you. I am quite sure it will go up, and I have ordered a thousand in the faith that my hopes will be realised.

In regard to your next push, I should like to make a few suggestions, so I hope you will not make a start until you have received from me a general scheme which I am at present preparing.

Briefly, I do not wish you to make any attacks along the dunes. The type of shell I am turning out is wholly unsuitable for this kind of attack. Also, I am opposed to your employing the 72nd Army, which contains a large number of my constituents. These should be kept in the rear in comfortable billets.

If you desire to attack in the neighbourhood of Nieuport, I have instructed Geddes to give you every assistance with My Monitors, which are now even more efficient than they were before, thanks to My Shells.

We are, of course, in need of a striking success just now, and, as I have impressed upon Balfour, there must be no negotiations until that success is secured.

I have arranged for Balfour to keep you posted as to the political situation, and I have instructed Derby, the Army Council, and Sir William Robertson to let you have all the supplies you require without consulting me. I strongly advise you to continue your pressure upon the Arras front, and I am sending you herewith the rough draft of a scheme which should enable you to reach Douai by August 4th.

By the way, what do you think of my suggestion (made to the War Council this morning on the spur of the moment) of repeating on a bigger scale a surprise attack upon the defences of the Dardanelles?

Personally, I think it is a legitimate gamble. Once we reached Gallipoli we should be within a few miles of a world-shaking decision. These and other thoughts chase themselves rapidly through my busy mind.

Just one other matter has struck me. I feel that Fisher should come back. Have you a place on your staff for him. I have offered him the post of Chancellor to the Duchy of Lancaster, but he has turned down that offer, although I pointed out that Lancashire has a very large seaboard, and it might be taken as a naval appointment.

I am just off now to see Law about my Premium Bond Scheme.

All kind regards,

Yours as ever,
Winston Churchill, Colonel

PS. I bear no malice about that little matter of a Brigade—perhaps you were right, and I should not have made a good Brigadier-General.

WC

Lord Derby to Sir Philip Sassoon:[1] *extract*

(*Derby papers*)

22 July 1917

War Office

Now, as to things political. Strictly between ourselves, Lloyd George made a *coup-de-main* when he appointed Geddes,[2] Winston Churchill and Montagu. I never knew a word about it until I saw it in the paper and was furious at being kept in ignorance, but you can judge of my surprise when I found that the War Cabinet had never been told. Lloyd George had acted on a prerogative, which is undoubtedly his, to make any appointment he likes without consulting his colleagues, though I believe they did know about Carson leaving the Admiralty. The latter, however, did not know that Geddes was going to succeed, till he was informed the evening before.

Myself I do not think the appointments are so very bad. Winston Churchill is the great danger, because I cannot believe in his being content to simply run his own show and I am sure he will have a try to have a finger in the Admiralty and War Office pies. We have an assurance that he will not do so, and I do not think that Geddes or I would stand for it for one moment, but I feel convinced he will try it on. The appointment of Montagu, a Jew, to the India Office has made, as far as I can judge, an uneasy feeling both in India and here, but I, personally, have a very high opinion of his capability and I expect he will do well.

There is no doubt that the appointment of Winston and Montagu is a very clever move on Lloyd George's part. He has removed from Asquith his two most powerful lieutenants and he has provided for himself two first-class platform speakers and it will be platform speakers we shall require to steady the country which is at present very much rattled by that distinguished body the House of Commons.

[1] Philip Albert Gustave Sassoon, 1888–1939. Of Jewish decent. Succeeded his father as 3rd Baronet, 1912. Conservative MP, 1912–39. Private Secretary to Sir Douglas Haig, 1914–18. Parliamentary Private Secretary to Lloyd George, 1920–2. Trustee of the National Gallery, 1921–39. Under-Secretary of State for Air, 1924–9; 1931–7. First Commissioner of Works, 1937–9.

[2] Eric Campbell Geddes, 1875–1937. An engineer on India railways before 1914. Deputy Director-General of Munitions supply, 1915–16. Director-General of Transportation, British Expeditionary Force, France, 1916–17. Director-General of Military Railways and Inspector-General of Transportation, in all theatres of war, 1916–17. Knighted, 1916. Honorary Major-General, and honorary Vice-Admiral, 1917. Conservative MP, 1917–22. First Lord of the Admiralty, 1917–18. Minister Without Portfolio, 1919. Minister of Transport, 1919–21. President of the Federation of British Industries, 1923 and 1924. Chairman of Imperial Airways and of the Dunlop Rubber Company.

Lord Reading[1] *to David Lloyd George*

(*Lloyd George papers*)

22 July 1917
Confidential

My dear LG,

On *quite reliable* authority I hear that BL is sore about the Winston appointment—his point being that he was not told it was to be made before it was actually given to the Press. He is not complaining of it but nevertheless is aggrieved.

I think it right to let you know.

Yours always
Rufus

Sir Maurice Hankey: diary

(*Hankey papers*)

22 July 1917

Quiet day at home in garden until the evening when Winston Churchill, who has just become Minister of Munitions, rang up from his house near Lingfield & asked Adeline & self to come over to tea, he sending a car for us. We went right enough & I had an interesting walk & talk with him, rambling round his wild & beautiful property. Lloyd George had given him my War Policy report & he was already well up in the whole situation and knew exactly what our military plans were, which I thought quite wrong. He had breakfasted with Lloyd George that morning.

On the whole he was in a chastened mood. He admitted to me that he had been 'a bit above himself' at the Admiralty, and surprised me by saying that he had had no idea of the depth of public opinion against his return to public life, until his appointment was made. He was hot for an expedition to Alexandretta[2] but I put all the objections and difficulties to him.

[1] Rufus Daniel Isaacs, 1860–1935. Liberal MP, 1904–13. Knighted, 1910, Solicitor-General, 1910. Attorney-General, 1910–13. Entered Cabinet, 1912. Lord Chief Justice, 1913–21. Created Baron Reading, 1914. Viscount, 1916; Earl, 1917. Special Ambassador to the USA, 1918. Viceroy of India, 1921–6. Created Marquess, 1926. Secretary of State for Foreign Affairs, 1931.

[2] The idea of a combined naval and military attack on Alexandretta, a Turkish port in the eastern Mediterranean coast, had been one of the earliest proposals of the war. Its aim was to have been the cutting of all Turkish road and rail communications with Syria, Palestine and Arabia. The scheme had first been advocated by Lord Kitchener at a meeting of the War Council on 8 January 1915, when Churchill had supported it. But it had been eclipsed by the Dardanelles operation, and was never tried, either while Churchill was at the Admiralty, or at any subsequent time during the war.

Lord Esher to Winston S. Churchill

(*Churchill papers: 15/155*)

24 July 1917 Paris

My dear Winston,

I am full of hope that you, with your fiery energy and keen outlook, will presently take all aeroplane construction into your Dept.

If you do not obtain control of this branch of munitions we shall have the worst possible time next year.

The story is a deplorable one, and, one of these days, LG and Cowdray will get all the discredit for what is not their fault.

All good luck to you, from yours affectionately

Esher

Lord Derby to David Lloyd George: extract

(*Lloyd George papers*)

25 July 1917 War Office

I saw Freddy Guest yesterday. He volunteered to me that the loyalty of the Unionists was above reproach; they were very sore about Winston but notwithstanding that they rallied to a man. The real truth is this, that when the Government put down their feet the whole party will rally to them.

W. H. Cowan[1] *to Winston S. Churchill*

(*Churchill papers: 15/155*)

25 July 1917

Dear Mr Churchill,

At a meeting of the Liberal War Committee[2] held this afternoon, I was requested to convey to you the thanks of the Committee for the valuable

[1] William Henry Cowan, 1862–1932. Liberal MP for Guildford, 1906–10, and for East Aberdeenshire, 1910–22. Chairman of the Liberal War Committee, 1916–18. Knighted, 1917. Joined the Conservative Party, 1922. Conservative MP for North Islington, 1923–9.

[2] The Liberal War Committee was a group of some forty Liberal MPs who wanted Parliament to take a more active part in war policy. Churchill had been a member since his return from the western front in April 1916. Among its other members was Sir Alfred Mond. The first Chairman of the Committee, Sir Frederick Cawley, had joined Lloyd George's Cabinet as Chancellor of the Duchy of Lancaster in December 1916.

services you have rendered on that Body, and to congratulate you upon your appointment as Minister of Munitions.

I am, Dear Mr Churchill, Yours sincerely
W. H. Cowan

Winston S. Churchill to W. H. Cowan

(*Churchill papers: 15/155*)

26 July 1917 Ministry of Munitions

Dear Mr Cowan,

I am extremely grateful to you and to the Liberal War Committee for the congratulations which you have sent me upon my appointment as Minister of Munitions.

I hope the Committee will not hesitate to send for me whenever they want to discuss any matter connected with this Department.

I think it is of high importance that the work and organisation of the Committee should be preserved in full activity, and so far as it is in my power to give them support and assistance, I shall not fail to do so.

Winston S. Churchill to Sir Laming Worthington Evans[1]

(*Churchill papers: 15/155*)

26 July 1917 Ministry of Munitions

Have you explored the question of the British Government securing a complete monopoly of one of the deep sea cables to America for the speedy transmission of all communications between Departments, or a Bureau focusing Departments on this side and the British Embassy and Northcliffe Mission on the other.

During my absence[2] please make some informal inquiries on this subject, both from PMG's Office and Foreign Office, and be in a position to advise me when I return.

[1] Laming Evans, 1868–1931. Admitted solicitor, 1890; retired, 1910, Conservative MP, 1910–18, 1918–29 and 1929–31. Inspector of Administrative Services, War Office, 1914–15. Controller, Foreign Trade Department, Foreign Office, 1916. Assumed the prefix surname of Worthington, 1916, and known as 'Worthy'. Created Baronet, 1916. Parliamentary Secretary Ministry of Munitions, 1916–18. Minister of Blockade, 1918. Minister of Pensions, 1919–20. Minister without Portfolio, 1920–1. Secretary of State for War, 1921–2 and 1924–9.

[2] Churchill was about to go to his constituency, Dundee, where, as a newly appointed Minister, it was necessary for him to be re-elected to Parliament. He had first been elected to Dundee in 1908, and had subsequently held the seat in the two General Elections of 1910.

Winston S. Churchill to Sir Laming Worthington Evans and Sir Arthur Duckham[1]

(*Churchill papers: 15/155*)

26 July 1917 Ministry of Munitions

It will be necessary next week, beginning from Thursday, to survey the whole field covered by the new programme.

The competing demands should be assembled on one hand, and on the other the chief limiting factor, whether they be steel, skilled labour, ball bearings, stampings and castings etc.

Please endeavour to furnish me with short tables showing the main features on both sides.

We have already got a steel distribution in considerable detail, and are in a position to make broad adjustments upon it, subject to Cabinet decision.

I want to know how the different classes of skilled labour, which are potentially transferable, are at present distributed between the various Munitions Services.

The Admiralty should also be brought under review so far as the statistics in our possession render that possible.

Heads of Departments who are liable to be affected by adjustments involving the curtailment of a portion of their programme should consider what suggestions they should make, what relief should be afforded for other Services, and what the consequence would be in their Department.

The Advisory Committee should, on Monday, consider in what way effect can best be given to this Minute, the necessity of which is self-evident.

It is not necessary to go into minute details at this stage, but only to obtain certain broad and practical data which allow a general view to be taken.

Winston S. Churchill to Sir Arthur Duckham and Sir James Stevenson[2]

(*Churchill papers: 15/155*)

26 July 1917 Ministry of Munitions

A regular system of leave for the staff of the Munitions Ministry, and especially the higher branches, should be brought into existence. A roster

[1] Arthur McDougall Duckham, 1879–1932. Chemical engineer and inventor. Deputy Director-General of Munitions Supply, 1916–17. Member of Council (Supply and Engines), Ministry of Munitions, 1917–18. Knighted, 1917. Member of the Air Council, 1918–19. Director-General of Aircraft Production, 1918–19. He published *Atlantic Letters of World Affairs* in 1932.

[2] James Stevenson, 1873–1926. Managing Director of John Walker & Sons, Distillers. Director of Area Organization, Ministry of Munitions, 1915–17. Vice-Chairman, Ministry of Munitions Committee, 1917. Created Baronet, 1917. Ordnance Member of the Munitions Council, 1918. Surveyor-General of Supply, War Office, 1919–21. Member of the Army

should be prepared, covering the Summer and Autumn months, which will secure to each Head of Department from ten days to a fortnight complete relief. But this must all be fitted in so as to avoid too many being away at one time, or continuity of work being broken. This can be done if everything is prepared beforehand, so that each Head of Department knows when he is going to get away and arranges his business and selects his Deputy accordingly. Pray let me have your observations on this. It is not intended to take any action on this until other matters of organization have been adjusted.

Winston S. Churchill to Sir Douglas Haig

(*Churchill papers: 15/155*)

26 July 1917 Ministry of Munitions

My Dear Field Marshal,

I take this early opportunity of writing to you to tell you how earnestly I shall endeavour to study your wishes and sustain the efforts of the Army by every means which fall within the scope of the Ministry of Munitions. I hope you will rely upon me to do this, and will let me know at once if there is any way in which I can serve you.

There are many difficulties here, both with labour and materials, especially steel, and at this stage of the War it will often become necessary to choose between desirable things and to throw special emphasis on this or on that branch of production.

If you have any suggestion which will improve the liaison which should be maintained between certain branches of this Department and the Army you will, I hope, let me know them.

Later on, when I am better informed and you are less busy, it would be a good thing for us to have a talk in order that I may carry out the general direction with regard to supply which I receive from the War Office with a complete and sympathetic understanding of your needs and wishes.

I was tempted to tell you when we met what was in store for me, but I thought on the whole it was better to wait for the fait accompli.

With all good wishes for the success of your operations,

Believe me, Yours
Winston S. Churchill

Council, 1919. Member of the Air Council, 1919–21. Personal Commercial Adviser to Churchill at the Colonial Office, 1921–2. Created Baron, 1924. Chairman of the Standing Committee of the British Empire Exhibition, 1924–5. In an obituary notice in 1926 Churchill described him as 'the most ingenious and compulsive manager and masterer of difficulties . . . with whom I have ever served'.

Winston S. Churchill to Lord Curzon

(*Churchill papers: 8/104*)

26 July 1917
Private

My dear Curzon,

I send you herewith an early copy of the Memorandum which has been prepared on the Steel question in this Department.

I am sorry that I shall not be able to be with you on Friday afternoon; but I feel I ought to go to Dundee to-night and give personal attention to the contest on Friday and Saturday.

I think you will feel that the position disclosed in the Steel papers is fairly conclusive against the possibility of giving full and immediate effect to the new Admiralty demand. On my return I will make a further effort to overcome the difficulties and see if better proposals can be put forward. But, broadly speaking, I hope you will decide to remit the general question of principle to the further consideration of the War Cabinet having regard to the facts which are now disclosed. It is worth noting by the way that the July import of Ore is now estimated at 550,000 tons, or nearly 200,000 tons drop on the corresponding month of last year.

Do you not think also that the Admiralty use of steel for other purposes than merchant shipbuilding requires to be reviewed. For instance, we started the War with a fairly good supply of ammunition for every class of gun having regard to the character of sea battles. During the three years that have followed, we have been enormously increasing our stocks, and apart from practice ammunition, have been firing very little away. In my time the advance was very great, and standing orders were given as to production, which I know Balfour long kept in operation. The reserves now accumulated will be found to be out of all proportion to what would be necessary to sink the German Fleet even under the most unfavourable circumstances. The American Navy has come in, etc, yet you will see that the Admiralty demands for shell steel are increasing month by month.

Again, an important proportion of the steel involved in the enlarged Admiralty demand is no doubt for the construction of destroyers for anti-submarine warfare. Here it is important to ask what kind of destroyer is being built for this purpose. The 1912–13 destroyer, for which I was responsible, lifted six or seven knots on its predecessor, attaining the immense speed of thirty-six or thirty-seven knots without sacrifice either of gun-power or sea-keeping capacity. These boats, which are almost miniature cruisers, were designed to catch and hunt down the best destroyers of the German Navy in their own waters across the broad distances of the North Sea. It is obvious that quite a different class of destroyer, much smaller and more humdrum, is required for submarine hunting far out of reach of all German surface ships. Twenty-five knots for instance with all the economies in money and material that follow from a sacrifice of speed would be quite sufficient for such a purpose. Yet, if I am rightly informed, we continue to reproduce the highest type although the War object for which it was created has been largely rejected.

It would be easy to add to these examples, but I only mention these two in the hope that this aspect of our Steel expenditure will not be lost sight of when it comes to adjudicate with inevitable severity between the competing claims of various services.

Yours sincerely
Winston S. Churchill

Winston S. Churchill to Lord Milner:[1] *extract*

(*Churchill papers: 15/155*)

26 July 1917
Private

Dear Lord Milner

. . . The abolition of the State veto on strikes in Controlled Establishments is a very serious proposition. There are no doubt disadvantages in maintaining it, and it now looks as if it were a mistake to have instituted it. On the other hand, the alienation of the Trade Union fund from strikers during the War is a substantial fact and the public withdrawal of the veto at the present time would either be viewed very ill or very well, and more probably the former. As at present advised I am opposed to it.

Broadly speaking, I am inclined to think that we must make up our minds, whether in regard to munitions work, national service, or recruiting for the Army, either to rub along on the existing basis, getting what we can by small expedients and recognising that no great new resources will be open to us, or, on the other hand, to undertake a great national campaign in order to extract the final percentage of effort from the people.

It seems to me that America, if properly handled, could far more easily

[1] Alfred Milner, 1854–1925. Under-Secretary for Finance, Egypt, 1889–92. Chairman of the Board of Inland Revenue, 1892–7. Knighted, 1895. High Commissioner for South Africa, 1897–1905. Created Baron, 1901. Created Viscount, 1902. Member of the War Cabinet, December 1916–18. Secretary of State for War, 1918–19; for the Colonies, 1919–21.

yield the men who are needed for all purposes than any political campaign would secure from this already almost fully extended country.[1]

I have to go to Dundee to-night for a couple of days electioneering, but I shall be back on Monday and hope to have an opportunity of a further talk with you.

All the papers I have seen show that it will not be easy to increase the intensity of national effort without a great national campaign, creating an entirely different atmosphere, and that, even then, the results which are open are not comparable to those which could be obtained in America.

Yours sincerely
Winston S. Churchill

Winston S. Churchill to the Electors of Dundee

(*Churchill papers: 5/19*)

26 July 1917

Gentlemen,

I have accepted the office of Minister of Munitions in the present National Government, and I therefore, for the fourth time, invite your support at an election.

I regret the constituency should have been put to the disturbance and exertion of a contest at a time when every ounce of strength should be concentrated on beating the enemy. But since the issue has been challenged, it behoves every man to choose his part and act with decision.

All the great parties in the State—Liberal, Conservative and Labour—are resolved to prosecute the War and to support the Government which is responsible for its conduct.

This is no time for domestic controversy. Every party in the last three years has consented to lay aside many of its strongest political convictions. Liberals have voted for Conscription, Unionists have laboured for an Irish Settlement, Trade Unionism has laid upon the altar of public duty its deeply valued customs and privileges. This is due to a profound and ever-present realization of the fact that we are fighting for all that is most dear, whether it be honour, or safety, or life.

Although our Fleets and Armies and those of our Allies have during these three years of peril held the extreme violence of war far from our bounds, it

[1] A year later there were more than 2 million American troops in Europe, and a further 1½ million in camps in the United States. During that year, 50,000 had been killed in action or died of their wounds, and 25,000 had died of disease.

is only by intense and hourly exertion that this position is maintained. France and Russia have borne the brunt for us during many months of intense suffering and unmeasured sacrifice. To-day, they look to us to be the prop and mainstay of the cause of freedom until the great Republic of our kith and kin across the Atlantic can bring its mighty and decisive force to bear. Never was such a crisis! Never was such an obligation! Never was such an opportunity! Compared to it, political, party and personal issues fade into utter insignificance. We have only to look at Russia to see the perils of want of unity, of a babel of voices, of visionary fanaticism, of even the natural yielding to real and heavy grievances. We see the Revolutionary forces in Russia—the men who have won her freedom, striving valiantly to obtain that control and discipline of national effort, without which in times like these there can be nothing but ruin.

Britain has never failed at any period in her history, and of all parts of the United Kingdom in this supreme hour of our fate, Scotland has shown the most steadfast countenance. Her manhood have sprung to arms; her soldiers—the civilians of yesterday—have confronted, attacked and beaten in the bitterest forms of war the best troops which forty years of Prussian militarism had produced. The brains of the Scottish race are guiding and governing our counsels, our industries, our armies and our fleets out of all proportion to its numbers. The wealth of Scotland, her wisdom, her craftsmanship, above all her unchanging and unconquerable will-power have sustained this righteous conflict at every point and at every stage.

I am confident that every elector will at this grave moment record his vote so as to strengthen our Government, to back our Armies, to inspirit our Allies, and to confound our Prussian foes. This will be in true accord with the long history and wide-spread reputation of Dundee.

Sir Douglas Haig to Winston S. Churchill

(*Churchill papers: 15/1*)

29 July 1917 General Headquarters
Private

Dear Mr Churchill,

Many thanks for your kind letter of 26th July and for the wishes which you express to help us.

We are now very well off for ammunition of all natures except 6-inch Howitzer. The supply of this, however, is now becoming more satisfactory. But the supply of guns of most natures to fire the ammunition is not equally satisfactory. The scale asked for in June 1916 has not been reached, and the number of guns for replacement of casualties has not been sufficient to maintain even the Batteries which have been supplied. The result is that operations are cramped at present for want of guns rather than ammunition. Full details of this have been supplied to the War Office.

The supply of guns and ammunition also seems to require co-ordination. Our demands for ammunition are, and must be, based upon the supposition that guns will be replaced as they become worn out. If there is any deficiency in the supply of guns while the full supply of ammunition continues to be manufactured, there is a surplus of ammunition. Moreover, if there is a deficiency of guns of any particular nature, additional work is at once thrown on other natures and increased supplies of ammunition of these other natures are required. This has been exemplified in the cases of the 18-pr. and 6-inch Howitzer. The supply of 18-prs. has not been sufficient, consequently we have now a large surplus of 18-pr. ammunition. On the other hand owing to the lack of 18-prs. and 60-prs. the 6-inch Howitzer has had to be used more extensively, and we have had to continually increase our demands for 6-inch howitzer ammunition.

As regards liaison, we are in the closest touch with the Munitions Design Dept. as regards design. As regards supply of munitions, all our demands must of course go through the War Office. The closest liaison between the War Office and the Ministry of Munitions is essential.

The difficulties with regard to labour and material are fully realised, and the authority responsible for the choice as to what should be supplied is a most important point. The only correct and satisfactory method is for the Commander in each theatre, assisted by his Staff, to work out his requirements according to his plans and submit them to the War Office, who can then co-ordinate demands in accordance with the general plans for the conduct of the war. It is then for the Ministry of Munitions to supply in accordance with the demands of the War Office.

We will all be very pleased to see you out here whenever you can spare the time to visit the British Forces in France.

Yrs very truly
D. Haig

Walter Long to Andrew Bonar Law: extract

(Bonar Law papers)

29 July 1917

My dear Bonar,

. . . I am greatly relieved by your assurance: I think if WC were to join the Cabt or if he tries to control policy & interfere in other Depts there will be very serious trouble. Already there are uneasy rumours current among sensible men who do not listen to mere canards.

The real effect has been to destroy all confidence in LlG it is widely held that for purposes of his own quite apart from the war he has deceived & 'jockeyed' us. The complaints come from our very best supporters, quiet steady, staunch men, & WC has made things worse by stating at Dundee that the opposition to him springs from his political opponents. This is a 'terminological inexactitude' & he knows it.[1]

Yours ever

Walter H. Long

Winston S. Churchill to Sir William Weir[2]

(Churchill papers: 8/104)

30 July 1917

Your paper on the limitations of aeroplane output—

It seems to me that the first thing in this field is a clear view of war policy in the Air, and that until this is decided all subsequent decisions are obstructed and may be vitiated. So far as I understand it, there are, at present the following main requirements—

(a) the Armies in the Field;

(b) Home Defence;

[1] On 22 February 1906 Churchill told the House of Commons of the system of Chinese indentured labour in South Africa (which three months earlier the Liberals including Churchill had described as slavery): 'It cannot in the opinion of His Majesty's Government be classified as slavery in the extreme acceptance of the word without some risk of terminoogical inexactitude.'

[2] William Douglas Weir, 1877–1959. Shipping contractor; his family won its first Royal Navy contract in 1896. A pioneer motor car manufacturer. Majority shareholder in G & J Weir Ltd, manufacturers of machinery for steamships. Scottish Director of Munitions, July 1915–January 1917. Controller of Aeronautical Supplies, and Member of the Air Board, 1917. Knighted, 1917. Director-General of Aircraft Production, Ministry of Munitions, 1917–19. Created Baron, 1918. Secretary of State for Air, April–December 1918. Adviser, Air Ministry, 1935–9. Created Viscount, 1938. Director-General of Explosives, Ministry of Supply, 1939. Chairman of the Tank Board, 1942.

(c) the Admiralty;
(d) the Air Service proper.

We require to know what war purposes are being pursued under each of these heads and to make a complete distribution of our resources between the heads. This can only be done in the light of military knowledge; for instance, suppose that under (d) an immense scheme of bombing machines is to be developed both by day and night, it should be possible to make a forecast of the proportion of loss which would arise in such enterprises. That proportion of loss might be quite different from that in ordinary Air fighting such as is proceeding on the Western Front. It might be vastly less. It does not follow that bombing machines, if properly complemented by fighting machines, would require the full number of machine guns or, in any case, that their employment should be held up for want of machine guns. It is possible that automatic rifles or rifles firing grenades might be a substitute. Therefore it is not possible to say without a knowledge of the War conditions that the machine gun is a limiting factor.

Further, the conditions of aerial warfare under all the four headings and its intensity must be forecasted and attempts must be made to ascertain the proportion of machines that will fall damaged in our own lines, on which

(a) the engine will be repairable; and
(b) the machine guns will be uninjured or repairable.

I should have thought myself that the number of machine guns you contemplate as necessary is much beyond what will, in fact, be needed; that every service on which aeroplanes are sent will not indispensably require machine guns; and that the wastage of aeroplanes under all conditions is out of all proportion to the wastage of machine guns.

I think we require, without delay, to have a conference with the Air Board under the presidency of a member of the War Cabinet—say General Smuts—at which the War policy in regard to Aviation for next year should be broadly decided.

The business of supply will then fall easily into its place. We shall avoid waste of material and misapplication of effort, and many problems which now seem difficult will be found capable of solution.

The making of munitions of all kinds in this and every other sphere, except in relation to a clearly comprehended forethought, are bound to be attended with a waste of our limited resources.

Pray illuminate this subject for me at your earliest convenience

Winston S. Churchill to the Munitions Advisory Committee

(*Churchill papers: 15/155*)

31 July 1917

Urgent

It is urgently necessary that the Rolling Mills should be fed to their full capacity. Please let me know how and when this can be done; what steps should be taken; and what the consequences will be.

Sir Glynn West,[1] who heard the discussions of Lord Curzon's Committee, can appraise you of the reasons.

I shall not come to any decision till I have your report, but two days is the most I can give you for the general outline of your proposal.

General Smuts to Winston S. Churchill

(*Churchill papers: 2/90*)

31 July 1917 Savoy Hotel

My dear Churchill,

Could you dine with me here tomorrow night at 8 pm? I shall try and get Guest too as there are many things to be talked over. Now that you are well in the saddle (and with such a majority!)[2] you must not ride too far ahead of your more slow-going friends.

Yours sincerely

J. C. Smuts

[1] Glynn Hamilton West, 1877–1945. Civil Engineer. A Director of Armstrong, Whitworth & Co. Deputy Director-General of Munitions Supply, 1915–16. Knighted, 1916. Controller of Shell Manufacture, 1916–17. Member of the Munitions Council (Guns), 1917–18. Returned to Armstrong Whitworth, January 1918; subsequently Chairman. Also Chairman of Armstrong Siddeley Motors Ltd, and Director of McMichael Radio Ltd.

[2] On 30 July 1917 Churchill had been re-elected for Dundee with 7,302 votes, as against 2,036 votes for his only opponent, the Prohibitionist candidate Edwin Scrymgeour.

August 1917

Winston S. Churchill to A. J. Balfour

(*Churchill papers: 15/51*)

2 August 1917 Ministry of Munitions

My dear Mr Balfour,

During the last few days I have been thinking about the proper organisation of our non-diplomatic communications with America, which, as you know, are being considered in several aspects at the present time.

There seem to me to be three distinct stages:—

(1) The Inter-Allied Council called for by Mr McAdoo[1] to settle a united demand on America on the basis of shipping and credit, and to divide up the total agreed upon between the respective Allies. This is already well on the road.

(2) The organisation within each British Department for the detailed formulation of their needs and for the day to day conduct of their business with America. At present a variety of persons communicate through various channels with their Agents and opposite numbers in America. This cannot be a good way of carrying on business and must lead to gaps, contradictions and over-lapping. I am arranging that all communications for America from this Office are collated and despatched by one man with a proper Staff.

(3) The inter-departmental organisation on this side of the business communications with America from the various Departments. This is also en train, and I attach the proposals which have been prepared here by my directions in response to the request of the Prime Minister for

[1] William Gibbs McAdoo, 1863–1941. American lawyer and politician. Established the New York and New Jersey Railroad Company, 1902. Vice-Chairman of the Democratic National Committee, 1912. Appointed by Woodrow Wilson Secretary of the Treasury, 1913; active in working out the Federal Reserve Banks system. Favoured strict neutrality, 1914. After America's entry into the war, floated four Liberty Loans amounting in all to $18,000 million. Instrumental in creating the Bureau of War Risk Insurance, first for shipping, then for all soldiers and sailors. Director-General of Railroads, 1917. Resigned from the Treasury in December 1918. Unsuccessfully sought the Democratic nomination for the presidency, 1920 and 1924. As his second wife he married one of Woodrow Wilson's daughters.

> the creation of what is called an 'American Board'. It is undoubtedly necessary that such co-ordinating machinery should exist, and it ought to be possible to create it and set it in motion without either interfering with the departmental responsibility and initiative, or introducing a new element of delay. You will see that we proposed in the beginning that the 'American Board' should only have copies of the cables which are passing, but that as they get into their stride they should take over the whole business of their despatch.

If this three-fold organisation is established all our business communications with the United States will pass through one transmission point on this side, and will be received at the same point for distribution to the various Departments. But do you not think that there should also be one transmission point and addressee on the other side? Ought not the Northcliffe Mission to be organised as a regular department and all communications, for whomsoever intended, be addressed to the Secretary of that department for distribution under the authority of the Head of the Mission to the various Agents and persons affected and for collateral information? I should be quite prepared to place all our business agents in America directly under Lord Northcliffe in exactly the same way as departmental officers are under a Minister here.

Although this system looks a little cumbrous I do not see how any of the stages can be omitted. A strict routine may, here and there, cause some inconveniences, but these are not comparable to those which arise when a considerable number of persons push ahead cheerily on their own affairs without knowledge of what others are doing or concert with them.

Yours very sincerely
Winston S. Churchill

A. J. Balfour to Winston S. Churchill

(*Churchill papers: 15/51*)

3 August 1917 — Foreign Office
Private

My Dear Winston,

Many thanks for your letter of August 2nd with regard to the organization of our business communications with America.

I quite agree that it is of great importance that a proper machinery for co-ordination between the various departments should be established here. The question is by what methods this can be best accomplished.

I think the present proposals for an American Board may be open to some criticism and I hope shortly to put forward for consideration some further suggestions.

The question of the Inter-Allied Council shows very clearly the necessity for a co-ordinating body.

With regard to the point which you raise as to the organization on the other side, I agree generally.

It seems to me that as Northcliffe is the head of the various departmental missions in the United States, all telegrams intended for such missions ought to be addressed automatically to him and he should arrange for their distribution to the persons immediately concerned.

Northcliffe is, however, responsible to the War Cabinet and not to the Secretary of State for Foreign Affairs and therefore any suggestions as to his organization must, I think, come from the Prime Minister.

Yrs ever
Arthur James Balfour

Winston S. Churchill to Walter Layton[1]

(*Churchill papers: 15/42*)

3 August 1917 Ministry of Munitions

Let me have on a single sheet of paper the following broad facts about the Tank programme, actual and prospective. How many tanks, and of what patterns, are to be ready month by month for the next 12 months? By whom, and to what extent, have these programmes been approved? How much steel do they require? How much do they cost? How much labour skilled and unskilled do they require in these 12 months? What are the principal limiting factors in material and class of labour? Apart from the number of Tanks, what quantity of spares, and what maintenance plant are required? Give the money value or weights of materials or proportion of labour required or whichever of the three is the most convenient and representative. Let me know the number of people in the Tank Department, the principal salaries

[1] Walter Thomas Layton, 1884–1966. Lecturer in economics, University College, London, 1909–12. Represented the Ministry of Munitions on the Milner Mission to Russia, 1917. Statistical Adviser, Ministry of Munitions, 1917–18. Unsuccessful Liberal candidate at the Elections of 1922 and 1923. Editor of *The Economist*, 1922–38. Knighted, 1930. Chairman, *News Chronicle* Ltd, 1930–50; Vice-Chairman, *Daily News* Ltd, 1930–63. Head of the Joint War Production Staff, 1942–3. Director, Reuters Ltd, 1945–53. Created Baron, 1947. Vice-President, Consultative Assembly of the Council of Europe, 1949–57. Deputy Leader of the Liberal Party in the House of Lords, 1952–5. Director, Tyne-Tees Television Ltd, 1958–61.

paid, and the aggregate of salaries paid per annum. Show particularly any part of Tank production which overlaps aeroplane production, ie any transferable margin, whether of skilled mechanics or of ball bearings, etc in which these two branches of production are clashing competitors. Show also the proportion of steel, of money, and of skilled and unskilled labour proposed to be absorbed in Tank production in these 12 months compared with the general Budget of the Ministry. I shall be quite content if many of these figures are approximate only.

Winston S. Churchill: departmental memorandum

(*Churchill papers: 8/104*)

3 August 1917

The whole question of reserves must be re-considered in conjunction with the forthcoming programme. With a small Army or a small production the percentage of reserves must be much higher than under present conditions. As the size of the Army and the number and variety of guns in the field increase, it is permissible largely to reduce the margin of reserve. Although no doubt the Military Authorities would like to have sure and constant surpluses in each variety of gun and of ammunition, they can undoubtedly if put to it make a surplus in one type meet to a certain extent a temporary deficiency in another. Also with the great means of production we have at the present time, we ought to be able to make very rapid adjustments in the character of our output. It seems to me very probable in view of the great expanse which has been taking place and the feeling that every demand can be met and that the safe thing to do was to make the biggest possible demand, that Military Officers and different estimating authorities have at every stage allowed an additional margin for safety, and that the aggregate of these margins far exceeds what is necessary to maintain the Army in the field well supplied under all imaginable conditions. We are now approaching at every point the limits of possible production, and any excess of precaution in providing for one Service means a direct and undoubted deficit in another. Looking at the immense shell production and programme which are now before us, I should have thought that it was possible to eliminate reserves altogether, and simply work on existing stocks, and weekly consumptions until we have got well ahead with guns, making all the time preparations to open the throttle of shell production again as soon as the gun difficulty is surmounted. It is obvious that this involves very nice calculations and arrangements beautifully foreseen to enable the required contraction or expansion of shells or gun programme to be made. My feeling is to close down in shells for the next 6 or 8 months, keeping everything ready to expand again thereafter. Meanwhile, open out on guns at the expense of shells, having as many factories as possible capable of being used for the production of either. These general principles are, however, of course subject to the necessary exceptions in regard to particular types of guns in which we have a surplus, and particular types of shell in which we have a special deficiency.

Winston S. Churchill to Sir James Stevenson

(Churchill papers: 15/155)

4 August 1917 Ministry of Munitions

(1) What proportion of our total explosive or propellant output could be based upon 10 million gallons of whiskey?

(2) What proportion do 10 million gallons bear to the whole existing stock of whiskey?

Winston S. Churchill to Sir George Newman[1]

(Churchill papers: 15/155)

5 August 1917 Lullenden

Dear Sir George Newman,

I am working through the various Departments by degrees, and the urgency of war services is such that it may be a few weeks before I can give 'Welfare' the attention it deserves. In the meanwhile I wish you to carry on. I see great advantages in the drafting of the short handbook summarizing the various White papers. I am anxious that this should be ready for circulation in the Winter to Managers and others concerned in the health of the Munition Workers. This work should have precedence of the Final Report, which, though no doubt of permanent value as a record of the Committee's work will, I expect, be rather bulky for these rough times.

I should like to see a proof of the Handbook when it is ready, and I hope every endeavour will be made to keep it short, simple and practical, and that

[1] George Newman, 1870–1948. Bacteriologist. Demonstrator at King's College, London, 1896–1900. Chief Medical Officer, Board of Education, 1907–35. Knighted, 1911. Chairman, Health of Munitions Workers Committee, 1915–18. Medical Member, Central Control Board (Liquor Traffic), 1915–19. Chief Medical Officer, Ministry of Health, 1919–35. Author of several medical works, including *Hygiene and Public Health* (1917).

the various points will be brought well out in the printing by the use of special types and plenty of spacing.

I attach the highest value to your work, and you may count on my active assistance.

Yours very truly,
Winston S. Churchill

Winston S. Churchill to Sir Graham Greene[1] *and Walter Layton*

(*Churchill papers: 15/42*)

5 August 1917 Ministry of Munitions

I propose to make arrangements to deal generally with the Tank position in a series of conferences, the details of which I will settle later, to be held during the week of the 19th instant. Meanwhile I am continuing to study the question by papers and interviews, and am endeavouring to ascertain the true proportion of labour and materials which can be allocated to the Tank programme of 1918 in relation to other requirements. Please inform me whether there are any questions, and if so which, whose urgency requires an earlier settlement. Advise me as to the persons who should be consulted. I am also awaiting Mr Layton's figures.

The decisions on the general programme clearly govern Tank policy in every aspect.

Winston S. Churchill to Sir Stephenson Kent[2]

(*Churchill papers: 15/155*)

6 August 1917 Ministry of Munitions

Please furnish me with a report of the amount of Sunday work now being done under the Munitions Department throughout the country.

[1] William Graham Greene, 1857–1950. Entered Admiralty, 1881. Private Secretary to successive First Lords of the Admiralty, 1887–1902. Principal Clerk, Admiralty, 1902–7. Assistant Secretary, Admiralty, 1907–11. Knighted, 1911. Permanent Secretary, Admiralty, 1911–17. Secretary, Ministry of Munitions, 1917–20.

[2] Stephenson Hamilton Kent, 1873–1954. A contemporary of Churchill's at Harrow. In the Coal Trade before 1914. Director-General, Munitions Labour Supply, 1917. Knighted, 1917. Went on a Munitions Mission to the United States, 1917. Member of Council (Labour Group), Ministry of Munitions, 1918. Controller-General of Civil Demobilisation and Resettlement, Ministry of Labour, 1918–19. High Sheriff of Sussex, 1924.

I am in principle strongly opposed to Sunday work, except in emergencies. It usually results in workmen receiving double wages for working on Sunday, and taking Monday off.

Let me have your views as to the consequences and practicability of a general or partial abolition.

Shane Leslie[1] *to Lady Randolph Churchill*[2]

(*Churchill papers: 28/129*)

8 August 1917 St Johnsbury
Vermont

We are equally glad and surprised at Winston's return to office. It shows that he was built for success that he should have declined to withdraw and sulk over a superficial failure. In America the conviction is that his big strategy over Antwerp and Gallipoli was right but that he was ill served. If either expeditions had succeeded the war would now be over.

The appointment to office has pleased Americans who look on Winston as ⅞ Yankee and ⅛ Blenheim. It is a pledge that senility has not the last way in everything.

Winston S. Churchill to Sir John Hunter[3]

(*Churchill papers: 15/42*)

9 August 1917 Ministry of Munitions

M Thomas,[4] in his interview with me yesterday, informed me that there were no less than 700,000 tons of steel which had been paid for by the French

[1] John Randolph Shane Leslie, 1885–1971. Son of Sir John Leslie and Leonie Jerome. Author and lecturer. Contested Derry City as an Irish Nationalist, 1910, but defeated. Served in British Intelligence in the United States, 1915–16. Succeeded his father as 3rd Baronet, 1944.

[2] Jennie Jerome, 1854–1921. Daughter of Leonard Jerome of New York. Married Lord Randolph Churchill, 1874. Mother of Winston and Jack Churchill. Editor of the Anglo-Saxon Review, 1899–1901. Married George Cornwallis-West, 1900; marriage dissolved, 1913. Married Montagu Porch, 1918.

[3] John Hunter, 1863–1936. Engineer and Contractor; Chairman of the Rivet, Bolt and Nut Co, Ltd, Glasgow. Director of Factory Construction, Ministry of Munitions, 1915–17. Knighted, 1917. Member of the Munitions Council (Group S: Steel and Iron), 1917–18.

[4] Albert Thomas, 1878–1932. A leading French Trade Unionist. Elected as a Socialist Deputy in 1910. Put in charge of railway organization, September 1914. Under-Secretary for Armaments, May 1915–December 1916. Minister of Munitions, December 1916–September 1917. During a mission to Russia in 1917 he persuaded Kerensky to undertake a further military offensive. Director of the International Labour Organization, Geneva, from 1919 until his death.

lying stranded for want of shipment in America. Surely the lifting of this steel, whether to France or to this country, should be a first-charge on our shipping resources. I presume the ships which carry ore from Northern Spain would not be capable of carrying steel across the Atlantic, but it seems the poorest economy of tonnage, labour and dollars not to transport this vital commodity to Europe. If you are in agreement with this, you should state a strong case for the Shipping Controller and for the information of the Admiralty and the War Cabinet.

It also seems very probable to me that the best plan we could make for the utilization of our resources in the new Programme of 1918 would include the carrying of all this steel to France and Great Britain as one of its fundamental features.

Winston S. Churchill to Sir Auckland Geddes[1]

(*Churchill papers: 8/104*)

12 August 1917

My dear Geddes,

I am strongly of opinion that the whole Man-Power question requires to be reviewed in conjunction with the Munitions Programme 1917–18, and both in relation to war plans by land and perhaps by sea also. The piecemeal handling of either subject has already led to waste, friction and confusion. I wish to approach the new decisions which are called for step by step with you. I recognize no divergent or particularist departmental interests. The sole question is the realization of the ultimate war effort in the best forms, and at the highest economy; and whether that effort is expressed in soldiers, or appliances, or ships, or political stability and to what extent in each case cannot be settled on Departmental grounds. Unity of conception over the whole field in harmony with war plans, and their simplicity in execution are the features at which we should aim. I am as you know preparing the date on which a general survey of the Munitions Programme can be obtained. I

[1] Auckland Campbell Geddes, 1879–1954. A distant relative of Lord Haldane. On active service in South Africa, 1901–2. Doctor of Medicine, Edinburgh, 1908. Professor of Anatomy, Royal College of Surgeons, Dublin, 1909–13. Professor of Anatomy, McGill University, Canada, 1913–14. Major, Northumberland Fusiliers, 1914. Assistant Adjutant-General, GHQ, France, 1915–16. Director of Recruiting, War Office, with the rank of Brigadier-General, 1916–17. Knighted, 1917. Conservative MP, 1917–20. Minister of National Service, 1917, 1918 and 1919. President of the Local Government Board, 1918. Minister of Reconstruction, 1919. President of the Board of Trade, 1919–20. Ambassador to Washington, 1920–24. Chairman of the Rio Tinto Company, 1925–47. Commissioner for Civil Defence, Kent, Sussex and Surrey, 1939–41. Created Baron, 1942.

presume you will be doing the same in regard to man-power. I should like to keep you apprised of every aspect of my work in this respect, and I should welcome similar co-operation from you. Meanwhile I am trying to keep the whole position open and not to complicate confusion further by partial expedients. Let us have a talk during this week; and will you kindly read the attached file which deals from our standpoint with matters with which you are no doubt in principle familiar.

Yours very truly
Winston S. Churchill

Winston S. Churchill to Sir Laming Worthington Evans

(*Churchill papers: 15/51*)

12 August 1917 Ministry of Munitions

I must leave the direct care of this business in yr hands during this week, as I shall be fully occupied with other matters. Pray do not hesitate to come to me if you feel in difficulties; but be masters of the question & formulate yr own policy.

Winston S. Churchill: departmental minute

(*Churchill papers: 15/42*)

12 August 1917 Ministry of Munitions

What steps have been taken to bring the bomb supply into line with the great expansion of aeroplanes now in progress? Evidently very large quantities of explosives will be required for strategic bombing, and all our resources will be involved.

Winston S. Churchill: departmental memorandum

(*Churchill papers: 8/104*)

15 August 1917

I am impressed with the unsatisfactory character of the arrangements in regard to Admiralty priority which obtain at the present time. It is not right that one department should claim and secure priority for all its work, however unimportant some classes of that work may be, over the most important work of all other departments. Priority should clearly go by the importance of services and not by any special privilege of any department. I have noticed several papers coming before me lately which show the need of a change of system and I contemplate first addressing the Admiralty and subsequently the War Cabinet on the subject. I wish therefore a case to assembled showing (a) the enormous share of our resources in material and skilled labour absorbed by the Admiralty (b) the inconveniences of the present system of priority, with examples of the harshness with which the Admiralty privilege is asserted and (c) the advantages which would follow from a unified system of supply and production, or, if this is too ambitious, from the regulation of both branches of production through the agency of an inter-departmental Committee surveying the whole field and endeavouring to promote harmonious and economical arrangements.

Winston S. Churchill to Walter Layton

(*Churchill papers: 8/104*)

15 August 1917

Pray consider the following in regard to the reserve of guns:—

In a small army engaged in what is believed to be a short period of intense war, as was our original expeditionary force, a reserve of guns was rightly provided and kept idle on the communications in order to replace gun casualties and losses in batteries. But now that the war is maintained on the front of very large armies only fractions of which are heavily engaged at any given time, and when it is carried on continually year after year as a regular business, no reserve of idle guns is needed. The ultimate gun reserves of the army should be a repairing organization in the highest state of activity and on the greatest scale. The emergency reserve of guns consists in putting a greater strain upon the lives of the existing guns through keeping them in the line for short periods after they should normally be withdrawn. From this it would appear that the reserve of guns to be provided in the programme of 1918 should not be taken as an arbitrary figure like 25% but should be that figure which is required to flush and feed the repairing organization to its utmost capacity. Let me see calculations worked out from this latter basis. The experience of the present offensive should yield the data and the programme of guns in the field, and their ammunition provided at present for 1918 should give the scale.

Winston S. Churchill: departmental memorandum

(Churchill papers: 8/104)

[15] August 1917

We must now be asking ourselves the question, 'In what direction are great expansions of our war-making machinery possible in 1918?' Artillery will remain a fairly constant factor and the steel situation must exercise its limiting power. Ought we not then to look to a gigantic expansion of trench mortars and their organization to a pitch as high as that now attained by our Artillery? Would it not be possible for the trench mortars properly concerted to take the whole trench pounding business off the hands of the Artillery and leave them free for attacking lines in rear, for counter battery work and all services of manœuvre? Could we not greatly increase our supply of explosives? Have we not already got large surplus and expansive power in this field? Could we not use cast iron carcases to pass these explosives over to the enemy? I am imagining an expansion in 'short range artillery' 10 or even 20 times as great as anything yet witnessed, and the whole organized by telephones, etc to the same high standard of action as our present artillery. You should look into this field from the point of view of materials available.

Side by side with this 'short range artillery' we must explore the provision of very long range guns, and long range howitzers. I have asked Sir Glynn West to report upon the possibilities of utilizing old naval guns which may be placed at our disposal. There must be at least 80—12″, and perhaps 20—9·2″ guns available from ships which have been, or will be laid up almost immediately. To make these guns effective for land service, railway mountings or other carriages will be necessary. Which are the best pattern? How long would they take? What would be saved in time by adapting naval guns to land service as against building guns specially? Secondly, assuming there were a saving of time in utilizing existing naval guns, could the ammunition for these guns be got ready so as to make the saving of time effective? Thirdly, what can be done to prolong the life of these guns? (a) by reducing the charges and working out new range tables accordingly; (b) by providing new 'A' tubes. Is it not possible to devise and organize rapid relining plants? Would it not be possible to put a tube like a 'Morris' tube in a 12″ gun and make it fire a 9″ or 10″ shell and to arrange for the rapid replacement of such tubes? This after all is only applying the sub-calibre principle to actual service. We ought not to be prepared to take 'No' for an answer on this question of extending the firing capacity of long range guns. The reason that their lives are short is that the inner tube wears out. That is the difficulty which has to be got over, and is not the obvious solution to have light rapidly replaceable inner tubes? It is for invention to solve this difficulty.

The above is without prejudice to the development of long range 6″ gun fire.

The development of aeroplanes is now clearly before us as a great expansive feature of the campaign of 1918 and preparations to that end are far advanced. Are we sure they are thoroughly concerted between all departments concerned? Is the bombing programme keeping pace with aeroplane construction and projective construction? Can our explosive supply stand at once the double increased demand (a) of an enormous trench mortar expansion and (b) of an enormous aerial bombing programme? In my opinion the manufacture of explosives should be pushed to the extreme limit, this being the governing factor. When this governing factor is ascertained it will then become encumbent upon us to find means of delivering the explosives to the enemy, and if the existing methods of distribution do not suffice to get rid of the explosives, new methods of conveying them must be developed. Do not let us be worried about having too much explosives on our hands. There is plenty of storage room behind the German lines.

I will deal with the Tank programme—ie mechanical infantry, on separate papers shortly.

The above is only to assist you in your survey of the resources and possibilities, and of course I am very imperfectly informed as to what these may be.

Lord Derby to Sir William Robertson

(*Derby papers*)

15 August 1917
Strictly Confidential

Dear CIGS,

As I particularly want to carry Curzon with us in our protest, I showed him the proposed letter. He pointed out to me that it was not perhaps best calculated to secure us a favourable reply, and was good enough to go through the draft with me. I have altered it so as to be able to secure his support if the matter comes before the Cabinet, and though it is perhaps milder than you and I should together have written, I think that more is to be gained by sending a letter which will secure us the support of most of the Prime Minister's colleagues, rather than by writing a letter to which they could not subscribe.

I send the letter to you to sign, if you approve, and to post to the Prime Minister. If you do not approve, will you return it to me here.

Yours v sincerely
Derby

Sir William Robertson to Lord Derby

(Derby papers)

15 August 1917

Dear Lord Derby,

I have signed & sent the letter. All I want is to be allowed to do my own work without interference by Winston & others.

Yours
WRR

Lord Derby and Sir William Robertson to David Lloyd George

(Derby papers)

15 August 1917
Secret

Dear Prime Minister,

There is, however, a matter in connection with the way in which the decision was reached to which I must ask leave to call your attention. I refer to the fact that the Minister of Munitions, instead of confining himself to the expression of his opinion on the points which, as head of that Department, he had very properly been summoned to the meeting of the War Cabinet, took an active part in the discussion of policy, and even voted on that aspect of the case.

I submit that, as he is not a member of the War Cabinet, and as his functions are really those of supply of munitions to the War Office and other Government Departments, subject to the approval of the War Cabinet, such a procedure on his part is not only inconvenient, but also quite irregular.

I am responsible, with the assistance of the CIGS for advising the War Cabinet as to the best allocation of artillery and other munitions between the different armies in the field, whether our own or our allies, and, if that advice is over-ruled, it ought surely to be by the opinions and votes of the War Cabinet rather than by those of other members of the Government. CIGS and I express our views on behalf of the military authorities and, when over-ruled, express our dissent, but loyally carry out the decisions arrived at, recognising that those given by the War Cabinet are supreme.

But we are both convinced that, if interference on questions of military policy is allowed to Ministers who do not happen to be in the War Cabinet, an entirely new position is created, and friction, which brings in its train inefficiency is sure to arise.

I feel sure that we have only to represent this to you to secure the protection of CIGS and myself, who were placed in a very difficult position this morning, from the recurrence of any similar incident in the future. We are both signing this letter, as we are in entire agreement on the subject.

Yours sincerely
Derby
W. R. Robertson

Sir Eric Geddes to David Lloyd George

(*Lloyd George papers*)

16 August 1917

My Dear Prime Minister,

At yesterday afternoon's meeting of the War Cabinet a Committee was appointed with General Smuts in the chair, and with Mr Churchill the only other named member of the Committee—

> to investigate whether any guns and ammunition could be released by the Admiralty for Military use, and to report the results of their inquiries to the War Cabinet.

This matter had already formed the subject of discussion earlier in the day between the Admiralty and War Office, and was being dealt with. I myself discussed it with the MGO[1] and was taking a personal interest in it. In these circumstances, I was at a loss to understand why the War Office should have brought the matter up at the Cabinet the same afternoon when they knew I was doing everything I possibly could to help them. On enquiry however, I learned that it was raised by the Minister of Munitions, to the complete surprise of the War Office.

I confess that I am a little disturbed at Churchill's action in this matter; at his being a member of the Committee; and at the terms of reference.

My fears as regards the Minister of Munitions are somewhat fortified by what has passed in conversation with him upon several occasions, and at recent meetings of the War Cabinet and Cabinet Committees. He has shewn that he contemplates an extension of his functions beyond what I have ever understood them to be, and an infringement of mine which I should view with great concern. When serving on the Committee appointed by the Cabinet to deal with the subject of Steel and men for Shipbuilding, of which Lord Curzon was chairman, I was obliged to make representations to him on the subject of Churchill's concern in purely Admiralty matters. I subsequently discussed the matter with Churchill, and it is quite clear that he considers

[1] From 1916 to 1919 the Master General of Ordnance, War Office, was Major-General Sir William Furse (see page 17).

that he is acting within his functions if he makes direct and indirect representations on such matters as—

The suitability of the design of destroyers ordered by the Admiralty, and the use to which those destroyers are put.

The adequacy or otherwise of the gun ammunition provision made by the Admiralty.

The use made of the 10th Cruiser Squadron.

The retention in commission of the older battleships and cruisers.

The manning of the Fleet and the use made of Naval ratings,

and lastly,

The withdrawal of guns from warships.

These are all matters of vital interest to whoever is First Lord, but it appears to me that the whole structure of departmental responsibility is destroyed if Ministers not in the Cabinet deem it their duty to particularly concern themselves in matters for which they are not responsible in another Department, and if the present procedure continues, I can foresee the certainty of great friction, with its consequent waste of valuable time.

Were it not that such dealings as I have had with Churchill have been most cordial, I would almost feel that there was a personal aspect to his interference in Admiralty matters since I have been appointed First Lord, but I am quite sure that such a feeling would be wrong, and that it is only due to his keenness and previous knowledge of the Admiralty that the difficulties which I foresee may arise.

As I have understood the position of First Lord under the existing form of Cabinet procedure, it is his duty to inform the War Cabinet (after consultation with the Board of Admiralty) on whatever Admiralty subject the War Cabinet may require information, to assist them in forming decisions on matters of Naval policy, and otherwise to be responsible for Admiralty administration, which responsibility he cannot share with others.

I hope that the draft minute can be altered to a request that the Admiralty shall investigate the suggestion put forward and that the Cabinet (through General Smuts if you wish) shall be informed of the result of their investigation.

As regards the future; I feel so strongly on the subject, and it is so evident that Churchill does not take the same view of the duties of the Minister of Munitions as I do, that I feel that I must ask for your assurance that his functions as the supplier of munitions to the War Office, and of certain raw materials to all Departments, should not be exceeded in so far as I am concerned.

Yours sincerely
E. Geddes

Winston S. Churchill to Sir George Ritchie[1]

(*Churchill papers: 15/155*)

16 August 1917 Ministry of Munitions

My dear Sir George,

Now that I have got settled down to the work of my Department I must, in addition to what I have already said to you personally, and in an interview in the press, send you a letter expressing my grateful thanks to the Committee and to all those who by their efforts helped to secure that great majority at Dundee for the National Government.

The election came at a very awkward time—during the hard-won holiday of the workers of Dundee. A small poll and a small majority would have been interpreted abroad as a sign of apathy and flagging energy. The sacrifice of those who curtailed their holiday to take part in the election has not been in vain.

Members of the Unionist Party and many members of the Labour Party have loyally subordinated every other consideration in order to strengthen the hands of the National Government in this time of crisis. When the dark shadow has lifted from the world we shall not be forgetful of the lessons all parties have learned in common sacrifice and in common effort.

Yours sincerely
Winston S. Churchill

Sir Maurice Hankey: diary

(*Hankey papers*)

17 August 1918

Who should turn up then but Lord Derby, who had just come from Geddes, and I will be jugged if he wasn't talking of resigning too! All because Churchill, during a discussion at the War Cabinet on the supply of guns to Russia had dared to say that Haig was better off than had been calculated for as regard 6″ howitzers, owing to the longer life of these weapons, and that a few guns could be spared! 'What right has he to express an opinion? He is only an ironmonger.' Here was a pretty kettle of fish! However, I soothed him

[1] George Ritchie, 1849–1921. Grocer's apprentice, 1865. Opened his own wholesale grocery and provision business in the 1880s. Elected to the Dundee Town Council, 1889. Finance Convenor, 1892–3. City Treasurer, 1895–1906. President of the Dundee Liberal Association, 1907–21. Knighted, 1910.

down too—by telling him I was tired and wanted a rest at Eastbourne, begging him to keep Geddes from resigning before Monday etc. Like setting a naughty little girl to mind the baby. This plan worked splendidly, and by 8.30 I slipped off to the station, arriving Eastbourne after midnight. . . .

Winston S. Churchill: memorandum

(*'Official History of the Ministry of Munitions'*)[1]

18 August 1917

The conditions under which the Ministry of Munitions was created were those of intense war emergency. The vital need of supplying the armies in the field with adequate, abundant and finally overwhelming supplies of ammunition, guns and war material of all kinds, necessitated and justified every expedient and the suspension of all ordinary rules. The immense and then unmeasured resources of the United Kingdom afforded an ample field for the enterprise and energy of departmental direction and for the organising capacity and bold initiative of British business men. Supplies were freely drawn from all parts of the Empire, and purchases from neutral States were used to supplement any deficiencies. As new needs arose they were met. Department was added to department. Military requirements were not only satisfied but anticipated. Vast programmes were successfully carried through. The British armies became the best equipped and most formidably armed in Europe. This process still continues and will become increasingly pronounced.

But after these great efforts, and in the fourth year of the war, we are no longer tapping the stored-up resources of national industry or mobilising them and applying them for the first time to war. The magnitude of the effort and of the achievement approximates continually to the limits of possibility. Already in many directions the frontiers are in sight. It is therefore necessary not simply to expand, but to go back over ground already covered, and by more economical processes, by closer organisation, and by thrifty and harmonious methods, to glean and gather a further reinforcement of war power.

It is necessary for this purpose that the Minister of Munitions should be aided and advised by a Council formally established. The time has come to interpose between more than fifty separate departments on the one hand and the Minister on the other, an organism which in the main will play a similar

[1] This volume, prepared at the Government's request during 1919, was never officially published, but during 1923 copies were sent to the principal British libraries. The official reference given for this particular memorandum was 'Hist Rec R/200/27'.

part and serve similar needs as the Board of Admiralty or the Army Council. It has been decided therefore to form the departments of the Ministry into ten groups, classified as far as possible by kindred conditions, placing in superintendence over each group an experienced officer of the Ministry, and to form these officers into a Council for the transaction of business of all kinds in accordance with the general policy which the Minister receives from the Cabinet.

It is believed that this can be accomplished without impairing the responsibility or hampering the initiative of the heads of existing departments of the Ministry. It is after all modelled on the only system by which it has been found possible to exercise the control of great armies in the field. The functions of superintendence are distinct from those of direct executive and administrative action, and, wisely exercised, are not a hindrance to it but a stimulus and support. It is indispensable that persons near the heads of very large organisations should not be smothered by detail or consume themselves in ordinary day to day business, but that they should have opportunity and freedom to take wide and general views, and to search resolutely and anxiously amid the incidents of business for the dominant truths. With a proper comprehension of their respective functions, there should be no conflict between the fullest simultaneous exercise both of superintendence and action.

Another indispensable feature of office organisation lies in the development of a trained and efficient Secretariat. The direction and distribution of the flow of official papers among all the departments, and the means taken to concert the action of the various departments and authorities concerned in each class of businesss, the recording of action and the circulation of information of all kinds, constitute a sphere second only in importance to decisions on policy and merits. Experience shows the value for these purposes of a strong element of trained Civil Servants, thoroughly acquainted with official methods and inter-departmental relations. Recourse at this juncture to a Council of business men already closely associated with the development of the department together with the strengthening of the Official Secretariat, should enable the Ministry, in spite of the increasing difficulties and strain of the war, to continue to render good and remarkable service to the State.

Lord Derby: memorandum

(*Derby papers*)

18 August 1917
Very confidential

RECORD OF WHAT HAS PASSED IN THE LAST FEW DAYS IN REGARD TO MR WINSTON CHURCHILL

On Wednesday the 15th a War Cabinet was held in my room at the War Office at which there was a discussion on guns for Russia. In the opinion both of the CIGS and myself, Mr Winston Churchill out-stepped his province by giving his views and voted on the policy to be pursued.

Directly after the meeting the CIGS and I agreed that although it was a small matter in itself the principle was a great one and could not be allowed to go unchallenged. We therefore decided to write a joint letter to the Prime Minister drawing his attention to the fact that there had been such interference and saying we felt perfectly certain after bringing it to his attention that he would protect us from being again put in the very false position we had been in the morning.

There was a War Cabinet in the afternoon which I did not attend but CIGS on his return told me that the question had arisen with regard to the giving up by the Navy of some guns for the use of the Army and that a Committee was to be formed to go into the matter. I left the matter there but the next morning I sent for General Furse to explain what had gone on as I knew that he had personally spoken to Sir Eric Geddes the day before asking him to enquire into the matter. General Furse told me that he was very much surprised when Mr Winston Churchill brought the matter forward, especially as there was nobody from the Admiralty present, and he told me he was so afraid that Sir Eric Geddes would think that he (Furse) had behaved badly in bringing the matter forward before the War Cabinet in view of the fact that he had spoken to him privately the day before and had been promised every possible assistance.

Almost immediately afterwards Sir Eric Geddes came over to see me and told me that he thought he had cause for complaint at our having brought this matter up at the War Cabinet. In fact what General Furse had feared was realised. I sent for General Furse who then explained the circumstances and Sir Eric Geddes was quite satisfied. I must mention here that the letter sent by CIGS and myself was signed by me late on Wednesday night and I left it myself at York House for CIGS to sign. This he did and sent it up early on Thursday morning before proceeding to France.

Sir Eric Geddes told me that he resented the idea of a Committee and that he was going to remonstrate about it. He also told me at the time that he had grave cause to complain of Mr Winston Churchill's interference in Naval matters and that he proposed to make a remonstrance to the Prime Minister. I saw Sir Eric Geddes late on Friday when he showed me a letter he had written to the Prime Minister making the protest and he then told me of his interview with the Prime Minister in which the Prime Minister told him that the letter was an unjustifiable one and Mr Winston Churchill had a perfect right to interfere and make the suggestions that he had done.

On asking Sir Eric Geddes what he intended to do he told me he intended to resign but that he would think it over till the next morning.

Saturday morning. He came over to see me and showed me a letter in which he tendered his resignation. After consultation he went over to see Mr Bonar Law as leader of his Party in the House of Commons, in the same way as I had previously consulted Lord Curzon as my leader in the House of Lords. I suggested an alteration in Sir Eric Geddes' letter which would give a loophole for the Prime Minister and which words Sir Eric Geddes inserted.

I then told Sir Eric Geddes what I thought my position was, as follows: If he received an assurance that Mr Winston Churchill would not be allowed to interfere then naturally that protection would be given to the War Office representatives. If on the other hand the Prime Minister accepted his resignation refusing to give the assurance then I should write another letter to the Prime Minister. The first letter I had written did not invite a reply and I had no reason to complain that one had not been sent. It was just meant to show what the CIGS and my feelings were on the subject and as a warning that if it happened again we should have to consider our position. My next letter however would be to ask for distinct assurances that we should not have any interference and if the Prime Minister did not give us these assurances, and if he refused them to Sir Eric Geddes there was no reason why he should give them to me, I should pursue exactly the same course as Sir Eric Geddes and ask to be relieved at once of my post.

Winston S. Churchill to David Lloyd George

(*Churchill papers: 15/31*)

19 August 1917 Ministry of Munitions

My dear Prime Minister,

It will I think be necessary for the War Cabinet to give a decision on the relations of the Ministry of Munitions & the Admiralty & War Office.

My view is that the M of M has nothing to do with strategy & tactics & that he shd express no official opinion on such subjects unless he is invited to be present as a Minister of the Crown at a meeting of the War Cabinet where such matters are raised, or is authorised by the Prime Minister to draw up a paper dealing with them.

On the other hand in the sphere of *materiel* the Minister of Munitions is entitled to review & examine the whole of our resources and to express his convictions as to the best use that can be made of them. For instance if the new shipbuilding programme requires a large cut to be made in the quantities of shell steel provided for the Army, it is right for the M of M to know what the Admiralty position in shell steel & ammunition is, & to state the facts statistically & comparatively to the War Cabinet. Or again if long range guns are urgently needed by the army, it is open to the M of M to draw attention to the very large reserves of such guns now being discarded by the Admiralty, & to indicate the use that could be made of them on land. Or again if the Admiralty claim entire control of the oxygen supplies & use oxygen for purposes far less refined & important than some of those under the charge of the M of M with consequent peril to our whole aeronautical supply, it shd be open to the Minister to draw attention to the relative merits of the competing services & to use all such arguments as may be necessary in that connexion. It is of course for the War Cabinet to judge: & there is certainly no harm in their hearing the facts on both sides.

At present the Admiralty claim a super priority upon all supplies; not only as respects the most urgent and vital parts of that immense business, but even in regard to comparatively commonplace needs. They assert the doctrine that the least important Admiralty needs shd rank before the most urgent claims of the Army or of Aeronautics. In my view there shd be a frank & free discussion on the merits in each case & a loyal & friendly effort by departments—even after a little plain-speaking—to do the best they can by the public cause. This may well involve some comment on the relative activities & responsibilities of the three services, & on the war effort each produces compared to the materials & human resources they consume.

You are well aware of the precedents wh exist in regard to the scope of the M of M & of the good results which are on record. If it shd be decided to limit & curtail the functions of that office, I trust I may be permitted to express an opinion upon the question before it is finally settled.

Yours vy sincerely
WSC

Winston S. Churchill to David Lloyd George

(*Churchill papers: 2/90*)

19 August 1917

Lullenden
East Grinstead

My dear Prime Minister,

With regard to the subject you mentioned to me today:—I met Admiral Sims[1] at dinner on the 16th. The conversation turned in to usual topics. The company of six persons was entirely official & well acquainted with state affairs of a secret character. Admiral Sims opened out upon a number of extremely confidential Admiralty matters. He told us of the latest methods of dealing with submarines, of the projected usual programmes both of this country & the United States, & of the discussions & decisions of the recent Paris naval conference.

I conceived myself entitled to speak with the freedom of a private & confidential circle. I used some general arguments in discussion to express the gravity of our position, & the evil consequences wh have flowed from prolonged naval failure to surmount the torpedo difficulty. I used no argument & stated no fact that I shd not be prepared to repeat in Parliament or that cd not be repeated in Parliament without disclosure to the enemy of anything they do not know already.

I have no means of knowing what fragment or travesties of this conversation have been repeated to the 1st Lord [Sir Eric Geddes] nor how far they resemble the truth. But if any section has been mischievously repeated, the 1st Lord's obvious course assuming he thought it worth while was to write or speak to me about it & give me an opportunity of telling him what had passed, and what were the circumstances.

Certainly nothing that was said reflected upon him or on his Board.

In ten years of official & nearly twenty years of Parliamentary life, this is the first time I have seen such a point raised in discerning the relations of ministers of the Crown.

Yours vy sincerely
Winston S. Churchill

[1] William Sowden Sims, 1858–1936. Naval cadet, 1876. Inspector of Target Practice, 1902–8, and Naval Aide to the President (Theodore Roosevelt), 1907–8. Captain, 1911. A staunch advocate of Anglo-American solidarity, and a fierce critic of naval inefficiency. Commander of the Atlantic Destroyer Flotilla, 1915–17. Rear-Admiral, 1917. Head of the Naval Liaison Mission to Britain, April 1917, he was a forceful advocate of the convoy system. He also persuaded the United States Government to despatch an anti-submarine force overseas. President of the Naval War College, 1917–18. Vice-Admiral, May 1918. Commander of the United States Forces Operating in European Waters, June–December 1918. Admiral, December 1918. Honorary knighthood 1918. Retired from the Navy, 1922.

Winston S. Churchill to Sir Graham Greene

(*Churchill papers: 15/155*)

20 August 1917 Ministry of Munitions

It is now necessary to consider the geographical allocation of the various departments and members of the Council in relation to the new scheme. It is desirable that the Council should be gathered in the Central building not too distant from my room, and I wish to be connected from my desk to all of them by telephone or metaphone as at the Admiralty. I shall want at least 20 switches on my table, probably in two separate sets. . . .

A Council room must be provided on the same floor and probably in the same suite as my room. The big bow window at the end seems to have considerable advantages.

Andrew Bonar Law to Sir Eric Geddes

(*Lloyd George papers*)

21 August 1917 11 Downing Street
Private

My dear Geddes,

With reference to your conversation with me I have spoken to the PM who assures me that he has already told Mr Churchill that he must avoid anything in the nature of interference with the work of the Admiralty and that he (the PM) will make sure there is no such interference.

Yours sincerely
A. Bonar Law

I am sending a copy of this letter to the PM.

Winston S. Churchill to Sir Graham Greene

(*Churchill papers: 15/42*)

22 August 1917 Ministry of Munitions

Remember that from tomorrow morning onwards I shall be sitting every day on the New Programme 1918, and I hope by this means to make a complete survey of all branches of the Department. Mr Layton should submit a scheme of procedure for my consideration which will cover the whole ground: all the special points to which I attach prominence coming in in their proper rotation eg aeroplanes, Tanks, shipbuilding, etc.

Walter Long to Andrew Bonar Law

(*Bonar Law papers*)

23 August 1917 Colonial Office

There are some ugly rumours about WC & interference in *War* policy—believe if this materialises it will end this Gov.

The feeling here & *in France* is very strong. . . .

Winston S. Churchill to Sir Graham Greene

(*Churchill papers: 15/42*)

23 August 1917 Ministry of Munitions

Sir Ernest Moir,[1] Sir Glynn West, and Mr Hunter should sit together in sub-Committee under Sir Ernest Moir's Chairmanship to consider the questions connected with the 700,000 tons of French steel awaiting shipment in the United States. What alternative courses are open to us in regard to this? How can we obtain relief from this source? For instance, could the French arrange with the Americans to use a part of this steel for the heavy shell of the American army and work up a proportion of new steel into the lighter varieties for France? If they did so could we obtain priority for carrying these lighter varieties when finished, or could we make the French carry them themselves so as to reduce pro tanto the French demand on our 75 steel? Alternatively, could we utilize any part of this French steel for our own purposes without affecting the dollar position and with corresponding relief to our own total steel resources? This must be considered in connection with British steel in America now awaiting shipment. This may be so much more convenient that it would deserve priority over any French steel in America turned over to us.

Secondly, why should not the French be forced to take a certain proportion of their own heavy steel from America and work it up into the 75 steel they principally require, with corresponding relief of our contribution of such 75 steel? This last question turns of course on the amount of waste and inconvenience involved in the process of conversion.

[1] Ernest William Moir, 1862–1933. Articled as an engineer, 1885; in charge of the southern cantilevers of the Forth Bridge. Resident engineer, Hudson River Tunnel, New York. A Director of Lord Cowdray's firm, S Pearson & Son Ltd, from 1900. Before 1914, a member of the Admiralty Engineering Committee; he also carried out the construction of the extended defence works at Dover harbour. Founded the Inventions Branch of the Ministry of Munitions, 1915. Represented the British Government in the United States, 1915–16. Created Baronet, 1916. Materials Member of the Munitions Council, 1917–18. President of the Inter-Allied Non-Ferrous Committee, 1918.

These notes will serve as some illustration of the questions I wish this sub-Committee to consider, but it is quite possible they will find a better variant than any I have set out.

Winston S. Churchill to Walter Layton

(*Churchill papers: 8/104*)

23 August 1917

I want the following facts for my meeting with the Cumberland miners to-morrow:—

50,000 tons of iron ore have been lost in consequence of the fortnight's strike and holidays. This 50,000 tons of ore would have made 50,000 tons of steel. How many ships of the Board of Trade standard pattern could have been made from 50,000 tons of steel? How many tons of wheat could those ships have brought to this country in the year 1918?

Again, during the last few months the German submarines have been devoting every effort to sinking iron ore cargo upon the seas and in the last 2, 3, or 4 months they have succeeded in sinking—how many tons? I believe I am right in supposing that the fortnight's cessation of work on the Cumberland field has inflicted more injury on our shipping and food supply next year than all the efforts of the German submarines have been able to inflict in 1, 2, or 3 months as the case may be.

Pray have these figures checked for me by to-night.

War Cabinet: minutes

(*Cabinet papers: 23/3*)

24 August 1917

THE MINISTER OF MUNITIONS . . . strongly favoured the formation of an Air Ministry, but he foresaw that many problems would have to be faced which could not be easily solved. Speaking from his own considerable experience, he was confident that there were natural and intimate bonds linking the two Services. He anticipated no great difficulty in combining the principle of a uniform Air Service with the recognition of the special needs of the Navy. When the two Services were merged into one the personnel would consist of:—

(a) Men who would make it their life-long profession.
(b) Soldiers and sailors who would be lent temporarily to the Air Service, but would return in due course to the Army and the Navy.

MR CHURCHILL said that he fully agreed as to the technical differences in the training of military and naval airmen. He was in accord with the view of the First Lord, that the specialised training of naval airmen demanded a longer period of tuition. Our American Allies inclined to the view that victory would be achieved by the side which obtained complete command of the air. The War Cabinet had approved (War Cabinet 173, Minute 25) a great and increasing extension of aircraft manufacture. In order to enable that expansion to be realised, he was arranging to give special priority to the output of aeroplanes, and he was diverting skilled workmen, as well as material, from shell production to this end. He considered that this development should be subject to, and guided by, the advice of a special Air War Staff, as adumbrated in the report of the Prime Minister's Committee, who would evolve a definite air-war plan of operations. Reverting to the question of the future of the *personnel* of the unified Air Service, he thought a large proportion of officers and men must look to the Army and Navy for their ultimate careers. The two Services could, however, be closely interwoven, and the exchange and seconding of all ranks could be arranged without prejudice either to their interests or to those of the State.

Winston S. Churchill to Lady Roberts[1]

(*Churchill papers: 15/155*)

24 August 1917 Ministry of Munitions

Dear Lady Roberts,

My attention has been drawn to a letter from you dated August 10th which was published in *The Times* on August 11th suggesting that Prismatic Compasses were wanted at once for a special purpose for the Army, and inviting the public to lend such instruments for the use of officers in the Field. The object with which you published your letter is undoubtedly prompted by excellent motives, but it appears from facts which have been placed before me that the Ministry of Munitions is already supplying these instruments, and can supply them to any extent without difficulty.

[1] Nora Henrietta Bews. Daughter of Captain John Bews, 73rd Regiment. In 1859 she married Captain (later Field Marshal Earl) Roberts, who died in 1914. Their son Frederick Roberts died of wounds received in action in South Africa in 1899.

The instruments to be of any practical use must be accurate. All Prismatic Compasses have to be made as a definite military store, coming under an Order in Council restricting the sale unless the instruments are clearly marked by a Government mark as being up to Army standard or not. You will see, therefore, that, even if your appeal to the public meets with an adequate response, it is possible that many of the instruments so supplied will not come up to the desired standard, and their use will not be permitted.

Upon this point may I venture to draw your attention to the importance of first communicating with myself or the Secretary of State before inviting the public to volunteer to make contributions towards the needs of the Army. It is only the War Office, or the Ministry of Munitions, who would really know whether any particular need existed, and whether there was any objection to an invitation being addressed to the public on the subject.

If you would be good enough to tell me the grounds which led you to issue your notice to the Press, it might perhaps be possible to set the matter on a satisfactory footing.

Winston S. Churchill: War Cabinet memorandum

(Churchill papers: 15/31)

MAN POWER AND MATERIALS

26 August 1917
Secret

The Ministry of Munitions is affected at every step by the treatment of the man-power problem.

The distribution of man power between the different services can only be settled by the War Cabinet. The War Cabinet cannot decide unless they know the effect of any particular distribution on munitions, agriculture, shipbuilding, &c. It would be easy for me, in conjunction with Sir A C Geddes, to afford the Cabinet all the necessary data; and after they had decided it would be easy for me to agree with Sir A C Geddes upon the best way, or the least injurious way, to carry out the decision.

But to do this it is indispensable that I should only have to deal with one authority. If the man-power question is split up among a variety of Departments out of touch or at variance with each other, and each cutting in on the labour market and on labour sentiment at numerous points, a continuance of the present friction, confusion, and inefficiency is certain. The greatest cause of irritation in the labour world at the present time is, in my opinion, the recruiting muddle. The questions which are arising every day among munition workers can easily be settled between two closely allied Departments. They are insoluble under present conditions.

I trust that in this war emergency a simple clear-cut policy will be followed, viz, that all material should be supplied by one Department and all men by another, and that these two Departments shall work in the closest concert. Every divergence from this, however tempting or persuasively argued, can only weaken our war-making capacity.

Robert Donald to Lady Randolph Churchill

(Churchill papers: 28/129)

28 August 1917 The Daily Chronicle

Winston is going very strong. I was discussing his work with the Prime Minister on Sunday and he has already made a great impression on the Ministry.

Winston S. Churchill: departmental memorandum

(Churchill papers: 15/42)

I want the sub-Committee on the Iron and Steel Programme, which has met under Sir John Hunter's chairmanship, to consider and report whether there are any measures which can be taken by the Ministry of Munitions in order to increase the total output of finished steel products from the 9,144,000 tons mentioned in the sub-Committee's Report of the 28th August 1917, to an output of 10,000,000 tons during the twelve months ended 1st September 1918.

I should like the sub-Committee to indicate (a) what measures should be taken to achieve this result; and (b) to what extent these measures will affect shipping tonnage, labour requirements and the present programme in connection with blast furnaces and steel works extensions.

Winston S. Churchill: circular letter[1]

(*Churchill papers: 15/155*)

29 August 1917 Ministry of Munitions

Confidential and not for publication

Sir,

After profound consideration we think it indispensable for the bringing of this struggle to a close within a measurable period of time that the output of aeroplanes should be largely increased. The defence of this country against the bombing raids by which the enemy is constantly endeavouring to kill and terrorise our civil population, the carrying of the war effectively into his own territory, and the proper support and protection by aircraft of our Army at the Front make the increased supply of aeroplanes a matter which requires your earnest efforts.

A Committee has been sitting to consider the system of the remuneration and conditions of employment of woodworkers engaged on aircraft work, with a view to securing the necessary development in output. I understand that a satisfactory suggestion has been put forward by this Committee, and that it is to be immediately brought before your Executive Council.

I trust that the significance of these matters will not be lost upon you, and that your Council will, in the national interests, see its way to adopt the suggestion of the Committee, and thereby liberate and concentrate all our available resources upon this highly important purpose.

I am Sir, Your obedient servant
Winston S. Churchill

[1] This letter was sent to the following:

W J Wentworth, Wood Cutting Machinists Society.
A E Smith, London & Provincial Coachmakers' Society.
A G Cameron, Amalgamated Society of Carpenters and Joiners.
A N Findlay, Patternmakers' Society.
A Gossip, Finishing Trades.
James Nicholson, United Kingdom of Coachmakers.
W Matkin, General Union of Operative Carpenters & Joiners.
G Ball, Wheelwrights & Coachmakers Operatives Society.
C Collier, Organ Builders Society.

Winston S. Churchill to Major-General Bingham[1] *and Sir Keith Price*[2]

(Churchill papers: 15/155)

30 August 1917 Ministry of Munitions

I presume you are constantly searching for new forms of Containers for the explosives which will drop from aeroplanes. I understand that at present nothing but what is called 'semi steel' is in view and that much resistance in the Container is required to produce the best explosive effect. This appears to militate against porcelain or glass for explosive bombs. Surely these substances while in a liquid form could be delivered in glass or porcelain, thus providing an alternative which does not trench upon our supply of iron or steel.

Pray let me know what are the facts.

Winston S. Churchill to Sir Arthur Duckham and Sir James Stevenson

(Churchill papers: 15/155)

31 August 1917
Private

I am disquieted about the Steel Department. I do not feel sure that its organization is good or that our available supplies are put to the best advantage. Considering the great importance of feeding the Rolling Mills and the positive orders that have been given on this subject as the result of War Cabinet decision, it is unsatisfactory that the comparatively small quantity of Steel necessary to feed these Mills should not have been forthcoming in spite of the Strike in Cumberland. I am quite certain that it is possible to keep the Rolling Mills fed to their full capacity in spite of such accidents if there is a good enough organization. This is the foundation of our whole position in regard to the Admiralty for if it can be shown that we are not discharging

[1] Francis Richard Bingham, 1863–1935. Son of the 4th Earl of Lucan. Entered the Army, 1883. Lieutenant-Colonel, 1910. Chief Instructor, School of Gunnery, 1911–13. Colonel, 1913. Deputy-Director of Artillery, War Office, 1913–16. Member of Council (Design), Ministry of Munitions, 1916–18. Knighted, 1918. Chief of the British Section, Inter-Allied Commission of Control, Germany, 1919–24. Lieutenant-Governor of Jersey, 1924–9. Colonel Commandant, Royal Artillery, 1931–3.

[2] Keith William Price, 1879–1956. Chairman of Price & Pierce Ltd. Joined the Explosives Department, War Office, 1914; Director of the Raw Materials Section, 1915. Deputy Director-General, Ministry of Munitions, 1916–17. Knighted, 1917. Member of Council (Explosives), Ministry of Munitions, 1917–19. Deputy Director-General, Ministry of Supply, 1939–45.

our obligations in this respect we should be greatly to blame. Out of an estimated Steel production of nearly 9,000,000 tons per annum we do not expect to produce more than about 1,200,000 or 1,300,000 tons of plates at the rate of 25,000 tons a week. Considering that plates are to have the first claim on our Steel resources, which are of such large dimensions, it is difficult to understand why there should be local shortages of supply at particular Rolling Mills.

What I have seen of the Steel Department's action and point of view in the Cumberland Strike, and generally in regard to statistics, does not give me sufficient assurance at the present time to fight a pitched battle on their Rolling Mill figures unless these have been subjected to most careful independent scrutiny.

Please speak to me about this.

Winston S. Churchill: departmental minute

(*Churchill papers: 15/136*)

31 August 1917

(1) Let me have a table showing the output of ships' plates from every individual Rolling Mill week by week for the last 20 weeks compared to the maximum possible output of each Mill if it were worked continuously night and day to its fullest capacity. If statistics for 20 weeks are not forthcoming, let me have them for as many weeks as possible, including, of course, the latest weeks.

(2) Let me have the fullest possible list of all the 'other services' for which plates are required, taking at least 10 pages and giving brief and easily understood explanations of the kind of uses to which they are put under each general heading. Then show for 8 or 10 weeks the amount allocated to and demanded by each of these services.

(3) Let me have a list of arrears of demands for plates which have not yet been met but which are still current and considered necessary.

(4) I wish in future to receive every week a detailed statement showing the output in plates of each Rolling Mill or group of Mills compared to their maximum output, together with a full explanation of any restriction of output due to lack of raw material. These returns should be collected by telegraph and should be described as 'The Minister's weekly Plate Return'.

(5) With regard to the Rolling Mills which are employed in making smaller varieties of plate, let me have a detailed list of at least 3 pages of the services for which these are required at present and the amounts demanded by and

allocated to them during the last 8 or 10 weeks. Report to me how long it would take to convert these Rolling Mills, or any of them, to roll the larger sizes of plate and whether arrangements could be made at any other Mills not now used for plate rolling to roll the smaller sizes, and how long such arrangements would take.

September 1917

Winston S. Churchill: Cabinet memorandum

(*Churchill papers: 15/31*)

2 September 1917 Ministry of Munitions
Confidential

1. The Departments of State most directly concerned in the prosecution of the war may be divided into two classes:—

(*a*) Supply Departments.
(*b*) Consuming Departments.

2. There are three Supply Departments:—

(i.) The Shipping Controllers Department which provides tonnage.
(ii.) The National Service Department which provides man-power.
(iii.) The Ministry of Munitions which provides material.

None of these three Departments should have any Departmental opinion on merits, ie, they should have no partisan feeling upon or responsibility for the use made of their resources. Their task is to show exactly what will be the consequences of any given distribution of available resources. These Departments should work in the closest accord, and for this purpose the three Ministers responsible should form a Standing Committee under the Presidency of a Member of the War Cabinet. Thus any difference between them could be immediately adjusted, their work could proceed in concert, and the whole body of information necessary for War Cabinet decisions would be assembled and kept constantly up to date. There is no room for special Departmental policies or rivalries between the Supply Departments.

3. The principal consuming Departments are:—

The War Office.
The Admiralty.
The Air Service.
The Food Production Department.

All these make vital demands on our limited available supply of tonnage, men, and material. These Departments naturally and legitimately pursue competitive policies. Each has its point of view and its own plan, for the fullest realisation of which it requires the largest possible share of available resources. This competition, however severe, is beneficial so long as adequate machinery is provided for appraising the relative importance of their demands in proportion to their war-making services, and for fitting all together into a general scheme. The responsible Ministers at their head should also be grouped together in a Standing Committee under the Presidency of a Member of the War Cabinet. And when necessary the Supply Group and the Consuming Group should meet together.

4. Thus there would be a clear formulation of the Wholy Supply on the one hand, and the Whole Demand on the other.

5. It would be for the War Cabinet to decide the final allocation. This can only be done with reference to definite War plans and with full knowledge instantly available of the consequences of any particular decision upon the whole aspect of demand or supply.

6. If the arrangements outlined here were adopted, it would follow, so far as practicable and as soon as possible:—

First, that everything relating to tonnage should come within the purview of the Shipping Controller, not merely those vessels which he manages directly, but our whole resources in carrying capacity, and, so far as possible, those of our Allies.

Secondly, that everything relating to man-power should come within the purview, and, as far as possible, within the control of the Director of National Service. The importance of this fact exceeds political or Departmental considerations.

Thirdly, that the whole business of material supply, whether for the Army or the Navy or the Air Service, should come within the scope of the Ministry of Munitions.

Winston S. Churchill to Sir Graham Greene

(*Churchill papers: 15/155*)

2 September 1917 Ministry of Munitions

Please draw attention to Minute 8 of the War Cabinet Meeting of August 39th relative to the 14″ and 16″ guns which are being made by Vickers for Russia. A Council Committee with Sir Glynn West presiding, members Sir

Charles Ellis,[1] Sir John Hunter, and Mr Layton, should assemble to deal with this point and to make recommendations as to the policy of the Ministry on this subject. My own view is that it is useless to send naval guns to Russia as the Russian Fleet is totally demoralized and much too weak to face the Germans in the Baltic in the absence of British naval activity in that sea. Therefore these guns might be of value on our front and ammunition might be made for them if they were retained in the West.

Another very pertinent point is, how is it that Messrs Vickers have been using up our limited steel and labour to build these guns without the Admiralty or the War Office or the Ministry of Munitions realizing what they were doing? No doubt Vickers gets a larger profit on war material when sold to Russia than when sold at home. Are we sure there are no other unsuspected orders of this nature being executed? Fullest information about all business of this character done by British Armament firms should be obtained, but the report of the Committees should not be delayed until this information is received.

Winston S. Churchill: Cabinet memorandum

(*Churchill papers: 15/31*)

3 September 1917 Ministry of Munitions

1. I have caused a statement of the Master-General of the Ordnance appended to Lord Derby's minute of the 16th August (GT–1771) to be examined in this Department, and I append a note upon it prepared by Mr Layton. I desire to make the following observations:—

1. That the heavy artillery in France exceeds by more than one-fourth what the Commander-in-Chief expected when the plans for the present offensive were made.
2. That the wastage in 6-inch howitzers is less than one-fifth of what was anticipated, and the output is rapidly providing an increasing establishment of heavy artillery which will continue progressively to surpass all early expectations.
3. The Master-General of Ordnance recognises cordially the effort made by the Ministry of Munitions to feed this augmented artillery to the full

[1] Charles Edward Ellis, 1832–1937. Barrister, Inner Temple, 1878. Director, John Brown & Co Ltd, shipbuilders, 1890. Joined the Ministry of Munitions, July 1915; Director-General of Ordnance Supply, 1915–17; Member of Council, 1917–18. Knighted, 1917. Chairman, Labour Committee of the Munitions Council, 1917. Member of the Royal Commission on Awards to Inventors, 1919–27. Vice President of the Institute of Naval Architects. A Director of the Great Eastern Railway.

during the present offensive, and his complimentary reference to this subject has been communicated to the officers concerned. The augmentation of fillings of 6-inch howitzer shell has been prodigious, having been raised in three weeks from under 250,000 to over 500,000. It is, of course, true that this effort has not been achieved without drawing upon our resources for later periods in the year. On the other hand, the elasticity of our filling processes is such that minor variations, such as the despatch of a few guns or a few thousand rounds to this or that foreign country, are not appreciable at any given period of effort.

Winston S. Churchill to Edwin Montagu

(*Churchill papers: 15/155*)

3 September 1917 Ministry of Munitions

My dear Edwin,

Many thanks for your letter of August 30th in which you point out that there is no representative of the Ministry of Munitions on the Committee appointed by the War Cabinet to consider the Air Service.

I am asking for a representative on the Committee. We have no intention of parting with the control of manufacture.

Winston S. Churchill

Winston S. Churchill to Sir James Stevenson

(*Churchill papers: 15/156*)

9 September 1917 Ministry of Munitions
Private and Personal

I am sure it is not possible to modify the Excess Profits Tax. What you gained in extra effort from the manufacturers you would lose, and more than lose, in the disaffection of labour. I do not however exclude the possibilities of a special bonus, presumably tax free—I will not say on 'output' but on 'achievement'. There is no reason why you should not discuss this possibility with Sir Herbert Hambling[1] and with Sir William Weir. I cannot however feel convinced at present that it is necessary.

[1] Herbert Hambling, 1857–1932. Entered the service of the London and South Western Bank at the age of 18; General Manager, 1911. Member of the Financial Advisory Committee of the Ministry of Munitions, 1916–17. Knighted, 1917. Finance Member of the Munitions Council, 1917–18. Deputy Chairman of Barclays Bank from 1918 until his death. Director of several marine insurance companies. President of the Institute of Bankers, 1923–5. Created Baronet, 1924. Government nominated Director of Imperial Airways, 1923–30.

Winston S. Churchill to David Lloyd George

(*Churchill papers: 15/46*)

9 September 1917
Secret
Ministry of Munitions

My dear Prime Minister,

There are one or two points on which I want to know your views before acting.

(1) Stern has rendered very good service in the past about Tanks, but I am sure he is not the man to carry this job further. It is in a very bad condition. The Tank Supply Department and the War Office are at loggerheads and this is particularly true of Stern and the soldiers. You know I do not set undue store by their opinion, but I am sure that the development of Tanks is prejudiced at this stage, however much it may have gained in the past, by Stern's methods and personality. Personally I like Stern and should be very sorry to hurt his feelings, but I have no doubt whatever that the moment has come for him to go and that he could be replaced by a far more efficient successor and that the whole development of Tanks would gain in consequence. It would be very difficult for me to find him another suitable job, but he has certainly deserved a KCMG or something of that sort.[1] Have you a strong view against his being superseded, and if not, can I count on giving him the honour?

(2) I am very inadequately staffed in the Labour Department and have been nearly let down two or three times already. Kellaway[2] is very knowledgeable, industrious, and sympathetic; but he is clearly not up to the task. If you had some other vacancy for him, Jack Hills[3] would carry far more guns and relieve me from a number of very tiresome and very ticklish questions which are now taking far more of my time and thought than they ought to. I quite recognise that Hills would be a Tory appointment, and Bonar Law, with whom I have had a talk, told me that there were many others on

[1] Albert Stern, who had received the CMG in 1917, was knighted (KBE) in 1918.

[2] Frederick George Kellaway, 1870–1933. Began work as a journalist in Lewisham, 1898. Liberal MP for Bedford, 1910–22. Joint Parliamentary Secretary, Ministry of Munitions, 1916–18. Deputy Minister of Munitions, 1918–19. Secretary, Department of Overseas Trade, 1920–1. Postmaster-General, 1921–2. Chairman and Managing Director, Marconi International Marine Communication Co, 1924–33. Vice-Chairman and Managing Director, Marconi's Wireless Telegraph Company. Deputy Governor, Cables and Wireless Ltd.

[3] John Waller Hills, 1867–1938. Admitted a solicitor, 1897. Conservative MP, 1906–18, 1918–22 and 1925–38. A Director of the Midland Railway Company, 1910–22. Captain, 4th Battalion, Durham Light Infantry, 1914; Major, 1915. Acting Lieutenant-Colonel, commanding the 20th Battalion, Durham Light Infantry, July 1916. Wounded, 30 September 1916, and returned to his Parliamentary duties. Chairman, West Midland Commission on Industrial Unrest, 1917. Financial Secretary to the Treasury, 1922–3. Privy Councillor, 1929.

his list before Hills. He suggested that I should give him a non-political post and this I will do if you think nothing can be done on the lines I have indicated.

(3) The Munitions Inventions Department requires invigorating. I am quite sure Goold-Adams[1] should go and I am inclined to appoint Henry Norman,[2] who though not very agreeable is very nearly a first-class man with immense energy and a great deal of special knowledge and valuable connections both here and in France in this class of subject. Do you see any objection on political grounds to my giving him this Department?

Please write on each of these points a few words to let me know your opinion and your wishes, if you have any, or whether you wish me to settle them as I think fit within the scope of my authority.

I was delighted with your Speech which in the language of buoyant optimism carried its grave message to this country and to Russia. I think it will do no end of good and was exactly the right note to strike.[3]

Some of the younger soldiers have been speaking to me about Henry Wilson's plans for a Supreme War Direction. Something like this is vitally necessary though the moment for inaugurating it wants careful choosing.

I propose to go over to France on Wednesday to see Haig about some of my Munitions affairs, and I shall then go on to Paris for a couple of nights to settle up with Thomas about Steel and nitrates on which in consultation with the Shipping Controller we have got rather a helpful proposal to make. If you want me to say anything to anybody while I am there please let me know. I shall only be able to be away 4 or at the outside 5 days. This is a very heavy Department: almost as interesting as the Admiralty with the enormous advantage that one has neither got to fight Admirals nor Huns! I am de-

[1] Henry Edward Fane Goold-Adams, 1860–1935. Entered army, 1879. On active service in China, 1900–1, Colonel, 1911. Temporary member of the Army Ordnance Board, 1914. Controller of the Inventions Department. Ministry of Munitions, 1915–18. Knighted, 1918.

[2] Henry Norman, 1858–1939. Journalist. Assistant editor, *Daily Chronicle*, 1895; resigned from journalism, 1899. Liberal MP, 1900–10 and 1910–23. Knighted, 1906. Assistant Postmaster-General, 1910. Chairman, War Office Committee on Wireless telegraphy. Created Baronet, 1915. Liaison officer of the Ministry of Munitions with the Ministry of Inventions, Paris, 1916. Chairman of the Imperial Wireless Telegraphy Committee, 1920. Member of the Broadcasting Committee, 1923. Subsequently a Director of several colliery companies.

[3] On 7 September 1917 Lloyd George had received the Freedom of the Borough of Birkenhead. During his speech he declared: 'I am confident with regard to the future. They will not be able to beat down the strength of this Empire, by means of all the efforts that they can make with their submarines. . . . There is no use disguising the fact that the news from Russia is disappointing. I have always believed in telling the truth and the whole truth to my countrymen, because I know full well that that is the way to get the best out of them. . . If Russia were defeated and humiliated under the leadership of a Revolutionary Government, large territories in Russia would be over-run, as they have been. . . . I am convinced, I know that in all this the Revolution is at stake—the credit of democratic government in Russia and elsewhere is at stake. . . .'

lighted with all these clever business men who are helping me to their utmost. It is very pleasant work with competent people.

When are you coming to London? The 'Referee' is eating very humble pie![1]

Yours always,
Winston S. Churchill

Winston S. Churchill: departmental memorandum

(*Churchill papers: 8/104*)

9 September 1917

It ought to be possible to make a Tank which could easily traverse the kind of inundations that are found on the Flanders Front. It appears to me likely that no alterations to the structure of the Tank would be required. All that would be necessary would be to make the belts which carry the track run round a rather larger circumference and to utilize this increased circumference to obtain (a) height to the extent of about 4 feet, and (b) length as far as may be necessary to provide for unseen submerged ditches and cavities in the ground. In other words, it would be like putting a bogie under a Tank and making the moving track run round the bogie as well as the tank.

An amphibious Tank is no substitute for this. It may have its place in some other tactical scheme but it does not meet this particular need. Please therefore concentrate on the definite problem of fitting an under-body to existing Tanks which will enable them to cross the shallow inundations which protect the enemy on considerable and important sectors of the Front. Inundations are supposed to be most effective from 18 inches to 2 feet deep, but as a matter of fact on the Flanders Front they very often run to 3 and even 4 feet, and of course there are holes and ditches underneath. The irregularities of the ground cannot however compare with those which exist on any of the battle-fronts and I am confident that this is a problem that can not only be easily but swiftly solved.

If this note does not convey a clear impression to your mind, pray consult me. I wish the subject to be examined, and plans and drawings to be made as quickly as possible with a resolute intention to solve the problem.

[1] In the first week of September the *Referee* had abused the Labour delegates to the Stockholm Conference as 'pro-German' pacifists. But the Trade Union Congress had quickly rejected the Stockholm call for a negotiated peace, and on September 9 the *Referee* accepted in its editorial that the Labour leaders had adopted a 'patriotic' attitude to the war.

Winston S. Churchill to the Chairmen of all Steel companies

(*Churchill papers: 15/136*)

10 September 1917 Ministry of Munitions

Gentlemen,

I am told that in some works in the Steel Trade there is an idea that the supply of Steel, and of all kinds of Steel material, is not a very urgent matter nor one directly connected with winning the war. My Council have therefore asked me to write to you and point out how absolutely false and dangerous such a view would be.

It is in fact the exact reverse of the truth.

This is a Steel War. The immense supplies which Germany has of Steel, and the way in which she has succeeded in grasping nearly all the great Steel centres in Europe, is the principal cause of her being able to maintain the struggle. With the exception of our own country and Northern Italy, there is hardly a single important Steel Works which the Germans have not siezed in this or previous wars; and but for the fact that the resources of America are to some extent available to us, the German Steel output each year would largely exceed the whole production of the Allies.

The foundation upon which all our chances of Victory stand is Steel. The greatest possible quantities are required not only to hurl at the enemy in the form of shells, but to build the cargo ships vitally needed to replace those sunk by submarines and so safeguard us against famine and ruin.

Apart from these two paramount demands for Steel, there is a host of other prime necessities for the successful conduct of the war and for the maintenance of our industrial life. Railways, locomotives, wagons, lorries, ploughs, tools, all depend on Steel production. The ships which feed ourselves and our armies, the shells and guns our soldiers fire, the rifles they wield, the loop-holes through which they fire, the revetments which uphold their trenches, the dug-outs which afford them shelter and protection, the light railway lines that bring up food and ammunition, all depend on Iron and Steel. Not only do we have to supply ourselves, but we have largely to aid our Allies, particularly the French, who were robbed of their best Steel Works at the first German onslaught.

Steel is not only our principal means of war, but it is our best chance of saving the lives of our soldiers. This is a war of machinery; and generalship consists in using machinery instead of flesh and blood to achieve the purposes of strategy and tactics. Every man or manager who is engaged in Steel Production is directly engaged in smiting down the enemy and bringing the war to a speedy close. And although he may not share the perils and sufferings of the fighting troops, he can win for himself the right to share their honour when victory is attained.

You are at liberty to post this letter, if you think it useful, in any portion of your Works, and I urge you to impress the facts to which it refers upon all helpers in the Cause.

I am, Gentlemen, Your obedient Servant
Winston S. Churchill

Winston S. Churchill to Lord Derby

(*Churchill papers: 15/156*)

11 September 1917 Ministry of Munitions

My dear Derby,

I have gone very closely into the question of spare parts for motor transport which you raised in your letter to me of the 10th August.

I think I am right in saying that the supply of these parts in sufficient numbers has presented great difficulties even since the outbreak of the War, and that the stock now in hand is very much larger than it was a year ago when the Ministry took control. You can feel assured that this question has at all times received the greatest attention on our part, but our motor works are designed to make a finished article with the comparatively small proportion of spares required in peace time, and the machinery has been balanced accordingly. Your war requirements on the other hand include very large demands for particular parts, which means that new machinery must be installed specially, and devoted to these parts, or else that the output of completed vehicles must be reduced and some machinery left idle. In order to meet the difficulties of the position, I would like to make the following suggestions:—

(1) that the War Office should carefully re-examine their stores of spare parts, reducing their demand when they find they have large stocks of certain classes.
(2) that they should let the Ministry have a fortnightly list of the most pressing spares.
(3) that the worn parts removed from lorries in England and France should be returned to the Salvage Department for repair or other utilisation.
(4) that no new motor vehicle should be accepted from manufacturers unless a proper proportion of spares is supplied with it. I suggest that the

necessary equipment of spares should be discussed between your officers and mine, but that before such consultation takes place, you should ask your Department to look once more into the possibility of economising the use of spares in France.

(5) that a higher priority be given for spares than for finished vehicles. If you concur, I propose to give instructions to the Priority Department to this effect. I am also taking up the question of the price to be paid for spares compared with the price of complete vehicles.

There is one more aspect of this question in which I think you may be able to help us. It appears that in spite of repeated requests from this Department we still have only a very indefinite programme for complete vehicles to work upon and no programme at all for spare parts, the demands for which reach us spasmodically. I am confident, and indeed it is obvious, that if we had a properly formulated programme, both for complete vehicles and spare parts, we should be able so to arrange our manufacturing capacity that we could meet your demands for both classes of supplies with much greater regularity and smoothness of working than is the case at present.

Winston S. Churchill

Winston S. Churchill to Louis Loucheur[1]

(*Loucheur papers*)

17 September 1917 Hotel Ritz
Paris

My dear Monsieur Loucheur,

I share your views about the extreme importance of accelerating the formation of the Inter Allied Council in order to facilitate the munitions supply of both countries. I am very grateful to you for the sympathy and energy with which you have aided the solution of this problem. You must not however suppose that I am authorised to deal on behalf of the British Govt with the arrangements for the Council or for its composition. That must be settled through the Foreign Office, as it is wholly outside the scope of the duties entrus-

[1] Louis Loucheur, 1872–1931. Engineer, contractor and munitions manufacturer. One of the first French businessmen to receive political office during the war. Under-Secretary of State at the Ministry of Munitions, December 1916–April 1917. Minister of Munitions, 1917–20. Elected to the Chamber of Deputies, 1919. Helped in the drafting of the economic section of the Treaty of Versailles, 1919. Minister for the Liberated Areas, 1921; Minister of Trade, 1924; Minister of Finance (for seventeen days), 1925; Minister of Trade, 1926; Minister of Labour, 1928. Author of the 'Loucheur Law' of 1928 to help deal with housing crises by building low-priced houses with the help of public funds.

ted to me. Nor have I the knowledge to enable me to express a decided opinion upon the character of the arrangements outlined in your draft telegram.

I will do everything in my power to facilitate the settlement of this matter. But I recommend you to put the proposition before the British Government through the regular channel of the Foreign Office. The question is most urgent and should be pressed from day to day, with the sole object of presenting to the US the joint agreed proposals of the Allies, in whose decision the accord of England and France should play a dominating part.

I shall be available between 10 & 11.30 tomorrow morning in case I can be of any service to you.

Yrs vy sincerely
Winston S. Churchill

Winston S. Churchill to Sir Joseph Maclay[1]

(*Churchill papers: 15/156*)

21 September 1917 Ministry of Munitions

My dear Joseph Maclay

. . . I have received from Monsieur Thomas the attached list of ships in French ports, which the French say a very small quantity of ship-building material would render useful in a short time. Does this matter come within your purview? Clearly these ships ought to be repaired and at work at the earliest possible moment, especially those which require such small quantities of material. Would it not be possible to supply the French with the material, additional to what we are giving them in the ordinary course, on condition that the use to which these ships were put should give us a proportionate relief? Can anything be done in this direction, and how can we do it?

I want to have another talk with you next week. The French have accepted my terms about the American Steel, and a very considerable advantage has been secured in consequence.

Winston S. Churchill

[1] Joseph Paton Maclay, 1857–1951. Shipowner. Member of the Glasgow Town Council. Commissioner for Taxes, City of Glasgow. Created Baronet, 1914. Shipping Controller (later Minister of Shipping), 1916–21. Member of the Committee on National Expenditure, 1921. Created Baron, 1922. Of his five sons, two were killed in action, Lieutenant William Strang Maclay (born 1895) in 1915, and Lieutenant Ebenezer Maclay (born 1891) in 1918.

Winston S. Churchill: departmental minute

(*Churchill papers: 15/31*)

22 September 1917 Ministry of Munitions

1. There is no reason to suppose that the immense programme of Aeroplane Construction which has been sanctioned cannot be achieved. The estimates of progress have so far been substantially confirmed by results. I append a statement which Sir A Duckham, Member of the Munition Council for this group, has prepared by my directions. This deserves to be studied. All necessary action will be taken, so far as it lies within the power of this Department.

2. The Aeroplane Programme will of course be frustrated if its requirements in skilled labour and material are not met, as they certainly can be. Still more is this true, if the claims of the Admiralty or of the War Office involve large withdrawals of skilled labour from munition supplies. . . . If Admiralty requirements for skilled labour are to be accorded super-priority or 'Admiralty Priority' without regard either to the effect upon munitions programmes or to the possibilities of internal economies in the Admiralty use of their present appropriation of skilled labour and materials, the obvious consequences will follow. The matter is one entirely for the Cabinet, and any decision they may take can be easily given effect to. It must, however, be remembered that a decision to give priority to one class of supply is *ipso facto* cancelled by a subsequent decision to give priority to another class of supply. It will be no use complaining afterwards when the inevitable consequences of such decisions mature.

The Zeppelin Programme for the Navy is another case in point.

It is suggested that all Departments engaged in the prosecution of the war should receive an equally searching investigation in order to ascertain the use they are making for effective war purposes of the labour and material at their disposal. It is impossible for any one Department to judge the relative importance of its own claims. That can only be done by the War Cabinet as a consequence of their General War Plan for 1918, which is not known to individual Departments.

It was to this point of view Sir William Weir's Memorandum to the Air Board, circulated by General Smuts, was directed.

3. I have examined General Smuts' proposal that Sir John Hunter, Member of the Munitions Council for the Steel Group, should superintend and be responsible for the construction of the aerodromes and sheds required to carry out the new Programme. I find that this gentleman had already, under the Ministry of Munitions, erected seven aerodromes in Lincolnshire and Shropshire, accommodating in all twenty-one squadrons, and numerous

auxiliary buildings. These aerodromes have all been finished and were occupied many months ago.

We learned in July that the War Office intended to carry out the New Programme Buildings themselves. The reasons for this decision were not imparted to us.

If it is now decided to reverse it and entrust the completion of the New Programme Aerodromes to Sir John Hunter and the Ministry of Munitions, we are willing to accept the responsibility; but it is necessary to draw attention to the lateness of the season, which prejudices rapid building operations.

I should deprecate the withdrawal of Sir John Hunter from the Ministry of Munitions, as he is at the present time personally directing the extensions of steel works which are vital to the execution of the Ships' Plates Programme described in my recent paper on that subject. The two tasks can conveniently be combined.

Winston S. Churchill to Lord Derby

(*Churchill papers: 8/104*)

25 September 1917

My dear Derby,

Herewith our Gas project in outline. If you still like it, the sooner action is taken the better. Every day is precious in war—and deadly. Thuillier[1] if available should come at once.

Yours very sincerely
Winston S. Churchill

Winston S. Churchill to Lord Derby

(*Churchill papers: 8/104*)

25 September 1917

In consequence of our discussion at GHQ I make you the following proposals for the re-organization of our Gas-Services at home—

[1] Henry Fleetwood Thuillier, 1868–1953. 2nd Lieutenant, Royal Engineers, 1887. On active service, Chitral, 1895. Brigadier-General, 1915. Director of Gas Services, GHQ France, 1915. Controller of Chemical Warfare, Ministry of Munitions, 1915–18. President of the Chemical Warfare Committee, 1917–18. Major-General, 1917. General Officer commanding the Thames and Medway Area, 1919–23. Director of Fortifications and Works, War Office, 1924–7. Knighted, 1930.

(1) The existing gas-services now under the Ministry of Munitions, whether of research or supply, should be amalgamated with the anti-gas services now under the War Office, whether of research or supply.

(2) A Committee of five or six soldiers, scientists, and others, should be formed with representatives of the present Gas and Anti-Gas Committees, and with additional members, representing both the General Staff and the Army in the field. This Committee should be called the Chemical Warfare Committee. It should be under the Ministry of Munitions. Its President should be appointed by the Minister of Munitions with the approval of the Secretary of State for War. The representatives of the General Staff and of the Army in the field should be appointed by the Secretary of State for War with the approval of the Minister. This Committee should be responsible to the Minister of Munitions for the whole business of research, experiment, design and supply of everything connected with Chemical Warfare.

(3) The Committee should form three Sub-Committees, styled the Gas, Anti-Gas and Gas Services Supply Sub-Committee. The Sub-Committee should be presided over by members specialized in their respective branches.

(4) It is proposed considerably to increase the number of scientists engaged in research and experiment for Chemical Warfare. This will be done by adding both to the Committee and the Sub-Committee an indefinite number of 'Associate Members' who will not take part in the administration of the gas-services, but who will be made acquainted with all that is necessary for them to know, and will work independently but in association. It is proposed by this means to connect allied scientists, particularly French and American, with the British development of Chemical Warfare.

(5) I heard with great pleasure your opinion that Major-General Thuillier should be President of the Chemical Warfare Committee. I thank you cordially for this offer, and I should be willing to appoint him immediately. I hope also that General Foulkes[1] may, without prejudice to his existing duties in France as Director of Gas-Services, become a member of the Committee. I should propose myself to select a scientist for Vice-President.

[1] Charles Howard Foulkes, 1875–1969. Entered Army, 1894. On active service in South Africa, 1899–1900. Played Hockey for Scotland, winning an Olympic Medal, 1908. Major, 1914. General Officer Commanding the Special Brigade, and Director of Gas-Services, GHQ, France, 1914–19. Deputy Chief Engineer, Southern Command, 1924–6. Chief Engineer, Aldershot Command, 1926–30. Retired with the rank of Major-General, 1930. In 1934 he published *Gas! The Story of the Special Brigade*. Colonel Commandant, Royal Engineers, 1937–45.

October 1917

J. L. Garvin to Winston S. Churchill

(*Churchill papers: 15/156*)

3 October 1917 The Observer

My dear Winston

. . . Do lets have a quarter of an hour together next week—the earlier the better anywhere. I hear much confidential talk of you for the Air Board; in speculative brilliancy nothing touches it but the real Bank of England in politics is where you are.

Yours ever
J. L. Garvin

Winston S. Churchill to Lord Derby

(*Churchill papers: 15/157*)

4 October 1917 Ministry of Munitions

My dear Derby,

The existing arrangement about the promotion of military officers serving under the Ministry of Munitions is not satisfactory and is not being interpreted by the War Office in a spirit which will render it satisfactory. You share, I know, my desire that the liaison between the War Office and the Ministry of Munitions, which is almost entirely occupied in serving the War Office, should be as perfect and as intimate as possible. It is necessary that a proportion of military officers serving under the Ministry in the interests of the vital supplies of the Army, should be active men fresh from the Front, liable and likely to return there before the end of the war. We cannot expect to secure a proportion of good men if a veto is placed on their advancement by the War Office, and if service under the Ministry of Munitions is to be regarded as a slur upon their military career.

There is no just reason that I can see for discriminating between officers of the professional army and temporary officers, now that the war has lasted so long. I have no sympathy for persons above the military age who do not hold permanent commissions but who desire to wear uniform for uniform's sake. There are however three classes of officers whose cases require to be provided for—

(1) A very small class. Officers holding permanent commissions who are employed at the heads of important departments largely or mainly military in their character and who require to have rank which is not wholly disproportionate to the importance of their functions.

(2) Officers brought back from the Front to keep our military departments fully abreast of Trench Warfare Research and Invention and cognate services. This second class whether holding permanent or temporary commissions requires to be safeguarded or we shall not get good men.

(3) Men of military age liable to the Military Service Act who have obtained commissions as Lieutenants and 2nd Lieutenants since the war or who holding commissions as Lieutenants or 2nd Lieutenants before the war have, because of their special aptitudes—scientific attainments, business abilities, and so forth—been retained at home in the interests of the Army. These are, I consider, entitled to the protection of the uniform and to a certain reasonable measure of advancement, having regard to their age and the importance of their duties, from the incongruous rank of 2nd Lieutenant at any rate as far as the rank of Captain, each case being judged on its merits.

At present practically every request which we put forward on all these three classes is refused and I am continually embarrassed by complaints which are not personal in their character but arise from incongruous circumstances detrimental to administrative efficiency.

I should be very glad if we could have a conference at which I think you and I should both be present, so that matters could be adjusted satisfactorily. As you know, owing to the Committee over which you asked me to preside, I am not unacquainted with the difficulties of the problem or with the great abilities of the officers in the War Office to whom its detailed conduct is entrusted.

Yours vy sincerely
Winston S. Churchill

Winston S. Churchill: departmental memorandum

(*Churchill papers: 8/104*)

4 October 1917

The munition factories in the bombing area should be furnished with dug-outs or other shelters. Many of the private firms have already taken such steps and the rest, together with the national factories, must be made to conform without delay. Materials where necessary can be supplied by the State. The labour must be found on the spot by the people working in the factories. They may be given on two or three successive days two hours off in each shift on full pay, conditional on their doing the rest of the job in their own time. It should not take long. The loss on output must be accepted; it will probably be more than made good by the confidence of the work-people and the fact that they will not scatter to their homes when an alarm is given but will instead remain close by in the dug-outs.

There are two important features to be aimed at in affording shelter against aeroplane bombs:

(1) The over-head cover should be at least two layers deep with as wide an air space as possible in between the upper or detonating platform and the lower or actual roof. The detonating platform need not necessarily be very strong. Bricks or rubble loosely packed on a layer of sand-bags are at once a good detonator and absorber: two or three courses of sand-bags ten feet below this should afford a considerable measure of protection from a small or medium bomb.

(2) Unless shelters can be made absolutely bomb-proof (in which case it does not matter how many people they contain) they should be divided up at short intervals by light sand-bag traverses like stalls in a stable to localize the limit and effect of any explosion. The entrances should always be covered by a sand-bag parados.

These principles are to be taken as a guide and not as a rule.

Winston S. Churchill

Winston S. Churchill to the Committee on Dug-outs

(*Churchill papers: 8/104*)

5 October 1917

(1) Surely one of your first steps should be to draft a letter to the munition factories in the bombing areas, setting forth in general terms the policy of the Ministry in regard to dug-outs, the general characteristics of the kind of

protection which is desirable, and the scope of the Government assistance which it is expected can be afforded, and asking them to furnish schemes for the protection of their workers, together with a statement of any useful material they may have or know of in the neighbourhood.

(2) You must be careful not to overweight this job at the start by seeking after perfection. Any shelter is better than none. A deep narrow zigzag trench in an open field is extremely good protection, and it is almost certain that it would not be hit directly. All kinds of odd material can be worked in to the making of over-head cover. At one factory they have already used empty shell cases. It might be possible to utilise for the purpose of giving immediate shelter material which is not wanted till later in the year and could be replaced before that by other things. Above all, we want to avoid anything like a sealed pattern with an engineer officer coming along to reject it because it does not come up exactly to his ideas. Anything is better than nothing; speed is better than perfection; makeshift and improvisation must animate the work.

(3) You must of course form a small Organization here to deal with the correspondence which will arise on this subject. In this matter you should refer to the Secretariat.

The original letter to the factories should be drafted to-morrow and should, if possible, go out to-morrow night, and your Organization must be in working order by the time the answers are received.

Remember that all these factories are full of highly competent engineers and practical men with plenty of tools and power handy and materials of all kinds lying about.

Winston S. Churchill: Cabinet memorandum

(*Churchill papers: 15/32*)

PROTECTION FROM AIR RAIDS

5 October 1917 Ministry of Munitions
Confidential

1. I have given directions that dug-outs and shelters are to be immediately provided under approved schemes in the whole of the munition factories in the bombing areas. Many private firms have already taken these measures with great advantage. The labour will be found from the people employed in the factories. The work should not take long. The loss on output must be accepted; it will certainly be much less than the loss caused by the people

scattering to their homes whenever an air-raid alarm is given. There will also be a great gain in the feeling of confidence imparted to the workers. I hope these arrangements will be complete within ten days.

2. I consider that, generally speaking, people are entitled to a safe shelter within reasonable distance of their homes or their work. I consider that in or near each street a house or houses should be prepared which affords reasonable security to the residents, and that in the vicinity of all large works, whether munitions or other, an adequate provision should be made for everyone. This, of course, would vary in each case with the facilities and materials available. I am impressed by the rapidity by which shelters have been provided in some of the munitions areas already, and I do not believe the task will be found a very formidable one. I expect the Germans are already hard at work providing proper shelters in the cities likely to be attacked. It is especially important to the confidence of the population that in working-class areas consisting almost entirely of frail two-storey dwellings there should be sufficient shelters prepared. Where there are larger houses an issue of sand-bags and of leaflets containing clear printed directions as to the parts of the house which are safe, the dangers to be avoided &c, should meet the case. I do not see why the work should not be done by volunteers working under the local authorities, assisted by the military forces in the country. There are scores of ways of giving efficient protection. There are thousands of officers and others in this country thoroughly acquainted with the methods. As long as people have a safe place to go to when firing begins and are compensated for the damage done to their houses they will stand a great deal of hammering and get back to their work promptly when it stops. All the defences can be improved gradually.

3. The best way to deal with the supply of guns for the London defences is to treat all the 3-inch 20-cwt AA guns as if they were on one list and under one service, and spread the wear evenly over them all by arranging for a constant interchange between the groups of guns on which the undue strain falls and the practically unused guns of the Merchant Service and the Fleet. This, in addition to an active system of relining, should greatly improve our margins of supply. It is, of course, important that none of the guns should be used up to the point when they are completely worn out, and that all guns should be removed to quieter stations while they still have 200 or 300 rounds of life in them.

Winston S. Churchill to Lord Northcliffe: telegram

(*Churchill papers: 15/52*)

9 October 1917 Ministry of Munitions

I have obtained the following statement from the War Office and Haig. It carries the highest authority and you can use it confidentially as you think necessary. Begins—The prospect of a reduction in the supply of 6″ Howitzer shell from America is causing grave anxiety and the War Cabinet urge that you will make every endeavour to induce the United States Government to authorise the placing of the contracts asked for by the Ministry of Munitions. The supply of this nature of ammunition is of vital importance for the common Allied cause and Sir Douglas Haig reports as follows—

> Situation is causing me concern in regard to 6″ howitzer ammunition. This howitzer is more generally used than any other weapon and has for all descriptions of artillery work proved itself invaluable. Recent successes have been due to a large extent to the ample supply of ammunition which has hitherto been available but any reduction as forecast in previous telegram will seriously hamper present offensive operations. If offensive is to be undertaken by British Army in the spring as regards 1918 amounts already demanded are absolutely necessary. Estimate of expenditure during winter was calculated at a very low rate to economise gun lives and I calculate that if reduction mentioned by you is made even if the expenditure during winter is considerably reduced which I cannot recommend there will only be enough ammunition in France by the 1st April next to complete the field echelons. End of Haig's message.

Your 358. My statement was very carefully guarded and of course we shall only come through safely if the greatest exertions are made in shipbuilding and the most stringent economy practised in food. Difficulties of combining truthful statement of position giving confidence here and discouragement in Germany with needs of working up vigorous shipbuilding campaign in America are inherent in situation. There are too many different publics to consider. Surely case for a great American fleet to carry and supply a great American army is self-contained and the diminution actual and prospective of the worlds tonnage a glaring fact. It ought to be possible to emphasize these without suggesting that we are not making good headway in our efforts against the submarines or that results of submarine campaigns have not been a great disappointment to the Germans. The Government here seemed rather upset at your pessimistic interview though they quite understood its object. It is all a question of emphasis and we must each keep each other's point of view in mind. Many thanks for telegraphing.

Lord Robert Cecil[1] *to Winston S. Churchill*

(*Churchill papers: 15/85*)

9 October 1917
Confidential

My dear Churchill

When I was over in France last week I was taken to the Headquarters of the Tanks & found the people there in a rather critical frame of mind. They complain that the tanks now being sent out to them are too short to be useful. The new German trenches are so wide that the tank cannot get out of them. They represent that weeks or even months ago they put forward six requirements—including greater length—none of which have been complied with. In despair they are beginning with very inadequate equipment to try to lengthen a tank experimentally for themselves. They shewed me their experiment which was not yet complete. They also shewed me two devices, one a baulk of timber & the other a bundle of faggots, which they had arranged in such a way that when the driving bands of the tank would not grip these things would come round with them & enable the machine to start again. But the defect was that these could only be put in gear by someone coming out of the tank for the purpose, which was of course impossible in battle conditions. I was also shewn some 'sledges' or heavy wooden trays constructed to be drawn by steel ropes behind the tanks. It was said that in this way a weight of 25 tons! could be drawn by a tank thus greatly facilitating the movement of guns & ammunition over rough ground.

A complaint was made that though these had been asked for months ago none had been sent & they had been forced to manufacture them for themselves. In this connection I was also shewn a large number of iron drums designed to convey ammunition by rolling. It was pointed out that they were absolutely useless for shell-marked country since they would be more trouble to move than the ammunition they were meant to carry. I feel it right to pass these statements on to you without in any way making myself responsible for the criticisms contained in them which may be ill or well-founded. Please forgive me if you already knew all about it—as is most probable.

Yours very sincerely
Robert Cecil

[1] Lord Edgar Algernon Robert Cecil, 1864–1958. Third son of the 3rd Marquess of Salisbury. Conservative MP, 1906–10. Independent Conservative MP, 1911–23. Under-Secretary of State for Foreign Affairs, 1915–18. Minister of Blockade, 1916–18. Assistant Secretary of State for Foreign Affairs, 1918. Created Viscount Cecil of Chelwood, 1923. Lord Privy Seal, 1923–4. President of the League of Nations Union, 1923–45. Chancellor of the Duchy of Lancaster, 1924–7. Nobel Peace Prize, 1937.

Leopold Amery: diary

(Amery papers)

10 October 1917

There was considerable discussion[1] between Churchill and the War Office themselves as to what the figure of guns available would be. Generally speaking, it was decided to fulfil our promises except in 8″ howitzers to Russia and Rumania, and the enormous Russian demands for machine guns. I talked with Churchill coming away. Under the influence of a successful speech to a large meeting of munitions workers the night before, he was very sanguinistic about the labour situation, and inclined to think that the great thing was to keep the machinery oiled by satisfying them, as regards pay etc, even if it involved progressive depreciation of all their money values.

Winston S. Churchill to Lord Robert Cecil

(Churchill papers: 15/85)

10 October 1917 Ministry of Munitions

My dear Cecil,

I am extremely obliged to you for your letter. I have been giving a good deal of attention to the Tanks lately, and have held two conferences with the representatives of the War Office and of the Tanks Corps, as the result of which I hope matters will be put on a sounder basis. Broadly speaking, I consider a year has been lost in Tank development, and the most strenuous efforts will now be made to repair this melancholy state of things. A very complete agreement was reached at our conference last Monday between all concerned.

Apart from the defects in supply, and the lack of concord between the users and the makers, there has been a failure to use the Tanks under conditions which are favourable to their action, or for which they were originally conceived. It is hoped that under the new arrangements we may secure (a) a better supply of Tanks, and (b) a better use made of the supply.

I should be very glad to have a talk with you about the details you refer to, with which I am fairly well acquainted. Could you come and lunch to-morrow Thursday at 33 Eccleston Square, 1.45?

Yours sincerely
Winston S. Churchill

[1] At the Allocation of Guns Committee, held at the War Office with Lord Curzon in the Chair. Amery was the Committee's Secretary.

Winston S. Churchill: statement to the War Cabinet[1]

(*Cabinet papers: 23/4*)

12 October 1917

One of the great industrial anomalies of the war was that higher wages were being earned by semi-skilled men on repetition work as compared with the wages earned by skilled timeworkers, some of whom had been teachers of the semi skilled. On the 15 August, just before Parliament rose, he had indicated that an attempt would be made to remedy this anomaly. . . . On the 21st August he had appointed a committee, under the Chairmanship of Major J W Hills MP to draw up a scheme of remuneration. . . .

His hope had been that the Committee would be able to recommend a lump sum in relation to output, [but] the extension of payment by result was highly controversial, and the Trade Unions would certainly be offended if an attempt were made to spread it by indirect means. . . .

He had therefore decided to attempt in principle the proposal to grant a bonus of 15% on earnings of certain scheduled workers. . . . He had discarded an alternative suggestion to embrace a larger class of workers and make the advance 12% instead of 15%.

Winston S. Churchill: departmental memorandum

(*Churchill papers: 8/104*)

RAILWAY WAGGON SUPPLY

14 October 1917

Be careful not to cut in upon munitions in the permanent peace time interests of the railways which are important *only as they affect war making capacity.*

It may be necessary to wear them out in winning the war.

We must not aim at too high a standard at the expense of munitions. Every demand we make on the War Cabinet must have its due relation to every other munitions demand.

[1] Among those present when Churchill made his statement were A J Balfour, Lord Robert Cecil, Lord Derby, Sir Eric Geddes and Sir William Robertson.

Winston S. Churchill to Walter Layton and General Thuillier

(*Churchill papers: 8/104*)

16 October 1917

. . . What are the factors which impose limits on the chemical supply? How much labour—and what classes of labour—is now engaged in the existing chemical supply? How quickly and to what extent could it be increased and what labour would be involved in such increase? I am anxious to consider the possibility of a supply on the largest possible scale of cast iron chemical shells to all or almost all natures of guns to be fired with reduced charges so as not to affect the lives of the guns and so to be a definite addition to the offensive power of our artillery. At present we are limited by steel and the lives of guns. If we can devise a type of ammunition which affects the lives of guns to a far less degree than ordinary shell and does not require steel, we shall have entered a new field of expansion which expansion should only be limited by the labour involved and by the special materials required in chemical manufacture. Both in the case of high explosives and lethal chemicals we must push our production to the maximum and devise methods of conveying it to the enemy. I have derived the impression that we are so far only trifling with chemical warfare and that we have got to prepare ourselves for action on an entirely different scale. I look to General Thuillier in the first instance to make proposals for very great increases and it will then be possible to see how far these plans can be reconciled with other needs. Chemical warfare must be one of the three or four leading features of our campaign of 1918.

Winston S. Churchill to Sir Francis Lloyd[1]

(*Churchill papers: 15/156*)

17 October 1917 — Ministry of Munitions

Private

My dear Sir Francis,

There is an officer under your command—Captain Ivor Rose,[2] Grenadier Guards, who was formerly in this Department, and rendered valuable ser-

[1] Francis Lloyd, 1853–1926. Entered the Army, 1874. Served in the Sudan campaigns of 1885 and 1898, and in South Africa, 1900–2, where he was severely wounded. Brigadier-General Commanding the 1st Guards Brigade, 1904–8. Major-General, 1909. Knighted, 1911. Commanded London District, 1913–19. Lieutenant-General, 1917.

[2] Ivor Sainte Croix Rose, 1881–1962. 2nd Lieutenant, 1901. Retired from the Army, 1907. Returned to the army, 1908. Captain, Grenadier Guards, 1914. Served on the western front, 1914–15. Employed in the Ministry of Munitions, October 1917–October 1918.

vices in the early development of Trench Mortars, and particularly the Stokes Gun. His help is particularly sought by us in connection with the re-organisation and expansion of Trench Warfare which is now in contemplation. I have applied to the War Office for him to be placed at my disposal, and I am informed that the request has been forwarded to you. I therefore venture to write to you to explain that real importance attaches to his coming here, on account of his special knowledge and aptitudes. He will be employed in capacities which will give him a considerably wider scope than he could obtain in his Regiment, with whom he has already seen much hard service. I shall be very much obliged if you can assist me in the matter.

Alas I remember how all those splendid fellows you gave me at the beginning of the war for the Naval Division vindicated the reputation of the Brigade of Guards, mostly at the cost of their lives.

Yours sincerely,
Winston S. Churchill

Sir Francis Lloyd to Winston S. Churchill

(*Churchill papers: 15/156*)

18 October 1917 Headquarters London District
Horse Guards

Dear Mr Churchill,

The Grenadiers don't want Rose to go because of course he is very useful but you must have him and Streatfeild[1] agrees.

There is only one thing he will lose his chance of being 2nd in command. However I have no doubt what you have got for him is better.

If you could spare a moment I should rather like to see you before you take him not to stop him but to tell you one or two things.

I conclude I shall hear when you want him.

Yours sincerely
Francis Lloyd

[1] Henry Streatfeild, 1857–1938. Joined the Grenadier Guards, 1876. On active service in South Africa, 1899–1900. Private Secretary to Field Marshal Earl Roberts, 1901–4. Equerry and Private Secretary to Queen Alexandra, 1910–25. Colonel commanding the Grenadier Guards, 1914–19. Knighted, 1916.

Winston S. Churchill to Sir Graham Greene

(*Churchill papers: 15/157*)

STRIKES AND THE MILITARY SERVICE ACT

18 October 1917 Ministry of Munitions

I am at present having a discussion with the War Cabinet on this subject and my recollection is distinctly that it was understood that the Secretary of State for War should act in consultation with the Ministry of Munitions who would be actually watching the Strike and endeavouring, possibly successfully, to prevent it. I certainly understood that Lord Derby assented to this. The distinction between a grave strike involving a serious situation of difficulty which has actually broken out and seems likely to continue on the one hand, and the frequent scares and temporary cessations of work which occur and are speedily put straight on the other, is extremely important. We are in full agreement with the War Office view that in the former case the soldiers should be withdrawn, but we think that a cut and dried order put automatically into operation on the smallest provocation by the military authorities without any reference to the Labour situation in the particular district, would be harmful. There ought to be no difficulty in adjusting these two points of view. I suggest that Major Hills should go and see Lord Derby himself upon the subject and thus avoid the necessity for a further reference to the War Cabinet.

Winston S. Churchill: departmental minute

(*Churchill papers: 15/157*)

18 October 1917 Ministry of Munitions

The whole of this Trench Mortar scheme must of course be considered in relation to the increased Chemical Warfare Programme and both are dependent with other things on tonnage. The method to be adopted is to work both out to their fullest extent on the assumption that the requested tonnage will be forthcoming. Secondly, to adjust the two programmes of Chemicals and Explosives between the services, and thirdly, to ascertain the final limits of the shipping we can get. This may again entail reconsideration.

I am not content with the modified programme proposed by Mr Layton. I am aiming at 40,000 or 50,000 tons of additional Trench Mortar ammunition to be stored ready for use in an offensive period apart from current requirements which naturally would be kept at a minimum.

The Trench Mortar is essentially a weapon of offence and operates much too close to the front line to be effective in defensive warfare. It is therefore not much use to the Russians while on the defensive who require principally machine guns and field artillery firing shrapnel. We should endeavour to retain as many as possible of the 9.45 Russian bombs and Mr Layton should make the best fight he can, reporting to me before reaching any agreement.

This matter now stands referred to the 'Clamping Committee' on the New Programme, who are fully apprised of the main line of policy which it is desired to pursue.

Winston S. Churchill to Lord Derby

(*Churchill papers: 15/156*)

19 October 1917 Ministry of Munitions

My dear Derby

The War Office has long recognised that the Ministry of Munitions, which in the course of its daily work has to handle detailed questions of priority both of labour and materials, cannot carry out its task intelligently unless it has readily accessible precise information as to consumption, stocks and shipment of munitions. We receive regularly a very large number of returns from your Department and these have enabled us to follow the gun and ammunition situation very fully. Arrangements have quite recently been made with your officers to fill up certain lacunae which have been revealed in these figures in the course of recent fighting. I am also arranging to have regular information on the aircraft situation.

There are, however, certain directions in which our regular information is not so good. I am told, for example, that since April our figures for stocks of Trench Warfare materials in France have only related to the quantities on the Lines of Communication. This may be a very misleading figure, as munitions in front of rail head may fluctuate very considerably. The point is of some importance as the stock figures are, I believe, the only means available for calculating the consumption of this class of munitions. We fully realise the difficulty of taking stock of these minor munitions and suggest that a quarterly stocktaking would be sufficient. If the first return were made to the end of September it would enable us to estimate how much Trench Warfare munitions had been used during the present offensive.

You have already very kindly arranged to supply us with certain figures as regards Tanks. These would be very much increased in value if we might have separate figures for Tank armament, with some additional information as regards the Tanks themselves. Our suggestions are shown in the blank schedule attached.

Finally, a regular return for motor transport on the lines of other munitions would afford a much better basis for formulating a mechanical transport budget than has hitherto been available.

Winston S. Churchill to Edwin Montagu

(Churchill papers: 15/157)

19 October 1917 Ministry of Munitions

My dear Edwin,

My inquiry relates solely to 9·2 inch guns, of which there are certainly six mounted at Bombay, and others at Calcutta. Reference to the coast fortifications handbook would probably confirm this; but you must have the information in the India Office.

Whether any of these guns could be liberated raises of course several difficult points. But even half of them would be a very useful contribution.

Yours ever,
Winston S. Churchill

H. W. Massingham[1] to Winston S. Churchill

(Churchill papers: 15/157)

20 October 1917 'The Nation'

My dear Churchill,

I haven't forgiven you for joining this rotten Government, but I must thank you, now that the ban on 'the Nation' has been taken off, for the fulsome & brilliant defence of our cause. It was really a very handsome act.[2]

[1] Henry William Massingham, 1860–1924. Journalist. Began work on the *Eastern Daily Press*, 1877. Editor of the *Star*, 1890. Editor of the *Daily Chronicle*, 1895–9. Forced to resign because of his opposition to the war in South Africa. Editor of the *Nation*, 1907–23. In 1909 he wrote the introduction to Churchill's volume of speeches, *Liberalism and the Social Problem*. In 1933 he joined the Labour Party.

[2] On 17 April 1917 the House of Commons debated the Government's suppression of a series of articles in the *Nation*, in which it was asserted that the British troops on the western front had been outmanoeuvred by the German tactical withdrawal. Churchill, then in Opposition, attacked the suppression, warning Lloyd George and his Government of the dangers of 'a universal harmonious chorus of adulation from morning to night about whatever was done, until some frightful disaster took place'. The suppression, he declared, indicated 'an undue love of power and an undue love of the assertion of arbitrary power' on behalf of the Government.

The ban practically made 'The Nation' into a good commercial proposition. I'm quite sorry to lose it.

Yours
H. W. Massingham

Winston S. Churchill to Sir William Weir

(*Churchill papers: 15/157*)

24 October 1917 Ministry of Munitions

A dangerous feature in the last Zeppelin raid has been masked by the disaster which overcame the raiders on their way back.[1] It is clear that the Germans counted on the height at which the Zeppelins of the newest pattern can now fly as a means of resisting all forms of existing aeroplane attack.

Apparently this calculation is at present well founded. If that is so, we ought to find without delay a means of sending aeroplanes up to even greater heights at night. I presume this point is being studied. Evidently they thought they could fly here with safety and certainty at altitudes where they could not be touched. It appears to me very important that experimental work to secure greater height records in aeroplanes should be pressed on.

Winston S. Churchill: War Cabinet memorandum

(*Churchill papers: 15/157*)

25 October 1917 Ministry of Munitions

I observe that the War Cabinet at its meeting of October 24th discussed the question of the publication of the second Report of the Dardanelles Commission and that the discussion was adjourned without any decision having been reached.

The Act of Parliament constituting the Commission directs that the Report should be laid before Parliament and there is no doubt that strong objection will be taken if it is withheld. There is no good reason for publishing the first Report and not publishing the second. Such a course would be unfair to individuals concerned. They have a right to claim that if a story of this kind

[1] An attack by Zeppelins took place on October 19. The public were depressed by the absence of anti-Zeppelin gun fire, but later exulted when it was learned that the raiders had been blown off their course while returning to Germany, and four had been forced to land behind the Allied lines in France.

is to be told in public in time of war, it should be told in its integrity and not simply those parts made public which prejudicially affect some individuals whilst shielding others. The fact that the first Report covers the period for which one political party was responsible while the second Report affects the period where both parties in a Coalition Government were responsible, is also material, and it would be invidious to pick and choose in a matter of this kind.

It must be remembered that the Commander-in-Chief of this expedition, Sir Ian Hamilton,[1] was removed from his command and has been since excluded from all employment. It would be very unjust to this officer, who has been the victim of so much ill-usage at the hands of his superiors, that the truth should not be known and that he should continue to be the scape-goat of the extraordinary delays and neglects on the part of the whole Government which led to the failure of the enterprise.

Of course I recognize that reasons of State in this formidable time may well induce Parliament to postpone the publication, but if so, it would be an obligation on the Government advocating such a course to make sure that the Commander-in-Chief whose military character has been impugned should suffer no injustice or lose from that course.

Finally, it is in any case premature to decide against publication until the actual text of the Report is in the possession of the Cabinet and can be studied.

Winston S. Churchill to David Lloyd George

(*Churchill papers: 15/157*)

26 October 1917 Ministry of Munitions

My dear Prime Minister,

The Secretary of State for War, the First Lord of the Admiralty, the Secretary of State for the Colonies, the Secretary of State for Foreign Affairs, and the Secretary of State for India each and all have the right of submitting direct to the King the names of officers whom they desire to recommend for recognition in the Orders of the Bath, the St Michael and the St George, or the Indian Orders respectively. The Minister of Munitions has however no

[1] Ian Standish Monteith Hamilton, 1853–1947. Entered Army, 1872. Major-General, 1900. Knighted, 1900. Chief of Staff to Lord Kitchener, 1901–2. General, 1914. Commander of the Central Force, responsible for the defence of England in the event of invasion, August 1914–March 1915. Commanded the Mediterranean Expeditionary Force, March–October 1915, after which he received no further military command. He published *Gallipoli Diary* in 1920.

such facilities. For any Baths he requires he has to apply to the Secretary of State for War, for any CMGs of which he stands in need he must have recourse to the Secretary of State for the Colonies, and for the Order of the British Empire he must apply to the Prime Minister. This causes great inconvenience. There is no office, as you know, which is more dependent than the Ministry of Munitions upon gratuitous and voluntary service and it is necessary and right that special recognition should be given to persons who are not paid, who are not pensionable, who are not permanently employed, but who nevertheless are rendering indispensable services and making the most strenuous exertions. It also happens from time to time that changes take place in the personnel which are smoothed over and facilitated by recognition in an Honours List or sometimes in the intervals between the appearance of Honours Lists. If I have on each and all occasions to apply to you personally it must involve you in considerable labour and pending your being able to give the necessary attention to the case or cases I am left in an uncertainty which is embarrassing. The result is that I have been forced to commit myself, subject of course to the King's approval, in certain cases on telephonic inquiries from your Private Secretaries. Would you therefore consider whether you cannot make me a definite allocation yearly, half yearly or quarterly of appointments to the Order of the British Empire in regard to which I may make recommendations direct to the King either for inclusion in a general list or when necessary on special occasions. If on any occasion my requirements exhausted the limits of what was considered the normal Departmental allocation I would recur to you for a further draught from the fountain.

Winston S. Churchill to David Lloyd George

(Churchill papers: 15/157)

27 October 1917 Ministry of Munitions

My dear Prime Minister,

I was surprised to see the Report presented by the Select Committee on National Expenditure which appeared in to-day's papers. So far as it affects the Ministry of Munitions, we had no idea that the investigations of the Committee had reached a point where they were in a position to make a Report. They had not thought it worthwhile to examine any of the principal witnesses in the Ministry, including the two Parliamentary Secretaries[1] or myself. Had

[1] Churchill's two Parliamentary Secretaries were Sir Laming Worthington Evans and Frederick Kellaway. On 30 January 1918 Worthington Evans was appointed Parliamentary

they done so, several of the principal points to which they refer could have been explained to them.

I feel fairly confident of my ability to deal with this matter in Debate should occasion arise, and I should welcome the opportunity. You will note however that they recommend the creation of a Financial Secretary to the Ministry of Munitions responsible to Parliament in the same way as are the Financial Secretaries of the War Office and the Admiralty. Both the existing under-Secretaries are very hard worked and there would be undoubted advantages in the appointment of an additional Parliamentary officer charged with the duties of Financial Secretary. The opinion of the House of Commons has hitherto been adverse to any addition to Ministerial Representation, but in view of the Report of the Committee it is difficult to see how Parliamentary opposition to an additional appointment could be maintained. It would also be very convenient should a Debate occur to be able to announce that we have met them in this respect. I therefore suggest to you the appointment of some Member of Parliament as Financial Secretary to the Ministry of Munitions. If you approve of such an appointment, I can furnish you with a detailed statement of the legal and Parliamentary steps which are necessary.

---

and Financial Secretary (but no separate appointment was made to the Financial Secretaryship). When Major-General J E B Seely replaced Worthington Evans as Parliamentary Secretary in July 1918, the post of Financial Secretary was dropped. It was subsequently restored in January 1919.

November 1917

Winston S. Churchill: Cabinet memorandum

(*Churchill papers: 15/32*)

1 November 1917 Ministry of Munitions
Secret

I circulate to the Cabinet a paper I have prepared on the supply of munitions of all kinds in 1918.

The situation is very serious. Our labour, skilled and unskilled, is being drafted away at a time when we need a largely increased supply. It is not possible unduly to press the workmen at the present time. Our dollar credits in Canada have been severely curtailed. Our importations of iron ore are scarcely two-thirds of our requirements from overseas.

At the same time, the Commander-in-chief in France and the War Office demand an artillery programme nearly half as large again as that provided for this year. The Admiralty demand double as much shipbuilding materials as last year. Their claims upon every kind of material, including especially the rarest, are rapidly increasing; and at the present time they already absorb between 35 and 40 per cent. of the entire labour supply of the country available for munitions of war. The Air Board have laid down a programme which requires our supply of aeroplanes to be at least tripled, in addition, of course, to the Admiralty airships. Meanwhile the maintenance of the railways of this country and other civil services essential to its war-making capacity has fallen heavily and dangerously into arrears; and the demands of the Allies become more insistent every week.

We cannot expect to give our armies next year any appreciable superiority in numbers over the enemy. We cannot expect, even if all the demands of the Commander-in-Chief are fulfilled, to give them a superiority in guns. Any superiority in ammunition which we may achieve depends on an improvement in tonnage of ore. We must expect a continuous attack in the spring of next year from the air, which, even if we obtain a general mastery, will hamper production in many important centres. We are sure to have additional demands made upon us in consequence of the Italian disaster.

In spite of the difficulties, it should still be possible by taking the proper measures of organisation, by enforcing the necessary economies, and by utilising to the full the resources of every department without exception, to meet and satisfy the main demands which are made upon us.

Sir Reginald Barnes to Winston S. Churchill

(*Churchill papers: 15/1*)

1 November 1917 57th Division

Personal & Private

My dear Winston

I am writing you this letter because I am *very* anxious to impress one fact on your mind, which I know is only rubbing in what you already realise.

My lot have been in the big show for the last ten days,[1] and the convinced impression I get from it is that the winning or losing of this war (bar submarines) depends on one thing, & that is real supremacy in the air. The reason is, that I am sure *bombing from the air*—now really only in its infancy—is going to make it *impossible* for the weaker side in the air to fight. You can fight and possibly hold your own with fewer infantry & guns, but if the other side gets command in the air & can really bomb you hard, it will be impossible to fight, because all your formation will be broken up & destroyed before they get into line. I am convinced it is vital that we should *concentrate* on (a) bombing machines; (b) fighting machines & in that order, because the bombing can if necessary be carried on a good deal at night. If you were here now, I know you would agree with me, as it is *the* striking development of the war.

Last night we were bombed continuously with hundreds of bombs, and it fairly opened one's eyes, & mark you there is *no* protection possible.

You will be doing your Country a great service if you open people's eyes at home to this, because we shall have to be quick—and concentrate.

I am writing this as an old friend, who would not do so if he did not feel strongly about it.

I hope you are fit, & that you like your job.

[1] The battle for the village of Passchendaele, which had opened on 12 October, and ended on 10 November. After nearly a month of fierce fighting, a quarter of a mile of ground had been captured, but at enormous cost. On 10 November alone 3,000 British troops had been killed and 7,000 wounded.

Glyn (R G)[1] sends you his salaams, he is on my staff.

My new lot are going pretty well I think in their first big show.

My best love, Yours ever
Reginald Barnes

Winston S. Churchill to Frederick Guest

(*Churchill papers: 15/157*)

3 November 1917 Ministry of Munitions

My dear Freddie,

I strongly support Sir Henry Wilson's election to the Other Club. I do not think either of the other two names you mention are desirable.[2] You will spoil the character of the Club if you bring in numbers of people simply because they are well-known and who are not in any sense friends or even acquaintances of ours. Tuft-hunting for tuft-hunting sake is much to be deprecated. You are not making a Company Prospectus but a small intimate gathering of friends most of whom move in the same world. One does not want to go there to meet strangers.

Winston S. Churchill to Herbert Samuel[3]

(*Churchill papers: 15/157*)

3 November 1917 Ministry of Munitions

My Dear Samuel,

I was surprised to read the Report which appeared in last Saturday's papers from the Sub-Committee on Munitions expenditure. I had no idea

[1] Ralph George Campbell Glyn, 1885–1960. Lieutenant, Rifle Brigade, 1904. Secretary Unionist Reorganization Committee, 1911. Employed at the War Office, 1912–14. Captain, on Missions to Serbia and Bulgaria, 1914–15. Liaison Intelligence Officer between the War Office and GHQ France, May–August 1915. Served Gallipoli and Salonika, 1915–16; France, 1917–18. Major, 1918. Conservative MP, 1918–22; 1924–53. Joint Parliamentary Private Secretary to Ramsay MacDonald, 1931–7. Created Baronet, 1934. Created Baron Glyn of Farnborough, 1953.

[2] The two others suggested were the painter Augustus John, and the novelist Arnold Bennett. Bennett was elected, John was not.

[3] Herbert Louis Samuel, 1870–1963. Liberal MP, 1902–18; 1929–35. Chancellor of the Duchy of Lancaster, 1909–10. Postmaster-General, 1910–14. President of the Local Government Board, 1914–15. Home Secretary, January–December 1916. Chairman of the Select Committee on National Expenditure, 1917–18. Knighted, 1920. High Commissioner for Palestine, 1 July 1920–2 July 1925. Home Secretary, 1931–2. Created Viscount, 1937.

that their inquiries had reached a stage when they were in a position to make a pronouncement of this character. The six people at the Ministry of Munitions who are chiefly responsible for past and present policy are myself as Minister newly taking office and responsible for a certain reorganization of the Department, secondly the late Minister, whose knowledge is of course much greater than mine, thirdly Worthington Evans and Kellaway, the two Parliamentary Under-Secretaries (the former of whom has habitually dealt with financial questions and both of whom have been there for more than a year); and finally Sir Arthur Duckham, the Chairman of the late Advisory Committee (out of which the present Council sprang) and his principal colleague Sir James Stevenson.

Not one of these officers, any of whom could have spoken with authority on the whole of the questions under discussion, was summoned before the Committee. Instead the staple of the evidence has been provided by a number of witnesses from the Finance and Contracts Department occupying subordinate positions. Sir Herbert Hambling, the head of the Finance Department, who was of course examined, has, as you know, only been in office for about two months. The same is true of Sir Graham Greene, the Secretary to the Ministry, and Masterton Smith[1] who has only been there six weeks.

At the time when I formed the new organization of a Council about two months ago, I had of course to refuse numerous requests from the heads of the forty or fifty departments in the Ministry to be included on the Council. Of these requests the most pressing came from members in the Finance and Contracts Group who felt their position prejudiced by the appointment of a new Chief in the person of Sir Herbert Hambling. Very considerable passages in the Report of the Sub-Committee followed almost word for word the representations as to the position of finance and contracts which were made to me by these gentlemen and which they seem to have repeated to the Committee. There is nothing to object to in this provided that the evidence taken is not one-sided and that the head of the Department whose organization is impugned as well as his Parliamentary colleagues and principal advisors in authority in the Department are also summoned and examined on the points which have been raised. But simply to rely upon the evidence of subordinate officials who however loyal are naturally dissatisfied at being placed under a Council member instead of directly under the Minister, without securing from that Minister or from any of the persons principally

[1] James Edward Masterton Smith, 1878–1938. Entered Admiralty, 1901. Private Secretary to five First Lords: McKenna, 1910–11; Churchill, 1911–15; Balfour, 1915–16; Carson, 1916–17; Sir E Geddes, 1917. Assistant Secretary to Churchill, Ministry of Munitions, 1917–19; War Office, 1919–20. Knighted, 1919. Permanent Under-Secretary of State, Colonial Office, 1921–4.

responsible a statement of their side of the case and of the reasons which have actuated them, is a course which surely cannot be defended. I should have thought that I as Minister responsible for certain changes in organization had a right to be examined before that organization was subjected to criticism, and to be given an opportunity of at least laying before the Committee the reasons which had actuated my policy.

As an example of the disadvantages of the course pursued, I would draw your attention to the reference made by the Sub-Committee to the fact that there was no representative of Finance on the Committee of Council appointed by me to consider the New Programme. This was a Committee appointed by me to deal with matters very largely of a technical character and also I must admit as a means of educating myself in regard to the different classes of supplies with which we were providing the Army. It was not intended to deal with any financial questions: its work has been entirely exploratory: it has not so far raised financial issues of any kind. On the other hand its proceedings have been laborious, and some of the supply members have I know felt the drain upon their time considerable. It would have been unreasonable to have kept the Finance Member sitting day after day through all these technical discussions not affecting Finance when he had only just taken over his new duties and when every minute of his time was required in mastering the very great difficulties of his Group of departments. But you will see from my minute constituting the Committee which I enclose that the two equally vital aspects of Labour and Finance were both to be associated with the work of the Committee as soon as the more technical aspects had been disposed of, and that there was no question of excluding the Finance Member from full and timely consideration of the Programme.

Of course it is possible that had these facts been laid before your Sub-Committee they would not have altered their opinion, and no doubt this is the view that they will now take; but at any rate it is usual when it is desired to criticise the administrative action of a Minister in some steps for which he alone knows the reasons and for which he is personally and solely responsible, to ask him what he has to say and to endeavour to understand his point of view before hurrying into print to condemn it.

I found, as you no doubt know, on coming into office the finances of the Ministry in an unsatisfactory state. But this was due to the conditions of emergency under which the whole of our munitions supply was called into being and to the overpowering demand for output at all costs. As the emergency was gradually met and output on a gigantic scale was achieved, the attention of my predecessor, Dr Addison, was increasingly directed to the financial aspect of the business of the Ministry. He saw with grave anxiety that the practical processes of supply had very largely outstripped the regular machinery of finance and contracts. He therefore took certain measures which have been extremely beneficial, though their results have yet only partially been obtained. These measures I have continued, but I was not satisfied and I am not satisfied with the position. I therefore superseded Mr Mann,[1] the former head of the Finance Department and relegated him to the Contracts Branch, for which he has special aptitudes. I have drawn Sir Herbert Hambling's attention to the situation that exists and requested him to make a complete survey of all the departments in the Finance Group and have invited him to make me proposals for further action. This he is now engaged in doing. But the business is very large and complicated: the daily pressure is also heavy and he has scarcely been in office two months. I think it is only fair to him to give him the time to make matured proposals, and I am sure he has not yet really had the chance to which any man charged with such responsibility is entitled. Meanwhile I have strengthened the Financial Advisory Committee. But I feel that my work in this very important sphere of the Ministry's functions is yet to do, and I should certainly welcome any assistance that could be afforded me by a Parliamentary Committee so long as it is loyal in intention and fair and instructed in its methods. I feel however very strongly that they have been precipitate in condemning on such a very partial, incomplete and one-sided examination of the question the spirit and organization which I have endeavoured to impart to the Ministry, and that before doing so they should at least have summoned me before them.

May I say that I write with greater freedom to you as the financial situation at the Ministry and the accumulation of arrears developed mainly during the year 1916 when you were yourself in the Cabinet, while my connection with these matters has scarcely lasted three months. Considering the enormous scope of Munitions Finance, the immense sums of money and the intricate character of the questions involved. I should have been very glad if you yourself had taken charge of this branch of your inquiry instead of entrusting it to a Sub-Committee which cannot claim to be very experienced. I should still be very glad if you could give your attention personally to this aspect and would place every facility at your disposal.

[1] John Mann, 1863–1955. Chartered accountant. Director of various engineering companies. Worked mostly in Glasgow. Interested in experiments in workmen's housing, public management of the liquor traffic, commercial education and industrial psychology. Financial Adviser, Ministry of Munitions, 1915–16; Head of the Finance Department, 1916–17; Controller of Munitions Contracts, 1917–19. Knighted, 1918.

Winston S. Churchill: departmental minute

(*Churchill papers: 15/157*)

3 November 1917 Ministry of Munitions

A Luncheon Club should be formed for the senior 60 or 70 officers of the Ministry. This would enable them to meet in twos and threes in *quiet* and agreeable surroundings daily. Everyone will get to know the other. 'Shop' could be talked under good auspices. Let a plan for this be elaborated. The arrangements require to be very carefully considered by some competent and understanding person. Time would be saved and many advantages gained. Accommodation must be found within the Metropole. There must be no crowding and no hustle. But everything very simple. Pray make me proposals.

Winston S. Churchill to Sir Arthur Duckham

(*Churchill papers: 15/157*)

5 November 1917 Ministry of Munitions

I observe that this week the aeroplanes are 20 per-cent below forecasts and that the engines from home are also below forecasts, the improvement in this respect being due only to importations. Pray let me know what is holding you up.

Winston S. Churchill to Sir Glynn West

(*Churchill papers: 15/157*)

5 November 1917 Ministry of Munitions

Our gun and carriage deliveries seem now not only to be below the long dated forecasts on which the 1918 programme is based, but they are below the latest monthly revised estimates sent to the War Office at the end of September. Deliveries of *new* guns to proof in October are less than in September: deliveries of *repaired* guns are far below the estimate, especially in the case of 4·5 and 60-pounder. What is the cause of this? Is it due to lack of guns to repair? Please let me have a report.

Winston S. Churchill: memorandum for the War Cabinet

(*Churchill papers: 8/104*)

DUPLICATION AND WASTE OF EFFORT

6 November 1917
Confidential

If we are to realise the full war effort of this country in 1918 and in 1919, it is indispensable that the most searching economy of men and material should be practised in every direction and by every Department; that no services should be duplicated; that no more should be taken for any service, however necessary, than is required; and that one central and superior view should regulate every portion of our defensive and offensive system. Unless we are to be confronted with a failure in munitions and shipbuilding, and with a very serious diminution in our potential war-making capacity, it is necessary that there should be a general stocktaking.

Those members of the War Cabinet or Government who were members of the Committee of Imperial Defence in the years before the war are, of course, familiar with every aspect of the 'Invasion' argument. I will, therefore, content myself with drawing attention to a few simple facts.

During the early months of the war, especially at the beginning, when Germany had the greatest incentive to try to throw a raiding army across the North Sea, we had as our defence against invasion:—

1. The Fleet, with a margin of eight Dreadnoughts.
2. Our submarines and flotillas.
3. Two and then one, and finally no regular divisions.
4. The Territorial Army, newly mobilised, with hardly any machine-guns, with 15-pounder artillery and scarcely any reserves of ammunition, gunners almost unskilled.
5. No coast fortifications and only a few guns in open batteries at the defended forts.
6. No mine-fields.
7. Practically no aircraft.

In these circumstances the Germans did not choose or did not venture to make an oversea attack.

We now have:—

1. The British Fleet, with a margin of about twenty Dreadnoughts.
2. The American Battle Fleet (the third strongest in the world) if we require it.

3. Enormous mine-fields, covering the German debouches and hampering the movement even of submarine craft.
4. Submarines and flotillas multiplied manifold.
5. The coast-line fortified from end to end with powerful batteries mounted at every port *and still being increased*. Powerful aeroplane forces and a perfect system of coastal watch.
6. A defence scheme devised by Lord French himself, according to the latest experience of this war.
7. A Home Army mostly in its actual battle stations, aggregating a quarter of a million men and supported by a powerful field artillery of upwards of 500 modern guns and howitzers, with boundless supplies of ammunition and enormous numbers of organised, mobile or sited machine-guns.
8. A million and a quarter other armed and uniformed men behind these.
9. The Volunteers.

Security is no doubt vital, but it must be remembered that if the factor of safety is exaggerated in any one part of our organisation, other parts may be exposed to fatal peril; and that if our strength is dissipated in making sure three or four times over in one direction, we may fail to have the strength available for the general offensive war, and may consequently be compelled impotently to witness the defeat of our Allies one by one.

The very serious situation of the war and the impossibility on present lines of securing any effective numerical superiority or any sufficiently large mechanical superiority over the German armies in the field compel me to bring these aspects of our present arrangements to the notice of the War Cabinet.

Winston S. Churchill to Lord Derby

(*Churchill papers: 15/157*)

7 November 1917 Ministry of Munitions

My dear Derby,

I venture to return to the topic I raised last week in the War Priorities Committee. At the present moment we are engaged in putting up a large number of buildings for the Army; you are also engaged in putting up a certain number for yourselves: but whether these buildings are put up by us or by you, they all have one object, viz, the service of the Army. It is therefore obviously absurd for either of us to commandeer certain classes of material against each other. Anything that you take for the works for which the War Office is responsible comes off other work in which you are equally interested. You are in fact only deranging your own supply which is proceeding in accordance with the relative degrees of importance attached to different classes of work by you.

You have shown yourself very broad-minded in all dealings between the Ministry of Munitions and the War Office, and I am very anxious not to appear 'acquisitive'; but the principles which should be followed are clear and ought to be stated, viz, (a) the War Office decides policy and assigns the relative importance of various classes of work and (b) the Ministry of Munitions executes and provides for the supply in accordance with the War Office decisions. Every step directed to this end, in spirit as well as in letter, will be beneficial and will promote the efficiency of supplies and the economy of material. Every step which falls short of it must be regarded only as a concession to Departmental feelings and as a sacrifice of general productiveness.

At the present time the War Office is building a number of aerodromes, aeroplane sheds, etc similar to and in some cases the same work as we are doing for military purposes and have been doing on a very large scale all over the country. The Air Board are anxious lest the War Office aerodromes, etc will not be completed *pari passu* with a very large delivery of machines which must be expected early next year. They therefore nearly two months ago moved Smuts to recommend that the construction of these aerodromes should be taken in hand, as so many others had been, by Sir John Hunter and be pressed forward with all the large resources and experience at the disposal of the Ministry of Munitions. Smuts accordingly so advised the Cabinet in a Memorandum. Your people however wanted to keep their own part of the construction in their own hands. It is very natural that they should, considering how much of pre-war War Office business has at one time and another been transferred to the Ministry of Munitions. But none the less it is not a good arrangement.

I am told that the work has not progressed at the rate which was expected, and that the apprehensions of the Air Board are very likely to be fulfilled. Certainly from a careful study of the statistics I think the output of machines in the early part of next year will be substantially ahead of the War Office arrangements for their utilization, and the source of the deficiency will then become plainly apparent. These tendencies being felt strenuous efforts are made by your people to catch up, and in consequence competition for materials and labour, rivalries between sub-departments and separatist tendencies instead of the pooling of materials have arisen. The instances we discussed last week are symptomatic of these. It would, I am sure, be much better if we were to undertake the whole of this class of work, and if there were only one authority serving the War Office in this matter. All the materials and labour which are available would then be employed to the best possible advantage under one direction in accordance with the policy prescribed by the War Office.

After all, we are not in the same relation to you as any other separate department of State. We are really your Supply Department, and exist almost exclusively to fulfil your needs and study your wishes. A thoroughgoing division of functions as between Policy and Supply, combined with the closest possible liaison, is clearly the only course to pursue.

This is not to suggest any immediate action, but for your general consideration.

Winston S. Churchill to Lord Milner

(*Churchill papers: 15/157*)

10 November 1917 Ministry of Munitions

. . . Although disputes and stoppages, when collected together in a weekly report, make a gloomy picture, it must be remembered that they are only the comparatively small exceptions to the vast mass of production which is flooding steadily forward. Demands of the workers for increases of wages are not, in my opinion, disproportionate to what is natural and reasonable in all the circumstances of the present situation, and certainly they are not in excess of the increases either in the cost of living or in the degree of effort which has been forthcoming.

Sir Maurice Hankey to Winston S. Churchill

(*Churchill papers: 15/157*)

14 November 1917

Dear Mr Churchill,

I cannot say how much I regret that you were seriously inconvenienced by the course of events at the War Cabinet this morning.

An important parliamentary question of great urgency was raised, which entirely dislocated the time table. One result was that, in an interval, while those concerned in one of the other questions were being awaited, General Smuts raised the War Priorities question, which was decided with only a short discussion, although particular note was taken of your protest. This occurred just before your arrival, and I had no opportunity to telephone to let you know that your question had been dealt with. At the moment you arrived the Cabinet were pressing on with the other questions in order to gain time to consider the Prime Minister's statement this afternoon. The Prime Minister asked me to say that he greatly regrets that the heavy pressure on the War Cabinet's time this morning prevented them from awaiting until you could be warned that this question was coming up. He particularly regrets that you should have come to feel that there was any discourtesy which, I need hardly say, was not intentional.

Yours sincerely
M. P. A. Hankey

Winston S. Churchill to Sir Reginald Barnes

(*Churchill papers: 15/157*)

15 November 1917 Ministry of Munitions

I did not answer your letter about bombing as I hoped I should have had an opportunity of seeing you during a flying visit to France. I hope if I come over again, as I may have to do in the next week or so, to look you up at your headquarters.

I am in entire agreement with the views which you put forward. Hitherto both the Naval and the Military Authorities have altogether underrated bombing possibilities and steadily discouraged the construction of bombing machines. We have however in spite of them made a good deal of progress in materiel and I can assure you I shall do everything in my power to emphasize this development.

I am very grateful to you for your letter which confirms me in the views I have long held.

Hoping to see you soon,

Winston S. Churchill to Sir Joseph Maclay

(*Churchill papers: 15/157*)

15 November 1917 Ministry of Munitions

My dear Sir Joseph,

. . . With regard to concrete barges, you say they have been 'in the air' for a long time. My anxiety is that they should be in the water in a short time.

I was advised by Sir Ernest Moir, who is a great authority on these subjects, that there was a good possibility of vessels of this character being created to increase our tonnage without drawing seriously upon our steel resources and, in particular, without affecting our supply of ship-plates. I felt it my duty to explore this matter thoroughly and to promote action by every means in my power. I was, and I am still to some extent, uncertain as to where the responsibility in such a question lies, but I understood that, as regards the practicability of such vessels and of their construction, the Admiralty is primarily concerned. I therefore addressed myself to the First Lord, and the conferences, which were attended by representatives of your Department, took place.

As a result of these conferences, a considerable number of these vessels are now being constructed.

I am strongly of opinion that the number (which the First Lord tells me is 60 plus 10 additional) is inadequate, and that at least double that number should be taken in hand without a day's delay.

I am fully aware of the towing aspect, and am confident that this difficulty can and will be surmounted when the concrete vessels are ready.

I must impress upon you that the supplies of iron-ore from the North of Spain are a matter literally of life and death to the British army in the field and to the whole munition output by which that army is sustained.

The reduction which you are forced to suggest in the paper on Shipping, which you have so kindly sent me, would be fatal to our war effort alike in 1918 and in 1919, and I am confident that we cannot leave any stone unturned or any practicable expedient unresorted to which will mitigate the disastrous consequences which you so clearly apprehend. I certainly could never acquiesce in seeing the whole Munition programme ruined and the striking power of our army vitally affected. I earnestly hope that no question of departmental procedure will be allowed to stand in the way of a vehement effort being made, not only by this but by every other channel, to avert the catastrophe which you foresee.

War Cabinet minutes

(*Cabinet papers: 23/4*)

16 November 1917

THE CHANCELLOR OF THE EXCHEQUER [Andrew Bonar Law], speaking as the Leader of the House of Commons, said that certain Members of Parliament were anxious to have inserted in the Bill a clause excluding any individual who might have any financial interest in aircraft factories, or any business connected therewith, from sitting on the new Air Council.

It was pointed out that the new Council would require the best brains and experience available, and that such exclusion would deprive the State of the service of men of great experience and business capacity when such would be invaluable.

THE MINISTER OF MUNITIONS informed the Cabinet that, if such restrictions were placed on himself and his predecessors, his Department would have to forgo the services of many men of known integrity who were indispensable and irreplaceable. In this connection Mr Churchill stated that a condition of employment in his Department was that any men who had business interests of any kind should disclose them fully to the Secretary to the Ministry.

The War Cabinet agreed that—

A clause in the above sense was unreasonable, and authorised the Leader of the House to oppose any amendment excluding business men from a seat on the Air Council.

Winston S. Churchill to David Lloyd George: telegram

(*Churchill papers: 15/55*)

19 November 1917 Paris

Please see subjoined telegram drafted by Layton. Italian demands are of extreme urgency for re-equipment of second army and replacement of losses in others. I consider them on the whole moderate and I believe they can be met generally without serious detriment to our own programmes. Loucheur has been authorised by French Government to contribute an equal quantity and is prepared to do so immediately, subject to our taking similar action. Dallolio[1] is waiting here till tomorrow, Tuesday night. Question is one of policy, not of detail. If you decide in principle to give aid demanded jointly with the French I am sure details can be arranged satisfactorily.

I therefore recommend you to authorise me to promise this aid tomorrow in conformity with the French subject (1), to such arrangements of details and methods as may be convenient and (2), to provision for repayment of material next year, which Dallolio offers, on which however it is not well to count too much. A further conference on munitions will be necessary at

[1] Alfredo Dallolio, 1853–1952. Entered the Italian Army as an artillery officer, 1872; Major-General, 1910. Director-General of Artillery, Ministry of War, 1910–17. Represented Italy in London and Paris on the Allied Commission for Munitions, Fuel and Repairs to the Cargo Fleet, 1917. Senator, 1917. Minister of State for Arms and Ammunition, 1917–18. General Commander of Army Artillery, 1918–20. Lieutenant-General, 1923. President of the Committee for National Mobilization (later the Committee for Civil Mobilization), 1923–39.

end of this month in order to secure unity of production *pari passu* with unity of command. The loss of two million tons given to Clémentel[1] is incomparably more serious to us than these new Italian demands. I hope with Loucheur's aid to secure some abatement in the interests of munitions of tonnage which Clémentel has captured. Pray let me have answer tomorrow on immediate Italian demand.

Layton's telegram begins.

Italian Minister has made following urgent demands to meet immediate needs for equipment of three hundred thousand men whom he states are without arms.

1. 150,000 British pattern rifles with 75 million rounds of small-arms ammunition (Loucheur is supplying similar quantity of French pattern but cannot do more).

2. Two thousand machine guns with 20 million rounds of small-arms ammunition (Loucheur also supplying similar amount).

3. Three hundred eighteen-pounder guns with six hundred thousand rounds.

4. Three hundred medium guns or howitzers with three hundred thousand rounds.

5. Forty heavy howitzers or mortars.

6. Forty tanks. On these we suggest following considerations. 1. could probably be supplied from home stocks or stocks in France plus two weeks new deliveries. Net effect would be to postpone final completion of re-armament with service rifles of home and Indian forces and volunteers for a few months, say from January 1919 to May 1919. This period could be shortened by maintaining output of Standard Arms Company which was being discontinued. Small arms ammunition would probably have to be drawn from home forces. 2. could be met by Hotchkiss guns which are accumulating in advance of tanks. 3. can only be met by sending next month's output to Italy which must reduce establishment either in France or home forces. 4. Italians want six-inch howitzers. We are examining possibility of Italy making carriages to balance our surplus guns but immediate demand can only be met at expense of equipment in France. If demand is agreed to it is important that return of guns for repair should not be delayed. 5. Italians want ten-inch or over, but would accept eight-inch. Propose sending marks one to five which it was intended to send to Russia later, but which have not been promised. 6. would involve training personnel. All these demands are in addition to munitions supplied with British units.

[1] Etienne Clémentel, 1862–1936. Deputy, Puy-de-Dôme, 1898. Occupied several Ministerial posts between 1898 and 1924, including Minister of Colonies, 1898, and Minister of Commerce, 1916–20. Instrumental in establishing the Inter-Allied Wheat Executive, 1916, and the Inter-Allied Maritime Transport Council, 1917. Senator, 1918. President and founder of the International Chamber of Commerce, 1919. Minister of Finance, 1924.

Sir Laming Worthington Evans to Winston S. Churchill: telegram

(*Churchill papers: 15/55*)

20 November 1917 London

I spoke about your telegram 1303 to the Prime Minister at the Cabinet Meeting to-day and I asked for approval in principle. Lord Derby told the Prime Minister that he could not concur until demands were examined by him and that General Furse would be in Paris to-day. The Prime Minister said that no arrangement should be made with the Italians without the concurrence of General Furse. Lord Derby is telegraphing you direct. The Prime Minister approved his telegram.

Dr Christopher Addison to Winston S. Churchill

(*Churchill papers: 15/158*)

22 November 1917 Westminster

Dear Churchill,

I have read your Memorandum on Munitions Budget, 1918, with immense interest.

One thing, however, amazes me and that is—that you do not anticipate to produce in 1918 more than 8,500,000 tons of finished steel product. I do not know what the expression 'finished steel product' implies, but I thought that our output was already up to a figure which was equivalent to a rate of 9,000,000 tons or thereabouts and that there might be a substantial increase in the coming months from the new furnaces, etc.

I should be greatly obliged if, as a matter of information, you would ask Hunter or someone to give me a note of the Steel position as it now is.

I must congratulate you upon the arrangements which appear to have been made for the shipping of French Shell Steel from America.

I sincerely hope that you will press a modification of the Admiralty claim as indicated in Paragraph (a) at the top of Page 4. We know, of old, that they are one of the most wasteful employers of labour and, honestly, I have not seen many signs of improvement.

It is a great and clear Memorandum and I congratulate you most heartily upon it.

Yours sincerely
Christopher Addison

Winston S. Churchill to Lady St Aldwyn[1]

(*Churchill papers: 15/158*)

25 November 1917 Ministry of Munitions

Dear Lady St Aldwyn,

I am indeed grieved that you did not receive my letter written to you from the Front, of profound sympathy with you in your double loss of husband and son. I had the very greatest regard for Lord St Aldwyn and it was a source of deep pleasure to me to feel that I had in some degree inherited his friendship for my father.

The world is so full of sorrow now that it is hard to find words which convey feelings of sympathy to those who are so cruelly stricken in the loss of all they love; but the double loss which fell upon you in so short a space of time was cruel beyond the experience of these sad times, and only your great courage can have enabled you to bear it.

Will you let me assure you with what pleasure I have heard from you again, and with every good wish from my wife and myself.

Believe me,
Winston S. Churchill

Winston S. Churchill to Louis Loucheur: telegram

(*Churchill papers: 15/157*)

26 November 1917

I propose to your Excellency an inter-allied munitions conference at Paris on Friday and Saturday and if necessary on Monday also. I have a series of proposals for co-ordinating the inter-allied production of munitions which I desire to have discussed, and of which I will apprise you at the earliest moment. The presence of the Americans is indispensable. I should therefore be very grateful if you would convene this conference yourself asking them and Dallolio to attend using my name as well as yours. I will come to Paris by the night train Thursday. Pray let me have an answer at the earliest moment.

[1] Lady Lucy Catherine Fortescue, 1851–1940. Daughter of the 3rd Earl Fortescue. In 1874 she married Michael Edward Hicks-Beach, 1st Earl St Aldwyn, Chancellor of the Exchequer, 1885–6, and in 1895–1902, and a close friend of Churchill's father. St Aldwyn died on 30 April 1916, seven days after his only son, Viscount Quenington, Conservative MP for Tewkesbury, had been killed in action in Egypt. One of Lady St Aldwyn's brothers, Lord Lionel Fortescue, had been killed in action in South Africa in 1900, and one of her nephews, Grenville Fortescue, had been killed in action on the western front in September 1915.

Winston S. Churchill to Andrew Bonar Law

(*Bonar Law papers*)

27 November 1917 Ministry of Munitions

My dear Bonar Law,

I am very sorry to learn that the Restriction of Imports Committee which was fixed for today is postponed. It is impossible to work out any policy for munitions supply while these vital matters are not even discussed, & while no means exists for a regular interchange of views between Departments. Ministerial Heads of Departments do not know either what other departments are doing, or what they want to do. There is no organized consultation between Heads of Departments; for instance I only learnt yesterday and casually—of Albert Stanley's[1] plan for lending shipping to the American Govt in order to transport their army more speedily. Yet this has a most important bearing on everything we are doing here, & might conceivably be made to fit in with those ideas of unity of production in munitions of which I spoke to you today.

Two most necessary Committees have been appointed by the Cabinet to afford some measure of co-ordination in the return of executive departments—Smuts' War Priorities Committee, & the Restriction of Imports Committee. Both, after a few fitful meetings, are falling into practical desuetude. Policy is decided by the War Cabinet; but *method* surely ought to be concerted by personal & formal intercourse between Heads of Departments. It is quite easy for munitions production to flow along from day to day under the present system; but it is impossible to give the Army trustworthy estimates on which plans can be based, or to impart that element of design by which alone the higher economies of production can be attained.

I really hope this Committee can meet as arranged this afternoon or tomorrow, under whatever Chairmanship may be thought to be expedient in Milner's absence.

Yours vy sincerely
Winston S. Churchill

[1] Albert Henry Stanley, 1875–1948. General Manager, American Electric Railways, 1896–1907. General Manager, Metropolitan District Railway, London, 1907. Knighted, 1914. Director-General of Mechanical Transport, 1916. Conservative MP, 1916–20 (Lord Beaverbrook accepted a peerage to enable him to be elected for Ashton-under-Lyne). President of the Board of Trade, 1916–19. Chairman and Managing Director of the London Underground Railways, 1919–33. Created Baron Ashfield, 1920. Chairman, London Passenger Transport Board, 1933–7. Member of the British Transport Commission, 1947.

Lord Cowdray to Winston S. Churchill

(Cowdray papers)

28 November 1917

I left the Air Board with regret. Any one taking a pride in his work naturally likes to reap what he has sown, and cannot leave it especially during a great transition period, without deploring having to do so.

Yrs, with every kind regard and thankfulness for your devotion to the needs of the Air Services.

December 1917

Sir Henry Wilson: diary

(*Wilson papers*)

3 December 1917 Versailles

Layton (Munitions) came down to see me. Winston & he are starting an Allied Munitions Council in Paris and he wanted to know what his relations were to be to me. We arranged for very close relations.

War Cabinet: minutes

(*Cabinet papers: 23/4*)

6 December 1917

LORD DERBY drew attention to a letter from Field-Marshal Sir Douglas Haig, dated the 24th November, 1917, pointing out that, if matters were allowed to go on as at present, without a great legislative or administrative effort to obtain men, the British infantry divisions in France would be 40 per cent. below their present establishment by the 31st March, 1918. Since this letter very grave reports regarding the situation in France had been received from the front. There was no longer any question of our deciding what our military policy would be next year, as that will be decided by the Germans. Sir Douglas Haig was, at this moment, 100,000 men below his proper strength. So far from there being any question of our breaking through the Germans, it was a question whether we could prevent the Germans breaking through us. The Army Council looked to Sir Auckland Geddes to make suggestions as to how the very large number of men essential for the army could be met.

MR CHURCHILL stated that he agreed with Lord Derby that the position was one of great danger. He gathered that the deficit which required making up during the next six months amounted to approximately 500,000 men. He quite realised that, as far as the Ministry of Munitions were concerned, they had to find men for release for the army, only he hoped that if the Ministry of Munitions made the great effort which they were called upon to make, other Departments, such as the Admiralty, would, by means of combing out fit men and by the utmost economy in the use of man-power, produce a substantial quota: he also thought that the demand for 90,000 men put forward by the Admiralty should be most carefully examined. He thought that use might be made upon small craft for the 60,000 trained American sailors now available. He was examining the question of the number of men available for release from munition work in its relation to output, and he pointed out that 53,000 men had been released from such work since April 1917. He estimated that by slowing down the output of certain munitions and by methods of economy and dilution it might be possible to obtain as many as 120,000 further men from munitions during the course of the next twelve months. These figures assumed, of course, that the Trades Unions would be consulted in accordance with the pledge given by Mr Arthur Henderson[1] before skilled men were taken in addition to all dilutees.

In his opinion the Government would be well advised to face the question of man-power in Parliament by presenting simultaneously all their proposals for raising men. It would be fatal to deal with the matter piecemeal by raising successive storms over such questions as the taking of skilled men, the application of conscription to Ireland, and the raising of the military age. It appeared to him that the number of men retained for purposes of Home Defence was large, and that something might be done in the direction of giving the fighting troops a rest during the coming three months by the use in the trenches of garrison battalions composed of older and lower category men.

Winston S. Churchill to Sir Auckland Geddes

(*Churchill papers: 15/158*)

7 December 1917 Ministry of Munitions

My dear Auckland Geddes,

I have had a number of newspaper extracts brought under my notice, which give accounts of speeches delivered on the Cumberland ore fields by

[1] Arthur Henderson, 1863–1935. Labour MP, 1903–18; 1919–22; 1923; 1924–31. Chairman, Parliamentary Labour Party, 1908–10. Chief Whip, Labour Party, 1914; 1921–4; 1925–7. President of the Board of Education, May 1915–August 1916. Paymaster General, August–December 1916. Member of Lloyd George's War Cabinet, December 1916–August 1917. Government Mission to Russia, 1917. Home Secretary in the first Labour Government, 1924. Secretary of State for Foreign Affairs, 1929–31. President of the World Disarmament Conference, 1932–3.

some officers of your Department, viz Mr Williams, Mr Gilmour, and Captain Edge.[1] I enclose you copies of the papers in question, which will you please return.

These speeches have been greatly resented and have caused much embarrassment in the district; and I received yesterday a deputation of the Cumberland mine owners protesting strongly against the charges, of which they were the objects.

I have had a great deal of difficulty in dealing with this area, and have devoted much personal attention to it. The steady and continuous increase in the output is satisfactory, and I am very much obliged to you for the assistance which your Department has given in providing for the importation of outside labour. Mr Gilmour also has rendered much valuable assistance and has, throughout, taken a moderate and sagacious view; but, on the other hand, there are several passages in the speeches both of Mr Williams and Captain Edge, particularly the latter, which are quite unsuited to the official positions which they hold, and are not in accordance with the tone that is becoming to representatives of Government Departments.

I have found it necessary to order an inquiry into the charges which they have made against the mine owners, who, I must remind you, are an essential factor in the output, and whom I am bound to treat with loyalty and consideration. This inquiry will begin very shortly, and, if they are cleared of the charges, as I am assured they probably will be, it will be necessary that an apology of some sort or other should be tendered to them, either directly by the Ministry of National Service or, if you prefer it, by me on behalf of your Department.

I hear that Captain Edge and Mr Williams are going back to Cumberland on Sunday, and, for that reason, I write to express the hope that they will not make any further speeches—certainly no more of this character—and will bear in mind that agents of the Government must observe a certain air of impartiality in dealing with the rival interests of capital and labour.

Yours sincerely,
Winston S. Churchill

PS. Forgive my bothering you with this, but I am sure you will see that three speeches, however well meant, are injurious to any discipline the owner can maintain in the pits, & openly partisan.

[1] William Edge, 1880–1948. Liberal MP, 1916–23 and 1927–31. National Liberal MP, 1931–45. A Junior Lord of the Treasury, August 1919–February 1920. A National Liberal Whip, 1922–3. Knighted, 1922. A Charity Commissioner, 1932–5. Created Baronet, 1937.

Winston S. Churchill: memorandum

(*'Official History of the Ministry of Munitions'*)

8 December 1917

It is vital to us to have in the field at the opening of the spring campaign a British army stronger and better equipped than we have ever had before, because the burden thrown upon it is going to be greater than before. On the other hand this army, once raised and restored to its full efficiency and strength, must be husbanded and not consumed. It must be an army crouched and not sprawled; an army with a large proportion of divisions in reserve at full strength, resting and training; an army sustained by every form of mechanical equipment, including especially tanks and aeroplanes, and possessing the greatest possible lateral mobility.

Winston S. Churchill to Major Jack Churchill

(*Churchill papers: 15/158*)

8 December 1917 Ministry of Munitions

My dear Jack,

I was grieved not to be able to see you when passing through Dunkirk last week, and I hope my telegram did not cause you inconvenience. I had no idea that one could not procure a motor for such a short trip as that.[1]

Clemmie is much better, but has had a very bad time, and will require to go to Brighton for a week.

We shall be at Lullenden for Christmas, and you and Goonie[2] and all the children are expected there. So mind you get leave, and telegraph when we may expect you.

I do not refer to the situation here, as we can talk about it when you come home.

[1] On 3 December, while he had been in France, Churchill had visited the Royal Flying Corps Advanced headquarters at Fienvillers. On the following day Maurice Baring recorded in his diary: 'Winston Churchill came to dine and sleep. He said the war would last a very long time. "Of course if we gave in we could have peace tomorrow," he said.' (*Flying Corps Headquarters 1914–1918*, published by G Bell & Sons, 1920)

[2] Lady Gwendeline Teresa Mary Bertie, 1885–1941. Known as 'Goonie'. Daughter of the 7th Earl of Abingdon. She married Churchill's brother Jack in 1908. Her first son, John George, was born in 1909 (he published his memoirs, *Crowded Canvas*, in 1961). Her second son, Henry Winston, known as Peregrine, was born in 1913. Her only daughter, Anne Clarissa, was born after the war, in 1920 (and married in 1952 Anthony Eden, later 1st Earl of Avon).

Winston S. Churchill to Andrew Bonar Law

(*Churchill papers: 15/158*)

10 December 1917 Ministry of Munitions

My dear Bonar Law,

I understand that you wish to hear from me to what extent I propose to give effect to the recommendations of the Select Committee on National Expenditure. These recommendations touch upon the Ministry on the one hand and the relations of the Ministry to the Treasury on the other. Taking the former first, my views are as follows—

(1) With regard to the Parliamentary Secretary becoming charged with finance in the same manner as the Admiralty and the War Office, as you know, I am considering this matter in relation to the probable resignation of Sir Herbert Hambling as Member of Council for Finance.

(2) I agree with the Select Committee that the Finance Member should be responsible for the financial consideration of programmes and the other matters referred to in the Committee's report, and I have no reason to suppose that any fresh instructions on this subject are required. This point will, however, receive my careful consideration in connection with the appointment of Sir Herbert Hambling's successor.

(3) I see no reason for acting on the recommendation of the Committee that there should be a member of council responsible for contracts as distinguished from finance. Under the general administration of the Ministry the duties connected with contracts are divided between the Departments of Finance, Supply and Contracts. It would be difficult, without considerable and unnecessary duplication of staff, to separate the negotiation of contracts from the Supply Department, which has technical information as to the nature of the supply, the capacity and cost of work. And again, the Contract Department could not deal with the purely financial side of contracts without reference to the Finance Department. Under the present organization the Member of Council for Finance is responsible also for contracts, and therefore represents both in matters in which they are intimately connected.

The various Supply Departments are also represented through Members of Council responsible for their respective groups and these deal with contracts from the point of view of supply.

There would thus be no advantage from the point of view of financial control or of administrative finance that the Contract Department should be separately represented upon the Council.

(4) Having regard to what I have said before, while I agree that the relations of the Finance Member to the Heads of his Department should be

clearly defined, I am not aware that there is any necessity for any further definition of those relations. They are direct and close. The matter will, however, be reconsidered when settling the functions of Sir Herbert Hambling's successor.

(5) I agree that the officers charged with the control of accounts should be in close relation to the Finance Member and that their staff should be strengthened. Steps have been taken to add to their staff in order that they may discharge their duties effectively, and Sir Herbert Hambling has been throughout in the closest relations with those officers in the discharge of their duties. I do not think that any fresh instructions are required in this respect.

(6) With regard to the recommendations of the Select Committee as to Treasury control, I need scarcely remind you that the Treasury have already taken certain action in which the Ministry have concurred. It has been agreed that the Treasury should be applied to for sanction in the case of capital expenditure on works etc above £50,000. Action has also been taken through the Priority Committee of the Cabinet and the various committees subordinate to it to co-ordinate the action of the three Main spending departments and it is in contemplation to place in a more official position the joint committee which was instituted some time ago to reconcile prices paid for similar contracts in the Departments of the Admiralty, War Office and Ministry.

Two Treasury committees have also been set up to deal with aircraft finance and loans and grants against capital expenditure.

With regard to the other suggestions, I must strike a note of warning in regard to the proposal that the Treasury should determine the rate of profits and principles governing the conditions of contracts for the guidance of the Contract Department. If this means that the Committee are in favour of an extension of any system of time and line contracts to general supplies, this change, I think, would be most objectionable. Nothing has been more criticised in the action of the Admiralty than the manner in which they have placed contracts on these lines, as it means that the contractor has no object whatever in insisting upon economy inasmuch as a fixed rate of profit is secured for the firm whatever happens. It is, in my opinion, far better that there should be less check upon the rate of profit and leave the amount to be reduced by the action of the Excess Profits Duty.

I am ready to co-operate with any proposals of the Treasury to give support to the efforts of the Finance Department to promote economy, but I am confident that these efforts will not be advanced by any scheme which places Finance in a position of hostility rather than of assistance to the supply Departments.

My experience is that, whenever Finance is placed in what is naturally a false position in relation to Supply, friction and mal-administration follow.

Believe me, Yours sincerely
Winston S. Churchill

Lord Stamfordham[1] *to Winston S. Churchill*

(*Royal Archives*)

11 December 1917 Buckingham Palace

My dear Churchill,

The King desires me to say with what pleasure and satisfaction he has read the report of your speech delivered last night at Bedford.[2]

His Majesty agrees with all you said and feels that it will do much good especially at the present time.

Yours very truly
Stamfordham

Winston S. Churchill to Lord Stamfordham

(*Royal Archives*)

12 December 1917 Ministry of Munitions

My dear Stamfordham,

I am vy glad indeed to learn that the King was pleased by the account wh he read of my Bedford meeting; & it is a source of great satisfaction to me to receive yr vy kind letter.

There was an extremely good spirit both at the meeting & in the streets outside.

As you know I regard this as a vy critical period of the War when weakness of any kind wd be fatal. I am sure the people can be absolutely trusted.

Please convey to His Majesty my sincere thanks for the gracious message wh has reached me.

Yours vy sincerely
Winston S. Churchill

[1] Arthur John Bigge, 1849–1931. Entered Army, 1869. Entered the Royal Household, 1880. Private Secretary to Queen Victoria, 1895–1901. Private Secretary to George V, 1910–31. Created Baron Stamfordham, 1911. His only son was killed in action on 15 May 1915.

[2] Speaking at Bedford on 10 December 1917 Churchill had exhorted Munitions workers to make an extra effort of production in time for the next Allied offensive. 'Masses of guns,' he said, 'mountains of shells, clouds of aeroplanes—all must be there.'

Winston S. Churchill to Louis Loucheur

(*Churchill papers: 15/158*)

13 December 1917 Ministry of Munitions

I have made inquiries as to the causes of the delays in the supply of steel to which your Excellency refers in your letter of November 20th, and I find that they are the result of certain changes recently made by our steel Department in their working of the system of allocation.

The difficulties from which these delays have arisen are, however, entirely of a temporary character, due to the transition to the new method, and we have taken measures which, it is hoped, will obviate such delays in the future. I may, however, point out that the delay in the arrangement of the French Government's September orders has not meant a loss of gross tonnage under the different classes of material. Until the new orders are arranged, deliveries have been continued under the old, and the total deliveries for October (over 34,000 tons) compare not unfavourably with those of previous months.

May I suggest to your Excellency that it would be of considerable assistance to us in preventing delays in the arrangement of the manufacturing programme if you could make arrangements to forward, not later than the middle of each month, your detailed requisitions under the allocation for manufacture in the following month, and to modify these requisitions subsequently as little as possible.

Winston S. Churchill to Sir Eric Geddes: unsent draft

(*Churchill papers: 15/158*)

13 December 1917 Ministry of Munitions

My dear First Lord,

You asked me some time ago to let you know if there were any serious questions of Admiralty policy which I thought it necessary to raise with the War Cabinet, and without entering into any formal engagement I told you I was extremely anxious to meet your wishes in that respect. I therefore write to let you know that there are three large issues on which I most earnestly hope you will fix your attention. They are all matters which affect fundamentally the domestic policy of the Ministry of Munitions. They are not questions which I am approaching in any way from the point of view of strategy or tactics. On these matters I have, as you know, very clear opinions, but I have not expressed any such opinions since I joined the Government. The points I wish to bring to your notice arise solely from considerations affecting (1) man-power (2) materials (3) organisation of supply.

On the first—man-power. It seems to me that the demand which the Admiralty is making for 90,000 additional men at the present time, whether considered as a competitor to Munitions or to the maintenance of the armies in the field, is a very hard one. Before the war we had to fight for every man and every sovereign for the needs of the Navy, and every naval officer has been brought up with the feeling that it was his duty to do his utmost to screw as much out of the Treasury and the House of Commons as possible. There was a great deal to be said for this in time of peace, and I myself profited enormously in wringing from Parliament and the Cabinet the necessary provisions. But now it is no longer a question of extracting from peace-time indulgence or Treasury thrift the greatest possible supply for the upkeep of the Navy, but rather a question of draining the last drops of blood from the soldiers in the trenches and the last ounces of energy from the munition factories.

It would be a grave wrong done to this country in its most critical situation, for the Admiralty to ask for more than is absolutely necessary to discharge the precise duties and functions which are imposed on it and accepted by it. I suggest to you that if owing to the submarine having been allowed to develop, as it has in former years, you are now compelled to make these immense demands for merchant shipbuilding and for anti-submarine craft, with which I am in entire accord, it should be an obligation to cut all other services to the absolute minimum; indeed, it should be a point of honour to release every man that can be spared to aid our military effort already so much weakened by the untoward turn of naval affairs.

Secondly, the Grand or Blue Water Fleet which has to be kept ready to fight the German High Seas Fleet, ought also to be kept at the minimum compatible with security. Considering that the great strength of the American Navy is now thrown into the scale, it surely should be possible to be content with something like the standards which were accepted for the battle fleets in the early and more critical periods of the war. At any rate, it would be a very wrong thing, on which in time the Nation would have to pronounce, if it were found that our supply of munitions was greatly affected and our armies greatly weakened through an excess of caution in regard to the margin of superiority required for the battle-field, and through keeping a force greatly in excess of what sound policy required. The tendency for every Commander and every administrative officer to pile up demands for the particular class of vessel or product in which he is interested, irrespective of the provisions which other departments are making to meet the same need, is one which can only be corrected by criticism which however loyal in intent must appear controversial in form.

Thirdly, I have heard with astonishment that since the beginning of the war the Admiralty have actually raised to 120,000 the standard of the number of men who can be landed on these shores from the 70,000, which was always considered the maximum of pre-war days occurring under conditions before the Fleet were mobilised, and without any of the present advantages of mines, submarines, and intelligence. This figure has been taken by the Home Defence Authorities of the War Office as the foundation for their estimate, and is one of the causes for keeping in this country the enormous number of men in khaki who are eating up our mutton without serving any effective military purpose. Ever since the year 1911 I have been in the closest touch with every aspect of this invasion problem, and I am quite sure, though I will not burden you here with the reasons, that there has in this respect been a very great departure from the sound and manly principles of war policy on which we acted in the crisis of 1914.

I trust most earnestly that this may receive your attention. A fresh mind like yours looking at facts from a commanding point of view, without prejudice, and studying the process by which opinion is being built up as well as the assertions which are being made to-day, would, I am confident, be able to render very great services to the country in this respect. Mr Balfour and Mr Asquith are saturated in this subject which we all studied together literally for years, and I am sure you would gain great advantage if you discussed the matter with them.

My second point is materials, and this arises largely from the same set of considerations as I have put before you in regard to man-power. I am told that the construction of light cruisers of the largest kind, and battle cruisers, and the manufacture of heavy guns, is actually being proceeded with at the present time on a large scale, having regard to the fact that every ton of material and every hour of skilled labour, can only be obtained at the expense of vital services. It seems to me a very grievous thing that any warships for other than anti-submarine purposes, should be proceeded with at the present time. The accession of the American Fleet to our resources, already so much greater relatively than they were at the beginning of the war, ought to have put the final quietus on further construction for Grand Fleet purposes. It is to me shocking beyond words, knowing what I do of the relative strength of the British and German Navies, and indeed, of the Allied and enemy Navies, that we should be actually robbing our Army of shell and other vital equipment for the sake of still further piling up an enormous surplus of Blue Water craft that will be left on our hands at the close of the war. We have reached a point where every ton taken by the Navy directly reduces the battery which protects the British troops in the field. If these matters could be debated in public and if the facts and figures could be laid before the nation, I am confident the Navy itself would recoil from the harshness of its action in regard to the general interest of the country. But in the present circumstances of secrecy, where there is neither Parliamentary nor Cabinet discussion in the old sense, there is no force but your own which can exert an effective control over such proceedings.

It is not only in the region of the construction of new warships for other than anti-submarine purposes that the Admiralty seem to be inconsiderate in their demands for material of the general interest at this time. The general super-priority claimed and in practice asserted by officers serving under the Admiralty, for all classes of material and for all kinds of work, produces repeated dislocations and waste. Two instances which have been brought to my notice in the last fortnight show the kind of thing that is going on. In the first case, the Admiralty overseers at [ ][1] seized the steel bars rolled for gun barrels for the Army on the grounds that they were required to make propeller shafts for the Navy, thus causing widespread dislocation when in fact it was afterwards discovered that these steel bars were not suitable for the purpose to which the Admiralty wished to put them. In another case, the work of a large shop at [ ][1] has been deranged by the super-priority accorded to potato-peeling machines for the Fleet, which are thus made to rank higher than aeroplane engines.

My third point is, of course, the water-tight Departments in which the Ministry of Munitions and the Admiralty Supply Departments work. You probably know far more about this than I do. What it means in waste, in friction, in undue accumulation of separate reserves, both of men and of material, to have these two great sets of Departments competing against each other in the same field without sympathy for each other's needs, cannot be measured. There ought, of course, to be one Supply Department serving the three fighting Departments in accordance with their needs as approved by the Cabinet. Supply on a vast scale is a civil function. It is the business of sailors, soldiers, and airmen to say what weapons they want and see that they get them and use them when they have got them. But supply should be dealt with from a single standpoint, and that a civilian one covering the whole area of the resources of the country. I do not consider that such a great matter could be decided without many weeks of careful examination, but that it is right in principle and necessary in fact if we are to realise to the full our remaining resources next year and the year after, I have no doubt.

I put these issues before you because I shall feel bound to raise them as and when opportunity occurs, and you pressed upon me your wish to have full notice in such matters. I earnestly hope they may be considered by you in the same spirit in which I put them forward, viz, the desire to see this country realise its highest war effort in the supremely critical period which lies before us.

[1] The names of both places were left blank in Churchill's draft.

General Dallolio to Winston S. Churchill: telegram

(*Churchill papers: 15/158*)

13 December 1917 Rome

Absolute Priority

I have duly informed you in Paris of the very serious situation which Italy finds itself as to what regards its supplies of coal and raw materials, and special measures were considered in this connection. But up to now nothing has arrived because France despite her much larger stocks of coal in comparison with Italy, awaits the arrival of coal from England before giving us what is most urgently and imperiously needed by us. I have to insist again, in the common interest and for the common purpose, on all arguments contained in the different memorandums I handed you in Paris,—the situation being, I repeat, of the utmost gravity, while our armies are fighting and holding the Piave line.

Winston S. Churchill to General Dallolio

(*Churchill papers: 15/158*)

14 December 1917 Ministry of Munitions

My dear General

May I draw your Excellency's attention to the question of purchases in the United States by the Allies, of acetone, acetate of lime and acetic acid. I understand that, in view of the importance of eliminating competition in the purchase of these materials, sanction was obtained to the principle that the British Ministry of Munitions should negotiate for the combined requirements of Italy, France and Great Britain.

In order to give effect to this sanction, the following procedure has recently been proposed both to the French and the Italian Governments, viz:—

(1) A combined contract would be entered into in the name of the British Government for the total supplies required, or as much of them as may be obtainable.

(2) In the event of supplies falling short of requirements, as seems more than probable, the matter shall be submitted to the Inter-Allied Council, or to the permanent Munitions Council in Paris, for allocation.

(3) The French and Italian Governments shall give an undertaking to the British Government to the effect that they will pay for their respective

portions in dollars in the USA out of their own dollar credits as payments fall due under the contract.

Further, an essential part of the scheme is that no independent inquiries should be put forward in the States by France and Italy, otherwise the advantages of joint purchases as regards price and distribution will largely be nullified.

The French Government have already agreed to the proposals indicated above, and have given the necessary undertaking as to the prohibition of independent negotiations. I understand, however, that, although your Government have notified their requirements of acetone, they ask for an absolute guarantee that all their requirements will be met, and so far have given no undertaking either that they will submit to allocation, pay for quantities allocated out of their own dollar credits, or will refrain from any independent negotiations.

I think you will agree with me that it is important that the Italian, French and British Governments should all act together in the purchase of these materials, particularly as the United States Government press this point. I therefore hope you will now be able to secure the consent of your Government to the proposals indicated above.

War Cabinet Committee:[1] *minutes*

(*Curzon papers*)

14 December 1917 War Office

MR CHURCHILL reported that Mons Loucheur had put forward a demand for an increased allocation of Vickers Machine guns, on the ground that these were urgently required for certain highest class services such as fighting aeroplanes; he anticipated that our output of these guns would exceed previous forecasts, and urged that we should not take the line that no allocation should be made to our Allies before all British services, of whatever character, were provided for, as in his opinion, some of our services could be met by Lewis guns, of which we have at present a large surplus.

[1] The Committee on Allocation of Guns. Its members were Lord Curzon (in the Chair), Lord Derby and Churchill.

Winston S. Churchill to General Dallolio: telegram

(*Churchill papers: 15/55*)

17 December 1917 Ministry of Munitions

We have arranged to send you from this country the following:—2,000 Lewis Guns, 50,000 Rifles complete with equipment, 20 million small arms ammunition packed for machine guns: 10 million small arms ammunition for rifles. All these are ready and shipment has commenced. We have also arranged to send you from FRANCE 40—8″ Howitzer equipments and 40—6″ Howitzer equipments to be despatched this month if possible; 40 more 6″ Howitzers will probably be sent in January.

We also hope to send you Field Guns, but there are difficulties in the way. Towards those asked for we at present propose to send some 140 15-pdr gun equipments with 75,000 rounds Shrapnel and 75,000 rounds HE, but it is not certain whether this number of equipments is available. 40 are already to go and the rest require overhauling and repair. Every effort is being made to expedite the work.

I trust your Excellency will be pleased to get the 6″. They are very precious.

War Cabinet: minutes

(*Cabinet papers: 23/4*)

24 December 1917

MR CHURCHILL stated that the perpetual agitation for further increases in wages was due very largely to the fact that the wage-earners were convinced that enormous profits were being made both by the employers and by profiteers engaged in trade and exchange. He was convinced that one of the only means of stopping these demands would be for the Government to take the whole of the excess profits instead of only 80 per cent. The only way to face the present situation was for the Government to make a proclamation stating that they meant to deal drastically with the question of profits, and to place the whole question of profits and wages upon a broad basis of justice and security, which would appeal to both capital and labour alike. Whatever increases were approved by the Cabinet should be announced by the Government, and not by one Department. It was being generally said that the war was being kept going by persons who were interested in making profits out of the war, and he felt that the very existence of excess profits being received by individuals was wrong both in principle and in morals.

War Cabinet: minutes

(*Cabinet papers: 23/4*)

26 December 1917

MR CHURCHILL stated that the Ministry of Munitions were doing all they could to damp down the production of Russian war material, but they did not at present intend to regard Russia as an entirely 'gone' concern, so that it seemed desirable to keep a nucleus going in order that the production of material for Russia might be restored in the event of a change taking place in the situation.[1]

MR CHURCHILL said he understood that a number of Russian officers were most anxious to be kept together, either in France or England, as a Russian unit to form a rallying point for those Russians who remained loyal to the *Entente*. In his opinion such a nucleus would be a valuable political asset.

Winston S. Churchill to G. N. Barnes[2]

(*Churchill papers: 15/111*)

28 December 1917 Ministry of Munitions

My dear Mr Barnes,

Thank you very much for your kind letter of the 27th. I am deeply grateful to you for all the aid and counsel which you have given me in Labour matters since I took office, and I am glad to think that we have been substantially agreed on every important step that has been taken.

At the same time, I must now state that the present position of the Ministry of Munitions in relation to the new War Cabinet Committee is one of difficulty. The Minister of Munitions is endowed, by Act of Parliament, with certain powers for the exercise of which he is personally responsible. What-

[1] In November 1917 the Bolsheviks, led by Lenin and Trotsky, had seized power in Russia. One of their first acts had been to remove Russia from the war, and to open peace negotiations with the Germans at Brest-Litovsk. By the end of 1917 several former Tsarist Generals had raised the standard of anti-Bolshevik revolt in South Russia and the Ukraine; but these forces seemed little able to challenge Bolshevik power, let alone reopen the eastern front against Germany and Austria-Hungary.

[2] George Nicholl Barnes, 1859–1940. Apprenticed as a machine tool worker at the age of eleven. Worked in the London Docks as a construction worker. General Secretary, Amalgamated Society of Engineers, 1896–1908. Chairman, National Committee of Organized Labour for Old Age Pensioners, 1902. Labour MP, 1906–22. Minister of Pensions, December 1916–August 1917. Member of the War Cabinet, May 1917–January 1919. Minister without Portfolio, August 1917–January 1920. He published *From Workshop to War Cabinet* in 1923.

ever is done in the way of Wage Orders must be done in my name, and it is quite impossible for me to regard this charge as a mere matter of form. I should not complain if an amending bill were passed transferring the powers now vested in the Ministry of Munitions to you or your Committee—a laborious and difficult task which no one can envy. But while I am responsible for the exercise of the statutory powers confided to me, I cannot escape from the burden. I saw, for instance, the recent Order of the 11th December for the first time when I visited your Committee on Friday last.

I am fully sensible of the need of co-ordinating the action of the various Government Departments, and I agree that the continuance of your Committee is necessary. But that Committee should continue not as an executive body taking the daily affairs out of the hands of the Departments or relieving Ministers of their own lawful responsibilities, but as an advisory body cognisant of what is being done, and offering collective advice to the War Cabinet in regard to any new proposal that may be made by the departmental Ministers which is in itself of sufficient importance to require Cabinet attention.

I should propose therefore to resume the full administration of the Wage questions within the scope of the Ministry of Munitions according to my statutory powers and duties. Secondly, to keep your Committee informed betimes of all that takes place; and thirdly, to consult the Cabinet on any departure of serious importance. It would also be open to your Committee, or to yourself personally as a member of the War Cabinet, to raise any question connected with the administration of the Munitions of War Acts which you thought necessary.

Meanwhile I should like to strengthen the representation of the Ministry of Munitions on the Committee by adding Sir Stephenson Kent who has now returned from America.

Winston S. Churchill to G. N. Barnes

(*Churchill papers: 15/111*)

28 December 1917 Ministry of Munitions

The policy which the Ministry of Munitions will follow in general agreement with the views of your Committee is as follows—

(1) *Piece-workers.*—No public announcement should be made about an increase of their rates. Employers should be pressed to revise the rates in cases where they are not of sufficient inducement to men to go on piece-work, but this can be done by circularising the employers, by conferences with

them, or by other forms of private negotiation. In each case the arrangement should be come to locally between the employers and the workpeople. It may be that we shall be confronted with such large numbers of claims that general and public directions will be necessary but, at this stage, I do not think any formal announcement is called for.

(2) *Time-workers.*—I deprecate also at present a public announcement in regard to time-workers. We have newly issued our Order of December 11th, and I think we had much better watch the developments which will arise from that before finally making up our minds. It seems to me inevitable that the outlying engineers, whether semi-skilled or unskilled, will eventually make good their claim to be included, but there is no need to anticipate this position at present.

The iron and steel trade have accepted an invitation to a conference on Thursday at the Ministry of Munitions. It is believed that work will be continued meanwhile. They will be asked to offer suggestions as to how their time-workers can receive the advance without disturbing the rest of the trade. I have no doubt we shall have to settle on the inclusion of the time-workers almost immediately.

The building and construction trade should be dealt with on similar lines, ie the onus should be put upon them of explaining how the claim for maintenance builders can be met without affording grounds for extending the advance to the trade as a whole. I do not propose to see them till later.

The woodworkers in the engineering shops can be left for the time being, but they will eventually have to be dealt with on the same basis as the iron and steel and building trades, ie by a bargain arrived at at a trade conference limiting, as far as possible, the application of any increase.

There is no need to move in any of these cases except when trouble actually arises.

The public utilities, including the electricians, should be referred to the Committee on Production through the Ministry of Labour, and we shall answer any requests we get from these trades in that sense.

I propose also to tell the chemical workers, should they make a demand, that they are entirely outside the scope of these awards, and that if they have any complaint to make, they must refer it to the Committee on Production.

Similarly, any application from the railway workshops must be met by the answer that their wages are dealt with by the special railway agreements.

There are certain miscellaneous industries in which difficulties have arisen, and, where these do not affect the general principle, the employers will be encouraged to pay the advance.

To sum up, the general principle is to stand for the present on the Order of December 11th, but to make its application complete, wherever possible, without making new difficulties. Secondly, to invite the three trades intimately interwoven with engineering, viz iron and steel, building (repair and maintenance), and woodwork (engineering section) to enter into trade conferences with us. And, thirdly, to refer all others, except certain miscellaneous trades, which can be dealt with without compromising the situation, to the Committee on Production.

These views are only interim views, and it is probable that more general action will be forced upon us in the near future. I do not think, however, that we should finally take up our position until the extent of the difficulty is more clearly defined than at present.

(3) I am deeply sensible of the value of the work of your Committee, and the need of a body taking a general and inter-departmental view of wage questions is obvious. At the same time, it is important that the administrative discretion of the Ministry of Munitions should not be fettered, and, of course, nothing can relieve the Minister of Munitions of the responsibility and the powers which attach to him by statute.

I propose to work in the closest accord with your Committee and to keep them constantly informed of everything that is done. I presume other Departments will do the same. The Committee will then be in a position to advise both the Cabinet and any individual Department on the inter-departmental aspects of any wage question which may come up, and you, as a member of the War Cabinet, will be able to draw their attention to any point which requires it.

(4) Finally, I should like to add Sir Stephenson Kent to your Committee in addition to Mr Wolfe.[1] You will, I am sure, recognise how much more important and how much larger our share in this business is than that of any other Department, or, indeed, of all the other Departments put together, and how indispensable it is that our departmental action should be thoroughly co-ordinated with the views of your Committee. It is for these reasons alone that I wish to add an additional representative of the Ministry to your body and certainly with no reflection upon Mr Wolfe or the manner in which he has discharged his work.

[1] Humbert Wolfe, 1886–1940. Born in Milan, of German-Italian Jewish parentage. Educated at Bradford Grammar School and Wadham College, Oxford. Entered the civil service, 1908. At the Board of Trade he played a leading part in the organization of Labour Exchanges and Unemployment Insurance. Controller, Labour Regulation Department, Ministry of Munitions, 1915–18. Director of Services and Establishments, Ministry of Labour, 1919–21; Head of the Department of Employment and Training, 1934–7; Deputy Secretary, 1938. A poet and literary critic, his first volumes of poetry were published in 1920 and 1924. He wrote or edited over forty books, and did translations of Greek, German and French poems and plays.

Winston S. Churchill to Sir Archibald Sinclair

(*Thurso papers*)

29 December 1917
Private

My dear Archie,

I had been anxiously looking for a letter from you & was delighted to receive one.

The cavalry myth is exploded at last & there is every prospect of these splendid regiments being given a fair opportunity on the modern field. I am strongly pressing that the cavalry shd be put by regiments into the Tanks both heavy & chasers & this view is meeting with a great deal of acceptance. I advise you to apply for Tanks, & I will assist in any way I can to further yr wishes. It wd be a thousand pities if the Cavalry were simply dispersed as drafts among the infantry. The future life of this arm after the war depends upon their discarding the obsolete horse, & becoming associated with some form of military machinery having a scientific & real war value. It is not fair to blame the cavalry. I blame those who assign impossible tasks & absurd conditions to brave men.

It looks as if the failure of the Submarine attack as a decisive factor must leave the Germans no resource but a great offensive in the west. In spite of their reinforcements from the Russian front they will be inferior in a. number, b. morale & c. ammunition & d. reserves. I wish them the joy of it. An elastic defence with strong 'one-day battle' counter blows, at other points, & tank led counter attacks on the flanks of hostile salients; a good army of manœuvre behind our front; & steady influx of Americans ought to make in combination a singularly cheerless outlook for the Hun general staff. Thank God our offensives are at an end. Let them make the pockets, let them trapse across the crater fields, let them rejoice in the occasional capture of placeless names & sterile ridges: & let us dart here & there armed with science & surprise & backed at all points by a superior artillery. That is the way to break their hearts & leave them bankrupt in resource at the end of the 1918 campaign. I look forward with good hopes to the coming clash; & to the opportunity of a good peace at the end of it.

We must not be done out of our world victory by wordy generalities. France has got to win & know that she has won, & Germany has got to be beat & know that she is beaten. I do not think there will be any weakness here or in America. For me Alsace Lorraine is the symbol & test of victory.

Arm yourself therefore my dear with the panoply modern science of war. Make catsmeat of these foolish animals, who have broken your hearts so far. Embark in the chariots of war & slay the malignants with arms of precision.

I will try vy hard to come to see you when next I come to France: or give you rendezvous in Paris. At present I am submerged by Labour difficulties—& have to fight for breath. I hope they are looking after Salonika, wh might otherwise well be a cause of offence.

We are Christmasing here with the children at Lullenden & I go each day to town. Clemmie sends her love & so does Goonie, & so as you know does yr sincere & devoted friend

W

Winston S. Churchill to Louis Loucheur

(*Churchill papers: 15/27*)

30 December 1917 Ministry of Munitions

Dear M Loucheur,

I have carefully reconsidered your renewed request for an allocation of 200 tanks of the latest model by March 1918. We shall not by that date have succeeded in equipping the Tank battalions we have organised and are organising with the new model or, indeed, fully even with the old. I doubt whether, even if the tanks could be supplied, there would be time for France to organise and train the necessary personnel. It would therefore be better, if the French Army needs a force of tanks for its March operations, that the matter should be settled as between the General Staffs, and that British tanks, if they can be spared, on which naturally I can express no opinion, should be assigned to the French Commander-in-Chief[1] complete with their personnel. I could, no doubt, find a small number of tanks of the existing pattern, say 15 or 20, for training purposes if it is desired to form units for handling them. Meanwhile, I am doing everything in my power to expedite the construction of tanks in France by the Inter-Allied Factory. But I am finding very grave difficulties on account of the demands made on similar material by the British Admiralty.

With regard to your letter about the food tonnage, of which I have already sent you a grateful acknowledgment, I am not yet able to make a further reply. Arrangements have been made, and are being carried out, to transport 500,000 tons of French steel, which had been lying in America, to France in place of the shell steel we had hitherto given, but I recognise that

[1] In May 1917 General Pétain had replaced General Nivelle as the Commander-in-Chief of the French forces. He remained Commander-in-Chief until the armistice (recognizing, as did Sir Douglas Haig, the supreme authority of Marshal Foch from March to November 1918).

you will wish to have a further allocation of shell steel and other steel for various purposes during the year 1918 similar to that which you have had in 1917. Although I cannot yet tell to what extent I shall be able to provide for this need, you may rely upon my doing my best with my limited and continually narrowing resources and increasing difficulties to serve you. I cannot yet however get any solid estimates of the tonnage on which I can count for the importation of steel and iron-ore, and, pending that, it would be impossible for me to enter into any agreement.

Is there any chance of your Excellency coming over here? If so, I trust you will let me know in good time, so that I may have some opportunity of returning the gracious hospitality with which I have always been treated when on French soil.

Winston S. Churchill: War Cabinet memorandum

(*Churchill papers: 15/112*)

31 December 1917 Ministry of Munitions

The Government find it necessary to place certain facts plainly before the nation at the beginning of the New Year.

The collapse of Russia has released a large part of the German and Austrian armies on the Eastern front, and several hundred thousand men and several thousand guns have been or are being moved across Germany to attack the British, French, and Italian armies in the West. The recent severe defeat of the Italian army has forced the British and French to send strong reinforcements of men and munitions to Italy, thus weakening our own reserves in France and Flanders.[1] The American armies are not yet ready and will not be a decisive factor for some time. Meanwhile our shipping tonnage has been seriously reduced by the submarines, and the new ships we are building are not yet coming into the water at the full extent. Scarcity of food and fuel in France and Italy has made it necessary for us to make substantial contributions from our own resources to aid these loyal Allies. The general war position is not therefore free from difficulty and even danger.

On the other hand, the Germans and Austrians are themselves hard-

[1] On 24 October 1917 the Italian Army under General Cadorna had been defeated at Caporetto, on the Isonzo river. In three days, more than 200,000 Italian soldiers had been captured, and the Italians were forced to retreat eighty miles westward, to the Piave river. Five French divisions under General Fayolle, and five British divisions under General Plumer, were at once sent to the Italian Front to help hold the new line, and had begun to take up their positions on 10 November, at the very climax of the battle for Passchendaele on the Flanders front.

pressed, and the Turks very much weakened and exhausted. The submarines are being well grappled with. The Americans are pressing forward with their preparations on a gigantic scale as rapidly as possible. The resources and reserves in men, money, and all kinds of materials on our side are vastly greater than those of the enemy. Practically the whole world has ranged itself with us in the struggle against Prussian militarism; and once the difficult and dangerous period into which we have now entered has been tided over the means of victory and of peace will be at hand.

The present position of the war, therefore, requires the entire strength and resources of the nation in order to win. More men must be found to strengthen our armies and enable them to hold the front in France, and aid our Allies where necessary. More ships must be built to bring in food and other supplies, and to aid in transporting the American armies across the ocean. More munitions of every kind, including aeroplanes and tanks, must be provided to equip the British armies to the highest perfection, and thus husband the lives of our men.

All this can be done, provided all work together in good comradeship. We have not suffered in this island losses nearly as great as those of the Germans. We have not had to face the scarcity and privation which they have had to endure almost from the beginning of the war. Our people are not weakened by want of food or unduly overstrained. Our output of ships, aeroplanes, and artillery is continuously increasing. We have many young men who can now be spared to help at the front those who have borne the main burden so long. It would be dishonouring to our race and name if we were at this critical period to fail in our clear duty. Though our responsibilities are very great, though our task is very hard, we have the strength and all that is needful for the emergency.

This is no time either for wage-scrambling or for profiteering. The idea that any class has a right to make an excess profit out of the war must be combated wherever it appears and by every means open to the State. Under the existing law four-fifths of the excess profits are taken by taxation. It is impossible to rest satisfied with this provision, and every practicable means will be employed by the Government to secure to the service of the country all excess profits made during this time of suffering.

Advances of wages have recently been given by the Government to definite sections of workmen in the engineering and shipbuilding trades. These advances arose out of an intention to remedy the contrast between the wages of skilled time workers in certain munitions industries which had grown up during the war. But in practice it was found impossible to keep the grant within the original limits, and as soon as one class was satisfied another felt entitled to make demands. The Government cannot, in the interests of the country, go further on this road. To do so would be to throw an undue burden on British finance, and if applied all round would lead to a rise of prices deeply injurious to the poorer classes of workers, and only wipe out the benefit of those who had received the advance. The only choice open is between cancelling the advances already made or coming to an immediate stop. It is inevitable that any line which is drawn in such matters must cause heartburnings to those left out, especially when their case sometimes appears to differ only slightly from others who have benefited. But this is better than taking back what has already been given, and in consequence leaving unremedied a well-recognised grievance which had long been felt by a large and deserving class of workmen. The situation must therefore be frankly faced.

There are a number of cases of small classes of workmen to whom the existing advance applies, but who have not yet received it. These are being dealt with on their merits as speedily as possible by the War Cabinet Labour Committee. There are also two or three large trades—notably the Iron and Steel Trade—certain classes of whose members are affected by the changes that have been conceded. The Minister of Munitions has been directed to convene Trade Conferences in these cases in order to ascertain whether and to what extent any consequential change is called for. Apart from this, it must be made clear that no further extension of the Orders already issued is possible.

While the war lasts Advances of Wages can only be given on proof of increased cost of living, or in the form of payment by results, or for some very exceptional cause. This applies equally to private employers, who must not consider themselves at liberty to make unauthorised advances to their workpeople, the cost of which in many cases is thrown on the State. The best way in which the mass of the British people can be helped through the present grave period in our national fortunes is, not by raising wages all round, but by keeping down the cost of living by every means in human power. It is to this that the efforts of the Government in the New Year will be constantly directed.

January 1918

Winston S. Churchill to Louis Loucheur: telegram

(*Churchill papers: 15/27*)

1 January 1918 Ministry of Munitions

I have received your Excellency's request for an additional supply of nitrates during the months January February and March amounting to practically ninety thousand tons. In October last at M Thomas' request I supplied forty thousand tons to France from our reserves receiving a personal and definite promise that this amount would be restored in January and February. Instead of this I am confronted with the very serious requests of your letter of December 23rd. Meanwhile the British reserves of nitrates have fallen during the last year from three hundred and fifty thousand tons to approximately one hundred thousand tons at the end of January. This is the sole reserve of nitrates on this side of the Atlantic Ocean and I cannot accept the responsibility of seeing it dissipated at this stage of the campaign.

It is to the United States and not to Great Britain that France should look in this matter. According to the existing programme the artillery of the British Army will not be so large nor so well supplied as that of the French Army in 1918. The American demand for nitrates aggregates nearly one half of the entire Chilean supply although a very small proportion will be required for the maintenance of the American artillery in the field. I trust therefore that your Excellency will address yourself to the United States and demand from them both the nitrates and the shipping which are required. Once this has been definitely guaranteed I should be prepared to assist your Excellency in the immediate emergency but I can only do so upon an American guarantee of repayment within four months of the date of any delivery made from here to France.

I sympathise profoundly with you in the difficulties of the position and with a view to diminishing the immediate difficulties I have agreed to the diversion to France of two ships now on the sea carrying approximately twelve thousand tons between them. I must add that I have received extremely unsatisfactory advices from the shipping controller in regard to the importations of ore from Spain through the scarcity of tonnage and from the Treasury in regard to the purchase of steel in America on account of the shortage of dollars and in these circumstances I shall write in the course of the next few days to your Excellency upon the general steel position.

Winston S. Churchill to Thomas Perkins:[1] *telegram*

(*Churchill papers: 15/27*)

1 January 1918 Ministry of Munitions

Nitrate of Soda position about which Sir Keith Price spoke to you and Mr Crosby[2] when you were in London has become most critical. The French stocks will be exhausted by end of January and Italian stocks by middle of January. Italian requirements are 15,000 tons per month, French requirements are 37,000 tons per month. No shipping is allocated for Italian Nitrate of Soda and only 18,000 tons per month for French Nitrate of Soda. Owing to shortage of tonnage British stocks have fallen from 325,000 tons a year ago to 100,000 tons which means that as British consumption is 45,000 tons per month there is only one month's stock of Nitrate of Soda in Europe against a round voyage of nearly five months.

We lent France 40,000 tons last October under promise of replacement during January or February which promise cannot of course be fulfilled. French now ask for 30,000 tons per month during January, February and March out of British stock in order to tide them over and give them a very small working reserve. I consider it out of the question to comply with any part of this request as I consider this reserve of 100,000 tons for Europe as dangerously small. I have told French Government that I cannot agree further to deplete British stocks unless US Government will give a guarantee to replace with American tonnage the amount provided out of British stock for 3 months.

In view of your large supplies and of French need I strongly urge that you should press your Government to give this guarantee and arrange for immediate shipments of Nitrate of Soda to this side in American tonnage.

[1] Thomas Nelson Perkins, 1870–1937. Chief Counsel to the American War Industries Board, and Assistant Director of Munitions, 1917–18. United States representative on the Reparations Commission, Paris, 1924–6. A Director of several companies, including General Foods, American Telegraph and Telephone, and South Pacific.

[2] Oscar Terry Crosby, 1861–1947. United States explorer, and an authority on electrical subjects. President of the Inter-Ally Council on War Purchases and Finance, November 1917–March 1919.

Winston S. Churchill to Sir Joseph Maclay

(*Churchill papers: 15/160*)

2 January 1918 Ministry of Munitions

My dear Sir Joseph,

Your letter of December 31st explains the position; but it was not unnatural that I should have been misled. Your memorandum of November 2nd confronted me with a deficit of 8,000,000 tons of which 2,000,000 tons was specifically mentioned as allocated to the Allies. It was to meeting this deficit that we addressed ourselves and I imagined that if the French demands were reduced there would be a relief similar to that which is afforded when our own demands are reduced. It now appears that the 2,000,000 tons mentioned by you and calculated precisely in your 8,000,000 deficit was not a definite figure but only an estimate of what you thought the French and Italian food requirements might eventually be squeezed down to, and that in spite of the changes which have been made it still stands as the figure for which we have accepted responsibility.

I cannot entirely accept the doctrine you enunciate in Paragraph 3. There is no such thing as an absolute food minimum. It is surely open to France to squeeze herself a little more than the Allies if she wishes to have certain additional munitions. At any rate the leverage I can exert through refusing munitions is a real and valuable factor, and any result that grows from its existence should surely be credited to munitions for how else can I fulfil the bargain? Meanwhile however I have to face the facts of the situation caused by the disastrous reductions in the tonnage available for munitions. Not only are the importations of ore from Spain quite inadequate to our military needs or to our manufacturing capacity, but I am also restricted by dollars from purchasing steel in the United States and from purchasing shells in Canada. The food, cotton, etc are made to rank in front of our shell supplies. The Commander-in-Chief's increased requirement for ammunition has been refused. The original programme of July on which he was counting has been reduced by half a million tons. Further large reductions are threatened. It is therefore clearly my duty to suspend altogether the exportation of steel from this country to France. This does not affect the 500,000 tons of French shell Steel which is being shipped from America, but it must affect all new allocations. I shall therefore notify M Loucheur in this sense without delay. I should propose, if you have no objection, to enclose a copy of your letter of December 31st as this explains the position in the clearest manner.

The nitrate position is also causing me grave anxiety. The shipping provided so far from Chili[1] is wholly inadequate to our needs. Great Britain needs

[1] Since the First World War, usually spelt Chile. The name is said to have derived from the Quichua words *chiri* (cold) or *tchili* (snow).

next year 46,000 tons a month as an absolute minimum, France 30–33,000 tons a month after allowing for a certain amount of home production, while Italy wants about 15,000 tons a month, or say 91,000 tons a month from Chili in all. This gives a reduced programme both for Great Britain and for France and the same programme for Italy as in 1917.

British ships are steaming at the present moment at the rate of 40,000 tons a month and French ships are expected to bring in an average of 18,000 tons a month. I must therefore point out (1) that you are falling down on British requirements (2) that you cannot escape some responsibility for seeing that the Allies' demands are met. Moreover our reserves have fallen in the last six months from 350,000 tons to about 100,000. The French and Italians are bankrupt. The French so far from being able to pay back the 40,000 tons which I loaned to them in October are now demanding 30,000 tons a month from us in the next three months as a matter of extreme urgency, claiming that their munitions factories will be completely stopped unless this is supplied. This would totally exhaust the British reserves and leave the Allies with no reserves whatever in Europe for emergencies. I must therefore refuse the bulk of this demand also unless I can receive a guarantee of extra importations to make it good in the immediate future.

I presume you realise that the conveyance of these decisions to the French will cause them serious embarrassment and will provoke immediate outcry.

It ought, I think, to be remembered that the imports assigned to the Ministry of Munitions are not used by the Ministry of Munitions for their own purpose but solely and exclusively for the supply of the armies in the field during the most critical campaign of the war.

Winston S. Churchill to Lord Derby

(*Churchill papers: 15/160*)

12 January 1918 Ministry of Munitions

My dear Derby,

I hope you will have noticed the extremely disquieting document circulated by Bonar Law yesterday in which apparently it is taken for granted that the Treasury and Austen Chamberlain are practically to suppress all Munitions imports from the United States during the next few months. This will affect you and Rothermere in all sorts of vital ways if it is persisted in, and I think it extraordinary that decisions of this kind should be taken without allowing the fighting departments concerned or the Ministry of Munitions which supplies them even to be heard. Just as every Service seems to have priority over the Army so far as men are concerned, Munitions are everywhere being side-tracked to the claims of food, of civil imports, of Allies, and of dollars.

I do hope that you will help in this matter and insist upon a fair consideration of our needs relatively to those of other Services.

Winston S. Churchill to Admiral Lambert[1]

(*Churchill papers: 15/160*)

13 January 1918 Ministry of Munitions

Dear Admiral Lambert,

Many thanks for your letter in which I was much interested.

The torpedo and the under-water weakness of modern ships against it has been the obstacle which in this war has robbed the British Navy of its due.

But for the fear of under-water damage the use of the British Fleet would have yielded satisfactory results to all concerned.

Instead of taking the obvious mechanical remedies against this paralysing threat, we have been content to remain on a complete defensive. The consequences have been disastrous to the country, and will long react unfavourably upon the Naval service.

Tactical and strategic schemes conducted by vessels suitably protected would have enabled us to realise and liberate the splendid qualities of our seamen; and would have denied to the enemy the opportunity to develop his own under-water offensive to the fullest extent.

We have had neither the tackle nor the will to use it: and your letter only reveals the heartburnings, and I hope the heartsearchings of many a brave and skilful Naval officer at this present juncture.

Let us hope however that the new organisation at the Admiralty will produce the war-policy which is required, and that it will eventuate before the struggle is otherwise determined.

With good wishes, Believe me, Yours very truly
Winston S. Churchill

[1] Cecil Foley Lambert, 1864–1928. Entered Navy, 1877. Captain, 1905. Fourth Sea Lord, 1913–16. Rear-Admiral, 1916. Knighted, 1920.

War Cabinet: minutes
(*Cabinet papers: 23/5*)

16 January 1918

MR CHURCHILL said that a position had been reached when a choice had to be made between importing one commodity rather than another, although both were in a high degree necessary for the prosecution of the war. The decision must rest with the War Cabinet. He was bound to point out that the munitions position was very serious. In 1918 the Germans would become more powerful than we were in artillery. A series of decisions had been taken by the War Cabinet prejudicial to the supply of fighting material. There had been a cut of 500,000 tons of steel. We were not getting more than two-thirds of the ore programme from Spain. In America we were held up by want of dollars. Nevertheless, cotton was still being imported, and on a higher scale in 1918 than in 1917. The cumulative effect would be to make a great military effort impossible. His Council were alarmed at the absence of any definition of limits within which the purchases of the Food Controller were to be exercised. In the past we had given 40,000 tons a month of shell steel to France, and were continuing this for the month of January, but it would be now necessary to refer the French to the United States. The French had nearly exhausted their supply of nitrates. The Italians had exhausted their stock. Our reserve of 350,000 tons had been brought down to 100,000 tons, which was very low in view of the long voyages entailed. If the United States Government were going to fail us in the air and with men, the least they could do was to provide us with dollars, so as to furnish munitions for our fighting forces. . . .

MR CHURCHILL urged that it was very difficult to apply a satisfactory standard to military requirements. The greater the munitions available, the greater and more frequent were the attacks that could be made upon the enemy. With food it was different, because a minimum standard of subsistence could be laid down.[1]

[1] Churchill reiterated his appeal on 29 January. The War Cabinet minutes for that meeting recorded: 'Mr Churchill then drew attention to the position of the Ministry of Munitions. . . . It was becoming increasingly difficult to maintain the supply of munitions to the army owing to the fact that priority of tonnage was now being given to food.' (*Cabinet papers: 23/5*)

David Lloyd George to Winston S. Churchill

(Churchill papers: 27/32)

18 January 1918 10 Downing Street
Highly Secret & Confidential

My dear Minister of Munitions,

The Admiralty have a secret and special project in hand which must be pushed forward with all speed. I understand that it will take something under 10,000 tons of expanded metal and rods. Details will be given you.

It is undesirable that anything should appear on official papers about this, but I wish it treated as a matter of very special importance and urgency, and the War Cabinet, although not recording this on any minutes which are being circulated, have agreed that it is of the very greatest importance that this matter should be dealt with without delay.

The steel should not be given to the detriment of the first priority awarded to warship construction and mercantile marine, and I shall be glad if you will consider at once what you can do to enable this expanded metal to be obtained as fast as is wanted.

I do not wish it to be referred to in any official correspondence, and it should simply be dealt with as steel handed over to the Admiralty Works Department.

Ever sincerely
D. Lloyd George

Winston S. Churchill to David Lloyd George

(Churchill papers: 27/32)

19 January 1918 Ministry of Munitions
Private

My dear Prime Minister,

I hope you are not closing your mind to these facts. The war is fought by divisions, & I think that is a true way of counting forces. Next to that 'rifles' ie fighting infantrymen are the test & with them guns, light, medium & heavy. I do not like the tendencies displayed in these paras which show very serious accumulation of forces & still more possibilities in the future.

I don't think we are doing enough for our army. Really I must make that point to you. We are not raising its strength as we ought. We ought to fill it up at once to full strength.

It is very wrong to give men to the Navy in priority to the Army. To me it is incomprehensible. The imminent danger is on the Western front: & the crisis will come before June. A defeat here will be *fatal*.

Please don't let vexation against past military blunders (which I share with you to the full) lead you to underrate the gravity of the impending campaign, or to keep the army short of what is needed. You know how highly I rate the modern defensive compared with offensive. But I do *not* like the situation now developing and do not think all that is possible is being done to meet it.

Fancy if there was a bad break!

Look what happened to Italy. One night may efface an army—men at once—at all costs, from Navy, from Munitions, from Home Army, from Civil Life. Stint food and commercial imports to increase shells, aeroplanes & tanks.

Wire and *concrete* on the largest possible scale.

A good plan for counter blows all worked out beforehand to relieve pressure at the points of attack when they manifest themselves.

If this went wrong—everything would go wrong. I do not feel sure about it. The Germans are a terrible foe, & their generals are better than ours.

Ponder & then *act*.

Yours always
W

Winston S. Churchill to David Lloyd George

(*Lloyd George papers*)

21 January 1918 Ministry of Munitions
Private

My dear Prime Minister,

Why shd *Goeben* & *Breslau* try to get loose now? Why shd they be ready to court destruction in order to enter the Meditn? They must have known that their life in the Meditn cd only be a short one. In 10 days a stronger British battle cruiser cd get there from home: & then they wd be hunted down, say a month of life at the outside. Yet they were valuable pieces, very well placed on the board.

They influenced Cple perhaps dominated it—they ruled the Black Sea.

Why? Why then did they try to enter the Meditn at all costs?

What cd these ships do in a month wh wd make it worth while to throw them away? Obviously nothing by themselves. Therefore it can only be *part* of a plan; a plan wh is going to operate quite soon; a plan so important that

Goeben & Breslau are only pawns in it. The important thing is to know what plan.

I cannot see what good they wd do by going into the Adriatic & being cooped up at Pola or Cattaro. Clearly they cannot get through the Straits of Gibraltar & if they did there is nothing but death outside. They cannot do any harm to Allenby[1] who is not in need of reinforcements.[2] Therefore by exhaustion I come to the only other point where danger may threaten: & I think you shd expect very soon a heavy prepared offensive against the Salonica front, wh will go on in spite of the fact that Goeben & Breslau can no longer harry our reinforcements as was hoped.[3]

Yours always
W

Winston S. Churchill to David Lloyd George

(*Lloyd George papers*)

22 January 1918 Ministry of Munitions
Private

My dear Prime Minister,

Really you ought to put the winding up of this 12½% business in my hands. I am sure I can do it with better chances of success than any other department. It is an odious job; but it ought not to be shirked.

At the employers deputation you spoke to me of the importance to *me* of reaching a good settlement & then immediately afterwards you handed all over to the unsympathetic hands of the Ministry of Labour who have neither the staff nor the capacity to handle it.

We are steadily getting through our difficulties in the enormous munitions

[1] Edmund Henry Hynman Allenby, 1861–1936. Entered Army, 1882. Major-General, 1909. Commanded 1st Cavalry Division, British Expeditionary Force, 1914. Commanded the Cavalry Corps, 1914–15. Commanded 5th Army Corps, 1915. Knighted, 1915. Commanded 3rd Army, 1915–17. Lieutenant-General, 1916. General, 1917. Commander-in-Chief, Egyptian Expeditionary Force, 1917–19. Received the surrender of Jerusalem, 11 December 1917. Created Viscount Allenby of Megiddo, 1919. Field-Marshal, 1919. High Commissioner for Egypt and the Sudan, 1919–25. His only son was killed in action in France in 1917.

[2] As a result of the German breakthrough on the western front in March 1918, many of Allenby's troops were transferred to France, and his final offensive did not begin until 19 September 1918, when he defeated the Turks at Megiddo, the biblical Armageddon (after which his cavalry advanced 550 miles in 38 days, entering Aleppo on 26 October).

[3] The Central Powers made no major attack on the Allied positions at Salonika during 1918; indeed, the first offensive on that front during 1918 was the one launched by the British on 1 September. By the end of the month British troops had entered Bulgaria, and both the French and Serbian forces had made considerable advances.

area, & with a fair chance I am confident we can deal with the shipyard cases.

After all this is a fair offer & a bold one. If you do not let me help you in a difficulty of this kind I shall soon cease to be of much use—if indeed I am not a burden already.

Now do I beg you take a short & simple course. Say 'The Minister of Munitions began this & he must settle it up'.

Give me the power & I will settle it up. But if it is simply to be muddled away by Barnes & an understaffed Labour Department, then I shall have to publish the true facts of the original order.

How many people know for instance that Milner & Barnes took the *crucial* decision to widen the schedule before any public announcement *in my absence*.

Yours always
W

War Cabinet: minutes

(*Cabinet papers: 23/5*)

23 January 1918

. . . the War Cabinet had before them a memorandum by the Minister of Munitions, together with the views of certain officers of his Department (Paper GT–3417), conveying the following suggestion as an alternative to the action proposed by the Committee on Production—

> 'Piece-work prices and premium bonus-time allowances, which do enable the men concerned to earn amounts reasonably in excess of those earned by time-workers in receipt of the 12½ per cent bonus, shall be revised.'

MR CHURCHILL recalled the discussion which had taken place at the War Cabinet on the 7th January, 1918 (War Cabinet 317, Minute 1). It was not then known what view would be taken by the trade union leaders. Since then, the Trade Union Advisory Committee had passed a resolution in favour of extending the 12½ per cent over the time-workers, against a uniform advance to all piece-workers, but favouring the revision of low piece-rates. The Ministry of Labour had been impressed by this resolution, and had made a public statement of the policy which they intended to follow. It was with surprise therefore, that he (Mr Churchill) had read the decision of the War Cabinet on Monday last (War Cabinet 326, Minute 3) agreeing to an increase of 7½ per cent. to piece-workers generally. That was a very serious decision, and a reversal of the policy announced to the public. It would cost the country between 30 and 35 million pounds, and would immediately react, not only on time-workers, but on women workers, who always shared in piece-work advances. It was important that the Cabinet should remember that shipyard labour, which it was specially desired to appease, was a small fraction of the total number of workers affected by the decision. Whereas only some 900,000 were being given the advance of 12½ per cent, the extension to piece-workers would raise the number to over 3,000,000. There was no general demand for the advance which the Cabinet was now offering; the leaders were against it, and large numbers of men who would receive it did not deserve it.

He recommended the Cabinet to adhere to the policy which had been publicly announced, and to deal with special cases as they arose, and particularly to make an attempt to revise low piece-rates. The general labour position was infinitely more manageable than it was five weeks ago, and with care, patience, and the provision of the necessary machinery, a gradual solution of the present difficulties could be achieved. There was a further reason why the Cabinet should not grant an advance at the moment; the Government was on the eve of serious trouble with the labour movement in connection with the Military Service Bill. The present grant should be kept in hand as a means of mollification later on.

Winston S. Churchill: message to the people of Dundee[1]

(*Churchill papers: 15/160*)

24 January 1918 Ministry of Munitions

The visit of the Tank gives Dundee an opportunity of showing in a new form the wealth and patriotism of the city. This powerful weapon of war is a thoroughly British conception and has proved on numerous occasions a method of saving life and winning victories. Let its arrival in Dundee be the signal for a rally of Dundinians of every rank and station, all united in their resolve to support by every means in their power and to the limit of their resources, the public cause in this time of danger and perseverance.

[1] This message was sent to the editor of the *Dundee Evening Telegraph and Post*, for publication in connection with the War-Savings campaign.

Winston S. Churchill to Lord Rothermere

(Churchill papers: 15/58)

26 January 1918 Ministry of Munitions

My dear Rothermere,

The future development of the Aircraft supply can be arranged in accordance with your wishes. It will be possible, if you so desire it, to concentrate on a very few types. But this will take time, and meanwhile, the existing production must not be sacrificed. We are now producing about 2,000 aeroplanes in the present month, and we expect to work up to about 3,000 machines and 4,000 engines in June. It is possible now to give a proportion of orders which will be effective from June onwards. These orders can largely be placed in accordance with the policy of your Ministry. It will not, I imagine, be possible immediately to concentrate only on three or four types without a large drop in the aggregate production. I do not think that the production ought to be allowed to drop below at least 4,000 engines a month, and it may well be considered worth while to raise production to 5,000, or even 6,000 engines per month. You could not for more than a year get so great a supply if production were confined to so few types. But a continuous reduction of types and an increasing concentration on selected types will take place, and it is now possible to draw out a programme which by June 1919 will combine the largest possible numbers with fewest types.

I enclose you lists of the existing orders and programmes on which we are working, and which, I suggest, it would not be right to disturb except in cases where machines ordered by the late Air Board have, before completion, become obsolete. If you will take these tables and have the story carried on, as your people wish it to be carried on from a tactical and strategic point of view, to (say) June 1919, I will then have your project studied to see how it can be made to fit in with the possibilities of supply, so that we may continue to approach your ideal without a drop in the aggregate monthly totals.

It seems to me that we ought to go on building up the size and scale of our Air Forces, and that we must not run the risk of a sudden curtailment of supplies to get a simplification of type, provided the machines or engines are serviceable. Provision would, no doubt, have to be made, in order that we should not be hide-bound in our development, in any of your forecasts for new types, either arising from new inventions or from new war conditions, which it may be necessary to meet. I suggest, therefore, that you should fill in a certain proportion of the programme with the types not yet specified—you might call them 'X'.

February 1918

War Cabinet: minutes

(*Cabinet papers: 23/5*)

AIRSHIP SHEDS

1 February 1918

The War Cabinet had before them a memorandum by the War Priorities Committee (Paper GT–3488).

MR CHURCHILL said that, although this question had once been decided by the War Cabinet, new conditions had been found to exist since that decision. The new feature was the diminishing supply of steel. This coincided with an enhanced demand for production in which steel formed a main element. He admitted that the cut in steel imports could not be resisted, as that was the only import that could be cut. But he pointed out that the Admiralty demands for steel were the only demands protected from any sort of proportional reduction. He asked that there should be a fair examination of the Admiralty demands, in order that the whole reduction, required by the necessity of the situation, should not be only at the expense of the Army and Air Service. If the sheds could not be dispensed with, was it not possible for the Admiralty to effect an equivalent diminution of its demands for steel in some other department? On the merits, he doubted the validity of the claim for these sheds, when considered in relation to the whole situation. The three sheds required could not be completed according to the Admiralty estimate, for 15½, 18½ and 20½ months respectively. He was advised that these figures were unduly optimistic. The same kind of steel and of skilled labour required for this work was, in his view, needed for more urgent undertakings. It was for the War Cabinet to decide what was to be cut.

Winston S. Churchill to General Dallolio

(*Churchill papers: 15/160*)

4 February 1918 Ministry of Munitions

My dear General,

You are of course aware of the great difficulties in providing tonnage to meet all the requirements of the Allies, and it has been found necessary, in order to meet the food requirements of Italy, France and Great Britain, to curtail very drastically the supply of tonnage available for the production of British munitions.

Moreover it is not economical from the shipping point of view that ore should be shipped from Spain to Great Britain and sent back as steel to Italy, while it is possible to import steel direct from America to your country. With the reduced tonnage at my disposal I very much regret that it will not be possible for me indefinitely to continue supplying you with shell steel, which I am at present doing, at the rate of 14,000 tons a month, and I should be glad if you would take steps to replace this supply at the earliest possible moment from America.

These circumstances have compelled me to adopt a similar course in regard to French shell steel, and after discussion with M Loucheur, I have already reduced production from 40,000 tons a month to 10,000 a month and shall have to stop the latter altogether at the end of February.

In the case of Italy, however, I am aware of the difficulties that have previously attended you in your efforts to get a satisfactory supply from the United States and should like to give you as long as possible to get your contracts going. I cannot, however, see my way in any case to keep those 14,000 tons going after the end of June.

War Cabinet: minutes

(*Cabinet papers: 23/5*)

5 February 1918

MR CHURCHILL said that a number of engineers were now volunteering. It should be possible to obtain from the great munition areas a stream of resolutions in favour of the vigorous prosecution of the war. Such resolutions should appear in increasing numbers day by day in the newspapers for at least a fortnight. They would have a marked effect on the disaffected elements. While much could thus be done by way of propaganda, it must not be forgotten that the engineers could paralyse every munitions industry for a time, but, fortunately, there were sufficient reserves to stand a short strike. It was necessary to consider in advance what steps should be taken in the face of a general dislocation of industry. It was most important that, should a trial of strength with the engineers take place, it should not be complicated by other issues, such as the shortage of food. It would be far better, during the critical weeks of the struggle, to draw on any available reserves of food. He was in favour of a small Special Committee being set up to prepare for emergencies.

Viscount Grey of Fallodon to Winston S. Churchill

(Churchill papers: 1/129)

6 February 1918 Fallodon

Dear Churchill,

This is upon a small matter of private business. Now & then a telegram comes to me re-directed from an office near Eccleston Square, and I should be glad if you could instruct your people to tell the telegraph boy, when he brings any telegram for me, that I have no address at 33 Eccleston Square & that the telegram therefore cannot be delivered & should be returned to the sender. The only people from whom I might care to have a telegram will not address one to Eccleston Square.

The last telegram thus sent me was from a place called Milano & was entirely in Italian: as neither I nor my servants understand Italian the contents did not worry me, but I had to pay 1/6d. on it.

You gave me a shock, when I last heard from you, by saying it was good of me to congratulate you on joining 'this Government'. Are people in high places in London still thinking in terms of party politics?

Living alone as I do one's mind is free to follow its own natural bent & gets to strange places, some of them interesting, but to publish my thoughts would not help the war, so I make no speeches. My agent has died & private affairs give me some forced occupation, more in fact than I desire. I still feel the war to be very depressing: I remember you reproached me once at the outset for not showing a sufficiently elate spirit, but it was my instinct before it came that it must be a huge world catastrophe.

On the other hand in the light of after events it has become increasingly clear that the war was inevitable & that we could not keep out of it & I have no questions. The Russian revolution is very interesting; I wish it could have come in time of peace, so that we might have had the intense interest of watching its development, undisturbed by the inconvenience & anxiety that it must be causing us now.

I am going off on railway business[1] tomorrow & then shall be in London for a day or two, but I keep out of the way of busy people. You must be very hard worked, but I never think of you as overstrained by political work any more than I am overstrained by doing what is congenial to me such as living at home in the country.

Yours sincerely
Edward Grey

Winston S. Churchill: War Cabinet memorandum

(*Churchill papers: 15/112*)

JANUARY SHIPBUILDING OUTPUT

8 February 1918
Secret

My attention has been drawn to a paper circulated by the Admiralty on the causes of the failure of the shipyards to reach their expected output in January. In this it is shown that, while holidays, weather, housing, and general labour unrest have tended to reduce output, the principal adverse factor has been disputes arising out of the 12½ per cent bonus. It is, of course, very difficult to appraise the influence of individual factors of unrest upon the general labour situation. I must, however, draw the attention of the War Cabinet to certain serious inaccuracies in fact—

For instance, an example is quoted that as the result of a 'Stay-in strike' policy 'in one engineering establishment the output of the month was reduced by 40 per cent of the normal output of that establishment'. This statement was also made to the War Cabinet when they were considering the 7½ per cent bonus of piece-workers, and appeared greatly to influence their decision. I therefore asked the Admiralty the name of the firm in question, and was informed it was G and J Weir, of Glasgow. This firm manufacture pumping machinery for all classes of ships; they are, at the present moment, well ahead with their deliveries. Pumping machinery for ships is invariably delivered three to six months ahead of the completion of the ships. It is therefore difficult to see what relevance the present situation in G and J Weir's shop has to the failure to realise the shipbuilding output for January. The introduction of this example is extremely misleading, and, even if the

[1] In 1898 Grey had become a Director of the North Eastern Railway Company. He subsequently became Chairman, but resigned his Chairmanship in 1905, on entering the Cabinet as Foreign Secretary. He was re-elected to the Board in 1916.

facts at G and J Weir's were as stated, they would afford no explanation of the short fall in Admiralty output during January.

I am advised that it is not correct to state that the strike in the shipbuilding yards on the Clyde towards the end of last year was caused by the 12½ per cent bonus. It was initiated by the boilermakers, who definitely struck against a Committee on Production award. Of 11,500 men who were on strike, 10,000 were boilermakers; and the boilermakers' dispute had no relation whatever to the 12½ per cent bonus. Sir Thomas Munro,[1] who visited Glasgow in January, after careful enquiry, reported that the 12½ per cent advance was not, in his opinion, an active factor in the situation, and that the unrest was due to the activities of a pacifist and revolutionary section of the men industriously working on the general dissatisfaction which existed. This element has been present in the Clyde area more than in any other district during the whole course of the war.

In Belfast, again, the strike which occurred was, as in the case of the boilermakers on the Clyde, a strike against a Committee on Production award. The workmen and employers had agreed together on a 7½ per cent advance. The Committee on Production would not recognise this, and awarded 5 per cent; but a month later gave the award on which the workmen and employers had previously agreed.

The Admiralty Memorandum dwells also upon the housing accommodation in Glasgow. The Glasgow housing conditions have long been unsatisfactory, but the acute difficulties which now exist are due to the Admiralty's desire to draft immediately large numbers of men to the Clyde for whose reception no previous arrangements have been made. This should surely have been foreseen in estimating future outputs.

With regard to the holidays and the weather, these also might have been foreseen. Holidays are usual in Scotland from the 1st to the 12th of January, and it is well known that all outputs are profoundly affected thereby. The weather also in these regions is usually bad at this season of the year.

The estimate that approximately 120,000 tons of shipping would be produced by the shipyards in January was always considered by the officers of this Department to be an impossible one, having regard to the above inevitable conditions and to the general capacity of the shipbuilding yards. We have for a long time pointed out that these inflated estimates would not be achieved, and I have deprecated, as strongly as possible, the diversion of steel plates to the shipyards from urgently-needed services like the tanks and locomotives without any true relation to the capacity of the yards to build them into ships.

[1] Sir Thomas Munro, Chief Labour Adviser at the Ministry of Munitions (see page 430, note 2).

There would, I think, be no difficulty this year in supplying the Admiralty, as and when they require them, with all the plates they are able genuinely to build into ships. But it is surely wrong that these precious plates should be taken away from services of the highest consequence and war urgency only to be hoarded in shipyards for long periods before there is any means of using them.

The output of plates is steadily increasing, and we have delivered to the Admiralty during the five months of last year nearly 70,000 tons more than we undertook to do. Their consumption has been much less than their expectation, and the First Lord has stated in his recent Memorandum on Shipbuilding Requirements that 'steel is no longer a limiting factor'.

Winston S. Churchill to Lord Beaverbrook[1]

(*Churchill papers: 15/160*)

12 February 1918 Ministry of Munitions

I understand that it is proposed entirely to supersede the special arrangements which have hitherto obtained between my Department and Colonel Buchan's[2] Department as to the sending of parties of munition workers to the Front by other arrangements suggested by an Inter-Departmental Committee whereby two parties each of twelve men drawn from miscellaneous trades will be sent out on five days of the week.

May I say at once that I fear this will be a serious mistake.

Our deputations have always been arranged with strict regard to two special points:—

(i) that the men comprising each party should be of outstanding personality and influence in the locality from which they are drawn; and

(ii) that each party should be accompanied by the local representative of the Ministry responsible for conducting labour negotiations in that locality, and that it should be sufficiently small in size to enable that officer to come into the closest personal contact with all the men during the period of the tour.

Our reasons for insistence on these two points are that we have always found that the best way of influencing the rank and file has been to influence

[1] Sir Max Aitken had been created Baron Beaverbrook in 1917. From February to November 1918 he was both Chancellor of the Duchy of Lancaster and Minister of Information.

[2] John Buchan, 1875–1940. Author, historian and novelist. Private Secretary to Lord Milner in South Africa, 1901–3. Lieutenant-Colonel, GHQ France, 1916–17. Director, Department of Information, 1917–18. Conservative MP, 1927–35. Created Baron Tweedsmuir, 1935. Governor-General of Canada, 1937–40. His brother Alastair served in Churchill's battalion on the western front in 1916, and died of wounds in 1917.

the really controlling spirits, and our experience shows convincingly that the facilities for close and intimate association in unique circumstances which these deputations have afforded enable an officer of tact and intelligence to get on such sympathetic and intimate terms with the men, that subsequently on his return he can enlist their active co-operation and support in dealing with the disputes arising from time to time in the districts from which they come.

I suspect that the system proposed by the Department of Information is intended to deal with the rank and file of working men. I am sure that it would meet with a scant measure of success applied to men of the calibre with whom we have hitherto dealt—men often of unusual intelligence and education, needing to be handled with particular skill and judgment.

I feel that we must retain our old arrangements without change unless we are to be deprived of perhaps our most valuable instrument for influencing the men who really count in the munitions labour world.

I should be glad if you would look into the matter, and let me know that this can be arranged. I need not point out how peculiarly close the connection is between the men who make the munitions and the men who are using them, which seems to me to justify the existence of special arrangements for the munition workers.

Winston S. Churchill to Lord Jellicoe[1]

(*Churchill papers: 2/103*)

13 February 1918 Ministry of Munitions

My dear Jellicoe,

I was glad to see that you corrected a passage in yr Hull speech wh had been wrongly reported. It is no doubt quite true that we none of us believed before the war that the Germans wd sink merchantmen at sight.[2] Apart from any qn of morality, the risk they wd run of embroiling powerful neutrals

[1] John Rushworth Jellicoe, 1859–1935. Entered Navy, 1872. Captain, 1897. Knighted, 1907. Vice-Admiral, 1910. Second Sea Lord, 1912–14. Commander-in-Chief of the Grand Fleet, 1914–16. Admiral, 1915. First Sea Lord, 1916–17. Chief of the Naval Staff, 1917. Created Viscount, 1918. Admiral of the Fleet, 1919. Governor-General of New Zealand, 1920–4. Created Earl, 1925.

[2] Speaking in Hull on 8 February 1918 Jellicoe declared that when, in 1911, Lord Fisher had submitted a memorandum on the danger of submarines attacking merchant ships 'he recollected that memorandum going to the Board of Admiralty after he joined it as Second Sea Lord, and there was nobody in a responsible position who agreed that the German navy would really do such a thing as Lord Fisher expected. Lord Fisher was right, as he had been right in many cases.'

seemed to most people in authority an effective deterrent. That was certainly the view of Prince Louis,[1] & I always understood you were in full agreement with it. At any rate, you were a member of the Board, & I have no recollection that you or anyone in a responsible position at the Admy ever drew attention to this danger. But even if we had regarded it as a certainty, I do not now know what measures cd have been taken, under peace conditions, to prevent it. Certainly no measures cd have been taken before the war comparable to those which have been taken—so far without decisive effect—since the war. Therefore I do not think the pre-war Bd of Admy lies under any reproach in this matter; & I do not think it is possible to draw a distinction between 'the Admy' & 'the Navy', the one arising almost wholly out of the other so far as professional matters are concerned.

It is also true no doubt that during the first months of the war the anchorages of Scapa & the Firth were not s/m-proof. This wd not be true of Sheerness, Dover or Portland. In these latter cases the only danger was a torpedo F—not a s/m—through the entrance; & that was easily remedied.

But never did I receive from any member of the Bd, or from the COS, or any naval officer at the Admy, or the C in C Home Fleets, or yourself as C in C designate, any recommendn in that sense.[2] On the contrary, the point which sticks most in my memory is the unanimous & written recommendn of the four Sea Lds sitting together, in favour of the abolition even of the torpedo nets, in face of my formal warning of the serious character of the decision, in wh however I eventually concurred.[3]

On the other hand, I do not think we need even here reproach ourselves too severely. I have yet to learn that the currents of Scapa Flow did not prove an impenetrable protection during the early months against underwater navigation; & after all, the boom defences at all points were vy quickly organized. There is no evidence to show that the Germans forecasted the future any more accurately than we did; & it is certain that by the time they were ready with their submarine attack on harbours, we were ready to meet it with our defences.

When we remember the numerous grave perils against which we took effective precautions without which disaster wd certainly have occurred, it

[1] Prince Louis Alexander of Battenberg, 1854–1921. A Cousin of George V. Naturalized as a British subject in 1868, when he entered the Royal Navy. First Sea Lord, 1912–14. At the King's request he discontinued the title of Prince and assumed the surname of Mountbatten, 1917. Created Marquess of Milford Haven, 1917. Admiral of the Fleet, 1921. Father of Earl Mountbatten of Burma.

[2] In 1914 the Chief of Staff at the Admiralty was Rear-Admiral Sir Frederick Sturdee, and the Commander-in-Chief of the Home Fleets was Admiral Sir George Callaghan.

[3] In 1914 the four Sea Lords were Prince Louis (1st), Jellicoe (2nd), Rear-Admiral A G H W Moore (3rd), and Captain C F Lambert (4th).

seems unduly severe to select a single danger, which even if it was to some extent unmet, led in the end to no mishap.

I shd prefer to rest our case upon facts & results: ie that on the outbreak of war, after a hundred years of grace, every man & every ship was in station & ready; that the merchant cruisers of the enemy were bottled up from the outset, & his fleet penned in; that before the first year was over his flag had ceased to fly in any quarter of the globe; & that his first s/m attack on commerce, altho' unexpected, had been so effectually coped with that von Tirpitz[1] was forced to resign for wishing to renew it.

I am sure you also will find more satisfaction in dwelling upon these memorable triumphs, in which you had yr share, than upon any omissions, however partial & excusable, for wh you too shared a collective responsibility.

Believe me, Yours vy sincerely
W. S. Churchill

War Cabinet: minutes

(*Cabinet papers: 23/5*)

15 February 1918

MR CHURCHILL pointed out that if it came to a question of closing down cotton mills or munition works, of the two choices it should be cotton and not munitions that should be restricted, having regard to the fact that the reduction in munitions import would also cause unemployment without a direct war result. . . .

MR CHURCHILL and LORD RHONDDA[2] called attention to the generous scale of meat rations prevailing in the services as compared with the civilian rations. It was suggested that the ration scales should be revised from the point of view of services rendered by the individuals.

[1] Alfred von Tirpitz, 1849–1930. Entered the Prussian Navy, 1865. As Chief of Staff of Supreme Naval Command 1892 he laid down plans for a powerful German Navy; as Secretary of State for Naval Affairs 1897 he supervised the construction of that Navy. He saw the Navy as an important instrument of diplomacy; not as a weapon of war. Favoured a fixed ratio for the Anglo-German Navies; wished to give up supplementary estimates in return for an Anglo-German Naval Agreement, 1912; in 1914 he advocated an early naval engagement to decide the war as quickly as possible. He resigned all offices on 15 March 1916. Entered politics as a Nationalist Member of the Reichstag 1924–8; urged German co-operation with Britain and the United States 1925–30. His eldest son, a naval officer, was taken prisoner by the British in August 1914.

[2] David Alfred Thomas, 1856–1918. Liberal MP, 1888–1910. President of the South Wales Liberal Federation, 1893–97. Managing director of several South Wales colliery companies. Created Baron Rhondda, 1916. President of the Local Government Board, 1916–18, and Food Controller, 1917–18. Created Viscount, 19 June 1918; died 3 July 1918.

Winston S. Churchill to Sir George Ritchie

(*Cabinet papers: 23/5*)

16 February 1918 Ministry of Munitions

My dear Ritchie,

Many thanks for your letter of the 12th. I agree with you that an election is inevitable once the new Register is complete. No one can tell at the present time how the issues will define themselves. If, as is probable, the war is still in progress I imagine that the only issue will be its vigorous prosecution as opposed to some form of pacifism or surrender. You will not, I think, be in any doubt as to the course I shall recommend to the electors in such an eventuality: it will be to fight on till a genuine victory is obtained no matter how serious may be the measures which we may have to take in that endeavour. I should hope that this issue would not be complicated by Party or personal differences and that the Liberals who support Mr Asquith will in the main act under the existing arrangements of the Party truce with the Conservatives, Liberal and Labour men who support the present Government. Should this occur the character of the election in Dundee would not be dissimilar from that of the bye-election in which very good results were obtained. If the Pacifist movement should in the meanwhile become stronger we may also hope that the rally to the national cause will be consequently stimulated. In the meantime everything should be done that is possible to keep our organisation lively and intact so that Dundee Liberals will be in a position to make their will effective against Kaiserism on the one hand or Bolshevism on the other. I have great confidence in my ability to put this case in all its amplitude before the electors when the time comes.

I send you a copy of a statement which has been prepared in the Ministry of Munitions by Major Hills, MP on the circumstances which led up to the granting of the 12½% bonus. I have been tempted to make them public in response to various questions, but I am never fond of exculpating myself at the expense of others, and I think on the whole that matters are settling down and will probably be forgotten in the general press of events. You are, however, at liberty, to show this paper privately and in confidence to any of my own principal supporters or others who may ask you questions.

I also enclose you for your *very private* information a copy of a letter which I have written to Lord Jellicoe in consequence of his speech at Hull. I do not think you need fear at all the verdict which history will pass upon the Naval administration which prepared for the war and carried us through its first 12 months.

I quite understand all you say about the dissatisfaction at the Government and particularly at the influence of the Northcliffe press. We are passing through a time of extraordinary difficulty, and all Governments are proving more or less unequal to the strain which is put on them. There are many things I see which I do not like and think could be better done. It is for instance a thousand pities that Mr Asquith cannot join hands with Mr Lloyd George and restore the national unity in these deadly times. I shall still hope that this may be achieved in one form or another. Meanwhile if we suffer so do our foes.

With every good wish, Believe me, yours very sincerely,
Winston S. Churchill

Winston S. Churchill to Clementine Churchill

(Spencer-Churchill papers)

17 February 1918 Tramecourt

My darling,

This vy clear weather & the state of the moon will certainly expose you to danger. I do wish you wd not delay to send the children out of town & of course I shd greatly desire your not sleeping in London during the raid period except when absolutely necessary.[1] It made me feel vy anxious last night to see how bright & quiet the night was. The motor is ready any time you like to go. You have only to tell Eddie.[2]

I am just getting up at Tramecourt—near the field of Agincourt—to begin a fairly long day on ammunition, tanks & gas with the different people who we supply. Tonight I hope to sleep at General Barnes' HQrs. Tomorrow I shall probably move down Southwards to the Cavalry Corps. I shall not go to Paris this time. I will let you know if anything shd occur to delay my return.

Darling onc I send you my fondest love. It is vy nice getting out here—without a care—except that I do not like to think of you & the kittens in London. Better be sure than sorry.

You will need to go down to Lullenden anyhow one day to see how it is all getting on. Smith will drive you.

With tender thoughts & vy best love, Yr devoted
W

[1] On 16 February 1918 six German aeroplanes had attacked London, killing 3 men, 5 women and 3 children. In a further air raid on London on February 17, 13 men and 3 women were killed. On March 7 a seven-aeroplane raid over north and east London left 11 dead and 46 injured.

[2] Edward Marsh, who had again become Churchill's Private Secretary in July 1917 (see page 9, note 4).

Winston S. Churchill to Clementine Churchill

(*Spencer-Churchill papers*)

21 February 1918

My darling,

Only a line to tell you we have had a long jolly day roundabout the Vimy district, & seen a lot of vy interesting & famous country.

Beautiful weather & the enemy extraordinarily quiet. I sleep tonight in a chateau hitherto untouched by shell fire, & tomorrow go to see Jack, Plugstreet & finish up for the night with Reggie Barnes.

Saturday I go to the Cavalry Corps & Monday night Paris where I shall stay for two days returning to England Thursday night (DV) in time for dinner.

I have been walking in mud for 5 hours & no lunch! Now I am going to snooze before dinner.

This clear weather will make London dangerous again. Tender love & many thoughts my own darling pussy,

Yr devoted
W

Winston S. Churchill to Lord Beaverbrook

(*Beaverbrook papers*)

23 February 1918

My dear Max,

Many thanks for your letter about the visits of munition workers to France. I have told my people to accept the arrangements you propose which appear quite satisfactory to me.

I am increasingly convinced that there can be no more valuable propaganda in England at the present time than graphic accounts of the Bolshevik outrages and futility, of the treacheries they have committed, and what ruin they have brought upon their country and the harm they have done to us and to our fighting men. It seems to me that the papers should be encouraged to give much publicity to all the news which reaches us of the chaos and anarchy in Russia. There is a strong feeling among British workmen that these wretches have 'let us down', and without overdoing it I think this absolutely true conception should be sustained by a constant stream of facts.

Yours, etc
Winston S. Churchill

Winston S. Churchill to Clementine Churchill

(*Spencer-Churchill papers*)

23 February 1918

My darling one,

I have been enjoying myself so much—& have had such vy interesting days & pleasant evenings. I spent one day with General Lipsett as I told you, & the next I came on here to General Barnes where we were vy warmly welcomed. I went all round my old trenches at Plugstreet. Everything has been torn to pieces & the shelling is still at times severe. The British line has moved forward about a mile, but all my old farms are mere heaps of brick & mouldering sandbags. The little graveyard has been filled & then smashed up by the shells. I missed Plugstreet's church. We ran past the place where it had stood without recognising it! My strong dugout however wh I built at Lawrence farm has stood out the whole two years of battering, & is still in use. So also are the cellars of the convent wh I drained & called the 'conning tower'. Otherwise utter ruin.

Jack came with us on this expedition & we lunched at Birdwood's[1] HQ before starting. Birdwood told me that he expects & hopes any day to see Jack's name in the Gazette for a DSO.[2] He is much appreciated where he is, & seems to have a lot of varied & interesting things to manage.

We had a jolly dinner at Gen Barnes' HQrs—George Paynter[3] (who commands one of his Brigades) & 'Sainty' Clowes[4]—I think you know him.

Yesterday I worked till noon with my shorthand writer & polished off two bags. (He is returning with them this morning.) Then we went out to see the Ypres salient. I had not been in Ypres for 3 years. It has largely ceased to exist. As for the country round & towards the enemy—there is absolutely nothing except a few tree stumps in acres of brown soil pockmarked with shell holes touching one another. This continues in every direction for 7 or 8 miles.

[1] William Riddell Birdwood, 1865–1951. Lieutenant, Royal Scots Fusiliers, 1883. General Officer commanding the Australian and New Zealand Army Corps (ANZAC), 1914–18. Lieutenant-General commanding the ANZAC landing, 25 April 1915. Commander-in-Chief of the Allied Forces at the Dardanelles, October 1915–January 1916. Knighted, 1913. Field-Marshal, 1925. Commander-in-Chief, India, 1922–30. Master of Peterhouse, Cambridge, 1931–8. Created Baron, 1938.

[2] Jack Churchill did receive the DSO. He was also awarded the Légion d'Honneur and the Croix de Guerre, as well as the Order of Avis of Portugal.

[3] George Camborne Beauclerk Paynter, 1880–1950. Entered the Scots Guards, 1899. Major, 1915 (severely wounded). ADC to Sir John French, 1915–16. Colonel, 1922. Commanded the Scots Guards and Regimental District and the 167th Infantry Brigade, 1923–7. An Equerry to the King, 1927–30. Assistant Director, Ministry of Fuel and Power, 1943. Knighted, 1950. Churchill wrote of him in a private letter on 18 December 1915: 'he has killed a lot of Germans with bare steel & pistol; but you wd not think he wd hurt a fly'

[4] George Charles Knight Clowes, 1882–1941. In 1911 he married the daughter of the Archdeacon of Sarum. On active service, 1914–18 (DSO). Lieutenant-Colonel, London Scottish, 1918. Hon. Colonel, London Scottish, 1939. Chairman, William Clowes and Sons Ltd, Printers and Publishers.

Across this scene of desolation wind duckboard tracks many of them in full view of the enemy; & all about it as we walked now here now there occasional shells were pitching or bursting in the air, & our guns hidden in mud holes flashing bright yellow flames in reply.

We stopped our motor for lunch on the Ypres–Menin road & I was eating sandwiches & drinking beer when General Hunter-Weston[1] drove up coming back from a tour round the line. He is an old acquaintance of mine: a tremendous chatter-box & vy much chaffed in the Army for his ornate manner. He is the general who made the speech in the H of Commons the other day beginning, 'I am a plain blunt soldier'. Also you remember when the man was drunk in the trenches & they hid him from the general by putting him on a stretcher covered with a blanket, he said 'Hunter-Weston salutes the honoured dead', & passed on—hoodwinked. Well—anyhow he commands an Army corps in this neighbourhood, and took much trouble to explain the terrain to me. He got into my car & we lunched together. Meanwhile howevery the Huns began to fire. The spot is a favourite one—& is called 'Hell-fire corner'. Big shells whined overhead & burst with vy loud bangs behind us. Nobody paid the slightest attention. The soldiers went on mending the roads & cooking their dinners & the traffic rolled to and fro. As we left the car to begin our walk a shell came just above our heads and burst about 20 yards away. Only one man was hurt a little further up the road.

Then we walked for miles (I have walked five hours at least each day) over these duckboards till finally we got to Glencorse wood & Polygon wood. These consist of a few score of torn & splintered stumps only. But the view of the battle field is remarkable. Desolation reigns on every side. Litter, mud, rusty wire & the pock marked ground. Very few soldiers to be seen mostly in 'pill boxes' captured from the industrious Hun. Overhead aeroplanes constantly fired at. The Passchendaele ridge was too far for us to reach but the whole immense arena of slaughter was visible. Nearly 800,000 of our British men have shed their blood or lost their lives here during 3½ years of unceasing conflict! Many of our friends & my contemporaries have perished here. Death seems as commonplace & as little alarming as the undertaker. Quite a natural ordinary event, wh may happen to anyone at any moment, as it happened to all these scores of thousands who lie together in this vast cemetery, ennobled & rendered forever glorious by their brave memory.

[1] Aylmer Hunter-Weston, 1864–1940. Entered Royal Engineers, 1884. Served on Kitchener's staff in the Sudan, 1898. Chief Staff Officer to Sir John French's Cavalry Division in South Africa, 1900. Brigadier-General commanding 11th Infantry Brigade, August 1914; promoted Major-General for distinguished service in the field. Commanded the 29th Division at the landing on Cape Helles, April 1915; promoted Lieutenant-General for the successful landing. Commanded the VIIIth Corps at the Dardanelles and in France, 1915–18. Knighted, 1915. Conservative MP, 1916–35. Known as 'Hunter-Bunter'.

One vy odd thing is the way in wh you can now walk about in full view of the enemy & in close rifle shot. Both at Avion (near Lens) & yesterday at Polygon wood we were within a few hundred yards of the German line & partially or wholly exposed. Yesterday in fact the duckboard track led us to within 500 yards of a vy strongly held Hun position at Polderhoek Chateau. It was like walking along a street—not a scrap of cover or even camouflage. Still people kept coming and going & not a shot was fired. In my days at Plugstreet it wd have been certain death. But I suppose they are all so bored with the war, that they cannot be bothered to kill a few passers by. We on the other hand shoot every man we can see.

On the way back we passed the lunatic asylum blown to pieces by the sane folk outside!

A vy nice young officer[1] acted as my guide—he had the VC & MC and was a vehement pro-Dardanellian where he had fought.

I saw one other vy remarkable sight wh I must tell you of tho this letter is becoming far too long. I saw what looked like an enormous cloud of dark smoke in the air, wreathing & twisting & curling & uncurling, & darkening & thinning out again. It was millions of starlings. They feed on the battle-fields and collect every evening into this swarm, and dance their ballets till dark. I have never seen anything like it.

Now my sweet one—I must really finish—I am off to the Cavalry Corps right down South, where I shall stay tonight, tomorrow & tomorrow night. They are in the line. I shall see Jack Seely & Archie S.

I hope I reach Paris if all goes smoothly Tuesday and leave by train late Wedy night. I have to go to *Montreuil* for business on Thursday & also to the Gas HQrs, then I hope to come by a destroyer and reach you latish on Thursday I hope for dinner.

Wd you care to come to B'ham with me on Friday morning 9.10! and see Tanks & munitions workers etc—& Mr Dudley Docker?[2] If so it wd be easy to arrange, & I shd like it so much.

Tell Eddie if you will come & he will put it all in train.

Your ever loving & devoted

W

PS. I have thought of lots of things out here.

[1] Robert Gee, 1876–1960. Enlisted as a private, Royal Fusiliers, 1893. Served in the ranks for over twenty-one years. Commissioned as a 2nd Lieutenant, May 1915. Served at Gallipoli, 1915. Captain, September 1915. Served on the Staff of the 29th Division, 1915–18 (thrice wounded). Awarded the Military Cross, 1916; the Victoria Cross, 1917. Conservative MP, 1921–2 and 1924–7. Much to the embarrassment of the Conservative Whips, he 'disappeared' in 1926, only turning up several years later, in Western Australia.

[2] Frank Dudley Docker, 1862–1944. Chairman of the Metropolitan Carriage, Wagon & Finance Company, Birmingham. Director of the Birmingham Small Arms Company Limited, and of the Midland Bank Ltd.

Mary Borden:[1] *diary*

(*Mary Borden papers*)

28 February 1918 Paris

Winston was amusing at Ritz. He said that French had told him that during the retreat he had several times thought of throwing himself with Mauberge but that he had remembered a precept of old Hansley 'A retreating force wh throws itself into a fortress is like a Captain who, when his ship is sinking, lays a firm hold of the anchor'.

Talking of Grey, he mentioned Grey's love of his tame squirrels . . . One day LG & Winston were discussing him & Winston said 'he is a firm sort of a chap, supposing the Germans turned up at his house suddenly & put a revolver at his head telling him to sign peace he wd not do so. LG said—that's not what the G's w^d^ say—they w^d^ say, if you don't do it we will skin your bloody squirrels—& Grey w^d^ probably capitulate.

Lord Bertie to Lord Stamfordham

(*Royal Archives*)

28 February 1918 Paris
Private and very confidential

My dear Stamfordham,

I dined on the 26th with Sir Charles Ellis and sat next to W Churchill his Chief. The latter talked a lot of rot at and after dinner to the effect that as we did not go to war to obtain Alsace Lorraine for France it ought not to be continued a single day beyond what might be necessary to obtain from Germany the evacuation of Belgium with necessary guarantees, of the occupied Provinces of France and the restitution to France of such *portion* of Alsace Lorraine as may be requisite to prevent our being open to the accusation of deserting France and consequently throwing her into the arms of another friend; that from Hertling's[2] speech and the march of the Germans

[1] Mary Borden, 1886–1968. Daughter of William Borden of Chicago, and wife of George Douglas Turner. She married General Spiers (as her second husband) on 30 March 1918. She published over twenty books, including her first novel in 1924, and *Passport for a Girl* (set at the time of the Munich Conference) in 1939. Head of the Hadleigh–Spears Mobile Field Hospital Unit, France, 1939–40.

[2] Georg Hertling, 1843–1919. Leader of the Centre (Catholic) Party in the Reichstag, 1909. Foreign Minister of Bavaria, 1912–14. Elevated to the rank of Count, 1914. Chancellor of Germany from November 1917 to 30 September 1918. His memoirs, *Erinnerungen aus meinem Leben* were published shortly after his death.

towards Petrograd and from other indications it does not seem likely that Germany will make peace on the conditions which he had named and the war must therefore go on; that we are gaining superiority over the Germans in Air warfare; that there is good prospect of being able to deal successfully with the submarine danger; that the supply of munitions and the attitude of workers and the public spirit in England have never been so good as now.

I asked W Churchill whether he thought that our Colonial fellow subjects would consent to restore to Germany the Colonial Possessions which have been taken or that Japan would retrocede to Germany Kiachao. He said that the war is a European war to settle the fate of Europe; that the decisions must be regarding Europe. I suggested that what he meant was that the decision of the battlefields would be in Europe.

W Churchill avoided any answer as to the action of Japan; but said that our South Africans might come to an arrangement with Germany to keep German South West Africa in exchange for some other conquered German Colony.

I then asked whether he considered that it would be safe to give up to Germany Dar es Salaam which lies on our road to India and might be used as a naval base for submarines, and German East Africa. He said that submarines do not require bases; that Germany cannot be restricted to Europe, that she must have coaling stations and Colonies; but that *if* she means to break up Russia we must break up Turkey. The inverse of this is that if Germany restore to Russia the provinces which she now appears determined to detach from her we must give up to Turkey Mesopotamia and Palestine and desert the King of the Hedjaz and the Arab cause.

I did not argue with W Churchill for it would have been loss of time. His notions seemed to me to be very strange and crude. Has he a longsighted eye on the leadership of a Labour–Pacifist Party with eventual Premiership?

Clemenceau[1] told me that W Churchill paid him a visit and had talked nonsense and he, Clemenceau, had told him 'tout court' that England is fighting for France and France fighting for England and that their interests are inseparable. I suppose that W Churchill had dilated on our sacrifices for French interests which are not entirely British ones. If so it was foolish to use such language to Clemenceau.

Yours ever
Bertie

[1] Georges Clemenceau, 1841–1929. Mayor of Montmartre, 1870. Member of the Chamber of Deputies, 1876–93 and 1902–29. Radical journalist; editor of *Justice*. Minister of the Interior, 1906. Prime Minister, 1906–8. Prime Minister and Minister of War, November 1917–January 1920. Known during the war as 'the Tiger'. In *Great Contemporaries* (1937) Churchill wrote of him: 'Happy the nation which when its fate quivers in the balance can find such a tyrant and such a champion.'

March 1918

Winston S. Churchill to G. N. Barnes

(*Churchill papers: 15/113*)

5 March 1918 — Ministry of Munitions

Dear Mr Barnes,

I have been studying the speeches which you delivered last week in the House during my absence in France.

I think it very surprising that, after I had responded to your strong appeal not to publish a full and connected account of the events leading up to the granting of the 12½% bonus, you should have embarked without notice upon a statement, which was not called for by any Parliamentary necessity, and which, owing to its partial nature, was misleading. More especially do I think it wrong of you to attribute the whole falling-off in the Shipbuilding programme in January and February to this cause, which imports an element of prejudice into the matter.

The Cabinet papers in your possession show that this is not true. The Admiralty themselves have stated that after the termination of the Scottish holidays on the 12th January, the weather conditions were such that until the 22nd there was only one day when outside work was possible. Moreover, as you know, although the 12½% bonus was operative for good or ill over the whole of the Munitions industries, an area five times as great as the Shipbuilding yards, our outputs have been extremely good, and in many cases above the estimates, and indeed above all previous records. This is especially the case with aeronautical supplies; for although these have been affected by a whole series of labour disturbances arising from various causes, the output for January exceeds the estimate of last August, far exceeds the intermediate estimate which we gave to the Cabinet in November, and constitutes a large advance upon the highest previous record.

Besides, I do not at all understand how you can allow yourself, simultaneously with an admission of formal responsibility, to assume an air of detachment in regard to this matter. For what has been done no man is more responsible than you. You are a member of the War Cabinet and not a departmental Minister. You were *the* Member of the War Cabinet specially charged to advise them in Labour matters and to watch the action of Departments accordingly. You were the first to proclaim officially 'the skilled man's grievance'. You directed attention to it publicly in your reference to the Commissions on Industrial Unrest; and seven out of eight of those Commission referred to it, and to the Leaving-certificate, in their reports. This was before I joined the Government at all, and it governed the situation which I inherited.

Further, you have been consulted and informed from week to week on every detail; and at every stage the policy adopted by the Cabinet has been that which you not only approved but recommended. It was to you that Major Hills submitted his report, before any proposal was made to the Cabinet at all. He has preserved the record of your spontaneous and cordial assent. The proposal which was made to the War Cabinet was the exact proposal which you had approved beforehand; and you supported it strongly there. It was, as you told the House, in its original form not a proposal for a 12½% bonus including the moulders, etc but, as you omitted to tell them, a proposal for a 15% bonus *excluding* the moulders, etc. This latter was the proposal of the Ministry of Munitions, and in justice to my official advisers I am bound to place on record the fact that they were throughout in favour only of the narrower schedule.

The Cabinet referred the question to the decision of yourself and one other Cabinet Minister. I placed the two alternatives before you both at the request of the Chairman. You heard all the opinions from the Departments concerned and from the Chairman of the Committee on Production. You decided in favour of the wider schedule and the 12½% bonus. I was not even present when the decision was taken, being summoned away on other urgent public business. I concurred in the decision after it was taken; but it was your decision and a decision of the Cabinet, and not mine.

The story does not end there. You became the Chairman of the Departmental Committee, of which I was not a Member, charged with the administration of the 12½% Order; and the Ministry of Munitions cannot therefore be held responsible for the delays which attended the settlement of the numerous outstanding points in dispute, or for the failure to deal with the claims of the low-paid piece-workers, the satisfaction of which had been an integral part of the original policy. Finally it was your policy and not mine to make a general extension of the 7½% bonus to piece-workers, irrespective of the rate of earning.

It astonishes me that in the face of these facts, every one of which is upon record, you should have felt yourself in a position to make the speech you did at Glasgow, or that having retracted that speech and so relieved me from the necessity of an immediate Parliamentary statement, you should have returned to the subject in the manner you did in the House of Commons last week.

Whether the increases of wages which have been granted in consequence of the 12½% decision over the whole area of Munitions and Shipbuilding industries, and which may well amount to between 30 and 40 millions sterling, will gain their reward in the ultimate contentment and wellbeing of the workers, cannot yet be decided. All that can be said is that the 2,600,000 munition workers, whom you described as a 'veritable volcano' a month ago, are at present in a higher condition of productive efficiency and uninterrupted work than at any previous period in the history of the Ministry of Munitions.

G. N. Barnes to Winston S. Churchill

(Churchill papers: 15/113)

6 March 1918

Dear Mr Churchill,

I am sorry that you think it necessary to renew the wages controversy, and that you should have committed yourself to the statements made in your letter of yesterday's date. In justice to myself, I must deal with your points, and I will do so, in the order as given.

First, you say that you had responded to a strong appeal by me not to publish a full and connected account of the events leading up to the 12½%. I made no such appeal. Just let me refresh your memory. On the 7th January, a certain decision was given by the Cabinet in regard to pieceworkers, and its prosecution, as well as the adjustment of all questions about wages, was turned over to the Ministry of Labour. The mandate about the pieceworkers was found to be then unworkable. After talking the matter over with the Ministry of Labour, and the whole of the Committee on Production, I suggested to the Cabinet that the Ministry of Labour should be given authority to give an increase to the pieceworkers up to 7½%. This was on the 21st January. You had not been consulted—not because of any discourtesy on my part—but because the thing had been turned over to the Ministry of Labour.

You, however, felt aggrieved, and demanded a rehearing which was given you on the 23rd, when the decision of two days before was reaffirmed. You had circulated certain documents that morning including a prepared statement, and in a covering letter you said that if the Cabinet did not reverse its decision of two days before and hand over wage adjustments to your Department, you proposed making a statement to Parliament. As soon as I had read it—which was not till three or four days later, as I had gone away to Nottingham immediately after the Cabinet meeting—I wrote a letter to the Prime Minister telling him that if you made the statement, I should be under the necessity of making a counterstatement. I enclose a copy of my letter and you will find there is no appeal made therein.

Major Hills saw me, I think, more than once in the days following, and questions appeared on the notice paper. Major Hills wanted to agree a statement with me on the basis of your prepared document, and out of respect to him (having regard to the peculiar position in which he was placed) I made certain suggestions upon which I thought an agreed statement might be made. Nothing came of it, and I understood you had turned it down. The questions disappeared without answer. Then you saw me a week or two later and I said then, so far as my memory serves me, that you had a perfect right to say that you had consulted everyone concerned in regard to the wage advance question about the amount, and to whom it should be given, and that you had been guided by their advice. I had no right to make any objection to your stating that anywhere, because it was a fact; but beyond that, I said that I thought it was unwise to go.

That is all that has happened so far as I am concerned about any appeal.

I am not aware that I said that the whole of the falling off in the shipbuilding programme was due to the $12\frac{1}{2}\%$, nor can I find any such overstatement in the official report of my speech.

The next point of substance in your letter is that I had been the first to proclaim officially the skilled man's grievance. I am somewhat at a loss in regard to what you mean there; but probably it has reference to my letter to the Press on the 27th August last, in the course of which I said that substantial progress had been made in the direction of giving effect to the recommendations of the Labour Commissions, and I gave particulars of them, such as housing, Compensation Act Amendment, and so on, with which I was dealing. But in regard to the discrepancy between the earnings of skilled time workers and unskilled pieceworkers, I said that the matter had been referred to a special committee, comprising representatives both of Trade Unions and Employers. That was a simple fact, I could not say more and I could not say less, and as a matter of fact, the statement was agreed to by your Department. The purport of it was that the thing had been taken out of my hands, and was being dealt with by your Committee consequent upon your pledge. The Labour Commission report never figured in a subsequent discussion here or elsewhere, and as you know there were many such discussions. The Labour Commission's reference to the skilled man's grievance went entirely out of my mind in connection with the proposed wage advance, and it was not until it appeared in your statement already referred to on the 23rd of January this year, that it came into the picture at all. That was the main objection to the statement.

It is quite true that you inherited the skilled man's grievance and I don't for a moment suggest that you could have done otherwise than promise to deal with it. I am only stating the facts when I say that your promise was the governing factor in the whole situation afterwards, and that the method of giving effect to the promise was one which was the result of a Committee set up by yourself with which I had nothing to do until it actually reported about the latter end of September.

You say that I had been consulted and informed from week to week of every detail. That is true as from the date just given above; and it is also true to say that Major Hills very kindly submitted his report to me before it went to the Cabinet. I don't know what you mean by having preserved a record of my spontaneous and cordial assent. I don't want to get out of anything which I did on that occasion, and if you have any record, I have no objection to your making what use you like of it. My assent, however, to the report was given, as I subsequently explained to the Cabinet as the report contained proposals in contradistinction to other proposals that had been made by the employers (and I believe other people) about an overhead bonus and the laying down as a condition of such bonus that the men should work piecework where it was possible for them to do so. In other words, I was against coercion and in favour of the report submitted as an alternative. If any doubt exists as to my position on those points, they may be cleared up by reference to the Cabinet proceedings on the 11th October. The document which I had prepared on the 9th, was then submitted, and you will find that it repeatedly mentions the promise made by you as the ground upon which the rise of wages must be given.

I enclose a copy of this document along with a copy of my letter to the Prime Minister.

The 12½% was given, as you might truly say, after examination subsequently by Lord Milner and myself, and in my answer to Mr Watt[1] last week in the House of Commons, I was perhaps less than fair to you or to myself in not making a fuller statement on that point. It was less than fair to you because you had been in favour, as I had been, of giving a larger percentage to a smaller body of men, and I should have said so. I say so now. On the other hand, it was less than fair to myself because the matter

[1] Harry Anderson Watt, 1863–1929. Barrister. Liberal MP for Glasgow Maryhill, 1906–18. Unsuccessful Liberal candidate, Argyll, 1922 and Glasgow Govan, 1923. A well-known athlete, he was for three years Champion of Scotland in the hurdles.

of a rise of wages had already been settled by the Cabinet, and Lord Milner and I were simply asked to say to whom it should be given and what it should be.

We called a conference of all the Departments—Ministry of Labour, Shipbuilding, as well as the Committee on Production, and representatives of your Department—and after hearing all of them, we were guided to the 12½% instead of 10% or 15% owing to the advice of the Chairman of the Committee on Production and because we were led to believe that subsequent readjustment might be made in dealing with a general demand for a rise of wages over the engineering trade which was then in hand. In that we were disappointed afterwards, and also disappointed to find that the 12½% was not to be confined to even the larger body of men than you had had in your mind, but had led to demands from all and sundry, from all over the industrial world.

But experience shows, I think, that it would have made little difference whether we had decided upon 10%, 12½%, or 15%. It was not the rise of wages given to munitions workers, who were skilled men, but the subsequent demands made outside of munition workers altogether, as well as outside of the engineering area of munition workers, which led to the subsequent trouble. I never blamed you for that, and that was the main trouble,—it has been throughout.

I note that you say you were not present at the conference when the decision was given, and of course to that extent you are absolved from any share of responsibility in that decision. I don't know that I have said anything to the contrary.

I am glad to know from your letter that there is such a highly satisfactory condition of things now prevailing in the munitions areas, and I believe that also applies to the industrial world generally; but I cannot help saying that I believe that is largely due to the increase of wages given to the pieceworkers, and that if the pieceworkers at the lower end of the earning scale had been dealt with earlier, we might have had that happy position of things much sooner. You, as well as myself, were in favour of that. You were in favour of a narrower schedule, as I was. Your promise was made as a well-meant effort to adjust an admitted anomaly; but the unfortunate thing was that in adjusting such anomaly we were landed in trouble over a much larger field than you ever had in your mind.

I have been desirous of doing you full justice, but at the same time the statements made in the House of Commons a fortnight ago, and in the course of which, as I thought, undue responsibility was put upon myself, left me no other alternative than to speak last week. That was my reason, and as it seemed to me, my justification for speaking on the spur of the moment, and therefore without full preparation or an adequate opportunity for dealing with the subject in a comprehensive way.

Yours sincerely
George N. Barnes

Winston S. Churchill to G. N. Barnes

(*Churchill papers: 15/113*)

7 March 1918 Ministry of Munitions

Dear Mr Barnes,

Many thanks for your letter. We need not quarrel about the word 'appeal'. I understood you to object to the statement of fact which I proposed to make. It now appears that you wrote to the Prime Minister and also saw Mr Bonar Law upon the subject. At the same time you declined to concur in any agreed statement, although Major Hills had several conversations with you on the subject. No statement was in consequence made. I did not wish to be drawn into public controversy with you, for such a proceeding would be improper between colleagues, and as you would not agree to any form of statement, I decided to bear in silence the criticisms which your Glasgow speech had directed upon me. On no occasion whatever have I in public mentioned your name or referred to your action, and in view of all these circumstances I was painfully surprised to read your renewed animadversions in the House of Commons.

The whole effect of your speech last week, though I readily believe it was not your intention, was to make out that the 12½% was the cause of the falling off in the shipbuilding output in January, and in your zeal to emphasise this point you even went so far as to declare the February output was no greater than that of January, whereas it now appears it was doubled.

The reference to the Royal Commissions on Industrial Unrest were, I believe, drafted by you, and they point directly to the disparity between the earnings of the skilled time-workers and the less skilled but much more highly paid pieceworkers. Coming into office as I did on the 17th July, with only a few days between my election and the end of the Parliamentary Session, I inherited the situation created by the Reports of the Commissions, for whose setting up you had been chiefly responsible; and I was also committed largely by your statement at Newcastle to the abolition of the leaving certificate. This was the situation in which my speech on the second reading of the Munitions of War Amendment Act was made. I did not then and have never since considered that that speech constituted a formal or binding pledge. Certainly it left everything open as regards method, time, or degree.

On the rest of your letter I am in substantial agreement and recognise fully the spirit in which it has been written.

Please do not suppose that I at any time have been seeking to throw blame on you. I should have been quite content to take my share—and it is a very important share—in the general responsibility. You would never have heard a word of reproach from me had you let the subject alone. It is contrary to the whole principle of Cabinet government to divide up individual responsibilities in matters of general policy, and obviously it is very unfair to do so. Members of a Government defend each other and defend the policy of the Government, and if they cannot do so they remain silent or, in very serious cases, they resign. That is the rule, and that is the only rule. It seems to me that it applies still more strongly in a Government formed like the present, where the members of the War Cabinet have taken upon themselves the prime responsibility for the conduct of affairs. It would seem to be obligatory upon them not to throw blame on Departmental Ministers serving under the War Cabinet. This would apply to a Cabinet Minister even if he had disagreed with the policy which a Department had recommended to the Cabinet and had resisted it at every stage.

As it is, nothing but harm has resulted from what has occurred. I have been subjected to an immense amount of hostile comment, largely based on misunderstanding, which I could not answer without appearing to throw the blame on others. You have suffered both through what you said and what you unsaid; the Government as a whole has certainly suffered in authority and reputation.

War Cabinet: minutes

(*Cabinet papers: 23/5*)

7 March 1918

The War Cabinet had before them a Memorandum by Lord Rothermere (Paper GT–3727) on the proposed increase in the Air Force Programme.

MR CHURCHILL expressed the view that production would soon outstrip the man-power requisite for utilising its results. By the 1st July, according to present estimates, 10,000 additional fighting machines would be delivered. A big indent had been made for machine guns, and it would be carried out. In the next six months 27,000 more aircraft machine guns might be expected, but they would not be needed as fast as they were made. Wastage in aeroplanes, moreover, had proved to be only 75 per cent., and in engines only 50 per cent. of the estimate. It followed that by the end of June there would be a large stock of material ready without the man-power to handle it.

GENERAL TRENCHARD[1] agreed that there would be a surplus of machine guns, but did not agree that there would be a surplus of aeroplanes, in view of the greater enterprises that would be undertaken. and of the need of keeping a reserve. It was never possible to foresee which type of machine would fare best; there might at times prove to be a surplus of some types, but, as a whole, there would be no excess. He agreed, however, that if the man-power asked for in the Memorandum by Lord Rothermere (Paper GT–3727) were not forthcoming, much of the material would perforce remain idle.[2]

G. N. Barnes to Winston S. Churchill

(*Churchill papers: 15/113*)

8 March 1918

Dear Mr Churchill,

I much appreciate the kindly tone of your letter just to hand, and I can assure you that the recent controversy has caused me much trouble and searching of heart. Nothing puts me out more than quarrelling, and the worst of all quarrelling is with one's colleagues.

I, of course, accept your position of the rule that applies, and should apply, in regard to resignation, and it was my firm intention of taking that course at the end of January when I wrote the Prime Minister. I wanted to say no more, and at the same time, I wanted no more to be said by anyone. Even then, I felt that my reputation as well as yours had suffered, and the least said by either of us the better. Time alone can justify one, and I wanted nothing better, and I am sure you wanted nothing better, than to be left alone to do one's work. I should have said nothing more about it but for the discussion a week or two later in the House of Commons, and I am afraid that my hurried and ragged speeches didn't add anything to clarity. How-

[1] Hugh Montague Trenchard, 1873–1956. Entered Army, 1893. Active service, South Africa, 1899–1902 (dangerously wounded). Major, 1902. Assistant Commandant, Central Flying School, 1913–14. Lieutenant-Colonel, 1915. General Officer Commanding the Royal Flying Corps in the Field, 1915–17. Major-General, 1916. Knighted, 1918. Chief of the Air Staff, 1918–29. Air-Marshal, 1919. Created Baronet, 1919. Air Chief Marshal, 1922. Marshal of the Royal Air Force, 1927. Created Baron, 1930. Commissioner, Metropolitan Police, 1931–5. Created Viscount, 1936. Chairman of the United Africa Company, 1936–56. Trustee of the Imperial War Museum, 1937–45. Order of Merit, 1951. His elder son, and both his stepsons, were killed in action in the Second World War.

[2] The War Cabinet approved the proposed increase of the Air Force Programme by 40 squadrons, as proposed in Rothermere's memorandum.

ever, I am glad to know that you have taken up the position you have, which, as I understand it, is to let the whole matter drop, and I hope that no estrangement will result; and that Major Hills especially, for whom I have a great regard will not be prejudiced in any way.

Yours sincerely
George N. Barnes

Sir Eric Geddes to Winston S. Churchill

(*Churchill papers: 15/1*)

8 March 1918 Admiralty

My dear Churchill,

I have been most interested in reading your inspiring paper on *Munitions Programme, 1919*.

I hope it will bring great thoughts to the minds of those who dictate our tactics. You have a great gift of expression and to one who has not studied the problem your arguments are very convincing.

I wish you every success in trying to get a decision for 1919.

Thanks for letting me see your paper.

Yours sincerely
E. Geddes

Winston S. Churchill to Sir Eric Geddes

(*Churchill papers: 15/1*)

10 March 1918 Ministry of Munitions
Private

My dear Geddes,

I am very glad indeed that you were interested in the views on the war which I have put forward, and I am much obliged to you for your kind note.

I have been pondering over the definition of the duties of a Supply Ministry and will send you something in a day or two. I quite understand your view and am anxious to meet it. But I do not want to cut myself off from being able to write such a paper for instance on the war as that which you have just seen with approval. Whatever office I held, or even if I were out of the Government, I should do that. If I thought the Cabinet were going seriously wrong I should remonstrate with them and if that proved useless or unwelcome, I should resign and say what I had to say in the House of Commons. I could never divest myself of that general responsibility. After all, the object is to find out what is the best thing to do, and counsel and criticism are necessary processes to that end.

But on the other hand a Supply Department would have to treat all its customers with impartial goodwill, and not attempt to use its special position and opportunities to force a particular view of war policy on the fighting services. That assurance you should certainly have in plain terms. Still more is it important that in any such arrangement the persons concerned should feel that they are working together, and that they mean to work together. I do not think we differ very much in opinion whether about the war in general or the Admiralty. On the contrary, the language you use on many aspects is in complete harmony with my convictions reached by considerable and hard experience.

Yours sincerely
Winston S. Churchill

War Cabinet: minutes[1]

(*Cabinet papers: 23/5*)

11 March 1918

. . . the attention of the War Cabinet was drawn to a suggestion in Mr Churchill's Munitions Programme for 1919 to supplement our military preparations in 1919 by provision for a gas attack on a very large scale. The Chief of the Imperial General Staff[2] stated that he had the whole of the questions raised in Mr Churchill's report under consideration. Limitations, he pointed out, were placed on the offensive employment of poison gas by the fact that the force employing it was prevented from penetrating into the gassed area for a period of time sufficient to enable the enemy to organise its defence. . . .

With reference to the discussion on tanks which took place at 10, Downing Street, on the 8th March, the Chief of the Imperial General Staff pointed out the difficulties which the defence would oppose to tanks. Low-flying aeroplanes might be defeated by our own aeroplanes; 'camouflaged' guns might be circumvented by smoke and night attack; but land mines presented a problem of the utmost difficulty.

[1] Churchill was not present at this meeting of the War Cabinet. Lloyd George, Curzon, Milner, Barnes, Bonar Law, Smuts, Balfour and Derby were the Ministers present. Sir Henry Wilson (Chief of the Imperial General Staff) represented the War Office.

[2] Sir Henry Wilson had become Chief of the Imperial General Staff on 18 February 1918, replacing Sir William Robertson, who had disagreed with Lloyd George both about General Allenby's proposed Palestine offensive, and about the creation of an Allied general reserve on the western front under the chairmanship of Marshal Foch.

Winston S. Churchill to Major Spiers

(Spears papers)

12 March 1918 Ministry of Munitions

Private

I had a long talk with HW[1] on your affairs and understood from him that in any case he would make no immediate change in your appointment. He said that Foch[2] was uneasy at the great influence you had acquired with the French Ministers and your ready access to them; but I pointed out the advantages to the British Government which resulted from this and which made you so valuable an agent. All the same, I think you ought to manage to re-assure Foch and make him feel at his ease. Let me know promptly if there is any difficulty, as I will not fail to go immediately to HW, with whom I get on very well and am in general agreement on war policy. I hope to be over in Paris again shortly, and will let you know in good time.

War Cabinet: minutes[3]

(Cabinet papers: 23/5)

13 March 1918

The War Cabinet had under consideration the question of the allocation of steel for the extended British tank programme as compared with the Anglo-American tank programme. . . .

MR CHURCHILL drew attention to War Cabinet 318, minute 13, and the Appendix thereto, in which the agreement between the British and American Governments is set out as regards the building of American tanks, and under which the latter undertakes to give priority as regards material, shipping, etc and to replace the armour plates for the United States tanks in the form of ship plates, on or about the date of delivery of the armour plate to

[1] Sir Henry Wilson.

[2] Ferdinand Foch, 1851–1929. Lieutenant, French Army, 1873. Professor, Ecole Superieure de Guerre, 1894–1900; General Commanding the Ecole, 1907–11. Commanded the XXth Corps, based on Nancy, 1913–14. Commanded the 9th Army, at the battle of the Marne, September 1914. Deputy to the Commander-in-Chief, during the 'race to the sea', October 1914. Honorary knighthood, 1914. Commanded the Group of Armies of the North, 1915–16. Deprived of his command after the battle of the Somme. Recalled, Generalissimo of the Allied Forces, France, March–November 1918. Marshal of France, August 1918. Appointed British Field-Marshal, 1919.

[3] Bonar Law was in the Chair at this meeting. The other members of the War Cabinet present were Lord Curzon, George Barnes and General Smuts. Churchill attended only for the item with which he was concerned as Minister of Munitions.

the factory, on the basis of ton for ton. Mr Churchill added that, if the United States failed to be punctual as regards deliveries in this matter, the armour plate that had been provided for their tanks would be diverted for the construction of British tanks under our extended programmes at a greater rate than trained *personnel* could be made available for manning the tanks.

H. E. Cooke[1] *to Winston S. Churchill*

(*Churchill papers: 1/131*)

13 March 1918 86 Eccleston Square

Dear Sir,

Lullenden Estate, Lingfield.

I beg leave to acknowledge the receipt of your letter of the 11th inst, and by direction of the Surrey Agricultural Executive Committee to send for your perusal copy of a report received by them from the Godstone District War Agricultural Committee, from which it will be seen that apart from the additional arable area required the general condition of the estate needs immediate attention, especially as a preliminary step the hedging, ditching, and clearing of bramble and thorn bushes.

The Executive Committee, dealing with cases of insufficiently cultivated land over the whole of Surrey, cannot assume over this wide area, as I am sure you will realise, the responsibilities belonging to owners and occupiers of actually getting the work done, but they are glad to offer any facilities in their power as set out in the enclosed circular letter. An effort is being made by the Executive Committee to get a gang of German prisoners for the Godstone district, in which case labour, in addition to the soldier labour named in the circular, will be available.

If you have time, and would like to discuss the question of labour, I shall be pleased to call by appointment.

I am, Sir, Your obedient Servant
H. E. Cooke

[1] Executive Officer of the Surrey County War Agricultural Committee.

Winston S. Churchill to H. E. Cooke

(*Churchill papers: 1/131*)

15 March 1918

My dear Sir,

I am very much obliged to you for your letter. Of course I am willing to do everything in my power to fulfil your requirements. At the same time reasonable regard must be had to practical difficulties. I have only had possession of this place for about 11 months. It had been left completely derelict in an agricultural sense for a large number of years. There was no stock; there was no hay; there was no farm plant of any kind or buildings; there was no manure; the hedges and ditches had been completely neglected, and the soil permitted to go entirely out of cultivation to such an extent that several of the fields are almost completely overgrown with thorn bushes. Had it not been wartime it would have been easy to have obtained the labour necessary at a moderate expense to put the land in proper order; but even so, several years and a considerable expenditure of capital would have been required before it was raised to the level of an economic proposition. Early last year I obtained the services of three German prisoners at 25/- a week, whom I housed. These men were employed on draining and on trenching a field for potatoes. Their labour was not at all satisfactory, and the experiment was very unpopular in the neighbourhood, and after 4 months I decided to send the men away, and since then I have not succeeded in obtaining, except at short intervals, adult labour capable of making any real impression. We were not able in consequence even to get in the hay this year. Such of it as had been cut rotted on the ground, and in these circumstances the feeding of stock through the winter was a matter of considerable anxiety. I have, however, purchased seven bullocks who have now been 4 months on the land and have got through the winter quite well.

Another difficulty is buildings, the cost of construction of which in wartime is practically prohibitive. Nevertheless, I am endeavouring to get both a cow shed and further pig-styes built, to plough up about three-quarters of an acre for potatoes in addition to the garden, and I have every intention of substantially increasing the stock during the course of the present year. That is really all that can be done with the resources that are available, namely, one gardener, one very old and crippled man, and two boys. If any serious effort is to be made to plough up land for crops, to clear the fields which are overgrown and dirty, to grow crops, to drain, hedge and ditch the fields, it is indispensable that proper labour should be found. I should be perfectly ready to employ as many German prisoners as could reasonably be used on this work if they are under proper control and can be lodged in Godstone, and to pay all reasonable charges in connection therewith. I accept the fullest responsibility for putting the land in good order by every reasonable and economic means; but I cannot accept that responsibility without regard to the limitations which physical circumstances impose. I hope this may be recognised.

I am, Sir, Your obedient servant
Winston S. Churchill

Lord Wimborne[1] *to Winston S. Churchill*

(*Churchill papers: 2/103*)

16 March 1918 Vice Regal Lodge
Dublin

My dear Winston,

I keep wondering whether the conditions you surmised are in any way maturing. The Compton-Rickett[2] speech has set the world a speculating.[3] It is even reported that *all* the allied prime ministers are in London!

You know my strong conviction, to which I think your own views now incline to share.

I tremble lest another chance be lost through obstinacy, over-confidence, or personal vanity. I cannot feel that Russia has any claim upon us, or see why we all should ruin ourselves on behalf of Bolshevism. As to any accumulation of German power in the end it is more than set off by the English speaking solidarity.

I really *earnestly* pray you use your influence in the direction of sane

[1] Ivor Churchill Guest, 1873–1939. Conservative MP, 1900–6. Liberal MP, 1906–10. Created Baron Ashby St Ledgers, 1910. Paymaster-General 1910–12. Lord in Waiting, 1913–15. 2nd Baron Wimborne, 1914. Lord Lieutenant of Ireland, 1915–18. Created Viscount Wimborne, 1918.

[2] Joseph Compton-Rickett, 1847–1919. Chairman of several coal trade companies, 1890–1902. Liberal MP from 1895 to his death. Knighted, 1907. Privy Councillor, 1911. President of the National Council of Evangelical Free Churches, 1915. Paymaster-General from December 1916 to October 1919.

[3] On 14 March 1918 *The Times* published an account of a speech made by Compton-Rickett on the previous day to the National Free Church Council. During the course of the speech he said: 'if they knew all the circumstances of the crisis of the moment they would agree that whoever was Prime Minister should have the undivided support of the nation. We were at a moment when, within the next week or so, and possibly the next few days, decisions of the utmost gravity might be taken affecting the whole life of the Empire in the time to come. . . . The German Federation and their friends were contesting with the British group, and it was hanging in the balance. It would be solved more rapidly, perhaps, than many of them thought.'

accommodation. How disproportionate, to calm reflection, do all human quarrels appear in contrast to their shattering results. A ruined world will curse this frenzied age in years to come!!. . .

Affectionately yours,
Ivor

Winston S. Churchill to Lord Wimborne

(*David Satinoff collection*)

18 March 1918 Ministry of Munitions

Alas My dear Ivor for yr hopes.

C Rickett's speech had no such significance; nor has the gathering of the Prime Ministers any other object but the prosecution of the War, wh it seems to me will certainly continue on a gt scale; for we are reinforced by America, & Germany by the capture of Russia.

The Germans are in no mood for reason and I shd greatly fear any settlement with them unless & until they have been definitely worsted. At present they think they have won. . . .[1]

Yours always
W

Winston S. Churchill to the 'Sunday Times', Sydney, Australia: telegram

(*Churchill papers: 15/155*)

[23] March 1918

I cannot do better than repeat what I said in the Guild Hall in August, 1914—

'We have only to endure to conquer.'

This is the hour above all others for Britain to show the cool and dogged tenacity which in every foreign country is recognised as the great character-

[1] On 18 March 1918 Churchill began his fifth official visit to France since he had become Minister of Munitions the previous July. On 19 March he worked at GHQ St Omer, and at Tank HQ Montreuil. On 20 March he went to see the commander of the IXth Division, General Tudor, at Nurlu, where he stayed the night. On the following morning, Thursday, 21 March, the Germans launched their first offensive since 1915, and at once broke through the British lines. Churchill returned that morning to St Omer, and throughout 22 March was in conference at the Chemical Warfare School, St Omer. He returned to London on 23 March.

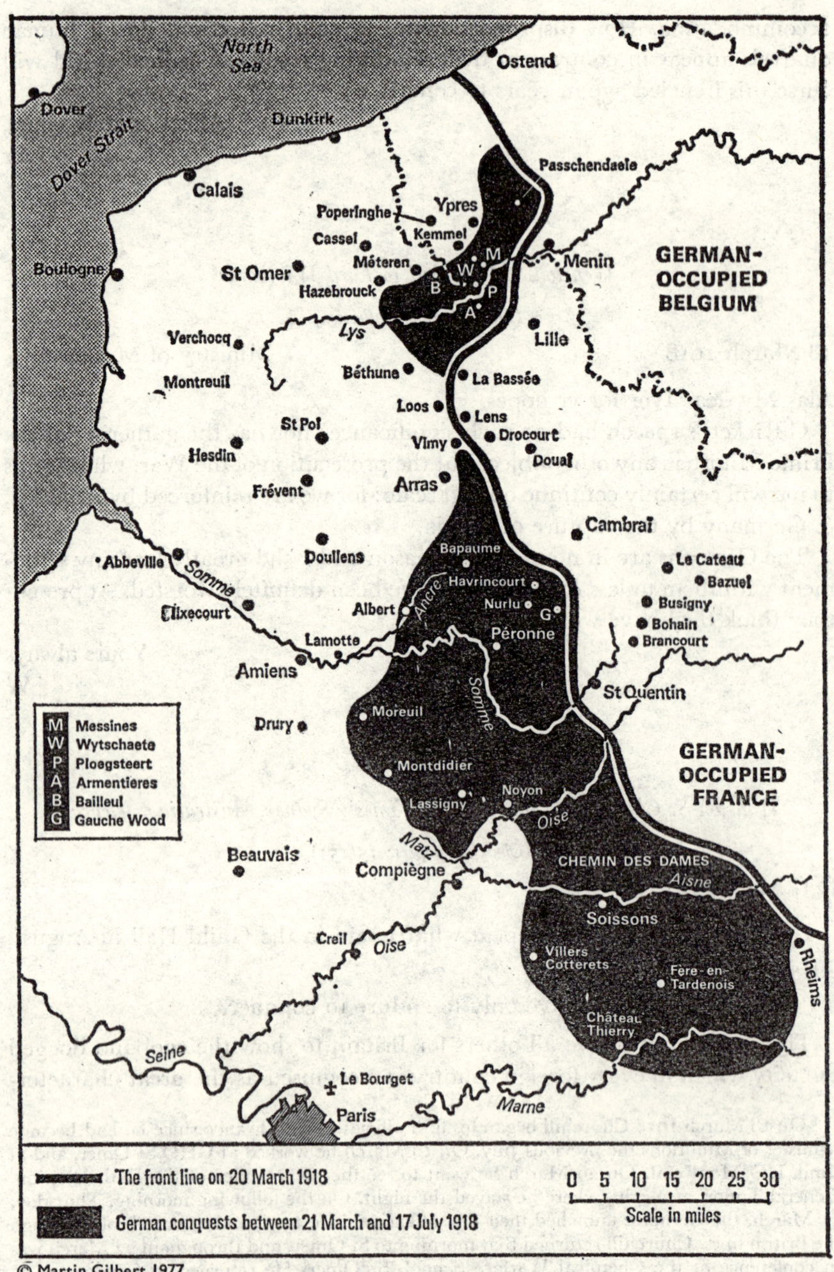

THE WESTERN FRONT DURING 1917 AND 1918

istic of our race. In the months that lie before us, every temptation towards weakness and compromise in the guise alike of good and bad motives, will be presented to us, and our empire must prove itself the rock on which our Allies in the old world can be upheld till our Allies, who are also our kith and kin and long separated brothers from across the Atlantic, can bring their irresistible force to bear, and so secure an honourable and a lasting peace.

Sir Henry Wilson: diary

(*Wilson papers*)

23 March 1918 London

An anxious day. The 5th Army seems to be beaten & has fallen back behind the Somme. The 3rd Army is retiring but is fighting well. Telephoning at 7 pm to me from GHQ, Lawrence[1] said the French had agreed to take over up to Peronne but that this would take 3 days which would be critical days. There is roughly the situation tonight.

I was about 5 hours with LG. I lunched at Bonar's with him & LG & in the garden of 10 Downing St till 4 o'c when we had a War Cabinet till 6 o'c. For hours I insisted on the importance of taking a long, broad view of the future of conscription on *everyone* up to 50 & of course on Ireland. I think I did good & Winston helped like a man. Smuts was good but more cautious, Milner disappointing. BL ditto. AJB rather uninterested. Curzon not there. We took following steps:

I telegraphed early to Reading asking him to press on Pres Wilson[2] the vital importance of sending over Inf. . . .

At the War Cabinet we decided to send out the 50,000 boys (trained) of 18½ years & up to 19, and some other lots which will make up 82,000 which with the 88,000 returning from leave will mean 170,000 in the next 17 days if we can ship at that rate.

[1] Herbert Alexander Lawrence, 1861–1943. 4th son of the 1st Baron Lawrence. Entered the Army, 1882. Served as an Intelligence Officer at the War Office and in South Africa, 1897–1902. Retired from the Army, 1903, and entered the City. A Member of the Committee of the Ottoman Bank, 1906 and a Director of the Midland Railway, 1913. Rejoined the Army, 1914. Major-General, 1915, on active service at Gallipoli, in command of the 127th (Manchester) Brigade. In the summer of 1916 he commanded the troops that drove the Turks from Sinai. Commanded the 66th Division at Passchendaele, 1917. Knighted, 1917. Chief of Staff, GHQ France, January–November 1918. Lieutenant-General, 1918. General, 1919. Considered as a possible Viceroy of India (1920) and as a possible Chief of the Imperial General Staff (1922), but chosen for neither. Member of the Royal Commission on the Coal Industry, 1925. Chairman of Vickers, 1926. Chairman and Managing Director of Glyn Mills & Co, merchant bankers, 1934–43. Both his sons were killed in action, Lieutenant Oliver Lawrence in May 1915 and Captain Michael Lawrence in September 1916.

[2] President Woodrow Wilson (see page 289, note 2).

Kirke[1] flew over to GHQ & back again. A good deal of fog. He says his impression is that the 5th Army is partly broken.

I asked Lawrence on telephone if DH was satisfied with Gough[2] & he said 'entirely'.

Paris was shelled! at 108 kilometres. Amiens also shelled. . . .

Sir Maurice Hankey: diary

(*Hankey papers*)

23 March 1918

News kept coming in all day of the increasing seriousness of the position on the Vth army front. . . . The War Cabinet met at 4 pm. They were rather inclined to be panicky, and eventually decided to send the 18½ to 19 year old men to France. . . .

Philip Sassoon to Lord Esher

(*Esher papers*)

23 March 1918 GHQ France

This is the biggest attack in the history of warfare I wd imagine . . . The situation is a very simple one. The enemy has got the men and we havn't. For two years Sir DH has been warning our friends at home of the critical condition of our manpower; but they have preferred to talk about Aleppo & indulge in mythical dreams about the Americans.

[1] Walter Mervyn St George Kirke, 1877–1949. Entered the Royal Artillery, 1896. Major, 1914. Served on the western front, and at Salonika, 1914–18. Colonel, 1917. Brigadier-General, 1918. Deputy Director of Military Operations, War Office, 1918–22. Major-General, 1924. Head of the British Military, Naval and Air Force Mission to Finland, 1924–9. Deputy Chief of the General Staff, India, 1926–9. Commander-in-Chief, Western Command, 1933–6. Knighted, 1934. Director-General of the Territorial Army, 1936–9. Inspector-General of Home Defences, 1939. Commander-in-Chief of Home Forces, 1939–40.

[2] Hubert de la Poer Gough, 1870–1963. Entered Army, 1889. On active service in the Tirah, 1897–8 and South Africa 1899–1902 (severely wounded). Professor, Staff College, 1904–6. Major-General, 1914; Lieutenant-General, 1917. Knighted, 1916. Commanded the 3rd Cavalry Brigade, 1914; the 2nd Cavalry Division, 1914–15; the 1st Army Corps, 1915–16; the Fifth Army, 1916–18. Chief, Allied Mission to the Baltic, 1919. He published *The Fifth Army* (1931), and *Soldiering On* (1954).

Sir Henry Wilson: diary

(*Wilson papers*)

24 March 1918 London

At 5 o'c a telephone message to say Combles & Peronne had fallen & our troops were retreating to the Ancre. I telephoned at once to LG at Walton to come up. At 5.30 Foch telephoned to me asking what I thought of situation & we are of one mind that someone must catch a hold or we shall be beaten. I said I would come over & see him.

At 7 o'c meeting at 10 Downing St of LG, BL, Smuts & me. We discussed & I said I was going over. There is no mistaking the gravity of the situation nor the entirely inadequate measures taken by Haig & Pétain in their mutual plans for assistance. While we were discussing, a telegram from Haig to say 3rd Army was pulling back to the Ancre & asking me to go over. So I go by special 6.57 tomorrow & then Destroyer.

I dined with Winston & Mrs Winston & LG also there & Hankey after dinner.

Winston backed me up *well* when I pressed LG *hard* to really conscript this country & Ireland. I finished by saying to LG 'You will come out of this bang top or bang bottom' and Winston cordially agreed. I want LG to summon Parliament, conscript up to 50 years of age & *include* Ireland. I am not sure that he sees the full gravity of the situation yet.

A moving day. We are very near a crash. LG has, on the whole, been buoyant, BL *most* depressing, Smuts talked much academic nonsense, Winston a *real* gem in a crisis, & reminded me of Aug: 1914.

War Cabinet: minutes

(*Cabinet papers: 23/5*)

24 March 1918

With reference to War Cabinet 371, Minute 8 (V), as regards a further supply of men, the Adjutant-General[1] stated that—

(a) Approximately 25,000 men, who had served as soldiers, might be withdrawn from munitions.

With regard to the proposal to take these men away from munitions, Mr Churchill said that he considered it very unsound. Of this number 7,000 were employed in shipyards; 3,000 were in blast-furnaces, on which the

[1] Lieutenant-General Sir Nevil Macready (see page 13, note 4).

output of steel-plate absolutely depended. This left 15,000 men, fit for general service, to be found from other sources, and he was firmly convinced that it would be folly to move key men from gun industries, and the manufacture of tanks and aeroplanes. Having in view the fact that the Ministry of Munitions was at present releasing 100,000 men for the army, he urged that no steps should be taken to withdraw a further 25,000 until the matter had been thoroughly gone into to see what fit men could reasonably be spared from the several industries under the Ministry of Munitions.

Winston S. Churchill to David Lloyd George: unsent draft

(*Churchill papers: 27/32*)

24 March 1918 33 Eccleston Square

My dear Prime Minister,

The following steps seem appropriate to the situation:—

1. 50,000 trained men from the Fleet including the bulk of the Marines.
2. The age raised to 55.
3. Ireland like all the rest of us.
4. The American army to form on existing British & French *Cadres* in so far as it is unable to enter the line by divisions.
5. The King shd be allowed to go to the Front.

These steps are additional to the obvious administrative measures wh are indicated by the Ministry of National service. You must not accept any statement that 10,000 men a day is the limit of cross-channel conveyance. It is quite untrue. There are a score of expedients that can be adopted.

The above also applies to the transport of munitions. Whatever is available & needed can & must be carried to France.

Parliament shd be called together with the utmost despatch & on yr initiation; & shd then be told *that practical measures are being taken* & must be insisted on.

There are of course two problems, (a) the immediate reforming of a front & (b) the enduring through the summer. I do not think the first insoluble if the *lift* is given, and proper steps are taken.

The second will be still harder to surmount; but after all the forces are not hopelessly unequal:

Violent counsels & measures must rule.

Seek the truth in this hour of need with disdain of other things. Courage & a clear plan will enable you to keep the command of the Nation. But if you fall below the level of the crisis, your role is exhausted. I am confident you will not fail. Lift yourself by an effort of will to the height of circumstances & conquer or succumb fighting.

I am sure this situation can be retrieved.

Even if the land war collapsed the sea, the air, & the United States will give us the means of victory.

But now is the time to risk everything; & to run risks for the very sake. You can count on the support of yr fellow countrymen in all forms of vehement action.

Your sincere friend
W

Sir Maurice Hankey: diary

(Hankey papers)

24 March 1918

LlG had gone off to dine with Winston Churchill, so I pursued them, and found Gen Wilson also there. The news was about as bad as it could be.... There was nothing to be done, but Churchill, supported by Wilson, was heavily bombarding the PM with demands for a 'levée en masse'. Eventually the PM went off to Walton Heath and the bombardment was transferred to me.

Philip Sassoon to Lord Esher

(Esher papers)

25 March 1918 GHQ France

The enemy is concentrating *the whole of the Central Powers* against us; now we see the criminal folly of all these side shows.

Sir Maurice Hankey: diary

(Hankey papers)

25 March 1918

This has been a really terrible day . . . our troops are everywhere being driven back and must be extremely exhausted. . . .

The War Cabinet met at 11 am, an anxious meeting. . . .

I had a walk with the PM before dinner; the news seemed better and we both felt more cheerful—in fact Balfour & Churchill whom I found in company with the PM were ridiculously optimistic—but on getting back from the usual round of St James Park we met Gen Macdonogh,[1] who told us that Courcelettes had fallen. All day I kept thinking of Briand's[2] saying during the drawn out Verdun attack—'Nous sommes crucifiés'.

Winston S. Churchill: War Cabinet Memorandum

(*Cabinet papers: 23/5*)

26 March 1918 Ministry of Munitions

1. The following are my revised figures for guns and carriages complete available by the 6th April, including those in reserve in France and England, or in transit or at proof:—

18-pr	797	Total equipments 1,915
4·5-inch Howitzer	399	
60-pr	164	
6-inch Howitzer	292	
6-inch gun	74	
8-inch Howitzer	141	
9·2-inch Howitzer	29	
12-inch Howitzer	19	

These figures are in advance of my previous estimate in each class—field, medium, and heavy—though the details are varied. They differ from the revised figures given in the printed minutes by including the current fortnight's output, which can be handed over immediately without waiting for proof.

2. There have been heavy expenditures and still heavier losses of small arms ammunition in this moving warfare, and General Headquarters has asked us for 230 million rounds at once. This can be supplied.

Winston S. Churchill

[1] The Adjutant-General (see page 471, note 3).

[2] Aristide Briand, 1862–1932. French politician. Minister of Public Instruction and Worship, 1906–9. Prime Minister, 1909–10. Minister of Justice, 1912–13. Prime Minister, January–March 1913. Minister of Justice, 1914. Prime Minister, October 1915–March 1917. Prime Minister and Minister of Foreign Affairs, January 1921–January 1922. Minister of Foreign Affairs, 1925. Prime Minister, November 1925–July 1926. Minister of Foreign Affairs, 1926. Awarded the Nobel Peace Prize for his part in the Locarno Agreements, 1926. Prime Minister for the sixth time, July–October 1929.

Sir Maurice Hankey: diary

(*Hankey papers*)

26 March 1918

After the Cabinet LlG asked Lord French (who is attending regularly) & myself & Winston Churchill to stay behind & discuss the situation. French was most bitter about Haig, who, he said, was no judge of men, had surrounded himself with stupid people & bad Corps Commanders. . . . He considered Haig had badly let down the army in shattering it in the hopeless Flanders offensive.

Sir Henry Wilson: diary

(*Wilson papers*)

26 March 1918

Doullens at mid-day. Poincaré,[1] Clemenceau, Loucheur, Foch, Pétain, Milner, Haig, Self. . . . Milner, Haig & I had preliminary talk, & Haig agreed to my proposal for Foch to coordinate. Then meeting of Poincaré, Clemenceau, Foch & Pétain, Milner, Haig & Self. After discussion in which I fell out with Pétain for contemplating a retreat, Milner put up proposal for Foch to co-ordinate & all agreeing, Clemenceau & Milner signed the document. Then I discussed removal of Gough & told Haig he could have Rawley[2] & Rawley's old 4th Corps Staff from Versailles to replace Gough. Haig agreed to this. Both Haig & Lawrence are delighted with this new arrangement about Foch. So is Foch & so, really, is Clemenceau who patted me on the head & said I was 'un bon garçon'. . . .

Back to Montreuil for tea. I saw DH just going out for a ride & he told me he was *greatly* pleased with our new arrangements. I told him & Lawrence at Doullens that *much* would now depend on the Officers he chose for liaison with Foch & that of course he could have anybody he liked. DH is 10 years

[1] Raymond Poincaré, 1860–1934. Minister of Public Instruction, 1893 and 1895; of Finance, 1894 and 1906. Prime Minister, 1911–13. President of the French Republic, January 1913–February 1920. Prime Minister and Minister of Foreign Affairs, January 1922–June 1924. Minister of Finance, 1926–8. Prime Minister, 1926–9. Between 1913 and 1934 he published ten volumes of memoirs.

[2] Henry Seymour Rawlinson, 1864–1925. Entered Army, 1884. On Kitchener's staff in the Sudan, 1898. Brigadier-General, 1903. Major-General commanding the 4th Division, September 1914; the 7th Division & 3rd Cavalry Division, October 1914; the IVth Corps, December 1914–December 1915. Knighted, 1914. Lieutenant-General commanding the Fourth Army, 1916–18. General, 1917. Created Baron, 1919. Commanded the forces in North Russia, 1919. Commander-in-Chief, India, 1920–5.

younger tonight than he was yesterday afternoon. Milner & I over by Destroyer (Mermaid) at 7 o'c Boulogne. Got back to Victoria ¼ to 11 o'c. Found Whigham[1] & Maurice[2] & Winston waiting for me. Milner, Winston & I to 10 Downing St & we told LG & BL & Hankey result of our labours & as I summed it up for LG 'the chances are not slightly in favour of us'.

Winston S. Churchill to all munitions factories: telegram

(*Churchill papers: 15/116*)

27 March 1918[3] Ministry of Munitions

A special effort must be made to replace promptly the serious losses in Ammunition which are resulting from the great battle now in progress. It should be our part in the struggle to maintain the armament and equipment of the fighting troops at the highest level. Our resources are fortunately sufficient to accomplish this up to the present in every class of Munitions. But it is necessary to speed up the completion of important work in hand. There are certain classes of shells which are specially useful now which can be released in large additional numbers in the next few weeks. I rely upon everyone concerned in the manufacture of 6″ shells to put forward their best effort, there should therefore be no cessation of this work during the Easter holidays. I acknowledge with gratitude the spontaneous assurances already received from the men in many districts that there will be no loss of output. Now is the time to show the Fighting Army what the Industrial army can achieve.[4]

[1] Robert Dundas Whigham, 1865–1950. Entered Army, 1885. Fought at the battle of Omdurman, 1898 and in South Africa, 1899–1902. Major-General, 1916. Deputy Chief of the Imperial General Staff, 1916–18. Knighted, 1917. Commanded the 62nd Division in France, 1918. Lieutenant-General, 1921. Adjutant-General to the Forces, 1923–7. General Officer Commanding Eastern Command (England), 1927-31. His only son was killed in action in 1914.

[2] Frederick Barton Maurice, 1871–1951. Entered Army, 1892. Colonel, 1915. Director of Military Operations, 1915–18. Major-General, 1916. Knighted, 1918. Principal, Working Men's College, St Pancras, 1922–33. Professor of Military Studies, London University, 1927. Principal, Queen Mary College, London University, 1933–44. Author of many historical works. In 1899 he married Edward Marsh's sister Helen Margaret.

[3] By 27 March the Germans had advanced 10 miles beyond the line which they had held before the Battle of the Somme, and having captured Albert, Chaulnes and Roye, were within 10 miles of Amiens. On the evening of 27 March they captured Montdidier, an important Allied railway junction, from which their guns threatened the Amiens–Paris railway.

[4] Among the many replies which Churchill received was one which read: 'Your wire received. The munition workers of Liverpool assure you that there will be no loss of output and are ready to show the fighting army what the industrial army can achieve.' (*Churchill papers: 15/116*)

Sir Henry Wilson: diary

(*Wilson papers*)

27 March 1918 36 Eaton Place

Breakfast with LG & Winston. I warned him that if now we blocked the Boches in their attack they would turn on Italy in May or June, & then come back to us in the autumn. Winston agreed.

Then to see the King, tell him of my trip & advise him to go out for a few days. Stamfordham *against* but I carried my point & the King goes tomorrow.

Then War Cabinet. Described my visit & wound up by saying the chances were in our favour now. . . .

The Boches pushing on & now threatening Montdidier.

David Lloyd George to Georges Clemenceau

(*Churchill papers: 27/32*)

[28] March 1918

Now that General Foch is practically in charge of the combined operations on behalf of the Allied Gov^nts^, the Prime Minister & the War Cabinet are anxious to be in the closest touch with him during these critical days. They have therefore deputed Mr Churchill to proceed to Head Q^rs^ to-day where he will remain for the present, so that, should there be any form of assistance which in the judgement of Gen Foch could be rendered by the British Gov^nt^, he can immediately communicate direct with the British Government.

Sir Henry Wilson: diary

(*Wilson papers*)

28 March 1918 36 Eaton Place

Winston telephoned he wanted to see me as he was off to France. I caught him in the train at Ch X. He was *being* sent out to Foch by LG! I told him I *could* not agree, & I must have this changed & he must go to Clemenceau *not* to any soldier. LG did change this during the morning & before I spoke to him at lunch at Derby House the Boches have taken Montdidier. . . .

Lunched at Derby's with LG also. I told him Winston could not go to Foch's HQ but he told me he had already changed this to Clemenceau &

J T Davies[1] later showed me the wire in which LG said BL & I were opposed to his (Winston) going to Foch so he was to go to Paris to Clemenceau. LG said he was sending Winston there as Bertie was no use. I think Winston will advise LG to send Derby to Paris & put him (Winston) into the WO!

David Lloyd George to J. T. Davies: telephone message

(*Lloyd George papers*)

28 March 1918

Find out which station Winston Churchill has gone to (Dover or Folkestone) & send a phone message to be delivered to him telling him that 'on reflection' I have come to the conclusion he had better stay in Paris & not at French Head Quarters. He had better therefore go straight to Clemenceau ascertain position & report here. If Clemenceau agrees he could then visit French GHQ but not stay there. Bonar Law & Wilson 'strongly take this view'.

Leopold Amery: diary

(*Amery diary*)

28 March 1918 Paris

Then to Ritz to meet Winston and give him LG's message which I had got over the telephone to stick to Paris and not go directing strategy at French GHQ.[2]

We had a good talk while he wallowed in a hot bath and then went to bed. (Winston is an extraordinary shape and wears a long nightgown!) He had found our GHQ very worried about Montdidier and the French, and down in the mouth generally—also evidently without information of what the French were doing. His own preoccupation was whether the French were only counter-attacking piecemeal or were getting everything together for a really big stroke.

He reports well of the War Cabinet, though they are still very worried

[1] John Thomas Davies, 1881–1938. Private Secretary to Lloyd George from 1912 to 1922. Knighted, 1922. A Director of the Suez Canal Company from 1922 until his death. Also a Director of the Ford Motor Company.

[2] Some years later Amery added in the margin at this point: 'Needless to say he paid no attention & careered about the front the whole time.'

about Ireland, mainly because LG doubts if Irish conscripts will fight. Bonar too was facing the storm all right, though, as WC said, he is a vessel with very low free board and the deep waters roll over his soul very easily.

Mary Borden: diary

(Borden papers)

29 March 1918

Winston has arrived to see what's going on. Bertie has put Clemenceau against him rather. B helping him. Enormous wires and telephones with Lloyd George. . . . Strong measures being brought into force in England. Raising age of conscription to 50. Conscription in Ireland. Winston says that Lloyd George says the point is that he doesn't know which way they'd shoot. Might go over to the Germans.

Winston S. Churchill and David Lloyd George: telegram

(Churchill papers: 27/32)

29 March 1918 Paris
Noon
Personal and Secret

Firstly, saw Lawrence, Chief of Staff, and Birch,[1] Artillery at GHQ on my way through yesterday. My impression was that the British Front was holding well in spite of continuous heavy attack, but that the strain was great, the resources narrowing, and there was serious anxiety to know when and how the French will intervene in real force. The movements of British divisions behind our Front seem to be proceeding with ease and celerity and I was assured that good arrangements have been made to interpolate the large drafts that you are sending in the battered divisions as soon as these are withdrawn from the battle and before they go into the trenches again. Even sedentary home service divisions will be useful to fill up sectors which however quiet cannot be left untenanted. Every fighting division will be needed

[1] James Frederick Noel Birch, 1865–1939. Entered Army, 1885. Served in the Ashanti War, 1895, and in South Africa, 1899–1902. Brigadier-General, the Royal Artillery, 7th Division, 1915. Artillery Adviser to Sir Douglas Haig, 1916–19. Major-General, 1917. Knighted, 1918. Lieutenant-General, 1919. Director of Remounts, 1920–1. Director-General of the Territorial Army, 1921–3. Master-General of Ordnance, 1923–7. General, 1926.

in the battle for the German reserves are by no means exhausted and their roulement has not yet begun. Marine gunners are especially needed because the guns will be far in excess of the gunners.

Secondly. Since arriving in Paris I have seen Generals Spiers and Sackville West.[1] There is no doubt the French realize the gravity of the next ten days and we need not assume that they are not exerting themselves. Accounts are conflicting of the rate at which their divisions will arrive and in any case the infantry coming by motor will often not have their artillery and impedimenta with them. There is therefore according to my present information, no immediate prospect of any strong French punch developing on a great scale as we had hoped from behind their present covering troops. Statements like Franklin-Bouillon's[2] which you read relate apparently to what should be and not to what is.

Thirdly. I sent Spiers to Clemenceau this morning to explain to him the purpose of my visit. I am to see Clemenceau at six o'clock. Do you observe that Loucheur has been deputed by the French Government to remain at General Foch's Head Quarters for purposes similar to those which you had in view in sending me. I shall see Loucheur today as he is in Paris. I will wire you later when I have learned more. Meanwhile you must take these impressions as provisional. I should like you to show this as all else that I send you to Henry Wilson.

Winston S. Churchill to David Lloyd George: telegram

(*Lloyd George papers*)

29 March 1918 Paris
Very Urgent
Personal & Secret

I had a most satisfactory talk with Clemenceau as I told you on the telephone and every personal facility will be accorded to me.

Spiers has been very helpful. I also saw Loucheur who has been continually with the armies.

[1] Charles John Sackville-West, 1870–1962. Entered Army, 1889. Served as a Captain in South Africa, 1899–1900. Twice wounded on the western front, 1914–16. Major-General, 1917. British Military Representative on the Allied Military Committee, Versailles, 1918–19. Knighted, 1919. Military Attaché, Paris, 1920–4. Lieutenant-Governor of Guernsey, 1925–9. Succeeded his brother as 4th Baron Sackville, 1928.

[2] Henri Franklin-Bouillon, 1870–1939. French journalist. Founded *La Volonté*, 1898. Entered the Chamber of Deputies, 1910. Minister of State in Charge of Propaganda, 1917. In charge of the secret French negotiations with Mustafa Kemal, 1921–2. Known to the British in Constantinople as 'boiling Frankie'.

The real intentions of the French Government are known to these men and I am completely re-assured as to their policy. It is quite right.

What I cannot judge is whether they will be able to carry it out.

But at any rate, a clear bold policy is being pushed to the utmost limit with all available resources and with the agreement of all concerned. But briefly it is the upwards punch of which I spoke to you.

The number of Divisions to be employed is given in Spier's telegram of this afternoon.

I cannot yet tell how far fact will correspond with intention.

The plan which I have been shown is worthy of the French Army. I do not know what the Hun is going to do.

II. Foch is delighted with his interview with Haig.

His object was to persuade Haig to reinforce debris of 5th Army S of the Somme. In return portions of the 5th Army including 2 Cavalry Divisions are being released from the French line for recuperation. Apparently it is intended to pull 5th Army out and re-constitute it in the neighbourhood SE of Amiens. I think that there is a great task for you to see that the rebuilding of the Army is backed by all the power of the State.

Munitions will be abundant but gunners, technical troops, Officers, Sergeants, as well as the enormous drafts must be found by you. It is a problem deserving your personal study because in a month or six weeks this Army such as it is though now counting for very little might well be the army of reserve and a great factor.

III. They are in good confidence here. Clemenceau of course a tower of strength and courage.

I will get him to back your admirable telegram to Rufus by a message to-morrow and by his seeing Baker.[1]

This is a vital matter.

Loucheur asserts that the Germans have a million men to replace casualties this summer and the conclusion is inevitable unless we can draw on the manhood of America.

[1] Newton Diehl Baker, 1871–1931. Lawyer; City Solicitor, Cleveland, Ohio, 1902–12; Mayor of Cleveland, 1912–16. United States Secretary for War, 1916–21. Member of the Permanent Court of International Justice at The Hague, 1928. In 1936 he published *Why we went to War*.

Winston S. Churchill to Georges Clemenceau

(*Churchill papers: 27/32*)

29 March 1918 Ritz Hotel
Paris

My dear President,

Here is the text of the telegram to America.

The Prime Minister wishes us to appeal to you to back it all you can by a message of your own. He also asks that, if you approve, you still see Mr Baker, American Minister of War, and persuade him to telegraph in support of these proposals.

Yours sincerely,
Winston S. Churchill

Clementine Churchill to Winston S. Churchill

(*Churchill papers: 1/125*)

29 March 1918 33 Eccleston Square

My Darling Winston

I long for news. Montdidier looks bad. Please do not go even within shell-fire range. I am sure it will not help your mission. . . .

Major Spiers to Sir Henry Wilson

(*Spears papers*)

29 March 1918 10 pm
Personal

1) Clemenceau has told G^{n} Pétain that for political reasons he insists that the American Div available should be engaged at the earliest possible moment.
2) G^{n} Pershing has informed G^{n} Pétain that all the American Army in France is at his disposal to do what he likes with.
3) M Clemenceau is most optimistic, his moral is superb, he is convinced that the Germans are now held but states he would fight if necessary every foot of the way back thro' Amiens & then thro' Paris. He has adopted Foch's point of view that no more ground must now be given.
4) Mr Churchill has made a good personal impression on Clemenceau.

Sir Henry Wilson: diary

(*Wilson papers*)

30 March 1918 36 Eaton Place

A good deal of rain which is *good.* LG came to my room again this morning at 10 am for gossip. The news is not so good as the Boches have pushed the French out of Montdidier & have got nearly into Moreuil. Winston, from Paris, reports well on the Tiger, & on the pace at which the French are coming up. . . .

At this morning's Cabinet LG read out portions of 2 wires rec[d] from Winston. Tonight in our walk, Milner referred to this & said he was going to tell LG that either he (M) must have LG's full confidence or else he would leave the Gov[t] I agreed with Milner. This sending Winston over—first, with the idea of his going to Foch which I killed, & then to Clemenceau is a direct snub to Milner who, after all, represented the Gov[t] at Doullens & has, all along, been the Cabinet Member at Versailles.

Philip Sassoon to Lord Esher

(*Esher papers*)

30 March 1918 GHQ France

But what does it matter that we are at bay before Amiens when we hear that in 'Mesopotamia our prisoners now total nearly 4000 and the pursuit has been continued beyond Ana'!! It makes me blind with rage. As the M Post put it rather well: 'what boots it that the English are crossing the Jordan if the Germans are crossing the Somme'. We have been promised 170,000 men from home—of which 80,000 are leave men. The remainder will not fill our losses—& then—*basta. Nothing* to fall back on. It is serious. . . .

DH saw Clemenceau yesterday. He is a fine old fighter, & what luck it is to have him there instead of some straw Painlevé or some fathomless Briand. A shell dropped on a church in Paris—from this long distance Krupp gun—& killed *80.* Clemenceau said it was a good thing as it had knocked all this peace talk out of them!

Clementine Churchill to Winston S. Churchill

(*Churchill papers: 1/125*)

30 March 1918 Lullenden

My Darling

The Prime Minister rang me up last night on the telephone to tell me your news—I am so relieved that you are confident as the newspapers tho' repeating again & again that we are 'holding them' are rather depressing.

I was grieved to read of all the people killed in Church on Good Friday. I do hope that when the long range guns start firing that you take cover. . .

Winston S. Churchill to David Lloyd George: telegram

(*Lloyd George papers*)

30 March 1918. Midnight Paris
Secret & Personal

All day I have been on the Somme Montdidier front with Clemenceau and have seen all the commanders including Pétain and Foch. The battle from Moreuil to Montdidier and round the corner to Lassigny has been very heavy. Both east and south enemy gained some ground employing 13 division including 5 fresh ones on the Moreuil Montdidier front alone. His artillery has now again become powerful. Very heavy attacks Moreuil Montdidier twice repulsed but some ground gained third time.

General Debeney[1] the commander here hopes to complete during to-morrow regular line of battle, but owing to haste with which they were transported his divisions are short of artillery and still shorter of shells. Units of 5th Army not seriously attacked on sector Somme Moreuil. The troops are worn out and deadened by what they have gone through. They hold the front and obey orders but are not doing much fighting. In many cases the divisions are only skeletons. There are many stragglers. However they have several hundred guns and cavalry corps which has not been much knocked and has preserved its strength about is near by. That this front

[1] Marie-Eugène Debeney, 1864–1943. Entered the French Army, 1886. Chief of Staff of the 1st Army, 1914–15. Général de Brigade, commanding the 57th Infantry Brigade, 1915; the 25th Infantry Division, 1915–16; the 38th Army Corps, 1916; the 32nd Army Corps, 1916. Général de Division commanding the 7th Army, 1916–17. Major Général of the Group of Armies of the North and North-East, 1917. Commanded the 1st Army, 1917–19. As a result of his methods, the verb 'to deb' came to mean the method of timing your own advance in such a way that your neighbour advanced first, thereby lessening the pressure on your own section. Chief of the General Staff (in succession to General Buat), 1924–6.

will be heavily attacked tomorrow is considered probable. All these facts certainly justify evident anxiety of Debeney and Rawlinson. The next few days must be critical like phases of the 1st battle of Ypres.

2. French are doing their very utmost sending whole available reserves as fast as they can come up to west and south of invasion angle. Nothing more can be done than what they are doing. German forces are, however, very strong though tired. They have more than 30 divisions in angle Somme–Montdidier–Noyon and fresh divisions pushed forward at special points. My impression, having regard to the weakness of 5th Army and its growing exhaustion, is that even when all French reserves are up the most we can expect at present is to slow down and stop the advance. Tomorrow I will go again and perhaps with more knowledge I shall form a more encouraging view. At Moreuil Seely distinguished himself.[1]
3. Enemy, from his present position, can shell Amiens and long (group omitted) of Amiens–Paris railway by bringing up medium long-range guns. He will certainly do this in a few days. Amiens has already been much damaged by bombs, and is largely deserted. I do not expect we shall get much more out of it anyhow as a railway centre or base.
4. Our armies require strengthening by every conceivable means. I wonder if there are any spare brigades of Home Defence troops. In the VG schools there are a great many officers and men. You ought to scrub your whole Military organisation and the Navy also, in order to diminish the enemy's superiority.
5. Clemenceau will prepare his telegram to Wilson[2] to-morrow 31st. He is favourable and so is Loucheur. Baker is no longer in Paris. I will press this point again to-morrow morning. Clemenceau is extremely cordial and confidential with me, and splendid in his buoyancy and resolution. He insisted on smelling blood and powder to-day, and only my prudence prevented him from doing more.
6. He is evidently moving towards proposing an enlargement of Foch's charter by adding the word 'direct' to 'co-ordination'. I told him I would let you know what was in his mind, so that you might think it

[1] During 30 March Seely and his Canadian Cavalry Brigade recaptured the Moreuil Ridge, which had fallen into German hands, and which had offered the Germans a chance to cut the Amiens–Paris railway. On 1 April they captured yet more German-held areas. During the course of this second day's fighting two of Seely's horses were killed under him, and he himself was so severely gassed that he was unable to return to active service.

[2] Woodrow Wilson, 1856–1924. President of the United States, 1912–21. In December 1916 he sought to persuade the belligerents to negotiate peace, but in April 1917, following repeated German sinkings of US ships, he obtained a declaration from Congress that a state of war existed with Germany.

over. He does not intend to propose anything new immediately. The first thing is to get out of the present scrape. Perhaps you will tell me what your views are.

Winston S. Churchill to David Lloyd George: telegram

(*Lloyd George papers*)

31 March 1918 9 am Paris
Personal & Secret

However immediate battle goes it seems certain that Huns intend grinding down our armies all through the summer and that there will be no respite. Their superiority in divisions gives them decided advantage. If you deduct 100 divisions from both sides for holding the line, it leaves them with 90 to 60 in the battle areas. Although *roulement* can proceed on both sides, this is a formidable preponderance and it tells more and more as reserves are used up. The decisive factor is the margin. This reflection is my own. I wonder if Wilson thinks it's sound. Loucheur says that Huns have one million men to replace casualties. Tremendous efforts are required not only to replace losses, but to increase the number of formations.

I return to my point about sedentary divisions or brigades, especially the latter which can be rapidly improved and can be put into quiet sectors safely while enemy's effort is fully employed elsewhere. The Belgians and Portuguese can hold line, so can our older men. The machine gun schools must have large numbers of very useful machine gunners. The Royal Naval Air Service is full of technical people. There are very large training establishments in England, the personnel of which should be scrutinized. There are swarms of unwounded officers. Remember the Navy increased its complements after I left by 25% above the full approved War establishment. Their whole use of man power is luxurious. The fighting lines is the weakest part of our immense organisation.

Fighting men are the need. I am told that one of the reasons for the break through was that though very fine trenches and second and third lines had been dug all over the place there were too few men to occupy them.

Winston S. Churchill to Clementine Churchill

(*Spencer-Churchill papers*)

31 March 1918 Ritz Hotel
Paris

My darling,

I hope LG will show you my telegrams wh give the best account of my activities.

Yesterday was vy interesting, for I saw with Clemenceau *all* the commanders:—Haig, Foch, Pétain, Weygand,[1] Rawlinson etc; & heard from each the position explained. The old man is vy gracious to me & talks in the most confidential way. He is younger even than I am! and insisted on being taken into the outskirts of the action wh was proceeding N of Moreuil.

Seely's Brigade had just stormed the wood above the village & were being attacked by the Huns there. Stragglers, wounded horses, blood & explosives gave a grim picture of war. I fiinally persuaded the old tiger to come away from what he called '*un moment délicieux*'.

We dined with Pétain in his sumptuous train and I was much entertained by Clemenceau. He is an extraordinary character. Every word he says—particularly general observations on life & morals—is worth listening to. His spirit & energy indomitable. 15 hours yesterday over rough roads at high speed in motor cars. I was tired out—& he is 76!

He makes rather the same impression on me as Fisher: but much more efficient, & just as ready to turn round & bite! I shall be vy wary.

'This battle fares like to the morning's war,
When gathering clouds[2] contend with growing light'

(You shd read the passage in Henry VIth part III) I think we ought to hold them for the time being, but a most formidable prolonged tremendous struggle is before us—if we are to save our souls alive.

This afternoon after I have finished my business with Clemenceau (about the American troops) I shall go to other parts of the battle front between Montdidier & Lassigny wh I did not see yesterday & I hope to see Generals

[1] Maxime Weygand, 1867–1965. Entered the French Army as a Cavalry Officer, 1887. Chief of Staff to General Foch, 1914–23. French Military Representative at Versailles, 1918. He received an honorary knighthood in 1918. Head of the French Military Mission to Poland, 1920. French High Commissioner in Syria, 1923–4. Commander in Chief of the French Army, 1931–5 and May–June 1940. Minister of National Defence, June–September 1940. Governor-General of Algeria and Delegate-General of the Vichy Government in French Africa, 1940–1. Prisoner of the Germans, 1942–5; liberated from prison by the Allies, but subsequently imprisoned in France, 1945–8. A military historian, he published a biography of Foch in 1947.

[2] Shakespeare actually wrote: 'dying clouds'.

Fayolle & Humbert[1] both of whom I know & who command there. I shall run no unnecessary risks.

Beloved it is yr birthday tomorrow. This I fear will not reach you in time—so slow are the couriers now that the train service is interrupted. I send you my fondest love and my dearest wishes for long & happy years. Do write to me & let me know all about our affairs. . . .

Tender love, Your devoted
W

Leopold Amery: diary

(*Amery papers*)

31 March 1918

Motored up to Paris to see Churchill. Having first suggested myself to join him on a trip he was doing round the Front I afterwards thought I wouldn't, as these stray tourists are not popular with staffs in a crisis. I found Bendor[2] shared that view very strongly and was going to ask me not to come. He said Churchill couldn't realize that he wasn't popular on these occasions, just because people received him reasonably politely.

We lunched at the Ritz and I talked over Irish conscription with Churchill who is sound on it—complained that if only my party had not insisted on hounding him out of the front rank he might have saved the country from so many disastrous hesitations. He showed me a very good wire from LG to Wilson asking for 120,000 American infantry a month. He is full of admiration for old Clemenceau with whom he spent 15 hours in a car yesterday, going right up into the fire zone and walking about.

Winston S. Churchill to David Lloyd George: telegram

(*Churchill papers: 17/15*)

31 March 1918 Midnight — Paris

Personal & Secret

I visited today 3rd French Army, General Humbert, also General Fayolle commanding group of armies in battle area, and dined with Pétain. Since

[1] Georges Louis Humbert, 1862–1921. Entered the French Army, 1883. Served in Indo-China, 1885; Madagascar, 1895 and Morocco, 1913–14. Général de Division, 1914. Commanded the 32nd Army Corps, 1914–15; the Army of Lorraine, 1915; the 3rd Army, July 1915–June 1919. Inspecteur Général (Paris), 1919. Governor of Strasbourg and Commandant of Alsace, 1919–21.

[2] The 2nd Duke of Westminster (see page 9, note 3).

yesterday's battle we have virtually gained 24 hours. No serious attack took place to-day, which can only be due to heavy Hun losses, yesterday and on Southern side of angle, namely Montdidier–Lassigny. French are now well established and solidly backed with guns. Southward thrust does not now cause anxiety.

Time has been very valuable on Montdidier–Somme sector and whole position should be greatly strengthened by to-morrow morning. Fifth Army has lost a little ground and French are grumbling. There is always some friction at junction of Armies and when this junction is critical point of hostile attack difficulties become pronounced.

Rawlinson wishes to withdraw his men to re-organise, and the French declare that he should hold on to the very small portion of the front in his charge. I think these difficulties will settle themselves. General Fayolle expects battle to continue in critical condition for good many days, but every day gained adds to our advantages. The enemy, however, is already shelling various Railway stations on the main Amiens–Paris line. Every phase of a battle like this brings its own problem—first, men; then, field guns; then, heavy guns; then, munitions. Now roads are coming into view. These difficulties are however present on the other side too.

Winston S. Churchill to Georges Clemenceau

(*Churchill papers: 27/32*)

31 March 1918

My dear President,

I should like to be able to tell Lloyd George what you will do about the American telegram. This is the moment to press Mr Wilson. It will be all the better if your telegram strikes a different note and comes from a different point of view, so long as it has the same object namely 120,000 Americans a month. Let us strike while the iron is hot. I don't see how else we can get the life energy which the armies will need this summer. I propose starting out again this morning at about 10.30, but of course I can put this off if you want to see me. It was a memorable day yesterday in your company & I was touched by the kindness and confidence with which you have received me.

Yours sincerely,
Winston S. Churchill

April 1918

Winston S. Churchill to David Lloyd George: telegram

(*Lloyd George papers*)

1 April 1918 Paris
9 am
Secret & Personal

Last night General Pétain explained to me the system by which he was thinning his line, so as to secure the greatest possible number of divisions for battle action.

Territorial regiments of older men which correspond to our brigades, are interpolated between ordinary divisions in the line and covered by their artillery. By this means on the front of every three or four divisions one division is set free for battle.

Surely some such system should be adopted by us. I have repeatedly urged the creation of divisions or brigades of older men. The volunteers are full of excellent material for this purpose. The organization of, say, sixty battalions of older men and men of lower categories if started now ought not to take more than two months. They would thus come into the line to relieve mobile troops during critical months of June, July and August. It is held as certain that the Germans will pursue this struggle to a final decision all through the summer and at present their resources are larger than ours. It would be fatal to be lulled by the talk about depression in Germany leading to peace. If we are to escape destruction every effort must be made.

I am thankful to see you are firm on the question of Ireland.

Sir Henry Wilson: diary

(*Wilson papers*)

1 April 1918 36 Eaton Place

Long wire from Reading saying that Pres: Wilson would accede to our request of 120,000 Inf: for 4 mos: (each month) but the fool put in a warning in his final para that if conscription is passed for Ireland the position in America would become *very difficult*. Of course LG fastened on this as a sort of excuse of having Ireland out of his Bill. . . .

Since March 21st we have lost some 140,000 Inf & have only got some 101,000 to replace with. France can take a punishment of 200,000. Germany of 500,000. I am now taking 20,000 BI men from Home Defence leaving 39,000 untrained boys. Rather a risk!

Winston S. Churchill to David Lloyd George: telegram

(*Lloyd George papers*)

1 April 1918 Paris
Midnight
Personal & Secret—Not for circulation

To be given to Prime Minister as soon as he is awake.

Clemenceau wants you, if you can, to come here at once. Considerable difficulties about the high command which you will readily understand have arisen. There has been a serious misunderstanding between the three commanders Foch, Haig, Rawlinson about the responsibility for the front at the junction of the armies. The point of junction is always delicate and when it is also the point of main hostile attack now impending extremely important questions are raised. To-day Clemenceau has personally adjusted some of the difficulties, but he now asks me to remind you of your promise to come and appeals to you to do so. I think it very desirable. You and he together can make a good settlement and no-one else can. It will be also a good thing for you to take a view of the British situation from a different stand-point.

Please telephone me what you will do, early to-morrow. I shall remain here meanwhile. Many congratulations on your American achievement.

Sir Henry Wilson: diary

(*Wilson papers*)

2 April 1918

Winston wires from Paris urging LG to come over at once. Much talk with LG, & telephoning to Winston, Tit Willow,[1] Spiers & Lawrence at GHQ. . . .

[1] Major-General C J Sackville-West (see page 284, note 1).

Telephoned Winston to meet us at Boulogne 7.30 am tomorrow. I am anxious to get Winston back, he is doing mischief in France. A charming note from Miss Stevenson[1] to LG on this subject!

Sir Henry Wilson: diary

(*Wilson papers*)

3 April 1918

Left Folkestone (*perfect* morning) at 7.15 am. . . . Met Winston at Boulogne. . . . Winston came nearly to Montreuil with us. LG, Winston & I in the car. Agreed Gough must be recalled. Winston said Clemenceau wanted Foch's position strengthened. I agreed but not up to C in C especially as the Tiger wished this principally to allow Foch to coerce Pétain & not Haig who was working smoothly.

We picked up Haig at Montreuil Winston having got out before we arrived there. . . . LG told Haig that Gough must go.

Lunched Beauvais. 1.30 pm. The Tiger came & sat with us & after lunch the Tiger, LG & I had a talk. Tiger produced a note as follows: 'Les Gouvernments Britannique et Français conferent au Gen: Foch la direction stratigique des operations militaires sur le front occidental. . . .'

Motored back to Boulogne, having dinner on the roadside before Montreuil. Then Winston & Ben d'Or joined us at Boulogne. . .

Winston S. Churchill to General Dallolio: telegram

(*Churchill papers: 15/48*)

5 April 1918

I am grateful to your Excellency for your true hearted message of comradeship and encouragement.[2] I shall send it to all the Munition Works of Great Britain and Ireland. Mr Gladstone many years ago made our people understand the cruel wrongs done by Austria to Italy and the fine part played by

[1] Frances Louise Stevenson, 1888–1972. Schoolteacher. Private Secretary to Lloyd George, 1913–43. She married Lloyd George in 1943. Countess Lloyd George of Dwyfor, 1945. She published her memoirs, *The Years That Are Past*, in 1967. Her brother, P W J Stevenson, was killed in action on the western front in May 1915.

[2] On 2 April General Dallolio had telegraphed to Churchill from Rome: 'In following with eagerness the heroic fight I send to you best wishes and cheers with heart both of soldier and ally.'

your gallant nation in this struggle for right and freedom is appreciated and admired by our workers no less than by our soldiers. The hand of the spoiler is stretched out over Europe and the foundations of our existence as free peoples are challenged. We recognise that this is the supreme effort of the Hun Empires to secure world domination. We are sure we shall break their purpose. Our resources in munitions will be sufficient for all the needs of the armies and it will not be necessary to reduce in any particular the supplies with which we have promised to furnish you and on which you are relying.

Ministry of Munitions message to The Press Bureau

(*Churchill papers: 15/116*)

5 April 1918

The following telegram has been sent by Mr Churchill to Mr Brindley, the Manager of the Ponders End Shell Factory in reply to a telegram informing him of the output of 6″ shells and 6″ howitzer guns from the Factory during the week from the 27th March to the 3rd April—

Considering the very high standard of production consistently maintained at Ponders End in ordinary times the results of your Easter effort by which your weekly output of shells and guns was nearly doubled are really wonderful. There is no more popular shell in the British Army than the 6 inch and no better weapon than the 6 inch Howitzer. The effects of this shell with a very sensitive fuse upon the German masses in the present battle have been extraordinary. I was told that near Albert last week 150 of these shells wrought indescribable havoc upon a heavy German column. So when you are turning them out in so many thousands you are playing a very direct part in the struggle. Give my hearty thanks to all and be careful not to let the women overdo themselves.

Winston S. Churchill

War Cabinet: minutes

(*Cabinet papers: 23/6*)

IRISH CONSCRIPTION

6 April 1918 10 Downing St

MR CHURCHILL: . . . The enforcing of conscription on Ireland is a rupturing of political associations, and involves a complete new orientation of antagonisms, and therefore it is folly not to see how grave that decision is. I could not agree to that unless our Unionist friends come with us on the other measure, which profoundly affects opinion here, in Ireland, and in the United States. It is hard that we should commit ourselves to conscription unless we can count on cordial agreement among our Unionist colleagues that they will go forward in support of Home Rule with equal energy.

DR ADDISON expressed concurrence with what Mr Churchill had said.

THE PRIME MINISTER: That is the policy of the Government. . . .

MR HERBERT FISHER:[1] Are you definitely satisfied that there is a military advantage in applying conscription to Ireland? I feel absolutely with you as to the bad effect on English public opinion of continuing to exempt Ireland; but we should look at it as a cold military proposition. English public opinion is sound. Our artisans will do their duty. You have to decide whether it is worth your while to enforce conscription in Ireland and thereby perhaps obtain disaffected elements for your army.

LORD DERBY: They will be distributed through the army.

THE PRIME MINISTER: That is the one consideration that chiefly worried me. Is it worth while, in a military sense? You will get 50,000, at any rate, at a minimum, who will fight. These five divisions will be made up of excellent material, of young men up to 25, at a time when we are taking old men.

MR CHURCHILL: I have not met one soldier in France who does not think we shall get good fighting material from Ireland. I think the decision of the War Cabinet is a battlefield decision, but a wise one.

H. A. L. Fisher: diary

(*Fisher papers*)

6 April 1918

Bob Cecil doubtful whether he can accept a Home Rule Bill which he has not seen! I raise question whether I think conscription will really produce

[1] Herbert Albert Laurens Fisher, 1865–1940. Historian. He published his first book, *The Medieval Empire* in 1898, and a further seven works by 1914. Member of the Royal Commission on the Public Services of India, 1912–15 and of the Government Committee on alleged German outrages, 1915. Liberal MP, 1916–18 and 1918–26. President of the Board of Education, 1916–22. A British delegate to the League of Nations Assembly, 1920–2. Warden of New College, Oxford from 1925 until his death. He published his *History of Europe* in 3 volumes in 1935. Governor of the BBC, 1935–9. Order of Merit, 1937. He published two volumes of memoirs, *Pages from the Past* (1939) and *An Unfinished Autobiography* (1940). He died after being run down by a lorry, while on his way to preside over an Appeal Tribunal for conscientious objectors.

the desired military result. LG says that after a week's anxious doubt he has come to the conclusion that it can. Derby says we shall get 50,000 good troops. Churchill vehement for the immediate forcing through of the proposal —'a battlefield decision'. Barnes says he can only agree to Conscription if Home Rule is really carried. We agree, however, that while the Government is to press both measures, it cannot treat them as interdependent.

Dr Addison: diary

(Addison papers)

6 April 1918

. . . The opposition to conscription for Ireland is vehement and strong as it is and, although from what we hear, it will not be much minimised by the prompt introduction of the Home Rule proposal, it appears to me to be not only the only possible, but the only just accompaniment of the Man-Power proposals as well as the redemption of what is a binding undertaking to give effect substantially to the general findings of the Convention.

I am glad to say that both Churchill and Barnes took a firm line on this question, but there is a dangerous and difficult point ahead of us. We must wait and see how the debate goes in Parliament, but obviously not a moment must be lost in bringing forward the Irish proposals.

Winston S. Churchill to H. H. Asquith

(Churchill papers: 2/103)

6 April 1918 Ministry of Munitions
Private

My dear Asquith,

I think it will be quite easy to arrange things so that Oc's[1] appointment throws no burden of any kind on his recovery of strength. Bridges[2] held the position for some time before he was able to take effective control. But he read up the papers & was fully informed of what was going forward. Anyhow

[1] Arthur Melland Asquith, 1883–1939. Known as 'Oc'. Sudan Civil Service, 1906–11. In business, 1911–14. Enlisted in the Royal Naval Volunteer Reserve, 1914. Served in the Royal Naval Division at Antwerp, Dardanelles and western front, 1914–16. Four times wounded. Controller, Trench Warfare Department, Ministry of Munitions, 1918. Member of Council, Ministry of Labour, 1919. Company director.

[2] Major-General Tom Bridges (see page 583, note 1).

I am delighted Oc will come, & I am writing to ask him to come & see me when he is next in town, so that the matter can be settled.

I have just got back from the French battle-front which I have been watching for the last week on behalf of the Govt. I saw all the generals & was given the fullest information. The position is for the moment quite stabilized. The line of battle is now regularly formed & satisfactory arrangements have been made at the junction of the armies. The main strength of the French army stands between Paris & the further advance of the enemy. Amiens of course will be under long range fire, & its extremely important communicns are compromised tho not at present interrupted. Both sides are now supremely interested in resolving the battle in their southern area & will make it a trial of strength like Verdun only more so. We must also expect to be attacked from La Bassée to Arras. If the enemy succeeded there it wd be vy unpleasant. If he does not succeed, at least he wd keep our reserves tied down. These are the most likely developments.

The American troops—as soldiers & not as divisions—will be needed in large numbers if we are to survive the summer, & so will every man we can claw out of these islands.

I have been able to replace everything in the munitions sphere without difficulty. Guns, Tanks, aeroplanes will all be ahead of personnel. We have succeeded in pulling the gun position round so completely since last summer that we can deliver 2000 guns as fast as they can be shipped.

It has been touch & go on the front. We stood for some days within an ace of destruction.

Winston S. Churchill to Louis Loucheur

(*Churchill papers: 15/48*)

6 April 1918 Ministry of Munitions

I am much concerned at the attitude taken by the French representatives at the Conference held last week on the Red Cross suggestion of the willingness of the German Government to abandon the use of poison gas. Apparently France is strongly in favour of our offering to give up this form of warfare, or at any rate of accepting a German offer. I do not believe this is to our advantage. I hope that next year we shall have a substantial advantage over them in this field. Anyhow I would not trust the German word. They would be very glad to see us relax our present preparations, allow our organisation to fall into desuetude; and then after an interval, in which they had elaborated new methods, they would allege that we had broken the arrangement and, perhaps even without this pretext, resume gas-warfare on the largest scale.

I am on the contrary in favour of the greatest possible development of gas-warfare, and of the fullest utilisation of the winds, which favour us so much more than the enemy.

The report of the Conference will soon be received, presumably by the French and British Foreign Offices. I hope before any decision is taken upon it, or any answer is given to the Red Cross, the French and British Ministers of Munitions and the General Staffs of the two countries may be given the fullest opportunity of expressing their considered opinions.

Winston S. Churchill to Sir Douglas Haig

(*Churchill papers: 2/103*)

12 April 1918

I cannot resist sending you a message of sympathy and sincere admiration for the magnificent defence which you are making day after day[1] and of profound confidence in the result.

Sir Douglas Haig to Winston S. Churchill

(*Churchill papers: 2/103*)

13 April 1918 General Headquarters
Personal

Heartiest thanks for your friendly telegram. Army is in a most determined mood and good spirits. Your old division under Tudor has been doing wonders.[2] Many thanks for the splendid assistance given by your Department.

[1] On 9 April 1918 the Germans had broken through the British lines on the Laventie front, between Ypres and La Bassée. But although they captured Ploegsteert and Messines, Ypres itself remained in Allied hands, and although on 12 April the main force of the advance reached the Forest of Nieppe, by 30 April the line was stabilized.

[2] The 9th (Scottish) Division, under Major-General H H Tudor (under whom Churchill had served in 1916), had lost more than half its fighting strength at the time of the first German breakthrough in March. Nevertheless on 10 April 1917, while still in the process of refitting, it bore the brunt of the German attack on Messines. On 16 April the Division was again at the centre of a German poison gas attack, but held out against superior forces. On 26 April it was withdrawn into reserve.

Winston S. Churchill to David Lloyd George: unsent draft

(*Churchill papers: 2/103*)

15 April 1918 Ministry of Munitions

My dear Prime Minister,

I do not often write to you because you are always so ready to see me & talk things over. But there are some things it is better to write than to say. Last time I wrote was in Jany to warn you about the danger of the reduction of the Army on the eve of the new campaign & in the face of the immense German concentration in the West. If you re-read that letter now you will perhaps be inclined to weigh this one.

I am sure you wd be wise to form a regular Cabinet. The Irish question cannot be faced without a political organisation of the Govt, & real comradeship & collective action among those concerned in it. If you try to carry a Home Rule Bill through the House of Commons with yr present system, you will run a vy great risk of defeat, which at this unfavourable war moment wd produce decisive results to yr Administration. On the other hand you are absolutely committed to such a Bill, & if it were abandoned the Government wd lose some of its members. You ought to fortify yourself by a proper Cabinet of responsible Ministers.

On even wider grounds I think the present system is condemned. It is quite right to have a War Council for the day to day settlement of military & administrative business relating to the war, & to relieve other Ministers of their responsibilities in these respects. But the high policy of the State ought not to be settled by so narrow & unrepresentative a body as yr War Cabinet, & I am certain that it will not be long accepted on such a basis.

Take for instance the Emperor Charles'[1] letter, wh I have been reading with growing sorrow that it shd have led to nothing:[2] or the winter decisions about man-power. These were supreme matters, & I am sure that they ought to have been dealt with by a representative Cabinet, & that they wd have gained in treatment had they been so dealt with. Now you are confronted

[1] Charles, 1887–1922. Heir presumptive to the throne of Austria-Hungary from 1906. Commanded the XXth Corps in the 1916 offensive against Italy. Succeeded his great-uncle Franz Josef as Emperor of Austria and King of Hungary on 21 November 1916. Following Austria-Hungary's defeat, he renounced his imperial powers, on 11 November 1918. In exile in Switzerland. In 1921 he twice crossed into western Hungary in an unsuccessful attempt to regain his throne, first in March and then in October. In November 1921 the Hungarian Parliament passed a Dethronement Act, abrogating all his rights. Refused the right of asylum by Switzerland, he was taken by English warship to Madeira, where he died in April 1922.

[2] In April 1918 the tension between Germany and Austria-Hungary reached its height with the publication of a letter which had been written by the Emperor Charles more than a year before, on 24 March 1917, in which he had told his brother-in-law, Sixtus of Parma, that he was ready to support, even in Berlin itself, 'the just claims of France to Alsace-Lorraine'.

with a first-class political issue, involving every section of the House of Commons, & at a time when opinion there is far from good. You have much greater knowledge & political insight than I, & I have no doubt all these things are in your mind. But I am convinced that the moment has come to form a political instrument for definite purposes, & that failure to do so will lead to grave risk of collapse.

Yours always
W

Winston S. Churchill to Dudley Docker: telegram

(*Churchill papers: 15/116*)

17 April 1918 Ministry of Munitions

Express again to all hands my satisfaction at the admirable deliveries. Tell them confidentially not for publication that the losses of tanks have been larger than previously reported but that they have exacted a heavy toll from the Huns in many cases and helped our infantry notably. Explain to them that during the uncertainty of the battle and its intense fierceness, it is not possible for the Tank Corps to make deliveries regularly. The roads are congested, depots are moving, everyone is involved in the fight. When the lull comes there will be a general refitting and that is the moment for which we must have ready the largest possible numbers. I am watching for this moment very carefully. They must not be put off their efforts if tanks accumulate temporarily. The Army is fighting for its life and we are standing by to put new weapons in their hands the very instant they turn to us. Let there be no misunderstanding therefore but only confidence and full steam ahead.

Winston S. Churchill to Duke of Westminster

(*Churchill papers: 2/103*)

22 April 1918 Ministry of Munitions
Private

My dear Benny,

I am delighted you are going to Spain & it will be vy kind of you to give my best respects & very sincere good wishes to the King.[1] I remember the

[1] Leon Fernando Maria Jaime Isidoro Pascual Antonio, 1886–1941. Posthumous son of King Alfonso XII of Spain, he was proclaimed King at birth (as Alfonso XIII). He married

deeply interesting talks I had with him in the spring of 1914, & have often thought about them & all he said to me then. I have watched all through the war with its ups & downs & perils to everyone the admirable skill & prudence with wh he has steered the ship. We have I think understood in England the difficulties of the Spanish position. I am sure I understand; & U have never underrated them. Still I believe in the end the force of events & the march of history will sweep away the difficulties, & offer a great & splendid opportunity to Spain & her wise Sovereign.

I hope you will tell the King that I am absolutely confident of the final result. I do not think there will be any compromise. It will be a clear-cut result. Everything shows that the English-speaking world is settling down to war & becoming more fiercely devoted to it month by month. Presently the British will be more bitter than the French. Later on the Americans will be more bitter even than the English. In the end we shall beat the heart out of Prussian militarism.

It is such a good thing my dear Benny that you shd be in Spain. I only wish I cd accompany you; for it wd indeed be a pleasure to me to meet once again a Prince who has been guided & preserved through so many dangers for the accomplishment of the highest form of service to the world.

With every good wish for the success of yr journey

Believe me, Yr sincere friend

W

Sir Henry Rawlinson to Winston S. Churchill

(*Churchill papers: 15/145*)

22 April 1918

Headquarters
Fourth Army

My dear Winston,

Can you give me any idea when we may expect to have available shell filled with Mustard gas? I ask because we have had very severe casualties lately from this form of projectile in the Villiers Bretoneaux area, the enemy having put over some 15,000 rounds of varying calibres during the night of 17–18 April. We had some 1400 men gassed and there can be no doubt that this form of projectile is very effective especially in a defensive battle. The

---

Victoria Eugenie, a granddaughter of Queen Victoria, in 1906. Narrowly escaped death in a bomb incident in Paris, 1905; and again on his wedding day in Madrid, 1906. Fired at three times, but escaped unhurt, in Madrid, 1913. He was outlawed, and fled the country, following the Republican majority in the 1931 elections. He died in exile in Rome.

men naturally feel that the enemy has a distinct advantage over us in possessing mustard gas and the contention of our chemists that our own lethal shell are still more effective, a contention with which I do not agree, is no satisfactory answer. We feel that we are at a disadvantage in this respect and morale suffers in consequence. The mustard gas should be used in conjunction with lethal shell. The Bosche puts them in mixed and in bursts of fire lasting 5 or 10 minutes with some 70 or 80% of mustard gas in each burst of fire.

I am very anxious to get this form of shell, for with it we can make a selected area of ground impossible to attack over. In defending Amiens the power to do this would be of the very highest value, for there are only certain avenues of approach open to the Bosche and if one could deny him these his chances of success would be zero.

Yours sincerely
H. Rawlinson

War Cabinet: minutes

(*Cabinet papers: 23/6*)

24 April 1918

MR CHURCHILL stated that, in order to secure the release of the largest possible number of men for the army and to maintain the greatest possible output of munitions, it was indispensable that there should be a greater control of the residuum of labour left behind in the workshops. It was necessary to bring great pressure to bear on everyone to enrol as a War Munitions Volunteer. Those who refused, and were not available to be moved about as required, should be made to understand that they stood a greater chance of being recruited for the army. This proposal had been put to the Trade Union Advisory Committee, and they were whole-heartedly in favour of steps being taken to increase the mobility of the men remaining available for the munitions industry.

He did not ask the Trade Union officials to commit themselves to an approval of what might be called 'industrial conscription'; he contented himself with the general resolution set forth in the memorandum before the Cabinet. The Advisory Committee were in favour of prompt action being taken. Mr Churchill added that the removal of absolute protection from trades and groups of workmen had resulted in very striking improvement in output and in methods of production. The proposals which he now was putting forward included the power to regulate and restrict employers in the use of labour of important types of which there was a shortage, and of controlling the engagement of labour by firms who are using labour uneconomically.

MR ROBERTS[1] said that he was in favour of the proposals, provided only moral pressure was used to secure enrolment. If there were any open threat of compulsion there was sure to be trouble. He thought the present moment propitious, and, if action were taken promptly, the proposals might be accepted without much opposition.

MR CHAMBERLAIN[2] suggested that the public announcement, as drafted in the memorandum, was rather in the nature of a threat to the men who did not enrol. It would be better so to word it as to provide a special encouragement to the man who does enrol, and has shown himself willing to place himself at the disposal of the State.

The War Cabinet decided—

> To approve the proposals of the Minister of Munitions, subject to the modification in phrasing suggested by Mr Chamberlain.

Winston S. Churchill to Sir Auckland Geddes: telegram

(*Churchill papers: 15/107*)

26 April 1918 Ministry of Munitions

Voluntary enlistment from certain firms has attained such serious proportions as to endanger output of certain vital munitions. I press you very strongly to agree that your officers be instructed refuse voluntary enlistments from certain firms where recruitment should be confined to releases under MARO scheme. Am convinced necessity of this measure. Fear otherwise it may be necessary instruct cessation of releases till numbers and effect voluntary recruitment ascertained. I cannot possibly release men except by a definitely organised process. If output is in danger of being deranged by promiscuous volunteering the regular recruitment will be prejudiced.

[1] George Henry Roberts, 1869–1928. Son of an agricultural labourer. Joined the Independent Labour Party, 1886. Labour MP, 1906–23. Parliamentary Secretary to the Board of Trade, 1916–18. Minister of Labour, 1917–18. Food Controller, 1919–20. Unsuccessfully contested Norwich as a Conservative candidate, 1923.

[2] Austen Chamberlain had entered the War Cabinet on 18 April 1918, as a Minister without Portfolio, in succession to Lord Milner (who became Secretary of State for War).

General Tudor to Winston S. Churchill

(Churchill papers: 2/103)

27 April 1918

My dear Winston,

May I call you that, I have known you so many years now—thanks so much for your letter, and all the kind things you say. I personally have done so little. The stouthearted Jocks & S Africans have done it all. It is very good of you to write as you must be full of work. The C in C has been most kind to us, & it has had a great effect in helping the men to endure, when really almost at the limit of endurance.

The Hun owes his success mainly to 2 factors, numbers and a skilful use of fog or smoke shell, without which numbers could have only meant more slaughter. M. guns don't get a shot until he is 20 or 30 yds off in large numbers. He makes a gap, his numbers pour through and are round in rear of the troops, who have held their front. There *ought* to be a future for *fast* tanks in this fog fighting, on the roads anyway. I wish we had had some whippets here: I have not believed in them, except originally as a great surprise used in large numbers. But I feel sure a few fast ones could have done great work here, especially if constructed to give good observation. In fog fighting artillery fire is negligible, as the Hun doesn't know where his men have got to once the attack starts.

So the tank ought to have a look in. Do come & see us if you can. You know I am never too busy, even with a battle on. We are out of the line now since this morning, but I have not actually moved my HQr. 2 of my brigades are out. Their morale is as high as ever, & if we get rest & reinforcements, we shall soon be all right again. When the yanks level up numbers, so that our line is shorter, and our divisions can get rest & training we shall be safe. Then when we have preponderance in numbers, we too can do the smoke attack trick and crumple him up. I hope we shall not stop till we do. It is marvellous the way you have replaced all the guns. Things will get worse before they get better, but that they will get better I am convinced.

Yrs ever
H. H. Tudor

May 1918

Winston S. Churchill to Louis Loucheur

(*Churchill papers: 15/48*)

1 May 1918 Ministry of Munitions

I send you herewith copies of two telegrams which have reached us from the United States which appear to me to be of equal importance and urgency.

In my view, we must do everything in our power to encourage the United States to pour troops into France as rapidly as possible, by making them feel that there will be no lack of artillery from one source or another to sustain American infantry when they enter the line of battle.

It will be a great mistake to depart in any way from the broad principles which we agreed to work on at the Paris conference in November last. It was then arranged that the Americans should look to France for Field Artillery, and to England for the heavier natures. The question of the French 155 or the British 6″ Howitzer was not finally decided. The French 155 is the weapon at present adopted by the American Army, for the manufacture of which you are largely responsible: but we have also an available supply of 6″ Howitzers, and if the Americans wish to increase the numbers of these medium guns available there would be no insuperable objection to their using both types.

As the result of these discussions, you undertook to supply a large number of Field guns: we undertook to supply 208 8″ and 9·2″ equipments; and we both have resources available to meet the requirements of medium natures.

Since then various events have happened. The Italian disaster has made large inroads on our joint stocks. The heavy losses of guns in the present battle have also exposed the British Ministry of Munitions to unexpected strains. Still, I am glad to say that we have every reason to believe that after replacing all losses and providing for the steady carrying out of our programmes of increase till they reach our full establishments, including the 25% reserve, we shall be able to carry out punctually and fully our undertaking to the Americans in respect of the 208 heavy guns. I have no doubt you are in a similar good position in regard to the 75's and 155's.

The question now arises—What can we do in response to these American telegrams *additional* to what we have already undertaken? I have considered this matter very carefully. I do not think it is worth while offering them any British field artillery. I have not got any very large amount, and they can get these weapons much better from you. I am best off in regard to the 6″ Howitzers, of which I can provide by the 1st November, if desired, 225 equipments; ie the quantity required to arm 9 divisions (180 equipments) with 25% (45 pieces) in reserve. Thereafter I could maintain the establishment thus created for an indefinite period. Thirdly, in addition to the 208 heavy guns which we have promised, I could supply, if need be, 50 additional equipments by the 1st November and 50 more by the 1st January.

I propose to telegraph to our Ambassador at Washington in this sense, and I attach a copy of the telegram. I shall be glad if you will let me know what supplies of Field artillery you can provide beyond what you have already undertaken.

The moral which we want to convey to the Americans is 'Come over as quickly as possible; we can provide you with plenty of artillery for all the men you send.'

I have set out this full exposition of my views being sure we shall be in general accord. Pray let me hear from you at your early convenience.

I am looking forward to seeing you and other French colleagues and friends when I come over for the Inter-Allied Conference later in this month.

With all good wishes to you personally, and very great confidence in the general situation.

Believe me
Winston S. Churchill

Winston S. Churchill to David Lloyd George

(*Churchill papers: 2/103*)

4 May 1918 Ministry of Munitions

My dear Prime Minister,

I always do my very best to help you & to give you my true opinion & advice when you ask for it. But I cannot undertake any responsibility for policy. Under the present system the War Cabinet alone have the power of decision & the right of regular & continuous consultation. Their burden cannot be shared by departmental ministers occasionally invited to express an opinion on particular subjects or phases.

Certainly I will never accept political responsibility without recognised regular power.

I do not seek this power. As you know I do not think the new system which Carson invented of governing without a regular Cabinet is sound or likely to be successful. But I am quite content in this war crisis to continue to serve you & the Government to the best of my ability in an administrative capacity, without troubling myself about political or party combinations, & to offer you personally in your intense labours for the national safety every aid & encouragement that a sincere friend can give.

It was a very warm-hearted & courageous act of yours to include me in yr Government in the face of so much Conservative hostility, & I have ever had yr interests at heart. But I shd fail in the frankness which our long & intimate friendship requires were I not—in view of our serious conversation yesterday—to make my position clear.

Yrs always
W

Winston S. Churchill: message to munitions workers[1]

(Reported in 'The Times', 8 May 1918)

7 May 1918

If we win, the cruel system which has let loose these horrors on the world will perish amid the execrations of those who are its dupes or slaves. Then and only then will there be a lasting peace.

Winston S. Churchill: Cabinet note

(Churchill papers: 15/33)

8 May 1918 Ministry of Munitions
Secret

The Secretary to the War Cabinet has circulated a paper (GT 4434) dated the 4th May urging Departments to settle differences among themselves before circulating memoranda to the War Cabinet. This has always been done by the Ministry of Munitions. The only cases where memoranda are circulated to the Cabinet are those in which there is no prospect of obtaining any agreement between Departments. Since the Ministry of Munitions came

[1] This message was addressed to the National Brassworkers and Metal Mechanics.

into existence the divergence of policy between the Admiralty and the Labour Department of the Ministry of Munitions has been a fertile cause of difficulty. The Admiralty, fortified by a War Cabinet decision according them absolute priority and immunity, have steadily declined to assimilate their practice in dilution and substitution to that of the Ministry of Munitions. No means exist for carrying the discussion any further.

Quite recently Mr Barnes suggested a conference on this very subject between the Admiralty, the Ministry of Munitions, and the Ministry of Labour; but was unable to get any acceptance from the Admiralty for his proposal. Meanwhile the War Cabinet themselves decided that the whole question was again to be brought before them, and it is in consequence of this decision, to which, I may add, no effect has yet been given, that any memoranda have been circulated by my authority.

No great demands have been made upon the time of the War Cabinet in this connection. Beyond a quarter of an hour's discussion a fortnight ago, I do not remember any occasion in the last three months when these questions have been discussed. The evil, however, has been continuous and progressive, and the paralysis of remedial action complete. In these circumstances it is necessary (a) the facts should be laid before the War Cabinet, and (b) that individual Ministers should have an opportunity of placing their views on record. It would be quite impracticable to rule that no memorandum should be circulated to the War Cabinet without its text having previously been discussed with other Departments concerned. The only consequence of such a ruling would be additional friction and delay.

Winston S. Churchill

Winston S. Churchill to Sir Douglas Haig

(*Churchill papers: 27/32*)

10 May 1918 Ministry of Munitions
Private

My dear Field-Marshal,

It wd be a convenience to me if I cd have a permanent lodging assigned to me in France somewhere in the zone of the armies. I do not like trespassing on yr unfailing good nature & hospitality each time I come over, tho' I shd hope you wd always let me come to see you when I am there & you are not too busy.

My liaison officer might be allotted a few rooms or a small house somewhere in the neighbourhood of GHQ & I cd stay there in ordinary circumstances when I had occasion. If you have no objection the arrangements cd vy easily be made. Perhaps you will let me know.

Of course I do not want to visit the Army on any other footing but that of your guest with all that that implies: but I shd like to be a guest who is never likely to be a burden.

I hope you will feel the debate yesterday did justice to yr own phase in the settlement about taking over the line. I know the Cabinet were extremely anxious to make a really just & adequate statement.

I am sending you a note about (a) Renault Tanks & (b) MG Pill boxes with which I do not encumber this letter.

Yours sincerely
Winston S. Churchill

Sir Douglas Haig to Winston S. Churchill

(*Churchill papers: 27/32*)

12 May 1918 General Headquarters

Dear Mr Churchill,

Many thanks for your letter of 10th inst. My QMG[1] is now looking out for a suitable residence for you in this neighbourhood, and will communicate with your Priv Sec regarding details. Houses are now difficult to find, and we officers have to pay high rents! Let me know if there is anything else I can do to help you.

Yours very truly
D. Haig

Winston S. Churchill to Sir Douglas Haig

(*Churchill papers: 27/32*)

15 May 1918 Ministry of Munitions
Private

My dear Field Marshal,

Thank you very much for your letter & for the arrangements wh you have authorized.

[1] Travers Edwards Clarke, 1871–1962. Entered the Army, 1891. Served on the North-West Frontier of India, 1897–8, and in South Africa, 1900–2. Lieutenant-Colonel, 1914; Major-General, 1917. Quartermaster-General, British Armies in France, 1917–19. Lieutenant-General, 1918. Knighted, 1919. Quartermaster-General to the Forces, 1919–23. Chief Administrator, British Empire Exhibition, Wembley, 1923–5.

I have to go to Paris next week for an I-Ally Munitions Confce & I will venture to propose myself for a night at yr HQ on the chance that you have room for me & that it is otherwise convenient. I will let Morton[1] know. I can then see yr QMG abt details.

I see from the War Cabinet record that you apprehend a truly terrific attack in the near future. All our thoughts are with you & the army. I cannot shake my profound conviction that the Germans are making a mistake, & that the end of the campaign will reveal the magnitude of their miscalculation to themselves as well as to the world.

Everything is vry solid here,
Yours sincerely
Winston S. Churchill

Winston S. Churchill to Louis Loucheur

(*Churchill papers: 15/48*)

15 May 1918 Ministry of Munitions

I cordially agree with your suggestion that we should create an inter-allied artillery of high calibre, capable of firing distances of 60 kilometres and over. I think you have already been informed to a certain extent of what we are doing in the way of producing such weapons, but I had better perhaps recapitulate the tentative programme which I am authorising, and to carry out which I should be very glad of your assistance.

At the present minute we have no guns. Naval or Land Service, which would fire at a greater range than 36 kilometres.

(1) With a view to obtaining a really long-range gun quickly, we are retubing a 16-inch gun to a calibre of 8·1 and are also adding to the length of the gun. It will fire a shell weighing 250 lbs. With this gun it is calculated that we should get a range of approximately 110 kilometres. This weapon weighs 136 tons, its length is approximately 92 feet, and it is a very serious

[1] Desmond Morton, 1891–1971. Second Lieutenant, Royal Artillery, 1911. Converted to Roman Catholicism shortly before the First World War. Shot through the heart while commanding a Field Battery at the Battle of Arras, April 1917, but survived the wound. Later awarded the Military Cross. ADC to Sir Douglas Haig, 1917–18. Seconded to the Foreign Office, 1919, where, with Churchill's support, he established the Industrial Intelligence Centre with its emphasis on the need to collect information about Bolshevik Russia (and subsequently about Germany and Eastern Europe). A close friend of Churchill's during the inter-war years. Director of the Industrial Intelligence Centre, 1930–9. Principal Assistant Secretary, Ministry of Economic Warfare, 1939. Personal Assistant to Churchill throughout the Second World War. Knighted, 1945. Economic Survey Mission, Middle East, 1949. Seconded to the Ministry of Civil Aviation, 1950–3.

matter for transportation, both on the railways and bridges and in the tunnels in England, and I presume in France.

(2) We are also retubing a 14-inch gun, which, with the 700-lb projectile, we hope will obtain a range of 66 kilometres. This equipment can be conveyed by railway, but would have to be lowered into a concrete emplacement to obtain the necessary elevation and traverse.

(3) We are also retubing a 12-inch gun, which was made for our Navy some time ago, with which, with a 700-lb projectile we should also obtain a range of 66 kilometres.

(4) We have before us a proposition for a 10-inch gun firing a 460-lb projectile, with an estimated range of 75 kilometres.

(5) If we can obtain from our Admiralty—but on this point I cannot speak for certain, as they are battleship guns—one or two 12-inch guns of the latest pattern, by retubing them and using a 450–500-lb shell we should obtain a range of approximately 66 to 68 kilometres. One of our armament firms has a design of mounting for this gun in existence, and I am giving orders for the manufacture.

I am sure that your experts will have informed you that it is difficult to estimate exactly the ranges that will be obtained, but, so far as calculations go, the figures I have given you should be approximately correct.

I think that possibly, as you have had great experience in the provision of railway mountings for heavy guns, your collaboration would be of the greatest help. I should like to suggest that if you send over an officer or officers to consult with mine, we could come to conclusions as to the best way of producing the necessary weapons to retaliate for the bombardment of the German long-range guns.

I attach a list which has been given to me of German towns within 110 kilometres of the French front line. Perhaps the officer or officers you send over could bring us information as to what you think would be your objectives of attack, which might help us considerably in deciding the ranges which we should attempt to reach.

Winston S. Churchill to David Lloyd George

(Churchill papers: 2/103)

15 May 1918 Ministry of Munitions

Secret

My dear Prime Minister,

There are no doubt a number of awkward difficulties in the elaboration of the scheme which we discussed on Monday night, & I do not at all underrate them. Officers have increased in numbers through war exigencies to such an extent that a Cabinet of Heads of Departments would be impossibly unwieldy. On the other hand, picking & choosing would be a nasty job, particularly when no uniform principle could be applied. There are certain men who ought to be in as politicians, & there are certain offices which must be in as offices; but some of the men who hold the greatest offices have no political value, while some of those whom you would want on political grounds hold offices of a minor character, the inclusion of which would open the flood-gate to other minor offices not filled by persons of political consequence. As between Liberal & Tory, all the traditional great offices except the India Office are filled by Tories, while the Liberal representation you would require is only to be found in the new or subsidiary posts. For instance, Fisher is a man you would probably want on personal grounds; but if the Board of Education were included, the other pre-war Cabinet offices, LGB, B of T, B of A, Post Office, & even Works, would be offended if left outside.

Similarly, if you wanted me in on political grounds, all the other new Ministers, eg Food, Shipping, National Service, Blockade, Pensions, which are held to be, I understand, of Cabinet rank, would expect to be in. This would bring you to nearly thirty, which is absurd. On the other hand, if you leave out, as would be quite logical & reasonable, the new Ministries, you would be shorn of your Liberal representation.

Clearly therefore you would have to use two different principles at the same time, viz picking Tories mainly by offices and Liberals mainly by men. So far as offices are concerned, the Lord Chancellor, the six Secretaries of State (including Air) the First Lord & the Attorney General are indispensable, total nine, plus the War Cabinet, six = fifteen. If you then picked three or at the outside four Liberals or Labour men you would be full up, ie 18 or 19, of whom 6 or 7 would be Liberals & Labour. That wd be about the minimum representation of Liberals that you could afford to put up with.

It would greatly facilitate your task, both from the point of view of offices & persons, if I remained outside. This I should be quite ready to do. You would then be able to say to the minor Tory offices, 'How can you claim to come in when the Ministry of Munitions is out?' Other Liberal Colleagues cd not be offended if they were left outside with me. I should not take such an arrangement in any way as a slight. I am quite content to serve during the war as an official in a purely administrative post without involving myself in political cares or party bitterness.

My only desire is to take part in the war, & I shall always be very grateful to you for giving me such interesting work. It wd be a great relief to me to be freed from the necessity of coming to decisions in political & party matters which would be at once premature & final. That is why I have so often disappointed you when our conversation has turned on party organisation & election preparations. I shd therefore be very glad to facilitate the creation of a political Cabinet by remaining exactly as I am.

That such a step is necessary both to the national interests & to your own, I am absolutely sure. How can you expect to form a party capable of real political action, without fusion of groups & an effective sense of corporate responsibility? At present you have two collections of non-responsible office holders, who never mingle as colleagues, who rarely meet as officials, & who have to be breakfasted in separate cages for fear their mutual prejudices shd overcome them; while you pass anxiously & with soothing & deprecative words from one to the other. As long as the war issue is the sole one on wh Parlt has to vote, you may keep the thing going by your personal efforts & by debating triumphs; even so you have to fight for yr life from month to month. But such an arrangement wd never stand the test of a political issue, nor would it be possible to build up any new effective party machinery behind it.

Winston S. Churchill to Sir Archibald Sinclair

(*Sinclair papers*)

16 May 1918

My dear Archie,

I am vy sorry indeed not to be able to present myself at yr wedding on Saturday. I have no legitimate official reason for crossing before Tuesday. . . .

My dear this is a splendid event in yr life and I wish you from the bottom of my heart lasting happiness. That you may be preserved through the dangers that surround you is my intense desire & I have also good confidence in yr fortune, & that this joyous event will renew it. God Bless you both & guard you always is my prayer. May you both see many golden summers together in the North & may all yr life be lighted by true love & sweet companionship.

I have been casting about in my mind for some token to mark this occasion, but I have decided to wait till you both return to these shores and can help me to find something that you wd like to keep & use in yr home.

Clemmie sends her vy best love & sincerest good wishes. She looks forward so much to meeting Marigold.[1]

[1]Marigold Forbes, daughter of Lieutenant-Colonel James Stewart Forbes. She married Sir Archibald Sinclair on 18 May 1918. After the war they lived at Thurso Castle, Caithness (one of the most northerly points in the United Kingdom, 661 miles from London). They had two sons and two daughters.

With every wish of friendship & wish every hope of fortune my dear friend believe me ever

Yours affectionately
W

General Tudor to Winston S. Churchill

(*Churchill papers: 2/103*)

16 May 1918

My dear Winston,

Thanks so much for your letter. I was so sorry to miss you when you were over. If you come next week you will find us back & I hope will stay a night. If we can squash the submarines, I think the rest is certain. The Hun has owed his success to only 2 things. One is using mist & fog & thickening it with smoke shell. 2. Finding *very* weak spots in our line & exploiting that. Watching the training here, I am convinced the way for us to save life is to insist on only holding so much line, that our infantry—& artillery can be trained. The men are good & only want training. Musketry hasn't been sufficiently encouraged in a lot of divisions, but that, though essential, is not enough. Men must have tactical field training. No mere instruments of war will make up for that. The division has had 9,500 casualties since you left us at Nurlu that morning. But if filled up & given a fortnight or so more good training, we should be as formidable as ever. The moral[1] is very high. By the bye though my 1st name is Henry, I have all my life used the other, why I don't know! Hoping to see you

Yrs ever
Hugh Tudor

Winston S. Churchill to Lord Fisher

(*Fisher papers*)

19 May 1918 Ministry of Munitions
Private

My dear Fisher,

Vy glad to get yr letter & its abundant evidence of yr health & energy.

I spoke to the PM as I said I wd, & he referred vy kindly to you & ex-

[1] Only after the First World War was the word 'moral' replaced in common usage by the word 'morale', with which it was synonymous.

pressed a desire to meet you at breakfast or dinner. This he wd no doubt have done but for the crush & scramble of events. Why don't you go to see him? He wd welcome you. But give a little notice.

I don't think you lost anything by not making yr speech. A speech from you is a card that you must not play improvidently. It shd be a long written statement *grave measured impersonal*. And the moment as well as the topic must be rightly chosen. You do not want to get 'Mauriced'.[1]

I do not think the M Guardian's criticisms require an answer. We did all in our power in the autumn of 1914. But I increasingly feel that the troops wh French had wd not have been sufficient or anything like sufficient; *& I agree* with you that no operation there without troops will yield first class results. On the other hand the inconvenience has turned out to be less than we apprehend. The Belgian coast is not the base of submarine warfare, but only a handy advanced base. The Elbe & the Ems are their real bases—always have been, always will be.

I agree with you that the Navy does not render a full return for the drain it makes on our resources. It cd do much more. But the successes they are having (thank God) in choking submarines are now becoming vy remarkable, & Zeebrugge[2] has given them back the '*panache*' that was lost at Jutland.

The past is full of sadness & the future of anxiety. But to-day Bank Holiday! In my sunlit garden I have the joy of the present. May it be yours also.

With my best regards, Yours vy sincerely

Winston S. Churchill

[1] On 9 May 1918 the House of Commons had debated a public letter written by the outgoing Director of Military Operations, Major-General Sir Frederick Maurice, in which Maurice accused Lloyd George of deceiving the House about the strength of the British Army on the western front. As a result of his speech in the debate, Lloyd George was left in undisputed control of the war-making machine, while the position of the Asquith Liberals, who had attempted to gain advantage from Maurice's letter, was much weakened. Maurice himself was at once retired from the Army, and refused both a court martial and an enquiry.

[2] On 22 April 1918 British naval and Royal Marine forces attacked two German submarine bases on the Belgian coast, the one at Zeebrugge, the other at Ostend. The Zeebrugge raid was largely successful, but that at Ostend failed. Such was the severity of the fighting, and the gallantry of those who took part in it, that nine Victoria Crosses were awarded. Two hundred men were killed in the two attacks.

Winston S. Churchill to Sir Ian Hamilton

(*Ian Hamilton papers*)

22 May 1918 Ministry of Munitions
Private

My dear Ian

I had an interview with Lord Milner last week & he asked me to tell you that he was 'favourable to yr reemployment'. He expressed himself generally in friendly terms, & recognised that the non-publication of the D'lles Report was a hardship to you.

I was pleased at his attitude, & am hopeful that he will act.[1]

Yours always
W

Winston S. Churchill: Cabinet memorandum

(*Churchill papers: 27/37*)

AERIAL ATTACKS ON GERMANY

30 May 1918 Ministry of Munitions

I must put on record my protest against the decision of the War Cabinet to make a formal and public promise not to bomb Germany during the course of a Roman Catholic religious festival.[2] The discouragement and misconception which a step of this kind causes throughout the country is out of all proportion to its actual importance. A unilateral engagement of this kind is altogether wrong in principle. If it was necessary or desirable to reach such an agreement, stipulation should have been made prohibiting the transport of war material or troops over the Rhine bridges during the period in question and prohibiting the temporary movement of enemy aeroplanes from defensive positions in rear of the line to the actual battle front.

The fact that the advantages the enemy may gain by such a step are small is no answer. A Government whose soldiers are fighting a desperate battle, and whose population is being urged to submit to every sacrifice, has no right to give away even small advantages; nor has a Government which exists solely for the vehement and rigorous prosecution of the war any right

[1] Despite Churchill's intervention, Milner did not in fact offer Sir Ian Hamilton any military employment.

[2] The British Government had given a public assurance not to bomb Cologne on Corpus Christi day.

to alienate from itself the support of loyal and ardent masses, whose help and confidence will be more and more needed in the days which are at hand.

Winston S. Churchill to Lord Beaverbrook

(*Beaverbrook papers*)

31 May 1918 Ministry of Munitions
Private

My dear Max,

With regard to our argument last night. My first bet was £25 to £5 that Chateau Thierry was less than 50 miles from Paris. The discussion arose out of the military situation, and I naturally had in my mind the great mass of houses and buildings of which Paris is composed, and not any arbitrary point in the city from which distances are measured. My view, therefore, is that the bet should be decided on the distance either of the Municipal boundaries or of the walls of Paris from Chateau Thierry. I agree, however, that the question of the definition of 'Paris' in this connection should be left to the decision of an arbitrator, and I am quite ready to agree with you upon one.

There is confusion about the second bet. You, becoming very confident, asked for 2 to 1 that you won the first bet. I was about to agree to this when you raised for the first time the question of the definition of 'Paris', and wished to insert words making it clear that you meant the geographical point in Paris from which the distances were measured, or the centre of Paris, or something to that effect. I demurred, and you crossed out the first line of the record which you had made. Subsequently, you or I offered—I cannot remember which—an even £5 on the distance from Chateau Thierry to the geographical point in Paris or a point in the centre of the city. The bet was written down by you in the form of an even fiver, although all reference to the definition of Paris was omitted. In these circumstances there is confusion about this second bet, and, although my memory is very clear, I think it had better be off altogether.

Meanwhile perhaps you will let me know who your suggestion is for an arbitrator on the first bet. . . . I do not know to this moment what the exact distances are, nor the point from which geographical distances are measured. Rough measurements on the map seem to show that it will be very close, possibly a matter of a few hundred yards should the arbitrator's decision favour the geographical point. If it is the walls I think there is no doubt I have a couple of miles in hand.[1]

Yours sincerely
Winston S. Churchill

[1] It is not clear how the bet was resolved, nor is there any unanimity in the standard works of reference as to the actual distance involved. According to *The Encyclopaedia Britannica* (13th edition, 1926), Château-Thierry is 47 miles from Paris. According to *The Blue Guides: North-Eastern France* (1930 edition) the distance is 59 miles. The town fell to the Germans on 2 June 1918, but they made no further major advance towards Paris.

June 1918

Montagu Porch[1] *to Winston S. Churchill*

(*Churchill papers: 1/129*)

1 June 1918 Connaught Hotel

Dear Winston

I am very glad you are able to come to our Wedding[2]—It seems almost incredible that today, when the World is in anguish, I should be allowed so much happiness.

I would now assure you that this, the most important step in my life is not taken in the dark. I have carefully considered the position from every point of view—your Mother's financial affairs are understood.

I love your Mother, I can make her happy. Her difficulties and obligations from henceforth will be shared by me—so willingly.

I thank you for your kindness and consideration. We shall be good friends.

Yours very truly
Montagu Porch

[1] Montagu Phippen Porch, 1877–1964. Served with the Middlesex Yeomanry in the South African War, 1900. Graduated from Magdalen College, Oxford, 1902. Served with the Egyptian Exploration Fund, 1904–5, crossing the Sinai desert by camel to collect ancient stone implements. Assistant Resident, Northern Nigeria, 1906; 3rd Class Resident, 1912. Lieutenant, Nigerian Regiment, Cameroons Expeditionary Force, 1914–15. Acting Resident, Zaria (Nigeria), 1915–18. After his marriage to Lady Randolph, he resigned from the Nigerian Civil Service to live in London. Went to the Gold Coast on business, 1921. He married again in 1926, and lived in Italy until his wife's death in 1938. He subsequently lived in Glastonbury.

[2] On Monday 3 June *The Times* announced that Lady Randolph Churchill and Montagu Porch had married 'very quietly' at the Harrow-road Register Office on Saturday 1 June. 'The bride wore a grey coat and skirt and a light green toque and a soft plain veil.' The register was signed by Churchill himself, John Leslie, Clara Frewen, Clementine Churchill, Lady Islington, Miss Winifred Porch, Lady Gwendeline Churchill and Lady Sarah Wilson.

Winston S. Churchill to Clementine Churchill

(*Spencer-Churchill papers*)

3 June 1918

My darling,

I had a touching vision of you & yr two kittens growing rapidly smaller and the aerodrome & its sheds dwindling into distant perspective as I whirled away.

It was a vy beautiful & wonderful journey. We crossed the Channel at 7400 & in one hour from leaving you we reached Hesdin 6 miles away from GHQ.

Sunny arrived all right in the evening & we were hospitably entertained by the C in C.

I spent the afternoon with Jack, & had tea with the Oxfordshire Hussars.

Now I am off to my Conference & then on to Paris.

The Flying business is vy different now to those earlier days. Kenley near Godstone (not Penshurst) is the nearest aerodrome for Lullenden. I will send you a message when I return & you can motor in there to meet me if you will.

Tender love & many kisses from

Yr ever loving
W

PS. I shall learn the situation when I reach Paris. It is evidently a vy anxious one.[1]

Winston S. Churchill to Clementine Churchill

(*Spencer-Churchill papers*)

6 June 1918 Paris

Beloved darling,

An air raid is in progress & I am due & overdue for bed. So these lines will be few but to the point. Much work has come upon me here & I have found the days all too short. I have seen very many interesting & influential people & transacted a good deal of business satisfactorily.

[1] On 27 May 1918 the Germans had begun the third of their 1918 offensives, attacking French troops on the Chemin des Dames, and driving them back nearly 12 miles by nightfall. For six days they continued to advance, capturing Soissons on 29 May, and Château Thierry on 2 June. On 3 June the German front line was at one point less than 50 miles from Paris. On 4 June Sir Maurice Hankey wrote in his diary: 'I do not like the outlook. The Germans are fighting better than the Allies, and I cannot exclude the possibility of disaster.' (*Hankey papers*)

You can judge the general situation for yrself. On the whole I am hopeful. But the fate of the capital hangs in the balance—only 45 miles away. Next time I come here (if there is a 'next time') you must really try to accompany me. You must prepare a good cause under the shelter of the YMCA (*Y*'a *M*oyens *C*oucher *A*vec) (as Loucheur calls it) & spend a few jolly days in this menaced but always delightful city.

I shall not leave here finally till Monday morning & Monday, Tuesday & perhaps Wednesday I shall be with the Army. DV, weather permitting & the rest of it I purpose to fly to Kenley Aerodrome Wed or Thursday. I will send you notice. Try to be at Lullenden so that we can be together. Kenley is near Godstone.

Tender love to you & all dear & dearest ones

Yr devoted
W

Sir Arthur Hardinge[1] *to A. J. Balfour*

(*Churchill papers: 2/103*)

7 June 1918 British Embassy
Private and Secret Madrid

I have told him [Duke of Westminster] that Winston Churchill's visit would in my opinion be undesirable even if he could find time for it. His coming to Spain, in his position, would be deemed a grave political step on the part of His Majesty's Government, would be misinterpreted by Germans and might be construed by Spaniards as a bid for active Spanish assistance in the war.[2]

Winston S. Churchill to Clementine Churchill

(*Spencer-Churchill papers*)

10 June 1918 Midnight Paris

My darling one,

The vy critical and deadly battle on the Montdidier–Noyon front has raged all day, & the latest accounts (5.30 pm) are apparently satisfactory.

[1] Arthur Henry Hardinge, 1859–1933. Diplomat. Knighted 1897; Privy Councillor, 1913; Ambassador to Spain, 1913–19.

[2] Churchill did not in fact visit Spain during the war. His previous visit had been in the summer of 1914, when he had played polo in Madrid. His next visit was in 1934, when he stayed in Barcelona.

There is no surprise here, but a blunt trial of strength—the line strongly held with troops & good reserves at hand. If the French cannot hold them back on this sector, it is not easy to see what the next step on our part shd be. I am hopeful. Both the generals Fayolle & Humbert who I saw yesterday, & who are certainly vy capable men, were soberly confident & hoped they wd be attacked.[1]

I go to GHQ tomorrow & hope to return to you Wednesday. But it may be Thursday. If you are at Lullenden, I will come on there & spend the night of Wed. Thursday is my Air dinner.

I have brought you a little present in Paris, wh I shall shew you when I arrive.

The young flying officer[2] has won my heart. His wife was there the other day when we started. He is vy gallant, & vy *battered.*

Tender love my dearest soul to you & all yr chicks.

Two Bertha shells arrived within 150 yards today. They are pop gun affairs & not in the least alarming.

Your always loving
W

Winston S. Churchill to David Lloyd George

(*Lloyd George papers*)

15 June 1918
Private

My dear Prime Minister,

I trust you will continue to press with all yr strength for the marrying of American divisions to our shattered cadres. This is the true line; & also for afterwards the value will be immeasurable. If you insist I am sure you can carry it through.

Yours always
W

[1] On 11 June 1918 the French were able to launch their first counter-attack, after which the Germans made no further advances towards Paris.

[2] Cyril Patteson, 1888– . 2nd Lieutenant, Royal Engineers, October 1914. Awarded the Military Cross for bravery at Suvla Bay, Gallipoli, 1915. Lieutenant, 1st Battalion, South Wales Borderers, May 1916. Seconded to the Royal Flying Corps, February 1917. Served in France in No 60 Squadron, March 1917; then in No 29 Squadron. Temporary Captain (Flight Commander), October 1917. Served with No 7 Aircraft Acceptance Park, Kenley, 1918. Acting Major, Royal Air Force, October 1918. Commanded No 1 Communications Squadron, October 1918 to July 1919.

Winston S. Churchill to Admiral Moore[1]

(*Churchill papers: 15/87*)

15 June 1918 Ministry of Munitions

I arranged this morning with S of S for War that the Tank corps men working in the Tank shops shd be allowed to remain for a further period—say 6 months. But this will not prevent all under 23 being released in accordance with the recent decision of the WCPCte, the same as men not in uniform. Action accordingly.

Winston S. Churchill to David Lloyd George

(*Lloyd George papers*)

17 June 1918[2]

My dear Prime Minister,

Pray consider this

(1) It is certainly against your instinct & conviction to shift the Czecho-Slovak Corps from Russia to France.

(2) I am sure it is against your inclination to back down before German threats of reprisals about clearing German women & children out of China. What we are doing now is to take the wrong course in both cases, & to make the first mistake a kind of bastard excuse for the second.

You may not be able to carry your point about the Czechs, because of Clemenceau; but we have an absolute right to clear the Huns out of China.

[1] Archibald Gordon Henry Wilson Moore, 1862–1934. Entered Navy, 1875. Naval assistant to Fisher, 1907–8. Director of Naval Ordnance and Torpedoes, 1909–12. Rear-Admiral, 1911. Third Sea Lord, 1912–14. Commander of 2nd Battle Cruiser Squadron, 1914; present at the actions in the Heligoland Bight, 28 August 1914, and Dogger Bank, 23 January 1915, after which he was relieved of his command on Jellicoe's insistence. Knighted, 1914. Controller of Experimental Design, Testing and Despatch, Ministry of Munitions, 1918. Admiral, 1919.

[2] Attached to this letter was Foreign Office telegram 310 dated 7 June from A J Balfour to Sir J Jordan in Peking. The telegram stated that the Supreme War Council had decided that because of the urgent need of ships to bring the Czechoslovak troops at Vladivostok back to France it had been decided that the ships alloted to transport German and Austrian subjects from China to Australia should be diverted for that purpose. Some 60,000 Czechoslovak troops, captured by the Russians on the eastern front in 1915, had been released by the Bolsheviks in March 1918. Moving eastwards by rail towards Vladivostok, on their long way back to the western front via Japan, they had been attacked by Bolshevik units, whereupon they seized several strategic towns, including Omsk and Krasnoyarsk, which they proceeded to hold against all Bolshevik attempts to dislodge them. By June 1918 they controlled nearly a thousand miles of the Trans Siberian Railway.

This makes an enormous difference in the future. Preparations for it are far advanced. To give way just because the Germans threaten to ill-use Belgians is weakness.

I ventured to warn you about the way in which the Cologne Corpus Christi benefit wd be taken. Do put your foot down on this. It is *abject*.

Yrs always
W

Winston S. Churchill to[1]

(*Churchill papers: 1/129*)

18 June 1918

I am touched by the kindness of your letter which I regret until now I have not had a chance to answer. It is very nice of you to wish to shelter me, and I need not say how very attractive such a proposition would be. But I have now made my arrangements for living here at the Ministry, and I find that it has many conveniences from the point of view of getting work done. It enables me to work up till the last moment before dinner, to get papers when I come back after dinner, and to begin with shorthand assistance as early as I choose in the morning. In these circumstances I do not think I will make a change at present.

Louis Loucheur to Winston S. Churchill: telephone message

(*Churchill papers: 15/145*)

[?] June 1918

I wish to confirm to you that our manufacture of Yperite Mustard Gas is working very well. We have now reached a production of 12 tons a day. I am ready to send you over an engineer to visit your factories if you desire it. I offer you the free entry to our factories which are working at full pressure, where you will be able to obtain all the information you seek.

[1] There is no indication in the Churchill papers of the name of the recipient of this letter.

Winston S. Churchill to Louis Loucheur: telegram

(*Churchill papers: 15/145*)

[?] June 1918

Yperite: many thanks your offer gladly accepted send your engineer over here to see our plans and thereafter he can take one of my men back with him to see yours. We are making much better progress than I told you in Paris and I hope to begin firing before the end of July. Your engineer should come direct to me.

Winston S. Churchill: Cabinet memorandum

(*Churchill papers: 27/37*)

A NOTE ON THE WAR

22 June 1918
Secret

1. Before the war the British military authorities forecasted with accuracy what the German plan of campaign would be, and Sir Henry Wilson in particular, as early as August 1911, unfolded to the Committee of Imperial Defence a completely true picture of the German attack in the West, through Belgium towards Paris, and also of the Russian weakness and tardy mobilisation in the East. On the other hand, our military advisers took a far too sanguine view of the relative strength and efficiency of the French and German armies. On the outbreak of war, the over-powering need was to stem the German rush, first on Paris, and secondly on the Channel Ports, and no one could think of anything else on land till this was done. By the end of November, as the Chief of the Staff has explained, Paris and the Channel Ports were saved, and the German onslaught brought to a standstill. The first phase of the war, which may be called 'stemming the rush', thus came to an end.

2. The second phase covered a period of 18 to 20 months, viz, from the end of 1914 to the Battle of the Somme in July 1916. During the whole of this period the position in the West was that the Anglo-French armies were strong enough to hold the Germans, but not strong enough to attack them with any chance of piercing their fortified lines. The main theatre, ie, the theatre where the main forces are gathered, ceased to be for the time being the decisive theatre, ie the theatre where an important decision can be obtained. These conditions were clearly recognised in the British Cabinet.

They were disputed by both the British and French military authorities. The divergence of view arising from different estimates of forces and values led to the loss of opportunities which will never recur.

3. The politicians were in the main generally convinced that the deadlock in the West would continue until a great British army could be called into being, and equipped with a powerful artillery and plentiful munitions. They therefore immediately looked for other theatres in which our forces could gain decisive results in the interval. Two great operations, each involving the concerted action of our naval, military and diplomatic resources presented themselves: first, the rallying of the group of small States at the north-western corner of Europe, thus turning the enemy's right flank, obtaining command of the Baltic, and forming contact with Russia in the north; or secondly, rallying the group of small States at the south-eastern corner of Europe, striking down Turkey before Germany could organise her, and establishing contact with Russia from the south. Of these two policies, the first was clearly the more difficult, and was never, perhaps, possible, having regard to our resources. The second, however, was not only possible but easy of accomplishment if the proper measures had been taken. Turkey was isolated from Germany by the Balkan States. She was ill-organised and ill-prepared. She was menaced by Russia. We held better cards than the Germans in regard to every single one of the Balkan States. The partition of the Turkish Empire offered the means of satisfying every aspiration. Lastly, the naval situation was entirely favourable. Our margins in the North Sea had been greatly increased since the declaration of war. The German submarines had not become formidable, and the destruction of Von Spee[1] had completed the clearance of the German warships from the surface of the oceans. An amphibious operation to strike down Turkey before she could raise her head, and to unite the Balkan States against their natural foes, the Turkish and Austrian Empires, was well within the scope of the naval and military resources at our disposal, after providing an ample superiority over the Germans in the North Sea and sufficient forces to defend actively the front in France and Flanders. It was, therefore, towards the southern flank of the enemy's line, to Turkey and to the Balkans, that our operations were directed—but, alas, half-heartedly.

4. The natural tendency of the naval and military point of view is to confuse the main and the decisive theatres. Wherever the main part of the army or the main part of the fleet is assembled, always claims their partisan-

[1]Maximilian, Count von Spee, 1861–1914. Entered the German Navy, 1878. Chief of Staff, German North Sea Command, 1908–12. Commanded the German Far Eastern Squadron, 1912–14. On 1 November 1914 he defeated Admiral Cradock at Coronel, off the Chilean coast, but on 8 December 1914 he was himself defeated at the Falkland Islands by Admiral Sturdee. During the battle von Spee went down with his flagship.

ship. Accordingly, the professional opinion of the navy grudged and resisted the employment at the Dardanelles of every unit, even the most obsolete; and the professional opinion of the army delayed, grudged, and stinted the employment of every soldier and of every shell required for the Eastern campaign. These tendencies, which would have been controlled by success, became at the first check overpowering. The Eastern enterprise was therefore cast away, with consequences of measureless disaster.

Bulgaria, always the key of the Balkans, remained undecided while the fate of the Dardanelles hung in the balance. Her course was determined by the loss of the Battle of Suvla Bay. The destruction of Serbia followed immediately, and the destruction of Roumania a year later. Turkey was gripped and organised by the Germans, entailing great diversions of our forces to Egypt and Mesopotamia. Adding the loss involved by these diversions to the loss arising from the destruction of Serbia and Roumania, the paralysis of Greece, and the hostility of Bulgaria, our failure to prosecute the Eastern enterprise successfully, may well have equalled the addition of two million soldiers to the ranks of our enemies. Besides this we lost the means to succour and animate Russia by direct contact.

5. The third phase of the war supervened upon the second. After the year 1915, there were no hopes of gaining any good results in Turkey or the Balkans. The Germans were everywhere in complete communication and control. In consequence, Allied armies large enough to achieve success in those theatres, were too large for the carrying capacity of our seaborne tonnage. Moreover, the submarine had become formidable in the Mediterranean, and the military weakness of Russia was plainly apparent. Half the soldiers lost, and half the shells fired in Artois in May, and at Loos and in Champagne in September 1915, resolutely used against Turkey, would have achieved for us the whole south-eastern theatre of war in that year; but in 1916 four times their number could not have retrieved the position. The extinction of other possibilities left France, therefore, the only theatre open to us.

Meanwhile, however, a great British army had come into being, abundantly supplied with munitions. The third or as it may be called 'The Slogging Phase' then began. This lasted from the beginning of the Battle of the Somme, the 1st July, 1916, to the end of the Passchendaele attacks in November 1917. During the whole of this period the British armies, sometimes alone and sometimes assisted by the French, were hurled almost continuously, or with the briefest intervals for recovery, in assaults upon the fortified German lines. I have personally always held the view that at no time in this period were we strong enough, in the absence of some entirely novel method of attack applied on a gigantic scale, eg, tanks or gas, to break through the skilful German defence, reinforced as it always was, and still is, by the power of giving ground wherever necessary without serious consequence.

Still, such was the heroic gallantry of the armies, and the determination of their leaders, so powerful was the artillery of which they disposed, that the hope of victory and the sense of mastery were never quenched in the hearts of our troops until the mud deluge of Passchendaele. And of course it is impossible to suppose that we could have sat still with folded hands during that time without exposing the French & other allies to the gravest dangers.

The most hopeful climax of these operations was, however, probably reached at the end of the year 1916 in the later phases of the Battle of the Somme. At this time the enemy were at their greatest strain. They were weakened by their folly at Verdun. They were attacked simultaneously by the British and French armies astride of the Somme. Brusiloff[1] gained his great victories on the Austrian front, and Roumania plunged into the war. The exertions which the Germans made in this emergency should make us realise the strength of our foe. By dint of them they managed to reach the winter, striking down Roumania meanwhile.

6. The Germans did not feel themselves strong enough in the spring of 1917 to withstand the renewed onslaught of the British and French armies. They therefore ruptured the Anglo-French plans for combined action by suddenly withdrawing their line from the Somme battlefields almost to St Quentin and Cambrai. They thus placed a broad belt of devastated country between them and their would-be assailants and also between the British and French armies. By this manœuvre they avoided the kind of long-prepared accumulated blow they have struck at us this year, and only had to face through the rest of 1917 disconnected attacks by the British, and occasionally, the French. The campaign of 1917, therefore, became very disastrous to us. Although each military episode, taken by itself, wore the aspect of a fine success, with captures of ground and guns and prisoners, in reality we were consuming our strength without any adequate result.

7. Late in the year a false naval argument played its part in swaying military policy. The harbours of Zeebrugge and Ostend were represented as being the source of the submarine warfare, and their capture or suppression were alleged to be vital. As a matter of fact, these harbours, of course, have never been and could never be the main base of submarine warfare. That has

[1] Alexei Alexeievich Brusiloff, 1853–1926. Commanded the Russian Armies south of the Pripet Marshes, 1916–17. His successful offensive, launched on 4 June 1916, was halted in September through lack of artillery munitions, having at one point advanced 70 miles and captured 300,000 prisoners. Supreme Commander of the Russian Armies, May–July 1917. Put his services at the disposal of the Red Army during the Russo-Polish War, 1920; Inspector of Cavalry, 1923–4; Head of the State Horse-breeding Establishment, Moscow, 1924–6. He is said to have died in poverty.

only been directed and can only be directed from the permanent naval bases of Germany in the estuaries of the Elbe, the Weser, and the Ems. Ostend and Zeebrugge were serious annoyances, but as objectives they were utterly inadequate to the sacrifices demanded of the army in order to secure the Flanders Coast. Moreover, the season of the year was advanced. The Russian collapse had taken place; nobody else was fighting; the numbers of the enemy on the front attacked were almost equal to our own; the direction of the attack was perceived and thoroughly prepared against by elaborate semi-permanent fortifications. In these circumstances the amazing efforts of the British armies could have had no other result than to weaken themselves.

The incidental disaster which happened to Italy was not so harmful as it looked. That country had only been putting about three-fifths of its strength into the war, and the renewed effort which was extorted from her more than made up for the heavy losses sustained.

8. While our military advisers were intent upon the battle and in hopes of gaining successes in the nick of time, they do not seem to have realised the awful consequence of the collapse of Russia. But in November and December this apprehension grew with politicians and generals, both British and French. The flow of German divisions and batteries from Russia to the West was unceasing for many months until finally a power had been accumulated which, after marking down every division of which we could dispose, left the enemy with a punching force of nearly fifty divisions.

In attack the German uses Surprise, in defence he uses Concrete. Our defensive problem this year is far more difficult than that which the Germans solved successfully in 1917. On every occasion in 1917 (except at Cambrai) the Germans knew where the attack would fall. Every attack (except Cambrai) was indicated by several days bombardment, apart from every evidence of preparation. Every German position was defended by lines of solid shell-proof structures sheltering machine guns, and ample reserves were held in rear to arrest a successful advance beyond the limits of our offensive barrage. Lastly, the Germans could always afford to give up some of the territory they overran so easily at the beginning of the war.

Our position this year has been very different. The initiative has passed completely to the enemy. His attack is mounted actually or in dummy over practically the whole battle-front, and besides we can never exclude his irruption at some quite unexpected point. We, on the other hand, have at least four places—Calais, Amiens, Paris, Verdun—which we regard as capital. The enemy can therefore ring the changes on a succession of vital points, before each one of which we have little or no ground to spare. Meanwhile, the use of gas and smoke have given new facilities to the offensive, and our methods of fortifications are still wanting in thoroughness compared with those of the Germans.

In this dire situation nothing has saved us except the stamina of our armies and the physical difficulties of persevering in an offensive after a certain distance. The stubborn resistance which the enemy has encountered, the bloody repulses which, in spite of his successes, he has sustained on the greatest scale, and the resources in men and material which the threat of utter ruin has extorted from the Allies, have gone far to equalise the struggle. The British army has responded to the appeal of its Commander. It is even possible that we shall end this campaign of agony and disaster in far better posture than we began it. But what are we going to do then?

9. This is the question to which I have been leading up. If I have tried to pick out as I see them the salient points in the past, it is with the object of showing that there are now and in the immediate future just as vital decisions to be taken if we can only secure the necessary vision and command. It may be that the Imperial War Cabinet will be able to impart to the Allied conduct of the war that general design and true selection of vital objectives which we have never yet been able to obtain.

10. There are two perfectly simple things to do. They have long been staring us in the face. Everybody sees them, but they see so much else at the same time that nothing effective has yet been done: (1) Reconstitute the fighting front in the East; (2) make a plan for an offensive battle in France in 1919, choosing the period of climax and subordinating, as far as pressure of circumstances will allow, every intervening event to that supreme purpose.

If we cannot reconstitute the fighting front against Germany in the East, no end can be discerned to the war. Vain will be all the sacrifices of the peoples and the armies. They will only tend to prolong the conflict into depths which cannot be plumbed. We must not take 'No' for an answer either from America or from Japan. We must compel events instead of acquiescing in their drift. Surely now when Czech divisions are in possession of large sections of the Siberian Railway and in danger of being done to death by the treacherous Bolsheviks, some effort to rescue them can be made? Every man should ask himself each day whether he is not too readily accepting negative solutions. May we not assume that President Wilson will regard the rescue of the Czechs as an obligation of honour? Who can rescue them except the Japanese? But even if President Wilson will not move himself, means must be found to move the Japanese. There are many means at the disposal of the British Empire.[1]

[1] On 2 July 1918 Lloyd George and Clemenceau appealed jointly to Woodrow Wilson to give military support to the Czech forces in Siberia. Three days later the United States Government agreed to send American troops to Russia in order to help the anti-Bolshevik

11. Secondly, we must organise the offensive battle for 1919. It will be no use thinking about this in the winter when (we may hope) our present anxieties will be at an end. It will be too late then. Unless while we are fighting for our lives all this summer we can look ahead and plan for 1919, we shall be in the same melancholy position next year as we are this.

In this war the initiative can only be seized as the result of plans made nearly a year ahead, and through the successful overcoming of some great difficulty. Is it not possible at the present time to conceive and visualise a victorious offensive battle in the summer of 1919, to manufacture all the apparatus necessary to that battle, and to subordinate intervening arrangements, as far as daily needs will let us, to bringing about a situation favourable to that battle? Do the means of beating the German armies in the West in 1919 exist? Can the men be procured? If so, the mechanisms can be prepared. We still have the time. Have we the will-power and the command to look ahead and regulate action accordingly?

War Cabinet: minutes

(*Cabinet papers: 23/6*)

26 June 1918

THE MINISTER OF MUNITIONS pleaded for equal treatment for all Departments, and said that it would be very invidious if any distinction were made. Mr Churchill instanced the serious difficulties which were occurring, owing to the clean cut, in various Departments under the control of his Ministry. A resolution had been received from the Metropolitan Carriage, Wagon, and Finance Company (Limited), which was the firm most responsible for turning out tanks, in which a protest was recorded against the young men being taken before suitable men had been provided to take their places. In this firm there were from 200 to 300 men involved, and the effect of taking these men would be that the output of tanks would be reduced from 50 to 15 a week.

MR CHURCHILL quoted from reports which he had received from other industries, including the chemical industry employed in making poison gas, the manufacture of breech mechanism for guns, and the steel department, where the effect of calling up 558 men of the ages of 19 and 20 from the ore mines of Cumberland would involve the loss of 2,000 to 2,500 tons of ore. Mr Churchill said that if the War Cabinet ruled that the decision should

---

forces. By the end of July over 7,000 British, American, Italian, French and Japanese troops had reached Vladivostok. The Japanese Government, which showed no reluctance to send troops to Russia, eventually contributed the largest single contingent.

stand, but that exceptions would be allowed in cases which were serious and where numbers were small, it would be most unfair to apply those exceptions to one Department only, and that the only terms on which his Department had agreed to the decision were that there should be universality in the contract. He made a suggestion that the Admiralty and Ministry of Munitions should be allowed a discretion each to retain 1,000 men.

July 1918

Sir Archibald Sinclair to Winston S. Churchill

(*Churchill papers: 1/129*)

3 July 1918

Winston,

I feel deeply ashamed of myself that I have never written to thank for the perfect letter which you wrote me when I got married: I missed you awfully at the wedding but I knew you would have been there if you could.

Now we have got a quite delightful little flat at Le Touquet. Next time you are over here, you must go & see Marigold & our little home—Les Aeroplanes, Paris Plage, only half an hour's drive from Montreuil.

I want to see you, too. I heard of you quite close by the other day & reproached you silently for never coming to see me. If you were to appear in a large & luxurious automobile on a Friday or (Saturday very early), I might be able to take you down to Le Touquet to see Marigold.

I was hugely interested to see that your mother had married again. Please give her my best love & heartiest good wishes: please remember to do that, Winston. Does one call her Mrs Porch or Lady Randolph now? Do you like Porch? I've been simply working all day long and have just had to ignore every single one of my marriage letters—yours is the first I have answered. The Battalion is going strong & when we get our motors we shall be as proud as peacocks. I'm delighted with my company & should like to show it to you at work one of these days.

There is much I should like to say about politics & the war but it would take too long & it would be futile unless I heard your reply, but the Government still seem to be in hot water about man power, in a terrible mess over Ireland & without any policy in Russia. I should like to see a few of the Ulster rebels sent to join the Sinn Fein 'rebels' & a belated but generous measure of Home Rule given at once. As soon as it was working you could demand your recruits or conscripts but not before. The Government wants new blood, & good, strong, Radical blood too of the John Simon, Samuel & Arthur Henderson type, more in sympathy than the present Cabinet with the democratic aspirations & ideals of America & the Dominions as well as of this country, and its high time you went to the War Office or Downing Street. You are hiding your light under a bushel with hardly a crack in it, through which any light ever escapes.

I'm so glad that Jack Seely has joined you[1]—please give him my love—Also to Clemmie & to Randolph[2] & Diana & Sarah[3]—bless them; I wish I could come down to Lullenden for the week-end!

Yrs always
Archie

PS. *Do write*, if you have time.

Lord Beaverbrook to Winston S. Churchill

(*Churchill papers: 2/103*)

4 July 1918 Hyde Park Hotel

My dear Winston,

I am overjoyed at your wonderful success. You have done immense service.[4]

Yours ever
Max

Lord Beaverbrook to Winston S. Churchill

(*Churchill papers: 2/103*)

6 July 1918 Ministry of Information

Dear Mr Churchill,

May I, as Minister of Information, convey to you my warmest thanks for consenting, amidst the pressing duties of your present office, to address a

[1] In June 1918 Major-General Seely had become Member of Council for the Welfare Group of the Ministry of Munitions. In mid-July he was appointed Deputy Minister of Munitions and Parliamentary Under-Secretary to the Minister.

[2] Randolph Frederick Edward Spencer Churchill, 1911–68. Churchill's only son. His godfathers were F E Smith and Sir Edward Grey. Conservative MP, 1940–5. Major, British mission to the Yugoslav Army of National Liberation, 1943–4. Journalist and historian; author of the first two volumes of this biography.

[3] Sarah Milicent Hermione Spencer Churchill. Born while her father was returning from the siege of Antwerp, 7 October 1914. Edward Marsh was her godfather. An actress, she published *The Empty Spaces* (poems) in 1966, and *A Thread in the Tapestry* (recollections) in 1967.

[4] On 4 July 1918, on the 142nd anniversary of the declaration of American Independence, Churchill had been the principal speaker at a meeting of the Anglo-Saxon Fellowship, held at Central Hall, Westminster. During his speech he declared: 'When I have seen during the past few weeks the splendour of American manhood striding forward on all the roads of France and Flanders, I have experienced emotions which words cannot describe.' As for Britain, Churchill said, the great reward of the war would be the 'supreme reconciliation' of Britain and the United States. 'That,' he added, 'is the lion's share.'

great Meeting of Anglo-Saxon Fellowship in the Central Hall on July 4th, and at the same time offer my heartiest congratulations upon the historic speech with which you signalised the occasion. You yourself must have been conscious of the extent to which you moved and stirred your great audience, and it must be a source of keen gratification to you personally to feel that you were the chief contributor to the success of such a great occasion.

The verbatim report, together with a brief account of the proceedings, and the names of some of the guests present, will shortly be issued by this Ministry in pamphlet form for distribution in the United States, and elsewhere. I hope to send you a copy.

With kind regards, believe me,
Yours faithfully
Beaverbrook

Sir Archibald Sinclair to Winston S. Churchill
(*Churchill papers: 2/103*)

[?] July 1918

Winston,

I've been reading your 4 July speech—I haven't had time till last night—and though I don't flatter myself that my opinion interests you very much, I feel that I must write & tell you what a splendid utterance it appeared to me to be & how absolutely I agree with almost every word you uttered & every sentiment you expressed.

I remember sounding you upon the possibility of drawing closer to the States on that first walk we took together at Maxine's years before the war. How delighted I was when you treated the idea seriously & not as an impracticable dream. It was certainly absolutely true of all Englishmen & Scotsmen with recent American connections & probably of the vast majority of thinking men in our country that they will be willing to regard the complete understanding & co-operation with America as our highest reward—'the lion's share'.

Next to that sentiment I liked best the insistence on the necessity of victory and the impossibility of compromise: and especially I was delighted (and not a little surprised, I confess!) at the declaration that the principles, for which we are fighting, will be Germany's (and Russia's, Winston!) protection when the final peace comes to be made. Of course, I remember you used to say that 'Germany for the Germans' was our battle cry, but lately I have thought that you had gone over to the camp of the 'practical statesmen'. This splendid declaration of democratic ideals thrilled me. It is the best counterpart of the President's utterances which has proceeded from Europe. Just off to my little home in Le Touquet, so in haste.

Archie

Winston S. Churchill: War Cabinet memorandum

(*Churchill papers: 27/38*)

THE GERMAN COLONIES

7 July 1918
Secret

I have read with great interest Mr Balfour's paper on the German Colonies, and Mr Long's comments upon it. There appear to me to be two dominating considerations:—

1. We could never allow any question connected with the disposal of the German Colonies to be the sole obstacle to the conclusion of peace.
2. We must not press British territorial claims to such a point as to alienate the sympathies of the United States.

It is evident that the application of these two considerations cannot be judged apart from the actual circumstances in which the Peace Conference assembles. It seems likely, however, that a decisive victory, such as Mr Long rightly contemplates, will only be attained after the United States have made sacrifices of the first order, and have developed a preponderating military power. The course of the struggle will then have drawn the British and American peoples very closely together; and it may well be that solutions altogether superior to any that are now open will present themselves.

War Cabinet: minutes

(*Cabinet papers: 23/7*)

ALIENS

8 July 1918

Attention was called to the demands of the public that persons of enemy origin should not be employed in Government offices, while no objection was taken to their serving in His Majesty's forces. On the other hand, it was urged that such persons employed in Government offices might have access to important information, while opportunities of obtaining information likely to be of value to the enemy were rare in the great majority of cases of those serving in the forces. There was, further, a risk of leakage from Government servants through their wives or other relatives who might be in communication with relatives in enemy countries. It was urged that in time of war the State was bound to bear in mind that persons of enemy origin resident in this country might not be able completely to resist 'the call of the blood'.

MR CHURCHILL deprecated action on the lines of the Report of the Parliamentary group, which would react very detrimentally on the Ministry of Munitions, both as regards scientific experts and Civil Servants. He thought that persons in the service of the Government could be left to be dealt with by the responsible heads of the departments. In order to quiet the public feeling which had been aroused, he was in favour of a searching review being carried out, but he was strongly opposed to any injustice being perpetrated in response to a clamour in the press. No one had proved that the country was in serious danger, and he was convinced that our Secret Service was more efficient than that of the Germans. His experience when Home Secretary and First Lord of the Admiralty had shown that the dangerous agents were not enemy aliens, but members of other nationalities. In the Civil Service there were men of enemy origin occupying high positions, who throughout the war had been working most loyally, and who were held in the very highest regard by their colleagues. It would be most unfair to deal harshly with such men. There were, further, scientific men, chemists, and others, who were very valuable to the State at the present time. There were others in the munitions industries in positions which might be compared with those of regimental officers. Lastly, there were the cases of men of German origin who were coming over in the American Army. He was aware that the present agitation was widespread, and that particular cases would be ruthlessly forced on any tribunal set up but he was equally certain that any panic measures resorted to now would be much regretted by the Government later on. He hoped that it would be stated clearly in the House of Commons that the Government did not admit that they had been in any way censurable in their administration of the laws against enemy aliens.

Winston S. Churchill to David Lloyd George

(*Churchill papers: 15/164*)

9 July 1918 Ministry of Munitions

My dear Prime Minister,

I want you to read the enclosed[1] to which I attach importance.

I shall probably circulate it late in the week.

I am becoming seriously alarmed about the effects of so many withdrawals of skilled men. We cannot go on indefinitely without producing effects which will be bad and stupid. It is my duty to warn you as far as possible of difficulties and mistakes before they occur. I have done everything in my power to help the Man-Power Supply, but I am being pressed now to make releases which will be most injurious, and wasteful of our war effort. In some directions we have already gone too far.

Yours always
W

Winston S. Churchill to Lord Milner

(*Churchill papers: 15/164*)

9 July 1918 Ministry of Munitions
Private

My dear Milner,

I send you an advanced copy of a paper I am preparing for the War Cabinet. Perhaps you will be able to read it before we meet this afternoon.

You are pressing me too far in this matter, and the war effort of the country may already have been impaired by the withdrawals to which I have consented. To go further will require much caution. It distresses me very much to hear you say such things as that you are prepared to face reductions in output of tanks, etc. What can the few hundred men involved do in the Army compared to what the Tanks can do? But there are many other small intricate supplies involved.

Yours sincerely
Winston S. Churchill

[1] Churchill's memorandum 'Munitions and the Limits of Recruiting', circulated to the War Cabinet on 12 July 1918 (see pages 343–7).

Winston S. Churchill to David Lloyd George

(*Lloyd George papers*)

11 July 1918

My dear Prime Minister,

I see that the War Cabinet meeting to discuss the Aliens question was not confined to the members of the War Cabinet, but that departmental ministers also attended. No department is more seriously affected by the proposed Civil Service regulation than the Ministry of Munitions. I shd therefore have been glad if you had seen yr way to invite me to be present.

Yours always
W

War Cabinet: minutes

(*Cabinet papers: 23/7*)

ALIENS

11 July 1918

MR CHURCHILL deprecated action on the lines of the Report of the Parliamentary group, which would react very detrimentally on the Ministry of Munitions, both as regards scientific experts and Civil Servants. . . . In order to quiet the public feeling which had been aroused, he was in favour of a searching review being carried out, but he was strongly opposed to any injustice being perpetrated in response to a clamour in the press.

Winston S. Churchill to Sir Archibald Sinclair

(*Sinclair papers*)

11 July 1918

Archie dear—I was delighted to get yr letter. I tried vy hard to see you when I was at the HQ of the 57th Division. I cd not discover yr squadron, tho portions of the 2nd LG[1] were within the command.

I will come to see you, if it is possible—on my next visit—I hope week of 20th.

I have been allotted a small chateau at Verchocq[2] by the C-in-C as a

[1] The 2nd Life Guards, in which Sinclair was a Squadron Commander.

[2] The Chateau Verchocq, built in 1810 by the Marquis de Coupigny, had been restored by André de la Gorce in 1910. Near Agincourt, it was surrounded by trees and difficult to see from the air. In July 1918 it was just under 25 miles from the front.

permanent lodging—a little *maison-toleré*. But I expect if you can escape for an evening you will want to go nearer to the sea. I will try to let you know my movements in good time. Is there anything you want?

I flew all my journeys last time, & vy nearly finished an eventful though disappointing life in the salt water of the channel. We just fluttered back to shore. I have had better arrangements made for a good flight for communication purposes now. It only takes 1 hour from Lullenden to GHQ! But one must have careful engine supervision.

I will try to organise a plan by wh you can be transported for a few hours nearer to your heart's desire.

The life & death struggle will begin again soon. Here mainly stress & talk.

I hope you were pleased with my Independence day speech.

If all goes well England & US may act permanently together. We are living 50 years in one at this rate.

Best love

Yr affectionately
W

PS. We will also talk about a constituency

Winston S. Churchill: War Cabinet memorandum

(*Churchill papers: 15/34*)

MUNITIONS AND THE LIMITS OF RECRUITING

12 July 1918
Secret

I must direct the attention of the War Cabinet to the very serious consequences that will arise from the continual drafting of skilled men into the army from the munitions industries.

Since the beginning of this year we have released no fewer than 100,000 men, nearly all of whom are skilled men, for military service. We have been deprived of all the Grade I men of 19 and 20 without excepting even draughtsmen, men employed in making gauges, breech mechanisms, optical instruments, and vital pivotal men.

It is anticipated *inter alia* that the withdrawal of these men will reduce the output of iron ore. In the Cleveland iron-ore mines alone the consequent loss of iron ore is estimated at 6,000 tons a week; the number of youths affected is only 250, but they are practically all underground drivers, a class of young fit men who can only be replaced by young miners working at the face. It is estimated that the Cumberland hematite mines will lose between 250 and 300 youths, with a consequent reduction in output of some 2,000 tons of ore per week. Blast furnaces and steel works will also be seriously affected, for it is considered probable that not only will it be impossible to start the new extensions which have been constructed during the past years, but that, in addition, it may be necessary in some cases actually to shut down blast furnaces at present in operation and to close some of the existing steel mills.

Hitherto I have done everything in my power to support the policy of the War Office and the Ministry of National Service. But I consider the time has now come when that policy requires to be the subject of a general reconsideration. Last autumn it was obvious that Russia would be out before America could come in, and that consequently the most strenuous efforts should be made to enable our Army to meet the attacks which would come upon it in the spring. The disasters of the spring rendered it still more imperative to provide men to carry us through the summer. I consider, therefore, we were right to run very great risks in all other directions in order to maintain the fighting front.

We have now to take into consideration a period where the conditions are entirely different from those of last autumn and this spring. The immediate crisis is not over, and, indeed, the worst may have yet to come. But men taken from industry after July will not reach the battle-front in time to influence the decision. So far as man-power is concerned, the die is cast. Secondly, the Americans, who have ten million men between 20 and 30 on whom to draw, are now arriving in great numbers, more than 270,000 having disembarked in a single month. The main contribution to our manhood next year must be derived from them. If we are to obtain any effective superiority in numbers, it can only be by American aid. No contribution that we can make can substantially alter the situation in a numerical sense. The question for us, therefore, is how to use the last remains of our man-power so as to develop the greatest possible military effort. This will not necessarily be by making the largest possible number of infantry soldiers.

Since the subject was last considered, the American forces in Europe have risen to 1,000,000 men. It is stated that more than 2,000,000 Americans have already been enlisted, that 3,000,000 will have been enlisted by the 1st September, and that the War Department is preparing clothing for 4,000,000 as from the 1st January. It is evident that the solution of the man-power problem lies in the speedy transportation to France of these great numbers, their training and organisation on the battle-front, and, lastly, their equipment and supply. The first 1,000,000 who have come have been almost entirely equipped by Britain and France. But for the fact that we were able to supply them with artillery, machine-guns, rifles, trench mortars, &c, and to feed them with munitions of all kinds, no use in the present crisis could have been made of this first million. My latest report from America states that the American army in France will be almost entirely dependent during the whole of 1918 on British and French artillery production. If we are to continue to put, as we must do, the most extreme pressure upon the American Government to pour its men over, we must be in a position to guarantee them thorough and immediate equipment when they arrive, and ample supply thereafter.

The limiting factors are perpetually changing. During the rest of 1918 and the first half of 1919 the limiting factor on the employment of American troops will not be men or tonnage or food, but equipment of all kinds. For the time being the American munitions programme, particularly in guns and aeroplanes, is woefully behind their available resources in man-power. Unless we and the French are able to supplement promptly every deficiency in the American munitions programme, the despatch of very large numbers of their troops may be retarded from this cause. On the one hand, there are available in America enormous numbers of men in the prime of life; on the other, in Great Britain, for the sake of getting comparatively small numbers of men of inferior physique who will not be much use, or of superior skill who cannot be spared, we run the risk of endangering production of munitions on which not only our own Armies, but the rapid importation of American troops, depend. The situation has, in fact, undergone a very marked change, and we shall commit another of the great mistakes of the war if we do not adapt our policy to it in time.

When the Army Council are warned, as they have been for some time warned, that we are now reaching the limits of releases of man-power from munitions which can be made without endangering output, and vital output, they are accustomed to reply that they would rather have men than munitions; but at the same time they continually put forward to us, and endorse, the Commander-in-Chief's requests for new and large increases in the supply of munitions, and great disasters occur at the front which expose us to enormous and unforeseen demands. For instance, we have had in the last few months strenuous demands to increase the range of the artillery, which can only be done by a very considerable programme of rearmament; very large increases of small arms ammunition have been demanded; largely increased supplies of breech mechanisms; a large increase in the supply of tanks; great extensions of our poison gas plant.

American necessities will come on top of all these, and France may at any moment be unable to assist us in meeting them. Already I have had from M Loucheur demands for 6-inch howitzers for the Americans beyond anything that I am able to supply, and a large proportion of the American divisions are not yet provided with artillery.

Then come the immense demands of the Air Force. The aeroplane engine programme has in the last two months fallen off very seriously indeed, and the extremely good situation which I was able to report to the Cabinet at the beginning of the year no longer holds good. Last week the production was only 688 against an estimate of 1,132. In one firm making crank shafts for an urgently needed type of aeroplane engine they have already lost seven out of eight highly skilled mechanics engaged on one essential stage of manufacture. The consequent loss of crank shafts involved a loss of twenty-five aeroplanes per week.

The case of Messrs Barr and Stroud is another illustration of the wastefulness of recruiting skilled men. They are about to produce a new anti-aircraft height finder, the merit of which is that it is far more efficient, and also requires a smaller personnel to use it. The withdrawal of some thirty skilled mechanics from this firm will mean the postponement for many months of the commencement of deliveries of an instrument which, if the men had been left at their work, would in a very few months have made possible the release of thirty men many times over from anti-aircraft batteries in the field.

Most remarkable of all is the case of the tanks. A programme was approved, at a special meeting of the War Cabinet presided over in February by the Prime Minister, for the urgent construction of tanks. That programme represented what I then considered to be the maximum effort we could make in this field. It is rapidly falling into arrears. Meanwhile, however, the War Office, on the urgent demand of the army in the field, have demanded 400 additional tanks, and if the plans which are favoured by the Chief of the Imperial General Staff are to attain fruition, still larger increases will be required. In spite of all the opposition to tanks, and the mishandling of this policy at every stage, they have now taken a firm root, and every week affords further evidence of their immense utility. I have now received a most urgent demand through M Loucheur, from General Foch for 300 large tanks to be delivered to the French in July, August, and September. The only thing that has been done to assist me in this matter has been to take hundreds of men from the manufacture of tanks, thus dislocating the whole of the Metropolitan Works, with the result that for the sake of getting enough men to make a couple of companies of infantry, the equipment of perhaps four or five battalions of tanks will be lost. Considering that one tank is worth hundreds of men, and, properly used, may conceivably be worth a whole battalion, I must avow myself unable to comprehend the processes of thought which are at work.

It seems to me evident that we are now going too far and over-shooting our mark in regard to man-power. Once the emergency of this summer has been surmounted, we ought not to rupture our munitions supply, particularly our supply of vital modern appliances, for the sake of adding 20,000 men more or less to our Army of over 3,000,000. We ought, on the contrary, to make sure that our great plants here are kept working at their fullest possible capacity in order that our own Army may be equipped with the most perfect, scientific, and life-saving weapons, and in order that we may be able to place in the field the largest possible number of Americans.

I do not by this mean to imply that we shall not be able to find more men from the munitions industries. On the contrary, I earnestly hope to continue, though on a greatly reduced scale, a steady policy of releases which will aggregate many thousands by the end of the year; but I now ask that—

(*a.*) Pivotal and vital men of 19 and 20 who were called up at the end of June shall be returned at my discretion up to a number, not exceeding 1,500;

(*b.*) That in regard to men of 21, 22, and 23 a clean cut should not be proceeded with; and

(*c.*) That future releases of men from the munitions industries should take place as and when efficient substitutes are secured and trained.

Winston S. Churchill to Louis Loucheur: telegram

(*Churchill papers: 15/87*)

15 July 1918 Ministry of Munitions

All the Mark V Tanks of which there are only 400 have been issued to the British Tank Corps in replacement of Mark IV and losses in battle and are actually in use. It would obviously be impossible to take Mark Vs from the trained British units who now have them. No deliveries of Mark V2 Star have yet begun. My Tank production has been greatly delayed by the withdrawal of men for the Army and my outputs for June, July and August are greatly affected. In the emergency it is a great mistake to treat as valueless the Mark IV Tanks of which about seventy are already surplus. These Tanks won the battle of Cambrai and on any ground except the Flanders winter mud are effective weapons. Will you take some of these *en attendant* better. The fifty Mark V1 Star will be sent as promised if you desire them. I greatly regret my resources do not render any other offer possible at the present time.

War Cabinet: minutes

(*Cabinet papers: 23/7*)

15 July 1918

THE MINISTER OF MUNITIONS drew the attention of the War Cabinet to a protest which had been received from the German Government against the use of certain classes of bullets by the British Army. Mr Churchill explained that about a year and a half ago a Committee of the Ministry of Munitions met to examine the question as to whether any economy could be made in the use of metals in the manufacture of bullets. As a result it was decided to substitute paper for aluminium in the core of the bullet, and bullets in this way had been in use for about a year. The Germans had now challenged the using of such bullets, and some very striking correspondence had been captured, which gave fully the various reports made by regimental, brigade, divisional, and Army Headquarters.

MR CHURCHILL read extracts from this correspondence, and pointed out that the General Officer commanding the VIth German Army[1] had ruled that as the bullets presented outside a complete envelope, it was not possible to fasten on to individual soldiers blame for their use. The German Government, however, had entered a protest and said that these bullets inflicted wounds similar to dum-dum bullets, and were in contravention of article 23, paragraph 1 (c), of the Declaration of The Hague Convention of 1899. Mr Churchill said that these bullets were examined very carefully by the Master-General of the Ordnance and other responsible officials, who are all confident that they do not violate The Hague Convention in letter or in spirit, that they do not break up on striking, and that they do not inflict wounds more serious than any other high velocity bullet. The paper was a feature by itself: it had been examined and no bad germs had ever been found, but at the same time it would be easy to say that some foreign matter might be able to get into a wound if the envelope broke. The paste used to fasten the paper is antiseptically treated.

In reply to a question as to whether it was possible to revert to the old pattern type, Mr Churchill said that there was really no choice, as the whole army was armed with this type of bullet now, and it would not only weaken our case if we changed the bullets, but apart from the difficulty which must necessarily be experienced, the moral effect of our own troops, who might think they had been armed with a bullet which would render them liable to reprisals on the part of the Germans, would be very serious.

[1] General von Quast. In the German offensive of April 1918 his had been the principal offensive, planned to cross the Lys and advance to Hazebrouck. Although successful in crossing the Lys, his troops advanced only as far as Bailleul, and Hazebrouck remained within the Allied lines.

MR CHURCHILL said that a War Office Committee had drawn up an answer to the German protest, which dealt at length with the details of the manufacture of the bullet and with the reasons why it was not considered necessary to discontinue its use. This answer, Mr Churchill considered, was too long, and he suggested that a short reply should be sent, without going into details, categorically refusing to change the bullet, and saying at the same time that the British Government was acting fully in accordance with the paragraph of The Hague Convention, mentioned above. It was proposed also in the reply to say that if the German Government proceeded to take reprisals, the British Government would be forced to make use of counter-reprisals.

After a short discussion, in which it was suggested that the German Government should be informed of the particular care which was being taken that the paper should be sterilised, the War Cabinet decided that—

A reply should be sent in answer to the German protest to the effect that the British Government categorically refused to change the bullet now in use, giving as the reason—

That the bullet presented a complete outside envelope, and was strictly in accordance with article 23, paragraph 1 (c), of the Declaration of The Hague Convention of 1899.

The answer should also state that if the German Government used reprisals as a threat because of the continued use of this bullet, the British Government would be forced to make use of counter-reprisals.

War Cabinet: minutes

(*Cabinet papers: 23/7*)

16 July 1918

With reference to War Cabinet 415, Minute 15, the Minister of Munitions called the attention of the War Cabinet to serious labour disturbances which were threatened in Coventry, Manchester, and other engineering centres in connection with the working out by the Ministry of the War Munition Volunteer Scheme. In Coventry the shop stewards had taken exception to the embargo which had been laid on certain firms, which prevented them recruiting further skilled men. There was only a limited amount of skilled labour in the country, and it was essential, if dilution was to be extended, to have the power to move men from where they could be spared to where they were urgently needed. This policy had been approved by the War Cabinet on the 23rd May, and announced on the 8th June. In consequence, certain firms which were either unwilling to proceed with dilution or had a surplus of skilled men, had been told that they must desist from taking on additional skilled men. These firms had complied with the Ministry's request whereupon the shop stewards threatened to strike unless the Ministry dropped its policy. They had, in fact, that morning tendered a week's notice in Coventry and Manchester.

The position was one which the Government could not possibly tolerate, and it was essential that he (Mr Churchill) should be authorised to deal vigorously with the situation should a strike take place. He had prepared a draft statement indicating the policy which he thought the War Cabinet should endorse. (MR CHURCHILL read the draft.) He wished to be free to proceed against persons conspiring against the State, and to withdraw from them the protection, which they now enjoyed, from recruitment for the Army. He agreed that it would be an illegitimate use of the Military Service Acts to compel workmen to put up with industrial conditions against which they were striking in the ordinary way, but this was not an ordinary dispute between capital and labour. It was absurd to comb out men from workshops for the Army and to allow others to walk out of the shops and remain immune while engaged on a strike of the kind now contemplated. He thought the present a good occasion on which to enforce the principle that if a man refused to do the special skilled work for which he was protected, he should be conscripted if fit to fight. He reminded the War Cabinet that on the 15h August, 1917, when the Munitions of War Bill was before the House of Commons, and when Leaving Certificates were abolished, he had made it plain that the Ministry intended to use the Defence of the Realm Act to prevent poaching by employers of fluid labour. (Hansard, Vol. 97, No. 117.)

MR CHAMBERLAIN said that, according to his recollection in the negotiations which had been carried on with the Amalgamated Society of Engineers and other Unions by the Man-Power Committee on which he had served, it had been clearly understood, when exemptions were granted, that if the men ceased to be engaged on the special manufacturing work for which they had been protected, they would be liable to army service.

MR ROBERTS was of opinion that the policy laid down by the War Cabinet should be carried out, and an attempt should be made to secure the co-operation of the loyal section—the great majority—of the workmen. Mr Barnes, who was also a member of the Committee, confirmed Mr Chamberlain's recollection. There had undoubtedly been some misunderstanding, and some of the men's leaders contended that if greater trouble had been taken to define the Government's policy, they would have even got it accepted or have held the men in check. The men complained that they were not fully consulted or adequately informed. However, as notices had only been handed in that day, there was a week during which attempts might be made to secure a peaceful settlement. He was anxious that the announcement made by the Minister of Munitions should be in the nature of a warning rather than of a threat.[1]

General Harington[2] to Winston S. Churchill

(*Churchill papers: 15/164*)

16 July 1918 War Office

Dear Mr Winston Churchill,

The Tank operation Scheme is now with CIGS for signature *en route* to Gen Foch & I will send you a copy and a letter giving you our requirements. The Tank training Manual will be out during the next few days which we hope will be adopted by all Allies. . . .

Relations as regards Tanks in France have much improved and people who have been opponents are quietly removed. I think and hope we shall now get on. I am sure also that the new training arrangements for France & England which are just coming into force will improve matters considerably & were badly wanted.

I entirely agree with your paper on 'Munitions & the limits of recruiting' and think that if we have been stupid we should admit it. I see Gen Seely promised Gen Foch 300 Mark V^{xx} tanks this year. CIGS thinks we should keep all the xx for ourselves & let the French have Mark V if you can spare them.

Yrs sincerely
C. H. Harington

[1] In its conclusions the War Cabinet decided: 'To sanction the policy proposed by the Minister of Munitions, and Mr Churchill undertook to discuss with the Minister of Labour the language of the draft announcement, and to consider whether or not he should base the action he was about to take on the speech delivered by him in August last.'

[2] Charles Harington, 1872–1940. Known as 'Tim'. Entered Army, 1892. Served in the South African and First World Wars; Major-General, 1916. Senior Staff Officer to Lord Plumer on the western front, June 1916–November 1917 (including Passchendaele), in Italy, November 1917–March 1918 and on the western front, March–May 1918. Deputy Chief of the Imperial General Staff, May 1918–October 1920. Knighted, 1919. Lieutenant-General Commanding the Army of the Black Sea, 1920. General Officer Commanding the Allied Forces of Occupation in Turkey, 1920–3. General, 1927. Governor and Commander-in-Chief, Gibraltar, 1933–8. He published *Tim Harington Looks Back* in 1940.

Winston S. Churchill to General Harington

(*Churchill papers: 15/1*)

17 July 1918 Ministry of Munitions

My dear General Harington,

I am delighted at all the good news which your letter contains. I look forward to seeing the document.

1. Where did you see that General Seely had promised General Foch 300 Mark V (2 Star) Tanks? I enclose the two telegrams (Enclosure A) I have had from M Loucheur on the subject and the reply which I sent to the second one. I have not received from Lord Milner any reply to my various letters about the Tank workmen being returned. My production has now fallen very seriously, and I see no prospect of meeting the French request. I do not think that General Seely will have used any language inconsistent with these views.

2. I gave you some time ago a copy of my 'Munitions Programme, 1919'. I now send you an earlier paper 'Munitions Programme, 1918' (Enclosure B). I should be very glad if you would read the passage about Trench Mortar attacks on a large scale. We have completely neglected this method, and the inertia of opinion was so hard to overcome that I did not renew my advocacy of it when writing 'Munitions Programme, 1919'; but I understand that the Germans used Trench Mortars on a great scale for all the front line bombardment in their attack on the Aisne positions, and I see that in the present battle the French front line troops were withdrawn immediately before the attack from the front line positions in order to escape 'the zone of the German Trench Mortar bombardment'. Surely you ought to take this up in conjunction with your general scheme? We have to aim at the simultaneous employment of all methods and means of attack which can be harmonised with the object of developing the greatest intensity of offensive power within a given limited period of time.

I should be glad to see any reports that have come in about the German use of Trench Mortars in recent battles.

3. I also send you two papers (Enclosure C) about Gas, the first of which has been prepared by General Thuillier and the second by Colonel Harrison.[1] I do not know how far you are informed on these latest developments. The second paper by Colonel Harrison is extremely secret, and I shall be glad to have it back as soon as you have read it as I have no other copy, and do not wish to multiply them.

[1] Gilbert Harwood Harrison, 1866–1930. Entered Royal Engineers, 1884. On active service in South Africa, 1899–1900. Colonel, 1913. Deputy Director of Works, War Office, 1916–19. Deputy Chief Engineer, 1919. Chief Engineer, Eastern Command, 1919. Retired (medically unfit for further service), 1923.

I think the Man-power question will be decided in the sense which I desire. It is very important not to go on doing the right thing after it has ceased to be the right thing. The conditions of this war are perpetually changing every 3 or 4 months, and a new view has to be taken and re-adjustments made. As the gale blows now from this quarter and now from that a different setting of the sails is necessary, though the object of the voyage and the principles of navigation are unaltered. Therefore I consider now and for some time to come you ought not to withdraw men so as to weaken my production of munitions. The Irish should be conscripted; munition workers who go on strike should be conscripted; above all, the Americans should be brought in not only in their own formations but as battalions attached *en passant* to every British brigade for training. All these things can be achieved if enough people with knowledge go on pressing continually above all not taking 'No' for an answer.

Will you let me know when you are free for dinner? I think it would be a good thing if we had a talk.

Winston S. Churchill to H. E. Cooke[1]

(Churchill papers: 1/131)

17 July 1918

Dear Sir,

The two fields which I was directed to prepare for Autumn ploughing are now nearly cleared of trees. I have also had another 10-acre field cleared and cleaned. The Military labour employed has not been very efficient, though I have no complaint to make of the men personally. More than £100 will have been spent in wages. I am willing, as I told you, to have the two fields originally specified ploughed if that is insisted upon. At the same time I am advised that there is no prospect of getting a crop which will repay even a small fraction of the capital expenditure involved. There can be no doubt that from the point of view alike of the interest of my property and of immediate food production it would be much better to use these fields for grazing cattle. The difficulties and expense entailed upon the owner of a small property without farm buildings, cottages, or farm implements in ploughing approximately 15 acres of ground are very formidable; the prospect of a crop doubtful; the prospects of financial loss certain. I have observed that owing to the general changes in the labour situation caused by the war, the question of breaking up more land is to be re-considered. If this

[1] Executive Officer of the Surrey County War Agricultural Committee.

is so, I shall be very glad if my case can be included among those under review.

I have during the present year alone (the first complete year of my tenancy) provided considerable sums of money to reclaim the land which had been left completely derelict and to develop food production upon it. Apart from the heavy expense in wages to which I have referred, I have built a pigsty, a cow-shed, and am about to build two other pigstys. I have purchased a horse and cart, two cows, and seventeen bullocks. We have succeeded in making a small hay stack and manure heap, neither of which existed on the place last year. The vegetable garden has been enlarged and fully planted, and about three quarters of an acre of land has been dug and planted with potatoes. A great deal of fencing has been done, and other necessary work which had fallen into arrears on the land. Altogether, I have provided nearly £1,000 of capital for food production during this year.

In these circumstances I hope I shall not be called upon to embark on the absolutely unremunerative task of ploughing up the two fields in question and attempting to get a crop therefrom.

Winston S. Churchill to General Birch

(*Churchill papers: 15/1*)

17 July 1917 Ministry of Munitions

My dear General Birch,

Many thanks for your letter. I did not in the least resent the official communication which you made on the subject of increasing the range of the Artillery. On the contrary, both criticism and heart-searching are continually necessary if good progress is to be made. On the other hand, I think Bingham and Bland[1] produced a very solid answer, and I hope you will address yourself to it categorically and see exactly how far the facts are in dispute and what further steps we can take to improve things.

I do not think from all I can hear that you would be well advised to give up NC at the present time, or in limiting your gases to two types, against both of which the German mask is a complete protection. The Germans have very great difficulties in procuring the materials out of which good masks are

[1] William St Colum Bland, 1868–1950. Entered the Royal Artillery, 1887. On active service, Burma, 1891–2. Waziristan, 1894–5 and China, 1900. Major 1906. Superintendent of Experiments, 1909–13. Member of the Ordnance Board, 1914. Lieutenant-Colonel, 1914. On active service in France, 1914–15. Colonel, 1916. President of the Ordnance Committee, Ministry of Munitions, 1915–19 (with the rank of Brigadier-General). Controller of Munitions Design, 1919. Commandant of the Ordnance College, 1919–20.

made and are at a disadvantage in that respect. We must be continually endeavouring to penetrate their masks, and ought never to cut ourselves off from this important line of development.

Labour is at the present time causing me a great deal of trouble, both what has been taken away from the munition factories for the Army and what is still left behind.

I hope to come out in a week or ten days, as there are several things I should like to discuss with you and others.

War Cabinet: minutes

(*Cabinet papers: 23/7*)

19 July 1918

THE MINISTER OF MUNITIONS said that it was really impossible for him to release more men from his Department, except slowly by dilution. As instance of the effect of releases already made, he mentioned that at the present time the output of aeroplane engines was approximately 55 per cent. of the programme arrange, and the output of tanks had fallen by one-half. It was also impossible to meet the requests of the War Office for breach mechanisms. Mr Churchill said that his Department would, of course, go on and do the best it could under the circumstances, but he could not face any further large withdrawal of labour. The vexation now in industries under his Department was very great. The men were resisting dilution and delaying output, and there was considerable discontent.

THE FIRST LORD OF THE ADMIRALTY[1] urged that he had already put before the War Cabinet the views that Mr Churchill had just expressed, and entirely endorsed everything which had just been said.[2]

War Cabinet: minutes

(*Cabinet papers: 23/7*)

22 July 1918

. . . THE MINISTER OF MUNITIONS described to the War Cabinet the position in the chief engineering centres, as revealed by reports received

[1] Sir Eric Geddes (see page 107, note 2).

[2] Later in the discussion, Churchill suggested 'that it might be possible to utilise Indian troops during the summer months on the Western front'. But following the exertions of the Indian Corps on the western front in 1915, and the heavy losses which it had suffered at the battles of Neuve Chapelle, 2nd Ypres and Loos, it had been felt that Indian troops should be sent whenever possible to battle fronts elsewhere, and in particular to Mesopotamia.

during the forenoon, with regard to the trouble which had arisen out of the plan for rationing skilled labour. It had been decided in Manchester to hand in notices that night, and in Birmingham the men were insisting on the withdrawal of the embargo. No notices had been rendered in Leeds, Glasgow, Bristol, or Cardiff. A meeting of shop stewards held at Sheffield had been sparsely attended. In Coventry the position hung in the balance. There was evidence that certain individuals were systematically fomenting trouble, but no legal action had been taken against them up to the present, and he (Mr Churchill) had refrained from any official or public announcement that he would have recourse to the powers authorised by the War Cabinet on the 16th July. But it was clear that the Government had reached a point where to shrink from using those powers, if found necessary, would be disastrous to the whole future of their relations with labour during the war. If the present situation were firmly handled, those relations would, he believed, be immensely improved.

The issue which had been raised was one which the Government could join with every confidence of obtaining the full support of the public and of the press. As an example of the weakness of the men's case, Mr Churchill mentioned that, side by side with the embargo, there was an unsatisfied demand in the country for 60,000 skilled men.

MR ROBERTS expressed the opinion that the Coventry workmen, whose notices terminated that night, would probably not go to the length of a strike.

The War Cabinet considered a suggestion made by the Minister of Munitions that it might be desirable to have a statement of the Government's policy made in the House of Commons that afternoon on a motion for the adjournment of the House.

The War Cabinet decided—

> To postpone such a statement, in order to see what developments took place in Coventry at the termination of the notices.

War Cabinet: minutes

(*Cabinet papers: 23/7*)

24 July 1918

THE MINISTER OF MUNITIONS summarised the position in the chief engineering centres in relation to the embargo on the employment of skilled men. The reports indicated that in Coventry over 7,000 men had ceased work, some areas were threatening to cease work unless the embargo were removed, and others appeared to be undisturbed. The general impression conveyed by the reports was one of hesitation, as if the men were not quite certain of their powers. The promoters of discord were strenuously endeavouring to rouse the workmen, and the question which the War Cabinet was called on to decide was whether they should allow the movement to spread before taking action, or whether they should act at once before the movement became much stronger. On the whole he was prepared to advise the War Cabinet to act at once by issuing a notice to the workmen containing a declaration that men on strike would have their exemption certificates withdrawn (Mr Churchill read a draft of the proposed statement). The statement ought to be issued that day.

He had summoned the Trade Union Advisory Committee for tomorrow, but it was useless to expect that they would take a strong line. The men were out to oppose conscription and dilution, and no doubt wanted to take full advantage of the upward trend of wages. The actual application of the embargo was limited to a few firms, but the men saw therein a large issue viz, the threat of military conscription if they resisted industrial conscription. The only weapon the Government could use in the situation was the removal of the protection certificates, and the right of the State to use that weapon ought never to have been allowed to become an arguable question.

MR HODGE[1] suggested, and Mr Churchill concurred, that in the notice it should be clearly stated that the Military Service Acts would not be applied to men remaining at work.

MR ROBERTS urged that it was important to allow the men time to be fully seized of the implications on their conduct if they struck work. He was not sure that the patriotic elements amongst workmen had grasped the character of the strike in which they were asked to join. It was further important that nothing should be done which would throw the Trade Unions in to Opposition. For that reason he held that the Minister of Munitions should consult the Trade Union Advisory Committee before taking any drastic steps. He did not believe that that Committee would endorse the action of the Coventry strikers.

In reply to a question whether the issue of the proposed notice would have the effect of throwing those Trade Unionists who were hesitating against the Government, Sir Stephenson Kent said that on the whole there was no big movement in the country at the moment in favour of a strike. It was conceivable that many might be moved to strike if provoked by the threat of the Military Service Acts. On the other hand, if the shop stewards (whose executive was meeting that day in Sheffield) recommended a 'down tools'

[1] John Hodge, 1855–1937. President of the Trades Congress, 1892. Labour MP for Gorton, 1906–23. Minister for Labour, 1916–17. Minister of Pensions, 1917–19. He published his memoirs, *Workman's Cottage to Windsor Castle*, in 1931.

policy, we should see at least as many more on strike tomorrow as there were today. He was in favour of action being taken at once, as the strikers had defied their own local representatives, their Trade Unions, and the State. The organisation of the strikers was improving daily. The Amalgamated Society of Engineers had gone back on the position which they had taken up on Friday last, presumably because they were afraid of the strength of the shop stewards' movement.

THE PRIME MINISTER emphasized the importance of the State winning in the struggle with the strikers. If to put men into the Army would help the State to win, then they should not hesitate to use the Military Service Acts, but it was a mistake to extend unnecessarily the difficulties of the State. The present dispute bore a strong resemblance to the conflict which as Ministers of Munitions, he had with the Clyde workers' committee, in that case the Government had satisfied themselves that they could stand a strike of six weeks on the Clyde. Ultimately, industrial peace was secured by deporting several of the leaders and prosecuting others. That policy destroyed the nerve of the Shop Steward movement, and Glasgow had been comparatively quiet since. It was most desirable that the bulk of the workers should be on the side of the State, and that no provocative action should throw them in to the opposite camp. He was of the opinion that it was somewhat soon to take the step suggested by the Minister of Munitions. In the meantime it could be ascertained who were the leaders who were fomenting the strike, and if a little time were given for the strike to develop, it might be found that the workmen themselves would fall in to hostile groups. There was no question of the Government going back on its announced policy, but only of deciding the precise moment at which to make a counter-offensive.

MR CHURCHILL reminded the Cabinet that the strikers were calculating on the Government being afraid to have recourse openly to the Military Service Acts. In view of the course the discussion had taken with reference to the Advisory Committee, he was prepared to meet the Committee and to announce to them the policy of the Government. He would then invite them to endeavour to settle the dispute, which was a strike against them as much as against the State. They could assume the *role* of standing between the Government & Labour, and could point out to the men that, unless the embargo scheme were allowed to operate, the Government would have no alternative but to withdraw the exemptions from Military Service of the men on strike.

MR ROBERTS said that his objections were met by Mr Churchill's last suggestion and Mr Hodge concurred. Mr Barnes urged quick action to help the waverers and pointed out the Govt's failure to 'give statutory effect to its pledges to restore Trade Union conditions after the war'.

The War Cabinet decided that the Minister of Munitions should meet the Trade Unions Advisory Committee and announce to them the policy of the Government. He should then relate to them the proposal that they should endeavour to settle the strike themselves, otherwise the Government would have no alternative but to put its policy into operation. In his statement to the Committee the Minister should emphasize the distinction between the present challenge to the State and an ordinary dispute. The former involving a form of procedure quite inapplicable to the latter. Finally, he should point out the difficulty of recruiting elderly men, agricultural labourers etc, in order to maintain the essential needs of the army, when young men exempted from Military Service to do work for the State refused to work at all.

Manchester Women Munition Workers to Winston S. Churchill: telegram

(*Churchill papers: 15/117*)

26 July 1918

Resolution just passed by two mass meetings women at British Westinghouse Manchester this mass meeting of women munition workers indignantly protests against the strikes now taking place in the Midlands and elsewhere while our soldiers at the Front are in such urgent need of supplies. We pledge ourselves to carry on and to stand by the men at the Front until a real victory has been achieved.

Lord Rothermere to Winston S. Churchill

(*Churchill papers: 1/129*)

26 July 1918 Air Board

My dear Winston

How can I thank you sufficiently for your letter of sympathy![1] Of all the messages I have received none have touched me more than yours and what you say has been a real comfort to me these days.

Believe me I value what you say very highly and I hope you will understand the delay in answering your letter.

Yours ever faithfully
Rothermere

[1] Lord Rothermere's eldest son, Harold Alfred Vyvian St George Harmsworth (born 2 August 1894; joined the Irish Guards 11 August 1914; twice wounded; MC 1918) had died on 12 February 1918 of wounds received in action at Cambrai. His second son Vere Sidney Tudor Harmsworth, born 1895, had been killed in action 13 November 1916. Only his third son survived the war.

Winston S. Churchill: draft Press statement, never issued

(*Churchill papers: 15/117*)

26 July 1918 Ministry of Munitions

After the disastrous battles at the end of March, the Ministry of Munitions was directed by the War Cabinet to release a large number of men for the Army. The need for men to fill the gap before the Americans could arrive, or the winter came, was so urgent that the Military Authorities declared that they must have the men even if the output of munitions fell off.

In these circumstances the very greatest efforts were made by the Ministry of Munitions to find the men for the Army and yet at the same time to make up the heavy losses in guns and war material which had been incurred and keep up a full supply.

In order to achieve this, it was necessary that the Ministry of Munitions should first have at its disposal a large number of War Munitions Volunteers who could be sent to shops where there was a special need, and secondly that they should be able to prevent over-staffing without regard to general interests by particular firms. This policy was fully discussed with the Trade Union Advisory Committee in April and in June. The employers were also kept regularly informed. Finally, on June 8th the whole scheme was published in such a way as to give the clearest possible explanation.

By proceeding on these lines, we have succeeded in maintaining fully the supply of munitions and in making good all losses, in spite of the fact that nearly 100,000 of our experienced workers have been released.

For some weeks past, the Minister of Munitions has been of opinion that the limits of recruiting from the munitions factories were being reached, and that further large withdrawals of men would create serious injury to our means of producing essential war material. This view has been in principle accepted by the War Cabinet, and it was intended that releases of skilled men for the Army should proceed very much more slowly than heretofore. The worst of the strain is, therefore, over, and it has been met not only without any failure of output, but while maintaining abundant and growing supplies for the armies of all that they require.

It was inevitable that this intense effort, and the disturbance attending upon it in every workshop in the United Kingdom, should cause some soreness and unrest. It would be unfair to blame the Department which has successfully grappled with these extraordinary difficulties because of the irritation caused by the necessary measures to meet the needs. It would be a thousand pities, now that the result has been nearly achieved, and when the pressure of recruiting from munitions works is likely to be sensibly lessened, to mar everything by a widespread stoppage of work. Every effort must be made by loyal and responsible people on both sides to reach a friendly and workable arrangement. There is no room for pride or temper or unreasonable obstinacy on either side. Only what is absolutely necessary for the safety of the armies must be asked for by the Government, and everything must be done to make the enforcement of what is necessary as little unpalatable to the workers as possible. If that spirit is shown on both sides, it is certain that a good settlement can be reached.

On the other hand, workers must be on their guard against certain evil and subterranean influences which are at work and which are always ready to take advantage of any difficulty or natural irritation to which the hard necessities of the war give rise. There is an under-current of Pacifism, Defeatism and Bolshevism at work which it would be affectation not to recognise and folly not to mark down. The belief of these Defeatists is that they can stop the war by stopping the output of munitions even for a month. In this they are entirely mistaken. Stoppage of work, even for a month, would not bring the war to an end. It would prolong it. It would not mean that our soldiers would not be able to continue fighting. It would mean that they would have fewer shells to fire; fewer aeroplanes to protect them; fewer tanks to support them; fewer guns and machine guns to hold back the enemy with, and consequently, being robbed of so many of these live-saving appliances, they would have heavier losses, smaller chances of victory, greater dangers of defeat, and would have to lay down their lives in larger numbers to fill the gap. Therefore the defeatists would not succeed even in their own visionary purpose, but would only bring avoidable misery and suffering on our brave men and rob them of the fruits of their struggles at the moment when these may not be so far away. The women of the nation whose male belongings are under fire should understand these facts thoroughly.

The position of comparatively young men, already in receipt of very high wages, who lend themselves, however unwittingly, to a movement of this character is a serious one. Whatever grievances or annoyances they have to put up with are trifling compared with the sacrifices made by men old enough in many cases to be their fathers who are on active service at the front, or by men who have been fighting for years, often several times wounded, or by the families of the fighting men in their deep anxiety.

If these exempted men will not do the work they have been left at home to do they will have to go and fight. It is impossible for the Minister of Munitions to continue to protect them from the obligation to which all other citizens are liable.

The Minister, in pursuance of the authority given him by the War Cabinet, has decided to withdraw the exemption certificates of all munition workers who are on strike.

Winston S. Churchill: Press statement under Lloyd George's name

(*Churchill papers: 15/117*)

26 July 1918

The Prime Minister has directed the following announcement to be made on behalf of His Majesty's Government:—

Certain men in the munition workshops have ceased work in disregard of their duly accredited leaders, and have remained idle against the advice of the Trade Union Advisory Committee. They have ceased work, not in pursuance of a trade dispute, but in an endeavour to force the Government to change the national policy essential to the prosecution of the war. Whilst millions of their fellow-countrymen are hourly facing danger and death for their Country, *the men now on strike*[1] have been granted exemption from these perils only because their services were considered of more value to the state in the workshops than in the Army.

It is not necessary for the Government to declare that all men wilfully absent from their work on or after Monday the 29th July, will be deemed to have voluntarily placed themselves outside the area of munitions industries. Their protection certificates will cease to have effect from that date, and they will become liable to the provisions of the Military Service Acts.

[1] This phrase in italics was added by Lloyd George to Churchill's draft. Churchill had written 'the skilled munition workers'.

August 1918

Winston S. Churchill to Sir George Ritchie: draft letter, never sent

(*Churchill papers: 5/20*)

3 August 1918 Ministry of Munitions

My dear Sir George Ritchie,

The beginning of the 5th year of the war makes me desirous of communicating with my friends in Dundee upon the main situation of our affairs; and I am particularly prompted to do so by reading the letter wh Lord Lansdowne has just written for publication in the newspapers.[1] When a statesman so high in character, so pure in nature & so experienced in affairs offers to his fellow countrymen definite counsel on the supreme issue at a moment like this it is due to the intellectual dignity of our public life that his words shd receive sober & searching examination. It is also fitting that great constituencies supporting with constancy by every means and sacrifice the prosecution of this bloody & destructive war shd from time to time formally & deliberately take stock of our national position & of the requirements of our cause.

Lord Lansdowne's view is unmistakably expressed. He advises that we shd now endeavour to make peace with Germany upon honourable terms, & that for this purpose we shd treat as overtures of good faith the various references to a desire for peace & to a readiness to discuss peace wh have been made on different occasions by German & Austrian ministers in their rapid transits through power & that we shd now try to make a territorial bargain with Germany & her allies wh wd spare mankind the suffering & slaughter & economic waste through wh they must otherwise plough their way. Such a proposition is undoubtedly a serious one, but it is not one wh those who take the contrary view need be afraid of facing.

[1] In July 1918 the 5th Marquess of Lansdowne, a former Viceroy of India and Secretary of State for War, had publicly advocated a negotiated peace with Germany. Earlier, from May to November 1915, he had served as a colleague of Churchill's in the War Cabinet, at which time he was Minister without Portfolio (a post he held until Lloyd George became Prime Minister in December 1916). On 30 October 1914 his second son, Lord Charles Mercer Nairne, had been killed in action in France.

For what is the contrary view. It is in a sentence that *this war has got to be won & that it is not won yet.* These twin hard facts will be found to dominate every form of argument not arising from despondency or treason. Let us not pretend that we have won yet. Let us not delude ourselves by thinking that there is any substitute for victory. To enter upon a struggle like this, to proclaim that vital & sacred issues are at stake, to cast the flower of the nation's manhood into the furnace, to wage war by land and sea for four devastating years, & then to discover that the foe is so stiff that after all a reasonable accommodation is expedient, & shd be brought about as quickly as possible is not, however it may be disguised, anything wh resembles 'an honourable peace'. To set out to redress an intolerable wrong, to grapple with a cruel butcher, & then after a bit to find him so warlike that upon the whole it is better to treat him as a good hearted fellow & sit down & see if we can't be friends after all, may conceivably be a form of prudence but that is the very best that can be said for it.

But is it even prudent? To judge this we must look out upon the vast field of the war & try however inadequately to compute its awful balances. Stated vy broadly the following is the salient fact of the war situation:—The *Appearance* of power is with the enemy & the *Reality* of power is with us. Consider first the *Appearance.*

Germany has won scores of battles. She has conquered enormous countries: she has subjugated & pillaged nearly a dozen states or provinces. She has made millions of soldiers captive; she has overthrown Russia; she has broken into the East; she occupies the capitals of Belgium, Serbia, Roumania & Poland. Austria, Bulgaria & Turkey are gripped tight in her hands: And the Kaiser now rules over wider regions, larger armies, more millions of subjects & slaves than at any previous moment in the war. That is the *Appearance.*

But what is the *Reality*? The German people have been fighting at their extreme extension for four years. All this time they have been bleeding on a battle front averaging about 200 divisions constantly in action. All this time they have been making the intense exertions necessary to equip, feed & sustain their tremendous armies. All this time they have suffered the protracted & cumulative evils of bad feeding & underfeeding. The grown manhood of Germany at the beginning of this war did not exceed by much more than 4 to 3 the grown manhood of France alone. The strain upon the life energies of the German people cannot be less than three times what we in the British islands have yet been called upon to endure. It is impossible that this strain can be borne by Germany indefinitely. That we have often been disappointed in the past is no reason why we shd be disappointed in the future. If we are steadfast they must collapse.

Three terrible things have happened to Germany during the present year.

First although we have now reached the month of August, their desperate attacks on the British & French armies have so far produced no decisive result. Secondly their submarine warfare has been definitely controlled. Thirdly brave, ardent American armies are safely landing in France at a rate wh over many weeks has exceeded 10,000 soldiers each day. Nearly a million & a half Americans have already crossed the Atlantic. There is no apparent reason why this shd not go on until the allied strength is overwhelming. To these three terrible things we may perhaps add a fourth—the Allied domination of the Air. All the world is marching against Germany & her confederates. All the continents, all the oceans, all the men in all the lands are leagued against the guilty nation. We have but to persevere to conquer. That is the Reality.

This prodigious contrast between Appearance & Reality, between the war map at the moment & the forces that are on the move shd be in our minds when we consider the kind of counsel that Lord Lansdowne urges upon us. A Peace made now would for all time register & rivet upon the world the appearance of German power taken at its culminating point. It wd forever deny the other nations all their heritage in Reality. A peace upon the accomplished facts of German triumph, at the hour when German triumph is tottering would shut out for many years from mankind their native basic right. They have the right & they have the strength. Are they to forego the right, & disperse the strength before the hollow pomp of German military assertion. Are we to doom our children to accept for all time the Germans at their own valuation, at their highest valuation, at their most extravagant valuation; to stamp these false values forever upon the world & to blot out from the account our immense, and if we give them play, overwhelming resources. To do so will be to defraud & defile the destiny of man.

Let us found ourselves on *Reality* & not on *Appearance*. Why—after going through all we have done—shd we seek peace at the moment when Germany is declining but has not yet declined & when America has only just begun. Why again, shd we accept—& by accepting establish and set the seal on the relative positions of Germany & Russia. Germany was wrong: Russia was right. Germany stands at the summit of her power. Russia is in the deepest abyss. Nothing has ever been seen before like the blatant parade of German success. Nothing has ever been seen before like the awful misery & convulsion of Russia. But can anyone suppose that this is the end of the story? Is it not certain that the great Russian nation will arise. Is it not certain that the German military power will be abated? Ought we to build our lives & policy & the future arrangement of the world on the unreal basis of a smashed-up Russia & an invincible Germany. Ought we to seek to negotiate a treaty wh will brand for generations on the foreheads of our race a fictitious inferiority

& a sham defeat. Yet that is what Lord Lansdowne in effect earnestly & obstinately beseeches us to do. President Wilson with searching thought has spoken the only word wh in these days shd be heard in the councils & camps of the Allies. 'Force, free without restraint, force to the utmost limit.' And that is the path upon wh the people of the United States—themselves nearly double the population of Germany—have avowedly & whole-heartedly embarked.

We must keep in step with them. They are our kinsmen from across the ocean. They are our sons returned from a long estrangement. They are our comrades of the Great War & of the Greater Future. With every day that this strife endures the old misunderstandings are lessened & the ancient quarrels vanish away. When we count the fearful cost, let us not forget to count the precious gain. In the community of interest & union of spirit & brotherhood in arms now being recreated between the American people & the British race lies the most solid guarantee of our common safety, & in years to come & of the general peace & progress of the world. Let us therefore look steadily out upon that portion of our task we have yet to do.

Two separate conditions are required of the German people. First they must be decisively beaten in the field by the armies of the Allies. That shd be the indispensable preliminary to a cessation of hostilities. Secondly they should by their own free & spontaneous action, by a real act of self-regeneration make a definite break with the system wh has led them to do many fearful & monstrous crimes. Not till then shd they be allowed to take their vacant place in the League of Nations & be received into the new brotherhood of mankind. Only in this way can the wounds of Europe be healed, only in this way can the sacrifices of the valiant be made fruitful. Only in this way can the horrors & calamities of this present time come to an end once & for all.

Yours vy sincerely
WSC

Sir Henry Wilson to Winston S. Churchill

(*Churchill papers: 15/1*)

6 August 1918

My dear Winston,

I am a little worried as to the prospects for next year both as regards the output of Tanks and Mechanical Traction. As regards the former you have our programme which I know is formidable, but I also know you will do your utmost to meet it.

As regards the latter the General Staff will inform QMG of our requirements and he will take up the matter with you.

What I feel is that though our numerical superiority next year will not be very great, yet we can add materially to that by our lead in mechanical means.

If it is decided that we go for the Boche let us knock him out properly and in no half-hearted manner.

To do this we want all your help.

Yours,
Henry Wilson

Winston S. Churchill to Sir Douglas Haig: telegram

(*Churchill papers: 2/103*)

8 August 1918 Chateau Verchocq

I am so glad that it has all come right I was always sure it would this year please accept my sincere congratulations on todays brilliant event.[1]

Sir Douglas Haig to Winston S. Churchill: telegram

(*Spencer-Churchill papers*)

9 August 1918 General Headquarters
11.15 am

Many thanks for your welcome congratulations. I shall always remember with gratitude the energy and foresight which you have displayed as Minister of Munitions, and so rendered our success possible.

[1] On August 8 the British 4th Army (under Sir Henry Rawlinson) and the French 1st Army launched an offensive against the Germans near Amiens. The British broke through at the first assault, and cavalry and light tanks pursued the fleeing Germans, advancing 7 miles, capturing 400 guns and taking nearly 22,000 prisoners. Churchill wrote of Rawlinson in *The World Crisis* (1916–18 p. 507): 'It was, truly, *his* victory . . . He had put aside old fashioned ideas, he had used new weapons as they should be used, he had reaped swift and rich reward.'

Winston S. Churchill to Clementine Churchill

(*Churchill papers: 1/129*)

10 August 1918 Chateau Verchocq

My Darling,

We had a very pleasant fly over and passed fairly close to Lullenden. I could follow the road through Croydon and Caterham quite easily. We came down at Lympne Aerodrome and watched all the machines starting for France. About fifty were being sent off that night. We landed here in good time for dinner. The Chateau is very comfortable—simple but clean. I have a charming room, filled with a sort of ancient wood-carved furniture that you admire and which seems to me to be very fine and old. The grounds contain avenues of the most beautiful trees, beech and pine, grown to an enormous height and making broad walks like the aisles of cathedrals. One of these must be nearly half a mile long. The gardens are very pretty, though of course there are not many flowers. I am sitting now in the open air on a glorious evening writing this to you.

Yesterday we went to the battle-field, motoring through Amiens and Villers Bretonneux to a village you will see on the long straight road on the map called Lamotte. This was about 5,000 yards inside the lines which the Germans had held the day before. As they were shelling the village and trying to shell the road, we moved the car down a side road about half a mile where we found a safe place for it, and then we walked about on the battle-field, picking our way with discretion. The actual battle front had rolled on nearly four miles from where we were, and all our heavy batteries in this neighbourhood had just received the order to move forward again. Jack, who is with Birdwood in the neighbourhood of Verchocq, came with us and acted as escort and guide. The ground everywhere was ploughed up by shells, but nothing to the same extent as the Somme and Ypres battle-fields. The tracks of the Tanks were everywhere apparent. There were very few dead to be seen, most of them having been already buried; but generally speaking I do not think there can have been much slaughter, as the enemy seems to have yielded very readily.

On our way to the battle-field we passed nearly 5,000 German prisoners, penned up in cages or resting under escort in long columns along the road-side. Among them were more than 200 officers. I went into the cages and looked at them carefully. They looked a fairly sturdy lot, though some of them were very young. I could not help feeling very sorry for them in their miserable plight and dejection, having marched all those miles from the battle-field without food or rest, and having been through all the horrors of the fight before that. Still, I was very glad to see them where they were.

To-day I have been working at GHQ on shells. The German shells have false noses which make them go much further than ours, and the question is, Why have we not developed these earlier? There is no doubt we have fallen behind, and great efforts will have to be made in this class of supply if we are to catch up next year. I think they have been far too complacent in Bingham's department, and I am going to hold a conference here next Saturday at which they will have to justify the present position, if they can.

Tomorrow I think of going again to the battle-field if I can get horses. It will be very interesting to see the armies moving forward. The events which have taken place in the last 3 days are among the most important that have happened in the war, and, taken in conjunction with the German defeats on the Marne and at Rheims, entitle us to believe that the tide has turned. Up to the present there must be at least 30,000 prisoners in our hands, with several hundred guns. In addition, Montdidier is surrounded and the troops holding it are cut off. This may largely increase our captures. On the front of three armies, the fourth British and the first and third French, several hundred thousand men have been marching forward for several days through liberated territory. Our cavalry are still out in front, and in some parts of the line there are at the moment no Germans left. The Australian armoured cars rushed through the moment the front was broken and attacked the headquarters of the transport and everything they could find in rear. They have reached the headquarters of an Army Corps and shot four of the staff officers. At another place they found the German troops in a village at their dinners and ran down the whole street firing in through the windows upon them, doing tremendous execution.

I am so glad about this great and fine victory of the British Army. It is our victory, won chiefly by our troops under a British Commander, and largely through the invincible Tank which British brains have invented and developed. Haig has done very well, and it does not follow that we are at the end of our good fortune yet. There are great possibilities in the situation if they can be turned to account. One American regiment has taken part on our front in this battle. Would you believe it—only three American Divisions were in the line at any one moment between Rheims and Soissons. They certainly had a good press. That is one reason why I rejoice that we should have won a great success which no one can take from us.

I have to be in Paris on Tuesday and have conferences there Wednesday and Thursday, and possibly Friday. Saturday and Sunday I shall have to have conferences here on the various branches of the new programme, and as I cannot get back for the week-end I shall probably stay on here till Wednesday or Thursday week. It is only here that one can get direct knowledge and be able to form true opinions about what is required. How I wish you could come out here, but that, alas, is impossible.

I send you a copy of an extremely appreciative telegram which I had from Haig in answer to my congratulations. It is certainly very satisfactory to have succeeded in gaining the confidence and good-will of the extremely difficult and to some extent prejudiced authorities out here. There is no doubt that they have felt themselves abundantly supplied.

Tender love, my darling one
Your ever loving
W

Winston S. Churchill to David Lloyd George

(*Churchill papers: 27/32*)

10 August 1918 Chateau Verchocq

There is no doubt Haig has won a very great success which may well be the precursor of further extremely important events. I spent yesterday on the battle-field, from which the fighting troops were just rolling forward. There did not appear to have been much slaughter judging from the corpses. The Divisional General[1] in whose sector I was, close to Lamotte village on the Villers-Bretonneux road did not estimate the number of dead Germans on the front of his Division at more than 200. He himself had lost only 40 killed. On the other hand, the roads were crowded with prisoners, and I met no less than 5,000 in one enormous column. This looks as if the Germans were putting up their hands very easily. The few German dead I saw were principally round their machine-gun positions. Of course, there is always the danger that local impressions may be misleading, but everything I could see and hear inspired me with the very greatest confidence and pleasure. It seems to me this is the greatest British victory that has been won in the whole war, and the worst defeat that the German army has yet sustained. How thankful you must be after all the anxieties through which we have passed.

You will like to see the telegram I have received from Haig in answer to my congratulations. At the same time I am far from satisfied with several classes of our supply. There is no doubt that the Germans, by putting false noses on their shells, have gained a distinct advantage in range and that they are in front of us in this important field.

Then there is the mustard gas, which I hope has turned the corner after so many difficulties, but which we are still destitute of. Aeroplane engines,

[1] Probably Major-General Charles Rosenthal, commanding the 2nd Australian Division.

particularly the high-powered types, have not fulfilled Weir's expectations. Lastly, there are the tanks. The Admiral[1] has not been a success, and further very great efforts are needed. It is only by looking facts in the face, especially the unpleasant ones, that one finds the means to overcome the difficulties and avoid mishap. On the whole, however, the Army have found themselves abundantly supplied with all they require.

So far as tanks are concerned, it was not possible for me to reinstate Stern. Such a step would have involved me in endless difficulties with the Military. I am very hopeful that with Seely's authority and drive, and Maclean's[2] very high qualifications and experience, we shall realise the full programme which I promised you at the beginning of the year by the required date. Meanwhile there are plenty of tanks for the comparatively small numbers of officers and men which have hitherto been provided. To handle the tanks which we shall certainly make by next June, at least 100,000 men will be required for the Tank Corps. The tanks also will fail in their full effect if the cross-country vehicles are not simultaneously ready. I hope you will continue to study this aspect, which is all-important. I see no reason why, if we take the steps which are open to us now, we should not win a decisive military victory in the West next year.

I am going on to Paris on Monday, but shall be back at this Chateau next Saturday, and here I shall stay for the best part of another week. It is a very beautiful place, with the most lovely trees, and you might do far worse than spend a few days here.

Winston S. Churchill to Major-General J. E. B. Seely

(*Churchill papers: 15/123*)

10 August 1918 Chateau Verchocq

I had a conference today at the Artillery Office GHQ on the subject of:—

(1) False-nosed shells. They showed me a complete collection of German shells of this type which yield superior ranges to our corresponding natures. The German specimens comprised the 6″ Gun and 6″ Howr, the 4·2″ Gun

[1] Rear-Admiral Sir A G H W Moore, Controller of Experimental Design, Testing and Despatch at the Ministry of Munitions (see p. 326, note 1).

[2] James Borrowman Maclean, 1881–1940. Educated as an engineer. Worked for several years on the Clyde. Entered the Ministry of Munitions as Director of Shell Production, 1915. Subsequently Controller of Gun Manufacture and Technical Adviser to the Ordnance Group. Appointed by Churchill to be Controller of the Mechanical Warfare Department, 1917. CBE, 1918. Controller of Tank Production, and Chairman of the Tank Production Committee, 1918.

and Howr, and the German Field Gun. Our shells compared very unfavourably like with like to these in appearance and, as it was claimed, in result. The false nose of the 6″ screws on to the top of the shell. Our latest 6″, of which I am told there are only a few hundred as yet with the Army, is an improvement on the earlier type and obviously approximates to the German false nose but it is a very poor try at it, and I was told that the Germans have further developments in preparation which will leave even their present pattern behind. I must say I was dissatisfied with the situation disclosed. I do not see how it can be contended that the Germans have not stolen a march on us and are not definitely ahead of us in this respect.

(2) The question before us is, What can be done to make up for the loss of time? We cannot scrap our existing ammunition. It must all either be adapted or fired off. Can it be adapted, and to what extent? The capacity of our shell factories will next year be in excess of steel available for Army requirements so far as bulk supply is concerned. Is it then possible, agreeably with a certain reduction in the total volume of output, to introduce this improved ammunition and to adapt a proportion of the old? If a marked increase in range could be obtained by cutting screw threads round the shoulders of some of our present ammunition and screwing a false nose cap on over the fuse, this should certainly be tried, and plans made on a very large scale for effecting the change. But it may be that the nose by itself without alteration in the driving band and the rifling would not achieve the improvement sought for. It may also be that we have not yet discovered the proper shape and proportion of a false nose which could be fitted on our ammunition. In this case the disaster is more serious, and we shall have no means of repairing it except by the construction of new shell; and having regard to the volume of supply required it will be impossible to do this except gradually. This has, however, got to be taken in hand at the earliest possible moment and on a very large scale. It is not at all creditable to us that the Germans should be firing these shells in every nature as a matter of regular practice while we are still fumbling with experiments.

(3) Among yesterday's captures was a complete railway gun and train. The gun is a Naval 11″, firing pre-war ammunition from enormous brass cartridge cases 7 ft high. The shells have false noses but sensitive fuses. The sensitive fuse is made to act in spite of the false nose by a wooden stick extending from the fuse inside the false nose and projecting about an inch beyond it. This seems to dispose of the argument that you cannot use an instantaneous fuse with false-nosed shell.

(4) In addition, I was shown specimens of the German clock-work time fuse, a whole case of which has now been captured. Complaint was made that we have nothing equivalent at the present time of a satisfactory nature, only

70 having been delivered in the last few months, and these inferior to the German. It seems to me very important to take this German fuse and copy it exactly, with only such alterations as may be necessary to screw it into our shell. Pray let me have a report on how this can be done, how long it will take, and what deliveries are possible. The supply required is not a large one.

I hope General Bingham and General Bland will be armed on all these points when they come over for next Saturday's conference. It is desirable, if he could spare the time, that Sir James Stevenson should also come over for the conferences.

Lord Esher to Philip Sassoon

(*Sassoon papers*)

10 August 1918

By the way, *who* is Siegfried Sassoon?[1] Tell me, and do not forget. He is a powerful satirist. Winston knows his last volume of poems by heart, and rolls them out on every possible occasion.

Winston S. Churchill to Clementine Churchill

(*Spencer-Churchill papers*)

14 August 1918 Paris

My darling Clemmie,

What a dear letter you have written me wh has just arrived.[2] I think all the plans you have made with Goonie are advisable & I hope you will take every

[1] Siegfried Sassoon, 1886–1967. Of Jewish descent. Novelist and poet. A friend of Edward Marsh. Enlisted in the Sussex Yeomanry, 3 August 1914. Went to the western front in November 1915, with the Royal Welch Fusiliers. Awarded the Military Cross for his heroism in bringing back the wounded after a raid opposite Mametz, 1916. Fought in the battle of the Somme, 1916. Wounded in the neck during the battle of Arras, April 1917. While convalescing in Britain, June–July 1917, he made a formal protest against the war, and threw his Military Cross into the river Mersey. Served in Palestine, March–May 1918, and on the western front, July 1918. Wounded in the head, July 1918. He published his first volume of war poetry, *The Old Huntsman*, in May 1916, and *Counter Attack* in July 1918; it was the poems in the latter which Churchill knew by heart. Among his other books were *Memoirs of an Infantry Officer* (1930) and *Siegfried's Journey 1916–20* (1945). Awarded the Royal Gold Medal for Poetry, 1957. His younger brother was killed at Gallipoli in August 1914.

[2] On 13 August Clementine Churchill had written to her husband from The Manor House, Mells, where she was the guest of Katharine Asquith: 'There is a perfect "En-tout-cas" tennis court & an open air swimming bath. When we are rich we might have one at Lullenden. . . . The War news continues good but it seems to me that "the Victory" is now complete & that for the present nothing more is to be expected? I do hope we shall be careful not to waste our men in pushing now that the spurt is finished.' (*Churchill papers: 1/25*)

step to carry them out. I will write to Cornelia about Tenterden Street without delay. If this house is not available I can take another for the two months.

We passed another interesting day on the battlefield on Sunday. The Germans were hardly firing at all, while our batteries thundered away. There were more German dead lying about than in the other sector wh I visited, & all our dead cavalry horses dotted the country side & disfigured the scene. We saw one of our message balloons (like those at Richmond) brought down in flames, the observers just skipping out in their parachutes in time.

I have conferences all day and many people to see. I cannot tell what my plans will be for next week, but I am vy anxious to pass a few more days at Verchocq going out each day to see my friends in different parts of the Army front, & getting information.

Loucheur tells me that Foch thinks the Germans along the whole battle front from Rheims to Albert are 'en lambeaux & en miettes' [in shreds & in crumbs] and that their difficulties are vy serious. What a transformation since I was last here!

Your ever loving & devoted
W

Winston S. Churchill to Clementine Churchill

(*Spencer-Churchill papers*)

15 August 1918

My darling One,

I never saw anything like the tropical brilliancy of the weather here. Each day is more perfect than the other. It was provoking to be cooped up in a conference hour after hour. On the whole this organisation wh we are largely responsible for bringing into being, is working vy well. It is quite an impressive gathering—the 4 great nations assembled along the tables with their ministers & generals etc. We arranged that each gt power shd represent one of the little powers (so as to restrict numbers). France took Greece. Italy was given Serbia, the US Belgium, & we look after the Portuguese so we are like four kangaroos each with an infant in the pouch. Ours is rather a dirty brat I am afraid.

Last night Sunny,[1] Ivor & I dined at Voisins & invited Thomas &

[1] The 9th Duke of Marlborough who, on 18 February 1917, had entered the Government as Private Secretary to the President of the Board of Agriculture and Fisheries. He was in France with his younger son, Lord Ivor Spencer-Churchill (see page 63, note 5).

Loucheur. Very interesting & pleasant talk. Thomas is vy full of the Czecho-Slovaks, of whom he is a gt patron.

I am going this morning to try to arrange a really big deal with Loucheur—Stettinius[1] (the American representative) comprising steel, Liberty engines & guns for the 3rd American army, wh if well done shd be profitable to all concerned.

I am in gt difficulties about high powered aero engines & am trying every shift to get more.

Dearest & best loved let me know what plans you make for Lullenden next Sunday: or will you pay another visit.

Always yr devoted
W

Winston S. Churchill to Clementine Churchill

(Spencer-Churchill papers)

17 August 1918 Paris

Darling Clemmie,

I expect to leave Paris tomorrow (Monday) & to go to Verchocq for a few days. I have had a lot to do here, & as this is the only place where all the threads—American, French & Italian—come together it is possible to get things done. I have been seeing a good deal of Mr Stettinius the American representative in Europe of the War Department & have established excellent relations. We depend on them for so many things now & I think we are steadily winning their confidence. The Anglo-American Tank factory at Chateauroux for wh I was let in by that foolish Colonel Stern is in a fair way to become an international scandal. I cannot secure either the labour or the organisation necessary for its completion. Meanwhile the material for the Tanks is nearly ready, & the Tanks are badly wanted. It is causing me such embarrassment & may be the cause of bringing me back to Paris towards the end of the week.

I entertained the Italians at dinner one night & delivered them a speech in the kind of French they understand & speak themselves. They were deeply

[1] Edward Riley Stettinius, 1865–1925. United States industrialist; President of Sterling & Co, Machine Manufacturers (1905), and of the Diamond Match Co (1909). In charge of the J P Morgan & Co Agency for the Purchase of War Supplies, 1915–17. United States Surveyor-General of Purchases, 1917–18. Second Assistant Secretary of War, 1918. Senior United States War Supplies Purchaser in Europe, 1918. Retired from Government Service, 1919. (His son Edward R Stettinius Jnr was Special Assistant to President Roosevelt, 1941–2 and Secretary of State, 1944–5.)

moved! Yesterday Loucheur took us all including the American Representatives to see Chateau Thierry & the reclaimed area on wh the recent battle was fought. We lunched with General Mangin[1] who commanded the victorious French attack. He was '*destitué*' after Nivelle's failure[2] in April 1917, or '*sacrifié*' as others call it by Painlevé. Now he is put back by Clemenceau, & immediately wins a tremendous battle. Nasty for Painlevé!

Of course the General was confident the Germans were about to collapse. In fact he used exactly the same sort of language I heard almost on this vy spot (Villers-Cotterêts) from Sir John French almost 4 years ago! I hope it is less premature now. Your remark about not throwing away our men shows you to be a vy wise & sagacious military pussy cat.

I am lunching with M Tardieu[3] today & dining with Derby. Clemenceau who I saw two days ago was full of complaints about the British man-power plans. I also am disquieted by what I know & think we are not making sufficient provision.

Sunny & Ivor live here vy peaceably, & we keep each other company. . . .

This Sunday you are I suppose at St Margaret's Bay among the shrimps & kittens. I do hope the sea is doing them good. We must meet at Lullenden next Saturday. I don't expect to be home till then, but will endeavour to arrive that evening at Penshurst aerodrome.

With tender love my darling Clemmie I remain

Your ever devoted & loving

W

[1] Charles Marie Emmanuel Mangin, 1866–1925. Entered the French Army, 1888. Served in western Africa, 1906–12 and in Morocco, 1912–13. Général de Brigade, commanding the 5th Infantry Division, 1914–16. Général de Division, commanding the 2nd Army Corps, 1916; the 6th Army, 1916–17. Commanded the 9th Army Corps, December 1917–June 1918; the 10th Army, June–November 1918. President of the Consultative Committee for Colonial Defence, 1921–2. Inspector General of Colonial Troops, 1922.

[2] Having achieved a major success at the battle of Verdun on 24 October 1916, General Nivelle (a relatively junior General) had been selected by Joffre to succeed Foch as Commander-in-Chief of the French Army. He had at once set about planning a new offensive on the western front, but his plans were cast into disarray when the Germans undertook, at the end of February 1917, a substantial tactical withdrawal. The revised offensive was launched on 16 April 1917 and lasted for three weeks. It was a failure; the Germans were driven back less than 2 miles, and more than 100,000 French soldiers were killed or wounded. Mutinies at once occurred throughout the French Army—in sixteen separate Army Corps—and on 15 May 1917 Nivelle, having refused to resign, was dismissed.

[3] André Pierre Gabriel Amedée Tardieu, 1876–1945. Born in Paris. Attaché at Berlin, 1897. Secretary to the Council of Ministers, Paris, 1899–1902. Member of the Chamber of Deputies, 1914–36. High Commissioner for American Affairs, 1917–19. Minister of the Liberated Regions, 1919–20. French Plenipotentiary at the Paris Peace Conference, 1919–20. Minister of Public Works, 1926–8; of the Interior, 1929–30; of Agriculture, 1931–2; of War, 1932. Prime Minister and Minister for Foreign Affairs, 1932.

Winston S. Churchill to Louis Loucheur

(*Churchill papers: 15/59*)

18 August 1918 Hotel Ritz
Private and secret Paris

My dear Loucheur,

I think it is of great importance that you should obtain, as is suggested, authority from M Clemenceau to discuss with Lord Weir and myself the immediate and urgent problems arising out of the long-distance bombing planes, and their dependence in the immediate future upon Liberty engines. For this purpose it is necessary that the immediate practical needs for the next three months of our two countries should be set out in broad detail, showing the classes of machines it is proposed to equip with Libertys, and the actual work which will be expected of them. In this way it should be possible to divide up the work between the two countries so as to discharge the maximum quantity of bombs upon the enemy within the period in question, and secondly to distribute the engines as they arrive according to programme irrespective of whether they form part of French or British allocation. Nor is this a matter which, in my opinion requires profound military debate. It is a perfectly simple business arrangement which, after the main facts and figures have been assembled, should be settled by Ministers in a couple of hours of friendly talk across the table.

It will be disastrous if after having made for all these months immense preparations to bomb Germany—not only the Rhine but Westphalia—and having our organisation and plant perfected in all respects except one, the effort should be rendered abortive through the lack of that one, viz a comparatively small number of Liberty engines.

This is the moment to attack the enemy, to carry the war into his own country, to make him feel in his own towns and in his own person something of the havoc he has wrought in France and Belgium. This is the moment, just before the winter begins, to affect his morale, and to harry his hungry and dis-spirited cities without pause or stay. While the new heavy French machines, of which you were speaking to me will strike by night at all the nearer objectives, the British, who alone at the moment have the experience, apparatus and plans already made to bomb not only by night but in broad daylight far into Germany, must be assured of the means to carry out their role.

It is the next three months we are so anxious about. In November the bad weather will come on, and by the Spring the difficulties in regard to the Liberty motor will be largely removed, and both the British and French aviation will have acquired all the means necessary for the most extensive aerial offensive. But now is the precious moment. Now there is a fine chance to be used or thrown away. Not a day should be lost in coming to a decision; not a word should be said which complicates the discussion. If we British are so insistent on this point, it is really not out of any desire to win an undue share of distinction against the enemy, but because we are profoundly convinced that in the next few months we can do this long range and daylight job, owing to our previous preparations, and no one else can in that time do it so effectively.

Winston S. Churchill to Clementine Churchill

(*Spencer-Churchill papers*)

20 August 1918

My beloved,

What splendid letters you write me! I have now had four each better than its predecessor. Really it is a vy great joy & comfort to me to get them. An immense amount of work arrived last night in 3 pouches & I am sending this off with the more urgent matters by Lord Weir who starts immediately.

I have every hope & intention of returning to England on Saty afternoon at the latest & proceeding direct to Lullenden.

Till then with tender love

Your devoted

W

Winston S. Churchill to Clementine Churchill

(*Spencer-Churchill papers*)

23 August 1918

My darling,

A line only to tell you that unless the weather is bad I shall fly over to-morrow (Saturday) afternoon to Penshurst Aerodrome & hope to be with you for dinner. Do not be the least worried if I do not turn up as a landing in a field somewhere out of the way is always a possibility. If the weather is bad I shall not cross.

The battle is now general along the whole front from the Scarpe to Soissons & 3 British & 4 French armies are attacking.

Simon dined here with me last night. He is fairly well fed up!

Perhaps I shall dine with Archie & the 2nd Life guards tonight.

I am quite alone here. It is vy jolly moving about so freely with the armies, & yet being able to do my work regularly.

I look forward to the joys of Lullenden however with much delight.

Your devoted loving
(drawing)

Winston S. Churchill to David Lloyd George

(*Lloyd George papers*)

28 August 1918

My dear Prime Minister,

I most urgently require a head for the Reconstruction & Demobilisation Committee of the Ministry of Munitions. The great problems connected with this are not being adequately dealt with by any organisation I have been able to call into being. Personally & on the merits, I shd like to appoint Simon as Chairman. When I saw him in France last week, he told me that Addison had proposed to him the Chairmanship of a much less important C[tee] than this one, of which I had already spoken to him some weeks ago. I found him well disposed to the Government & to yourself, and quite ready to recognize the facts of the situation. I shd therefore propose to take this course unless you see reason to the contrary.[1]

McCurdy[2] is hopelessly at sea with his Committee, drifting over the whole Labour ocean and dipping his colours to every Bolshevik craft in sight. He is sitting every day, including Sundays, & all day; & Kent & my other people are absolutely worn out. He is a nice little man personally, but Labour politics come to him with all the charm of a new revelation. I am doing my best to look after him.

What glorious times! When are you coming back? I hope they won't go too far!

Yours always
Winston S. Churchill

[1] The appointment was not made.

[2] Charles Albert McCurdy, 1870–1941. Barrister, 1896. Liberal MP for Northampton, 1910–13. Food Controller, 1920–1. Coalition Liberal Chief Whip (Joint Parliamentary Secretary to the Treasury), April 1921–October 1922. Chairman, United Newspapers Ltd, 1922–7 (Managing Director, 1925–7). Director, London Express Newspapers Ltd.

War Cabinet: minutes

(*Cabinet papers: 23/7*)

30 August 1918

THE MINISTER OF MUNITIONS in reply to questions as to how the shortage [of coal] would affect his Department, said that he sincerely trusted that the Ministry of Munitions would not alone have to bear this burden. Undoubtedly pressure might result in economy without a proportionate falling off in munition output and such pressure should be exerted to the fullest extent. It might even be advisable to propose some system of rewards for the production of the same output with a less consumption of coal.

At the same time Mr Churchill strongly expressed the opinion that every branch must be equally taxed, and he strongly urged the claims of Italy to an increased supply for her requirements.

Sir Maurice Hankey: diary

(*Hankey papers*)

30 August 1918

I dined at the Club, where the PM was also dining with Winston Churchill. After dinner I went back to Downing St. . . .

I strolled with Winston Churchill round at midnight to the Ministry of Munitions, where he is sleeping. He was much perturbed at the mysterious arrival there of 5 large boxes of small arms ammunition, which had been dumped down in the hall.

September 1918

War Cabinet: minutes

(*Cabinet papers: 23/7*)

3 September 1918

THE MINISTER OF MUNITIONS said that, in his opinion, it was impossible to say what coal would be needed until the policy to be pursued as regards the war had been decided. It was proposed to take these men from the army and use them for bulk production. In his opinion it would be far better to take a smaller number of men to be utilised for highly skilled grades of production, such as gun mechanism, tanks etc, the contribution of such men towards the war effort next year being far greater.

MR CHURCHILL said that his department was prepared to make a cut on basic bulk production, and a reduction on the steel output. He had held a meeting with the First Lord of the Admiralty, who had agreed to consider carefully whether it was not possible to reduce heavy production in order to lighten the demand on coal. His department had asked for an increase in 5 million tons over the amount of some 80 millions which it had used last year. This extra amount had been asked for in order to produce steel from the new blast furnaces, and it had been hoped that the amount of 10 million tons of steel produced this year would be increased to 12 millions next year. In the circumstances he recognized that this extra amount could not be got. Mr Churchill said that he had come to the conclusion that, unless it was absoutely necessary, miners should not be withdrawn from the services. . . .

MR CHURCHILL said that he had been considering whether it was not justifiable now to use a certain portion of the reserve supply of ammunition. During the battle days of last year an average of 43,000 tons of ammunition was fired. During this year the average had been 38,000 and it would probably not be greater than that amount in the coming year. It might therefore be possible to allow the reserve of ammunition now in store to fall to two-thirds, or one-half of the present amount, but it would be necessary for the army to use up the stock now available, and drastically cut down bulk production. If it were decided to do this, it would be necessary to begin slowing down immediately the making of shell, which would naturally create considerable dislocation in the Labour Department of his Ministry.

Winston S. Churchill: War Cabinet memorandum, not circulated

(*Churchill papers: 27/39*)

THE MURDER OF CAPTAIN CROMIE[1]

4 September 1918 Ministry of Munitions

I have read Sir R Paget's[2] telegram No 2602 of September 3rd about the murder of Captain Cromie. I knew this officer personally before the war. He was a very gifted man, of exceptionally high professional attainments. He was one of the first to take a submarine into the Baltic, and after the British submarines had to be destroyed he remained at his post working with the very greatest devotion, and applying to Russian problems a keen and sympathetic intelligence. It seems to me that his defence single-handed of the inviolability of the British Embassy at Petrograd, to the loss of his life, constitutes an action deserving in the first place the special recognition of His Majesty's Government, if the facts as now known are confirmed. The courage of one man in withstanding a ferocious mob is of an even higher character than that which is so abundantly displayed in the field of battle; and I trust that at a suitable time it may receive the fullest recognition.

I earnestly hope that the Government, in spite of its many pre-occupations, will pursue the perpetrators of this crime with tireless perseverance. Reprisals upon various Bolshevik nonentities who happen to be in our hands are of no real use, though they should be by no means excluded. The only policy which is likely to be effective, either for the past or the future, is to mark down the personalities of the Bolshevik Government as the objects upon whom

[1] Francis Newton Allen Cromie, 1882–1918. Entered the Royal Navy as a midshipman, 1898; served in the China Expedition, 1900. Commanded the submarine E19, which forced a passage into the Baltic, September 1915. Brought German shipping in the Baltic to a halt for a whole week in October 1915. In command of the English Flotilla in the Baltic, 1916–18. Murdered by the Bolsheviks, 31 August 1918.

[2] Ralph Spencer Paget, 1864–1940. Educated at Eton. Entered the Diplomatic Service as an Attaché, Vienna, 1888. Knighted, 1909. Minister at Belgrade, 1910–13. Assistant Under-Secretary of State for Foreign Affairs, 1913–16. Minister at Copenhagen, 1916–18. Ambassador to Brazil, 1918–20. Privy Councillor, 1919. His telegram of 3 September 1918 contained an account of Cromie's death sent to Copenhagen by Harald Scavenius, the Danish Minister in Petrograd. According to Scavenius 'Captain Cromie's corpse was treated in a horrible manner. Cross of St George was taken from the body and was subsequently worn by one of the murderers. English clergyman was refused permission to repeat prayers over the body.'

justice will be executed, however long it takes, and to make them feel that their punishment will become an important object of British policy to be held steadily in view through all the phases of the war and of the settlement. The exertions which a nation is prepared to make to protect its individual representatives or citizens from outrage is one of the truest measures of its greatness as an organised State. The fact that men are dying in thousands in fair war must not deaden us to the entirely different character of an act of this kind.[1]

Winston S. Churchill: War Cabinet memorandum

(Churchill papers: 15/34)

MUNITIONS POLICY
1919 OR 1920

5 September 1918
Secret

1. The extremely important paper written by the Chief of the Staff on the 25th July affirms the conviction that the German armies in the West could be decisively defeated in the summer of 1919, provided that we selected a climax, concentrated every available resource upon it, and subordinated intervening events to it. The method of mechanical attack was also set out by the General Staff, and our preparations to produce the necessary vehicles are at hand. The brilliant successes which have been gained, almost without intermission, since General Wilson's paper was written, reveal the justice of the above conception, with which, I may mention, General Pétain seems to be in the most complete accord. No doubt it is right to exploit to the full the present favourable situation, and we need not exclude the possibility of results being achieved of a very far-reaching character. On the assumption, however, that these results are not decisive, and that the winter closes down with an unbroken German front in the West, we ought now to have reached definite conclusions as to the character of next year's campaign. The questions involved affect directly every arrangement for munitions supply and manpower. All these questions can be settled harmoniously if they are related to some central design, if for the first time we have a definite war policy towards which every part of our organisation contributes.

[1] The War Cabinet did not accept Churchill's suggestion, but at its meeting on 4 September 1918 (at which Churchill was present but did not speak) it was decided to send a telegram to the Bolsheviks 'threatening reprisals' against Lenin, Trotsky and the other Bolshevik leaders if the lives of British subjects were not in future safeguarded.

The first question, therefore, to be answered is: Are we to try for a decisive victory in the West next year as the Chief of the Staff advises, or alternatively are we to make our arrangements on the basis of carrying on as well as possible without running too great risks during 1919, and reserving the climax of the war till 1920? It is obvious that on this decision depends the treatment of almost every question, national and inter-Allied, pending at the present time. For instance, if we do not hope for victory next year, and resign ourselves to 1920, there is clearly no need to worry about a hasty development of the American armies in advance of their own domestic munitions supply. We ought to refuse to make any large commitments in the way of artillery or equipment. We ought to ease up the strain on our own population, civil industries, shipping, &c, so that in its modified form it may be borne as long as possible. We ought to press on with large works of construction and war projects which require 12 to 18 months for their execution. We ought to press continually and to the utmost the development of our mercantile marine. The objections which may be urged against the further increase of our immense naval superiority over the enemy would lose much of their force; and, lastly, our army should be promptly cut down to the limit of divisions which could be kept in the field to the end of 1920. Our munitions programmes could be fitted in with such arrangements, so as to pile up large reserves of all kinds in 1919, which could be used in 1920. This might enable further releases of munition workers to take place in the early months of 1920, while yet insuring adequate supplies for the reduced army.

Agreeably with the above, an increasing proportion of our war effort would be devoted to the East, to ensuring the defence of India, to endeavouring to rebuild the Russian fighting front, and to prosecuting our attacks upon the Turkish Empire. We should be content to play a very subordinate rôle in France, and generally in the Allied Councils, during 1919, and count on having solid forces and conserved resources available for the decisive struggles of 1920, or held in hand for the peace situation if our Allies break down meanwhile.

Now this, at any rate, whatever else may be said about it, is a clear policy, and it cannot be denied that, taking a particularist view of British interests, there are many features in it to which weight may be assigned. But if it is to be adopted it should be scientifically organised and deliberately pursued. This should be the definite theme in accordance with which our policy in every sphere of national activity should be shaped and developed. Having adopted it, we should not be drawn from it by flickers of success, or by the entreaties of our Allies. Home politics, foreign politics, trade, food, munitions, manpower, shipbuilding, Army, Navy, Air Service—all should be governed by these general conceptions. It is better to have a policy of this kind than simply to drift, the sport of circumstances and accident, and a facile tool of other Powers with a will and a plan of their own.

2. The alternative policy of aiming at victory next year would also carry with it a whole series of consequential decisions, which it is urged should be regarded as a designed whole, and not a mere accommodation of departmental aspirations.

This second alternative would appear to require, *inter alia*, the following measures:—

(*a.*) The bringing over of the largest possible number of American troops.

(*b.*) In order to encourage the above, we must do our very utmost to arm, equip, and clothe them in advance of their own war industries.

(*c.*) All works of construction which cannot yield a war result during the period of climax in 1919 should be rigorously pruned.

(*d.*) Every effort should be made during the winter to accumulate munitions, and further releases from the munitions works should be stopped during that period; but in the early spring of 1919 large releases should again begin from the munitions works, and for this purpose our reserves of ammunition, filled and unfilled, should be decidedly drawn upon.

(*e.*) From March onwards every effort should be concentrated in the shipyards on vessels nearing completion, and there should be a definite diminution in the starting of new work or of long-dated work. A substantial contribution of men from Admiralty industries of all kinds should be made in time for them to reach the field trained during the battle period.

(*f.*) The release of coal-miners from the mines should be renewed in the early spring, agreeably to the diminution in the output of munitions, and we should be prepared to run considerable risks in the winter of 1919 in coal supply in the effort of making victory certain.

(*g.*) It should be possible for the Navy to assist during the period of the decisive battle by releasing temporarily sailors and marines to strengthen the Army. There could be no better form for a naval contribution than to supply the men necessary to steer and manage, say, the last 2,000 British tanks to be completed before the battle.

(*h.*) The Air Force should conform in its development to the policy of a climax, ie, all establishments in this country should be cut down to the minimum during the decisive period. The Aerial Home Defence in all its forms should be temporarily cut down. The long periods of training and preparation which intervene between the handing over of machines and the formation of squadrons should in regard to the last batch of squadrons that can be completed in time be deliberately curtailed.

(*i.*) The people of the country as a whole should be taught to look for a climax and work for it. They would then be found to be ready to make very great sacrifices to secure victory, even if this involved a far harder state of life than anything we have yet experienced.

3. Although I have contrasted these two alternative courses for the purpose of showing how important it is to make a choice, it is obvious that a very large proportion of our action will be common to both courses. If we try our best to preserve as much strength as possible for 1920, it will weaken our war effort in 1919, but nevertheless that war effort will be a great one. Conversely, if we make every exertion to procure a climax in 1919, and then fail, we shall still have the means of continuing as a powerful factor in 1920. The question is not one of an absolute choice, but of emphasis. It seems to me that the War Cabinet ought to give an early and unmistakable decision on which side the emphasis is to be thrown.

War Cabinet: minutes

(*Cabinet papers: 23/7*)

6 September 1918

MR CHURCHILL expressed the view that we should under no circumstances allow the Allied control of the Trans-Siberian Railway to be forfeited.[1]

Winston S. Churchill to Clementine Churchill

(*Spencer-Churchill papers*)

8 September 1918 Verchocq

My beloved,

We sailed across the Channel through a fierce storm and were over the other side in about 11 minutes. We came down at Fruges aerodrome instead of Fauquembergues [six miles away], as the latter appeared to be deserted

[1] Following the murder of the Tsar on 17 July 1918, British, French, Italian, Japanese and United States troops all began actively to support the Czechoslovak troops on the Trans-Siberian railway, as well as the various former Tsarist officers who were raising anti-Bolshevik armies. Two British battalions, commanded by a Labour MP, John Ward, had actually been in action against the Bolsheviks near Omsk.

from the air. I got here in good time for dinner & delivered Johnnie's[1] letter to Jack. I am going to lunch with Haig today and am spending the morning in bed with my papers. (I only woke up at 9.30.)

It was so nice yesterday on the beach with you & the kittens. They all looked 'in the pink'. I do hope you were not cold going back in the car, or were not worried at my method of travel. It gives me a feeling of tremendous conquest over space, & I know you wd love it yourself. The Canary[2] is much alarmed by motor cars & thinks them far more dangerous than aeroplanes.

I am looking forward to receive a long loving delightful letter to wh I will endeavour to send a suitable reply. I am vy happy to be married to you my darling one, & as the years pass I feel more & more dependent on you & all you give me.

With tender love, Your own
W

PS. The thunder upset all the telephones last night so that I found it vy difficult to send word of my arrival. I hope the message got thro' eventually.

Winston S. Churchill to David Lloyd George

(*Churchill papers: 15/1*)

9 September 1918 Chateau Verchocq

My dear Prime Minister,

Before I can make definite proposals about steel, and consequently coal, I must first have the whole Munitions programme for 1919 worked out; and secondly I must know what the Americans are really going to require of us. The programme is now completed in draft, and I have made certain proposed reductions, the effects of which are being examined this week. I am to see the Americans in Paris on Wednesday or Thursday. When this is completed I shall be able to provide the Cabinet with a definite basis on which any necessary decision can be taken. Meanwhile, I understand the Coal Controller will be away for the next week or ten days.

I have, however, been looking into the question of ammunition expenditure out here under the new conditions which the war has taken, and I regret to say that, so far from offering hopes of reduction, there is every sign of increased demand. For instance, in each of the last two weeks of open fighting on the wide battle front they have fired over 70,000 tons, and they

[1] John George Spencer-Churchill, Jack Churchill's son (see page 207, note 2).
[2] Churchill's pilot, Captain Cyril Patteson (see page 325, note 2).

are now asking for a daily intake of over 9,000 tons against 5,000, 6,000 and 7,000 with which we have been able to satisfy them to date. It appears that although the prolonged bombardments, like Messines, etc, have been given up, the firing is now maintained by all the guns of the army over practically the whole front at once. The old limiting factor, namely, the fatigue of the gunners, which imposed a certain limitation on the concentrated local operations of last year, is no longer present when all, or almost all, the batteries of the army are able to fire over the whole front. It would, of course, be quite impossible to continue to supply ammunition at the present rate indefinitely, and I do not think that will be demanded of us; but in view of the hopes in which I indulged when we last discussed this matter, I thought you ought to know at the earliest moment that very heavy demands, backed by very solid reasons, will come from the army for next year. In addition to this, if the prospects of a forward move mature, we shall have a largely increased demand for rails. I do not think it is impossible to satisfy both demands within reason, provided the right measures are taken, and provided the Admiralty bear their share in the consequent reductions.

To a certain extent coal can be economised if more tonnage can be given. For instance, every ton of steel I can get from the United States will save at least 4 tons of coal and more if we use it in substitution of making steel from low grade British ores. It is really therefore impossible for me to make definite proposals about steel and coal without hearing definitely from the Shipping Controller what he is going to do for us next year. All this is going forward, and I deprecate a hasty decision on any one part of the programme until a general view can be taken. We are beginning these discussions much earlier this year than we did last year, and a fortnight or three weeks spent in getting all the cards on the table at once will certainly not be wasted. My own feeling is that there will be enough to meet all reasonable needs.

There is a considerable set-back here against the Air. There is no doubt that the demands of the Air Force on men and material are thought to be much in excess of the fighting results produced. There is no doubt that if Haig had to choose between 50,000 men for the Infantry and 50,000 men for the Air Force, he would choose 50,000 men for the Infantry. The reason is not that a man in the air is not worth more than a foot soldier, but that a man in the Air Force is not a man in the air, and that anything from 50 to 100 men are required in the Air Force for every one man fighting in the air.

The magnificent performances and efficiency of the squadrons cannot be accepted as the final test. Everything ought to pay a proportionate dividend on the capital invested, and it is from this point of view that the Air Force should be tested. How much flying, for instance, is done by the RNAS for the 45,000 first-rate fighting men and skilled men they employ? How many bombs are dropped? How many submarines are sunk? How many flights are made? How many Huns are killed for the enormous expenditure of national energy and material involved? Again, take the balloons and the airships. Let a similar test be applied to them. You really cannot afford to let any part of your organisation fail in this culminating period to produce continuously war results equal to its demand on the public resources.

I do not think Tanks would suffer by this comparison. At any rate, I am very ready they should be subjected to it. Up to the present there have only been about 18,000 men in the Tank Corps, and they have only had 600 or 700 Tanks to use in action. It is universally admitted out here that they have been a definite factor in changing the fortune of the field and in giving us that *tactical* superiority, without which the best laid schemes of strategists come to naught. It is no exaggeration to say that the lives they have saved and the prisoners they have taken have made these 18,000 men the most profit-bearing we have in the army. As for the demand which Tanks have made up to the present on material and skilled labour, it is indeed a very modest one. I am having graphics prepared which will illustrate these facts.

It has now been settled to raise the Tanks to 55,000 men. This is only about half what will be needed for the Tanks I shall actually have ready by the summer of next year. Although my outputs are only about half what I had expected, General Elles[1] of the Tank Corps tells me 'that the Tanks they have will see out the Tank men this year'. The Tank men are killed and wounded in considerable numbers, and the permanent wastage of the personnel is high, whereas the Tank in any victorious battle recovers very quickly from his wounds and hardly ever dies beyond the hope of resurrection. A few months sojourn in the grave is nearly always followed by a re-incarnation, so long, that is to say, as he is not snaffled by the powers of evil. Apart from the above, the fatigue on the Tank crews in action is very great, and the idea of the same crew working double relays of Tanks will certainly not carry us very far.

From the above it is clear to me that you will have large numbers of these invaluable weapons without the men to man them, and that therefore you will be faced with the need of handling these unique products of British ingenuity, which properly used would give us a great influence and control over war policy, to our Allies who will not understand how to use them nearly so

[1] Hugh Jamieson Elles, 1880–1945. Entered Royal Engineers, 1899. Served in the South African War, 1901–2. Deputy Assistant Quarter-master-general, 4th Division, 1914. Brigade Major, 10th Division, 1915. Wounded in action, 1915. Lieutenant-Colonel commanding the Tank Corps in France, 1916–19. Promoted Brigadier-General, 1917; Major-General, 1918. Knighted, 1919. Commandant of the Tank Corps Training Centre, 1919–23. Director of Military Training, War Office, 1930–7. General, 1938. Chairman of the International Sugar Council, 1938–45. Regional Commissioner for South-West England, 1939–45.

well as our officers and men would do. I do trust, therefore, that you will not quit the opinions which you held so strongly a few months ago, and in consequence of which preparations have already far advanced on an important scale. Although it is quite true that the Germans will develop their means of attacking Tanks by anti-Tank rifles as well as by field guns, land mines, etc there are four new circumstances which will tend to make the Tank an invaluable weapon next year. Here they are:—

(1) Greatly increased numbers. They will be able to afford to have a considerable proportion knocked out in each battle and yet have enough left at every point to secure success.

(2) They have never yet developed smoke appliances with which they are being fitted. Smoke as an aid to the attack, and particularly to Tank attack, is only in its infancy. It is going to receive an enormous expansion next year.

(3) They have never yet been used in darkness; but that was the original idea which I had when they were conceived. Hitherto they have not been capable of negotiating the accidents of ground by night, but with better Tanks and a proportion, though only a proportion, of larger Tanks, night operations will become possible at points where trench warfare has given place to open fighting.

(4) The tactical manœuvring power of the Tank and its combined training with infantry are developing fast and will yield immensely improved results. Tanks are not opposed to infantry: they are an intimate and integral part of the infantryman's strength. What has made it so difficult to develop a good policy about Tanks has been the repeated shifts of opinion for and against them. Every time a new success is gained by their aid, there is an immediate clamour for large numbers. The moment the impression of that success passes away, the necessary men and material are grudged and stinted. I repeat what I said to you in my last letter—that there ought to be nearly 100,000 men in the Tank Corps by the time the programme on which I am working by your express directions is completed.

I spent yesterday on the battle-front, and guided by General Lipsett of the 3rd Canadian Division, went over a large part of the ground taken by us beyond Monchy. I walked over the Drocourt–Queant line and went on up to the extreme high watermark of our attack. I noticed several remarkable things. The Drocourt–Queant trench was strongly held with Germans, and it was a very fine, strong, deep trench. In front of it was a belt of wire, nearly 100 yards broad. This wire was practically uncut and had only little passages through it, all presumably swept by machine guns. Yet the troops walked over these terrific obstacles, without the wire being cut, with very little loss, killed many Germans, took thousands of prisoners and hundreds of machine guns.

Three or four hundred yards behind these lines was a second line, almost as strong and more deceptive. Over this also they walked with apparently no difficulty and little loss. Behind that again, perhaps a mile further on, were just a few little pits and holes into which German machine guns and riflemen threw themselves to stop the rout. Here our heaviest losses occurred. The troops had got beyond the support of the Tanks, and the bare open ground gave no shelter. In one small space of about 380 yards wide nearly 400 Canadian dead had just been buried, and only a few score of Germans.

The moral appears to be training and Tanks, short advances on enormous fronts properly organised and repeated at very short intervals, not losing too many men, not pushing hard where there is any serious opposition except after full preparations have been made. It is the power of being able to advance a reasonable distance day after day remorselessly rather than making a very big advance in a single day that we should seek to develop. This power can only be imparted by Tanks and cross-country vehicles on the largest scale.

You would have been shocked to see the tragic spectacle of the ground where our attack for the time being withered away. It was just like a line of seaweed and jetsam which is left by a great wave as it recoils.

Winston S. Churchill to Clementine Churchill

(*Spencer-Churchill papers*)

9 September 1918

My darling one,

It is a day of sunshine & storm swiftly recurring. April in September. I am just off motoring to see the Naval Division & later Reggie Barnes. They are on newly conquered territory near—well perhaps it is better not to say. Afterwards I may go on through Bapaume to see Archie—if I can find him.

I worked yesterday here and at GHQ. I lunched with Haig & had a satisfactory talk with him. They are all convinced of the bad *morale* of the German army.[1] The demeanour of the prisoners toward their captive officers, the

[1] In the four weeks since 10 August 1918 the British had captured over 77,000 German prisoners and 800 heavy guns. 'There has never been such a victory in the annals of history. . . .' Haig wrote in his diary on 10 September. 'The discipline of the German army is quickly going, and the German Officer is no longer what he was. It seems to me to be the beginning of the end.' (Quoted in Robert Blake, *The Private Diaries of Douglas Haig.*)

demeanour of the officers themselves, the talk of the wounded etc, are all quite different from anything yet experienced here. One must always discount the sanguine opinions of the Army. Still there is an end to every task, & some day the optimists will be right.

Jack & Gen Tudor & Gen Fowke[1] dined here last night & we had long discussions on Gas & artillery. I am going to the Northern part of the line tomorrow & hope to stand again on Kemmel Hill—if the Hun does not want it as a target. Tomorrow night the Tank officers are coming & Wednesday I fly on to Paris.

I have every hope of reaching Lullenden on Saturday—*via* Penshurst. But the weather may be my master.

Tender love my darling one from yr ever devoted

W

Winston S. Churchill to Clementine Churchill

(*Spencer-Churchill papers*)

10 September 1918 Verchocq

My darling,

I was out all yesterday on the battlefield & went over the celebrated Drocourt–Queant lines under the guidance of General Lipsett. I will not weary you with the military lessons wh emerged, but they were vy interesting & instructive. Everywhere the soldiers received me with the broadest of grins & many a friendly shout or hand wave. I think I value the spontaneous & unmerited goodwill of these heroic men more than the Garron Tower estates.[2] But do not be alarmed. I am not going to renounce them. Why shd we not enjoy both?

The ruin of the countryside was complete. A broad belt of desert land stretches across the front in some places 30 miles wide without a tree that is not a blasted stump or a house that is not a heap of bricks. Everywhere pain &

[1] George Henry Fowke, 1864–1936. 2nd Lieutenant, Royal Engineers, 1884. Major, 1900. Director of Public Works, Transvaal, 1902–4. Attached to the Japanese Army in Manchuria, Russo-Japanese War, 1905. Brigadier-General, 1913. Engineer-in-Chief, British Expeditionary Force, 1914–16. Lieutenant-General, 1916. Knighted, 1916. Adjutant-General in France, 1916–19.

[2] Under the will of Frances, Marchioness of Londonderry (whose eldest daughter married the 7th Duke of Marlborough, Churchill's grandfather), Churchill stood to inherit the Garron Towers Estate, County Antrim, on the death of his cousin Lord Henry Vane-Tempest who had been born in 1862. In 1918 the estate was bringing in an income of more than £4,000 a year. Vane-Tempest was killed in a railway accident in Wales on 25 January 1921, whereupon Churchill came into his inheritance. He sold the estate in 1924, when it realized £57,000 (£5,000 of which he used to purchase Chartwell).

litter & squalour & the abomination of desolation. Everywhere too the enemy flung shells at random—now here now there, to wh the working, sleeping, eating, bathing, loitering, marching soldiers paid not the slightest attention. Most of our dead are already buried, but a number of German blue grey bundles still lie about.

These scenes produced a strange effect upon the Canary who accompanied me. The reappearance of scenes wh he had left for so long & his old terrible memories of the Somme upset him altogether. He did not get frightened. He got positively ill and almost incapable of thought or action. Is it not odd when he is so skilful & resourceful & fearless in the air!

My darling one—I remember that this letter shd reach you on the 12th September. Ten years ago my beautiful white pussy cat you came to me. They have certainly been the happiest years of my life, & never at any moment did I feel more profoundly & eternally attached to you. I do hope & pray that looking back you will not feel regrets. If you do it [is] my fault & the fault of those that made me. I am grateful beyond words to you for all you have given me. My sweet darling I love you vy dearly.

Your own unsatisfactory
W

Winston S. Churchill to Clementine Churchill

(*Spencer-Churchill papers*)

10 September 1918 Verchocq

My darling,

The days are wonderful & the news scarcely less bright. We took Layton out yesterday to see the new attack wh was launched between Arras & Albert. We were taken to a coign of vantage by the general[1] commanding the N Zealand division. At the time I left they had taken in this small part of the battle front several hundred prisoners without losing more than 50 men! Haig with whom I lunched was vy hopeful about the situation & vy appreciative in his references to Tanks & my share in them. It was & *is* substantial. Layton returns today by the aeroplane wh brings this letter & my pouches.

I am off to see A Sinclair who is rather near the line. Jack dines tonight as

[1] Andrew Hamilton Russell, 1868–1960. Educated at Harrow and Sandhurst. Colonel, New Zealand Expeditionary Force, 1914. Served, and wounded, at the Dardanelles, 1915. Knighted, 1915. General, commanding the New Zealand Division, 1918. President of the New Zealand Returned Soldiers' Association, 1921–4 and 1926–35. Inspector-General, New Zealand Forces, 1940–1, and member of the New Zealand War Council. One of his two sons was killed at the Battle of El Alamein in 1942.

last night. In the full moonlight the Hun airmen buzz continually & the heavy crash of falling bombs rattles our windows. We are however not likely to be molested in the chateau.

Tomorrow I have to see a battery of our new guns—the first yet made—in the line on its trial.

I look forward so much to seeing you all at Lullenden Saturday afternoon. Probably I shall arrive at Penshurst.

Your ever loving husband
W

Winston S. Churchill to Clementine Churchill

(*Spencer-Churchill papers*)

12 September 1918 Hotel Ritz
Paris

My darling,

Loucheur wants to spend a night with me at Verchocq & proposed to come Sunday. I fear therefore I shall not be able to return this week-end as I had hoped. I shall try to be back in London on Tuesday morning early. Let me know through Eddie where you will be that day & what yr plans for the week are.

I motored on here yesterday as the weather was too bad for the Canary. I was alone & took the road by Montdidier in order to see the ruin the war had brought on this unlucky town. For an hour we ran through devastated, shell-pitted facias—scraggy shreds of woods—along the road where Clemenceau & I had stood on that melancholy April day when the whole front was quivering & buckling back. Montdidier is a heap of ruins. But bad as it is, it does not reach the utter destruction of Bailleul & Méteren in the North. There the British artillery has been at work—regardless of expense—& nothing but red smears of brickbats mark the site of what was in the spring thriving townships.

This morning the Americans '*déclenchéd*' [launched an attack] towards Metz in overwhelming strength & according to my latest news have taken Thiaucourt—wh is important & registers an advance of 7 or 8,000 yards by noon. The position of the German troops in St Mihiel (look at the map) wd appear to be gravely compromised.

Who shd I meet in the foyer of the Ritz, but Muriel[1] & her husband! He is a

[1] Muriel Thetis Wilson, 1871–1964. Daughter of Arthur Wilson of Tranby Croft. In his early twenties Churchill had asked her to marry him, but she had turned him down. In 1917 she married Major Richard Edward Warde (1884–1932).

vy average specimen. But she seems quite happy with him. I did not discern any sign of kittens. She looked vy handsome & is over here on 'husband's leave'. The Ritz is chock-full again. Lady K & Emily Yznaga—Dudley Marjoribanks, Dick Molyneux & many others.[1]

I am dining with Spiers to-night—Painlevé is coming. '*On est très méchant pour lui.*' I shall try to console him.

I am trying also to arrange to give the Germans a good first dose of the Mustard gas, before the end of the month. Haig is vy keen on it & we shall I think have enough to produce a decided effect. Their whining in defeat is vy gratifying to hear.

Ten years ago my dearest one we were sliding down to Blenheim in our special train. Do you remember? It is a long stage on life's road. Do you think we have been less happy or more happy than the average married couple?

I reproach myself vy much for not having been more to you. But at any rate in these ten years the sun has never yet gone down on our wrath. Never once have we closed our eyes in slumber with an unappeased difference. My dearest sweet I hope & pray that future years may bring you serene & smiling days, & full & fruitful occupation. I think that you will find real scope in the new world opening out to women, & find interests wh will enrich yr life. And always at yr side in true & tender friendship as long as he breathes will be your ever devoted, if only partially satisfactory

W

Many kisses.

Winston S. Churchill to Clementine Churchill

(*Spencer-Churchill papers*)

15 September 1918

My darling,

Eddie received my instructions to convey to you my reproaches yesterday. Up to this moment I have not had a single letter. Really it is unkind. Mails have reached me with gt regularity & swiftness by aeroplane or messengers. They have comprised all manner of communications but never one line

[1] Lady Natica Lister-Kaye, a close friend of Lady Randolph's; her sister Emily Yznaga del Valle; Dudley Marjoribanks (1874–1935), whose mother was Churchill's aunt Fanny, and who later succeeded his father as 3rd Baron Tweedmouth; and Richard Frederick Molyneux (1873–1954), third son of the 4th Earl of Sefton, and Groom-in-Waiting to King George V from 1910 to 1936.

from the Cat. The Canary on the other hand receives each day through my bag a bulky screed from his mate. You have certainly given me no chance to *answer* yr letters. You have deprived yourself of any opportunity for accusing me of not having read them. When I reflect on the many and various forms which yr naughtiness takes, I am astonished at its completeness & its versatility. So there!

Having put down my barrage on yr trenches, let me explain further why I have not returned home. Loucheur has to visit Dunkirk today & on his way back proposes to bring his party (six) to dinner here. I have asked also Jack & Simon & the owner of the Chateau (he is a Count)[1] was likewise tactfully invited to the feast by me. Tomorrow I must return to Paris, where Mr Ryan (air)[2] has at last arrived. The US have now accepted my large artillery offer—more than 2,000 guns—out of wh they will be able to arm perhaps 15 additional divisions or nearly half a million men, in time for the crisis of next year. We must finish it then. On the other hand I am negotiating to get 2 or 3,000 Liberty motors for our air force, particularly for the bombing of Germany by the Independent force.

My days here have been fruitful in business & I have got a lot of things moving wh were otherwise stuck. The hamper of mustard gas is on its way. This hellish poison will I trust be discharged on the Huns to the extent of nearly 100 tons by the end of this month—in one dose. I find each day lots to do, & lots to see. Indeed I have not done half the things I wanted to do yet. In the mornings or afternoons I sit here quietly looking at my papers—or I can sally out in my car to some friend up in the line. Or I can get someone I want to talk shop to, to come & dine here. Meanwhile the work arrives in steady consignments, & the telephone & aeroplane keep me in the closest touch. It is just the sort of life I like—Coming out here makes me thoroughly contented with my office. I do not chafe at adverse political combinations, or at not being able to direct general policy. I am content to be associated with the splendid machines of the British army, & to feel how many ways there are open to me to serve them.

[1] André de la Gorce, 1878–1967. Son of a distinguished historian and nephew of Vice-Admiral de la Jaile. Lived all his life at the Chateau Verchocq; active in local politics; continually re-elected as Maire and General Counsellor for over fifty years.

[2] John Dennis Ryan, 1864–1933. Born in Michigan. Worked as a clerk in a general store, 1881–9, and as a travelling salesman (in lubricating oils), 1890–6. In charge of the interests of the Amalgamated Copper Company, Montana, 1900–9; President of the Company, 1909 (he changed its name to the Anaconda Copper Mining Company; at his death its assets were more than $700 million). Resigned the Presidency in 1917 to serve on the War Council of the American War Cross. Director of the Bureau of Aircraft Production, May–July 1918. Assistant Secretary of War, and Chairman of the Aircraft Board, August–November 1918. Chairman of the Board, Anaconda Copper Mining Company, from 1919 to his death. Appointed by Pope Pius XI a Knight of St Gregory the Great, 1923.

Two of our new guns—the ones I went to see fire—have been hit by shells —& the trial battery has been tested in earnest. They seem to like it—but there are still some difficulties. Gen Tudor has given me a captured German anti-tank rifle. It is a wopper! When the soldier fires it, it knocks him flat. If he was not so frightened of the Tank he wd never dare to let it off.

I have not been able to see the Guards, but I heard from one of them, that the Dove has done extremely well—using both beak & claws—& is recommended for the Military Cross.

Darling one, I do not expect I shall be home before Wednesday. Saturday we go to Edwin [Montagu]—do we not. All this makes me desirous of Lullenden news—Do write me by pouch all about it. I got rid of those Houtpoort shares too soon. By holding on I cd have made £500 more. . . .

My lovely one I will now close with fondest love & many kisses from

Your ever devoted though vilely neglected

Pig

The Duke of Westminster to Edward Marsh

(*Marsh papers*)

24 September 1918 Bourdon House

My dear Eddy,

You might tell Winston in answer to his wire that I only have a shut Rolls at present, if that is any use to him.

Will hand it over for his use in France. It is my last night tomorrow before returning to Spain. I wonder whether he and Mrs Winston would dine 8.15–8.30.

Yours ever

Bendor

Winston S. Churchill: War Cabinet memorandum

(*Churchill papers: 15/34*)

SUPPLIES TO THE UNITED STATES ARMIES

25 September 1918

Secret

The United States in response to our appeals are sending men to Europe far in advance of their general munitions programme. Their shell programme is hopelessly in arrear. Their gun programme is even worse. Not only in the main staples of equipment, but in a very large number of minor supplies, they will find themselves very largely deficient. Unless, therefore, the arsenals of Great Britain and France can supply these deficiencies, the Americans cannot be expected to continue pouring in men, and the armies available for 1919 must be proportionately reduced.

On the other hand, there is reason to believe that, working together, the French and British munition works can supply fully the needs of all the United States troops which can be brought by our maximum carrying capacity to Europe, and can supply them with good weapons and ample ammunition, provided only that the necessary raw materials are sent by America to be made up in our factories. No undue strain will be imposed upon our munition factories. The gun plants and the shell plants are running so smoothly now that, given raw material, they can easily meet their share of American needs. The processes of dilution and of releases of men will continue, in spite of this extra work, at a moderate rate.

I am, therefore, pursuing the policy of doing everything possible to equip the United States armies, and offering every assistance in my power. I have agreed to supply them with more than 2,000 guns in 1919, and to make the ammunition for all these guns if they will send the raw materials. By this deal alone, considerably more than one hundred millions of British indebtedness to America will be extinguished. It seems to me indispensable that this process to which we are deeply committed, should continue.

War Cabinet: minutes

(*Cabinet papers: 23/7*)

26 September 1918

THE MINISTER OF MUNITIONS said that the threat of cancelling protection certificates in the Coventry strike had been extremely effective; so much so, that everybody was back at work by the time named, except about 50 men, and of these, several had telegraphed regretting their absence, and saying they were making their way back.

MR CHURCHILL expressed the opinion that the cancellation of protection certificates was the proper course to pursue, and that when this action was taken at Coventry, it had received the warm approval of the country. It was necessary for the Ministry of National Service to make all preparations as was done there, so that the men would know the Government really meant to take action.

October 1918

War Cabinet: minutes

(*Cabinet papers: 23/8*)

1 October 1918

MR CHURCHILL said that the Inter-Allied Munitions Council, upon which he represented the British Government, had been examining the problem of food and munitions imports recently in Paris.

They had come to the conclusion that the best plan was to divide the year into two that, during the first half-year, while home-grown cereal stocks were high, munitions should have tonnage priority over food, and that, during the second half of the year, after cereal stocks have priority over munitions.

He urged that there should be no delay in the ratification of this conclusion by the Cabinet, because it was essential that the munitions stocks of the Allies, which had been reduced during the summer and autumn campaigns, should be increased during the winter in preparation for the next campaign in the following spring. So far from the new form of open warfare resulting in a small expenditure of ammunition, it had had the contrary effect. Recent firings had beaten all previous records, during fifteen days 10,000 tons had been used. As a proof that ammunition had not been wasted, an order of Ludendorff's[1] had been found, from which it appeared that 13 per cent of the German artillery had been destroyed in a single month, apart from the guns captured.

MR CHURCHILL then submitted figures in regard to Inter-Allied Munitions tonnage. . . . He understood that in view of the reduction in nitrate products from Chile, the tonnage available for food and munitions

[1] Erich von Ludendorff, 1865–1937. Entered the Prussian Army, 1883. Served on the German General Staff, 1894–1913. Quartermaster General of the 2nd Army, August 1914, when he took over command of the 14th Brigade of Infantry, whose General had been killed, and captured Liege. Chief of Staff to Hindenburg in East Prussia, 1914–15; First Quartermaster General of the German armies, 1916–18. With Hindenburg, he controlled the making of German war policy. Fled to Sweden, November 1918. Returned to Germany, April 1919. Published *My War Memories* in 1919. Joined Hitler's unsuccessful attempt to seize power in Munich, November 1923. Entered the Reichstag as a National Socialist, 1924.

would be about 40,000,000 tons of which 22,000,000 tons would be for food, and 18,000,000 for munitions.

He suggested that, dividing the year into two the allocation should be: 10,000,000 tons for food and 10,000,000 tons for munitions in the first six months, and 12,000,000 tons for food and 8,000,000 tons for munitions in the second six months.

Sir Douglas Haig to Winston S. Churchill

(*Churchill papers: 27/32*)

3 October 1918 General Headquarters
Thursday
Personal

My dear Mr Churchill,

Very many thanks for your kind letter of 1st Oct, and for your friendly remarks on the doings of our splendid army. I am more than grateful for the kindly sympathy which you extended to me during the anxious time we passed through in the spring and for the immense vigour with which you set about providing us with munitions of war. I have read the memoranda you enclose with great interest, and I hope everything will be done to *maintain* the army at full strength in order to beat the enemy as soon as possible. In my opinion it is of the highest importance to keep on pressing the enemy at every possible point; because, if we allow him any breathing time at all, he will be able to reorganise his forces, to construct new defences, to make new plans, and much of the work of 'wearing him out' will have to be started afresh.

Yours very truly
D. Haig

Winston S. Churchill to Major-General J. E. B. Seely

(*Churchill papers: 15/87*)

4 October 1918 Ministry of Munitions
Secret

I wish to have proposals submitted for the construction by February of 1,000 camouflaged or training Tanks.

The objects of these Tanks will be as follows:

(a) to create alarm and panic among the enemy;
(b) to divert and distract fire from the real Tanks;

(c) for instruction of infantry and other arms working behind the line with Tanks;
(d) generally to multiply the number of Tanks and give the impression that unlimited numbers are available.

The main characteristics of these Tanks will be as follows:

(a) They will resemble either the Whippet or the Mark V.
(b) They must be constructed of materials which do not clash with the existing Tank programme. A light steel framework covered by thin sheets of metal and driven by an ordinary lorry engine would appear suitable.
(c) Protection should be afforded inside the camouflaged shell to the driver by means of a strong steel cupola surrounding the driver's seat, and with enough room, if possible, for a second man standing behind him to fire a single Vickers gun. All other parts of the structure would be freely traversible by bullets.
(d) Crew: not to exceed two.
(e) Speed: whatever speed can be realized with the materials available.

NB The idea may be shortly stated as a Renault Cupola in the forepart of a Mark V dummy shape.

Lord Haldane[1] *to Winston S. Churchill*

(*Churchill papers: 2/103*)

10 October 1918

My dear Winston,

With the courage and chivalry which are always yours, you have spoken out about the pre-war work at Glasgow.[2] You have been worth to me all my late colleagues put together, I am grateful.

I send this line, but it inadequately expresses what I feel.

Ever yours,
Haldane

[1] Richard Burdon Haldane, 1856–1928. Liberal MP, 1885–1911. Secretary of State for War, 1905–12. Created Viscount, 1911. Lord Chancellor, first under Asquith, 1912–15; then under Ramsay MacDonald, 1924.

[2] Churchill had been speaking at a lunch given by Glasgow Corporation on 8 October 1918, after he had visited the Georgetown Filling Factory. During his speech he spoke of the importance of Haldane's pre-war Army reforms in preparing the Army for its wartime struggle.

Sir Maurice Hankey: diary

(*Hankey papers*)

13 October 1918

I motored home[1] with Winston Churchill, who was very friendly. He wants me to become High Commissioner for Mesopotamia after the war.

War Cabinet: minutes

(*Cabinet papers: 23/8*)

RESTORATION OF PRE-WAR PRACTICES BILL

16 October 1918

THE MINISTER OF MUNITIONS did not think there was any great or widespread pressure on behalf of a Bill. He had within the last few days met with no opposition when he had explained to bodies of workmen that it was impossible to redeem the Government's pledges. The War Cabinet was being asked to approve a Bill which was absurd and vicious. It was a Bill to entrench a number of small and close corporations in restraint of trade, and would probably meet with the resistance of the great majority of the unskilled and women workers.

When hostilities ceased, the State would be faced with the enormous task of bringing the armies home and of transferring the labour of women, and during that period the Government must retain control of industrial conditions. He should like to see an attempt made by the Government to come to terms with Labour for a reconstruction period of, say, two years, during which special conditions of control would be in force. This might be done by a National Conference, at which problems of wages and conditions of production might be examined, and a charter for Labour drawn up. If such a charter were secured and given a trial, he was satisfied that the resulting material prosperity during the transition period would be so great that there would not be the slightest desire on the part of anyone to revert to *pre*-war conditions.

If it were decided to proceed with the Bill, it should be put in charge of Ministers who believed in it. He himself did not, but the officers of his Department would give every possible help in advancing the Bill if it were decided to proceed with it.

[1] From Danny, in Sussex, where Lloyd George, Bonar Law, Balfour, Reading and Churchill had discussed Germany's likely acceptance of President Woodrow Wilson's armistice conditions.

THE SECRETARY OF STATE FOR AIR [Lord Weir] said that he spoke without political experience, and was only concerned with safeguarding the national interest. Whatever procedure was adopted, the dominating issue should be to preserve the great progress in productive methods brought about by the war. He agreed with Mr Churchill that an effort should be made to persuade Labour to take a larger view, both of their opportunities and their responsibilities.

November 1918

Winston S. Churchill to General Tudor

(*Churchill papers: 2/103*)

4 November 1918 Ministry of Munitions

My dear Tudor,

You will be amused to hear of our adventures on leaving Harelbeke. I ought to have enquired about the actual direction of the line, instead of proceeding on a general impression. I did not know that it 'jinked' in so very markedly towards Vive St Eloi, and consequently sailed along the Ghent Road until I got to Beveren, under the impression that I was running almost parallel to the Front, whereas apparently we were directly approaching it. We then luckily turned off, looking for a pontoon bridge across the Lys, and eventually found ourselves in the Village of Desselghem. Here I was puzzled to see a peasant suddenly throw himself down behind the wall of a house, and something seemed to be very odd about his gesture. Still, so strong was my impression that we were nearly 10,000 yards from the line that I did not draw any true conclusions from the incident.

The next moment, however, a shell burst about 50 yards ahead of the car, and women and children and soldiers began running about in all directions holding their hands to their faces. I then thought it must be an aeroplane dropping bombs, and as the explosion made such a very large cloud of whitish smoke, I thought they must be gas bombs.

Two or three seconds later a whole series of explosions occurred all round us. I had a momentary impulse, through being still under the impression that we were attacked by a low-flying aeroplane, that it would be better to stop in the village as we might be followed in our large and flaunting car and hunted down in the open country. Very luckily, however, I let the car run on, for the very spot where I had thought of pulling up to make enquiries was struck by another shell almost immediately.

In a few minutes we were in the open country and out of it. We then waited and watched the village being shelled from the banks of the Lys, and it was then clear that it was artillery fire and not bombs, as the shells could be

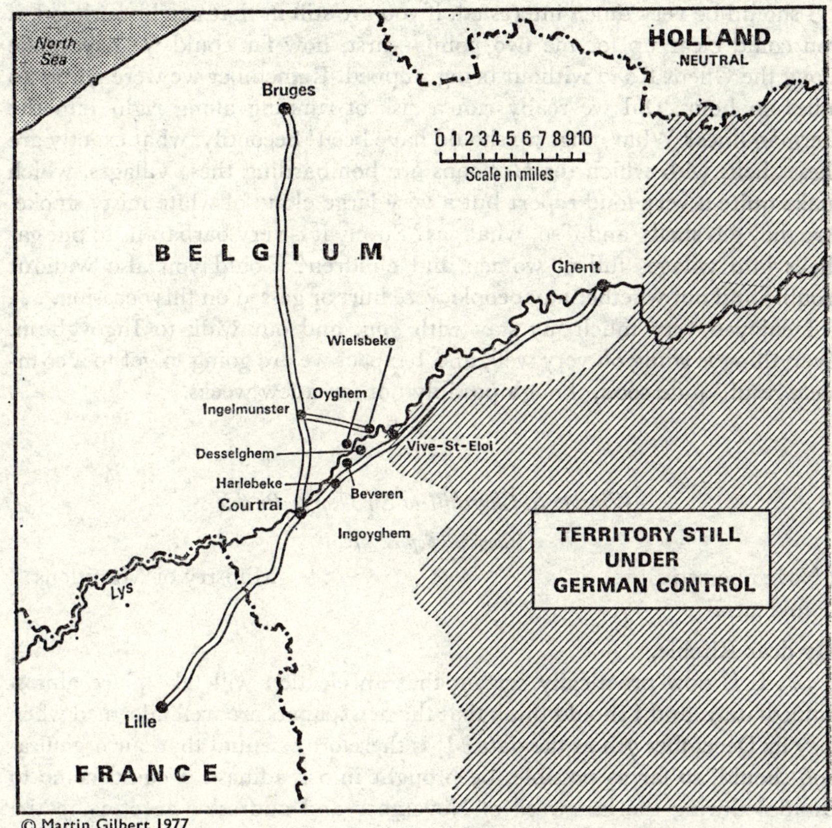

THE LILLE–GHENT SECTOR IN OCTOBER 1918

heard distinctly coming from the north. I continued to speculate stupidly upon the odd habits of the Huns in firing such a very long-range battery upon an obscure village 10,000 yards behind the lines, and we then proceeded, still with this in mind, to cross the Lys near Oyghem and work our way up towards Wielsbeke station, from which we turned west to Ingelmunster.

As far as I can make out, Wielsbeke station was very little more than 2,000 yards from the front line. At any rate, all down the first three miles of the Ingelmunster Road we had another rapid series of shell to enliven our journey, and it was not till I got to Bruges that I found out where the line actually ran. Really I would not have believed that after all these years one would be so stupid as to motor near the Front without knowing exactly how the line ran. However, all's well that ends well.

I should be very much interested, if you are still in that neighbourhood, if you could clear up for me two points—first, how far could we have gone along the Ghent Road without being stopped. Remember we were going 40 miles an hour. Did we really run a risk of running along right into the German lines? What mugs we should have been! Secondly, what exactly are these shells with which the Germans are bombarding these villages, which make quite a very loud report but a very large cloud of white misty smoke. Are they gas shells, and if so, what gas? Surely it is very barbarous to put gas shells into villages full of women and children? Could you also without trouble find out whether any people were hurt or gassed on this occasion. . . .

I enjoyed very much my stay with you, and our walk to Ingoyghem. Everything is going on very well, and I expect we are going to get to a complete result quite soon, though possibly not for a few weeks.

Winston S. Churchill to Sir George Ritchie

(*Churchill papers: 5/20*)

5 November 1918 Ministry of Munitions

Confidential

My dear Ritchie,

. . . It is now practically certain that an election will take place almost immediately, and I should think that the newspapers are well informed when they fix December 7th as the date.[1] It is therefore essential that our organisation should, so far as possible, be brought into readiness. I could come to Dundee during the last week of November and address a meeting in the Kinnaird Hall. Perhaps you will give me some suitable dates when the Hall is free. Opportunities should also be taken at the same time of addressing the women and of meeting the leaders of the Liberal Association. My expectation is that we shall go to the country as a Coalition Government, asking for power to deal on broad and non-Party lines with the problems of Reconstruction and Demobilisation. Those can obviously be much better dealt with after than before an appeal to the people. In these circumstances I should suppose Wilkie[2] would not be opposed by the official Labour Party and that I should receive the support of the Conservative Party; in other words, that the two sitting Members should be returned. I think it, however, most important that

[1] The General Election (the first since 1910) in fact took place on 14 December 1918.

[2] Alexander Wilkie, 1850–1928. Served his apprenticeship as a ship-constructor. Subsequently Secretary of the Glasgow Shipwrights Society and for seventeen years a member of the Glasgow Trades Council. General Secretary of the Shipconstructors' and Shipwrights' Association. Represented the Trade Union Congress at the Detroit Labour Convention, 1899. Labour MP for Dundee, 1906–22. Companion of Honour, 1917.

we Liberals should stand on our own foundation, ready to welcome support from any quarter which is freely given, but capable of holding our own, if need be, unaided.

I think it essential to come to an understanding with the *Dundee Advertiser*. I have secured—(this also is very private)—from Lord Rothermere a promise that, if necessary, he will publish during the election a special Dundee edition of the *Glasgow Record*, which can be placed in large numbers in the hands of the electors and will serve as a vehicle to report my speeches and champion our cause. I do not wish to do this, however, unless it proves impossible to obtain assurances of loyalty from the *Dundee Advertiser*. Did not I ask you in my last letter who were the persons owning the *Courier* and *Advertiser* with whom I should discuss this matter? Are the proprietors ever in London? If so, could an appointment be arranged? It is very much better to come to a friendly understanding if possible. Such an understanding may be much more easily reached when it is known that we are not entirely dependent upon their goodwill and can, if necessary, make newspaper arrangements which will secure our position while embarrassing theirs.

I have received a resolution from Lady Baxter's[1] Association of Women asking for 'No peace with the Hohenzollerns' and 'Unconditional surrender of Germany'. I am deferring answering this until the conditions which have been decided at Versailles have been definitely offered to the Germans by Marshal Foch. These conditions are very stern, and if the Germans submit to them, as they must be made to do, they will in my opinion give us all that we have been fighting for, and all we have a right to ask. It is quite possible that the Germans will refuse, and that a further period of struggle lies before us. In this case we ought to be able to crush them completely in the Spring. If, however, as is more probable, the Germans accept the conditions and give the guarantees, we may have peace before the end of the month.

Winston S. Churchill to David Lloyd George

(*Churchill papers: 2/103*)

7 November 1918 Ministry of Munitions
Private

My dear Prime Minister,

I am vy grateful to you for letting me do such interesting war-work at the M of M during the last sixteen months. I have tried my hardest to con-

[1] Edith, daughter of Major-General J L Fagan. She married Sir George Baxter, later the Chairman of the Dundee Unionist Association, in 1889. A Justice of the Peace for Forfarshire, in 1918 she was awarded the OBE for her wartime work on war pensions at the Ministry of Pensions, and on the training of disabled men at the Ministry of Labour.

tribute something towards the great result now being so fully achieved under yr energetic & sagacious leadership. If the end of the war comes now, I am of course quite ready to do anything wh may be necessary in the proper wnding-up of the Ministry & in the immediate resettlement of industry—provided that such shd be your wish.

It is not possible for me however to take the very serious & far-reaching political decision you have suggested to me without knowing definitely the character & main composition of the new Govt you propose to form for the period of reconstruction. I was vy glad to find that you take the view wh I hold so strongly that as soon as the war is over we shd return to the system of a regular Cabinet composed of the holders of the principal offices of State acting together with collective responsibility. Such a Cabinet shd I think especially at this time be primarily based upon the House of Commons & shd not contain unrepresentative or reactionary elements. Without wishing in any way to intrude upon yr decisions I feel that I cannot choose my own course without knowing who yr chief colleagues wd be.

There is also a personal aspect wh I cannot exclude. I am vy anxious not to be an embarrassment to you in any way. I do not wish to be pressed by yr good nature on reluctant Conservatives. Nothing but misfortune wd attend a Govt in the days & difficulties like these wh did not at the outset start in a spirit of loyal political comradeship. Please believe therefore that I shd make no complaint whatever on quitting the Govt now or at the end of the war, & that I shd leave with no other feeling but that of friendship towards you & of admiration for yr work in this supreme struggle & glorious outcome.

Yours always
W

David Lloyd George to Winston S. Churchill

(*Churchill papers: 2/103*)

8 November 1918

My Dear Winston,

After the conversation we had on Wednesday night, when we arrived at an understanding on questions of policy, your letter came upon me as an unpleasant surprise. Frankly it perplexes me. It suggests that you contemplate the possibility of leaving the Government, and you give no reason for it except an apparent dissatisfaction with your personal prospects. I am sure I must in this misunderstand your real meaning, for no Minister could possibly adopt such an attitude in this critical moment in the history of our country. I am confronted with a problem as great as that of the war—fuller of difficulties and as vital to the people of the country. If you decide to desert me just as I am entering upon this great national task—although you have been good enough repeatedly to assure me that no one else could in your judgment do it as well—the responsibility must be yours.

What is your grievance? It cannot be policy. You know that I have not invited you to commit yourself to anything on Economic issues or Home Rule to which Mr Asquith and his colleagues had not already committed the Liberal Party, without any protest from you either at the time or subsequently.

Is it your associates in the Government? If so, which of them? It is a Coalition Government; you knew that when you joined it. You joined the Asquith Government which was also a Coalition; and the only difference between that Coalition and the present is that for Lansdowne and Selborne have been substituted Milner and Cave.[1]

It cannot be that you will not serve in a Coalition Government of which I am the head and in which Mr Asquith is not represented, because you took that decision over a year ago. It cannot be that you consider that Coalition may be essential in war but that in peace you ought to revert to Party Government. For years you have urged the Coalition of Parties for reconstruction, and you have recognised that in the great task of reconstruction which confronts us a Coalition of Parties is essential to success.

You say that before you come to 'the very serious and far-reaching political decision' which I invited you to take you must know how the Government is to be constituted. Surely that is an unprecedented demand! The choice of the Members of the Government must be left to the Prime Minister, and anyone who does not trust his leadership has but one course, and that is to seek leaders whom he can trust.

If you are dissatisfied with your personal position, may I point out that it is better than your position in the Asquith Government. You know when there was a vacancy in the Ministry of Munitions Asquith was urged to appoint you to the post, but the position given to you was that of the Duchy of Lancaster.[2]

[1] The Marquess of Lansdowne and the Earl of Selborne had both served, together with other senior Conservatives, in Asquith's Coalition from May 1915 to December 1916, Lansdowne as Minister without Portfolio and Selborne as President of the Board of Agriculture and Fisheries. Neither were given Cabinet Office under Lloyd George, but two other leading Conservatives who had not been in Asquith's Cabinet took their place, Lord Milner as a member of the War Cabinet and Sir George (later Viscount) Cave as Home Secretary.

[2] A reference to the political crisis of May 1915, when Lloyd George had apparently urged Asquith to make Churchill Minister of Munitions. As Churchill later recalled it, Lloyd George had suggested that he should be made Colonial Secretary. But Asquith in fact gave Churchill the Chancellorship of the Duchy of Lancaster, and it was Lloyd George himself who became Minister of Munitions (the post he held until July 1916, when he became Secretary of State for War).

I have fully recognised your capacity, and you know that at the cost of a great deal of temporary dissatisfaction amongst many of my supporters I placed you in the Ministry of Munitions which during the war was one of the most important posts in the Government.

I should deeply and sincerely regret if anything came to sever a political and personal friendship which has now extended over fourteen years, but this is no time for half-hearted support.

The task I have in front of me when the war is over will require the whole-hearted loyalty, support and energy of all my colleagues. If you are assailed with personal doubts this you cannot give, and therefore it is right that you should make up your mind now.

Ever sincerely
D. Lloyd George

Winston S. Churchill to David Lloyd George

(*Churchill papers: 2/103*)

[9] November 1918 Ministry of Munitions
Private

My dear Prime Minister,

You have certainly misconceived the spirit in wh my letter was written. If you read the speech I made on the same day to the representatives of the Boards of Management you will see how far I am from contemplating any 'desertion' of you or yr Government during this critical period in wh my Department is so prominently concerned.

My difficulty arises from the fact that an election is about to be fought the result of wh will profoundly affect political relationships & political issues for several years to come, & that you have pointedly invited me to make a speedy & a definite choice in regard to it. It is just because I do not wish to be 'a half-hearted supporter' that I have ventured to ask for some further re-assurance from you. I do not feel that it is unbecoming in me to ask for this on public & on personal grounds. You have several times told me of yr intention when Peace comes to create a regular Cabinet on something like the Gladstonian model. You have not yet told me whether you wd wish me to become a member of it. Yet I must say quite frankly that once the war and the first crisis of reconstruction are over, I shd not feel able to take a part in political responsibilities no matter how interesting or important the office I held without a seat at the council table at wh we have sat together for so many years.

I do not think it wd be right for me to exercise any influence I may possess in Parliament or the country on political issues without a reorganised or legitimate share in political power. Rather than hold office without real responsibility I wd prefer to be a private member when you can dispense with my services, & in the meanwhile remain *politically* uncommitted in any special sense.

You are quite right in saying there is no present disagreement in policy between us. I consider the Government is entitled to claim full freedom of action within the scope of the Paris Resolutions during this extraordinary period whenever a case is made out on the merits. I have always shared yr view that Home Rule shd be given to that part of Ireland wh so earnestly desires it & cannot be forced upon that part which at present distrusts it. I agree also that an election is necessary at the earliest moment. I shall certainly say this at the election in any circumstances.

But do you not think I am justified in asking for some general description of the complexion of the Government you propose to form as to the balance of parties in it. After all the future depends at least as much on the character of the instrument as on the precise formulas used in regard to particular questions. Some measure of confidence & consideration might I think be extended by you to one who if he comes at all will come with heart & hand. I was distressed by the tone of yr reply on this point. You have never found me wanting in respect for the position of a Prime Minister.

Lastly—for I am afraid this letter is unconscionably long—am I unreasonable in wishing to feel that yr principal Conservative colleagues are genuinely willing to have me act with them? Do please remember what has taken place in the past, when yr Government was formed or later, when Lord Salisbury's[1] deputation waited upon you.[2] I do not desire to be brought simply by yr goodwill into a hostile circle. It wd only lead to much unhappiness. I understand fully the many difficulties you surmount with unfailing courage. May I not count on yr sympathetic comprehension of mine?

Yours always

W

[1] James Edward Hubert Gascoyne-Cecil, Viscount Cranborne, 1861–1947. Conservative MP, 1885–92 and 1893–1903. Succeeded his father (the former Prime Minister) as 4th Marquess of Salisbury, 1903. President of the Board of Trade, 1905. Lord President of the Council, October 1922–January 1924. Lord Privy Seal, 1924–9. Leader of the House of Lords, 1925–9.

[2] A reference to the two successful Conservative attempts to prevent Churchill being brought into Lloyd George's Cabinet, the first, in December 1916, the second in June 1917. On the first occasion the protesters had been Austen Chamberlain, Lord Robert Cecil, Lord Curzon and Walter Long.

War Cabinet: minutes

(*Cabinet papers: 23/8*)

10 November 1918

MR CHURCHILL said that we should not give up solid military advantages because we were dealing with a rabble. It was essential that we should hold the great strategic points. It was important that we should not attempt to destroy the only police force available for maintaining order in Germany. We might have to build up the German Army, as it was important to get Germany on her legs again for fear of the spread of Bolshevism.

THE PRIME MINISTER said that marching men into Germany was marching them into a cholera area. The Germans did that in Russia and caught the virus ie of Bolshevism.

Sir Henry Wilson: diary

(*Wilson papers*)

11 November 1918 36 Eaton Place

Dined with LG at 10 Downing St.[1] Only Winston & FE Smith. We discussed many things but principally the coming General Election! LG wants to shoot the Kaiser. FE agrees. Winston does not, and my opinion is that there should be a public expose of all his work & actions, & then leave him to posterity!

Winston S. Churchill to D. C. Thomson[2]

(*Churchill papers: 5/20*)

12 November 1918 Ministry of Munitions

Sir,

I have been following the comments and correspondence which have appeared in the *Dundee Advertiser* a few weeks ago on the series of speeches

[1] The armistice with Germany had come into effect at eleven o'clock that morning. All Germany's allies had already surrendered: Bulgaria on 29 September, Turkey on 31 October and Austria-Hungary on 7 November.

[2] David Couper Thomson, 1861–1954. Born in Dundee, son of William Thomson, Shipowner. Founder of the publishing company of D C Thomson & Co, 1905. Managing Director of more than twelve Scottish newspapers, including the *Dundee Courier*, the *Dundee Argus*, the *Dundee Advertiser*, the *Evening Telegraph*, the *Weekly Post*, the *Weekly Welcome*, *Red Letter* and the *Sunday Post*. In 1922 he started his first comic paper, the *Rover*. In the late 1930s he launched *Dandy* and *Beano*.

which I delivered during my tour of some of the munition centres. These speeches were intended solely to impress upon the munition workers and the Boards of Management directing them the paramount importance of prosecuting the war with the utmost vigour to a victorious conclusion, and of not slackening any preparation in consequence of proposals and rumours of peace. That was the intention of these speeches. That was the character of these speeches. That was the sense in which they were understood by those who heard them, and in which they were interpreted by the whole of the Press of the United Kingdom, with two exceptions. Out of many scores of newspapers which commented on these speeches, including some of the strongest Jingo organs in the country, only two commented unfavourably upon them. Those two were the Conservative and Liberal Newspapers of the City of Dundee, which, on the same day and in similar language, placed an interpretation on my speeches which no other journal throughout the country, Liberal or Conservative, Scotch or English, Metropolitan or provincial, had thought reasonable or true.

Owing no doubt to the restriction upon newspaper space in war time, no full report of any of these speeches has appeared either in the *Dundee Advertiser* or the *Dundee Courier*. Of this I cannot complain, because I know the difficulties; but the very fact that a full report cannot be given imposes an honourable obligation upon the editors of newspapers to make sure that their comment is a thoroughly fair one. To select a single phrase or a single passage apart from its context, and to make that the subject of hostile comment, without giving at the same time a full report, is not fair. Especially is this true when the passage, wrested from its place in the general argument, may be made to convey a wholly false impression, and an impression shared by no other newspaper in the country of any shade of politics. Perhaps I may therefore ask that some other passages from this same series of speeches, equally essential to my argument, should also be quoted *in extenso*. I set them forth hereunder:—

> 'I cannot help feeling that nearly everyone here will agree with me when I say that, in the face of facts like this, mere words will not do. We cannot accept smooth words as the expiation of foul deeds. Let me just give you an illustration of why I feel a sense of injustice at the proposals which are placed before us.
>
> 'The criminal stands over the body of the victim. The officers of the law have forced their way into the room, and all around are the evidences of the bloody deed, but the murderer says—"Good afternoon, policeman, I am very glad to see you. I entirely agree with you that all this bloodshed is very regrettable. I go further; I think it is very reprehensible. We must

make a concerted effort to stop it in the future, and let me say you may count on my loyal co-operation." Or take another case. The British or American infantry have gone over the top. They have marched into the deadly hail of bullets and artillery barrage, and of a whole company perhaps half have fallen killed or wounded, but the others pressed on in front of them. They see the German machine gun which have done the mischief. They rush at it. It fires upon them. Another dozen men fall dead or mutilated on the ground. The rest spring forward, their bayonets gleaming in retribution, and the German gunners, having loosed off the last belt, rise serenely to their feet, hold up both their hands, and say—"Kamerad, will you kindly take us to Donnington Hall?" It does not quite happen that way in this world' (Glasgow Oct 7th).

'We must obtain effectual guarantees that, if any discussions entered upon should not reach a satisfactory conclusion, everything connected with the military apparatus of Germany and the naval apparatus of Germany would have been put out of gear to such an extent it would not be possible for them immediately to leap out upon us and resume the war' (Sheffield Oct 9th).

'It is much better to have it finished now. The only way to have it finished now is to have effective guarantees which render the Germans incapable of resuming the struggle. That is not a matter which can be dealt with only by statesmen. The first man who has to be consulted on the subject of the guarantees which must precede an armistice must be Marshal Foch. When we speak of military guarantees, when President Wilson speaks of military guarantees, it is obvious that the word "military" in its general significance, includes as a special branch in which we must take a special interest, naval guarantees. Those are matters upon which the advice of the British Admiralty must be heard. And I would like to point out that this process of exacting guarantees is a merciful and not an unmerciful process. It really is taking the road which is going to get mankind out of its miseries in the quickest and the cleanest way. The more stringent the guarantees the more utterly impossible they render it for the German nation, the German militarists, to resume the war, the more we can relax our martial preparations and begin the transition of our industries from destructive purposes to productive and reproductive purposes and the more easily all the Allied countries—ay, and Germany herself—can bring their men back from the fighting fronts to try to revive the threatened economic prosperity of the whole world' (Manchester Oct 5th).

I should like to draw the attention of your readers to a rather remarkable fact emerging from these quotations. In his reply of October 14th, to the

German note, President Wilson used the following expression about military guarantees:—'They must maintain the present military supremacy of the armies of the United States and of the Allies in the field.' I ventured on reading this, to use an expression far more searching, viz, They must be such as to render the Germans incapable of resuming the struggle. I rejoiced to see that in his last reply of October 23rd, President Wilson reached the same conclusion, and had substituted for his original condition the following:—'They must be such as to make a renewal of hostilities on the part of Germany impossible.'

It is also perhaps worth while to notice that although I had to speak on these grave subjects without an opportunity of consulting my colleagues, I was the first person in this country to express the opinion that the mere evacuation of the invaded territories by the enemy would not suffice; that definite *Guarantees* must be exacted, and that these Guarantees must be of a nature to satisfy not only the Military but the Naval Authorities. This is the view which has been universally adopted by the Allied Governments, and it is one which would obviously have commended itself to all who face these serious questions earnestly and resolutely.

General Tudor to Winston S. Churchill

(*Churchill papers: 2/103*)

13 November 1918

My dear Winston,

You were a bit rash. I enclose the information you want: it has taken a day or 2 to get. We are off on the 17th to march to the Rhine. I am debating about leave! I think the march will be most interesting, but it is a long way from the Rhine home. I hope you will remember to touch Holland for about £1,000,000,000 compensation for the supply of concrete to the Huns! There is no sign of their having used it on roads. The amount about is colossal. I hope Germany will not fall to Bolshevism. I should think they have too much education. It won't be an easy job to command a Division in Germany. The relations with the inhabitants will cause trouble, & our men will be wanting to get home.

Yours ever,
H. H. Tudor

The shell you speak of may be sneezing gas, which is not deadly.

Winston S. Churchill to David Lloyd George

(*Lloyd George papers*)

19 November 1918
Private

My dear Prime Minister,

As soon as you are fit again you ought I think to give at least two mornings to considering in Cabinet the general ensemble of immediate demobilisation & reconstruction work; & you shd receive brief verbal statements from the different Ministers concerned, & ask searching questions, to ensure that action is proceeding on right lines & is properly coordinated. Frankly, I am anxious about it.

Although I am going very slow, and gaining time in every direction possible, I cannot help unloading from now onwards a continuous broadening stream of men and women workers. Others go on to short time, & all lose their high wartime wages & fall to a mere pittance & consequent discontent. Workmen say freely that if the Government were ready to spend £8,000,000 a day for an indefinite period to win the war, they ought not to grudge a much smaller sum to carry the country over the transition period.

I am this afternoon seeing both the Food & Coal authorities in the sense in which you wished; but I am sure you ought yourself to give directions as part of a general plan.

I am very anxious to feel sure that everything is working on good lines before Ministers disperse to the election, & you probably are involved in Peace business as well. I hope therefore you will at the earliest moment satisfy yourself that properly concerted arrangements are being made.

We had a satisfactory talk this morning about seats, & made some progress. We are to meet again this afternoon. I will tell Freddie to send you a report.

Yours always
W

Lieutenant-Colonel Bernard Freyburg to Winston S. Churchill

(*Churchill papers: 9/129*)

19 November 1918

A line to tell you that I had the most wonderful finish to my war—we heard at 9.15 that hostilities were to cease at 11 a.m. We were in the line doing an advance guard to the division. I decided to get in touch with the

Bosche and raid him with my Cavalry and cyclists one last time. We knew he was holding the crossing over the Dender at the Village of Lessines. We started at 9.50 and galloped 20 kilometres, rushed his outpost lines at the gallop at 5 minutes to eleven and charged into the village only 9 strong shooting up the streets with revolvers and chasing bosche round blocks of Buildings. We captured a bridge head at 2 minutes to eleven and mopped up the Village to the tune of 4 officers 102 other ranks and several machine guns. I thought this would amuse you.

The question is what should I do now to do with my life. Can you advise me about it, I come home on leave when peace is signed and I have led my brigade into Germany.[1]

Yours ever
Bernard

Winston S. Churchill: Cabinet memorandum

(*Churchill papers: 27/39*)

THE UNFINISHED TASK

19 November 1918 Ministry of Munitions

It is urgently necessary that the Peace Conference should assemble and that the business of settling the main out-lines of Peace should be concluded. No doubt there will be a great number of details, like the delimitation of frontiers in distant regions, which will require lengthy and careful treatment; but the important thing for all of us is that an agreement should be reached among the principal nations of the world which will enable us to regard the Great War as definitely finished. Until this has been achieved, the armies cannot be thoroughly demobilised, industries cannot be effectively restarted, credit cannot be liberated and revived, and, generally speaking, the healing process cannot begin.

The condition of the world at the present moment is tragic in the extreme. The vanquished nations, covering as they do the greater part of Europe and Asia, are plunged in anarchy, approaching in many regions to a complete dissolution of society. Over the four once mighty Empires of Russia, Germany, Austria and Turkey hunger reigns supreme. The structure of their governing institutions has been completely shattered; the whole system of their industrial life is paralysed, all those vast intricate processes by which great cities are fed and warmed, by which industries are maintained, by

[1]For Freyburg's subsequent career, see page 34, note 4.

which trains are made to run and ships to put forth upon their voyages, are either completely arrested or are working in feeble and in fitful spasms.

All the Rulers have been cast down, all the governing classes have been utterly discredited. New and untried men, destitute of experience, have been tossed by the waves of revolution on to this or that pinnacle of rock, where they cling precariously and desperately till they are engulfed in the surges of another billow. Meanwhile the masses of the people, without guidance or hope, lie prone in a sort of stupor or writhe in fury under the gnawings of famine. And the harvests of 1919 are still many months away!

These nations have been led by their Rulers into great crimes and by the evil systems of government which flourished among them they have drawn all the world into slaughter, but they have at any rate one right which they may claim from their conquerors, and that is the right to know their fate and to know it as soon as possible. Anything is better than an indefinite continuance of the present state of uncertainty. No terms that the victor could impose could be so harsh as an indefinitely suspended judgment. It is not their interests alone which are at stake. Our interests are profoundly affected by the fortunes of those from whom we have been sundered in this struggle. A permanently ruined Germany means a permanently impoverished Britain. Russia in anarchy means Europe in convulsion; and Europe in convulsion means Asia in disturbance and America in distress. Prompt and clear must be those great decisions which assign definite limits to the increasing confusion and miseries of the vanquished and above the tempest-torn waters light again the beacons of mankind.

The situation of the victorious Powers is infinitely less difficult than that of their defeated enemies, but it is none the less full of anxiety. We have made extraordinary efforts and we have secured tremendous results, but we are exhausted by the efforts and astonished by the results. Through all these months of struggle our eyes have been fixed upon the goal. It is now attained. The antagonists have been beaten to earth, stunned by the concussion of the final blow. But the victor who has struck it is breathless and bleeding; only his will-power has kept him going, and now that triumph has been gained, there seizes upon him an intense longing to throw aside his helmet and his weapons and cast himself on the ground beside his prostrate foe. But there is too much work to do.

The penalty of defeat is ruin. The reward of victory is responsibility. It is an awful recompense. The nations who have drawn the sword in the cause of right and justice, who have persevered together through all the vicissitudes of this fearful journey, whom no danger could appal nor hardship weary, have now become responsible under Providence for the immediate future of the world. They can no more divest themselves of this responsibility than they could in the first instance have stood out of the war. They can no more leave Russia to her fate at the end of the war than they could have left Belgium to her fate at the beginning of the war. The British Empire and the United States have come across the seas and oceans to rescue Europe from the oppression of militarism; they cannot leave her in a welter of anarchy. To do so would be to sacrifice at a stroke all the fruits which have been gained by an infinitude of sufferings and achievement. We should have won the victory only to cast it away. Not for the first time in British history should we have won the war and lost the peace. We should let slip from our relaxing fingers all the advantage which nearly a million Britons gave their lives to gain. We should leave our responsibilities undischarged, our task unfinished. In place of honour there would be dishonour; in place of order there would be confusion; in place of lasting peace there would be a reviving strife. And all for the sake of rest and repose! But such hopes themselves would be vain. We should get no rest and no repose from their indulgence. We might abandon Europe but Europe would not abandon us. Our unfinished task would follow us home. There is no way out of this task except by ploughing through it. Therefore we must at this juncture not only be prompt and decisive in our action, but steadfast and persevering as befits those to whom all the world is looking for guidance and example.

It is ridiculous to suppose that the war is over because the fighting between the armies has stopped. A man might as well work with might and main for a year and go away before pay day, leaving the premises on fire. We have got to make just as great an effort in the next six months as we should have made if the war had been going on at full blast: indeed in some ways we have got to make a greater effort. It is quite true that so far as we are concerned slaughter has stopped; the cutting off of men in their youth or in their prime, the maiming, the mutilating, the searing, the asphyxiating has come to an end.

Let us thank God for that. But apart from this, the difficulties and anxieties of the task are tremendous and there is no easy way through them.

In the first place there is Germany. What reparation ought she to make? What reparation can she make? How can she make it? When can she make it? How can we make sure that she will make it? Whom are we to deal with in Germany? Will those we should deal with this month be in power next month? Will the next Government be bound by any obligations contracted by this one? What will the next Government be? Will it be a Bolshevist anarchy completing the ruin of the German nation, or will it be a military government crouching for a spring at the Rhine? Evidently we must proceed with great care and vigilance, seeking so to influence matters that a government might be created in Germany strong enough to shoulder the burden of reparation and yet not capable of suddenly renewing the war. Such a problem will tax to the utmost limits all the resources of wisdom, of virtue and of statecraft which the victorious Powers command. It will never be solved unless they stand together armed and active, resolved not to be defrauded of their just rights on the one hand nor to be drawn into extravaganzas by the fullness of their victory on the other.

A wise and firm settlement of the outstanding questions against Germany may prove in the end the surest means of disentangling us from our responsibilities in Russia. Prompt action does not mean hurried action. Prompt action is needed: hurried action would fail in reaching a good result:—it would fail even in reaching a speedy result.

Our countrymen have paid too heavy a price in the war to grudge the patience and determination necessary to secure a lasting peace.

The Governments of the victorious states have solid claims upon the confidence of their respective peoples. They have not led them into any wrongful war, but only along paths which the conscience of all mankind has approved. They have not led them to disaster but to a victory beyond our dearest hopes. The great organisations which during the war have created and trained and moved the armies, have turned all Britain into one great arsenal; have fed its population from day to day with sea-borne food brought safely across submarine-haunted seas—these great organisations also deserve confidence. Their immense machinery is capable of dealing with all our immediate needs if it is not obstructed or deranged, and there is no other machinery in existence or which can possibly be called into existence which can help us through our difficulties. Already great progress has been made. Shipping has been liberated and British vessels are sailing unchallenged across the waters of the world in free quest of everything our island needs for its life and manufactures. Nearly three-quarters of the process of demobilising the munitions industries of the country has already been completed and this has been achieved with an absence of friction or violent shock little short of marvellous.

So too with the Army; the mighty machine which has carried our soldiers to victory will, when the fruits of the victory have been gathered, bring them safely and swiftly home. Although around us from day to day we see many annoyances and shortcomings, yet looking back over the course that has been travelled through we can only see succession of splendid achievements. While we are grumbling at the way our affairs are managed, all the rest of the world, most of all our foes, is full of envious admiration for the British system and the British way of doing things. And in a few months time, when a wise & a righteous peace has been secured, the work wh is now being done wh so much fault is found with will be seen to be a worthy part of the history of these great days.

May I say this? 'We only just got through.' The more one knows about the struggle the more one realises on what small narrow perilous margins our success turned. At the first onslaught France was within an ace of being destroyed. A vy little more & the submarine warfare instead of bringing America to our aid, might have starved us all into absolute surrender. Even after March the twenty first the danger was extreme both to Paris & the Channel ports. It was neck & neck to the very end. But because the whole nation worked together without flinching & because our race was sound as a bell in all the virile, valiant qualities & because we had world justice on our side we have at last come safely through. Let us be thankful. Let us never cease to compare any inconveniences or irritations we suffer at the present time, with what might so easily have come upon us, if we had been defeated or even if the war had been prolonged for another year.

The victory wh has been won amid these hazards does not belong to any party or to any class. It belongs to all. Every household in the land has borne its share; most bear its scars; many have gained especial honour. We have always moved forward together in a company of many millions of British men & women. The result of these labours is national property. It must on no account be squandered. It must be guarded as a sacred trust. Britons must stand together & hold for all what has been won by all.

Winston S. Churchill to David Lloyd George

(Lloyd George papers)

21 November 1918
Private & Confidential

My dear Prime Minister,

I send you herewith a copy of the Manifesto with the alterations in red ink which Bonar Law accepted from me; also a letter to Sir W Robertson which I think states the position in terms which can be thoroughly defended. It is certainly more advantageous to us vis-à-vis the Unionists than anything the Whips have yet been able to get.

I also send you a note on the need of relieving by prompt action the ebb tide of Munitions Employment. You must think of this.

I am telling Rothermere that you will receive him some time on Friday morning. Would it not be convenient if he came down & drove you up? (If so telephone.) I am sure he wants to come along. His principal complaint is that your programme is not sufficiently advanced & that you are being held back by reactionary Tories. Austen is his *bête noire* at present.

Will you consider whether something cannot be said about an enquiry into War-fortunes? The old Tories have nothing to fear from it, & everybody else except the profiteerers will be enchanted. Why *should* anybody make a great fortune out of the war? While everybody has been serving the Country, profiteerers & contractors & shipping speculators have gained fortunes of a gigantic character. Why shd we be bound to bear the unpopularity of defending old Runciman's[1] ill-gotten gains? I wd reclaim everything above say £10,000 (to let the small fry off) in reduction of the War Debt.

Yours always
W

James K. Foggie[2] *to Winston S. Churchill*

(*Churchill papers: 5/20*)

21 November 1918 Dundee

Dear Sir,

No doubt you have noticed the hostile attitude the Dundee Advertiser have taken up against you for some time. The reason of which you may not know being that the Advertiser is now controlled by the Proprietors of the Courier, a rank Tory paper.

Your last speech in which you declared you did not want *Unconditional Surrender* from the Germans, has certainly given you a set back in Dundee.

Now as one of your electors, & a worker who has always given his whole time to further your interests during an election, I am writing to give you an idea of the feelings in your Constituency.

Now that we have beaten the Germans we must deal with them as they did to the French in 1870–1871. You must be able in your address on Tuesday to explain 'Unconditional Surrender'.

I think the great card to play & one which will give you a huge victory, is that you declare, 'that Germany must pay this country & the other allied Nations, all expenses caused by the War'.

Germany started the War, & has been defeated, therefore it stands to reason she must pay. Had Germany beaten our Empire she certainly without any doubt, would have made us pay all expenses.

[1] Walter Runciman, 1847–1937. Shipowner. Created Baronet, 1906. President of the United Kingdom Chamber of Shipping, 1910–11. Liberal MP, 1914–18. Author of several historical works relating to the sea. Created Baron, 1933. Father of Walter Runciman (Churchill's Cabinet colleague from 1908–16). In his will he left £2,388,453, on which £1,176,130 were paid in death duties.

[2] James K Foggie, 1866–1947. A Dundee art dealer, active in local politics; for several years he was Liberal representative for Ward VIII on the Dundee City Council.

Dundee will stand nothing else. Dundee has given over 30,000 soldiers. Almost 20%, over 3,000, have been killed. Although we support the Coalition Government, I think I am right in saying we all prefer Asquith to Lloyd George. We feel Lloyd George is only the tool of Lord Northcliffe & we have not got over how he got his position.

I trust these few candid remarks will be useful. Hoping to see you on Tuesday.

Yours faithfully
James K. Foggie

Winston S. Churchill to James K. Foggie

(*Churchill papers: 5/20*)

22 November 1918 Ministry of Munitions

Dear Mr Foggie,

Many thanks for your letter. I look forward to seeing you when I arrive in Dundee on Tuesday next.

I am in cordial sympathy with your feeling that we must not allow ourselves to be deprived of the full fruits of victory. But do you think that you are quite right in saying that we ought to impose upon Germany the same sort of terms as they imposed upon France in 1871? Surely the forcible annexation by Germany of Alsace-Lorraine against the will of the people who lived there and who wanted to stay with France was one of the great causes at work in Europe all these years to bring about the present catastrophe. If we were now to take provinces of Germany inhabited by Germans who wished to stay with Germany, and held them down under a foreign government, should we not run the risk of committing the same crime as the Germans committed in 1871 and bringing about the same train of evil consequences?

Again with regard to payment for the war, I am entirely in favour of making the Germans pay all they can. But payment can only be made in one of three ways. (A) Gold and securities. This could only be a drop in the bucket. (B) Forced labour, ie Germans coming to work for us and our Allies in a state of servitude. This would take the bread out of the mouths of our own people, and, besides, we would rather have these Germans' room than their company. Or (C) Payment in goods. We must be careful not to demand payment in goods from the Germans which would undercut our own trade here. Otherwise we shall be creating by Treaty that very dumping against which our own manufacturers are so much up in arms. The Allies have demanded from the Germans Reparation, ie payment by them for the damage which they have done. This may easily amount to more than £2,000,000,000. They have not asked them to pay for the expenses of the war which I see have been calculated at £40,000,000,000. The reason why they have not done so is because they believed that it was physically impossible for them to pay, and that a Treaty drawn up on that basis would be found afterwards to be valueless.

Speaking more generally, I think that the Government which has conducted this country to this astounding triumph and has compelled Germany to accept the devastating conditions of the armistice, is entitled to claim some measure of confidence, and that the Allied Statesmen who are now going to meet together should be trusted, with their superior knowledge and experience, which cannot be shared by everybody, to do their best for the general future of the world. We must be very careful to stand firm upon those great principles for which we have fought and in whose name we have conquered. By adhering firmly to these through the darkest and through the brightest hours we shall preserve that glorious position in the eyes of all mankind which British Liberalism, not less than British valour, has won for our race and name.

Winston S. Churchill: letter to his constituents

(*Churchill papers: 5/20*)

23 November 1918 Ministry of Munitions

Ladies and gentlemen. All the Empires and Nations which broke the peace of Europe and took arms against us and our Allies have been shattered to fragments and beaten to the ground. Their Emperors and Kings are fugitives; their fleets are captive; their armies have surrendered or are in flight. Those proud races and rulers who had prepared so long for war, who were so confident of victory, have had to sue for peace and beg for mercy. The war is consequently coming to an end.

The National Government of Great Britain composed of men of all parties under the skilful and daring leadership of Mr Lloyd George now asks for a renewed expression of your confidence and loyalty to enable them to complete their task. That task will not be completed until, *first*, a Peace Treaty has been made which secures us the solid fruits of victory and vindicates the principles of freedom and justice for which we have been waging war: *secondly*, until the agriculture and manufactures of our island have been restored to a high condition of peaceful activity, and, *thirdly*, until our armies have been brought home and our soldiers and sailors replaced in civil life under conditions which enable them to earn a proper living for themselves and their families.

Do not under-rate the gravity and the difficulty of this three-fold task.

If you believe that a Party Government composed exclusively of Conservatives or of Liberals or of Labour men would have a better chance of discharging this tremendous business, it is your duty to choose them and to place them in power. But if, on the contrary, you believe that those strong forces in British national life which, by their union, have won the war, ought now to stand together and work together in the anxious and difficult years which lie before us, then I call upon you to give to the National or Coalition Government, and to the Prime Minister, your whole-hearted confidence and support.

This is no time for facing both ways. Whoever has the work to do should be given the power to do it. Whoever bears the load should have the backing. It will take all our united efforts, all our comradeship, all our loyalty, to lead the world back from the ruins of war to the shining fields of Peace and Plenty.

Neither is it a time for putting forward elaborate programmes of political and social reform. All men and women worth their salt have been night and day absorbed in fighting the war through to victory. Scarcely a week has passed since the enemy surrendered. You should distrust therefore those who come before you with showy and specious plans for social re-organization which they cannot have properly thought out and which they have only brought together to dress the political shop window. You should assure yourselves of the *spirit* in which these problems will be dealt with and the *principles* which will guide those whom you entrust with the responsibility. I would ask you particularly to read the joint declaration of policy signed by the Prime Minister and by the Leader of the Conservative Party, a copy of which I enclose herewith. I am in hearty agreement with this declaration and will do my best to give effect to it.

Anyone can see that after all that has happened and all that has been achieved, the world cannot be allowed to slip back and to settle down into the old narrow pre-war rut. The sufferings through which we have passed and the stern lessons of these terrible years must be made the means by which we can lift ourselves to a higher level. If all classes and parties will work together during the first five years of Peace with the same unselfishness and noble emulation and zeal for the true glory of our country as they have shown in these last five years of war, we shall make a new Britain so prosperous and so fair that our dead will not have died in vain.

British civilization has stood the test of war; it has safeguarded the freedom of the whole world; it has ruled the oceans in the name of humanity; it has defended the weak and poor; it has beaten Hun militarism into the dust;

and while putting forward the most superb manifestations of martial strength, it has not been false to the standards of honour and of mercy. The British name has never stood so high in the eyes of all mankind. In all these glories Scotland has played a leading part, and no city has won more distinction than Dundee. Let us then solemnly affirm our faith in the high destinies of our country and of the British Empire and pledge ourselves anew to the service of our age.

I am, Ladies and gentlemen, Your obedient servant
Winston S. Churchill

Lord Beaverbrook to Winston S. Churchill

(*Churchill papers: 2/103*)

26 November 1918 Hyde Park Hotel

My dear Winston,

Please believe me when I say that I am writing you this letter not in any ill-humoured spirit, but simply because I want to explain my position to you.

I understand that you have criticised me on the ground of the political attitude of the *Daily Express*.

I make no complaint of this, but at the same time I think it only fair to both of us to explain my own position.

I take an independent attitude. I am not bound to the Coalition Ministry in any way, since I resigned before the new departure began. Nor do I object in any way to the inconvenience caused by the Prime Minister's choice of the present moment for a General Election—since I advised him myself to dissolve. What I do feel is that it is unwise and wrong to ignore the public claims, based on service to the State, of many candidates who will not give all the Coalition pledges, and I claim the right to speak freely on this and other matters. I am in favour of the return to Parliament of the men who have best deserved it from their services in the War and indeed before the War. As a matter of fact, the great majority of those men are to be found in the ranks of the Coalition; but where there is a good man outside those ranks, I intend to support him.

In the same spirit I claim the right to criticise the Coalition leaders in their public capacity in the columns of a daily paper. Nobody is bound to me by more intimate ties of friendship and affection than Bonar Law. But, at the same time, I know that I can disagree with his public policy on occasion without forfeiting his friendship or, indeed, doing anything to forfeit it.

Does not the same argument apply to yourself and the Prime Minister? You are a close friend of mine. But surely you would not expect that fact to make a vital difference in any public comment I made on your policy in affairs of state? One supposes, of course, that we were honestly disagreed and that the comment was made without malice. Well, that is the case to-day.

I feel sure that you will realise the reasonableness of this comment on your public action and I should be deeply sorry if you did not. There is a vast difference between honest divergence and hatred and malice or uncharitableness. So much for the public aspect.

Speaking to you as a friend, I think you are making a mistake. You have accepted the Coalition compromise as a necessary expedient for carrying on the King's Government but not from the heart. Its policy is not really to your mind. Believe me, any man makes a great mistake who compromises on great issues of principle however pressing the necessity may appear to be, and I believe you would have been wiser to take the alternative course.

This letter is not a hostile one; in fact it is one which could only have been written by a friend.

Yours faithfully
Max

Sir Henry Wilson to Winston S. Churchill

(*Churchill papers: 2/103*)

27 November 1918 War Office

Dear Winston,

Well done. I am delighted with your speech about the Navy.[1] And it wants saying when so many people are talking rubbish about universal brotherhood.

Henry Wilson

[1] Speaking in his constituency on 26 November 1918, Churchill had warned of the need to keep Britain's naval power intact, in view of the many threats that might emerge in the post-war world. He also appealed for five years 'of concerted effort by all classes' to build a more prosperous and fairer society. His speech ended: 'The choice is in our own hands. Like the Israelites of old, blessing and cursing is set before us. To-day we can have the greatest failures or the greatest triumph—as we choose. There is enough for all. The earth is a generous mother. Never, never did science offer such fairy gifts to man. Never did their knowledge and organisation stand so high. Repair the waste. Rebuild the ruins. Heal the wounds. Crown the victors. Comfort the broken and broken-hearted. There is the battle we have now to fight. There is the victory we have now to win. Let us go forward together.'

Winston S. Churchill to Clementine Churchill

(*Spencer-Churchill papers*)

27 November 1918 Royal Hotel
Dundee

My darling,

Events are moving here in a satisfactory manner. The Unionist Party have unanimously resolved to support me and Wilkie by every means in their power, and Sir George Baxter[1] and his friends appeared on my platform last night. The Liberal Party, while adopting me unanimously as their candidate, are not decided yet whether to support Wilkie as well, or to plump for me, or, as a third alternative, to bring out a second Liberal. If a second Liberal is decided on it will certainly be a local man. I expect, however, that we shall ultimately reach the position of supporting Wilkie. Scrymgeour[2] is in the field again, but he will only take votes from the second Labour candidate assuming one is run, and will do me nothing but good. Whether a second Labour candidate will be run is not certain. The local Labour people are split on the matter, the Wilkieites being violently against it through fear of our coming into the field with a second Liberal, and the wilder spirits being ready to break away even against the advice of the Labour Party Headquarters. Our Liberal decision naturally waits in suspense on theirs.

Yesterday I saw Mr Thomson of the *Dundee Courier* and *Advertiser*, and had an hour and three quarters interview with him—for the first half an hour very hostile and daggers drawn great protestation of utter independence of political parties of all kinds and total disinterestedness in politics. I made it perfectly clear that if we were going to be treated unfairly by the *Dundee Advertiser* and the *People's Journal*, either in reporting or in comment, I should denounce the arrangement to the electors by which the Liberal and Conservative papers were both run in a single interest. After a while it emerged that the grievance is neglect.

It appears that two years ago Bonar Law failed to answer or answer satisfactorily some letters which Thomson wrote—I wonder on what subject—and this has rankled: 'Everything is done for the great newspaper kings in London, but who cares what happens to the little people of Dundee, etc.' I

[1] George Washington Baxter, 1853–1926. Chairman of the Dundee and District Liberal-Unionist Association, 1886–1910. Unsuccessful Unionist candidate, 1895, 1908 and 1910 (on the two latter occasions, against Churchill himself). Knighted, 1904. Chairman of the Dundee Unionist Association, 1910–19. Created Baronet, 1918. President of the Scottish Unionist Association, 1919.

[2] Edwin Scrymgeour, 1866–1947. The son of a pioneer of the Scottish Temperance Movement. Inaugurated the Prohibition Party in Dundee, November 1901, and fought six elections at Dundee as a Prohibitionist candidate. He was finally elected (by defeating Churchill) in 1922, and remained an MP until 1931.

pointed out that there was no reason why because Bonar Law had not answered letters, they should take it out of me, and this they fully admitted. After that the conversation got more friendly, and in the end a substantial measure of agreement was reached. At any rate, this morning's papers have both turned round, as you will see from the copies I am sending you, and I believe they mean to support me thoroughly during the election. It is, however, very unsettling not having any security except the moods of this extremely dour and politically erratic man. For the time being, however, I think that difficulty is solved.

The meeting last night was the roughest I have ever seen in Dundee. Usually at elections when each side has its champions, the opposition go to their own meeting and let off steam in cheering sentiments which they admire: but now, when there is practically no effective opposition or counter-case being unfolded, all the extremists crowded to my meeting, filling it an hour and a half before the advertised time, in order to make a demonstration on their own. Both outside and inside the hall there was a good deal of disorderly hostility, consisting almost entirely of Bolshevik elements. Another current was the discharged soldiers who pressed their own interests. I think I was very successful in dealing with one of the most turbulent meetings I have ever addressed, but I had to scrap entirely my speech and trust in the main to interruptions and rejoinders, a good many of which came off. We had a great struggle to get into the hall in a very hostile mob. I was afraid for a few moments that Sir George Ritchie would be knocked down. However with great agility he seized his assailant by the throat and succeeded in forcing him under the wheels of a motor-car, whence he was rescued by Archie with some difficulty. The only uncertain element is the great one, this enormous electorate composed of so many of the poorest people in the country. I am pretty confident, however, that we shall secure very large majorities indeed.

I shall return on Thursday and be with you in London on Friday morning, unless I stop to join Lloyd George en route at Newcastle. The women are all bidden to the meeting of the Association tonight. The two Associations are now inter-mingled without distinction.

There is no doubt that my handling of the meeting last night was a gt success & that the whole position is becoming orderly & solid. Tender love my darling one

from yr devoted
W

Winston S. Churchill to David Lloyd George

(*Lloyd George papers*)

29 November 1918

My dear Prime Minister,

. . . Seriously please reconsider John Maclean.[1] I hear from both Sir Thomas Munro[2] & MacCallum Scott[3] that they are much against it. It will I think depress friends, stultify our general position & make the Bolshevik rapscallions vy boastful.

The right time for Amnesty is when Peace is signed, & then there are many other captives who shd share in it. A general election is no reason. It will be vy difficult to let Maclean out & not de Valera[4] & Co.

I most strongly urge reconsideration.

An amnesty of military offenders is a really big thing & well worth doing. But Bolshies & Conshies shd now wait their turn.

Yours always

W

Can you not suspend action?

[1] John Maclean. A former teacher, and MA from Glasgow University, he was sent to prison for sedition in November 1915. In the spring of 1916 he was sentenced to a further 3 years penal servitude for encouraging strikes. In July 1917 he was released on ticket-of-leave. Appointed Bolshevik Consular Representative in Glasgow, January 1918. Imprisoned for 'seditious speechmaking', January 1918. Stood as an independent Labour candidate in the Gorbals, Glasgow, against the Coalition Labour candidate, and member of the War Cabinet, John Barnes, November 1918. Released from prison, 2 December 1918, after Barnes had brought the issue to the War Cabinet. Defeated by Barnes at the General Election (14,247 votes to 7,436). During his campaign in Dundee, having been heckled by Maclean's supporters, Churchill declared: 'If this country had been full of John Maclean's we would have been conquered by the Huns.' In the General Election of 1922 Maclean stood as an Independent Communist candidate, and was defeated.

[2] Thomas Munro, 1866–1923. County Clerk of Lanarkshire, 1904. Knighted, 1914, the first County Clerk either in England or Scotland to receive this distinction. Chief Labour Adviser, Ministry of Munitions, 1916–18. Adviser to the Demobilization Branch, Ministry of Labour, 1919. Treasurer of the Lanark Education Authority from 1919 to his death.

[3] Alexander MacCallum Scott, 1874–1928. Secretary, the Liberal League against Aggression and Militarism, 1900–3. Liberal MP, 1910–22. He published a biography, *Winston Spencer Churchill* in 1905 and a revised edition, *Winston Churchill in Peace and War*, in 1916. He joined the Labour Party in 1924.

[4] Eamon De Valera, 1882–1975. Born in New York. A leading figure in the Easter Rebellion, 1916. Sentenced to death; sentence commuted to life penal servitude on account of his American birth. Released under the general amnesty, June 1917. President of the Sinn Fein, 1917–26. Elected to Parliament as a Sinn Fein MP, 1918. Imprisoned with other Sinn Fein leaders, 1918; escaped from Lincoln Jail, February 1919. 'President' of the Irish Republic, 1919–22. Rejected the Irish Treaty and fought with the Irregulars against the Free State Army, 1922–3. President of Fianna Fail, 1926–59. Leader of the Opposition in the Free State Parliament, 1927–32. Minister for External Affairs, 1932–48. Head of the Government of Eire (Taoiseach), 1937–48, 1951–4 and 1957–9. President of the Republic of Ireland, 1959–73.

Margot Asquith[1]*: diary*

(Countess Oxford and Asquith papers)

30 November 1918[2]

Winston who was privately keen H should forgive & join LlG joined as usual with the mob of praise—but in his heart if he has any outside his family & 'Foyer' he feels very uncomfortable & guilty. He said to his Aunt Ly Sarah Wilson[3] 'if I had been a better fellow I wd have been at Asquith's side thro' this business'. But Winston will *never* be a 'better fellow'. I sometimes think he has no *soul*, or *heart*, or *age*, or *judgement* or even *Ability* (apart from a touch of *genius*).

Ll George can *walk round Winston in astuteness*! the latter always keeps the peace, the former breaks it with as much regularity as the man on the road breaks stones in front of a quarry. LlG has much more character than Winston; I dont mean a *better* character, or a better nature, but *much* more of both.

Winston is a *far* better fellow with a far nicer nature tho his genius is a clumsy one. A *very* good speaker but the worst debater for a flexible voluminous talker I ever came across! the bed rock of this inability to debate is a noisy inelastic mind. He is like a train of strength that runs on one line always passing the trains of strength never encountering or countering them & the lines he travels on are Himself! Any & every aim that ends with self is tiresome! Poor Winston is shallow of soul & boyish of heart with neither dignity or temper. Everyone he works with likes him & dislikes LlG—but the latter has made an amazing success of his life—charming & camouflaging & taking in quite remarkable men, the other takes in *no* one! Winston is like the bull & LlG (indeed much less dextrous men than LlG!) need not take either a very quick or a very long step to escape his charge!

[1] Emma Alice Margaret Tennant, 1864–1945. Known as Margot. She married H H Asquith (as his second wife) in 1894, and published four separate volumes of memoirs, including *The Autobiography of Margot Asquith* in 1921. Her son Raymond was killed in action in 1916.

[2] Churchill's 44th birthday.

[3] Lady Sarah Isabella Augusta Spencer-Churchill, 1863–1929. One of Lord Randolph Churchill's sisters. In 1891 she married Gordon Chesney Wilson, Royal Horse Guards. In 1899 she was taken prisoner by the Boers in South Africa, but was later exchanged for a Boer prisoner, and was sent to Mafeking, then under siege, where she joined her husband. While serving as a Lieutenant-Colonel, Royal Horse Guards, Gordon Wilson was killed in action on the western front on 6 November 1914.

December 1918

Winston S. Churchill to Sir Robert Perks[1]

(Brown Library Liverpool collection)

4 December 1918
Private

Dear Sir Robert Perks,

Many thanks for your letter of the 30th ult. The Government policy is that Germany should be made to pay to the uttermost limit of her resources, subject to such payment not taking a form which would be injurious to our own industry. An Inter-Allied Committee has now been set up to make a complete examination of the German resources with a view to ascertaining her full capacity to pay. I am in full sympathy with this policy, subject, however, to the following reservation—that I do not consider that we should be justified in enforcing any demand which had the effect of reducing for an indefinite period the mass of the working class population of Germany to a condition of sweated labour and servitude, as such a state of things would re-act on our own labour standards in this country in one form or another.

Yours sincerely,
Winston S. Churchill

Winston S. Churchill to Richard Lee[2]

(Churchill papers: 5/20)

9 December 1918 Ministry of Munitions

Dear Sir,

I am much obliged to you for your letter of December 6th. If the peace which we are going to make in Europe should lead, as I trust it will, to the

[1] Robert William Perks, 1849–1934. Railway lawyer, 1878–92. Liberal MP, 1892–1910. Treasurer of the Liberal League, 1902. Chairman of the Metropolitan District Railway, during conversion from steam to electricity, 1902–6. Created Baronet, 1908. First Vice-President of the union of Methodist Churches, 1932–3. A leading advocate of the Channel Tunnel scheme.

[2] The Reverend Richard Lee, a constituent.

liberation of captive nationalities, to a reunion of those branches of the same family which have long been arbitrarily divided, and to the drawing of frontiers in broad correspondence with the ethnic masses, it will remove for ever most of the causes of possible wars. And with the removal of the *Cause*, *The Symptom*, ie armaments, will gradually and naturally subside.

I cannot but think we have much to be thankful for, and more still to hope for in the future.

With regard to Russia, you have only to seek the truth to be assured of the awful forms of anti-democratic tyranny which prevail there, and the appalling social and economic reactions and degenerations which are in progress. The only sure foundation for a State is a Government freely elected by millions of people, and as many millions as possible. It is fatal to swerve from that conception.

Yours very faithfully,
Winston S. Churchill

Edward Marsh to J. T. Davies

(*Lloyd George papers*)

9 December 1918
Secret
Private

Dear Davies,

Mr Churchill thinks he ought to let you know that he was approached on Saturday, to his great surprise, by an acquaintance who shd have known better, with a suggestion that he should procure a baronetcy for a certain Hodge,[1] a Newcastle Shipowner, and receive £5,000 on delivery of the goods.

Naturally the intermediary received short shift—& Mr Churchill thinks you may wish to make a note, to be borne in mind if the idea of any honour for Mr Hodge is mooted again.

Yours
EM

[1] Rowland Frederic William Hodge, 1859–1950. A prominent Tyneside shipbuilder; founder and Managing Director of the Northumberland Shipbuilding Co Ltd. Created Baronet, 1921. A member of the Junior Carlton Club. He lived in later life at Churt in Surrey, where Lloyd George also made his home.

War Cabinet: minutes

(Cabinet papers: 23/8)

10 December 1918

THE PRIME MINISTER recalled that some time ago a Committee had been appointed, with General Smuts as chairman, to co-ordinate the work of the various Departments concerned with demobilisation. General Smuts had now resigned, and up to the present it had not been possible to make satisfactory arrangements for continuing his work. It was worth considering whether or not it would be preferable to have some one person appointed to act as the co-ordinating centre of the Government's policy, such a person to have supreme authority within the limits of certain main principles which would be laid down by the War Cabinet. At present no one person seemed to be in complete touch with the whole problem. He had received strong representations from Departments like the Irish Office and the Scottish Office as to the need for greater co-ordination.

MR CHURCHILL pointed out that there were serious objections to the appointment of any one Minister in a position to give orders to other Ministers and Departments. Such a system would tend to weaken Ministerial responsibility. It would be preferable to have a Cabinet Committee of four or five Ministers drawn from the Departments specially involved in demobilisation, with a chairman. Certain Departments were far more concerned with demobilisation than others, and this was specially true of the Ministry of Munitions. Under the old system of a large Cabinet the problem would have been assigned to a Committee of four or five Ministers. Inasmuch as principles of high policy were involved, he should like to see a Cabinet Committee of Ministers with political experience, the Chairman of which would report to the Cabinet. Underneath this Cabinet Committee would be a Committee of Experts. He was not sure that the War Cabinet fully appreciated the extent and number of the decisions already taken. The Ministry of Munitions had taken steps to prevent the discharge of workpeople by placing orders, for example, for the manufacture of railway material. The Ministry of Munitions was the most suitable machinery for the placing of orders, and was waiting to receive such orders from the Board of Trade and other Departments. It was important to place orders immediately to prevent unemployment, even at the risk of the Government later on having to sell some of the material manufactured at a loss.

Winston S. Churchill: letter to his constituents

(*'Dundee Advertiser'*)

13 December 1918

Ladies and Gentlemen,—

Saturday offers a great opportunity to the electors of Dundee, and no one should neglect the duty of recording a vote. The issues at stake in this momentous election have become very plain to the nation at large. But they are nowhere so plain as in this city. The choice is between those sentiments of patriotism and comradeship which have won the war and those cowardly conceptions which at every stage have urged a dishonourable peace. The choice is also between a patient and organised effort to rebuild and enlarge the prosperity of our country and a weak and futile Bolshevism which would ruin it. On the one hand, there is the union of the strong national forces whose steadfast perseverance through so many perils have led us to victory; on the other are the faint-hearts and feather-heads who were as eager to swallow defeat abroad as they are to excite disorder at home. There can be no doubt what will be the decision of Dundee.

But the times are too grave, and the issues too vital, for the electors to leave anything to chance. We are fighting a battle on the home front which is the natural consequence and conclusion of the battles which have been gained on the seas and in the field. It is imperative that all those who range themselves upon the side of the enduring greatness and true glory of Britain should act together and neglect nothing. Dundee must speak with an unfaltering voice. The larger the poll the larger the majority. The larger the majority, the higher will be the credentials of the Government which will represent the British Empire in the forthcoming Peace Conference. The mandate of a free democracy is needed to reinforce the victories of our Fleets and Armies, and to clothe our representatives at the World Council with the fullest measure of national authority. Let every man and every woman resolve by their vote and their influence on Saturday to set the seal on the triumphs of these four terrible years. Let them rally with energy to the cause in pursuit of which Dundee has suffered, and dared, and achieved so much.

This is no time for feeble compromises. Stern and strong decisions followed by downright action are required from all responsible citizens. Let a message go forth from Dundee which will resound throughout the land, which will inspire the friends of Britain all over the world with the conviction of her stable and broadly-founded power. Let that message sweep from the minds of our crouching enemies their lingering hopes that we are not united. Then let us go forward together against the foes of Scotland and of Britain, whether they be the Huns abroad or the pacifists, Bolsheviks, and Sinn Feiners at home, resolving that the victory which has been gained shall be enjoyed by all, and that the nation as a whole shall enter united upon its hard-won inheritance of peace, and power, and plenty.

I am,
Ladies and Gentlemen,
Your Obedient Servant,
Winston S. Churchill.

Winston S. Churchill to Clementine Churchill

(*Spencer-Churchill papers*)

13 December 1918 Royal Hotel
Dundee

My darling,

The situation here is, I think, increasingly satisfactory. I am sending you in tonight's pouch a bundle of newspapers in case you have not seen all that has appeared. I had a very remarkable meeting at Broughty Ferry, about 800 people practically unanimous, and evidently inspired by the most friendly sentiments. There is no doubt that these two new suburbs, Downfields and Broughty Ferry, which are now comprised in the constituency, are very favourable to the Coalition. So far as Party complexion is concerned, they are probably rather more Unionist than Liberal. On the present occasion, as far as can be ascertained, the opinion there is overwhelmingly in my favour. And these two suburbs together comprise more than 8,000 voters. This in itself will go far to neutralise the defection of the Irish vote. You will see that, according to instructions from the Irish Central Headquarters, this vote is to be given to the two wild-cat candidates.[1]

The Catholic clergy, headed by the Bishop of Dunkeld,[2] have had however various secret meetings, and have informed Sir George Ritchie that they propose to advise their people to vote for me, while at the same time avoiding anything like a public split with the Central Irish Organisation. I have hopes, therefore, that a very large proportion of the Irish vote may come right.

[1] The Prohibitionist candidate, Edwin Scrymgeour, and the Labour Candidate, James S Brown, a Member of the Dundee Trades Council, and subsequently President of the Dundee Trades and Labour Party. In the 1918 election Scrymgeour polled 15% and Brown 11% of the vote.

[2] John Toner, 1857–1949. Born in Glasgow. Educated at Scots College, Valladolid, Spain. Ordained, 1882. Served as a parish priest in Glasgow, 1890–1914. Bishop of Dunkeld, 1914–20. Active in the negotiations for the Education (Scotland) Act, 1918. Apostolic Administrator, Glasgow Archdiocese, 1920–2. He died in Dundee.

We had a big wind up last night in the Kinnaird Hall, and I made a most successful speech to an almost entirely friendly audience. The opposition were present, but their interruptions only gave me opportunities, of which I took the fullest advantage. Mr Scrymgeour is counting on some support from among the women, but our information is that this will not be formidable. Everything we can hear from the soldiers, and the demeanour of all Service men met with, indicates that their voting will be enormously Coalition. Brown, the second Labour candidate, is in full retreat from the Bolshevism of a fortnight ago. His placard today is 'Vote for Brown and bury Bolshevism'. I am contemplating a counter-placard 'Vote against Bolshevism and bury Brown'.

Altogether I think the chances of a great majority are very good, and it is not impossible that it may be the greatest majority ever yet recorded at a British election. Still, a majority of one is sufficient, Sir George Ritchie is quite satisfied with the course of the contest, and places the figure very high, so high indeed that I will not commit myself to it on paper before the event.

Asquith is having a very rough time in East Fife, and is being subjected to abominable baiting by a gang of discharged soldiers. I do hope it will be all right for the poor old boy.[1] I have been sorely tempted to take up the cudgels for him, but it would have caused many complications here and elsewhere. I think Mr Falconer[2] is quite safe for Forfarshire since I succeeded in depriving his opponent of the coupon.

Both the local papers have been working splendidly, and have shown the greatest cleverness in their advocacy. There is no doubt that my time has been in every respect well-spent. I shall drive twice round the constituency tomorrow morning and visit all the polling booths, and then catch the 2.47 to Edinburgh, where I shall dine. There is no use my remaining here after darkness sets in.

I went yesterday to see Leuchars Air Station, and have invited two of these young pilots over to lunch today. One of them is only 21, and has risen to Colonel by his ability rather than by any great prowess in the field. The other has killed 39 Huns, and has a very great reputation as an 'Ace'. It is rather strange for these youths having what undoubtedly must be the greatest and finest part of their lives, with all its tremendous experiences in the region of

[1] Asquith had represented East Fife since 1886. In December 1918 he was defeated by a Conservative candidate, Colonel Sir Alexander Sprot, who secured 8,996 votes against Asquith's 6,994. For more than a year he was without a seat in Parliament. In January 1920 he was elected for Paisley, which he held until 1924, when he was defeated by the Labour candidate (E R Mitchell).

[2] James Falconer, 1856–1931. Liberal MP for Forfarshire, 1909–18, and 1922–4. In 1918 he was defeated by the Conservative candidate, William Thomas Shaw, whose name was in fact inadvertently included in the final list of Coalition candidates, although as a result of Churchill's efforts he did not actually receive the 'coupon'.

action lying behind them while yet at an age when most young men are still at their books.

I am just off to address a midday meeting of the shipyard workers at the Docks. They sent and asked me to come to address them, and I have made an exception to my rule against open air meetings on their account.

Tender love my darling one, & with vy many kisses to you and the kittens,

Yr loving & devoted
W

Winston S. Churchill to General Travers Clarke: telegram

(*Churchill papers: 2/103*)

15 December 1918 Ministry of Munitions
Private and Personal

The Prime Minister is greatly disturbed by reports that election newspapers which have been sent out by various parties have not yet reached troops. Wimereux is specially mentioned. He also has no detailed information about the steps which are being taken to enable troops to vote and to ensure that they do so freely. The matter is of extreme importance as it affects the electoral rights of the soldier.

The Cabinet will in all probability send a Minister out to-morrow to enquire on the spot. I hope however that you will be able to reassure us. Please send me back as full an account as possible of what is being done and inform me when units will receive said newspapers. Secondly please telephone and telegraph whether you can take from Tuesday onwards about 300,000 copies each day of various newspapers and distribute them daily to troops thereafter for five days in succession. Will you kindly send me an answer by telephone through the Resident Clerk War Office which I can show Prime Minister by 11.30 am to-morrow Monday.

Lord Milner to Winston S. Churchill

(*Lloyd George papers*)

16 December 1918

My dear Churchill,

Our letter has gone to the Newspaper Association (Riddell) & arrangements are being made to distribute the papers on the other side. They are prepared for 50 tons (about 800,000 copies) a day.

What remains is to make sure that the friendly papers—Mirror, Express, Chronicle, as far as I know—avail themselves of the offer, & send out the right sort of stuff. The issues of to-night, to-morrow & Wednesday night are what matters.

As I understand, YOU ARE GOING TO LOOK AFTER THIS. I think it is the really important point.

GHQ wire that they would welcome a visit from a Minister to investigate & see all their records, & personally I should be very glad if you went, as I feel sure you would then realise how much had been done. But, though this would be a personal satisfaction, I feel that from the point of view of *results* you could do more useful work in looking after the papers here.

Yours very sincerely
Milner

Sir Henry Wilson: diary

(*Wilson papers*)

16 December 1918 36 Eaton Place

Winston came to tell me he was going to succeed Milner as War Minister. Whew!

Winston S. Churchill to David Lloyd George

(*Lloyd George papers*)

17 December 1918 Ministry of Munitions
Private & Personal

My dear Prime Minister,

Amid your great pre-occupations of the war, the election, and the peace, there are some aspects on the Demobilisation problem which have not been fully presented to you, or in their proper proportion. The major part of the problem falls entirely within the scope of the Ministry of Munitions, and is only capable of being dealt with through its machinery. Any attempt to side-track or supersede this machinery will result in a breakdown. The Ministry of Munitions employs nearly three million workpeople who have to change their job, and is in intimate touch with forty or fifty thousand firms employing the said workpeople. It has a staff of nearly 17,000 persons, grouped in 60 or 70 departments and headed by an administrative Council of the highest possible qualifications. The actual executive work cannot be done through any other machinery. And why should it be done through any other machinery? We are employing the workmen and dealing with the firms. We have got to turn off the workmen by acting through the firms, and we alone can place the orders for alternative work with the firms. We are not only the remedy; we are also the disease. Everything else in demobilisation is really ancillary and subordinate to the Ministry of Munitions' task at the present juncture. The demobilisation of the Army is a separate problem, which, although related, is not nearly so urgent. The Housing policy is required to feed the order books of the Ministry of Munitions. The Railway policy, the Electrical policy, are simply contributory streams to the needs of the Ministry of Munitions. No one else knows, or can possibly know, the problem as it is known here. The idea that the Ministry of Munitions is one of thirteen Departments of State all concerned in demobilisation is not in true proportion. It is in fact about 80 per cent. of the whole difficulty, and possesses 90 per cent. of the means of solving it.

Secondly, you have not been apprised of the immense progress which has been made or the power and excellence of the organisation which exists here, nor, I venture to think, do you realise the comparatively small number of main decisions of policy which are required to enable action to proceed freely. I send you enclosed a brief summary of the work done, and of some of the points on which decisions of policy are required. . . .

Please note that I have obtained an Act of Parliament which enables the Minister of Munitions to use for the purposes of the transfer of industry back to peace *every* power which he has hitherto enjoyed for the purposes of war. No one knows better than you how sweeping those powers are, for they are as you devised them.

My advice is therefore as follows: Make your *expert* Demobilisation Council around the existing Demobilisation Council of the Ministry of Munitions, by adding to it any representatives of other Departments closely involved that may be considered by them desirable, viz:—

Treasury and Board of Trade, if not already satisfied;
Kent transferred *en bloc* (with all he has accumulated);
A War Office representative. . . .
A National Service representative. . . .
A Shipping representative. . . .
An LGB representative.

No other Department requires a continuous representation; they can attend when their affairs are concerned. This Council should be responsible to the Minister of Munitions, whoever he is for the time being; but in practice you will find that it will work itself under the general authority of the Minister.

Stevenson is, of course, the main spring and would be the Chairman. This Council would possess at its immediate disposal the vast machinery of the Ministry of Munitions with its 70 or 80 departments, which is the only machinery in the country capable of handling the business. It would work out the whole plan and put up to the higher authority points of disagreement between Departments, or points which required political decisions.

What should that higher authority be? You will have to go off to settle the Map of Europe, apart from making a new Government. You must establish some organisation here that will function efficiently in your absence, and will be capable of taking all excepting the most crucial decisions and of compelling from day to day prompt obedience by all Departments. In my opinion that body can only be a Cabinet Committee composed of your principal colleagues who are not required for the Peace Conference and whose Departments are peculiarly involved. I should suggest the following:—Chamberlain, Montagu, Addison, Auckland Geddes, Barnes or Roberts, Stanley, and the Minister of Munitions. Of these, Austen Chamberlain, as one of the most experienced Ministers and the Senior Privy Councillor, would naturally take the Chair.

I would suggest that this body should exercise during the next few weeks the authority of the Cabinet, the principal Ministers being, of course, responsible for keeping in touch with you, ascertaining your general wishes, and studying the political interests of the administration. Of course, if Bonar Law wished to take the Chair, he, as Chancellor of the Exchequer and Leader of the House, would be beyond all question; but I am afraid he will not undertake it.

To sum up, in short my proposal is to group and create the whole of the expert Council round the existing Council of the Ministry of Munitions, with plenary control over its departmental machinery; to call upon that Council to do the work and make the plan under the general responsibility of the Minister of Munitions for the time being, and to refer to the Cabinet Committee as described for all decisions of policy, which the experts are incompetent to give; the Cabinet Committee also to be responsible, severally and jointly, for infusing the necessary energy into the administrative action of the Departments which they control, being empowered as a Committee within the scope of their reference to give directions to other Departments after discussing the matter with the Ministers concerned.

Believe me, in the above I have only been actuated by a careful consideration of your interests and the interests of the Government and by a desire to see a machinery erected which will actually work, and set you free for the grave tasks which lie before you. This business of demobilisation is one in which things will have to get worse before they get better; but I am quite certain the machinery I have indicated will grapple with the difficulties, and that it is very unlikely that any alternative machinery can be created which will not lead to a breakdown. Least of all do I think it possible to appoint a single man unacquainted with what has been done and is being done, and unacceptable to a large proportion of the essential people, and to endow him with powers which really ought not to be exercised by anyone short of the Prime Minister himself.

I beg you to give these matters yr early morning thoughts.

Yours always
W

Winston S. Churchill to Bernard Baruch:[1] *telegram*

(*Churchill papers: 15/54*)

17 December 1918 Ministry of Munitions

. . . as our task is now drawing to its close, I take this opportunity of expressing to you my heartfelt thanks for all the assistance you have given to me, to this country and to the Allied cause from the great position which you have filled. It has been a real pleasure to me to work with you. I appreciated more than I can say the compliment which you paid me in entrusting to me the large discretionary powers over our war purchases of nitrate, thus making me agent for the United States, whose financial interests in the closing phase of the war were, so far as the purchase of nitrate was concerned, five or six times our own. To give those great powers spontaneously and freely, and to support their use at all times by every act of confidence and consideration, was a measure of the large way in which Americans do things, and also of the high degree of co-operation which is possible between our two countries.

If, in order to secure complete victory, it had been unhappily necessary to prolong the war during 1920 and 1921, I am certain that Anglo-American co-operation would have become so intimate as almost to amount to a fusion in many respects of our war effort. It has been inspired throughout by the principle, How can we help each other best? and the only rivalry that existed was as to who could give the most to the other. If that spirit can continue to

[1] Bernard Mannes Baruch, 1870–1965. Of Jewish parentage; born in New York. Financier Chairman, Allied Purchasing Commission, 1917. Commissioner in Charge of Raw Materials, War Industries Board, 1917–18. Chairman of the War Industries Board, 5 March 1918–1 January 1919. Economic Adviser to the American Peace Commission, 1919. Member of the President's Agricultural Conference, 1922. American Representative on the Atomic Energy Commission, 1946. He published two volumes of memoirs, *My Own Story* in 1957 and *The Public Years* in 1960.

animate the great branches of the English-speaking family, their enduring fame and the future peace of the world will be placed upon unshakeable foundations.

I am quite certain that those men on either side of the Atlantic who, through their official duties, have been brought into relationship during these years of stress have a special duty laid upon them all their lives to keep in touch in public matters and work with the same aim. . . .

Sir Maurice Hankey: diary

(*Hankey papers*)

19 December 1918

Short War Cabinet at 11.45 to fix up the appointment of Sir Eric Geddes as principal demobiliser. Churchill sulky & hostile.

Sir Henry Wilson: diary

(*Wilson papers*)

19 December 1918

Dined alone with Winston. . . . We discussed again his being War Minister. He tells me LG now wants him to combine War Office & Air. I am not sure about this. What of the Navy & what of Commercial Air? It seems quite clear that Winston is going to succeed Milner and I have grave doubts about the situation.

Winston S. Churchill to David Lloyd George

(*Lloyd George papers*)

26 December 1918

My dear Prime Minister,

Here is the letter about the new Government wh you have asked me to write you.

I assume that Asquith & his friends will stop outside. I hope however that bitterness will be assuaged by his going to the Peace Conference. I consider that if you are the leader of the majority of the Liberals you shd become leader of the Liberal party & that this issue shd be raised as soon as possible. The two matters may perhaps be made mutually to help each other.[1]

Unless someone of real political consequence like Asquith becomes Lord Chancellor it does not seem to me necessary to include that office in the limited Cabinet you have in mind. The Lord Chancellor cd if you found it convenient be treated as a high judge & as Speaker of the House of Lords rather than as a politician.[2]

I assume secondly a Cabinet composed of the leading political figures who follow the Prime Minister holding between them all the principal offices of State. Having regard to the offices which must be represented I do not see how this can be less than 14 or 15. Of this I suppose the Unionists wd constitute at least half.

You wd no doubt wish to have near you 3 or 4 men of experience & party weights unburdened by departments &c & Bonar Law as Leader of the House (Query as 1st Lord of the Treasury) Curzon Lord President, Milner (or Rufus) Lord Privy Seal & Barnes Duchy of Lancaster.[3] Thus yr War Cabinet system wd be merged in the larger body required for peace purposes without being definitely abandoned. The old sinecure offices are intended to supply this non-departmental element in the Cabinet & by using them the foreign term 'Minister without portfolio' can be avoided.

The Secretaries of State are it seems to me fairly obvious now; but there is a point about Jews wh occurs to me—you must not have too many of them. Montagu represents the Indian policy of the Government & therefore counts for more than a mere administrator. After Peace is settled Balfour will probably retire & surely then Rufus shd be his successor at the Foreign Office. Indeed I shd like to see him join the Government now as Lord Privy Seal—a close & old friend at yr side. The advent of the Infant Samuel to the Home Office shd be considered in the light of the two above-mentioned facts. Three Jews among only 7 Liberal cabinet ministers might I fear give rise to comment.[4]

[1] Neither Asquith nor any of his Liberal supporters were given places in the new Government, nor was Asquith asked to go to the Paris Peace Conference. But he remained Leader of the Liberal Party, even after the 1918 election, when his followers won only 54 seats, as against 62 for the Lloyd George (or National) Liberals.

[2] On 10 January 1919 Lloyd George appointed Lord Birkenhead (then Attorney General) as Lord Chancellor. No 'limited Cabinet' was established, although the War Cabinet system continued until October 1919.

[3] On 10 January 1919 Bonar Law was appointed Lord Privy Seal, and Lord Milner Secretary of State for the Colonies. G N Barnes remained Minister without Portfolio and Curzon remained Lord President of the Council.

[4] Lord Reading (Rufus Isaacs) received no further Cabinet Office until 1931, when he became Foreign Secretary in the National Government. Balfour remained Foreign Secretary until October 1919, when he was succeeded at the Foreign Office by Lord Curzon. Herbert

It wd be a pity to move Montagu from India, but if you decide to send him to the Exchequer I suppose Austen wd succeed him. I understand he is friendly to Montagu's Indian policy. Milner wd be vy good at the Colonies. He ought to be given 50 millions a year to develop our tropical possessions, & at least 20 millions worth of orders for ironmongery ought to be placed promptly in the Munition works. Walter Long on this plan wd go to the Admiralty wh I expect he wd enjoy vy much. For the Home Office I suggest Fisher. You need a new man in the Cabinet & his political attainments are superior to those of any others now in sight. He wd strengthen the Government if he held an office of high rank. I think he is the best of all yr discoveries.[1] You tell me that you have destined for me the task of dispersing & liquidating our Armies & Air Force & of building from the residue the armies & the aviaries of the future. I had as you know other ideas but I will do my best to serve you as you wish. It is a vy important & difficult task & you do me honour in choosing me for it.

So much for the Secretaries of State.

About the Exchequer—the man of all others for that great & vital post wd be Rufus: but alas he is an Earl. It has occurred to me that possibly the intention wh you have to get ministers have the right to speak in either House might modify the objection. It is really wrong that the best man shd not fill the post of danger. In no other constitution wd such a barrier exist. But I only mention this idea in passing. Otherwise I presume you will choose Montagu. This in my judgment wd be the best course open.[2]

I hope you will find it possible to include the Attorney General in the Cabinet. He can help you vy much with the Tory democrats. His exclusion wd I think chill a loyal friendship. He can earn £20–25,000 a year from an entirely independent position.

Scotland will not stand having no Cabinet Minister, & if Scotland is represented Ireland wd follow. I consider however that French wd be an asset to the Cabinet. Thus the tally of 15 is completed of whom 7 are Unionists & 7 Liberal & French non-party.

I have only a few isolated suggestions to make about the non-Cabinet offices & Under-Secretaries.

Samuel received no Cabinet Office under Lloyd George, but was sent to Palestine as the first High Commissioner in July 1920. (In 1931 he entered the National Government as Home Secretary.)

[1] On 10 January 1919 Milner was appointed Colonial Secretary and Walter Long First Lord of the Admiralty. But H A L Fisher remained at the Board of Education, and Edward Shortt became Home Secretary.

[2] On 10 January 1919 Austen Chamberlain was appointed Chancellor of the Exchequer. Montagu remained as Secretary of State for India.

I cannot think of anybody for Labour. I do not myself hold with the existence of such a Ministry. *Arbitration & Conciliation* are the functions of an impartial department like the Board of Trade. *Factories* etc are well managed by the Home Office. Labour *policy* belongs to the Government. But since the office has been created and is looked upon as a sort of sop for Labour men, I cannot see why Roberts shd not continue. He is honest & plucky & loyal.[1]

Pensions wd be well filled by Jack Seely. The main policy is *Cash* wh comes from the Treasury on the decision of the Cabinet. Its execution requires a sympathetic figure—'one who knows what they went through', who understands how to talk to them, & someone who can stand Parliamentary badgering. It involves dealing with a mass of detail in a humane & warm hearted spirit—not entirely without knowledge of politics. MacCallum Scott wd make a good Under-Secretary for Pensions & a good counter to Hogge[2] so far as Scottish opinion is concerned.[3]

If you are not attracted by this plan perhaps you will consider Seely for Postmaster-General. I do not think he will take an Under-Secretaryship, now that Peace has come.[4]

I am perturbed about the Ministry of Munitions (or Supply). I fear you are gravitating towards Andrew Weir.[5] This wd mean the exodus of the best men I have got. Stevenson, Duckham, Layton, K Price, Alexr Walker[6] wd I am pretty sure take their departure. Their work is indispensable to our success in demobilising the Munitions industries; & that is one of the vital concerns of the Government during the next two or three months. My advice is Worthington Evans who wd keep the whole machine together. He has qualities both in the Administrative & Parliamentary sphere.[7] Anyhow I hand the business over in good order & you must absolve me from further responsibility connected with it.

[1] On 10 January 1919 Roberts was replaced as Minister of Labour by Sir Robert Horne, and was appointed Food Controller (an office, unlike Labour, which was not in the Cabinet).

[2] James Myles Hogge, 1873–1928. Liberal MP for East Edinburgh, 1912–24. President of the Edinburgh University Liberal Association. A persistent back-bench advocate of Scottish interests. Chief Whip of the Asquithian Liberals (the Wee Frees), 1922.

[3] Macallum Scott received no Ministerial appointment in 1918.

[4] Albert Illingworth remained Postmaster General, an office he had held since December 1916. Seely did agree to accept an Under-Secretaryship, to Churchill (in his capacity as Secretary of State for Air).

[5] Andrew Weir, 1865–1955. Shipowner. Surveyor-General of Supply, War Office, 1917–19. Created Baron Inverforth, February 1919. Minister of Munitions (later of Supply), January 1919–March 1921.

[6] Alexander Walker, 1869–1950. Brewer; Chairman of John Walker & Sons, Distillers. Served at the Disposal Board, Ministry of Munitions, 1918–19. Knighted 1920.

[7] Sir Laming Worthington Evans was appointed Minister of Pensions (an office not in the Cabinet).

I expect you will weigh vy carefully Selborne[1] before putting him out of court for Agriculture. Bathurst[2] is I am told vy much a farmer. I thought Ian Macpherson[3] an extremely good suggestion for the Chief Secretaryship to the Lord Lieutenant. This wd create a vacancy at the War Office, & I shd like to have either Londonderry[4] or Fitzwilliam[5] to represent the Department in the Lords as Under-Secretary. It is important when dealing with the Army to have the social side not entirely unrepresented. You yourself found Derby assistance in this respect. If these young men of great worldly position are sincerely desirous of aiding a democratic & progressive policy, I think it is right to associate them directly with the Administration.

I hope you will endeavour to gather together all forces of strength & influence in the country & lead them along the paths of science & organisation to the rescue of the weak & poor. That is the main conception I have of the Victory Government & from it we may draw the prosperity & stability of the Empire.

I appreciate vy much indeed your having wished me to write fully to you on all these interesting points.

Yours always
W

[1] William Waldegrave Palmer, 1859–1942. Liberal MP, 1885–6; Unionist MP, 1886–95. 2nd Earl of Selborne 1895. First Lord of the Admiralty, 1900–5. High Commissioner for South Africa 1905–10. President of the Board of Agriculture and Fisheries in Asquith's Coalition Government, from May 1915 to June 1916, after which he received no further Cabinet appointment. His second son, Robert, was killed in action in Mesopotamia in 1916.

[2] Seymour Henry Bathurst, 1864–1943. Succeeded his father as 7th Earl Bathurst, 1892. Owner of 12,000 acres. Master of the Vale of White Horse Foxhounds. A Conservative, he received no political office either under Lloyd George, or later. His eldest son, Lord Apsley (a Conservative MP 1922–9 and 1931–42) was killed in action at Malta in 1942.

[3] James Ian Macpherson, 1880–1937. Barrister. Liberal MP, 1911–18; Coalition Liberal, 1918–31; Liberal National, 1931–5. Under-Secretary of State for War, 1916–18. Vice-President of the Army Council, 1918. Chief Secretary for Ireland, 1919–20. Minister of Pensions, 1920–2. Created Baronet, 1933. Created Baron Strathcarron, 1936.

[4] Charles Stewart Henry Vane-Tempest-Stewart, Viscount Castlereagh, 1878–1949. Conservative MP for Maidstone, 1906–15. Succeeded his father as 7th Marquess of Londonderry, 1915. Served briefly on the western front as 2nd in Command, Royal Horse Guards, 1915. He held no Government office until appointed Under-Secretary of State for Air, 1920–1. Minister of Education and Leader of the Senate, Government of Northern Ireland, 1921–6. Returned to Westminster as First Commissioner of Works, 1928–9 and 1931; and as Secretary of State for Air and Lord Privy Seal, 1931–5. Churchill's first cousin.

[5] William Charles de Meuron Wentworth-Fitzwilliam, 1872–1943. ADC to Lord Lansdowne (the Viceroy of India), 1892–3. Liberal Unionist MP, 1895–1902. Married Lady Maud Dundas, daughter of the 1st Marquis of Zetland, 1896. Succeeded his grandfather as 7th Earl Fitzwilliam, 1902. Served on the Army HQ Staff, South Africa, 1900, and in France, 1914–15. Lieutenant-Colonel, 1912. Interested in mining engineering, and travel. He never held any Government office. (Viscount Peel was appointed Under-Secretary of State for War on 10 January 1919 and remained in office until April 1921.)

Leopold Amery to David Lloyd George

(*Lloyd George papers*)

27 December 1918 Offices of the War Cabinet

Don't put Churchill in the War Office. I hear from all sorts of quarters that the Army are terrified at the idea. What he needs is a field for adventure and advertisement, and the field that would give him most scope in both directions is the Air Ministry with its interesting potentialities, both commercial and strategical, or, failing that, the Colonial Office, minus the Dominions, where there is a great field for constructive administrative and economic policy.

Winston S. Churchill to David Lloyd George

(*Churchill papers: 2/103*)

29 December 1918 Ministry of Munitions

My dear Prime Minister,

I realise that you ought to have a speedy answer to the question you put to me this morning abt going to the WO or the Admiralty.

My heart is in the Admy. There I have long experience, & any claim I may be granted in public good will will always rest on the fact that 'The Fleet was ready'.

In all the circumstances of the present situation I think I shd add more weight to yr administration there than at the War Office.

There will be a good reason for connecting the Air with the Admiralty, for though aeroplanes will never be a substitute for armies, they will be a substitute for many classes of warships. The technical development of the air falls naturally into the same sphere as the mechanical development of the Navy; & this becomes increasingly true the larger the aeroplane grows.

There, I have no doubt what my choice shd be.

Yrs
W

January 1919

Sir Douglas Haig to Winston S. Churchill

(*Churchill papers: 1/132*)

1 January 1919
Personal

Kingston Hill
Surrey

My dear Mr Churchill,

Very many thanks for your kindness in writing. I heartily reciprocate your good wishes for the New Year, and I hope that it may be a bright & prosperous one for you personally.

I am greatly pleased that you should have found the map which I sent you so satisfactory, and I feel honoured that you shd think it worth framing.[1]

What rubbish *The Times* writes about our mutual friend Foch's Strategy!—As a matter of fact it resolved itself into two phrases which he repeated at most of the meetings I had with him viz '*Tout le monde à la bataille*' and '*on ait ce qu'on peut*'.

Again best of luck for 1919 & Believe me

Yours very sincerely
D. Haig

Edward Marsh to Lord Esher

(*Esher papers*)

1 January 1919

Ministry of Munitions

I'm still in slight suspense as to where Winston & I shall be this time next week—anyhow it will be somewhere that gives him a good chance.

[1] A map showing the disposition of the Allied and German forces on the western front on 25 September 1918, at the start of the final Allied offensive. Churchill was so impressed by it that in 1927 he reproduced it facing page 534 of the fourth volume of *The World Crisis*.

David Lloyd George to Winston S. Churchill

(*Churchill papers: 2/105*)

9 January 1919 10 Downing Street

My dear Churchill,

Under the authority which I have received from the King to form a new Government, I have submitted your name to His Majesty for the office of Secretary of State for War and Air. The King has been pleased to give his assent to your filling this office and I should be glad to know as soon as possible whether you will accept it, as I am leaving to-morrow for France.

Yours sincerely
D. Lloyd George

Of course there will be but one salary!

Winston S. Churchill to David Lloyd George

(*Churchill papers: 2/105*)

10 January 1919 Ministry of Munitions

My dear Prime Minister

I am willing to undertake the vy responsible duties of the office wh you have offered me, & I take this occasion to thank you for the renewed proof of yr confidence wh such an invitation implies.

I shall do my utmost to serve you & to sustain the interests of the Government.

yrs always
Winston S. Churchill

Sir Henry Wilson: diary

(*Wilson papers*)

10 January 1919 36 Eaton Place

War Cabinet. I sat between Milner & Winston, ex & present War Ministers. I brought up the necessity of some decision about Russia whether at Murmansk or in Siberia or in Poland or Ukraine or Caucasus. Absolutely *no* policy.

It was agreed that this must be our first subject in Paris on Sunday.

I had a long talk with Winston in the Ministry of Munitions this morning. He comes over to the WO on Monday. He is full of fight & of ideas. Wants to stop demobilization altogether! wants to bring home all reliable troops, ie Household & other Cavalry, Yeomanry, Home County Rgts: etc. I hope he and I may get on. Ominous letters from Rawley & others in France about the temper of the troops there. . . .

Winston is now S of S for War & for Air. I asked him where the Admiralty came in & he admitted—nowhere!

I also saw Jack Seely who is US of S for Air under Winston & he also agreed that the arrangement about the Admiralty & the Air was quite hopeless.

Lord French to Winston S. Churchill: telegram

(Churchill papers: 2/105)

11 January 1919 Dublin Castle

Enormous congratulations. I am delighted to see you at the head of the Army at last.

Winston S. Churchill to Sir Douglas Haig: telegram

(Churchill papers: 16/3)

11 January 1919 War Office
Personal and Private

Your very serious telegram of the 9th instant about demobilisation and morale has been read by me. Unless there is some reason which I do not know to the contrary, it would be advantageous if you could come over here for Tuesday, Wednesday or Thursday. In conjunction with Eric Geddes we can then survey the whole position and take definite decisions which are clearly needed. Secondly, on taking over this new office I want to let you know that I am heart and soul with you about providing for disabled Officers and I am sure that working together with Worthington Evans, the extremely able Minister of Pensions, we shall be able to arrive speedily at good results.

All good wishes.

Churchill

Winston S. Churchill: departmental note

(*Churchill papers: 16/1*)

12 January 1919 War Office

The Air Force will be maintained as a separate service from the Army & the Navy. It will comprise all Air activities military, naval or commercial. It will control its own technical & experimental Departments. It will be composed of officers, NCOs & men who are drawn from the Army & the Navy as well as of direct entry airmen. Flow will be maintained from & to both parent services so that future commanders of Army & Navy are thoroughly acquainted with air warfare, & so that a prolonged career may be open to high merit. An air staff college will be formed in two divisions:—juniors for specialised air work; seniors for combined war thought.

The defence of the coast & of marine fortresses will fall naturally to the Air Force, once it possessed the officers of combined knowledge & real status. The Air Force is the arm wh stands alone & midway between the land & sea services. Where they clash, it rules. Given superior thinking power & knowledge it must obtain the primary place in the general conception of war policy.

Sir Henry Wilson: diary

(*Wilson papers*)

14 January 1919 36 Eaton Place

Long talk with Winston who proposes to hold up de-mobilization for all men who have not completed 2 years in France. There is much to be said for his argument, & we meet with Lawrence & Fowke to examine his proposals.

We must do something drastic to stop the present stampede which is going on.

Winston S. Churchill to Viscount Midleton[1]

(*Sold at Christie's, 21.11.62, lot 215*)

14 January 1919 War Office

My dear Brodrick,

Nemesis no doubt has brought these old bones to life. It is poetic justice that after 20 years I shd find myself confronted with yr difficulties on a still larger scale. And if you take your revenge, you will not find me unconscious

[1] St John Brodrick 1856–1942. Conservative MP, 1880–5 and 1885–1906. Secretary of State for War, 1900–3; for India, 1903–5. Succeeded his father as 9th Viscount Midleton, 1907; created Earl, 1920. He published his memoirs, *Record and Reactions* 1856–1939 in 1939. In 1901 Churchill had attacked his military policy in a series of speeches published with the title *Mr Brodrick's Army*.

of the fact. But seriously I am vy grateful for the kindness of yr letter wh encourages me to hope that retribution may be tempered by mercy. It will give me great pleasure to hear from you if at any time there is some question or matter wh you think I shd look into to.

'It is by accident that we have become a military nation. We must endeavour to remain so.'

Yours vy sincerely,
Winston S. Churchill

Winston S. Churchill to General Allenby

(*Churchill papers: 16/3*)

14 January 1919 War Office
Secret

On assuming office as Secretary of State for War I wish to tell you that I hope you will not hesitate to write or telegraph personally to me on any matter in which you think I can be of assistance to you in your work. I have followed your brilliant victories with great admiration and the wonderful results which have followed from them. In the difficult tasks which lie before you I send you all good wishes for your further successes.

Winston S. Churchill to General Ironside[1] and General Maynard:[2] telegram

(*Churchill papers: 16/3*)

14 January 1919 War Office
Secret

Immediate attention is being given by me to the difficulties of your situation. Decisions must be taken within a few days by the Great Powers in

[1] William Edmund Ironside, 1880–1959. 2nd Lieutenant, Royal Artillery, 1899. On active service in South Africa, 1899–1902. Major, 1914. Staff Officer, 4th Canadian Division, 1916–17. Took part in the battles of Vimy Ridge and Passchendaele. Commandant of the Machine Gun Corps School, France, 1918. Brigadier-General commanding the 99th Infantry Brigade, 1918. Major-General commanding the Allied Troops, Archangel, October 1918–October 1919. Knighted, 1919. Head of the British Military Mission to Hungary, 1920. Commanded The Ismid Force, Turkey, 1920; the North Persian Force, 1920–1. Lieutenant-General, 1931. Quartermaster-General, India, 1933–6. General, 1935. Governor and Commander-in-Chief, Gibraltar, 1938–9. Head of the British Military Mission to Poland, August 1939. Chief of the Imperial General Staff, 1939–40. Commander-in-Chief, Home Forces, May 1940. Field-Marshal, 1940. Created Baron, 1941. In 1953 he published *Archangel 1918–19*.

[2] Charles Clarkson Martin Maynard, 1870–1945. 2nd Lieutenant, 1890. On active service in Burma, 1889–92, the Tirah, 1897, South Africa, 1900–1; and the Great War. Brigade-Commander, 1915–17. Commander-in-Chief of the Allied Forces at Murmansk, 1918–19. Knighted, 1919. Major-General, 1923. He published *The Murmansk Venture* in 1928.

Paris, and whatever policy is adopted will be carried out vigorously. My intention will be to secure you in one way or another the support necessary for whatever task you are called upon to carry out. Please communicate freely with me on any matter which is causing you anxiety, or in which I can assist you.

Lord Milner to Winston S. Churchill

(*Churchill papers: 16/3*)

14 January 1919

My dear Churchill,

... I have no doubt either that you agree with me in thinking that the withdrawal of our & the Canadian troops from Siberia at present would be a fatal blunder. It is not a question of their fighting value but of the moral effect. It would be better to risk a few thousand men (though there would be no risk if the railway could be put right) than to allow the whole fabric of Russo-Siberian resistance to Bolshevism to crumble. What sort of a Peace (!) shd we have, if all Europe & Asia from Warsaw to Vladivostock were under the sway of Lenin?

Yours vy sincerely
Milner

Sir Henry Wilson: diary

(*Wilson papers*)

15 January 1919 — 36 Eaton Place

Winston had his first Army Council meeting, & after that we had another meeting at which DH and Fowke & Robertson & Horne[1] & Auckland Geddes were present to discuss Winston's proposals for the formation of an

[1] Robert Stevenson Horne, 1871–1940. Lecturer in Philosophy, University College of North Wales, 1895. Examiner in Philosophy, Aberdeen University, 1896. Active at the Scottish Bar, 1900–14. Assistant Inspector-General of Transportation, with the rank of Lieutenant-Colonel, 1917. Director of Department of Materials and Priority, Admiralty, 1917. Director, Admiralty Labour Department, 1918. Third Civil Lord of Admiralty, 1918–19. Knighted, 1918. Conservative MP, 1918–37. Minister of Labour, 1919. President of the Board of Trade, 1920–1. Chancellor of the Exchequer, 1921–2. Declined office under Bonar Law and turned to the City for employment, where he became Chairman of the Great Western Railway Company, the Burma Corporation, the Zinc Corporation and the Imperial Smelting Corporation, and a Director of the Suez Canal Company, Lloyds Bank, the P & O Steam Navigation Company and the Commercial Union Assurance Company. Created Viscount Horne of Slamannan, 1937.

Army of Occupation. On the whole the wisest plan seems to be to form this Army of men of certain ages & of certain lengths of Services & a Committee under the AG was formed to thrash this out & to report in 48 hours. Another Comm^{ee} undertook to examine the cost of the extra pay involved for those who are held to serve on willy-nilly. Winston very clear & good. . . .

At 5 o'c I was present in Winston's room when Winston gave an address to 50 representatives of the Press. It was excellent. His points were:—

(a) Necessity of Army of Occupation which must be done by compulsion.
(b) Necessity of a Post bellum voluntary army.
(c) Necessity for keeping up our present forces in Russia.

After he had finished & Burnham[1] & one or two others had addressed the meeting, I made a short address about Discipline, about the waste of money & uselessness of an Army without discipline & about the reinforcements for Murmansk etc which consist of RAMC, Railway & Electic Light personnel. The whole meeting went off very well & we will see now what the Press will do. Of course Winston is diametrically opposed to LG with his 'no conscription'.

Winston S. Churchill to Sir Henry Wilson

(*War Office papers: 32/9299*)

15 January 1919 War Office

The present time is suitable for making certain important re-groupings of duties between Departments of State and within the War Office itself. The Government have determined in principle on the formation of a Ministry of Supply. Mr Andrew Weir has left the Supply and Contract Branch of the War Office and has assumed office as Minister of Munitions. He desires urgently to take over at once the Contract Branch of the War Office. In principle I am not opposed to this. I think, further, that the Ministry of National Supply should make for the War Office and to their order everything they require (including clothes) except only the provision of food and horses. All those engineering stores which were made by the QMG's Depart-

[1] Harry Lawson Webster Levy Lawson, 1862–1933. Conservative MP 1885–1906 and 1910–16. Mayor of Stepney, 1907–9. President of the Institute of Journalists, 1910. Succeeded his father (the principal proprietor of the *Daily Telegraph*) as 2nd Baron Burnham, 1916. President of the Empire Press Union, 1916–28. Created Viscount, May 1919. President of the International Labour Conference, Geneva, 1921–2 and 1926; of the Press Experts Conference, 1927 and 1929; and of the Public Health Congress, 1924 and 1927. He had no sons. One of his nephews, William Lawson (Lieutenant, Scots Guards) was killed in action in October 1914, at the age of 21.

ment should be made for us in the same way as shells and guns have been. Therefore, in principle, on this head I am disposed to meet the wishes of the Ministry of Supply and in so doing we shall be carrying out the policy on which the Government have embarked.

On the other hand I cannot think that the Army will regard it as satisfactory that during years of peace they should be deprived of the control of experiment, inspection and design in all matters relating to ordnance, tanks, etc. The same is true of the Air Ministry who require the return to them of the technical departments of aeronautical supply. With regard to fixing the true frontier of design between the user and the maker I consider the using department must predominate in weight and initiate action. The supply department, however, should act in a critical function of a secondary character in order to make sure that the designs ordered are not unduly hard or unduly expensive to make and are capable of being produced in great quantities, etc. It is the delimitation of this frontier between supply and design, between the makers and users, between the Ministry of Supply and the War Office and Air Office that now requires to be explored and I should not feel inclined to come to a settlement with Mr Andrew Weir about handing over these new branches to him except in conjunction with the satisfactory solution of the design side of the question.

The change which I have in mind would have the effect of restoring to the MGO the great function of experiment, design and inspection. It would relieve the QMG of a very large portion of his work; he would make nothing, he would buy nothing (except food and horses), he would have no contact with labour at any point. It seems to me quite arguable whether in these circumstances an amalgamation should not be made, when a convenient opportunity occurs, between the resuscitated MGO and the depleted QMG so as to have only one Member of Council dealing with the whole field of material. This is the arrangement which exists on the Air Board. I do not know enough of what the remaining duties of the QMG would be to form an opinion how far it could usefully be paralleled here in the War Office.

Another inroad on 'Q' should it seems to me be made by transferring all discipline to the Adjutant General. There should be only one discipline in the Army for which AG is primarily responsible. It is surely not a good thing to have RE and ASC units under different control.

Cognate to the above and worth considering at the present time are the relations between the Military Secretary's Department and the Department of the Adjutant General. My idea of a Military Secretary is an officer of high rank, greatly respected in the Service, who, as the intimate counsellor of the Secretary of State, advises him on high patronage. In the present case, however, the Military Secretary discharges the whole vast business of postings and minor appointments which really, I should have thought, would far better have fallen under the Adjutant General. This also requires consideration at the present time.

To sum up, my feeling is in favour of only three great departments within the War Office—'G' (General Staff), 'A' (Adjutant-General or Personnel), and a combination of 'O' and 'Q'. But, as I say, it may well be found that enough will be left to 'Q' to justify an independent existence.

Now as to the steps to be taken. The immediate action is limited, as follows, to negotiating with the new Minister of Supply the terms on which he shall receive the Supply and Contract services now gathered under 'Q' and shall restore to the War Office the experiment, design and inspection functions which were taken away when the Ministry of Munitions was formed. (A parallel negotiation is being conducted by the Air Office.)

I should like you to discuss with me generally the subject matter of this minute, and also to advise me on—

(a) A small Committee to draw the line in regard to our re-capture of design and our surrender of Supply and Contracts.
(b) To negotiate the exchanges with Mr Weir.

Sir James Stevenson can obviously play a principal part in (b), and I will, in the final stage deal with Mr Andrew Weir personally, but I want to know *exactly* what to give up and what to demand. Meanwhile, I have given instructions that no part of the War Office business is to be handed over to the Ministry of Supply and that Sir James Stevenson, in the first instance, shall succeed to exactly the same duties as were discharged by his predecessor.

Winston S. Churchill to Lord Curzon

(*Curzon papers*)

16 January 1919 War Office

My dear Curzon,

We have made good progress in recasting the military policy and towards the immediate formation of a strong well-disciplined Army of Occupation. I hope to have the general principles of the action which should be taken ready for circulation on Saturday. I should be very much obliged if they could be considered by the Cabinet on Monday morning? It would surely be better for the Cabinet in London to arrive at a clear opinion upon the scheme and if we are all agreed about it here I think it very likely that the Prime Minister will give his assent. At any rate time is very important and under the present pressure the Army is liquefying fast and if we are not careful we shall find ourselves without the strong instrument on which our policy in Europe depends in the next few months.

Yours sincerely
Winston S. Churchill

Lord Esher to Philip Sassoon

(*Sassoon papers*)

16 January 1919

What a Government! Winston's appointment is, of course, a gamble. It is mightily unpopular, but he possesses, as Macaulay said of Chatham, 'an impetuous, adventurous and defying character'. So that you may hope his turn will be to the right and not to the left.

Edward Marsh to Lord Esher

(*Esher papers*)

17 January 1919 War Office

We are settling down by degrees—it is rather a racket but W is bearing up well & I think he has made a good start.

Andrew Bonar Law to David Lloyd George

(*Lloyd George papers*)

17 January 1919 11 Downing Street

My Dear Prime Minister,

. . . We spent the whole afternoon today with regard to the Army Scheme. I started very anxious to avoid raising a question of this kind just now but after a prolonged discussion I came to the conclusion that something must be done and done quickly and that on general lines, Churchill's proposal, which has been concurred in by Horne, Auckland Geddes and Eric Geddes, is as good a proposal as is possible. He, of course, is taking all details with him.

His scheme is based on letting free all those enlisted before 1st January 1916. This involves taking all the young men who would be apprentices and would be going on with their education and also a very large number of those who can be least well spared from industry because they were the last to go mainly on that account. Such an arrangement will involve a kind of attack, the details of which it is easy to imagine, but on the other hand I could suggest no other scheme which would be less open to attack. I thought possibly of a scheme of selection by ballot from the whole force but probably that would be worse. In saying that I think something on these lines must be done, that does not involve my agreeing to making a proposal for an army of this size on the meeting of Parliament.

You will, I have no doubt, hear all they have to say and possibly you may yourself suggest some better method generally of dealing with it, but as the proposal stands, my view would have been to make whatever arrangement is necessary now apply for the immediate future without involving any additional powers of compulsion, making it plain when the proposal is made public, that whatever figures are given now are larger than what we expect will be necessary later and that we would have time to make proposals for compulsion before peace is signed and the existing Military Service Act comes to an end.

Yours sincerely
A. Bonar Law

Sir Henry Wilson: diary
(*Wilson papers*)

17 January 1919 36 Eaton Place

We had another meeting in Winston's room at 11 am of Winston, Eric Geddes, Horne, Kent, DH, Robertson, Macdonogh,[1] Fowke, Lawrence, Self & Burnett Hitchcock[2] & we finally settled on the men who are to form the Armies of Occupation. All men who have joined since Jan: 1st 1916 will give us about 1,600,000 which will do us quite well & leave us a margin. We also include no men above 40. When we want to discard we only discard pivotal men & then the oldest by years. Then those men we keep get good leave & substantial increase of pay probably 75 pc.

Everyone agreed to our scheme so it is being printed now in its final form. . . .

[1] The Adjutant-General (see p. 471, note 3).

[2] Basil Ferguson Burnett Hitchcock, 1877–1938. Entered Army, 1897. On active service in South Africa, 1899–1900. General Staff Officer, Bermuda, 1910–12. Major, 1915. Director of Mobilization, War Office, 1917–18; Director-General, 1918 (with the rank of Brigadier-General). Major-General, in charge of Administration, Aldershot Command, 1921–5. Commanded the 55th (West Lancs) Division, 1926–8; the 4th Indian Division 1928–30. Lieutenant-General, 1930. Knighted, 1932.

Long talk with Winston before dinner. I told him when we had our scheme through the War Cabinet on Tuesday both he & I ought at once to go over to Paris & get LG to agree to it & get it out without a moment's delay. We are sitting on the top of a mine which may go up at any minute.

Winston S. Churchill to General Thwaites[1]

(*Churchill papers: 16/15*)

17 January 1919 War Office

Let one of your officers, by a readjustment of duty, be detailed to look after my maps. These will presently be placed on rollers in the small anteroom next to my room.

The maps must be carefully selected to cover the whole field of interest, particularly the various Russian theatres of war and disturbance.

If the officer will go and look at the arrangement I had at the Ministry of Munitions he will see to what extent it requires to be supplemented.

The officer should be able to explain to me what the general position is at any time in any of the theatres.

Winston S. Churchill to Walter Long

(*Churchill papers: 16/3*)

18 January 1919 War Office
Private

My dear Long,

In a recent paper by the 1st Sea Lord[2] the Admiralty have taken up towards the Air Ministry exactly the line towards which everyone who

[1] William Thwaites, 1868–1947. 2nd Lieutenant, Royal Artillery, 1887; Lieutenant-Colonel, 1914. Served on the western front, 1915–18. Commanded the 141st Infantry Brigade, 1915–16; the 46th Division, 1916–18. Major-General, 1918. Director of Military Intelligence, September 1918–April 1922; Director of Military Operations and Intelligence, April–October 1922. Knighted, 1919. General Officer commanding the 47th Division (TA), 1923–6; the British Army on the Rhine, 1927–9. Director-General of the Territorial Army, 1931–3.

[2] Rosslyn Erskine Wemyss, 1864–1933. Entered Navy, 1877. Commodore, Royal Naval Barracks Devonport, 1909–11. Rear-Admiral in command of the 12th Cruiser Squadron, August 1914, charged with escorting the British Expeditionary Force to France. Convoyed the first Canadian troops to France, September 1914. Governor of Mudros, February–April 1915. Commanded the naval squadron at Cape Helles, April 1915. Acting Vice-Admiral at the Dardanelles, November–December 1915; directed the naval aspects of the evacuation of the Gallipoli Peninsula. Knighted, 1916. Second Sea Lord, 1917. First Sea Lord, 1917–19. Created Baron Wester Wemyss, 1919. Admiral of the Fleet, 1919. Known as 'Rosy'.

cares about the Air Force has been consistently working. I learned however from the 1st Sea Lord the other night that in consequence of the Secretaryship of State for the Air being held by the S of S for War, another paper was about to be circulated departing in important aspects from the satisfactory position adopted in the first.

I hope therefore that before any such step as this is taken you will give me the opportunity of talking the matter over with you. I feel that having undertaken at the wish & suggestion of the PM the dual responsibility for the WO & the Air Ministry I am entitled to a little breathing space & time to look round. I should feel it rather hard on me if, without any change in the status & organisation of the Air Force having occurred, & without my being given the time to formulate any policy, the Admiralty were to take alarm & commit themselves to a retrogressive policy.

I am fairly confident that I shd be able to propose to you arrangements wh both in form & fact will be satisfactory to the Admiralty; & as a colleague I ask that there shd be frank & friendly discussion between us before a difference between Departments is published to the wide circle of Govt Depts. With yr long experience of affairs I am sure you will recognise the reasonable nature of my request.

David Lloyd George to Winston S. Churchill

(*Churchill papers: 16/3*)

18 January 1919 Paris

My dear Winston,

I have just heard that you propose bringing before the Cabinet on Tuesday the question of continuing military service for an army of 1,700,000. I am surprised that you should think it right to submit such a scheme to my colleagues before talking it over or at least before submitting it in the first instance to me. It is hardly treating the head of the Government fairly. This is a question not of detail but of first class policy which may involve grave political consequences (it might even produce trouble in the Army) & I ought to have been consulted in the first instance. A memo ought have been sent to me by aeroplane which would have reached me in a few hours.

Please let me know something of your plan at once.

Ever sincerely
D. Lloyd George

Winston S. Churchill to David Lloyd George

(*Churchill papers: 16/3*)

19 January 1919 War Office
Secret

My dear Prime Minister,

I send you a file of papers which represent the results of my study of the demobilisation emergency. I do not think you will get the military authorities to function properly until they are re-assured that they are not going to be left without an Army. At present the discipline of the whole Army is being rotted—every platoon simultaneously—by the pulling out of people in ones and twos without any relation to what the ordinary man regards as fair play; and because the rate of discharge from France is necessarily limited by railway transport, etc, and the feeling is so bad, we are told that we cannot release the enormous numbers of men who are on our pay list in England whom we do not want and who want to go.

Once we get the Armies of Occupation settled and have these compact and strong forces of moderate dimensions to rely upon, it will be easy to concentrate our benefits in the way of pay upon those who have to stop and to push the others out of doors as fast as they want to go, or even faster.

You will see that, broadly speaking, I contemplate getting rid of three men out of four. The saving which will accrue from accelerating this process by even two months will more than pay the extra cost of rendering those who stop a contented and a privileged class.

I am very anxious about the state of the Army, both in France and at home: it is better now than it was ten days ago, and I hear from various quarters that the statement we prepared and which you issued before I came into office had a very steadying effect. The papers also have seen the red light and have been trying to help as much as possible instead of exciting discontent. But I hear bad reports from J H Thomas[1] about the railwaymen; from Haig about the general discontent of the Army in France; and from Robertson so far as home is concerned. French is very worried about the Irish situation, and I have had to slow down the rate of demobilising the few efficient troops we have in that country.

[1] James Henry Thomas, 1874–1949. Began work as an errand boy at the age of nine; subsequently an engine-cleaner, fireman, and engine-driver. Labour MP for Derby, 1910–31; National Labour MP, 1931–6. General Secretary, National Union of Railwaymen, 1918–24, and 1924–31. President of the International Federation of Trade Unions, 1920–4. Vice-Chairman of the Parliamentary Labour Party, 1921. Secretary of State for the Colonies in the first Labour Government, 1924. Minister of Employment and Lord Privy Seal, 1929–30. Secretary of State for the Dominions, 1930–5; for the Colonies, 1935–6. He published *When Labour Rules* (1920) and *My Story* (1937).

It is really of vital importance to me to get this large scheme of mine settled. A broad and bold handling of the whole problem is required, and I think I have succeeded in grasping it and in evolving a comprehensive and far-reaching plan.

You cannot do better than read the explanatory statement which I have prepared with my own hands and which, subject to certain minor alterations which discussion will suggest, represents the policy I recommend. This statement I want to publish in time to catch the Sunday papers at the end of this week, and I am arranging to prepare the Editors and Proprietors beforehand by conferences and personal interviews, which will occupy the greater portion of my time. I am asking Henry Wilson to go over on Tuesday with the scheme and to obtain your assent to it. If you see objections to it, I will come over myself and discuss it with you.

Sir Archibald Sinclair, who is the bearer to you personally of this packet, is, as you know, a great friend of mine and will I hope soon be contesting a Scottish By-Election on your behalf.[1] It will be nice of you to receive him.

Yours always
WSC

Winston S. Churchill: memorandum

(Lloyd George papers)

THE ARMIES OF OCCUPATION

19 January 1919 War Office

1. On November 11th, when the armistice was signed, there were nearly 3,350,000 Imperial British officers and soldiers on the Pay and Ration strength of the British Army. During the two months that have passed since then, rather more than half a million have been demobilised or discharged. The system of demobilisation which has been adopted aims at reviving national industry by bringing the men home in the order of urgency according to trades. There is no doubt that this is the wisest course, and it will continue to be followed in the large majority of cases. The time has now come, however, when military needs must be considered as well as industrial needs.

2. Unless we are to be defrauded of the fruits of victory and, without

[1] Sinclair did not find a constituency until the General Election of October 1922, when he was elected (as a National Liberal) for Caithness and Sutherland. Between 1919 and 1922 he served as Churchill's Military Secretary, first at the War Office and then at the Colonial Office.

considering our Allies, to throw away all that we have won with so much cost and trouble, we must provide for a good many months to come Armies of Occupation for the enemy's territory. These armies must be strong enough to exact from the Germans, Turks and others, the just terms which the Allies demand, and we must bear our share with France, America and Italy in providing them. The better trained and disciplined these armies are, the fewer men will be needed to do the job. We have, therefore, to create, in order to wind up the war satisfactorily, a strong, compact, contented, well-disciplined army which will maintain the high reputation of the British Service and make sure we are not tricked of what we have rightfully won. It will be an Army far smaller than our present Army. In fact, it will be about one third of the great armies we have been using in the war.

Our Military Commanders, who know what Marshal Foch's wishes are, say that 1,150,000 men of all ranks and arms will be sufficient to guard our interests in this transition period. Therefore, when this new Army has been organised and while it is being organised, nearly two and a quarter million men who were held to military service when the fighting stopped will be released to their homes and to industry as fast as the trains and ships can carry them and the Pay Offices settle their accounts. In other words, out of 3,350,000 it is proposed to keep for the present 1,150,000 and release all the others as fast as possible.

3. How ought we to choose the 1,150,000 who are to remain to finish up the work? When men are marked for release they obviously ought to go home in the order which will most quickly restart our industries, for otherwise they would leave their means of livelihood in the Army, relinquish their rations and their separation allowance only to become unemployed in great numbers. But, when men are kept back in the Service to form the Armies of Occupation a choice cannot be made simply on trade grounds. It must be made on grounds which appeal broadly to a sense of justice and fair play. Length of service, age, and wounds must be the main considerations entitling a man to release. The new Army will, thereupon, be composed in the first instance only from those who did not enlist before the 1st of January 1916, who are not over 40 years of age and have not more than two wound stripes. If anyone has to stay, it must be those who are not the oldest, not those who came the earliest, not those who have suffered the most.

4. We, therefore, take these broad rules as our main guide. According to the best calculations which are possible they should give us about 1,700,000 men out of which it is intended to form the Army of 1,150,000. If we find, as we shall do in all probability, that we have in the classes chosen more men than we actually require after dealing with a certain number of pivotal and compassionate cases, we shall proceed to reduce down to the figure of

1,150,000 first by reducing the age of retention to 39, to 38, to 37 and next releasing the men with two wound stripes.

As the time goes on we shall not require to keep so large an army as 1,150,000 in the field and it will be possible to continue making reductions on the principle of releasing the oldest men by the years of their age. When, however, the results of the war are finally achieved, the Divisions which have remained to the end will be brought home as units and make their entry into the principal cities of Great Britain with which they are territorially associated.

5. Volunteers for one year's service at a time for the Armies of Occupation will be accepted from men, who would otherwise be entitled to release, or who have been released and wish to rejoin if they are physically fit and otherwise suitable; and young recruits will be sent from home to take their turn and do their share. All these will be in relief of the older men. They will enable the age limit to be further reduced and the older men to be sent home. In particular the 69 Battalions of young soldiers of 18 years of age and upwards who are now at home will be sent at once to help guard the Rhine Bridgeheads. They will thus enable an equal number of men, old enough to be their fathers, to come home and they themselves will have a chance to see the German provinces which are now in our keeping and the battlefields where the British Army won immortal fame.

6. The new Armies of Occupation will begin forming from February 1st and it is hoped that in three months they may be completely organised. There will then be two classes of men in khaki, viz those who form the Armies of Occupation, and those who are to be demobilised. Everything possible will be done to send home or disperse the two and a quarter million men who are no longer required. But, they must wait their turn patiently and meanwhile do their duty in an exemplary manner. Any of these men who are marked for home who are guilty of any form of insubordination will, apart from any other punishment, be put back to the bottom of the list. There are no means of getting these great numbers of men home quickly unless everyone does his duty in the strictest possible way. It is recognised, however, that service in the Armies of Occupation is an extra demand which the State makes in its need upon certain classes of its citizens. The emoluments of the Armies of Occupation will, therefore, be substantially augmented, and every man will draw bonuses from the date of his posting to these Armies. . . .

These graduated bonuses[1] will be paid as a special addition to the pay of the Army during the period of occupation in recognition of the fact that the service is compulsory. The total cost of these additions in one year for an

[1] The bonuses began at 10/6d a week extra for Private Soldiers, 12/3 for Corporals and 14/- for Sergeants. 2nd Lieutenants were to receive 24/6 extra, Captains 31/6, Majors 35/-, Lieutenant Colonels 38/6 and all higher ranks 42/-.

Army of 1,150,000 men will be about £40,000,000; of this £34,000,000 will go to the rank and file.

8. Leave will be granted to men of the Armies of Occupation Home and Overseas Garrisons on as generous a scale as possible. No leave will be given to men marked for home and waiting their turn for demobilisation as it is desirable that all the facilities should be concentrated for the benefit of those who have to stay (except in cases of special urgency).

9. The Armies of Occupation will be as follows:—

Home Army.
Army of the Rhine.
Army of the Middle East.
Detachment of the Far North and of Siberia.
Garrisons of the Crown Colonies and India.

These forces will be varied as circumstances may require but no young soldier under 20 will serve elsewhere than at home or in the Army of the Rhine.

10. Besides the men of the classes mentioned who will be held to form the Armies of Occupation, and the Home and Overseas Garrisons, and who include the Regular Army and such SR & TF Officers and men as must be retained, there are a certain number of special services on the Lines of Communication, at the Bases, and here at home in which all men must be retained whatever their class, because like the Railwaymen, the necessary Royal Army Service Corps units and the Pay and Record Office staff, they are vitally necessary for demobilising and paying off all the others. These, not exceeding the numbers required, will therefore be deemed to be included in the Armies of Occupation as indispensables and will participate in the increased rates of pay. They will, however, be demobilised as soon as the great bulk of the two and a quarter million men, who are to be dispersed, have passed through their agencies back into civil life.

11. There remains the British Army in India. Many of the Territorial and Garrison Battalions who left England in the Autumn of 1914 to guard our Indian Empire or our Overseas possessions, have served 4 hot weathers in the East without either relief or the excitement of battle. Up to the present hardly any volunteers have come forward to take their places or those of the Home Garrisons, as part of the permanent after-war Army of the British Empire. It is therefore necessary while this 'after-war' or 'Old British Army' is being reconstituted that these men should remain abroad for another hot season. It is felt that in all the circumstances they ought to participate in the increased rates of pay which apply to the Armies of Occupation.

12. The effect of the general plan can perhaps best be judged by the following table.

	To be retained	*To be released*
11th November 1918		
Home Army 1,400,000	250,000	1,150,000
British Expeditionary Force 1,640,000	650,000	1,000,000
Armies of Salonika, Palestine and Mesopotamia (British troops only) 420,000	200,000	120,000
Detachments of the Far North and Siberia 14,000	14,000 (pending relief)	
Army of India (British) 96,000	76,000	20,000 (unfit)
Colonial Garrisons 12,000	12,000	
Total	1,202,000 to be retained	2,290,000 to be released

Regular Army being gradually reconstituted

13. The above arrangements seem to be the best that can be devised for the year 1919. During this year however we must remake the Old British Regular Army so as to provide on a voluntary basis the Overseas Garrisons of India, Egypt, the Mediterranean Fortresses and other Foreign Stations.

It is believed that volunteering for the Regular Army will greatly improve, as soon as the great mass of those who volunteered for the war against Germany in the early days have come back to the freedom of civil life and have had a chance to look round. It is upon the steady rebuilding of this Army that the relief of the Territorial battalions in India and various detachments in distant theatres now depends. Every effort will therefore be made to hasten its formation both by recruiting and by re-engagement.

14. It is not necessary at this stage to settle the conditions on which the National Home Defence Army for after the war will be formed. There are many more urgent problems which should be solved first.

15. The entire scheme of the War Office for dealing with the many difficulties of the present situation and for safe-guarding British interests is thus published to the Army and the Nation at large. It has been agreed upon between all the authorities and Departments concerned. The consent of Parliament, where necessary, will be asked for at the earliest possible moment. It remains for all ranks and all classes to work together with the utmost comradeship and energy to put it into force and thereby to safe-guard the best interests of each one of us and the final victory of our cause.

Winston S. Churchill to King George V

(Royal Archives)

19 January 1919 War Office

Your Majesty,
Sir,

It is with feelings of profound respect that I offer to Your Majesty & the Queen my sympathy in the grievous loss which Your Royal family has sustained by the early death of Prince John.[1] I fear that this break in the circle of Your Majesty's affections will be most painful, & it is indeed melancholy that this young life shd have closed so suddenly & so prematurely. The sympathy of the whole nation has been outspoken & if I venture to add these few lines, it is on account of the gracious kindness with wh your Majesty has always treated me for so many years, & wh King Edward used to show to my father & mother. I remain Sir

Your Majesty's faithful & devoted servant
Winston S. Churchill

Austen Chamberlain to Winston S. Churchill

(Churchill papers: 16/3)

19 January 1919

My dear Winston,

You are fortunate, if I may judge from your letter, in being able to concentrate on one problem for the moment. Here there are so many questions of equal urgency and so many people from outside the public offices whom it is my business to see that I cannot get on as fast.

Until I see the paper which you propose to circulate on Saturday, and which by the way will not reach me till Sunday morning, I cannot tell what issues are involved in it. But I would beg in any case for a little more time for their consideration before we come to a Cabinet discussion. Whatever the exact nature of your proposals, they will be of first class importance and they will merit, I think, much more than 24 hours consideration.

I have been turning over in my mind your suggestion of an official

[1] John Charles Francis, sixth and youngest child of King George V and Queen Mary. He was born at Sandringham on 12 July 1905. In 1917, having long been subjected to epileptic attacks, he was segregated from his family and contemporaries, and was looked after by a nurse, Mrs Bill, on the Sandringham estate, where he died, at the age of thirteen, on 18 January 1919.

residence. I hope you will not press it now. I recognise that there is a good deal to be said for it, but I think the trend of public opinion is against it and I do not think that the Cabinet would be likely to approve a departure from custom in that matter.

Yrs sincerely
Austen Chamberlain

Winston S. Churchill to David Lloyd George: telegram

(*Lloyd George papers*)

19 January 1919 War Office
10.15 pm

It was impossible to send an aeroplane across today on account of the weather and no boats are crossing. Archibald Sinclair, therefore leaves tomorrow morning and should reach you in Paris by nightfall. Bonar Law has been held up at Boulogne and cannot reach here till Tuesday evening. If on seeing proposals you approve them in general terms I would earnestly ask you to telegraph permission to Cabinet or me to make provisional examination of them on Wednesday. I could then if necessary come over to you Thursday with Henry Wilson, in order to reach a final decision. Situation in army causes great anxiety to all my advisers. A few more weeks on present lines and there will be nothing left but demoralised and angry mob, made up of men left behind on no principle that they consider fair and without the slightest regard to military formation. Only powerful and bold action can now retrieve a situation which as you know has been in suspense for many weeks. I am keeping Haig in order that he may report the gravity and the difficulty of the position to the Cabinet. Total figure of the army which it is proposed to ask for during occupation period is not one million seven hundred thousand (1,700,000) but one million one hundred and fifty thousand (1,150,000) and this includes India and every other theatre. My explanatory memorandum which I have only this moment finished should reach you to-morrow, and I feel confident that knowing your views it will please you. I do hope you will help me in these difficulties, for, without your approval, all action is paralysed.

Winston

Winston S. Churchill to David Lloyd George: telegram

(*Churchill papers: 16/3*)

20 January 1919 War Office

Your letter of the 18th instant wh I am very sorry to receive. I naturally supposed that you would wish the matter thrashed out here first as obviously the whole scheme had to be brought over to Paris for your consideration and I presume also for approval by Cabinet Colleagues there. Any discussion here could only be purely provisional and designed to clear the way for the case being put before you in the most convenient form and with preliminary difficulties swept away. Arrangements had been made to send the whole scheme to you tomorrow by aeroplane together with my full explanatory memorandum and either Henry Wilson or I or both of us proposed to come over Wednesday. Considering the number of departments involved and the all important share of the Treasury it would have seemed to me quite futile to come to Paris without obtaining preliminary agreement here. It never occurred to me for a moment that with the Cabinet split (halved) on both sides of the Channel the course I was taking would not be as much in accordance with your wishes as I am sure it would be with your convenience. I am sending you this afternoon all the material that has been prepared. It is still in an incomplete state and would no doubt have been modified in important particulars by the discussions which are still proceeding in this office on different aspects.

Briefly the scheme consists in releasing two men out of three and paying the third man double to finish the job. I am extremely anxious about the present state of the army and am serving you to the very best of my ability in preparing a comprehensive scheme for your approval.

Winston

Sir Henry Wilson: diary

(*Wilson papers*)

20 January 1919 36 Eaton Place

LG has written Winston a cross letter for getting out a scheme for Armies of Occupation without his seeing it. Winston has replied that it was no use showing him a half-baked scheme & he wanted to complete it before going over with it or sending me over with it to Paris.

Several interviews with Winston dined with him at the Turf. Some fortnight ago I wired to Knox[1] suggesting that John Ward[2] who commands a Batt^{n} at Omsk should wire in clear to Barnes his views on Bolshevism. An *excellent* wire from Ward arrived this morning but LG or someone in Paris has marked it 'Secret'. It must get out somehow.

Winston all against Bolshevism, & therefore, in this, against LG. I can't understand LG being such a fool.

Winston S. Churchill to General Macdonogh[3]

(*Churchill papers: 16/3*)

20 January 1919 War Office

Dear Adjutant General,

I am sorry to have to burden you by enquiries at a time when I can see how heavy your work must be, but the complaints which we see from all sides about the slowness—and, indeed, the paralysis—of the demobilising machinery and the absurdities which it perpetrates in so many cases make it indispensable that I should know whether it can or cannot be improved.

I want you to ask yourselves a few questions.

Are you sure that you have got a big enough machine at the top? How many officers of real authority presiding over great functions of demobilisation have you got in direct relations with yourself? Who are they? Are they able officers? You ought, it seems to me, to have six or seven quite important

[1] Alfred William Fortescue Knox, 1870–1964. 2nd Lieutenant, 1891. ADC to the Viceroy of India (Lord Curzon), 1899–1900 and 1902–3. Lieutenant-Colonel, 1911. Military Attaché, Petrograd, 1911–18. Major-General, 1918. Chief of the British Military Mission to Siberia, 1918–20. Knighted, 1919. Conservative MP for Wycombe, 1924–45. Author of *With the Russian Army, 1914–17*.

[2] John Ward, 1866–1934. Began work at the age of twelve as a railway navvy. Worked as a navvy on the Manchester Ship Canal. Fought in the Sudan Campaign of 1885. Joined the Social Democratic Federation, 1886. Founded the Navvies' Union, 1886. Member of the Management Committee of the General Federation of Trade Unions, 1901–29; treasurer, 1913–29. Labour MP, 1906–22. Served on the western front as a Lieutenant-Colonel, Middlesex Regiment, 1915–16, having recruited five labour battalions. In 1918, while he was at Vladivostok with two battalions of the Middlesex Regiment, he supported Kolchak's revolt, 1918–19. He was appointed CMG in 1918 and CB in 1919. Liberal MP, 1922–9, when he was defeated by the Labour candidate, Lady Cynthia Mosley (Sir Oswald Mosley's wife and Curzon's daughter).

[3] George Mark Watson Macdonogh, 1865–1942. Lieutenant, Royal Engineers, 1884; Major-General, 1916. Director of Military Intelligence, 1916–18. Knighted, 1917. Adjutant-General, 1918–22. Lieutenant-General, 1919. Member of the Royal Commission on Local Government, 1923–9. President of the Federation of British Industries, 1933–4. Member of the Central Committee for the Regulation of Prices, 1939–41. Member of the Finnish Aid Bureau, 1940. A Director of several companies, including Venezuelan Oil Concessions and the National Provident Institution. Chairman of Scammell Lorries Ltd.

people on this job alone reporting direct to yourself. Who is there besides General Burnett-Hitchcock in that position? He appears to me to be very much over-worked: indeed, he often looks as if he has been working all night long. That is not the way to do such big jobs as this. The man at the top should not be overloaded: there should be plenty of them, and each should have his sphere, and they should have leisure and a good deal in hand. You cannot possibly do it without wise delegation of powers and a really big machine at the top.

Let me see a picture of your demobilising machine, showing how your principal functions are divided and who fills the top post. Would it not be well, for instance, to form a demobilising group, over which you presided, consisting of six or seven Heads of Branches? That is the kind of organism that I have found very useful in such matters. An hour a day with the six or seven executive Heads of well-conceived Branches places the Head of a Department like yours in a position of enormous advantage.

Of course, it may be that all this is done already. At any rate, I want to know who are your principal officers and what their functions are; and I want to meet them personally with you on Wednesday next.

I suppose you realise that, once our Armies of Occupation at home and abroad are definitely announced and the process of forming them has begun, I contemplate pushing the best part of three-quarters of a million men in the United Kingdom out of the Army in about a fortnight. I cannot see any sense in holding these men, at our great expense and to their great discontentment, when they do not want to stop and we have nothing for them to do.

It will be indispensable to introduce some system of leave pending settlements of accounts, or some rough and ready system of adjusting accounts which a man may accept at his own risk if he wants his liberty the sooner. For instance, I am sure there are numbers of men who are being kept out of good incomes while the Army machine is making up its mind conscientiously to pay them £25. Such men would be very glad to say 'Give me my freedom and let me go'.

With regard to medical examinations of men on discharge in order to safeguard ourselves from subsequent claims for ill-health contracted in and by the Service, I am of opinion that we might possibly say that no man would be allowed to prefer a claim after discharge unless he has at the moment of discharge submitted himself to a medical examination. In other words, instead of our examining everyone to protect ourselves, we should insist on those who wish to take precautions for their future, in case of a subsequent outbreak of illness, taking the positive step. This would probably reduce enormously the labour of medical examinations.

I have not yet received the report about the officers. It seems to me that you ought to get rid of at least 30,000 officers in the next three months. There are swarms of them that want to go and that you do not want to keep. All these could go on leave 'TFO' or 'PFD' (Pending Final Demobilisation). Their accounts can be dealt with as the turn of each is reached without keeping the officer kicking his heels at some damp depot. Courage! Out with them. You will never get the volunteers for the new after-war Army till you have pushed very large numbers into the streets, and let them find their own level and see whether civil life is all they fancy it to be at the present time.

Pray take these observations as a guide for your assistance and not in any way as a reflection upon your work.

Yours sincerely
WSC

Winston S. Churchill to Lord Curzon

(*Churchill papers: 16/3*)

20 January 1919 War Office

My dear Curzon,

I should be very much obliged if you would arrange that I should be summoned to meetings of the War Cabinet when matters affecting the War Office are discussed. At present the Chief of the Staff is summoned at the beginning of your meetings, and I have to learn from him the views you and other Ministers express on matters like the reinforcement of the Caucasus.

Londonderry is very pleased with his new work and is throwing himself into it with zeal. He was gratified by the kindness of your letter to him, and spoke to me in warm terms about it. I have a feeling that he will do well now he has got his foot on the ladder.

Lord Curzon to Winston S. Churchill

(*Churchill papers: 16/3*)

20 January 1919 1 Carlton House Terrace

My dear Churchill,

Certainly I will, you have every right to be present on all such occasions.

But the question of reinforcing the Caucasus was not (so far as I remember) discussed at War Cabinet. General Thwaites talked it over with me in FO.

Yours ever
Curzon

Sir Henry Wilson: diary

(*Wilson papers*)

21 January 1919 36 Eaton Place

After lunch I went to see BL just back from France. He told me that LG was angry with Winston but I explained he had no reason to be. Winston went at 6 o'c & also explained to BL.

DH in to discuss our new scheme & he is in absolute agreement with me about necessity of carrying it out. . . .

I saw Winston at 7 o'c. He had just rec[d] a message from LG strongly objecting to our scheme. He must be *made* to agree.

LG won't let Winston place our scheme before the Cabinet tomorrow but has no objection to all the members meeting in 'conversations'. This will give him the chance of denying, later on, that we put our scheme before the Cabinet. I wired LG this morning, or rather the Lord[1] telephoned to P de B[2] to take my message of 'grave concern' to LG.

J. T. Davies to Winston S. Churchill: telephone message

(*Churchill papers: 16/3*)

21 January 1919
6.10 pm

With reference to your telegram, the Prime Minister thinks the figures are extravagant and far beyond the necessities of the case. If it were published to the Army that such numbers are to be compulsorily retained, there will be trouble.

If the German Army is to be demobilized, it is absurd to retain so big an Army, and German demobilization must be the first step.

The Prime Minister will be glad to see you on Thursday. Meanwhile the less haste, the greater speed.

[1] Vere Brabazon Ponsonby, Viscount Duncannon, 1880–1956. Known as 'the Lord'. Conservative MP, 1910 and 1913–20. On active service at Gallipoli, 1915. Personal Assistant to Sir Henry Wilson, 1916–20. Succeeded his father as 9th Earl of Bessborough, 1920. Governor-General of Canada, 1931–5. President of the Council of Foreign Bondholders, 1936. Chairman of the League of Nations Loans Committee, 1937.

[2] Major-General Percy Radcliffe, Director of Military Operations (see page 20, note 2).

Winston S. Churchill to Andrew Bonar Law

(*Churchill papers: 16/3*)

22 January 1919 War Office

My dear Bonar,

I am bringing my contingent at 3 to your room.

I suggest we keep two questions separate 1. The place now proposed to form the Armies of Occupation with increased pay. 2. The financial question of how much that increased pay should be. I am therefore not summoning my Financial people until 4, and am asking Macnamara[1] to come then. Unless you say to the contrary I shall carry on.

Yours very sincerely,
Winston S. C.

Sir Henry Wilson: diary

(*Wilson papers*)

22 January 1919 36 Eaton Place

At 3 o'c we had Cabinet 'conversations', Bonar telling us that no decision was to be taken. BL, Eric Geddes, Walter Long, Wemyss, Austen, Horne, Self, DH, Winston, Macdonogh & Burnett Hitchcock.

Winston stated the case for the necessity for our scheme. I emphasized the urgency of the situation pointing out that unless we carried out our proposals we would lose not only our Army of the Rhine but our garrisons at home, in Ireland, Gib, Malta: India—etc & that even now we dare not give an unpopular order to the troops & discipline was a thing of the past. DH said by Feb. 15th he would have no army in France.

Much talk round the plan but Winston & I stuck to it & in the end got an unwilling assent to our proposals. Austen very frightened of the expense. BL very determined not to express an opinion. Curzon not present so FO not represented. No secretary so no record of the proceedings as BL was so frightened of any decision.

[1] Thomas James Macnamara, 1861–1931. A school teacher for sixteen years, and subsequently editor of the *Schoolmaster*, 1892–1907. President of the National Union of Teachers, 1896. Liberal MP for Camberwell, 1900–22 (National Liberal, 1922–4). Parliamentary Secretary, Local Government Board, 1907–8; Admiralty, 1908–20. Minister of Labour, 1920–2.

Winston S. Churchill to Andrew Bonar Law

(*Churchill papers: 16/3*)

22 January 1919 War Office

My dear Bonar Law,

I do think you might write a line to the PM to tell him

(a) that there was a general feeling that something very like this would have to be done at once and that Eric Geddes & Horne from their end were in agreement with the scheme,
(b) that it is admitted that numbers must be scrutinized further, and
(c) that the pay must be largely increased above present rates but the exact amount is under discussion between the various Departments affected and the Treasury.

Please do your best to impart to him the impression which I understood you to have formed, viz, that action is imperative and that no one could suggest a less objectionable plan.

Please give me a nice and helpful letter to take. I guarantee you a triumphant success in the House of Commons, if nothing goes wrong elsewhere.

Yours ever,
W

Winston S. Churchill to Sir Eric Geddes

(*Churchill papers: 16/3*)

22 January 1919 War Office

My dear Geddes,

One of the first papers I saw on taking office was your 'Demobilisation Appreciation' of the 14th instant.

I was struck with the enormous mass of officers and men whom the Army apparently had on their pay lists when the fighting stopped on the 11th November. The contrast between these enormous numbers and those who had been demobilised was, particularly in the case of officers, most marked.

I took these figures as a starting point in my argument, never dreaming for a moment that they were inaccurate; and it was several days before I discovered what the real facts were.

I think it is very important that you should know this, because if you are misled, the Cabinet gets wrong information. For instance, your memorandum represents the total strength of the Army 'other ranks' on the 11th November as 5,353,000, but this figure includes oversea troops, Indian & African Natives, Egyptians, Local Forces and Natives other than troops and prisoners of war. The actual strength of the British 'other ranks' is 3,500,000 and it is with this figure that our demobilization returns are brought into relation. The number of officers on the 11th November is given as 558,000: it was actually 170,000. The figures I have given you cover the total strength of all the British troops to be dealt with by the demobilization machinery.

You will agree, I am sure, that the War Office have some ground for complaint that the facts should have been put before the Cabinet in this form without any explanatory note, and I hope the responsibility will be brought home to the official who prepared the report to which I have referred.

I have received a written protest from the Adjutant General against the circulation of such figures, which I am therefore bound to bring to your notice.

Many thanks for your assistance today.

Winston S. Churchill to Sir Reginald Brade[1]

(*War Office papers: 32/9300*)

23 January 1919 War Office

Please see the two sets of telegrams attached; one relating to the Caucasus and the other to Ireland.

I do not consider that telegrams of this character, which go far beyond the scope of routine military operations, should be dealt with without prior reference to me, or, in my absence, to the Under Secretary. It surprises me very much that a practice has grown up under which such a state of things is possible. These are not staff matters, but matters of high policy.

In regard particularly to the proposed proclamation of County Tipperary, please inform me whether the power to sanction such a step is vested by Statute in the Army Council or in the Secretary of State. If the latter is correct, please advise me what course to take. If the former is correct and the Army Council have the power by Statute, please inform me whether they met before sending the telegram No 74273.

Pray advise me generally on the constitutional aspect.

[1] Reginald Herbert Brade, 1864–1933. Entered the War Office as a Clerk, 1884. Assistant Secretary, War Office, 1904–14. Knighted, 1914. Secretary, War Office, 1914–20.

Sir Henry Wilson: diary

(*Wilson papers*)

23 January 1919 Villa Majestic
Paris

Winston, DH, Macdonogh & Self over by 11 o'c service. . . . I had long discussions on the boat & in the train with Winston, DH & the AG & we are all absolutely agreed that compulsion is necessary & that our total figure of about 1,200,000 is approximately correct & that no time is to be lost.

P de B tells me that LG is against our plan for Armies of Occupation so we shall have some fun.

Lord Esher to Winston S. Churchill

(*Churchill papers: 16/3*)

23 January 1919

My dear Winston,

You have made a splendid start from all I hear. Nothing but eulogy comes my way.

Everybody who matters is delighted!

What will that funny jealous little devil LG say at having a S of S who *acts* instead of talking. *Nous Verrons.*

Reduce your Army Council. It is too big. The old War Cabinet plan of a *small* number of permanent members, and calling in your departmental experts is sound.

Your Army Council resembles the old Asquith 23! However, you will soon form your own opinion. But it may be that the time has come for a complete revision of the plan of my old Committee.

The requirements of the State move in cycles. We have long outgrown this old Cabinet system. Hence many of our woes.

Perhaps post-war conditions may necessitate the abandonment of our Army Council altogether.

That you should plan an Army Establishment *before* consenting to Demobilisation is a stupendous feat, when, judged by the past activities of the War Cabinet! Have you read 'Schönbrunn'? If not tell E Marsh to get it for you.

Yours ever
Esher

Mary Spears: diary

(Spears papers)

24 January 1919 Paris

B[1] had long talk with Winston who said he had a row with LG (while the latter was shaving) about Russia. It seems it was LG's idea to invite Bolsheviks to Prinkipo & Wilson rushed in and took it all on himself. . . .

Winston told LG one might as well legalize sodomy as recognize the Bolsheviks.

Winston has got out his scheme for the Army and has asked Northcliffe to support him!!

Sir Henry Wilson: diary

(Wilson papers)

24 January 1919 Villa Majestic

Winston, DH, the AG & Self breakfasted with LG. He would *not* discuss our scheme for making Armies of Occupation but would only discuss how we could demobilize the Boches Divisions, take away more guns & mash up their munition works at Essen etc. All of which is quite sensible but not what we have come over to discuss. Then we had a meeting at Quai d'Orsay where we discussed this again & where Foch produced a paper asking us for 18 Divisions. I made a short speech which was afterwards much applauded by LG & Winston.

Then Winston, DH, the AG & I lunched with LG and we had a long discussion about our schemes which in the end LG agreed to our plans except that he wants us to keep only 10 Div^s in France instead of 15 & he wants rather less salvage men, & he wants everyone taken out of Russia including Omsk! Otherwise he agrees broadly with the whole of our scheme. So this is splendid.

Then at 4 o'c, Winston, DH, the AG & I had a 3-hour meeting in my room here when we settled all our procedure. AG & Vesey to go back to London tonight & see BL & Austen tomorrow & Winston & I to go back Mon: night, hold a Cabinet 3 pm. Tuesday, Press meeting 5 pm. Then all the Press to bring out 'puffs' on Wed:, & we follow with the AO Thursday, & then the great adventure of 'compulsing' a million men in the time of peace to serve abroad will have begun. There is not a moment to lose as all our power over the Army is slipping away.

[1] Beaucaire, Mary Spears' nickname for her husband, Brigadier-General Spears.

Winston S. Churchill to Clementine Churchill

(*Spencer-Churchill papers*)

24 January 1919 Ritz Hotel
Paris

Beloved one,

My friend [Lloyd George] wants me to stay here till Monday night. I am planning to reach London early Tuesday. I have made good progress with my business & the generals are quite content. I was taken by the PM to the Conference this morning & placed in a seat of honour among the great ones of the earth. I was appointed to represent England on a committee with Loucheur & General Bliss[1] (USA) to plan to destroy all the German munition works & to disarm them utterly. This will keep me for a few days. It is important.

I breakfast lunch & dine with the PM who is splendidly installed close by this hotel. It is a good thing to get in touch again. We were diverging a good deal. I think I influence him in a considerable degree, & there is no one with whom he talks so easily.

Dearest Clemmie I do hope all is well with you & with the kittens: & that yr house hunting will be fruitful & that you will have some propositions to make to me on my return.

Tender love my darling
Yr devoted
W

PS. I am keeping Archie here *à côté*.

I hope to launch my big scheme Thursday.

Sir Henry Wilson: diary

(*Wilson papers*)

25 January 1919 Villa Majestic

At 10 am Winston & Eric Geddes came to discuss some details of our new scheme & we got out another paper defining certain points & insisting on the

[1] Tasker Howard Bliss, 1853–1930. Entered the United States Army, 1875. Professor of Military Science at the Naval War College, 1885–8. On active service in Puerto Rico during the Spanish-American war, 1898. Brigadier-General, 1901. Assistant Chief of Staff, US Army, 1909; Chief of Staff, 1917. General, 1917. American Military Representative on the Supreme War Council, Versailles, 1917–19. American Commissioner, Paris Peace Conference, 1919. He received an honorary knighthood from King George V in 1918.

fact that no one in the Armies of Occupation will be allowed off except extreme compassionate cases.

Worked at papers all the morning. I think now our scheme for a Clear cut for Armies of Occupation is now complete. We shall get about a million men who will be compelled to serve for 12 mos: of course if these men really refuse to serve we are done, but I have no fear of this if the case is properly put to the men & if Winston & I can get the support of the press.

Winston sent me over a note he proposed putting in the tomorrow & I agreed with a couple of small alterations. Also a note he was sending AG recapitulating all our work here, & with this I also agreed except that I could not agree to Volunteers being allowed to come into the Armies of Occupation as substitutes—as I wrote Winston it would never do to allow men in the Armies of Occupation to cadge about for substitutes. He agrees. . . .

Andrew Bonar Law to David Lloyd George

(*Churchill papers: 16/3*)

25 January 1919 — 11 Downing Street

My dear Prime Minister,

The Adjutant-General has just come with the Memorandum explaining the decision to which you have come and he has told me exactly how it stands. I confess that I am very much afraid of this. As I wrote you before I quite agree that something of this kind must be done and done at once but the fear which I myself had as to the effect of either telling the public now through the press or of introducing a Bill immediately Parliament meets definitely creating a new Military Service Act will be very dangerous has been greatly confirmed by the conversations which I have had with any politicians whom I have met. They are only H A L Fisher, Worthington Evans and Baird[1] who all took the view that to do this right away would be regarded by the public as inconsistent with the speeches made by the candidates at the election. The Adjutant-General tells me that, in the Army

[1] John Lawrence Baird, 1874–1941. Entered Diplomatic Service, 1896. Acting Agent and Consul-General, Abyssinia, 1902. Conservative MP, 1910–25. Served as an Intelligence Officer (Major) on the western front, 1914–15. Parliamentary Secretary to the Air Board, December 1916–January 1919 (when he was succeeded as Parliamentary Under-Secretary by J E B Seely). Succeeded his father as 2nd Baronet, 1920. Parliamentary Under-Secretary of State, Home Office, 1919–22. Minister of Transport, 1922–4. Created Baron Stonehaven, 1925. Governor-General of Australia, 1925–30. Chairman of the Conservative Party Organization, 1930–6. Created Viscount, 1938.

Order which he has drafted for submission to the Secretary of State, it is only proposed to announce this as the steps which are to be taken until the statutory period ends, and my own impression is that if we could confine the public notice to this and add that whatever steps were necessary to take in order to secure the fruits of victory after peace would be considered later with the knowledge which would be gained in the meanwhile by the progress of the Peace Conference, that this would make all the difference in the political situation. In other words, it is simply a question of the right time for doing what is necessary.

No one is a better judge than you of the political dangers and if you were here I should not have any hesitation in agreeing to anything on this line which you thought safe, but I doubt whether you fully realise the political dangers of the course proposed.

I will have a Cabinet at three o'clock on Tuesday as Churchill asks but I wish you would seriously consider this with him if possible and let me know whether you still think that the notice given to the press should show our full intention, which I believe to be Churchill's idea and whether we should commit ourselves to a Bill immediately Parliament meets or whether the plan I suggest would not be better. I need not say that it is not on merits that I ask you to reconsider this for it would be far better to make quite plain what we mean to do now, but I think the political dangers are very great.

Macdonogh has told me that in the Army Order they are going to make an appeal for volunteers and he thinks it is possible that they may get the bulk of the soldiers by voluntary methods in the course of a few months. If there is even a chance of this it is a strong additional reason for not committing ourselves at this moment to a new compulsory Act. . .[1]

David Lloyd George to Winston S. Churchill

(*Churchill papers: 16/3*)

27 January 1919 Paris

Mr Churchill

Have just received this from Mr Bonar Law. Please consider very carefully.

D.Ll.G.

[1] Voluntary recruitment did indeed prove insufficient for the immediate post-war needs (see page 549, and page 597, note 1). But only volunteer troops were sent to Russia (see 23 April 1919). The Conscription Act itself did not finally lapse until 30 April 1920.

Winston S. Churchill to David Lloyd George

(*Churchill papers: 16/3*)

27 January 1919 Paris

Prime Minister,

I hope you will not allow the vague fears expressed in the note you have just sent me to paralyse necessary action.

Foch has accepted the small and reduced force of 10 divisions on Haig's explicit assurance that they would be solid divisions and not unstable and melting formations. Compared to the French and American forces, our contingent will be extremely small. We are thus reducing our burden by regularising our organisation. In addition to what we have to keep in France, there are the 70,000 men in India, the 100,000 agreed upon for all our widespread responsibilities in Mesopotamia, Palestine and Turkey, and the garrisons of our fortresses and Crown Colonies.

It is quite absurd to expect that these vitally necessary forces can be provided during the present year on a voluntary basis. They can only be provided on a compulsory basis pending the creation and organisation of voluntary forces, about which no time will be lost.

We are, therefore, up against harsh facts. The question raised by Bonar Law is whether we should boldly and frankly face this situation, proclaim it to the nation and ask Parliament to support us from the outset; or whether we should live from hand to mouth and from month to month as if we were nursing a guilty secret in the hopes of something turning up to remove the difficulties.

I pointed out to you three days ago that there was a great danger of making the duration of compulsion—albeit for a greatly reduced number—dependent upon the date of the signature of peace. As long as we are afraid boldly to demand from Parliament the necessary measures, the agitation to let everybody go will grow in strength, and if it thought that 'the interminable discussion at Paris', 'the peasantry of diplomacy', etc, are the solo limiting factors which are preventing the return of hundreds of thousands of men to their families, you will find yourself greatly harassed in conducting the complex deliberations which are indispensable to the re-settlement of Europe and Asia.

Besides, it is not true to say that the signature of peace affects the military problem of the British Army. That problem consists in the fact that we have got to find garrisons on the reduced scale proposed during the whole of this year, both for France and other theatres, and it is physically impossible to organise a voluntary army in that period.

Therefore, it seems to me that the manly course—and the honest course—is to take Parliament fully into our confidence and rely on the good sense of the nation, which, having won so great a victory, would never forgive us if we cast the fruits away.

Of course it would be made clear that we shall hurry forward our voluntary recruiting to the utmost, that our commitments will steadily diminish, and that for these reasons it will very likely be possible during the latter part of the year to reduce still further the number of men compulsorily retained both by substitution of volunteers and by contraction of responsibilities.

I therefore strongly press that a definite provision should be made by Parliament for the responsibilities for the army, and that we should not drift because we shrink from stating the true facts to the public. I believe myself that the issue will do nothing but good in the House of Commons, and that it will brace the majority returned to secure the fruits of victory and show a clear line between those who mean the same thing on these big matters and the feeble but well-meaning folk who at every stage have hampered action and would have lost the war.

It can, of course, be made perfectly clear that what we propose is not the continuance of conscription in time of peace, but the abolition of conscription and the substitution of a voluntary army for a compulsory army; but this obviously takes time, and John Bull is not such a fool as to be incapable of understanding a plain necessity when he sees it.

With regard to procedure, I do not contemplate an announcement on Thursday of our intentions to bring in a Bill immediately. I should propose to confine myself to the general statement in the memorandum that I have already given you, viz, 'the consent of Parliament, where necessary, will be asked for at the earliest possible moment'. We shall be able to see how this announcement is received by the press and the public generally and also the immediate effect of it upon the army.

The next step will be to put a sentence in the King's Speech, which can be considered in the light of our knowledge of the position in ten days, to the effect that we shall ask Parliament for the necessary measures to safeguard the interests of the State and our conquests during the period necessary to create a voluntary army.

A still further interval will elapse before it is necessary to introduce the Bill. It is probable that the actual legislation need not be brought before Parliament till the middle of March, and, as far as my present knowledge goes, I think it should simply be a part of the Army Annual Bill which carries the army forward only from year to year. There would be time to consider in this interval, as an alternative, a form in which the reduced contingent to be retained compulsorily should be maintained for, say, eight months after the final signature of peace instead of in an annual form. This, however, I should greatly deprecate, for the reasons I have given.

You realise, I suppose, that all the men of the present army are serving on one or the other of the following bases:—

either (a) 'the duration of the war', which means the signature of the Peace Treaty;

or (b) 'six months after the cessation of hostilities', and this is universally interpreted by the men as six months from November 11th, ie, May 11th.

We therefore automatically lose all authority over the whole of our armies in every theatre and in India if the Peace Treaty is signed at any moment after May 11th; or on May 11th if it is signed at any moment before.

It is this wholesale and immediate collapse of our entire military fabric at some uncertain date in the near future which constitutes the cause of the catastrophe which it is my duty to urge you to avert by timely measures.

The discipline of the soldiers who are to be retained depends upon their knowing that they have got to stay in their new units for a considerable number of months and possibly for a year, and that they are chosen for this on grounds which commend themselves to the army sense of fair play. They then make up their minds to go through with it; the sooner they jump this fence, the better; the sooner they put out of their heads the idea that they are going to get home by pushing and shoving, the better; the sooner they settle down to finishing up the job as men sharing an equal burden and as the men that ought to bear the burden if anyone has to, the sooner we shall be provided with forces on which we can rely.

I really think it a pretty strong order that the opinion of the late Under Secretary to the Air Board should be cited in this connection. I should have thought that Baird was sufficiently occupied in deciding whether he would or would not serve as Under Secretary for Munitions.

Sir Henry Wilson: diary

(*Wilson papers*)

27 January 1919 Villa Majestic

A long talk with DH after breakfast. He is clearly of opinion that our proposals for a clean cut & extra pay will produce a force which can be disciplined. Everything turns on this. . . .

DH is under no illusions as to the present state of the Armies but he has real hopes of our new scheme. A wire from WO which I showed him agrees to our proposal for doubling the pay of the men who are kept on. This is good, & it has been agreed to by a Cabinet comm[e] with Worthington Evans in the Chair.

DH went off at 10.30 to GHQ & I asked him to be up Cologne way on Thursday next when I hope our scheme will become public.

After he left, Winston sent me over a long letter BL has written to LG in which he shows he is terrified of our scheme coming out now because it is against 'election speeches'. Poor Bonar—always terrified.

Winston writes tonight before he goes off to dine with PM & says we must go on giving Denikin[1] what we can, & he also addresses a note to the PM in which he says he is very unhappy about Russia. I attached a short note saying that I had been writing about Russia for months but with no result, that I was in favour of clearing out of Omsk *now* if France would agree, & getting ready to clear out of Murmansk & Archangel next summer; but on the other hand I wanted to strengthen our position on the line Batoum–Baku–Krasnovodsk–Merv.

Winston S. Churchill to David Lloyd George

(*Churchill papers: 16/3*)

27 January 1919 Paris

Prime Minister.

I am distressed by the military telegrams from Russia. We have very small forces (about 14,000) there. They are exerting a great influence, particularly in Siberia, because they are thought to be the vanguard of Britain. They are nothing of the sort. Individual officers and soldiers are keeping large towns and districts up to their duty against the Bolsheviks by giving the impression that 'Britain is behind them'; whereas long ago Britain has quitted the field.

We are at the present moment heavily and indefinitely committed in all sorts of directions, and we have, as far as I can see, not the least intention of making good any of them.

[1] Anton Ivanovitch Denikin (1872–1947). Joined the Imperial Russian Army at the age of 15. Commanded the Iron Division in First World War. After the March revolution of 1917 he became chief of staff to General Alexeyev, supreme commander-in-chief, and later commanded the south-western front. Marched with Kornilov on Petrograd in September 1917, was arrested but escaped after the Bolshevik revolution to the Don Basin. By September 1918 he was sole commander of the White Army with the North Caucasus area under his control. By May 1919 he had occupied the whole Ukraine and in October penetrated as far north as Orel. In the autumn the Bolsheviks rallied and began to throw his army back towards the Black Sea. Early in 1920 the Red forces captured Rostov, the White Army broke up and he fled to Constantinople. After 1926 he lived in France. In 1945 he emigrated to the United States.

From the mere War Office standpoint, I object very much indeed to keeping soldiers in the field who are denied the transport, the technical services, the doctors, the hospital staffs and even the mules that they require according to their numbers. But that is what we are doing. These poor men are writing cheques on our account and in our name which we have neither the intention nor the means to honour. They have written a good many already.

It seems to me most urgent for us to frame and declare our *policy*. 'Evacuate at once at all costs' is a policy: it is not a very pleasant one from the point of view of history. 'Reinforce and put the job through' is a policy; but unhappily we have not the power—our orders would not be obeyed, I regret to say.

Therefore, we must confine ourselves to modest limits. I offer the following advice:—

(1) With regard to Murmansk and Archangel. Withdraw these forces as soon as the ice allows, using the interval to wind up commitments there and offering persons compromised there through working with and for us a refuge on our ships. Meanwhile, however, equip and sustain these forces with the small technical details and medical staff they require for their welfare, using discreetly for this purpose all our present powers under the Military Service Acts. All told the details needed do not exceed 1,000.

(2) South Russia, Transcaspia and Siberia. These comprise enormous regions into which it will be disastrous for us for Bolshevism to penetrate. Here we have called into being during the war, in reliance upon our promises and encouraged by our aid, Russian armies which are fighting themselve, in an indifferent manner with varying fortunes—but still fighting. We are very heavily compromised with Denikin and the Omsk Government. We have only got two battalions in Siberia, and they are everywhere being paraded as symbols of the British power.

I consider, in view of what you have told me, that the anti-Bolshevik Russians should be told that they have got to shift for themselves, that we wish them well, but that all we can do is to give them moral support by the presence of such volunteers—officers and men—who are ready to serve in these theatres, and material in money, arms and supplies.

I hold most strongly that, after all that has happened, we cannot cut these anti-Bolshevik Russian armies suddenly off the tap of our supplies. As long as they are able to go on fighting effectively, we should continue to aid them with arms, supplies and volunteers. We should fix now the quota of arms and supplies, but should give no guarantee as to the number of volunteers.

If they are suppressed or throw up the sponge, we should, of courses withdraw and disinterest ourselves in all that may follow.

North Sea
Murmansk
BRITISH
FINNS
Baltic Sea
Archangel
BRITISH
Irtysh
BALTIC STATES
YUDENITCH
Petrograd
Kotlas
Warsaw
POLES
Moscow
Volga
Viatka
Ural Mountains
WESTERN SIBERIA
Smolensk
Perm
UKRAINIANS
Kazan
CZECHS
Kama
Ekaterinburg
KOLCHAK
FRENCH
Kharkov
Samara
Ufa
Cheliabinsk
Petropavlosk
Omsk
Tobol
Ishim
Black Sea
DENIKIN
Volga
Orenburg
Ural
Kokchetav
COSSACKS
COSSACKS
COSSACKS
COSSACKS
Irtysh
Astrakhan
CAUCASIA
TURKESTAN
Batum
BRITISH
Caspian Sea
Lake Balkhash
TURKEY
Aral Sea
Baku
KHIRGIZIA
Krasnovodsk
BRITISH
Tashkent
TRANSCASPIA
Enzeli
Ashkabad
Merv
Meshed
PERSIA
AFGHANISTAN
INDIA

SIBERIA, 1918–1919

All the telegrams show that this matter requires your personal attention. At present we are extending our commitments, curtailing our contributions, and not even maintaining our own men, who have been sent there by compulsion, as British soldiers should be maintained by the Government responsible for their proper usage.

WSC

Sir Henry Wilson to Winston S. Churchill

(*Lloyd George papers*)

27 January 1919 Paris

Dear S of S,

With all you say I entirely agree. For *months* I have been writing papers about Russia with no result.

I know it is very difficult to come to a decision because the question is difficult & is enormously complicated by our Allies, and now I don't believe we *can* decide anything until the Prinkipo affair[1] is exploded.

I am in favour of being ready i) to quit Murmansk & Archangel next summer; ii) of quitting Omsk *now* if the French agree; iii) but of strengthening our hold on Batoum–Baku–Krasnovodsk–Merv line.

I will show you the papers we have written.

HW

Winston S. Churchill to Lord Northcliffe

(*Churchill papers: 16/3*)

27 January 1919 Hotel Majestic
Paris

For your secret and personal information, I send you a file of papers which in various stages will show you the military policy which I consider immediately necessary and which I am expecting to launch on Thursday.

I have found things in a very bad state. The demobilisation has been held

[1] The Allied proposal that a conference should be held between the Bolshevik and anti-Bolshevik Russians, under Allied auspices, on the Turkish island of Prinkipo (near Constantinople). At first the Bolsheviks seemed willing to attend, but the anti-Bolshevik Russians refused, and sought instead to enlist further Allied support for their military efforts to reach Moscow and Petrograd.

up and the armies on the Front are melting fast. The system that has been adopted caused unrest in every platoon simultaneously: men were everywhere drifting away in fives and sixes without regard to length of service, wounds, or age or other considerations which commend themselves to the ordinary soldier's sense of justice, but solely on industrial qualifications, about which there is a good deal of suspicion and humbug, if not actual fraud.

The consequence was that the whole morale of the army was being impaired and had already deteriorated.

It is necessary to take a plain and a bold course, to decide what is the smallest number of men that we need to finish the job; to choose these men on grounds of service, ie, those who had done the least service, and to make it clear to them that they will have to stop until things are cleared up, to form them into homogeneous units—solid units, not melting units—to give them much better pay as a compensation for having to remain, and to kill their hope of a speedy return to England. In other words, to separate the sheep from the goats, to make the sheep stay with proper provender and to let the goats go home as quickly as possible in the order of industrial convenience.

This policy has commended itself to all who have so far been consulted. It requires, however, repeated explanation to the public and to the troops. I am taking every step in my power to this end. I already, ten days ago, foreshadowed this policy to the Newspaper Proprietors' Association, and I have issued in to-day's papers a further preliminary announcement. I am to see the Newspaper Proprietors' Association on Tuesday, leaving 24 hours for them to consider the position and to prepare their articles for Thursday morning, when a full announcement will be made. Thereafter, there has been organised by General Swinton,[1] under the Ministry of Labour, a strong publicity campaign, of the War Loan type with heavy expenditure on advertisements, etc, designed to explain the position and obtain volunteers for the army under the new and improved conditions, in order to relieve and replace men who must be compulsorily retained meanwhile.

The second serious aspect of the situation is this. All our present armies are engaged on either 'six months after the cessation of hostilities', which the men interpret as six months after 11th November, ie, 11th May; or 'for the

[1] Ernest Dunlop Swinton, 1868–1951. 2nd Lieutenant, Royal Engineers, 1888. Commanded 1st Battalion, Railway Pioneer Unit, in South Africa, 1900–1. Assistant-Secretary to the Committee of Imperial Defence, 1913–14. Official 'Eye-Witness', GHQ, France, 1914–15. Colonel, 1915. Raised Heavy Section, Machine Gun Corps (tanks), 1916–17. Major-General, 1918. Attached to the Ministry of Labour, 1919, where he toured the country speaking for the Third Liberty Loan. Controller of Information, Civil Aviation Department, Air Ministry, 1919–21. Knighted, 1923. Chichele Professor of Military History, Oxford, 1925–39. Colonel Commandant, Royal Tank Corps, 1934–8.

duration of the war', which means the signature of the Peace Treaty. Therefore, at some uncertain date, which anyhow is rapidly approaching, the whole of our authority over all our armies in every theatre and in India would lapse automatically. There is no possibility of obtaining voluntary forces in the interval to take the places of the men we need, greatly though these men will be reduced in numbers. India, Palestine, Mesopotamia, Turkey, Malta, Gibraltar, and the Rhine, all have to be provided for: and 600,000 or 700,000 white soldiers in the very least that will enable us to hold our Empire and our conquests during the currency of the present year.

We cannot possibly get these numbers except by an interim extension over a much smaller area of the Military Service Acts. In other words, Parliament and the country have got to face the fact that if you let your compulsory army go before your voluntary army is created, you lose all you have been fighting for.

Therefore there must be created in the interval, from serving soldiers who have the least cause to complain, a military force to be maintained by compulsion during the present year.

I am very anxious that you should realise the difficulties with which I am confronted, because they are the difficulties of the country, and I am sure that you will do all in your power to help forward an honest and courageous policy of facing those difficulties and overcoming them.

I therefore send you these papers in confidence and ask you to do your utmost to further the measures which are necessary. I do not myself fear at all the course of such a policy, provided that a strong lead is given and that the reasons which make each step necessary are fully and frankly explained.

I was going to send Sir Archibald Sinclair down with this message, in order that he could give you a verbal explanation in addition, and I asked Harold [Lord Rothermere] to telegraph to you in that sense. I find, however, that I must take him back to London with me at the moment, and I therefore am only sending you this file under seal.

I hope you will let me hear from you by telegram or letter.

Sir Henry Wilson: diary

(*Wilson papers*)

28 January 1919 36 Eaton Place

We got to Boulogne at 8 am & had some breakfast, & pushed off 9.30 am. Winston wanted to fly but it was too rough. We got to London 2 o'c.

We had our Cabinet 3 o'c. BL in chair also Walter Long, Austen, Eric

Geddes, Milner, Winston, Horne. Winston explained our proposals but not very clearly. However it went off all right & at 5 o'c Winston & I saw the Press & Winston again explained to them & I added a few words about the great responsibility which was for the time being transferred from the Officers to the Press, for the men & Officers were strangers to each other, the whole Army was in a state of flux & the men took their colouring greatly from the Press. Robertson added some remarks in the same strain.

War Cabinet: minutes

(*Cabinet papers: 23/9*)

28 January 1919

THE SECRETARY OF STATE FOR WAR, resuming, said that 280,000 men were wanted in France for salvage purposes, in order to salve property, the value of which amounted to many hundreds of million pounds. This salvage work could, of course, be handed over to civilians, but only at enormous loss. Many of the salvage men might be found from the Demobilizables, who would be glad to continue to serve at higher rates of pay.

He estimated that we should need 200,000 men to hold the Rhine, 50,000 on the Lines of Communications, 280,000 (which might possibly be reduced to 120,000) for salvage work. If the reductions in regard to salvage men were found feasible, the total required for France would be 370,000. For the Middle East we should want 100,000 European soldiers and 250,000 native soldiers.

The European soldiers were estimated at the low number of 100,000, because the Prime Minister had represented that he hoped to be able considerably to reduce our commitments in those regions. The said regions comprised the whole of the Middle East, where our troops were at present, excepting India, and involved the evacuation of the Dobrudja and the Caucasus, and reducing our present garrison in Syria.

We had, in Siberia and North Russia, some 14,000 men. He would here remark that the situation of our troops in Russia was most unsatisfactory. Owing to our having an unsettled policy, it had not been possible to send out a sufficient supply of medical services or enough railway men, &c, in order to enable our troops to hold their own with confidence against the Bolshevik armies, which were growing in efficiency and audacity.

Winston S. Churchill to David Lloyd George

(*Churchill papers: 16/3*)

29 January 1919 War Office
Private

My dear Prime Minister,

The Cabinet yesterday made no difficulties at all about my Army proposals. Addison had thought that we were intending to re-open conscription and call up a new class, but, when assured on this point, he expressed complete agreement. Fisher, who was there, also concurred after hearing the case stated. Austen, Long, Milner, and Eric Geddes strongly supported me. Bonar put his point about the House of Commons, but the general feeling was overwhelming that we had better take them into our confidence boldly from the outset.

I stated to the Cabinet that you were not yet finally convinced as to the actual proportions of the forces to be maintained on the Rhine, and I pointed out to them the reductions which had been effected in our proposals at your wish. The general feeling of the Cabinet was clearly that the important decision of principle was the continuance of compulsion for the interim period, that this decision was inevitable, and that, once taken, the question of numbers to a hundred thousand or two one way or the other would not make any difference to our Parliamentary or other difficulties.

The opinion was generally expressed that we were cutting it too fine, and the Cabinet desired me to put the figure of 900,000 instead of the 800,000 which I had proposed. It was pointed out that it would be quite easy in practice to use no more than were actually required and to make any necessary reductions, whereas, if we had not something in hand and emergencies arose, there would be immense difficulties in going back to a higher figure. I have, therefore, put the figure at 900,000 as desired, but this need not affect the arrangements which you approved. In my forecast to the press I talked of 'about a million', in order that the real figure might appear somewhat more moderate than the surmise.

The newspaper men took it all like lambs. A P Nicholson[1] said he was surprised at the moderation of the figure and that we could get through with so few. I did not tell how the troops would be disposed between the different theatres, and they are naturally keeping Germany well to the front in their very helpful articles.

[1] Arthur Pole Nicholson, 1869–1940. Parliamentary Correspondent of *The Times*, 1908–13. Lobby Correspondent of the *Daily News*, 1914–19. Political Correspondent of the *Daily Chronicle*, 1920–3. Chairman of the Journalists Parliamentary Lobby Committee, 1921–2. Political Correspondent of the *Westminster Gazette*, 1924–9.

Everything is to be launched to-morrow and we must await the result.

The railwaymen and base details in Calais practically came out on strike yesterday, but all my information goes to show that the fighting troops are quite sound, and with firm clear leading I hope we shall get the Army into a good state in a few months.

I am having searching enquiries made through all the sources open to me into the conditions of German demobilisation. Even if they all go off into the interior of Germany, I should have thought it would be necessary to keep strong forces on the frontier ready to enforce the Peace Terms, especially the conditions of disarmament, to which you attach so much importance.

It would be a very serious decision for Great Britain to give up the Cologne bridgehead and hand it over to the Americans, the Belgians or the French. Such a step would, I should have thought, fatally weaken our position at the Peace Conference. It is only a little while ago that you were strongly impressed with the need of our being very strong while the discussions were proceeding, and Henry Wilson tells me that your view then was that all our 60 divisions should be kept at any rate in cadre formation. It is a big drop from that to 10. If there is to be another big drop in the immediate future, I doubt if we shall have sufficient men to garrison effectively the bridgehead which has been entrusted to us with its extensive perimeter. And I am quite sure that you will never get the Germans to give up anything more than has actually been taken from them unless you have effective forces at your disposal.

I do not expect them to make an attack upon us in the West. Their game is to adopt a *non possumus* attitude in regard to further demands, to lose as much time as possible in negotiations until our patience is exhausted and our armies have melted away, and then to regulate affairs on their Eastern Frontier and tell us to mind our own business about that.

If the Germans handle their situation well now and we handle ours badly, I see no reason why they should not be relatively more powerful than ever in a few years' time. The removal of the Russian menace, which as you used to say was their great pre-occupation before the war, goes far to compensate them for their losses of territory and population in the West. If the Austro-Germans affiliate with them, they will be stronger than ever. When the British and American Armies have disappeared, the French will be left face to face with an enemy twice as numerous as they are. The great crops of children which are coming forward in Germany every year are three times as great as those on which France will have to depend. I do not see what there is to prevent these facts from manifesting themselves in a few years' time; and it is from that standpoint that the work of the Peace Conference will be judged.

The difficulties of your task seem to be enormous, and I cannot understand how they could be handled successfully by you unless you had a strong army at your back. It seems to me that the great position you hold at the Peace Conference would be fatally undermined once it was known that you could not back your words by force of arms. Your strength at the present time is largely due to the fact that, whereas [President] Wilson relies on words, you deal in facts.

I do hope you will give consideration to these views, which are sincerely conceived in the interests of your Government. As you know, I should much have preferred going to the Admiralty, where there would have been none of these difficulties for me to try to solve and where I could have lived in comfort for a year or two.

I am confident that all the forces on which you will now have to rely in the new Parliament are vigorous patriotic forces, quite ready to go a long way in social legislation and in regard to property so long as they are assured that a strong national policy is being pursued and that we are reaping the fruits of victory.

I think this is the mood of the soldiers too. At any rate it is significant that they attack members of the Non-Combatant Corps whenever these are brought into the camps for demobilisation. This has occurred to such an extent that we have to exclude non-combatants from the present process. There are numerous instances of dispersal stations refusing to handle the affairs of these men. Give the soldiers firm leading and there are very good chances of everything going well.

I will come over on Saturday (not Friday) and I will endeavour to arrive in time for dinner, provided Saturday is equally convenient to you.

Bonar Law has just telephoned to say that he is very pleased with the form of announcement I propose for to-morrow, and that he was much relieved to find at the Cabinet yesterday such a complete measure of agreement, especially amongst our Liberal colleagues like Fisher and Addison.

I see we are not to have the pleasure of Major Baird's assistance.

Winston S. Churchill to Lord Milner

(*Churchill papers: 16/3*)

29 January 1919 War Office

My dear Milner,

I am very much obliged to you for your support yesterday. I have had a very busy fortnight, not only making plans, but running about explaining them and overcoming opposition and doubts. It is a struggle nowadays almost physical in its character!

We loose off tomorrow.

I hope you are refreshed by your rest.

Yours very sincerely,
Winston S. Churchill

Winston S. Churchill to Walter Long

(*Churchill papers: 16/3*)

29 January 1919 War Office

My dear Long,

Many thanks for your help yesterday. I am hopeful about the policy and *sure* of its necessity.

Yours very sincerely,
Winston S. Churchill

Winston S. Churchill: departmental minute

(*War Office papers: 32/5676*)

29 January 1919 War Office

Colonel Ward is doing admirably, but I do not think the publication necessary at this moment.

Our policy in Siberia is too nebulous & our prospects too gloomy for special attention to be invited.

War Cabinet: minutes

(*Cabinet papers: 23/9*)

GLASGOW STRIKERS

30 January 1919

MR CHURCHILL said we should not exaggerate the seriousness of the disturbance. . . . We should be careful to have plenty of provocation before taking strong measures. By going gently at first we should get the support we wanted from the nation, and then troops could be used more effectively. The moment for their use had not yet arrived. . . .

MR CHURCHILL said that before taking any action in dealing with the strikers, we should wait until some glaring excess had been committed. The moment the revolt advanced over the line of a pure wage dispute, and the strikers were guilty of serious breach of the law, then was the moment to act.[1]

Sir Reginald Brade to Winston S. Churchill

(*War Office papers: 32/9301*)

30 January 1919 War Office

S of S

You told me a few days ago that you wished to be kept more closely informed of the incoming and outgoing letters of importance.

I am arranging that the latter shall be sent up to you with the papers as they come for signature. I am afraid you may find the numbers rather oppressive at times, but, if you approve, I will exercise discretion and not trouble you with those that are not really important. It will also be necessary that the same procedure shall be followed in regard to telegrams.

As to the former, we have a daily list of important letters received, which is circulated to all Members of Council. During the war, we have had to curtail this list, and to suppress altogether the other list which we used to distribute of 'important decisions'. The reason was that, as the value of the list depended largely on a wide distribution, there was considerable risk of matters of great secrecy becoming too widely known. The lists have, however, now been restored.

The daily lists are type-written. A weekly edition is printed for wider circulation.

I annex copies of this week's and to-day's lists.

I suggest that, with a view especially to avoiding risk of delays, these lists should be shown to you every day, and that you should ask to see those that are of special importance at the moment. The letters come in at irregular intervals throughout the day and our object is to place them as early as possible in the hands of those who have to deal with them. Delays must arise if they are to be held up for you to see first.

It may interest you to know that the present daily intake of letters (our

[1] During the discussion, Bonar Law argued that it might be necessary to bring out troops, while Sir Robert Horne advocated seizing the strike leaders. By 1 February 8,000 troops had been sent to Glasgow.

Registry is centralized) amounts to over 40,000. The proportion of this number that is important cannot be stated, but I expect it is rather high.

R. H. Brade

Frederick Guest to David Lloyd George

(Lloyd George papers)

30 January 1919 12 Downing Street

You will be interested to hear that Winston's statement re an Emergency Army has been extremely well received; even the Daily News finds it hard to criticise.

Lord Northcliffe to Winston S. Churchill: telegram

(Churchill papers: 16/3)

31 January 1919 Menton

Thursday night letter just received. All my newspapers will do exactly what you wish on the subject. I have telegraphed to Dawson[1] and Caird.[2] Have health details from convalescent officers which make me anxious.

Winston S. Churchill to Sir Douglas Haig: draft telegram

(Churchill papers: 16/3)

31 January 1919 War Office
Personal & Secret

I have no information wh enables me to form a final opinion about the Calais situation. Will you kindly send me full & constant reports. In particular can you count on the fighting troops to enforce discipline along the line of communication & base details. Without local information it is impossible for me to advise specifically but on general ground the following points appear important.

1) Full explanation to the men of position & of the new scheme. Demobilisation is proceeding vy rapidly. Their comrades are dependent on them

[1] George Geoffrey Dawson, 1874–1944. Private Secretary to Lord Milner in South Africa, 1900–05. Editor of *The Times*, 1912–19 and 1923–41.

[2] Andrew Caird, 1870–1956. Administrator of the New York Headquarters of Lord Northcliffe's Mission to the United States, 1917–18. Knighted, 1918. Managing Director of the *Daily Mail*, 1918–26. Chairman and Managing Director of the *Calcutta Statesman*, 1927–8. Unsuccessful Conservative candidate for St Ives, 1928 and 1929.

for their return to their homes. Railway men must therefore do their duty by the fighting troops. As soon as the rush of demobilisation is over which will be by the end of March or middle of April large numbers of railway men will be demobilised by age & service classes and before that the opening of the Rhine will enable a good many to be released and

2) Meanwhile they are soldiers & the reputation of the British army is in their keeping. They must return to their duty & no bargaining or negotiation can take place between them & the Army authorities. The reason why no bargaining can take place is because it would be wrong and wd do harm to the Army & to the country.

Thirdly there must be a channel for expressing their grievances & once the men have returned to their duty the authorities must enter into these patiently and fully with representatives of the men chosen in an orderly manner. They shd be told this. Everything shd be done to lighten the strain on these men even if it means some slowing down of demobilisation but I shd personally deprecate agreeing to a definite number of hours per week as a bargain. I shd be glad to send over a skilled labour adviser to assist in any discussion about wages or hours with men who have returned to duty and I keep an open mind on the subject. I am however vy much inclined unless matters are far more serious than I know of not to give in to this kind of pressure.

I think it vy important for authority to be vindicated even if it takes time & involves risk & disturbance. Some of these affairs have to get worse before they get better. Above all a few days time is valuable & therefore I am for slow methods if possible showing unalterable determination and a readiness to see things drag on for a bit if necessary. We are in the right & the men are good British men & if they have time to cool & to think over the position they will see that we are right. I am very confident of this. Gradually if it is necessary & possible the disaffected area shd be surrounded & all communication cut off with the outside world. Pray let me know what you think.

Sir Douglas Haig to Winston S. Churchill

(*Churchill papers: 16/3*)

31 January 1919 GHQ, France
Secret

Dear Mr Churchill,

No doubt the AG of the Forces has kept you informed of the very serious Mutiny which occurred in Calais and was yesterday suppressed in the most satisfactory manner, without bloodshed and in such a way as to reflect credit on the Army as a whole. In due course I propose to forward a detailed report. In the meantime however it seems to me desirable that you should be in possession of the main facts of the case in order that you may realise at once

1) How critical the situation was, and that if we had failed to suppress the mutiny when we did the consequences wd have been most far reaching.

2) How much depended on the staunch behaviour of such troops as we were able to concentrate against the mutineers, and on the tact & courage of the officers to whom I entrusted the task of quelling the mutiny—and

3) How important in my opinion, it is that the ringleaders of the Mutiny should suffer the supreme penalty. If any leniency is shewn to them the discipline of the whole Army will suffer, both immediately & for many years to come.

Briefly the story is this—Last Monday the men of the Ordnance Workshops, MT and Transportation Troops at Calais stopped work.

One result of this was that there were no trains available to take away some 5,000 men who happened to arrive at this time from England.

The situation as regards the Ordnance, & Railwaymen gradually improved. On the other hand the attitude of the 'leave men' became quickly that of 'mutiny on active service'.

Every effort was made to ascertain and deal with any grievance which they might think they were suffering under. They demanded as a body to be sent back to England!—Their attitude was threatening, insubordinate & mutinous. I at once concentrated round their Camp the best part of two Divisions with machine guns, and placed General Byng[1] in charge of the whole situation at Calais. He took over command on Wednesday morning.

All preparations were finished yesterday (Thursday). The Camp was then surrounded by machine guns, and General Sandilands[2] at the head of his Brigade (104th) marched into the camp with fixed bayonets, drove the mutineers towards one end, and arrested the 3 ringleaders, after a few words of explanation.

The 3 prisoners will be tried. The rest have now been sent off by train to their Divisions.

[1] Julian Hedworth George Byng, 1862–1935. Entered Army, 1883. On active service in the Sudan, 1884; in South Africa, 1899–1902. Major-General, 1909. Commanded the Troops in Egypt, 1912–14. Commanded the 3rd Cavalry Division, 1914–15; the Cavalry Corps, 1915; the 9th Army Corps, 1915–16; the 17th Army Corps, 1916; the Canadian Corps, 1916–17, the 3rd Army, 1917–19. Knighted, 1915. General, 1917. Created Baron, 1919, and granted £30,000 by Parliament for his war service. Governor-General of Canada, 1921–6. Created Viscount, 1926. Commissioner, Metropolitan Police, 1928–31. Field Marshal, 1932.

[2] Henry George Sandilands, 1864–1930. Entered the army, 1884; Colonel, 1913. Served through the war on the western front (mentioned in despatches five times). Brigadier-General, Commanding the 104th Infantry Brigade, 1918. Retired, 1919.

I consider that the manner in which Gen Byng handled this most difficult situation is worthy of high commendation.

The condition of the workshops at Calais is having my attention, and I will report in due course what I think shd be done with the services concerned.

Yours very truly
D. Haig

Winston S. Churchill to Sir Douglas Haig: telegram

(*Churchill papers: 16/3*)

31 January 1919 War Office
Secret and Personal

I am very glad to hear that the disorders at Calais have come to an end. I have not yet received any full report of what occurred. Unless there was serious violence attended by bloodshed or actual loss of life, I do not consider that the infliction of the death penalty would be justifiable. The death penalty should be used only under what may be called life and death conditions, and public opinion will only support it when other men's lives are endangered by criminal or cowardly conduct. In this connection it is relevant to mention the Court Martial at Portsmouth published in Wednesday's papers sentenced to two years IHL sailors who not only refused to obey orders but actually ran up the red flag in place of the White Ensign on a ship of war at sea in time of war.

This seems to me to be a very flagrant case, but I suppose the feeling that life was not taken or endangered and that actual fighting has stopped at the present time influenced the Court to leniency.

I will, of course, await your full report before forming a final opinion.

Secondly, with regard to your telegram of yesterday about wage conditions of railwaymen, etc. When order and discipline have been thoroughly restored and the ringleaders punished with fitting severity, I should be quite willing to take up the question of working pay for technical units and overtime pay for railway work. If you thought well, I could send out someone like Sir George Askwith[1] who has great experience in such matters and who could go into the labour conditions on the spot and advise from that point of view.

[1] George Ranken Askwith, 1861–1942. Barrister, 1886. Industrial arbitrator. Assistant Secretary, Board of Trade, 1907. Chairman of the Fair Wages Advisory Committee, 1909–19. Knighted, 1911. Chief Industrial Commissioner, Board of Trade, 1911–19. Created Baron, 1919. President of the British Science Guild, 1922–5. Vice-President, Royal Society of Arts, 1927–41. President of the Institute of Arbitrators, 1933–41.

Winston S. Churchill to Austen Chamberlain

(*Churchill papers: 16/3*)

31 January 1919 War Office

My dear Austen,

I have succeeded, as you will have seen, in reducing my net to 1,300,000. I hope to push all except the retained 900,000 out in the course of less than two months, and thus save you all the money I can. You will see we are running now 38,000 a day, which is really very creditable to the organisation Milner set up.

I was wrong about the 70,000 white troops [in India]. The Total number out there is 96,000, of whom about 20,000 are coming home as invalids. I entirely agree with you in thinking that a further reduction will be possible in the near future, in consequence of the removal of the Russian menace, and the development of mechanical weapons of war. I must, however, have more time to consider the entire Indian situation with my military advisers, so as to make the air play its true part in relieving the expensive men we shall have in the future to keep across the seas.

On the whole the policy has been very well accepted, and I am much obliged to you for the broad view you have taken of our difficulties in the emergency in which we stand.

I hope soon to address you on the finance of the Army for this year, and a little later on to present you with a more durable scheme.

Yours very sincerely
Winston S. Churchill

Winston S. Churchill to Lord Curzon

(*Churchill papers: 16/3*)

31 January 1919 War Office

My dear Curzon,

Replying to your FO letter of Jan 23rd, we had already advanced far on the path of sending reinforcements, leave-men, and demobilised troops up the Rhine and Scheldt. They would of course carry their arms. The situation on the military railways is very serious. The railways are congested, the railwaymen over-strained and mutinous, and the journey imposes great hardships on the troops. Using Rotterdam and Antwerp, all these difficulties will speedily disappear.

The matter is therefore of the highest practical consequence to us.

Robertson's[1] telegram from the Hague of the 29th (344 and 346), however, seem to throw difficulties in the way. It is intolerable that the Dutch should crown their money-making achievements in the war by imposing a four-days journey in open trucks on the officers and men of the British Army to whose exertions their independence is due. If such an attitude were persisted in, it would rank with the sand and gravel, out of which the pill-boxes of Flanders, which cost so many British lives, were constructed.

I do hope that you will assist us to your utmost, and that my views may be conveyed also to Mr Balfour. The extreme urgency of the case arises from the fact that we wish to begin sending at once the 69 young battalions by the Rhine route.

Yours very sincerely
Winston S. Churchill

[1] Malcolm Arnold Robertson, 1877–1951. Entered Foreign Office, 1898. 1st Secretary, Washington, 1915–18. 1st Secretary the Hague, 1918–19. British High Commissioner, Rhineland, 1920–1. British Agent and Consul General, Tangier, 1921–5. Knighted, 1924. Ambassador to Brazil, 1927–9. Retired from the Diplomatic service, 1930. Conservative PM for Mitcham, 1940–5. Chairman of the British Council, 1941–5.

February 1919

Winston S. Churchill to Sir Reginald Brade
(*War Office papers: 32/9301*)

1 February 1919 War Office

Secretary

I wish you, before you go, to issue an Office Memorandum regulating the methods of dealing with papers, telegrams, etc, in the Department.

(1) *Letters.* Important letters which affect policy and may become the subject of Cabinet discussion should be submitted to me for approval before they are despatched. If I am absent they should be submitted to the Under Secretary of State. If the matter is of great urgency, ie if the public service will suffer in the interval before my approval or that of the Under-Secretary can be obtained, sanction is to be presumed, provided the letter is put forward on the authority of a Member of the Council. The letter should then be sent to my Private Office after action has been taken.

In cases where I am available the letters will come to me before the Under-Secretary in order to save time, but in all cases the Under-Secretary will see important letters after my approval has been given and action has been taken in ordinary circumstances, or before action (subject to urgency) if I am not available.

Arrangements will be made in the Private Office to scrutinise the daily lists of important letters received and despatched and to draw my attention to any omissions. I recognise that there must be a number of border-line cases about which reasonable doubt may arise. In such circumstances it will be better during the first few weeks to send the letters forward for my sanction. I shall thus be able to obtain a general view of what is passing.

Important letters which are received in the office should go straight to the authority who will have to deal with them, but simultaneously a copy should be furnished to me.

(2) *Telegrams.* Copies of all telegrams received or despatched will, of course, be furnished daily to the Private Office. I do not wish to see operational telegrams dealing with routine business until after they have been dealt with.

Telegrams which—

(a) affect or initiate policy;
(b) involve inter-departmental action;
(c) are likely to become subjects of Cabinet discussion;
(d) raise questions likely to form the subject of Parliamentary controversy; or
(e) convey rebuke or censure to Commanders abroad;

should be referred to me before despatch.

The Parliamentary Under-Secretary will see the telegrams after action for information, but in my absence, or if I am not available, the CIGS or his deputy will act for me with plenary authority.

(3) Official papers referred for my decision should not be addressed to the Private Secretary but to the S of S.

It should not in ordinary circumstances or under good arrangements be necessary for any paper to reach me except directly from a Member of the Army Council or someone acting for such member in his absence. In all cases the last minute should contain a definite recommendation for action, which can be approved simply by an initial.

WSC

Winston S. Churchill to David Lloyd George

(*Lloyd George papers*)

1 February 1919 War Office
Private

My dear Prime Minister,

Will you consider Freddie being made a Privy Councillor. Most if not all of those who have held his position through a victorious election have received this recognition. The Chief Whip is certainly 'Privy' to more counsels than most of those who are sworn. In fact he is Privy to a good lot. I know he wd like it.[1]

Gulland was thus honoured!

I wish I cd have got over; but I did not like to leave. The Calais meeting has had some serious consequences: & 8000 troops have been sent into Glasgow. Everything is however going vy well here & I do not see any reason for yr changing yr plans.

Yours always
W

[1] Guest did not become a Privy Councillor until 1920. In 1929 Churchill asked Baldwin to give Guest a peerage, but without success.

Walter Long to David Lloyd George

(*Lloyd George papers*)

1 February 1919 Admiralty

My Dear Prime Minister,

. . . There are all sorts of questions arising now as regards the Air Force, and we cannot even discuss them profitably, much less decide them owing to the fact that we have no accurate knowledge of what the future position is to be and also owing to the fact that all these representatives to whom I have referred are not prepared to accept the decision of the Secretary of State for War.

Dont misunderstand me: there is no hostility to Winston, on the contrary, the courage, the ability and the clearness of vision which have marked his treatment of army questions have already won him immense support and, as I told you in my last letter, I am confident he will have no difficulty in carrying his proposals through parliament; but everyone asks how can he be the head of two great departments?

I wont trouble you with the variety of arguments which are being effectively used, but I would most respectfully ask you to consider whether it would not be wise to frankly admit that the Secretary of State for War has more than anyone man can do in dealing with the extraordinarily difficult problems connected with the army with which he is confronted; and accepting this bare statement of fact would it not be well to restore the Air Ministry?

You have an excellent man in Seely—keen and knowledgeable—and if this were done hostility would disappear and, as time goes on, you could see what is the proper policy for the future. On the other hand if things are allowed to remain as they are there will be very serious difficulty quite early in the coming session. We shall no doubt be able to overcome it by temporising, but it will not diminish, and, in the meantime, the efficiency of our fighting services must suffer.

Very sincerely yours
Walter H. Long

Winston S. Churchill to David Lloyd George: telegram

(*Churchill papers: 16/4*)

3 February 1919 War Office
Secret & Personal

I have received a memorandum which is dated Jan 31st from CIGS about the safety of our troops in North Russia and it is no doubt now before you. For security I am forwarding another copy by to-night. I hope you will give it your earnest consideration. My view is as follows:—The policy of sending or withdrawing such expeditions must be decided by the Government and I presume in this case by the Allied Governments; but once they have been sent and while they are there the responsibility for their proper maintenance, nourishment and support rests with the War Office and I am bound to take whatever measures are possible to give effect to the military advice I receive and make sure that our troops are not ill-treated or cast away, always provided that the original scope of the operation as determined by the Government is not extended.

Do you realise that a disaster might easily occur on this front during the four months which must inevitably elapse before these men can be withdrawn if that is what the Government decide; and that in any case our men will be exposed to needless suffering without their proper railway units, medical attendance, electricians for the dark months and necessary supply of drafts? In these circumstances I ask that the Cabinet decision against sending more men to Russia shall be modified to enable the necessary reinforcements set forth in the General Staff memorandum to be sent. It will then be for me having regard to the military situation and the present state of discipline in the Army to take whatever measures are practicable.

The alarming rumours which are circulating in London about the safety of our troops in North Russia are not justified by the facts, but the situation may rapidly deteriorate and people will not tolerate their belongings being left to their fate on this desolate coast without resolute efforts being made to succour them. These measures will be equally necessary whether the decision of the Allied Governments is to withdraw in the summer or go on with the operation. The details will be explained to you by CIGS.

War Cabinet: minutes

(Cabinet papers: 23/9)

SINN FEIN PRISONERS

4 February 1919

THE SECRETARY OF STATE FOR WAR hoped that the Cabinet would not be in any way influenced by the possibility of the present authorities having to resort to forcible feeding. In the case of the suffragettes a few years back, the Government had stood firm, and they ought to do so in the present instance. The prison authorities ought themselves to be capable of keeping

THE ANTI-BOLSHEVIK FORCES IN EUROPEAN RUSSIA, 1919

order in gaols, and the Government should not be asked to arrive at an important decision because those authorities were afraid of disturbances. He himself did not contemplate any trouble in Ireland. In his view there was no place in the world where there was less danger at the present time, and he was satisfied that the troops there could be relied upon. He thought that the Cabinet could not be expected to come to a lightning decision on so important a political question.[1]

Winston S. Churchill to Austen Chamberlain[2]

(*Churchill papers: 16/4*)

4 February 1919 War Office

My dear Austen

It is important and urgent to settle the terms of enlistment in the 'after-war' army. Not a week should be lost if we are to be in a position to relieve our territorials detained in India during the Autumn of this year.

As the re-creation of the after-war army will have to proceed during the period when the armies of occupation are in existence on the new rates of pay, it will plainly be impossible to institute a different permanent rate. On the other hand, these high rates if universal would make it very difficult to maintain an after-war home defence army of a sufficient size without undue cost to the tax-payer.

I am therefore seeking to solve the problem along the following lines:—

There will be two after-war armies: one long service for our foreign garrisons, and the other short service with a long reserve period for home defence. The former will be as small as we can manage, and the latter as large as we can afford.

My immediate task is to re-create the former on a voluntary basis. The only source immediately available is the soldiers who have served, or are still serving, in the present war. These are trained, seasoned, veteran troops, fit to go to the East or to go into action in any theatre in the world. It would be quite unnecessary to pay young new boys, recruited for the first time, on whom we have to spend nearly two years feeding, training and so forth, the same wage as is rightly earned by these veteran soldiers.

I am inclined, therefore, to propose that the present rates should be paid

[1] Later, when the discussions turned to labour relations in Britain, Churchill told the War Cabinet: 'The curse of Trade Unionism was that there was not enough of it, and it was not highly enough developed to make its branch secretaries fall into line with the head office. With a powerful union either peace or war could be made.'

[2] Austen Chamberlain had succeeded Andrew Bonar Law as Chancellor of the Exchequer on 1 January 1919.

to the soldier only after two years service and when he is a fully trained man. Every man who has served or is now serving in the present war or armies of occupation will, if suitable, be allowed to volunteer up to the numbers required for the after-war army. He will, on joining this army, be credited with whatever time he has served during the present war, if that is over two years, and with two years service if he has served during the war for a period of less than two years. Thus he will be considered to be a war-trained man in the third year of his service. This should bring us the volunteers we need.

On the other hand, the young recruits will come in on a substantially lower scale for the first year, would work up in proficiency pay during the second year, and, if satisfactory, would reach their full scale only in the third year.

The distinction appears to me to be quite a just one and is, after all, that prevailing in many industries between the apprentice and the craftsman. It has the enormous advantage of on the one hand offering a real inducement to the war-trained man to volunteer for our garrisons abroad, and at the same time not unduly burdening our home defence army with expense.

I do not write this letter to you because any immediate decision is required from you, but in order to advise you early of the lines on which I am proceeding. A Committee is at work on all the details.

With regard to the letter which you have written to me about the Staff College, I really do not quite know what to do. The General Staff have pressed me very earnestly on this matter, and have convinced me that what they ask is just and in the interests of the Service. Indeed, General Harington was under the impression that he had convinced Sir Robert Chalmers[1] of the propriety of their request.

I am more concerned with the process by which such matters should be settled than with the particular instance. It seems to me that with these hundreds of millions of money to be managed, it is a thoroughly vicious arrangement which requires a Secretary of State for War to appeal personally in a lengthy letter to a Chancellor of the Exchequer over an extremely small matter of this kind, and which leads the Chancellor of the Exchequer to consume so much of his valuable time in entering into an elaborate argument on the subject.

I should have thought that all the while matters of far greater importance were pressing for attention. Add to this the fact that the results of this painful process lead only to a blank wall of refusal and that the subject in question

[1] Robert Chalmers, 1858–1938. Entered Treasury, 1882. Chairman, Board of Inland Revenue, 1907–11. Knighted, 1908. Permanent Secretary of the Treasury, 1911–13. Governor of Ceylon, 1913–16. Under Secretary for Ireland, 1916. Joint Permanent Secretary to the Treasury, 1916–19. Created Baron, 1919. Master of Peterhouse, Cambridge, 1924–31.

is really too small for a Cabinet decision to be invoked, and I think the unsatisfactory nature of our arrangements become clearly manifest.

Frankly I should have thought that in a matter of this kind the opinion of the Secretary of State should have counted and that he should be accorded a discretionary power within certain general limits.

The Treasury has often seemed to me to concentrate on small points of detail which they obstinately fight, while the great tide of expenditure moves forward altogether beyond their control.

Would it not be far better for us to try to reach a broad agreement on totals and general principles, instead of wearisome bickering over details?

The interests of the tax-payer are never absent from my mind. By the accelerated demobilisation alone we are saving you many millions of money. By an ingenious solution of the problem of the future army we can greatly lighten your burden in future years. By an harmonious inter-weaving of air and military forces in our foreign garrisons, we may be able to assist you further. And these, I submit, are the planes on which I think you and I should meet and discuss, rather than on points of the order concerned with whether a couple of officers shall be Colonels or Brigadier Generals when instructing at the Staff College.

It seems to me that in such a matter as that, I should not be forced to argue—still less to argue unavailingly—with you, but should be placed by you in a position to act for you as your colleague, having regard to the general interest.

Meanwhile, I am afraid I cannot agree to accept the refusal conveyed by your letter.

Austen Chamberlain to Winston S. Churchill

(*Churchill papers: 16/4*)

5 February 1919 Treasury Chambers

My dear Winston,

I hasten to send a reply to your letter of yesterday. Let me deal first with the second and personal question raised in it. As regards the rank and pay of the officers at the Staff College, this is a minor matter, but it is the only one which threatens trouble between us. Let me say at once that I am not going to allow it to develop into a quarrel even of the most friendly and 'official' character. You and I are both faced with an extraordinarily difficult task. We are out to help one another and not to get in one another's way. If after hearing what I have to say and giving your personal attention to the matter, you tell me that in your opinion the proposal put forward by the War Office is necessary in the interests of the Service, I will withdraw my objections, strong as I think my case is, and will accept your statement and give my sanction to your proposal.

And now let me say a few words on the merits of your suggestions. You say that it is irritating and wasteful that the time of people with such big problems in front of them as you and I should be occupied in discussing minor matters of this character. I need not say that I agree. Controversy about matters of this kind is most wearying and is apt to occupy a wholly disproportionate amount of time, but I am sure that if you were in my place you would find it impossible to adopt the suggestion which you make that the Treasury should confine itself to settling lump sum estimates with the Departments and allow them to spend within the limits of those lump sums at their discretion.

You will find it to be a universal rule that when Departments are spending very large sums and when indeed the national expenditure itself is on a very high scale, they are apt to become less careful in the minor matters. Yet it is when very large expenditure is in any case necessary that the greatest care is required to see that there is no waste. Apart from this, such latitude given to Departments would involve not only the Treasury but themselves in much subsequent trouble. There is no question on which the action of one Department more immediately affects the position and claims of another than that of the salaries paid. We are already criticised here by the Committee on Public Expenditure for having exercised an insufficient control and for having allowed divergencies to grow up in such matters between different Departments. It is no doubt true that we make our mistakes like other people, and that for want of complete knowledge we sometimes take wrong objections or object to the wrong thing. But to forego our right to examine such proposals and to criticise them if to us criticism seems necessary would, I feel sure, be considered as a dereliction of duty on our part.

Now as regards the particular case. Is not the real object of the War Office proposal to secure to certain individual officers whom they wish to appoint to the Staff College the rates of pay which they have drawn under war conditions? If so, I think that this is unreasonable. Yet I cannot make out that there is any other real ground for the proposal which your people have put forward. There is an argument as to the relative rank and rates of pay of the teachers and the taught, but as far as I can understand the situation, such an argument will not stand examination. The pupils at the College revert to their substantive rank and the relative rank of professor and pupil would be maintained. There is always a very natural tendency on the part of any of us to be kind-hearted to those who serve under us and to make their position as comfortable as possible. I submit to you that if you look into the matter yourself, you will find that no military principle and no military object is at stake. What is sought is merely a special advantage for particular officers and facts do not justify this special treatment.

There is my case. Examine it candidly and give me your answer. As I have said, I am not going to quarrel with you or haggle with you about this matter. If you are convinced after examination that it is necessary in the interest that these officers should have the rank which your people have proposed for them, I will yield my judgment to yours. All I ask is that you should not take the case of your officials for granted but should satisfy yourself that it is a fact.

Now may I say a word about the new Army scheme. It is of course a disappointment to me that the course of events has forced you out of your original position that the pay of the Army of Occupation was to be something entirely exceptional and temporary and not to be applicable to the new permanent Army. As you pointed out at the time, this pay was required as compensation to men who were not professional soldiers for undertaking a special burden from which the majority of the Army were to be released. The Army offers no permanent career for these men and no such advantage as would tempt them voluntarily to leave civil life for it.

The case of your new Army is of course quite different. They will all be volunteers. They will all be men who of their own motion choose a military career; and your object is, as I understand it, to make it, in conjunction with opportunities for civil employment after they leave the Colours, a career for a lifetime—ending on final retirement with a pension calculated on the combined military and civil service. If this be so, are you sure that it is necessary to abandon your original plan for a distinction between the terms which you would offer to them and the compensation which you pay to the Armies of Occupation?

In any case I quite agree with you that the soldier who has seen two years war service is entitled to a higher rate of pay than the raw recruit. But I would like to suggest to you that the two years probationary period suggested by you for the raw recruit of the future is not comparable with the two years active service which the men immediately enlisted from the existing armies will have. Would not something like four years of service be more nearly equivalent to two years war experience?

Please take these suggestions in the friendly spirit in which they are offered. They do not pretend to be anything more than first thoughts on the scheme which you have sketched to me. They deal, of course, only with that portion of your after-war army intended for the foreign garrisons.

Yours sincerely
Austen Chamberlain

Winston S. Churchill to David Lloyd George

(Churchill papers: 16/4)

5 February 1919 War Office

As you took such a strong line about our military position at Constantinople I think you ought to know that the General Staff believe that the French intend to vest the control of the armistice execution in hands of Franchet d'Esperey[1] who is due to arrive at Constantinople in a few days and will, it is rumoured, be made a Marshal in order to place him over Allenby. We consider that Turkey was conquered by British troops, & that the execution of the armistice & primary at C'nople shd rest with us. Matters can only be arranged between you & Clemenceau. I am sending papers by mail tomorrow.

Secondly I am strongly of opinion that no British interest is served by retention of our 26th Divn in Bulgaria. The French are always ready to cast us for these sterile jobs, while hastening themselves to pick out the plums. General Staff wish immediately to withdraw 7 Battns from Bulgaria & as soon as possible all the rest. This course is indeed practically forced upon us by the reductions wh we have agreed to make in the Army of the Middle East. Papers on this point are also being sent you. You will see how the two hang together. Clemenceau will of course press strongly for retention of our troops in Bulgaria.

WSC

David Lloyd George to Winston S. Churchill: telephone message

(Churchill papers: 16/4)

5 February 1919 Paris

Your telegram February 3rd. I consider that any details necessary to secure the health, comfort and nourishment of troops in Northern Russia should be sent without delay.

The Cabinet decision that no reinforcements should be sent to Russia was due to the fact that they were advised by their military advisers that there

[1] Louis Félix Marie François Franchet D'Esperey, 1856–1942. Born in French Algeria. Entered the French Army in Algeria, 1876. On active service in Indo-China, 1886. Attached to the multi-national Chinese Expeditionary Force, 1900. Général de Division, 1912. Commanded the Occupation troops in western Morocco, 1912–13. On active service on the western front, 1914–17, commanding the 5th Army, 1914–16; the Group of Armies of the East, 1916, and the Group of Armies of the North and North-East, 1916–17. Commander-in-Chief of the Allied Armies of the East, with his headquarters at Constantinople, June 1918–November 1920. Commanded the French forces in Odessa, 1919. Marshal of France, 1921.

was considerable unrest in the Army on the subject of Russia and that the despatch of further troops might have serious results.

I understand that you consider that specialists such as electricians, railwaymen and so forth can now safely be sent and I think you should do what is necessary immediately to improve the conditions of those serving in Archangel and Murmansk.

I do not think, however, that you should send out drafts to enable demobilisation to commence there without feeling assured of what the effect on the troops would be.

Winston S. Churchill to David Lloyd George: telegram
(*Churchill papers: 16/4*)

5 February 1919 War Office

Many thanks for your telephone message of the 5th. You may be sure that I will proceed with discretion in regard to any troops sent to Russia, and, avoid a regrettable rebuff by every means. Opinion here is that *morale* of Army is much improved now from what it was three weeks ago. Full reports are not yet available, but there is a growing feeling of confidence. I hope it will not be long before anxieties in this respect at least may be greatly diminished. Meanwhile I ought to tell you that, since my telegram of the 3rd, two messages have been received from Murmansk & Archangel of a more encouraging nature as regards the daylight, and, secondly, showing that medical conditions have been greatly improved by insertions made locally. I am therefore having the question of the strength of any drafts that may be required carefully re-examined.

Winston S. Churchill to General Harington,[1] General Radcliffe and General Thwaites
(*War Office papers: 32/5684*)

6 February 1919 War Office
Secret

It is highly important to know what the Russians can & will do for themselves.

[1] For all but three months of Churchill's two years as Secretary of State for War, General Harington served at the War Office as Deputy Chief of the Imperial General Staff. In his memoirs, *Tim Harington Looks Back* (London, 1940), he wrote: 'During that time I saw a lot of Mr Winston Churchill and his wonderful brain and capacity for work. How he got through it will always be a mystery to me. I used often to put twenty five important papers in his box at about 8 pm and so did other Army Councillors. They would all be back on our tables by 11 am next morning with his decisions written in his own hand in red ink. . . .'

If they can put up a real fight, we ought in my view to back them in every possible way. But without them it is no good our trying.

Be vy careful not to let our wishes colour our statements.

Winston S. Churchill to Walter Long

(*Churchill papers: 16/1*)

8 February 1919 War Office
Most Secret

My dear Long

Many thanks for sending me a note of your Admiralty desiderata.

It may perhaps simplify our discussion on Monday if I tell you in advance, for your own personal information, the main outline of the policy I have in mind.

(1) In the first place, the fact that I hold the seals of two offices in no way implies the absorption of the Air Force in the Army. This arrangement is in principle temporary. It is of great convenience during the process of demobilisation that the Air Force and the Army can be guided step by step from one point of view. The practical course of business is greatly simplified and expedited thereby.

Secondly, the whole future garrisons of the British Empire have to be reviewed in the light of the war and the increased responsibilities cast upon us by our victory. It is desirable that in this review the disposition of the Air forces and those of our garrisons should be regulated in harmony from a single standpoint, in order that the fullest use may be made of the new arm, especially—in the East and in the Middle East—and that economy of expense and personnel may be effected to the utmost.

(2) Meanwhile the future independence of the Air Force and Air Ministry will be in no way prejudiced. Nor will it be in any way 'militarised'. On the contrary, I propose deliberately to 'de-militarise' it and to enhance its distinctive character by every reasonable means.

For instance, I contemplate eliminating altogether all military ranks and titles and establishing new titles appropriate to a new service and a new element standing midway between the two parent services and catering for the needs of both.

The ranks in contemplation are as follows:—Air Marshal: Air Commodore: Wing Commander: Squadron Leader: Flight Leader: Flying Officer or Observer.

The exact terminology is, of course, being further studied and discussed, and

I quote the totals in order to illustrate the principle which it is intended gradually, and as convenience allows, to introduce through every aspect of the Air Service.

(3) I propose to make considerable changes both in the organisation of the Air Council and in the high personnel. It is proposed first of all to reduce it in size. Apart from Ministers, there will be a First, Second and Third Air Lord or Air Member, who will be responsible respectively for War Aviation, Civil Aviation, and Aircraft Production.

I propose to recommend to the Prime Minister the appointment of General Trenchard as First Air Lord and Chief of the Air Staff, and to ask General Sykes[1] to become the Second Air Lord in charge of civil aviation. The Third Air Lord will probably be General Ellington.[2]

I am particularly anxious to provide an increased naval representation in the high offices of the Air Ministry and in the commands. I am hindered only by the fact that there are very few naval officers associated with the flying service who have yet the requisite seniority and standing. While the war has been going on there have been more opportunities for men to reach high positions in military aviation than with the Navy. Time will correct this disproportion and enable us to maintain an approximate even balance between the two parent services.

For the present I propose, subject to further discussion, General R M Groves[3] as Deputy Chief of the Air Staff and Director of Air Operations. It is intended to make this post of much wider scope and importance than at present.

[1] Frederick Hugh Sykes, 1877–1954. Entered Army, 1901. Severely wounded in the South African War. Learned to fly, 1911. Commander, Royal Flying Corps, Military Wing, 1912–14. Major, 1912. Chief Staff Officer, Royal Flying Corps, France, 1914–15. Colonel Commanding the Royal Naval Air Service, Eastern Mediterranean, 1915–16. Brigadier-General, 1917. Deputy-Director of Organization, War Office, 1917. Served on the General Staff, Supreme War Council, Versailles, 1917–18. Major-General, 1918. Chief of the Air Staff, 1918–19. Knighted, 1919. Appointed by Churchill First Controller-General of Civil Aviation, 1919–22. In 1920 he married Bonar Law's daughter Isabel. Conservative MP, 1922–8, and 1940–5. Governor of Bombay, 1928–32.

[2] Edward Leonard Ellington, 1877–1967. 2nd Lieutenant, Royal Artillery, 1897; Major, 1914. Deputy Assistant Quartermaster-General, 1914–15. Lieutenant-Colonel, 1915. Major-General, Royal Air Force, 1918. Appointed by Churchill Director General of Aircraft Production (later Supply) and Research, Air Ministry, 1919–21. Knighted, 1920. Air Vice-Marshal, Commanding the Royal Air Force, Middle East, 1922–3; India, 1923–6; Iraq, 1926–8. Air Officer Commanding-in-Chief, Air Defence of Britain, 1929–31. Chief of the Air Staff, 1933–7. Inspector General, Royal Air Force, 1937–40.

[3] Robert Marsland Groves, 1880–1920. Joined the Royal Navy, 1896. Entered the Royal Naval Air Service as Wing Commander, 1914. Wing Captain, 1917. Served with Royal Flying Corps, 1917–18 (DSO, 1917). Brigadier-General, 1918. Deputy Chief of the Air Staff, 1919. Officer Commanding the RAF, Middle East, 1919–20. Killed in an air crash near Cairo.

I propose to offer the Directorship of the Directorate of Personnel to a Naval Officer. . . . Apart from this, I understand that Trenchard commands in a very considerable degree the confidence of the naval flying service as well as that of the army, and that his appointment to the first place will be in every way agreeable to the Board of Admiralty.

(4) I have given the papers you kindly sent me this morning to General Trenchard to study, and I am sure you will find him very desirous of meeting Admiralty wishes in every way possible without rupturing the central principle that united and independent Air Force.

It is clear that the officers of the Air Force must be drawn from three separate sources, viz, officers holding permanent Air Commissions; officers seconded from the Navy; officers seconded from the Army.

I contemplate—though all these matters are for discussion between us—that these last two classes will graduate with the Air Force and, after serving three or four years as airmen, will return to their parent services, carrying with them their experience of the air.

How else are the two parent services to have in future years in their high commands officers familiar with and having sympathy for the new element of warfare?

These officers may at a later period in their career return for a second tour in command or on the staff of the Air Force, and thus keep themselves apprised of the latest developments and at the same time support the Air Force with the experience and standing of the two older services.

It occurs to me as possible that what may be called Grand Fleet Aviation, by which I mean the fighting ships of the Grand Fleet and the ancillary seaplane ships, might be provided for by officers who had returned to the Navy after being seconded in the Air Force during, say, the first two years of their return. This principle may be found capable of meeting some of the admitted difficulties of the present position.

General Trenchard is very anxious that in the immediate future we should endeavour to preserve considerable distinction between the different classes of aviation services within the Royal Air Force. There are already four or five well-marked divisions similar to those which prevail in the Army between the infantry, cavalry, artillery and engineers, and it should be possible through this process also to cater for the special needs of the Navy without prejudice to the integrity and unity of the Air Force as a whole.

I hope that these notes, which I beg you to treat as entirely for your own eyes, may be of use to you before your talk on Monday.

Winston S. Churchill to General Sykes

(*Sykes papers*)

9 February 1919

My dear Sykes,

My predecessor Lord Weir left me his formal recommendation to divide the main functions of the Air Ministry into War & Civil Aviation branches, & to offer the War side to Trenchard & the Civil side to you. General Seely has also endorsed this. I have come to the conclusion after vy anxious thought that all arrangement on these lines will be in the best interests of the service. I propose therefore to recast the Air Council so that it will contain in addition to Ministers only three Air Members (or Air Lords perhaps) changed respectively with War Aviation, Civil Aviation & Aircraft Production. With the assent of the Prime Minister I propose to offer the first of these posts to Trenchard & I shall be vy glad indeed if you will undertake the sphere of Civil Aviation. It wd be essential to the success of such an arrangement that you & Trenchard shd be able to work together in goodwill & loyal co-operation. He has answered me that there will be no difficulty on his side & I am sure that if you place yr services at my disposal in this new post there will be none on yours. Thus we shd succeed in securing for the Air Force & Air Ministry at this critical period in its life a representation in its life wh wd comprise those who had served it best.

I shall look forward to seeing you at 1 o'clock tomorrow (after the Cabinet); & believe me yours vy sincerely,

Winston S. Churchill

Sir Henry Wilson: diary

(*Wilson papers*)

9 February 1919 36 Eaton Place

Winston said he had had a long talk with LG last night & there was no doubt that LG thought both railways & miners were coming out on great strikes, & that there was going to be a trial of strength between the GOV & the Bolshevists. So be it.

Sir Henry Wilson: diary

(Wilson papers)

12 February 1919 36 Eaton Place

The War Cabinet. We discussed food distribution in this country in case of coal & railway strikes & agreed that the Ports must be cleared & food well scattered. Then I raised the question of Russia & insisted that there was no policy & there was positive danger to our detachments. Winston backed me well & we made an impression. I promised to get out some notes on what we could do if we went to war with the Bolsheviks. LG agreed that if Prinkipo fell down then something else must be tried.

War Cabinet: minutes

(Cabinet papers: 23/9)

12 February 1919

THE SECRETARY OF STATE FOR WAR said that we were committed in various directions in Russia. We had forces both in the north and in the south of Russia, and in Siberia. The men there were entitled to know what they were fighting for, and were entitled to proper support from home. Our enterprises in all these directions were crumbling. The situation in the north was not yet serious, although it might very easily become so. The Bolsheviks were getting stronger every day. In the South, General Denikin's army had greatly deteriorated. Krasnoff[1] was discouraged, and believed the Allies had thrown them over completely. The situation in Siberia was exactly the same. There was complete disheartenment everywhere. The Great Powers were still delaying the decision on this matter. If we were going to withdraw our troops, it should be done at once. If we were going to intervene, we should send larger forces there. He believed that we ought to intervene.

THE PRIME MINISTER said he understood the military view to be that, if we were going to do any good, we should need a million men at least, and these should be despatched in the spring.

MR CHURCHILL, continuing, said that he did not suggest intervention

[1] Peter Nikolaevich Krasnoff, 1869–1947. A General in the Tsarist Army, he went to the Don after the October Revolution, and organized an anti-Bolshevik Don Army, receiving military aid first from the Germans, and then from the Allies. He twice attacked Tsaritsyn, but failed to capture it, and eventually put his Don Army under Denikin's command. In 1919 he emigrated to Germany. In 1945 he was captured by the Red Army, sentenced to death for collaboration with the Germans, and hanged.

on that scale, but we ought to try and keep alive the Russian forces which were attempting to make headway against the Bolsheviks.

THE PRIME MINISTER said there were various courses open. As regards intervention, in order to be successful it was necessary to have a million men advancing from Odessa or through Poland. Another policy was to supply the Russian forces with guns, equipment, &c, but every opinion he had heard expressed was to the effect that guns alone would be of no use, as it would be necessary to send in addition at least 150,000 men.

THE SECRETARY OF STATE FOR WAR said that he agreed that intervention on a large scale was not possible, but we ought to continue to help the anti-Bolshevik forces in Russia as much as we could. The alternative was to withdraw at once.

THE CHANCELLOR OF THE EXCHEQUER[1] said that, as he understood the position, the chances of any good results had greatly diminished in the last few weeks. The anti-Bolsheviks in Russia had expected far more help than the Allies had sent them. Our information now was that both Denikin's and Krasnoff's forces were untrustworthy. The English troops in Siberia were very tired, and the Czechs were less willing to fight. With regard to Archangel, the Russian forces there were useful as a fighting force only in conjunction with the Allies, and the position appeared to be serious. With regard to Odessa, he referred to a telegram from Lord Granville,[2] dated the 19th January, 1919, announcing the despatch of Greek troops to Odessa (No 55) M Venizelos[3] wished to demobilise his army, but, in order to retain the good will of the Allies, was prepared to allow them to serve in Russia. As it was, 41,000 Greek troops were under orders to go to Odessa, of whom 3,000 were already on the spot. If they got into trouble, it would be impossible for France and England to leave them to their fate, and we might be involved at any moment against our will.

THE PRIME MINISTER said that he would like to have the military point of view on the question of the various alternatives which were before the Government. He had already indicated two possible policies, namely, that of intervention and that of supplying the Russian forces with guns and money.

[1] Austen Chamberlain.

[2] Granville George Leveson Gower, Viscount Granville, 1872–1939. Succeeded his father as 3rd Earl Granville, 1891. Entered the Diplomatic Service, 1893. Councillor of Embassy, Berlin, 1911–13; Paris, 1913–17. Diplomatic Agent, Salonika, 1917. British Minister in Athens, 1917–21; in Copenhagen, 1921–6; at the Hague, 1926–8. Ambassador in Brussels, 1928–33.

[3] Eleutherios Venizelos, 1864–1936. Prime Minister of Greece, 1910–15. Forced to resign by King Constantine, May 1915. Prime Minister for the second time, August to October 1915. Subsequently Prime Minister 1917–20, 1928–32 and 1933.

He would like to know what this latter policy meant—how much money it would mean, and whether it would involve sending more forces. There was a third policy, namely, to withdraw altogether. He would like to know also what it would mean, from the military point of view, if we had to defend those States which would come under the protection of the League of Nations. In reply to a question, he said that Siberia was not amongst these States, as it did not now claim independence.

THE SECRETARY OF STATE FOR WAR said that the War Office would prepare a paper on this question. He thought that, if we came to the conclusion that if we had no effective means of helping these people, the sooner they were told the better it would be. On the other hand, if the Allies would not help Russia, Japan and Germany would certainly do so, and in a few years' time we should see the German Republic united with the Bolsheviks in Russia and the Japanese in the Far East forming one of the most powerful combinations the world had ever seen.

THE PRIME MINISTER said that the Russian non-Bolshevik armies were inferior to the Bolsheviks neither in men nor guns, and if the Russian population had been behind them they would certainly have made headway. For months the Bolsheviks had had none of the essentials of a disciplined army, yet the Russians had made no effective advance.

LORD CURZON said at present there was no doubt that the Bolsheviks were in the ascendant militarily, and we had to consider how far we were responsible for this. The Czechs maintained that the position was due largely to the lack of decision and uncertainty of the Allied policy. As regards the non-Bolshevist groups inside Russia, there was no doubt they considered the invitation to the Conference at Prinkipo as a recognition of the Bolshevik Government on an equality with themselves. The Prime Minister had put before them three policies. That of a determined and thorough-going intervention was held to be impossible. Before deciding on the other extreme, a complete withdrawal, the War Cabinet should be perfectly clear that they were doing all they could in what he would call the bolstering policy. In any case, we could only provide forces for Russia by means of volunteers, not only British volunteers but men of other nationalities. M Scavenius[1] had mentioned to him the possibility of getting Swedish volunteers.

THE CHANCELLOR OF THE EXCHEQUER said that the question of finance had to be considered. President Wilson had made it clear that he was opposed to intervention of any kind, and the United States would take no

[1] Erik Scavenius, 1877–1962. Entered the Danish Foreign Ministry, 1901. Foreign Minister, 1909–10 and 1913–20. Minister in Stockholm, 1924–32. Foreign Minister for the third time, 1940–2. Prime Minister and Foreign Minister, 1942–5. In 1948 he published a defence of his policies in *The Negotiation Policy During the Occupation*.

financial responsibility, so that France and Great Britain between them would have to sustain the whole cost.

THE FIRST LORD drew attention to a letter from Colonel John Ward, which had appeared in the press, and which he said had made a great stir in the country. It conveyed the impression that the men in Siberia had been forgotten.

LORD CURZON said that a Blue Book was being prepared at the Foreign Office, containing an account of the Bolshevik activities in Russia.

THE SECRETARY OF STATE FOR WAR said he thought the War Office should be definitely instructed as to the policy to be pursued. They should be told either to intervene or to help the Russian forces with guns and equipment, or to withdraw.

THE PRIME MINISTER said that no alternative plans had been submitted to the War Cabinet. He thought that a paper should be submitted showing the military effect of the alternative policies. In addition, he would like to know the extent of the obligation we had undertaken in promising the protection of such States as Poland, Esthonia, and Lithuania. This was an obligation which America had also undertaken.

THE CHANCELLOR OF THE EXCHEQUER said there was also a political factor to be taken into consideration. He understood that no one believed that the non-Bolshevik Governments in Russia could by themselves stand for a moment.

THE PRIME MINISTER, continuing, said he would like to have the War Office Paper, which the Cabinet had now decided to ask for, in time for discussion on the next day. A request could then be made that it should be discussed in Paris on Friday. He thought it was essential that this matter should be decided before President Wilson left for America on Saturday. It was a question which could not be decided here in London, but they could send an expression of their opinion to Paris.

The War Cabinet decided that:—

> The Chief of the Imperial General Staff should prepare a statement showing the military effect which would ensue from the adoption of each of the following policies with regard to Russia:—
>
> (i.) Intervention.
> (ii.) Evacuation.
> (iii.) A middle policy of giving all possible help by way of arms and money to the anti-Bolshevik Governments of Russia.
> (iv.) The defence of all those States which depended upon the Great Powers for their protection.

Sir Henry Wilson: diary

(*Wilson papers*)

13 February 1919 — 36 Eaton Place

Cabinet at 12 o'c. Russia. I refused to give any opinion of how much chance we should have of beating the Bolsheviks if we back the Esthonians, Poles, Denikin etc. There are too many unknown quantities for me to offer an opinion. After great arguments then & again between 6 & 8 pm at H of C it was clear that neither LG nor the Cabinet would throw their hearts into beating the Bolsheviks by means of the Esthonians, Denikin etc & so I insisted there was only one course left and that was to clear out. So Winston & I are off at 5.30 am tomorrow morning by special to Newhaven & then Destroyer to Dieppe to *force* a decision in Paris tomorrow afternoon. . . .

I am all in favour of declaring war on the Bolsheviks, but the others, except Winston won't.

War Cabinet: minutes

(*Curzon papers*)

13 February 1919 — 10 Downing Street

THE SECRETARY OF STATE FOR WAR stated that there was no doubt that the only chance of making headway against the Bolsheviks was by the use of Russian armies. If Russian armies were not available, there was no remedy. Large British and French Armies were not to be thought of. There were already considerable Russian armies in being, amounting in all to 455,000, composed as follows:—

Archangel	25,000
Finland	35,000
Esthonia	30,000
Poland	30,000
Gen Haller[1]	30,000
Gen Denikin and Krasnoff	150,000

[1] Jozef Haller, 1873–1960. A Pole. Born in Cracow (then part of Austria). Served in the Austro-Hungarian Army, 1891–1918. In February 1918 he led his troops, who were mainly Poles, into the Russian lines. In July 1918 he left Russia (via Murmansk) to command the Polish Army in France; returned with his Army (of 50,000 men) to Poland, April 1919. Officer Commanding the Polish Volunteer Army, July 1920; commanded the Northern Front, August 1920. Retired from the Army, 1926. Active in Politics, 1926–39. Minister of Education in the Polish Government in Exile (London), 1940–3. He died in London.

Kolchak[1]	94,000
„	13,000
„	18,000
British	14,000

One of the extraordinary factors of the situation was that, while Poland was being pressed on all sides by the Germans and the Bolsheviks, there were 30 divisions waiting in France under General Haller which the Allies were being hindered from sending to Poland by improper representations made by the German authorities who refused to allow them transport over the Danzig–Thorn railway. In addition to this, the Russians had plans for trying to increase their armies. They were aiming at an army of 1,000,000. He was unable to vouch for their troops or plans, but unless a definite policy were materialised there was no use going on. Unless the Russian forces could be made into an effective army, the whole undertaking was impossible. He would put the following question to the General Staff:—Assuming the British Government were not prepared to send masses of men to Russia, and subject to that limitation, did the General Staff consider there was a sufficient prospect of getting the Russian armies into a fighting condition?

While he was not prepared to guarantee results, because we had to deal with Russians and their *moral* was not good, he felt that if we did not decide upon a policy we should have a succession of disasters, followed by wholesale massacres and the extermination in one way or another of the whole of the people who had been supporting us. If we were unable to support the Russians effectively, it would be far better to take a decision now to quit and face the consequences, and tell these people to make the best terms they could with the Bolsheviks, than to leave our troops there and continue without a policy. Prinkipo, whatever was thought of it, was a plan. He did not agree with it, but if it had succeeded it would have led to something. Assuming the Prinkipo was at an end something must take its place. He hoped it would be possible, before President Wilson left for America, to arrive at a decision.

THE PRIME MINISTER read a letter he had written to the British Empire Delegation, in which he had insisted that the Russian question should be discussed and decided one way or the other before President Wilson left. He had stated that if the Prinkipo proposition came to nothing we must decide

[1] Alexander Vasilievich Kolchak, 1870–1920. A Crimean Tartar by birth. Served in the Russian Imperial Navy. Led an Arctic rescue expedition, 1903. Played a leading part in the siege of Port Arthur, 1905. Vice-Admiral, 1916. Commander-in-Chief of the Black Sea Fleet, 1916–17. Minister of War in the Siberian 'All Russian Government' (anti-Bolshevik), 1918. Declared himself 'Supreme Ruler', with dictatorial powers, November 1918. Resigned the leadership of the anti-Bolshevik forces in favour of General Denikin, December 1919. Shot by the Bolsheviks at Irkutsk, 7 February 1920.

what the alternative was to be. It was unfair to the Russian peoples not to make up our minds, and a decision should not be made in President Wilson's absence. He was averse from going to Prinkipo to meet the Bolsheviks alone. On the other hand, the other Russian groups would not confer and could not fight. If Prinkipo was to be abandoned, President Wilson ought to share the decision and face the responsibility. It was pointed out that one of the conditions of the Prinkipo scheme was that fighting should be stopped, but the Bolsheviks, while accepting the invitation to go to the Conference refused to stop fighting.

Winston S. Churchill to Sir Henry Wilson

(Lloyd George papers)

13 February 1919

Will you please supply me, for the information of the Cabinet, with the answers which the General Staff give to the following questions. In giving these answers you are entitled to assume—

(a) that the Prinkipo Conference will not take place and that the Allied Governments will instead make a united appeal to all loyal Russians to exert themselves to the utmost against the Bolsheviks;
(b) that no troops can be sent from this country by compulsion to carry on the war in Russia.

As a variant to both (a) and (b), you should also assume that all the great allied Powers, except the United States, agree in (a).

QUESTIONS

(1) Within the limits aforesaid, what means are there of aiding the Russian Armies to wage war upon the Bolsheviks?

(2) What are the actual measures which the General would propose, generally and in each of the theatres? (But see also hereunder.)

(3) What numbers of non-Russian soldiers, and particularly of British soldiers, would be required?

(4) At what do you estimate the cost

(a) of obtaining and maintaining the British personnel;
(b) of maintaining the Russian Armies that are in the field or are required to be raised?

With regard to question (2), the following points of detail arise.

(a) Ought we to evacuate Murmansk and Archangel, and, if so, when and how?

(b) What assistance can be given by the British Fleet and Army to the Esthonians, and what other means are there of bringing them aid?

(c) In what way is Poland to be aided? Should it be assigned to the French? What is to be done with General Haller's army? If it should be sent to Poland, what steps are necessary to secure its prompt arrival? What are the causes of delay and what should we do to remove them?

(d) What is the rôle of the Roumanian French and Greek troops at & in the neighbourhood of Odessa? Could they be employed elsewhere with advantage? Could they, or any part of them, be exchanged with British troops in the Dobrudja? Would this be wise? Are there other more useful spheres of employment open to the French and Greek troops in this area?

(e) What is the present situation of General Denikin's Army, including that of General Krasnoff?

Would it be better for the French and Greek troops at and in the neighbourhood of Odessa to proceed directly to his aid?

What aid does he require?

What are we doing to help him?

Is there anything more that we can do?

(f) What is the precise rôle and present situation of the British forces holding the Batoum–Baku Railway, and of the British naval forces holding the Caspian Sea?

Could these forces be more usefully employed elsewhere?

To what extent are they aiding General Denikin's army by their presence?

Could they aid it in any more direct manner?

Would advantage result from reinforcing them with the remaining British troops in the Dobrudja?

Would it be contrary to British interests and would it be in accordance with your general scheme to entrust the custody of this railway to two Italian divisions?

Is there any reason to believe that the Italians are willing to undertake this?

(g) How far is our Trans-Caspian force dependent upon the Batoum–Baku railroad and the command of the Caspian?

What would happen to it if this line were sacrificed?

Could it be maintained if this line were not sacrificed but entrusted to the Italians?

What is the situation of the British Trans-Caspian force?

What measure do you suggest to increase and animate the Russian and Turkoman forces available for fighting the Bolsheviks in this theatre?

To what extent do you consider Indian interests involved?

(h) What is your policy for Siberia?

Is it contrary to British interests that the Omsk Government should (a) against our will, and (b) with our encouragement, come to terms with the Japanese in order to procure effective Japanese intervention in Western Siberia?

In what form and to what extent could British aid be given to the Omsk Government with ten or twelve thousand volunteers employed in technical offensive services of the highest order?

When would these be needed?

When do you think they could be supplied?

What arrangements do you recommend to improve the working of the Siberian Railway?

How would you propose to relieve the British units now compulsorily employed in this theatre and to replace them by volunteers?

What course do you propose to take about the Canadians at Vladivostock?

Are they any use? Are they likely to be of any use? If not, how soon could they be sent home?[1]

What other means are there of succouring the armies of the Omsk Government?

(i) Any other detailed points which may occur to you as part of the concerted scheme for waging war against the Bolsheviks.

Generally, after a comprehensive and detailed survey of the foregoing factors, do you consider that, assuming your requirements are met by the Governments concerned, there is a reasonable prospect of animating the Russian armies so as to secure success in the Summer and Autumn of 1919? If so what kind of success do you contemplate as possible.

Do you recommend HM Government to urge their allies to take part in such a campaign and to contribute towards it to the best of their ability themselves within the limits aforesaid?

WSC

Winston S. Churchill to Major-General J. E. B. Seely: telegram

(*Churchill papers: 16/4*)

15 February 1919 Paris

Secret

Resist strongly any proposal to remove any form of flying from control of Air Ministry. You should point out that the whole future of Air Ministry

[1] At this point Lloyd George himself wrote in the margin of Churchill's letter: 'Borden told me the Canadians will not stay in Siberia.'

depends upon its having the necessary body and substance which can only be supplied if, so far as the Government is concerned, functions of all kinds connected with the air are vested with it. On no account allow an adverse decision of this kind to be taken in my absence here. Make a direct appeal to Prime Minister to give me an opportunity of making my case known.

Philip Kerr[1] *to David Lloyd George*

(*Lloyd George papers*)

15 February 1919 Paris

Mr Churchill arrived yesterday afternoon, and attended a Meeting of the Council of Ten at which he raised the question of Prinkipo. President Wilson explained his views, which amount in substance to two propositions: (a) That he could not see what good the Allied troops were doing in Russia; he did not know for whom or for what they were fighting. (b) That he wanted above all to get information about conditions in Russia, and that he was prepared to send representatives informally to meet Bolsheviks or anybody else in order to enable him to get information on which to found a decision. I enclose the Minutes of the Meeting which indicate the course of the discussion. At the conclusion Mr Churchill asked whether the President would support active assistance to the anti-Bolsheviks in the event of the Prinkipo proposal failing to produce a settlement. Mr Churchill gathered that the President said that he would agree to this, but the Minutes are not so definite.

After the Meeting we had dinner with the CIGS and after some discussion Mr Churchill decided that he was going to propose to Mr Balfour that the Council of Ten should come to two decisions: first to publish a further statement following up the Prinkipo proposal and stating that an Allied Commission would go to Prinkipo provided hostilities were stopped on all fronts throughout Russia within, say, ten days; second that an Inter-Allied Commission be set up immediately to work out what military and economic action should be taken in conjunction with the neighbouring peoples of the pro-Ally armies in Russia to bring the Bolshevik regime to an end. This Commission was to begin its work immediately so as to enable the Supreme War Council to decide upon whether it would adopt an active anti-Bolshevik policy in the event of the Prinkipo proposal having failed ten days hence.

[1] Philip Henry Kerr, 1882–1940. Worked as a Civil Servant in South Africa, 1905–8. Editor, *The Round Table*, 1910–16. Secretary to Lloyd George, 1916–21. Secretary of the Rhodes Trust, 1925–39. Succeeded his cousin as 11th Marquess of Lothian, 1930. Chancellor of the Duchy of Lancaster, 1931. Chairman of the Indian Franchise Committee, 1932. Ambassador in Washington from 1939 until his death.

Mr Churchill asked me to make a draft of a note to the Bolsheviks; he also made one of his own. The CIGS drafted a proposal for the appointment of the Inter-Allied Commission. This morning the drafts were compared. There was a considerable difference between the two. Mr Churchill's draft was a departure from the original Prinkipo proposition, in so far as it was really addressed to the Bolshevist Government alone and made it a condition of coming to Prinkipo that the Soviet Government should notify the Peace Conference that it had ceased hostilities and withdrawn its troops for a distance of five miles within a stated period in which case the Allied Governments would invite pro-Ally forces to do the same. My draft followed the lines of the original Wilson proposal in that it was addressed impartially to both sides. It stated that the Allied Commission would go to Prinkipo provided a truce had been signed within ten days on all fronts, and it declared that the refusal to accept a truce proffered by the other side would be regarded as tantamount to a severance of relations with the Associated Powers. Mr Balfour saw both drafts and preferred Mr Churchill's. This, therefore, is the proposal together with that for the appointment of the Inter-Allied Military Commission of Enquiry which is going to be put before the Conference this afternoon by the British Delegates.

I am inclined to think that Mr Churchill's line as regard Prinkipo is the right one, provided it is drafted in such a form as to give every inducement to the Bolsheviks to accept the Armistice. The defect of the original Prinkipo proposal was that the Allies, while actually fighting side by side with Kolchak & Co against the Bolsheviks suddenly assumed an attitude of complete neutrality when addressing Russia from the platform of the Peace Conference. It would have been wiser, I think, from the start if they had addressed themselves direct to the Bolsheviks and informed them that if they accepted the proposal they would see that the pro-Ally Governments made an armistice also. Mr Churchill's proposal puts the project on this basis and thus gives the Prinkipo proposal a fair chance, provided the statement contains no suggestions or conditions which will make it difficult for the Bolsheviks to accept.

I will telephone and let you know the decision. I think the proposal as it stands now will bring the Prinkipo issue to a head one way or another. I also think that it is a good plan to work out in practical detail what the policy of intervention means in practice so that the Supreme War Council can take a decision with a plan in front of it. But I cannot conceal from you that in my opinion Mr Churchill is bent on forcing a campaign against Bolshevik Russia by using Allied volunteers, Polish and Finnish and any other conscripts that can be got hold of, financed and equipped by the Allies. He is perfectly logical in his policy, because he declares that the Bolsheviks are the enemies of the human race and must be put down at any cost. Personally as I think you know, I am against such a policy because, to my mind, it must lead to the Peace Conference taking charge of Russian affairs, and if they do that it will end in revolution in the West. The question, of course, will not arise for decision unless the Prinkipo proposal fails and until the Report of the Allied Commission has been received, but I think you ought to watch the situation very carefully, if you do not wish to be rushed into the policy of a volunteer war against the Bolsheviks in the near future.

General Harington to General Ironside

(*War Office papers: 106/1153*)

15 February 1919 War Office

As question of Russia is still under discussion at Paris we cannot give you definite statement of policy. You should therefore make preparation for an active defensive on the Dvina River pending further instructions. . . .

Winston S. Churchill to David Lloyd George

(*Churchill papers: 16/20*)

15 February 1919 Paris

At the close of the conference this evening, Baron Makino[1] asked me rather anxiously whether I had any news about the position in Siberia. I thereupon spoke to him in general terms about the goodwill with which we regarded the Japanese and the excellent position they were in to afford assist in operations against the Bolsheviks.

I pointed out that while all the other countries were tired, they were fresh; and that while we had no direct national object to serve in Siberia which would justify us in sending men there on a compulsory basis, Japan had great national interests in that part of the world which might well justify the employment of a national army raised on a compulsory basis.

I also said that at the Cabinet on Thursday, as a result of which I had been sent over to Paris, I had heard very cordial expressions used about Japan and very sympathetic language had been used about her general position.

[1] Nobuaki, Count Makino, 1861–1949. Educated at Tokyo University and in England. Japanese Minister in Rome and Vienna. Subsequently Minister of Agriculture, Commerce and Foreign Affairs. One of the Japanese representatives at the Paris Peace Conference, 1919. Grand Keeper of the Imperial Seals.

On the other hand I said that the present situation in Siberia was most unsatisfactory. The Siberian railway was so ill-organised that only one train was coming through a day and there were evidently lots of misunderstandings which were hampering effective action.

I said that in regard to the special military enquiry which it is in contemplation to set up on the Bolshevik problem, it was essential that Japan should play an important part.

He seemed to me quite willing to go further into these matters, but I thought it better to confine myself to the above generalities, which are probably not worth putting on record.

Winston S. Churchill to A. J. Balfour

(*Churchill papers: 16/20*)

16 February 1919 Paris

My dear Mr Balfour,

I cannot feel any doubt that we ought to accept the 15th February as the date when the Prinkipo offer definitely lapsed. There is every ground of fair play and consistency for this, and if we open up further overtures involving further delays, we may destroy the last remaining chances of military action.

I can come round and see you this morning if you like. My only engagement is Clemenceau at ten o'clock; but really I have nothing to say beyond what is in this letter.

Will you not send a telegram to the Prime Minister saying that we do not feel that Prinkipo can be kept alive after to-morrow's meeting? If I know that you have decided on breaking it off, I will send him a personal telegram further explaining the position.

If Clemenceau had not stopped General Albi,[1] I think he was going on to say, on behalf of the French General Staff, that forces were already within our reach which, properly handled, would break up the Bolshevik power. Then there is Beneš[2] and the Czecho-Slovak project. Then there are the

[1] Henri Marie Camille Edouard Albi, 1858–1935. Born in Marseille. Entered the French Army, 1878; Général de Division, 1914. Commanded the 34th Infantry Division, 1914–15; the 13th Army Corps, 1915–16. Director of Communications of the 5th Army, 1916–17; of the 4th Army, 1917. Inspector-General of the Reserve, 1917–18. Chief of the General Staff, 1918–20.

[2] Eduard Beneš, 1884–1948. Born in Bohemia, the son of a farmer. Educated in Prague, Berlin and London. A leading member of the Czechoslovak National Council, Paris, 1917–18. Czech Minister for Foreign Affairs, 1918–35; Prime Minister, 1921–2. President of the Czechoslovak Republic, 1935–8. In exile, 1939–45. President of the Czechoslovak National Committee in London, 1939–45. Re-elected as President of the Republic, 1945. Resigned, 1948. Author of many books and pamphlets on the Czech question. He published *My War Memoirs* in 1928.

Japanese and all the possibilities that may be open there. There are also the Roumanians.

I have been asking myself whether the Bulgarians might not be given a chance to relieve their past misdeeds, placing an army at our disposal to undo some of the harm they did to Russia by their ingratitude. Such an army of, say, three Bulgarian double divisions could be brought into action across the Black Sea in conjunction with Denikin's troops and far removed from any contact with Greeks or Roumanians. The Enos–Adrianople–Midia line[1] might be their reward.

I only set these ideas down to show how many pieces there are on the board, which, if all set in motion effectively and in concert, might very speedily alter the present disastrous situation.

All these proposals and the whole field ought to be examined without delay by the special Military Commission for Russian Affairs, which we must labour to have set up to-morrow.

A. J. Balfour to Winston S. Churchill

(*Churchill papers: 16/20*)

16 February 1919 Paris
Private

My dear Winston,

. . . I am most ready and anxious to back you up in any policy which you may decide upon in regard to Prinkipo; but I am reluctant to take the lead. The policy to be pursued is difficult, and must be determined largely by political instinct. I see great merits in the Prinkipo scheme from the point of view of English and American Public Opinion, but I am not the inventor of it, and never felt as enthusiastic about it as the Prime Minister, who was its author *and to whom all the credit of initiating it is due*. He has sent you over here because, having been present at the Cabinet Meetings where the whole subject was discussed at length, you are not merely acquainted with the paper arguments on either side but are bathed in the atmosphere which prevails in Downing Street, and have received directions immediately from there. I will of course, give you all the assistance in my power; but I think in the circumstances detailed above, you have no choice but to take the lead in.

Yours sincerely
AJB

[1] See Map 13, page 1990-1.

Winston S. Churchill to David Lloyd George: telegram

(*Churchill papers: 16/20*)

16 February 1919 Paris

Wilson's last words before leaving on Friday were that whilst anxious to clear out of Russia altogether and willing, if necessary, to meet the Bolsheviks alone at Prinkipo he would nevertheless, if Prinkipo came to nothing, do his share with the other Allies in any military measures which they considered necessary and practicable for the Russian Army now in the field. I consider this a very satisfactory note for him to end on and I conceive that we are entitled to count on American participation in any joint measures which we may entertain.

Accordingly special meeting at the Quai d'Orsay took place at 3 o'clock today on the Russian situation. At this meeting, with Mr Balfour's approval, I made the following two-pronged proposals.

First to wireless the Bolsheviks the message which is appended.

Secondly, simultaneously with sending of the message I proposed the setting up of an Allied Council for Russian affairs with political, economic and military sections. This Council should have executive power within the limit of the policy defined for this by the Allied Governments. Thus, a continuous and concentrated study of the Russian problem will be secured and that unity of command and control introduced into the Western theatre.

I also asked that this agreed upon, the military section should begin functioning at once. Broadly speaking it would have to answer the kind of composite questions I put, by the direction of the Cabinet, to the General Staff and it should be asked to make a report within the shortest possible time. Therefore if Prinkipo fell through the Supreme War Council should be presented immediately with a complete military plan and an expression of opinion from the highest military authorities as to whether within the limit of our available resources there is a reasonable prospect of success. The Supreme War Council would then be in a position to make a definite decision whether to clear out altogether, or to adopt the plan.

In the discussion which followed Clemenceau argued strongly that we should regard the Prinkipo proposals as having definitely broken down. In this he was very effectively supported by Sonnino[1] and also by the Japanese,

[1] Sidney Sonnino, 1847–1922. Born in Alexandria, Egypt, of a Florentine father and an English mother. Italian Minister of Finance, 1893–6. Twice Prime Minister of Italy for a hundred days, in 1906, and 1909–10; Foreign Minister, November 1914–June 1919. Second Italian Delegate (Orlando was the First) at the Paris Peace Conference, January–June 1919. Senator, 1920. A distinguished Dante scholar and bibliophile. When the Fascists seized power in October 1922 he looked on their movement with sympathy, but died a month later.

all three of whom expatiated on the harm done to the military position. Balfour and I pointed out the advantages to British public opinion of having made it clear to the whole world that we were doing our utmost to seek a termination of the bloodshed in Russia and to promote a peaceful solution, and that we should not make a sharp turn which would appear to be breaking off negotiations abruptly. Lansing[1] and House[2] were with us in this and Clemenceau would, I think, have agreed to the telegram or something like it with a few verbal alterations. But then it was pointed out by Sonnino that in our original Prinkipo invitation we had specified the 15th February as the date by which not only should all fighting have stopped but the Russian representatives including Bolsheviks should have actually arrived at Prinkipo. I was not aware of this having come newly into the business but it was evident that everyone felt very strongly that a perfectly fair and reasonable breaking-off point had been reached, that the Bolsheviks had spent the month in attacking us and were advancing with success on all fronts, that they had sent us a baffling and in some ways an insulting reply, that they had not made any attempt to come themselves and that none of the pro-Allied Russian Governments would meet them.

In view of this consensus of opinion we asked to adjourn the matter till Monday when both my two propositions will be given consideration. The details of our proposals are appended. I will wire you again tomorrow after a further talk with Mr Balfour.

Note please that I have made it perfectly clear throughout that we can in no circumstances send men by compulsion to Russia. Also the Cabinet should read the General Staff Memorandum of the 11th instant which was prepared in the Military Section in Paris, and is available in the War Office. Lastly I am seeing Clemenceau on Sunday about Constantinople.

[1] Robert Lansing, 1864–1928. Admitted to the American Bar, 1889. Specialist in international law and arbitration. Counsellor for the Department of State, 1914–15. Secretary of State, 1915–20. A Commissioner to the Paris Peace Conference, 1919. He published two books, *The Peace Negotiations* and *The Big Four at the Peace Conference* (both in 1921).

[2] Edward Mandell House, 1858–1938. Born in Houston, Texas. Personal Representative of President Wilson to the European Governments, 1914, 1915 and 1916. Special Representative of the United States at the Inter-Allied Conference, Paris, 29 November 1917; at the Supreme War Council, Versailles, 1 December 1917; and during the Armistice negotiations, 1918. United States Peace Commissioner, Paris, 1919. Member of the Commission on Mandates (London), 1919.

Winston S. Churchill to David Lloyd George: telegram

(Churchill papers: 16/20)

16 February 1919 Paris
Personal and Secret

After further careful consideration I think that it will be better not to send any wireless message immediately about Prinkipo. The original invitation fixed as the time limit February 15th and that has now expired without any result having been achieved. I do not see that we are called upon to show our hand immediately. It will be a more prudent course to set up the Military Commission at once to take stock of the whole situation, to prepare out of the resources which are available a plan of war against the Bolsheviks, to submit that plan when completed to Supreme War Council together with an expression of authoritative military opinion, as to whether it has reasonable chances of succeeding or not. It is in the light of the decision that the Supreme War Council will then take, that any further communication to Bolsheviks and other Russian Governments should be framed. I do not prejudge what the result of military enquiry will be, it may show that we have no means at our disposal for continuing the resistance with any hope of success. In that case we shall have to quit. If however a reasonable prospect of success is disclosed and it is decided to adopt the plan, then will be the moment to proclaim that Prinkipo has already lapsed as from February 15th and hearten up our allies by every means we can employ.

I have received a message from Mr Balfour that he wishes me to continue to take the lead in this matter here and that he will assist.

Unless I hear from you to the contrary I propose therefore to act in the sense here indicated.

The military enquiry should not take long and until it is completed we really do not know where we are.

David Lloyd George to Philip Kerr: telegram

(Lloyd George papers)

16 February 1919
10.40 pm
Very Urgent

See Churchill and tell him I like the telegram which it is proposed shall be sent to Bolsheviks. As to alternative programme I trust he will not commit us to any costly operation which would involve any large contribution either of men or money.

The form of his telegram to me looked rather too much like that. I had understood from his conversation with me that all he had in mind was to send expert details who volunteer to go to Russia together with any equipment which we can spare. I also understood that our volunteer army was not to be drawn upon for that purpose, and that the effort made to secure volunteers would not be on such a scale as to arouse vehement opposition in this country, involve us in heavy expenditure and interfere with the growth of our own volunteer army. All these things ought to be made clear to all the other powers before an agreement is arrived at otherwise they might either depend too much on us or subsequently reproach us with having failed in our promises. The main idea ought to be to enable Russia to save herself if she desires to do so, and if she does not take advantage of the opportunity then it means either that she does not wish to be saved from Bolsheviks or that she is beyond saving. There is only one justification for interfering in Russia, that Russia wants it. If she does then Kolchak, Krasnoff and Denikin ought to be able to raise a much larger force than the Bolsheviks. This force we could equip and a well equipped force of willing men would soon overthrow the Bolshevik army of unwilling conscripts especially if the whole population is against them.

If on the other hand Russia is not behind Krasnoff and his coadjutors it is an outrage on every British principle of freedom that we should use foreign armies to force upon Russia a Government which is repugnant to its people.

David Lloyd George to Winston S. Churchill: telegram

(*Churchill papers: 16/20*)

16 February 1919 London

Am very alarmed at your second telegram about planning war against the Bolsheviks. The Cabinet have never authorized such a proposal. They have never contemplated anything beyond supplying armies in anti-Bolshevik areas in Russia with necessary equipment to enable them to hold their own & that only in the event of every effort at peaceable solution failing. A military enquiry as to the best methods of giving material assistance to these Russian armies is all to the good but do not forget that it is an essential part of the enquiry to ascertain the cost. And I also want you to bear in mind that WO reported to Cabinet that according to their information intervention was driving the anti-Bolshevik parties in Russia into the ranks of the Bolsheviks.

I had already drafted a reply to be sent to Philip Kerr about your first telegram. I am sending that reply along with this. I adhere to it in its entirety. If Russia is really anti-Bolshevik, then a supply of equipment would enable it to redeem itself. If Russia is pro-Bolshevik, not merely is it none of our business to interfere with its internal affairs, it would be positively mischievous: it would strengthen & consolidate Bolshevik opinion. An expensive war of aggression against Russia is a way to strengthen Bolshevism in Russia & create it at home. We cannot afford the burden. Chamberlain says we can hardly make both ends meet on a peace basis, even at the present crushing rate of taxation; and if we are committed to a war against a continent like Russia, it is the road to bankruptcy and Bolshevism in these islands.

The French are not safe guides in this matter. Their opinion is largely biased by the enormous number of small investors who put their money into Russian loans and who now see no prospect of ever recovering it. I urge you therefore not to pay too much heed to their incitements. There is nothing they would like better than to see us pulling the chestnuts out of the fire for them.

I also want you to bear in mind the very grave labour position in this country. Were it known that you had gone over to Paris to prepare a plan of war against the Bolsheviks it would do more to incense organised labour than anything I can think of; and what is still worse, it would throw into the ranks of the extremists a very large number of thinking people who now abhor their methods.

I sincerely hope you will stand by your first proposals, subject to the comment which I have passed on them.

Please show these messages to Foreign Secretary.

Winston S. Churchill: draft Press announcemen

(*Churchill papers: 16/20*)

16 February 1919 Paris

The Allied and Associated Governments instituted a special military enquiry to be undertaken in common into the present military situation in Russia, with a view to advising the Supreme War Council at an early date.

The governing principle of this enquiry will be that the regeneration of Russia can only be achieved by Russians, and that the function and duty of the allies is limited to assisting the Russian Armies called into the field by the allies during the war against Germany to maintain themselves against Bolshevik coercion.

David Lloyd George to Winston S. Churchill

(*Churchill papers: 16/21*)

17 February 1919
12.30 pm

Have consulted with my colleagues. They approve of my telegram. They urge you not to commit this country to anything beyond what is contained therein.

Winston S. Churchill to David Lloyd George

(*Churchill papers: 16/20*)

17 February 1919 Paris

There is no difference at all between my second telegram and my first so far as the military enquiry is concerned. The limited character of our assistance will be clearly stated in accordance with your views, which I perfectly understand on this point. Other Powers will presumably say what they can do. Perhaps the Japanese can do much more than any of us. When all the available information has been sifted and weighed by the military authorities, we shall have their recommendation as to whether there is or is not a reasonable military hope. It is with this recommendation clearly before them that the Supreme War Council, probably a week hence, will have to make up its mind whether to go on or quit.

On reflection it seemed to me more prudent not to send the telegram which in all probability finally disposes of Prinkipo until we knew what the result of the military enquiry was. Otherwise we might be in the position of being unable either to fight or parley. My second telegram is really more tender towards Prinkipo than the first, because I am afraid to shut that door without being sure that there is another one open.

You need not be alarmed about the phrase 'planning war against the Bolsheviks'. As you pointed out at the Cabinet, we are actually making war on them at the present moment. All that is intended is to assemble in a comprehensive form possible means and resources for action, and to submit this report to the Supreme War Council.

Believe me I realize perfectly all your difficulties. I only wish I could see a solution of them.

Sir Henry Wilson: diary

(*Wilson papers*)

17 February 1919 Villa Majestic, Paris

Peevish wire in early from LG to Winston saying that country was in a dangerous state, that war against the Bolsheviks was impossible etc, etc.

Winston quite calm. I fancy LG is getting jumpy about the strikes.

Later in the day Winston & I found that LG had wired to Philip Kerr to send copies of these telegrams to Colonel House. This was a low down trick, as this general tenor showed that LG did not trust Winston.

Winston was very angry.

At mid-day we had a meeting of our own Imperial Council here and much talk about Russia & of course nothing settled. Borden[1] plainly said that he was going to withdraw his Canadians from Vladivostock leaving our 2 poor Batt^{n} in the lurch at Omsk. . . .

Then Tit Willow & I lunched & we discussed Russia. I really believe we shall be unwise to march in against the Bolsheviks.

Then we had Supreme Council in Pichon's[2] room at 3 o'c. We discussed Russia & whether we should submit the problem to MRs at Versailles. House objected to this, AJB backed House, Clemenceau exploded. House said neither American men nor material would be allowed to go to Russia. Tiger said that being so the other Powers would discuss Russia without America. He said it was a pitiful thing to see the victors of the Boches afraid to refer the Russian problem to Versailles. Both Winston & I & Sonnino were entirely in sympathy with Clemenceau. I said nothing but Winston spoke a little & well.

And so in the end it was agreed that each country should ask its Military Adviser who should report separately, no Joint Note being allowed. I think this is the greatest depth of impotence I have ever seen the Frocks fall.

I advised Winston to go home as he was doing no good here & would get tarred, so he went tonight.

[1] Robert Laird Borden, 1854–1937. Canadian Prime Minister, 1911–20. Knighted, 1914. First Overseas Minister to receive summons to Meeting of British Cabinet, 14 July 1915. Representative of Canada at Imperial War Cabinet, 1917–18. Chief Plenipotentiary Delegate of Canada at the Paris Peace Conference, 1919. Represented Canada on Council of League of Nations. Chairman of Sixth Committee of the League Assembly, 1930.

[2] Stephen Pichon, 1857–1933. Radical Deputy, 1885–93. Ambassador to Haiti, 1894; to Brazil, 1896; to China, 1898–1901. Resident General, Tunis, 1901–6. Senator, 1906–24. Three times Foreign Minister: October 1906–February 1911; March–December 1913 and November 1917–January 1920. One of the signatories of the Versailles Treaty.

Philip Kerr to David Lloyd George

(*Lloyd George papers*)

17 February 1919

Your various telegrams and messages about the importance of not drifting into war against the Bolsheviks have been received and have I think had their effect. There was a meeting of the BED on the Russian situation this morning at which Mr Balfour set forth very much your view. The discussion showed pretty clearly that everybody was agreed that effective war against the Bolsheviks was probably impracticable because of public opinion at home, and that it was probably undesirable on its merits because it would strengthen Bolshevism at home. On the other hand there was a concensus of opinion, I think, that it would be very undesirable to allow the Bolsheviks to over-run Siberia and the small communities along its borders & so gain a great access of strength & a huge territory. There was also a general agreement that it was desirable to have a careful investigation made of what it would cost in men, money and equipment, to maintain the anti-Bolshevik forces more or less in their present positions.

In accordance with your instructions I showed copies of your telegrams to Colonel House. Colonel House said that he entirely agreed with your view, except that he was opposed even to the appointment of a Commission of Enquiry because it would certainly be boomed by the French as the beginning of an anti-Bolshevik war which in turn would produce anxiety among the working classes in England and America, which would force both the British and American Governments immediately to declare their Russian policy. He also asked me to say that the principal object of his policy was to prevent the Germans and the Russians being driven together for that would inevitably mean a great aggressive combination stretching from Yokohama to the Rhine. He thought the French anti-Bolshevik policy would drive straight to this result and he could not imagine what possessed them in advocating it. He was in favour of keeping in touch with the Bolsheviks with the object of gradually bringing them to terms, restoring Allied influence in Russia and so composing the peace.

I told both Mr Balfour and Mr Churchill that I was showing your telegrams to Colonel House because you wished him to know what your views were. Mr Churchill was very indignant at this on the ground that it revealed to the Americans the internal disagreement of the British Government and made it seem as if you had not confidence that he would represent your views. I told him that I was certain that there was no such idea in your mind, that you regarded Colonel House as a friendly member of a body which was responsible for working out the peace of the world and that you habitually communicated documents to the other members of the Conference. I said that I was certain that you had no idea of showing the slightest want of confidence in him, but that your sole object was that Colonel House should understand your personal attitude towards the whole question of intervention. The question is before the Conference this afternoon and Mr Churchill will probably return to London tonight. I have no doubt that the Conference will declare against an active Bolshevik policy. Mr Balfour is against it, so are the Americans and so is Clemenceau. The latter's idea is to maintain a barrage against the Bolsheviks on their existing line, because we have not the strength to do anything else.

Colonel House: diary

(*House papers*)

17 February 1919 Paris

Although Churchill had received his instructions from Lloyd George, he was persistent in pushing his plan for a military committee to examine the question as to how Russia could best be invaded in the event it was necessary to do so. I opposed this plan with some vehemence. . . .

Balfour told me yesterday that he intended to let Churchill lead on this question because he, Churchill, was sent over to Paris as a representative of the War Cabinet to do so. He said it could not do to have both Downing St and Paris handling the same question. It either had to be done by Paris meaning himself, or by Downing St, meaning Lloyd George and the War Cabinet.

Winston S. Churchill to David Lloyd George: telegram

(*Churchill papers: 16/20*)

17 February 1919
Personal and Secret

This afternoon I proposed the formation of a military commission to enquire into what measures were possible to sustain the Russian armies we had called into being during the war with Germany and to protect the independence of the border States.

The Americans who had had the advantage of reading your telegrams to me made difficulties even in this, expressing fears that even setting up a commission to enquire into the military situation might leak out and cause alarm.

Mr Balfour therefore proposed that no formal commission should be set up but that the military authorities might be allowed informally to talk together and, instead of presenting a report to the Conference as a whole, might individually hand to their respective representatives on the Conference a copy of the results of their informal and unofficial conversations.

After Clemenceau had commented on the strange spectacle of the victorious nations in this great struggle being afraid even to remit to the study of their military advisers at Versailles a matter admittedly of vital importance to Europe, this project was agreed to.

You are therefore committed at some date in the near future to receiving an informal document embodying certain military opinions bearing upon Russia. You are committed to nothing else.

Winston S. Churchill to David Lloyd George: unsent letter

(*Churchill papers: 16/21*)

17 February 1919 Paris

I understand perfectly your view as conveyed in your two telegrams, and nothing which I am doing or going to do will commit you to anything inconsistent with it or beyond it. But I do hope you realise that, as soon as the Military Commission has reported (which ought not to be more than a week) you will have to take a definite decision one way or the other.

As Secretary of State for War under the present arrangements, I am not responsible for anything beyond carrying out the policy you settle and providing you with the means for carrying out such a policy. If after receiving the military report you decide to clear out of Russia with or without your allies, orders will immediately be issued and action will follow as fast as is physically possible.

I will not dwell on the odious character of the events which will follow, because it is obvious. There will be no peace in Europe until Russia is restored. There can be no League of Nations without Russia. If we abandon Russia, Germany and Japan will not. The new States which it is hoped to call into being in the East of Europe will be crushed between Russian Bolshevism and Germany. Germany will regain by her influence over Russia far more than she has lost in colonies overseas or provinces in the West. Japan will no doubt arrive at a somewhat similar solution at the other end of the Trans-Siberian Railway. In five years, or even less, it will be apparent that the whole fruits of our victories have been lost at the Peace Conference, that the League of Nations is an impotent mockery, that Germany is stronger than ever, and that British interests in India are perilously affected. After all our victories we shall have quitted the field in humiliation and defeat.

This is an unpleasant prospect, and before embracing it I think you should be fortified by the strongest military opinion showing that no other course is open, that the situation is hopeless, that the Russian armies are quite useless and that there are no means at our disposal of animating and sustaining them—that there is nothing for it but to let things rip and take the consequences.

I think it quite possible that the military report will be to this effect, and that it will be clear that, as the great nations will not fight with large national armies to restore Russia, it is not worth while keeping alive the embers of Russian resistance. To do that would only be to prolong the agony.

On the other hand, the military report may show that there is a reasonable possibility of success. But still, in spite of that report, you may decide to quit. This would be, in my opinion, a decision more difficult to defend before history, but still it would be a decision quite open for you to take and which only you can take. What would be utterly indefensible would be to come to this truly awful decision without accurate, comprehensive and authoritative military advice. That I am sure you will not wish to do.

There is also a minor point on which the War Office is bound to have a direct responsibility, viz, if it is decided not to support John Ward and Co actively by every means in our power, they have got to come away at once.

I could not take the responsibility of leaving these men unsupported to their fate after the policy which sent them there had been definitely abandoned. Therefore, there seems to me to be no escape from the dilemma—fight or quit; get on or get out.

I think you will see that I am taking a level and detached view of the position. I am carefully avoiding forming any opinion on the military aspect, and I have told Henry Wilson to be on his guard not to let the wish be father to the thought. I have also, in order that your hands may be absolutely free, tried to keep Prinkipo from being finally ruled out until the result of the military enquiry is known. If we cannot fight, I suppose we ought to parley. Perhaps if we gave the Bolsheviks boots, clothing, food and money they might be willing to show mercy to Kolchak, Denikin and Co. I am not at all sure, however, whether the House of Commons would approve of this. It seems to me very probable that they will neither supply the means to fight nor the authority to negotiate.

I have also been doing my best to maintain a consistent line on your Prinkipo policy. It has no friends here now that President Wilson has gone, and Colonel House announced himself opposed to it. Sonnino and Clemenceau are infuriated with it. Makino deposed that it had prejudiced the military situation in Siberia. Balfour, in private, disowns it. All the military men without exception condemn it. But if we cannot fight or will not fight, it is no doubt logical that we should sue for peace on the best terms that we can get for ourselves and those we have brought into the field.

You must forgive me putting these cruel facts before you when you have so many anxieties and burdens to bear. I am sure your courage will not shrink from facing them in their ugliest aspect.

Winston S. Churchill to Sir Henry Wilson: telegram

(*Churchill papers: 16/21*)

19 February 1919 War Office

Yesterday I saw Prime Minister, who quite understands the situation. He did not intend that his telegrams should be shown to Colonel House but only that his general views should be explained to him. He does not wish to make war on the Bolsheviks. He is, however, quite willing to help the Russian armies on the lines specified provided that it is not too costly. On this point he wishes to be particularly informed. He was entirely in opposition to the cutting off of supplies from Kolchak, Denikin and Co as he considered that since we called them into the field for our own purposes in the German war we were bound to help them in this way. End of Prime Minister's views.

You must consider the effect on public opinion if the outrage on Clemenceau is traced to a Bolshevik source.[1]

I do not like any time limit being fixed to the support of Denikin and Kolchak. Denikin's victory appears to be of importance and surely it will not be honourable to sell these Russian armies in order to secure a frontier for the new states. In my opinion the two matters are wholly separate.

You may show this to Mr Balfour privately.

[1] On 19 February 1919 a 23-year-old Frenchman, Emile Cottin, shot at Clemenceau. Fearing a Bolshevik plot, the French police at once raided houses where French Bolsheviks were known to live. But during Cottin's trial, which began on March 15, it became clear that there was no Bolshevik connection. Cottin was in fact an anarchist who had been imprisoned three times for anti-militaristic speeches and inciting soldiers to disobey orders. He was sentenced to death, and shot.

David Lloyd George to Winston S. Churchill

(Churchill papers: 16/21)

20 February 1919 10 Downing Street

My dear Secretary of State,

I have read Sir Henry Wilson's paper on Russia and your covering Memorandum, & I quite agree with what you say in the latter as to 'how essential it is that the Allies should have a definite policy' and 'how indispensable it is that there should be some decision'. But may I remind you of one or two facts which are not irrelevant in this connection?

1. The War Office have repeatedly been asked to prepare a statement showing clearly to the Cabinet what any one of three alternative policies would mean in men, material, money. In spite of repeated requests no answer has been given to either of these three questions. The document that came to my hand late last night is only a partial reply: nothing is said about cost, and there are notable gaps even as to men and material. For instance, take (c):—

> '*Denikin's forces* . . . We may also find it necessary to help in the re-establishment of railway communications, both for military and economic reasons.'

What does that mean in men, material, money?

Take (d). This ignores altogether the proposal made by the military members of the Supreme War Council, that Italy should occupy this territory. Why is nothing said about that? The recommendation was made weeks ago.

As to the cost of the suggestions put forward, it is no use ignoring this all-important element in policy. The Treasury is experiencing the greatest difficulty in meeting essential demands for housing and land settlement for soldiers, and the burden of annual expenditure even on a peace footing will tax the resources of this country to the utmost. And the question of whether any given policy means millions or tens of millions or hundreds of millions ought to weigh in our decision. I have tried for weeks to get from the WO some estimate which would afford me any guidance. The Cabinet have urged the same consideration. It is no use clamouring for policy until the War Office, which alone is in possession of the facts and the technical experience, can supply us with this information.

May I also point out that in so far as a policy is possible without this information, very definite instructions in writing were given you when you went to Paris to represent the Cabinet at the Allied Conference on Russia. I understand that Mr Balfour left the matter entirely in your hands. You do not seem to have succeeded in securing any decision. I certainly suggest no blame to you. I am not even criticising the Allies. They also want facts & estimates of cost and it seems that they have so far been as unsuccessful in obtaining guidance for their military men as we have been with ours.

There is an extraordinary reluctance in the War Office to supply us with any information. A week ago the King asked me to obtain information for him as to what steps we were taking in Esthonia, and what support we were giving to *Kolchak*, *Denikin* and the other anti-Bolshevist forces. Surely there must be some ledger easily accessible to an intelligent clerk which will supply the necessary particulars as to guns, ammunition, rifles, medical supplies and other equipment which has been sent by us to these various forces.

Ever sincerely
D. Lloyd George

Winston S. Churchill to Sir Henry Wilson

(*War Office papers: 32/5383*)

20 February 1919 War Office

As I understand the position, we are about to confront Germany with the definite terms of a preliminary peace, which she will either have to accept or face the denunciation of the armistice with a corresponding advance of our armies into German territory; and this will take place in the course of the next ten days.

I can readily understand that it is right to keep the blockade going until we know one way or another what she will do, but surely if she submits to the conditions of the preliminary peace which we dictate, the blockade should be raised, and we have no right whatever to go on starving the great mass of German women and children.

I cannot at all agree that this is a right and proper thing to do once the conditions of the preliminary peace have been accepted. The reports which you showed me of the condition of the people in Hanover are particularly distressing, and there is a great deal of evidence of this sort from other quarters that I have seen.

It seems to me barbarous in the last degree to prohibit the German fishing fleet from going out to catch fish for almost starving people, and I am not prepared personally to make myself responsible for defending the continuance of this system indefinitely. Things must be brought to a head, and either the war must be resumed, or conditions of peace must be reached which are satisfactory for us and give the German people some chance of life and work. . . .

Winston S. Churchill to David Lloyd George

(*Churchill papers: 16/4*)

21 February 1919 War Office

I do not know how long it will be necessary to keep an army on the Rhine: that must be settled in Paris by the Allied Powers. I should think that our 10 divisions would be required to stay there for more than a year, perhaps two years. But of course the Cabinet can withdraw them at any time if they so desire it after notifying our allies. This would entail the handing over of the Cologne Bridgehead to the French, the Americans or the Belgians.

As long as we are represented in the armies of occupation, compulsion will be necessary. There is no possibility of maintaining 10 divisions in Germany on a voluntary basis. The first thing we have to do with our volunteers is to relieve the garrisons of India. Even that cannot be done for six or seven months at the earliest.

Naturally we are not going to keep an army on the Rhine until the indemnity is paid, but only till such time as the state of Europe and the execution of the Peace Treaty lead the Allied Powers to the conclusion that no international force is required.

(2) There is no chance of my creating a volunteer army to garrison the British Empire, to provide for Ireland and internal order at home before peace is signed. 300,000 or 400,000 men are required, and so far I have 35,000. Therefore quite apart from the army of the Rhine, I must retain men *after* the signature of the peace but in diminishing numbers and for a limited time.

(3) I do not contemplate an immediate transition from war to peace, but a gradual descent step by step while things are settling down. The basis of my policy is the practical requirements of the year 1919, nothing more and nothing less.

(4) With regard to Russia, you speak of my 'Russian policy'. I have no Russian policy. I know of no Russian policy. I went to Paris to look for a Russian policy. I deplore the lack of a Russian policy, which lack may well keep the world at war for an indefinite period and involve the Peace Conference and the League of Nations in a common failure.

All I am doing is carrying on from day to day, guided by such indications as I receive from the War Cabinet, for whose decisions I naturally have no responsibility beyond my departmental duty.

We have troops in various parts of Russia which were sent there before I came to the War Office. Whatever is settled, some of these troops cannot get away, as at Archangel and Murmansk, until July. Others cannot be withdrawn without grave risk of breaking up the Russian armies with whom they are serving and which were called into the field by us for our own purposes during the period of the war with Germany. This is the situation at Omsk. In the Caucasus we have 4 brigades, mainly composed of your Indians, holding the Batoum–Baku railway, and the Admiralty have 8 small armed ships on the Caspian, which it is believed secure the command of that great inland puddle. These troops are not in contact with the Bolsheviks, but they are a certain support for General Denikin's army, which you will observe has recently gained an important victory, taking 31,000 prisoners and much materiel.

Until I receive instructions to withdraw these various troops and let the Russian situation crash to the ground, I must do my best to nourish them and sustain them. But it is very difficult, in view of the indecision of the Cabinet and the ignorance of the public; and so far I am not responsible for sending a single man to Russia.

If it is decided that we are to go on helping Denikin, Kolchak and Co, I shall organise specially certain volunteer units to help the Russian armies with the technical services you mention, and I shall try to replace the conscript troops now in Russia by these technical volunteer units gradually and so as to avoid a sudden collapse.

I may add that it is clear to me that you are altogether failing to address your mind to the real dangers which are before us. As long as Russia is in chaos there will be no peace in Europe and no economic revival. Without Russia the League of Nations is a farce and no Peace Treaty can be anything but provisional. Russia will certainly rise again, perhaps very swiftly, as a great united empire determined to maintain the integrity of her dominions and to recover everything that has been taken away from her. While this process is going on Europe will be in a perpetual state of ferment. The belt of little States we are now calling into being will be quaking with terror and no doubt misconducting themselves in every possible way. Germany and Russia will have miseries and ambitions in common and their mighty national interests will be struggling for expression and restoration. When we have abandoned Russia, she will be restored by Germany and Japan, and these three Powers together will constitute a menace for Britain, France and the United States very similar to that which existed before the present war. The position of India in face of such developments is not an enviable one, and I wonder that with your vision you have not perceived the danger.

Sir Henry Wilson: diary

(*Wilson papers*)

21 February 1919 36 Eaton Place

I gave Winston my Russian proposals which, he said, were most cold blooded. He talked much wild nonsense about sending 6000 men each to Denikin & Kolchak. I believe my proposals are the sanest, & best that can be made in a very difficult & complicated case.

The King sent for me at 6.30 & talked about Russia for an hour & of the necessity taking & feeding Petrograd!

Sir Henry Wilson: diary

(*Wilson papers*)

22 February 1919 36 Eaton Place

Another talk with Winston about Russia. I saw Finlayson[1] this morning back from Archangel. He says Ironside must know end of March whether he is to quit Archangel or not otherwise he will get into a mess.

I told Winston that we really *must* be given a policy.

Winston S. Churchill to General Harington

(*War Office papers: 32/5679*)

22 February 1919 War Office

It is the business of the general staff to continually be exploring all the possibilities of a military situation without regard to the political limitations which Governments may find it necessary to impose on military action. . . .

We may live to regret bitterly the opportunities and resources we are losing through the present indecision.

[1] Robert Gordon-Finlayson, 1881–1956. Entered Army, 1900; Major, 1914. Served on the western front, 1914–18. Colonel, 1918. Served in North Russia, 1918–19. Military Assistant to Sir Henry Wilson, 1921. Brigadier-General, War Office, 1922. Major-General, Commanding Rawalpindi District, 1931–4. Knighted, 1937. Lieutenant-General, Commanding the British Forces in Egypt, 1938–9. Adjutant-General to the Forces, 1939–40. Commander-in-Chief, Western Command, 1940–1. Special Commissioner, Imperial War Graves Commission, 1942.

Sir Henry Wilson: diary

(*Wilson papers*)

23 February 1919 36 Eaton Place

Another talk with Winston about Russia. I am now putting up a further paper about all the theatres in Russia advising delimination in the west, evacuation at Archangel, instructional staffs *only* with Denikin & Kolchak & handing over Trans Caucasia to Italy.

Sir Henry Wilson: diary

(*Wilson papers*)

24 February 1919 36 Eaton Place

Winston cordially agreed with the whole of my Russian papers and proposals, & has now written a covering note & it is all printed & goes to the Cabinet on Wednesday. At the Cabinet this morning we did nothing but discuss coalminers & Railway strikes. I hope the miners strike as I think now they would have the whole country against them.

War Cabinet: minutes

(*Cabinet papers: 23/9*)

24 February 1919

MR CHURCHILL said that there were several questions, viz, Treatment of Conscientious Objectors, New Army Bill, and Policy in Russia, which, if practicable, he would like the War Cabinet to consider on the following day. The question of what was to be our policy in Russia was an urgent one, since the position in this connection was more or less the same as it had been six weeks before.

After a short discussion as to the urgent questions which had to be considered by the War Cabinet on the following day—

THE PRIME MINISTER said that, with reference to our policy in Russia, the matter had been discussed three times at Paris. It was not the fault of the British delegates that no definite decision had as yet been arrived at. The question was one which must be discussed at Paris, since it was not a question of coming to an agreement with one Government, but the views of the representatives of five different Powers had to be taken into account. The policy of the British Government had been agreed upon and actually stated in writing. The further discussion of the matter was being held over until his return to Paris, and he would then press for the adoption of the policy which had been decided on by the War Cabinet, in the first instance, as being the best to pursue.

MR CHURCHILL said that the Chief of the Imperial General Staff had prepared four proposals for giving effect to the Cabinet policy. What he wanted the War Cabinet to do was to approve of certain measures being taken. There might be a serious disaster at Archangel in the coming spring unless an early decision were come to.

THE PRIME MINISTER asked whether, if, as proposed, the question were discussed, the War Cabinet were to be invited to take a different view to that which they had already agreed upon. The question of our policy in Russia was one which could only be usefully discussed in conjunction with our Allies.

Winston S. Churchill to Sir Hugh Trenchard

(*Trenchard papers*)

24 February 1919

On no account *stir* till you are well. I have put off the Air Estimates till next week, & the other matters can wait or be adjusted in yr absence. Everyone is being bowled over.[1]

War Cabinet: minutes

(*Cabinet papers: 23/9*)

25 February 1919

THE SECRETARY OF STATE FOR WAR was of the opinion that our external debts in countries like the United States should be included in the claims for reparation. Our debt to America was over 1,000 millions. We had depended upon the United States for food and raw materials, and we had managed to get these commodities on account of the credit which we had built up in that country. The damage to our finances and our trade that had thus been incurred was just as real as the material damage to France and Belgium. He thought our external debts should have priority next to claims for reparation for concrete instances of destruction. France, too, was in debt to the United States, and he thought that it would be a good thing if Germany could take over our debt and the French debt to the United States.

[1] Trenchard was suffering from a severe attack of influenza, from which he nearly died. Later the influenza epidemic was to hit the Churchill household (see page 614).

War Cabinet: minutes

(*Cabinet papers: 23/9*)

26 February 1919

THE SECRETARY OF STATE FOR WAR suggested that our policy in Russia should be discussed before the return of the Prime Minister to Paris. The War Office had circulated a paper on the subject (GT–No 6885).

THE PRIME MINISTER thought it would be of very little use discussing this question here, since France, the United States, Italy, and Japan were all concerned. He knew the Cabinet's views, and he would press those views at Paris.

THE CHANCELLOR OF THE EXCHEQUER said there were one or two questions in connection with our policy in Russia which he would like to mention. The first was in connection with our troops in the Caucasus and at Baku. We went to these places in the first instance on our own initiative. From Admiralty reports which he had seen it was very doubtful if, from the point of view of oil and supplies, our occupation of Baku was likely to lead to any useful results, and he suggested that it ought to be terminated as soon as possible. The whole situation in the Caucasus was very mixed. The second point which he would like to mention was in connection with the support which we proposed to give General Denikin's army. There was a great deal to be said for our supporting Denikin, providing he undertook merely to fight Bolshevism, but he was also attacking Georgia. The proposal made by the CIGS was to send men to the number of one or two thousand; this was rather different to helping with military equipment and stores and a few experts.

LORD CURZON said that one of the conditions which we had made with Denikin was that he was to fight against Bolshevism and not against Georgia and Armenia.

THE SECRETARY OF STATE FOR WAR said that what he wanted was a definite policy laid down as to what our action should be in each locality.

THE PRIME MINISTER said the Cabinet was quite clear as to what policy should be pursued, but the cost was a determining factor, and it was for the War Office to say approximately what each of the alternative policies proposed by the Cabinet might cost. It was very important that he should have this information before returning to Paris.

THE SECRETARY OF STATE FOR WAR said that every effort was being made by the War Office to provide this information, and to estimate the cost of the minimum requirements in each case.

The War Cabinet decided—

That the War Office should submit, before the return of the Prime Minister to Paris, a paper showing the approximate expenditure which might be involved by each of the alternative policies suggested by the Cabinet.

Winston S. Churchill to David Lloyd George

(*Churchill papers: 16/21*)

27 February 1919 War Office

I send you herewith a statement of British assistance given to Russia, which, as you will see, is considerable. The criticism that may be passed is that it is related to no concerted policy, and that while it constitutes a serious drain on our resources it is not backed with sufficient vigour to lead to any definite result. There is no 'will to win' behind any of these ventures. At every point we fall short of what is necessary to obtain real success. The lack of any 'will to win' communicates itself to our troops and affects their morale: it communicates itself to our Russian allies and retards their organisation, and to our enemies and encourages their efforts.

With regard to your complaint that the War Office have not furnished you with information, I must point out to you that the War Cabinet have long been accustomed to deal direct with the Chief of the Staff and other military authorities, and they know as well as I do the difficulties of obtaining precise plans and estimates of cost from military men in regard to this Russian problem. The reason is that all the factors are uncertain and that the military considerations are at every point intermingled with political decisions which have not been given. For instance, to begin with what is fundamental, the Allied Powers in Paris have not decided whether they wish to make war upon the Bolsheviks or to make peace with them. They are pausing midway between these two courses with an equal dislike of either.

You refer to my mission to Paris. I proposed that a definite military enquiry should be set on foot and pursued from day to day by the Great Powers to frame a plan for making war on the Bolsheviks, utilising every available resource, and I thought that when this plan was made, the Governments would be in a position to decide whether they would adopt it and drive it through with all their strength and faith or whether on the other hand, they would reject it and boldly face the alternative policy.

You objected however even to the use of the words 'prepare plans for making war on the Bolsheviks'. Even armed with yr fullest authority & power this task wd have been a vy difficult one. The informal military enquiry evaporated without producing any tangible result. The military men are unable to deal with this Russian problem without the clearest political guidance.

I had previously, in a desire to secure for the Cabinet such information as our War Office can supply, drafted a questionnaire, a copy of which I have circulated to the Cabinet. I now send you a memorandum completed by the General Staff wh gives most of the information in a somewhat different form. Further, in order to reduce as far as possible the uncertain factors in this question, I have asked the Chief of the Staff to make definite proposals for action. These are now before you. You are aware that they do not embody the policy which I would pursue myself. They are only an attempt within the limits prescribed by you to meet the immediate practical needs of the situation so far as it affects British commitments and British interests in the absence of any decision being taken by the allies as to war or peace.

You now ask that the cost of these measures should be estimated, and I enclose herewith the best estimate which it is in the power of the War Office to make and which can only be put forward subject to the reserves which are clearly stated.

Lastly, I must quote the decision of the War Cabinet (515) of the 10 January in which it is clearly shown that you conceived yourselves to be fully equipped to obtain at Paris the main decisions from the allies on Russian policy, and that you realised that this was the first matter that should be dealt with. Since then nothing whatever has been decided. I recognise the necessary difficulties of the problem & the minimum pressure of events: but I do not feel that the War Office is to blame.

It is necessary in my opinion that you shd go to Paris & with the necessary War Office assistants hammer out a policy & force by yr personal authority the Allies or some of them to come to an agreement on the critical political & military aspects. No one below you can do it.

In the meanwhile I ask for approval of the makeshift policy put forward by the CIGS in the paper lately circulated.

War Cabinet: minutes

(*Curzon papers*)

28 February 1919 — 10 Downing Street

THE SECRETARY OF STATE FOR WAR said that the contents of the Papers had caused him some surprise, as the French apparently envisaged the permanent control of the Rhine bridgeheads. He noticed that Marshal Foch made no attempt to estimate the size of the International Force, and before the Government gave their considered reply to these proposals he suggested that it would be as well to find out:—

(a) What size the force was to be:
(b) Whether the United States would contribute.

The size of the force should, of course, be sufficient, in the event of a sudden German attack, to stem the avalanche long enough to enable the bridges to be destroyed and the main international Army to be mobilised. Mr Churchill then urged upon the Cabinet the necessity of winding up all military matters with the least possible delay. All the intelligence received by him was to the same effect, that cruel privations were being suffered by the German people at the present time. He himself wished to see Germany treated humanely and adequately fed, and her industries re-started. He had little patience with the cranks of various kinds who denied that Germany suffered any privations at all, and advanced exaggerated claims for indemnity. He thought that the step proposed by Marshal Foch might prove to be a wise one, subject to America bearing her share, but, as stated above, we must not, in his view, decide whether to endorse this policy until we had ascertained the intentions of the United States. It was highly desirable, in his opinion, that in handling this question we should show ourselves as sympathetic as possible to the French, for two reasons: first, in order that she might show herself accommodating in regard to our own Eastern policy; and, second, to enable us to acquire great influence over France and the Peace Conference generally, with a view to the adoption of a merciful policy towards Germany. Incidentally, he suggested that France might feel a greater sense of security if we would meet her wishes in regard to the construction of the Channel Tunnel.

THE PRIME MINISTER enquired whether it was conceivable that a force consisting of less than 150,000 men could hold the bridgeheads. Such a force must be able to withstand the enemy's onset for at least 48 hours, and if the United States, France and Great Britain made equal contributions to that force they would each have to supply at least 50,000 men. He doubted very much whether the country would be prepared to supply a permanent garrison of this size for the Rhine, when troops at any moment might be needed in India and elsewhere. He wished to ask what was the Foreign Office view of the proposition to set up a separate German Republic West of the Rhine, the Republic to be entirely disconnected from Germany East of the River; and also of the further proposition that Germany should be compelled to relinquish all idea of union with the Germans of Austria. His own mind had not been made up on the matter, and he would like to discuss the whole question with the Cabinet before he returned to Paris. At present he inclined to the view of the Secretary of State for War, that we should give France all possible support in respect of her claims and desires in the West, so long as those claims did not leave a legacy of injustice which would rankle as Alsace-Lorraine had rankled. M Clemenceau loved his own country just as he hated and feared Germany, and he was not particularly concerned about the East. One of M Clemenceau's ambitions was to see a small independent republic, which would comprise the whole of the coalfields, to be set up West of the Rhine, to be entirely independent of Germany and to be controlled, but not annexed, by France. . . .

THE SECRETARY OF STATE FOR WAR thought that Germany would get to work quietly producing munitions and completing her plans, but she would only come into the open when we and our present Allies or associates began to quarrel, as might unfortunately be the case in future. There was no doubt that the Republican Party in the United States was bent on disentangling their country from Europe, one result of which might be that one day they would start competition in armaments. He thought that there was a serious danger that, unless Peace came soon, Russia and Germany might make common cause. They were both in the pit of misery, which men in each country attributed to the folly shown in fighting each other. If they joined together it might have grave consequences in the future.

David Lloyd George to Winston S. Churchill

(*Churchill papers: 16/4*)

28 February 1919 — 10 Downing Street

Dear Secretary of State,

I have just seen a telegram from Constantinople, which rather suggests an intention on the part of Brough[1] to commit us to the responsibility for a debt of fifteen million roubles incurred by the Georgian Republic to the Corporation of Baku, and a further liability of three million roubles per month. This seems to me to be quite unjustifiable unless much stronger reasons are urged for it than appear in this telegram. But it is an indication of what I fear will inevitably occur if we continue to occupy and accept the responsibility for the government of these regions. Please let me know what reply you have sent to GHQ, Constantinople.

Yours sincerely,
D. Lloyd George

[1] Alan Brough, 1876–1956. Entered Royal Engineers, 1895. Major, 1914. On active service, 1914–18. Lieutenant Colonel, 1918. Served in South Russia, 1919–20 (awarded the CBE). Assistant Director of Engineering, War Office, 1927–31; Director of Mechanization, 1932–6. Retired with the rank of Major-General, 1936.

March 1919

David Lloyd George to Winston S. Churchill

(*Churchill papers: 16/5*)

1 March 1919 10 Downing Street

My dear Secretary of State,

You will have seen the disquieting telegram that has just come in from Admiral Webb,[1] Constantinople. The French are becoming quite intolerable. The third power in point of strength, they want to create the impression that they are the first in point of authority. We cannot allow our men to be ordered about in the East where prestige is more essential to us than in any other quarter of the globe. Franchet d'Esperey must be told quite peremptorily that if he meddles Milne[2] will be put under Allenby and will not even nominally acknowledge the former's authority. What did you tell Clemenceau about this business? . . .

Ever sincerely
D. Lloyd George

[1] Richard Webb, 1870–1950. Entered the Royal Navy, 1885; Captain, 1907. Director of the Trade Division, Admiralty War Staff, 1914–17. Commanded HMS *New Zealand* in the Grand Fleet, 1917–18. Rear-Admiral, 1918. Assistant British High Commissioner to Turkey, 1918–20. Knighted, 1920. Rear Admiral, 4th Battle Squadron, Mediterranean Fleet, 1920–2. Vice-Admiral, 1924. Head of the British Naval Mission to Greece, 1924–5. President, Royal Naval College, Greenwich, 1926–9.

[2] George Francis Milne, 1866–1948. Entered the Royal Artillery, 1885. Commanded a battery at Omdurman, 1898. Served on Kitchener's Intelligence Staff in South Africa, 1900–2. Brigadier-General, commanding the 4th Division artillery, 1913–14. He took part in the battles of Le Cateau, Marne and Aisne, 1914. Lieutenant-General commanding the British forces at Salonika, 1916–18. Knighted, 1918. Commanded the British Forces at Constantinople (Army of the Black Sea), 1919–20. General, 1920. Chief of the Imperial General Staff, 1926–33. Field-Marshal, 1928. Created Baron, 1933. He wrote no account of his military experiences, and destroyed most of his personal diaries.

Winston S. Churchill to David Lloyd George

(*Churchill papers: 16/5*)

2 March 1919 War Office

My dear Prime Minister,

I have to acknowledge your two letters of the 28th February and the 1st March.

You will see from the enclosed telegram that the point you raise in the first letter about Brough was dealt with spontaneously by the department as you would have wished.

Since you have written to me about this telegram, I should like to let you know that since I have been at the War Office I have studied very carefully all the telegrams that are passing, and I have asked that in important cases they should be shown to me before they are sent off. On the other hand, as you no doubt realise, the War Cabinet is accustomed to deal directly with the General Staff and that frequent consultations have taken place, both here and in Paris, at which I have not been present. Further, Curzon's Eastern Committee habitually consults the Chief of the Imperial General Staff and gives him direct orders which he executes. In these circumstances I consider that I have hitherto been an observer rather than a responsible actor.

I have no hesitation in saying that in my view we ought to clear out of the Caucasus as soon as possible. Having stayed there so long, we may as well wait until at any rate a provisional decision is given at Paris as to the fortunes of the Georgians. It is also important that our warships should remain on the Caspian until in any case Denikin has taken Astrakhan and has taken control of the mouth of the Volga. But once he is there, I really do not see why we could not come away, even if the Italians are not willing to take our place. If we came away, however, I think we ought to make it up to Denikin by sending him the strong mission of officers and sergeants which I have already advocated.

This is the policy which I should enforce if the matter were left in my hands, and for which I would in these circumstances take a full measure of responsibility.

On your instructions, I telegraphed a fortnight ago to General Milne ordering him to use every method of courtesy to the French but in no circumstances to give way to these improper demands. When I went to Paris, I saw Clemenceau and told him quite plainly what I had done under your direction. I also told him that we had conquered Turkey and not the French, and that it had been understood that we were to have the prime position in Constantinople during the peace negotiations. He fired up at this and asked me if there was any part of the world in which we did not think we should have the prime position. I replied that the Valley of the Sarre was one place at any rate. He then got quite friendly, handed me a long paper of complaints against our officers which he had already prepared, and asked that Balfour and I should meet him and Pichon the next day or the day after to come to a friendly arrangement about the whole business. I reported accordingly to Balfour, who said that all the documents relating to these matters were in London and that he knew nothing about it and could not argue the case, which could only be dealt with by Curzon from the Foreign Office. I therefore took no further action.

On my return to London I learnt from the Chief of the Imperial General Staff that he had been summoned over to the Foreign Office and had received from Lord Curzon certain directions, to carry out which he has gone to Paris and is returning to-day. I will let you know when I have seen him how the matter stands.

Again in this field the policy clearly is for you to come to a firm understanding with Clemenceau, linking the settlement of the French frontiers with the arrangements which should be made in the East.

I am making arrangements to come to Paris on Friday, but unless you require me at your side as your lieutenant in these quasi-military affairs, it would be better for me to stay here, where I have plenty of very interesting work to do.

I should be very grateful if you would let me come and talk to you to-morrow morning for about a quarter of an hour about my speech introducing the Army Estimates, which comes off to-morrow afternoon.[1]

What about those young fellows who are pressing me on Russian matters. Would it not be a very good thing for us both to lunch with them on Wednesday and have a friendly private talk? Are they not a class of your supporters with whom you ought to be in personal touch?

[1] When Churchill introduced the Army Estimates in the House of Commons on 3 March, he appealed to the House to support the Government in maintaining a strong Army on the Rhine until it could be seen more clearly how things were going to shape. He underlined the exceptional difficulty of framing the Army Estimates when the country was half-way between peace and war. As regards demobilization, he said that the Government's plan was to release three men out of four, and to pay the fourth man double to finish the job.

Sir Hugh Trenchard to Winston S. Churchill

(*Churchill papers: 16/5*)

3 March 1919
Confidential

Dear Mr Churchill,

Instead of being better I feel rather worse and I feel it would be better for the Air Force if I tendered you my resignation as CAS.

I do not think I have the guts to pull it through now. I am played out and I am sorry I took the job as it must be most inconvenient to you. It is worrying me very much indeed and I feel that there are many things not going right until you have put in my successor.

Perhaps in six or nine months time if I have recovered I can be of use in a small way again, but at present I feel I am not fit to do work. The doctor does not think I shall be fit for 3 weeks or a month or maybe longer.

Yours sincerely
Hugh Trenchard

Winston S. Churchill to Sir Hugh Trenchard

(*Churchill papers: 16/5*)

3 March 1919
Private

My dear Trenchard,

I appreciate warmly the motive wh prompts you to write as you have done. I think after all yr hard work you ought to take a month or six weeks leave & then let me know how you feel. There is not the slightest difficulty in carrying on for that time. In any case I cd not think of losing yr greatly valued services until I was satisfied you were physically unfit.

I do not believe for a moment that you will not be in good health & spirits long before the six weeks I prescribe are over.

I am looking forward so much to working with you; but you must really get quite fit before you come back.

Winston S. Churchill to Lord Birkenhead

(*Churchill papers: 16/5*)

[March 1919]

Advice to the Crown about the appointment of Ministers comes from the Head of the Government, and the question of the combination of one or more offices in the hands of a single Minister is likewise a matter for which the Prime Minister is responsible. It is therefore on his behalf, and in the name of the Government as a whole, that the present arrangement whereby the Seals of the Secretaryships of War and Air are held by a single Minister must be justified.

The policy of the Government is to maintain the separate and independent character of the Royal Air Force. Every step that has been taken in the course of the present year has been taken with that end in view. There is no question of subordinating the Royal Air Force to the Army or to the Navy or of splitting it into two and dividing it between the Army and the Navy. In order to emphasise the distinct and independent character of this branch of the fighting services, uniform and ranks and titles have been deliberately differentiated from those prevailing in the Army and the Navy.

The whole organisation of the Air Force as a separate force, and of the Air Ministry as a separate ministry, has proceeded without intermission. A complete scheme for the post-war organisation has been elaborated during the year and is now very far advanced. When the Estimates for 1920 are introduced it will be possible to lay before the House this scheme in full detail, and it will then be seen that all the varied functions of the Royal Air Force and its complex organisation have been fully provided for, including its work with the Navy, its work with the Army and its work as an independent strategic factor. We have aimed throughout the year at creating a separate permanent Air Service affording as good a career and as good opportunities of advancement to officers and men as either the Army or the Navy.

On the other hand, the Prime Minister decided, in forming the present Administration, that the scale, size and cost of the Royal Air Force in the years immediately following the great war would not be sufficiently large to justify the appointment of a separate Secretary of State. Many arguments have been used showing the importance of restricting as far as possible the number of Ministers forming the Cabinet. Already the complication of our business and the increase in the number of Departments has raised the total number beyond what many people thought would be desirable. A separate Cabinet Minister for a force which cannot in the immediate future be in size or cost more than a sixth or seventh the size of the Army or the Navy could not be justified. It may well be that in the years that are to come the importance of the Air Force will grow at the expense of the other two Services, until possibly, as some people think, it will take the prime place in our defensive organisation. The present arrangement would then naturally lapse, and nothing that has been done is inconsistent with a separation of the offices. The importance of economy and of modest establishments during these next few years is well known, and this entails the Air Force being restricted to limits which do not justify a separate Secretary of State. To have a separate Air Minister and to include him in the Cabinet would create an anomalous position in regard to at least half a dozen other offices which for practical purposes have just as great weight and importance at the present time, and this would make the organ of Government altogether unwieldy.

There are two other important reasons, special to the present year and the next year, which render the combination of the offices desirable. First, the demobilisation of the Army and the Air Force had to proceed simultaneously. They were intermingled in the fighting forces in every theatre of the war. Their general demobilisation problems were practically identical. Uniformity and simultaneity of practice so far as possible were indispensable. Differences in practice in such matters would have multiplied the already large but inevitable list of grievances and hard cases which the processes of demobilisation in so many different theatres of war all over the world has entailed. The Navy was in a different position. It was not mixed up with the Army, and, further, the Navy had only made a moderate expansion during the war, was entirely self-contained, and therefore differences of practice in regard to demobilisation did not cause hardship and complaint to anything like the same extent than as between the Army and Air Force. Even so, some difficulties have been experienced from this cause alone.

Secondly, we have not only to demobilise the Army and the Air Force. We have to reconstruct and redistribute the fighting forces by which our Empire is maintained. The garrisons of Palestine, Mesopotamia and India have to be reconsidered from the point of view of the new technical inventions which the war has produced and of the general advance in the science of war. This is a problem which must be studied in its integrity. If we are to derive the economies in man-power, and consequently in expense, which should follow the increase in the power of scientific weapons and especially from the great usefulness of aeroplanes in maintaining order and suppressing revolts in these large oriental regions, it is essential that the problem of the new distribution of our fighting forces, both on land and in the air, should be studied from a single point of view. It will be found when the Estimates for next year are presented and when the Government policy in regard to the

Army and the Air Force is laid fully before Parliament, that this combination of the Air Force and of the Army has been attentively studied and made fully effective.

Of course it may be said that this line of argument, carried to its logical conclusion, would involve the Navy as well as the Army and the Air Force. There are some who have criticised the present arrangements—indeed those who are the most perspicacious critics of the present arrangement point to such a combination of the three Services as the true solution. Incidentally, that is General Seely's point of view. It is not, however, possible to take all these steps at the same time. At any rate it may be said that the present arrangement goes two-thirds of the way on that road; and no step has been taken which is in any respect inconsistent with a complete scheme under which the Army, the Navy and the Air Force would all figure as separate Services within a common organisation of Defence, and would possess a joint Imperial General Staff, or War Staff, consisting of officers who would not look at war from a departmental point of view as land officers, sea officers or air officers, but would be able to increasingly tender advice to the executive Government on defence problems viewed as a whole.

Lord Haldane to Winston S. Churchill

(*Churchill papers: 16/5*)

4 March 1919 28 Queen Anne's Gate
Westminster

My dear Winston,

I have read your admirably conceived and executed speech.[1]

I am sure that it is right to proceed by carefully divided stages, and to take abundant time before deciding on the final stage. The form when that stage is reached will depend on a precise ascertainment of the purposes for which the Army is to be wanted, & this you cannot determine for some time to come. But you can lay down your method of procedure & this you have done with lucidity.

[1] On 3 March 1919 Churchill introduced the Army Estimates to the House of Commons. Despite the victory of November 1918, he said, Britain was still only 'half way between peace and war'. His speech continued: 'The greater part of Europe and the greater part of Asia are plunged in varying degrees of disorder and anarchy. . . . The victorious Allies, on whom there rests the responsibility for enabling the world to get to work again, are themselves exhausted in a very serious degree; and all these elements of difficulty and uncertainty vitiate or threaten to vitiate our calculations.'

On questions of fundamental organisation you have a very good reserve man to consult in Ellison,[1] if he has not forgotten his old cunning.

With best wishes, Yours vy sincerely
Haldane

Winston S. Churchill to Louis Loucheur

(*Loucheur papers*)

4 March 1919

My dear Loucheur,

I take great pleasure in the very beautiful medal which you have sent me. I shall value it both for its remarkable workmanship and as one more token of the lasting regard which we formed for one another during our long & fruitful association at the French & British Ministries of Munitions.

Yours very sincerely
Winston S. Churchill

Sir Henry Wilson: diary

(*Wilson papers*)

4 March 1919

War Cabinet. I gave my opinion on the Rhine frontier saying it was the strongest for the French but 80 miles longer than Lorraine & Belgian frontiers & requiring about 15 Div[s] of Allied Troops. Failing this frontier I thought the Rhenish Provinces ought to be de-militarized. The Cabinet were unanimous in writing the Rhine out of the question. . . .

Cabinet harmonious about clearing out of Archangel & Murmansk, & also Caucasus.

[1] Gerald Francis Ellison, 1861–1947. Entered the Army, 1882. Joined the Army Headquarters Staff, 1890; Staff Captain, 1894. On active service in South Africa, 1899–1900. Director of Organization, Army Headquarters, 1908–11. Staff Officer, to the Inspector-General of Overseas Forces, 1911–14. Major-General, General Staff, 1914–15. Deputy Quarter Master General, Gallipoli, 1915. Major-General, Administration, Aldershot, 1916–17. Inspector-General of Communications, and Deputy Quarter Master General, War Office, 1917–23. Knighted, 1919. Lieutenant-General, 1923.

War Cabinet: minutes

(*Cabinet papers: 23/15*)

RUSSIAN POLICY

4 March 1919

With reference to War Cabinet 537, Minute 2 THE SECRETARY OF STATE FOR WAR enquired whether the Cabinet were prepared to inform him more definitely as to the policy they intended to pursue with regard to Russia.

THE PRIME MINISTER said that he would take the earliest opportunity on his return to Paris to get the matter discussed by the Peace Conference. The general intention of His Majesty's Government was to withdraw the armies from every part of Russia as soon as practicable and then to supply Russian commanders who were friendly to the Allied cause with guns, aeroplanes, munitions and everything that might be of use, except troops and money.

THE SECRETARY OF STATE FOR WAR said that as regards Murmansk and Archangel, it would be impossible for climatic reasons for us to evacuate the Forces there until June. In the meantime, however, we must take steps to see that our Forces in both places receive proper reinforcements. Further we should have to supplement our detachments at those ports in order that the withdrawal, when carried out, should be properly conducted. It was most important that everything should be done to ensure a safe and orderly evacuation when the time came. With a view to his being in a position to make adequate arrangements he pressed for a decision on two points:—

(a) Were we to withdraw as soon as the weather permitted, and
(b) If we were to evacuate were we also to undertake the removal of inhabitants who were friendly to us?

As regards the Caucasus, how long were our troops to remain there? Was it to be until the League of Nations had decided the fate of Georgia? Further, in respect of the Caspian, what did the First Lord intend to do with the Fleet he was at present maintaining there? If we cleared out of the Caucasus how should we 'make it up to' General Denikin?

THE DEPUTY CHIEF OF NAVAL STAFF [Admiral Fremantle[1]] said

[1] Sydney Fremantle, 1867–1958. Entered the Royal Navy, 1881. Rear-Admiral, 1913. Served at the Dardanelles, 1915. Commanded the 9th Cruiser Squadron, 1916; the 2nd Cruiser Squadron, 1917; the Aegean Squadron, 1917–18. Deputy Chief of the Naval Staff, Admiralty, 1918–19. Knighted, 1919. Vice-Admiral commanding the 1st Battle Squadron, 1919–21. Commander-in-Chief, Portsmouth, 1923–6. In 1949 he published his memoirs, *My Naval Career 1880–1928*.

that the Admiralty fully recognised that whatever policy HM Government adopted, a heavy responsibility rested upon the Navy. A considerable flotilla, which includes six monitors, a repair ship, several special river craft, etc, with about 2,400 naval ratings, was to start at once for the northern parts of Russia in order to arrive at Murmansk by the 1st May, if possible. The composition of the Flotilla had been determined with a view to meeting either eventual evacuation or a further advance. Last year we had been overpowered on the river, and it was for this reason that a substantial number of river craft formed part of the flotilla. The dangerous period would be the five or six weeks following upon the 1st May when the river would be open but the White Sea would be closed.

THE PRIME MINISTER said that figures were an essential element when a Government was called upon to decide its policy in a case of this kind. He had only just been put in possession of figures showing the cost of all these various Russian commitments. It appeared that for our Military Forces only, including transport, no less than £73 millions were required for a period of six months. If the cost of naval requirements were added, the total cost would be 150 millions sterling per annum, for what were after all very insignificant operations.

THE CHANCELLOR OF THE EXCHEQUER [Austen Chamberlain] said that he would not challenge the charges for the naval purposes as our vessels would be required equally whether we decided to evacuate or advance. He himself felt that there was no question that we ought to withdraw from North Russia, subject to our Allies' consent. So far as the Caucasus and Caspian were concerned, we had no obligation to our Allies, and he could not see that any British interests were being served by our presence there.

THE FIRST LORD OF THE ADMIRALTY [Walter Long] agreed that an early decision was required as to whether we were to evacuate North Russia or not.

THE SECRETARY OF STATE FOR WAR said that he himself was not responsible for the present situation, and he was still uncertain as to what the Cabinet wished done. He understood that authority had been given to take whatever naval measures might be necessary for the protection of our naval forces in North Russia. He claimed that he equally should be authorised to take adequate military measures to support and reinforce the men we had in North Russia until they could be withdrawn. The sooner he was informed of the Government's policy the sooner he could start on the preliminary arrangements. Unless he was given the authority he required from the Cabinet, he was deeply apprehensive that the consequences might be absolutely disastrous. His own wishes were:

(a) To evacuate North Russia in such a way that a catastrophe would be avoided.
(b) To evacuate the Caucasus, subject to a date agreed upon in Paris.
(c) 'To make it up' to General Denikin, and for this purpose he proposed to send a Military Mission for the General's assistance. This would mean withdrawing about 30,000 men, and sending instead 1,800 NCO's and others who would act as instructors.
(d) To send a similar Mission to Admiral Kolchak and to recall the battalions now in Siberia under Colonel John Ward.

He regarded all these as reasonable propositions, and if our friends in Russia failed to maintain themselves with such assistance as he suggested, he did not think we could be blamed.

THE ACTING SECRETARY OF STATE FOR FOREIGN AFFAIRS [Lord Curzon] thought they were all agreed so far as North Russia was concerned, and suggested the Cabinet should authorise the naval and military authorities to take all necessary measures to ensure an efficient evacuation. As regards the Caucasus, he suggested that the Eastern Committee, which still survived in another form, should be instructed to submit to the War Cabinet a series of proposals as regards a possible evacuation, indicating its political and other consequences. The case of Georgia had been mentioned. He wished to point out that public opinion in Georgia was not unanimous in regard to the occupation of the country by Allied troops. He would remind the Cabinet that Armenia was trying to establish a Republic, whose precarious existence was only being sustained by the presence of British troops.

THE CHIEF OF THE IMPERIAL GENERAL STAFF said that he would be glad if the Acting Secretary of State for Foreign Affairs would obtain from our representatives in North Russia the numbers of such friendly inhabitants as it might be incumbent upon us to remove.

THE PRIME MINISTER said that he fully concurred with his colleagues in thinking that the evacuation of Murmansk and Archangel was desirable at the earliest opportunity. He would press this policy upon the Peace Congress on his return to Paris. As regards the Caucasus, he would welcome the suggestion of the Acting Secretary of State for Foreign Affairs that the matter should be discussed, and proposals put forward by the Eastern Committee, but he trusted that these proposals would be put forward in such a way that the hands of the British Delegates in Paris would be in no way tied.

The War Cabinet decided:—

(a) That their policy should be to press for the early evacuation of Murmansk and Archangel and to authorise the Secretary of State for War to make the necessary preliminary arrangements.

(b) To ask the Prime Minister to communicate the policy of HM Government as set out in the above discussion to the other British Delegates in Paris.

(c) To ask the Secretary of State for War to circulate to the War Cabinet the paper he had prepared showing the cost of maintaining our forces in the various centres in Russia.

Winston S. Churchill to Sir Henry Wilson

(*War Office papers: 32/5682*)

4 March 1919 War Office
Secret

CIGS

I am expecting to receive from you a statement of the forces you require to cover a withdrawal from Archangel & Murmansk & to maintain the full security of our troops there till we decide to go. Will you consult with AG & let me have definite proposals together with a time table.

I will then do my utmost to meet yr requirements.

Winston S. Churchill to General Radcliffe and General Harington

(*War Office papers: 32/5682*)

5 March 1919 War Office
Most Secret

I am extremely anxious about the Archangel position. In view of the Cabinet's decision yesterday that we are to prepare for evacuation in June, I wish to receive at the earliest date definite plans for such an operation prepared by the Generals on the spot and carrying with them the approval of the General Staff.

I wish the Generals on the spot to know that they are free to claim reinforcements, etc, for the purpose of covering the operation of withdrawal.

I wish to know what steps are necessary and possible with regard to removing the Russian population who have compromised themselves on our behalf. Where are they to go after they have been removed, and what are we to do for them when they have been so removed?

I wish to see a definite time table for this operation prepared with the necessary latitude.

What is the situation of the aeroplane attack which is to be made on the Bolshevik steamers on the higher waters of the Dwina? I understand that if a vessel can be provided on the 10th March at Sheerness, she could take the machines which the Air Ministry have provided. What are you doing about this? It is your responsibility in the first instance. Do not let it be said that these machines were held up because the Shipping Controller could not provide the ship. If I am informed that this is the difficulty, measures will be taken to secure that a ship is supplied; but unless I am warned in good time these delays occur. What is the time table of this air operation?

It seems to me that we ought to be preparing without delay a force of 5,000 or 6,000 men who could be sent if necessary to extricate these North Russian expeditions. What sort of force would be most useful? How would it be organised? Clearly it must be a first charge on the men who are now volunteering for general service in the volunteer armies.

The AG should submit a scheme, prepared in conjunction with the General Staff, which would enable the assembly of such a force to be begun without the slightest delay. It is not necessary even to wait for the reports of Generals Ironside and Maynard. I obtained the authority of the Cabinet yesterday to embark at once on the preparation of this force. If it is not needed subsequently, all the better. Having regard to the fact that men volunteering are entitled to leave, I wish to know whether we have as many as 5,000 or 6,000 now available. There is no need to tell these men where they are going at this stage. The thing is to form them into these special battalions and see that they are kept in the best of order and good spirits.

When would the first battalion be ready? I want a time table showing the dates at which these units will be respectively completed.

Ought we not to continue passing battalions from Murmansk to Archangel in a steady trickle according to the full capacity of the communications, and ought not these battalions to be replaced one after another by the new units we shall be raising which we could put into Murmansk?

What news is there of the special ships which can break the ice and go straight into Archangel? How does that matter stand? How many men could they carry? How many voyages could they make in the time available before we are to expect heavy enemy attacks.

I am certain that we are in increasing danger on this front. Do you observe that Trotsky[1] has stated that he intends to wipe out the Archangel and

[1] Lev Davidovich Bronstein, 1879–1940. Son of a Jewish farmer. Studied mathematics at Odessa University, 1896. Gave up his studies to devote himself to revolutionary activity. Exiled to Siberia, 1898; escaped to England, 1902, with a forged passport in the name of 'Trotsky'. Jointed the Mensheviks against Lenin, 1903. Returned to Russia, 1905. Again deported to Siberia, he again escaped, to London, in 1907. In exile in Vienna and Paris. Expelled from Paris, 1916, he went to New York. Returned to Russia, 1917, where he was

Murmansk forces and clear the coast? Sometimes such statements are all bluff, but in the present condition of the Bolshevik forces it might help them to say beforehand that they could do a certain thing—well knowing that they have the power to do it—and then to make good later on.

I am extremely anxious about this position, and from day to day my anxieties increase. We have now got our authority from the War Cabinet to go ahead making preparations, and I have announced to Parliament and pledged the War Office to leave no stone unturned, and therefore I wish that a most intense effort shall be made and pressed forward, having as it were a first charge on all our interests and resources, in order to secure the effective execution of the Government policy in a manner not incompatible with the honour of our army.

I should like also to be able to raise the morale of our men out there by promising them definitely in a message direct from me that they will either be relieved by volunteers from England or withdrawn altogether as soon as Archangel is open, but that in the meanwhile their safety depends upon their exertions, and that if they are to see their homes again they must, for their own salvation, observe the strictest discipline and fighting energy.

Let me have a full report, through the CIGS, on all this with the least possible delay. Let me have subsequently a weekly report of progress and of any items hampering progress.

Winston S. Churchill to Sir Henry Wilson

(*Churchill papers: 16/15*)

5 March 1919 War Office

We are to acquiesce in the withdrawal of the Canadian troops from Vladivostock.

I think a letter should, however, be drafted to Mr Borden which in courteous terms brings out clearly the fact that in this respect British troops have not received the support from their Canadian comrades in this adventure which they had a right to expect.

Perhaps you will think over this. It should certainly be put on record.

---

reconciled to Lenin and became head of the Petrograd Soviet. Directed the armed uprising of 7 November 1917. Commissar for Foreign Affairs, 1917–18; for Military Affairs, 1918–25. Expelled from the Communist Party by Stalin, 1927. In exile in Turkey (1929), Norway (1936), and Mexico, where he was assassinated, almost certainly on Stalin's orders.

Winston S. Churchill to General Seely

(*Churchill papers: 16/5*)

5 March 1919 War Office

My dear Jack

Trenchard continues seedy and so, I am sorry to say, do you.

I have to go to Paris on Friday, and shall probably be away during the week with the Prime Minister. I therefore told the Whips to put the Air Estimates off till Thursday, the 20th, which will give us more time to put our house in order.

I think the expense will cause a shock, following as it does upon the enormous demands of the Army and also the Navy Estimates, which touch nearly 150 millions. Everything must therefore be done to try to a reasonable figure. I have provisionally approved the estimates on a basis of 100 squadrons and 27 millions expenditure, apart from 37 millions liquidation charges.

I am very anxious that a start should be made with the Baghdad permanent air station, as well as with the Cairo and Karachi stations, and I think we ought to take money in the Estimates for these purposes, cutting off the set sum from other heads so that the aggregate is not exceeded.

I propose that you should introduce the Estimates, and I will keep myself in reserve to explain any general point that may arise in debate. It is essential that you should devote yourself in the first instance to showing the progress which has been made in liquidating the Ministry of Munitions production.

You will see the fuss that is being made in the 'Times' about civil aviation. I presume that it is due to the Treasury holding up the proposals. Will you give this matter your attention.

Interdepartmental Conference:[1] *minutes*

(*Foreign Office papers: 371/3661*)

6 March 1919 Foreign Office
Secret

MR WINSTON CHURCHILL said he was in favour of the quickest possible evacuation of our troops from the Caucasus, and at the same time of giving Denikin the support of a Military Mission, and of munitions and

[1] This Conference was held under the Chairmanship of Lord Curzon. Also present were Churchill, General Radcliffe, Admiral Fremantle (Deputy Chief of the Naval Staff), Captain Coode (Director, Operations Division, Admiralty), John Shuckburgh (India Office), G J Kidson (Foreign Office), J Y Simpson (Foreign Office) and S D Waley (Treasury).

arms, provided he did not pass a certain line which we could fix. In his opinion such definite support would be of far greater assistance to Denikin in his struggle against the Bolsheviks than the mere presence of our troops on the other side of the Caucasus.

But, before we evacuated, the situation at Astrakhan and in the Caspian must be cleared up, and measures must be taken to prevent the cutting off of our troops at Krasnovodsk. Once rid of the Astrakhan fleet our own ships could be handed over to Denikin as part of the mission. He would, therefore, like to see the Admiralty proposals with regard to Astrakhan brought off as early as possible, and hoped at the same time to see Denikin move up and hold the line (and especially the mouth) of the Volga. It would then be possible to hand over the ships and at the same time make a convention with Denikin as to the conditions on which he would continue to get our help. One of the conditions, of course, should be the guarantee of Georgia's independence. He thought that Denikin would be likely to accept the conditions laid down by us because, without our help in arms and ammunitions, and without our military mission, he would be found to fall. He considered that while these naval operations in the Caspian were going on, the War Office should draw up a plan for evacuation on, say, a 3 or 3½ months' scale, and proceed to carry it out. As to Georgia, Azerbaijan, Daghestan, and the other small States, he really did not see what British interests were involved. There seemed to be no doubt that as soon as Russia revived they would be reconquered, and once more form a part of the Russian Empire; what happened in the interval did not affect us, for we had no interests there.

THE CHAIRMAN [Lord Curzon] said the policy of the Secretary of State for War was clear and intelligible, but it appeared that he was really only interested in Denikin, and was indifferent to the New Republics of the Caucasus. Mr Churchill was inclined, in his opinion, to over-estimate our hold over Denikin; with Batum and Baku within his grasp it seemed unlikely that he would march north when he might stay at home and take the prize at his feet.

MR WINSTON CHURCHILL said he was afraid that unless we had a definite programme we should find ourselves still more deeply involved, but that with it we might be able not only to get out, but to get out in style.

GENERAL RADCLIFFE said the General Staff was in full accord with the Secretary of State's expression of policy. There was no great military difficulty in coming away from the Caucasus, but it would be a pity to leave until the situation at Astrakhan had been cleared up.

THE CHAIRMAN said the result of our attempts to establish the independence of these States seemed to be that *we* had a military Governor in every State.

MR WINSTON CHURCHILL said it was quite obvious that the longer we stayed the deeper our claws would stick in. It was very difficult to avoid sending out detachments when all sorts of events were developing all over the place.

ADMIRAL FREMANTLE said from the Admiralty point of view we had no purely naval interests in the Caspian. The naval operations there were subsidiary to the military. So long as our land forces, or Denikin, remained in the Caucasus, it would be essential for their safety that the command of the Caspian should remain under our control. But if, on the other hand, we were going to withdraw, there was no need for our fleet. The point seemed to be that if Denikin gave up his aspirations over Georgia he would be our friend and might rely on our help; but if not, not.

CAPTAIN COODE[1] said that in order to bomb the Bolshevist fleet at Astrakhan an advanced aeroplane base would be necessary, as the machines at present on the Caspian could not fly from Petrovsk as far as Astrakhan and back. Long-distance machines could not hope to reach the scene of operations before April; meantime, the ice might begin to melt any day, and if our bombing operations were to be carried out at all they should be undertaken at once. It was true that now we had got rid of the 'Russian flotilla' our ships on the Caspian were quite capable of facing the Bolshevist fleet at Astrakhan, especially as the northern waters, on account of their shallowness, did not suit submarine work, but destruction by bombing was preferable, as it involved less danger of loss than a naval battle.

MR SHUCKBURGH[2] said that India's political interest in the Caucasus was rather remote, especially if the Trans-Caspian situation disappeared, and the India Office had no strong views on the subject of evacuation. If Russia came back India would be no worse off than before the war. It was true that if Bolshevism got a foothold it might filter down, but the view taken by the India Office was that we must not push the *glacis* of India too far westward.

THE CHAIRMAN thought that withdrawal from the Caucasus would also involve an early withdrawal from the Hamadan–Enzeli line, which

[1] Charles Penrose Rushton Coode, 1870–1939. Entered Navy, 1883. War Staff Officer, 1912. Captain, 1913. On active service, 1914–18; senior destroyer officer at the Dardanelles (in charge of landing a part of the ANZAC forces north of Gaba Tepe), 1915; DSO, 1916. Director of the Operations Division, Admiralty, 1917–20. Retired with the rank of Rear-Admiral. He married, in 1904, Noel Callaghan, daughter of Admiral of the Fleet Sir George Callaghan.

[2] John Evelyn Shuckburgh, 1877–1953. Entered the India Office, 1900. Secretary, Political Department, India Office, 1917–21. Appointed by Churchill to be Assistant Under-Secretary of State, Colonial Office, 1921. Knighted, 1922. Remained Assistant Under-Secretary of State until 1931. Deputy Under-Secretary of State, Colonial Office, 1931–42. Appointed Governor of Nigeria, 1939, but did not assume office owing to the war. Worked in the historial section of the Cabinet Office, 1942–8.

would react on the Persian situation. With regard to Denikin's being unable to keep the undertaking proposed, it should be remembered that Paris felt very strongly on the question of the independence of the Caucasus States, and it looked as if the Georgians were going to receive recognition.

MR WINSTON CHURCHILL said if he thought there was any prospect of our keeping it permanently, he would personally like very much to annex the Caspian; but he was certain we could not keep it, and if we did it would only bring us into collision with revived Russia. Therefore he did not feel it was worth paying the price we were paying for a short stay; it would be much better to devote our energies to some place where we intended to remain.

MR WINSTON CHURCHILL said that in addition to deciding on the bombing of the Astrakhan fleet, and the preparation of a plan for evacuation, he thought the Conference should also advise His Majesty's Government to enter into a convention with Denikin to supply arms and munitions, a military mission and a naval support, on condition he did not invade Georgia, and that he respected a particular line of frontier in regard to the Caucasus States. The plan of evacuation would necessarily take time to execute—three or four months at least. A good deal could happen in that period; the Peace Conference would have reached its conclusions, and there would be opportunities to arrange for the future of Baku.

He also thought that it would be advisable to make it known beforehand that we were going to evacuate. The knowledge might have a wholesome effect on the attitude of the Georgians and other tribes to our well-meant efforts; it might result in our being asked by the people themselves to stay, so it was quite possible that the mere expression of our intention to withdraw might make it easy for us during the period of evacuation.

THE CHAIRMAN said that Denikin must not be permitted to invade Trans-Caucasia or to absorb the small States for the present. He attached great importance to the setting up of the present. He attached great importance to the setting up of the line of frontier which it was proposed that Denikin should respect, and considered that the Foreign Office should be consulted. The previous line demarcated had not been adhered to by Denikin, and steps must be taken to ensure that the same fate did not await the new proposal. With regard to the evacuation, it would obviously have to begin in the east. The first thing was to get Malleson[1] out of Trans-Caspia into Persia; Krasnovodsk would then have to be evacuated, and our fleet in

[1] Wilfrid Malleson, 1866–1946. Joined the Royal Artillery, 1886. Transferred to the Indian Army, 1904. Head of the Intelligence Branch, Indian Army headquarters, 1904–10. Colonel, 1908. General Staff, India, 1910–14. Chief Censor, India, 1914. Inspector-General of Communications, East Africa, 1914–15. Brigadier-General, 1915. Commanded the Imperial forces in East Africa, 1915–16. Major-General, 1917. Head of the British Military Mission to Turkestan, 1918–20. Knighted, 1920.

the Caspian disposed of, and the Caucasus line step by step, from east to west, withdrawn. A special arrangement might have to be made for Baku, and if possible it should be internationalised.

The Conference decided—

1. That the creation of an advanced air base for the purpose of carrying out bombing operations against the Bolshevist fleet at Astrakhan should be sanctioned.
2. To advise His Majesty's Government to enter into a convention with General Denikin, promising him the support of (a) arms and ammunition, (b) a strong military mission, and (c) the co-operation of the Navy in the Caspian till he has taken Astrakhan (for which operation a time limit should be set); such support to be conditional on his giving an undertaking to respect a stated frontier line with regard to the Caucasian States.
3. That this frontier line should be defined by the War Office in consultation with the Foreign Office.
4. That the War Office, in consultation with the Admiralty and the India Office, should prepare a plan for the evacuation of the Caucasus and the Caspian to begin at once, the evacuation to be from east to west (starting with General Malleson's force in Trans-Caspia), on the lines indicated by the Chairman.
5. To consult the military authorities as to the announcement to the Governments of the various States in the Caucasus of the intended withdrawal.
6. To submit the above programme, together with a report of the meeting, to the British Peace Delegation in Paris for their approval.

War Cabinet: minutes

(*Cabinet papers: 23/9*)

6 March 1919

The War Cabinet had under consideration a Memorandum by the Shipping Controller[1] (Paper GT–6922) with reference to the shipping which would be required to transport munitions of war to the Black Sea for the assistance of General Denikin, in which it was stated that additional tonnage to the extent of 150 per cent. of that hitherto indicated would be required,

[1] Sir Joseph Maclay, who had been appointed first Shipping Controller in December 1916, and held the office (which was not in the Cabinet) until it was abolished in March 1921.

involving the use of some twenty or more ships of 5,000 tons, that, owing to the shortage of tonnage, the Shipping Controller considered the demand as very serious, and that, if the work were to be undertaken, Italy and France should be called upon to give at least equal assistance, as an Allied responsibility.

THE SECRETARY OF STATE FOR WAR said that the shipping he asked for would not all be required at once, but he wished to avoid successive delays in obtaining ships from time to time as they were required. An Inter-Departmental Committee, which had just met under Lord Curzon's Chairmanship, had decided to recommend to the War Cabinet a threefold policy in the Caucasus—

(i.) To make preparations to withdraw;

(ii.) To compensate General Denikin for our withdrawal by supplying him with material and munitions of war, and with a military mission as proposed;

(iii.) To make it a condition of such support that General Denikin should not interfere with the Georgians and other independent States in the Caucasus.

He regarded the supply of arms to General Denikin as a lever, on the one hand, to enable him to fight the Bolsheviks, and, on the other, to prevent him from maltreating the Southern States; and the supply of this material was therefore an essential part of the scheme for removing our troops as quickly as possible. He proposed to spread the supply over the next few months, doling it out to General Denikin according to his requirements. It was necessary to retain the power to control him if he did not fall in with our wishes.

MR CHURCHILL hoped that the Shipping Controller would be willing to supply the shipping within the next few months, in order that the War Office might carry out a coherent policy with regard to the Caucasus. It was useless to invite either the French or the Americans to provide the shipping, as General Denikin came solely within the British sphere, though he agreed that the fact that we were supplying the shipping for the Caucasus was a point which should be raised in regard to other claims by the Allies for shipping assistance from this country; for example, the transport of General Haller's army to Poland. Moreover, the demand for twenty shipments of 5,000 tons did not involve the employment of twenty ships for more than a single voyage. The transport of this material would be spread over some months, and it was quite possible that only a quarter of that number of ships would be required, each ship making several journeys. The evacuation of the British troops could not take place for some months, owing to the necessity of withdrawing troops from distant points, such as Trans-Caspia and Krasnovodsk, and moving them along the Baku railway to Batum. Mr Churchill pointed out that the scheme advocated was the only practicable one to carry out the policy of evacuation consistently with our obligations to the Southern peoples, and the necessity for covering the withdrawal of our own troops. It was essential to support General Denikin, for if he were to break down ou troops would be cut off by the Bolsheviks. General Denikin was a great shield to our troops along the whole of the line.

LORD CURZON concurred in Mr Churchill's observations with regard to the evacuation of troops, and pointed out that it could not be carried out hurriedly, but must be progressive, and might be attended by disorder and bloodshed, owing to fighting between the local populations in consequence of our withdrawal. We were relying on General Denikin to fight and beat the Bolsheviks. He had shown a tendency, however, to turn southward and attack the States on the other side of the Caucasus as an easier target. He was a type of the old-fashioned monarchical Russian who regarded it as his natural *rôle* to bring back the Caucasus States under Russian rule. Lord Curzon said that he was entirely in agreement with the Secretary of State for War that it was necessary to retain control over General Denikin through the supply of material, which should be used to carry out his real object of attacking in the north, but not in the south.

THE SHIPPING CONTROLLER stated that the shipping position was becoming more serious every day. New proposals were continually being put up. Already eighteen ships were asked for to transport material to the Black Sea, and it was now proposed to increase this number by 150 per cent. He protested that the British Government should not be required to furnish all the ships needed for transport. Ships which had recently been taken from the Austrians by the Italians, and were intended to be under the control of the Allies, were being used by the Italians for a great Libyan expedition. There were heavy demands for tonnage for bringing wheat from Australia, and ships would shortly be required to supplement the wheat supply of India. In addition, there were over 400 ships round the coast requiring repairs, which it had not been possible to execute owing to the shipbuilding strike; while, owing to the possibility of coal trouble, it had been necessary to divert tonnage to build up stocks of coal in our coaling stations. It was quite impossible for him to carry out properly shipping programmes if constant new demands were sprung upon him suddenly by the War Office.

THE SECRETARY OF STATE FOR WAR protested that it was becoming increasingly difficult to carry out any coherent policy, owing to objections raised by the Shipping Controller and the Treasury. The War Office had tried very hard to devise a scheme within the limits laid down by the Cabinet. Moreover, with the withdrawal of our forces in the Caucasus, an enormous drain upon shipbuilding would be removed. All he asked at present was that the Cabinet should approve the continued despatch of these stores, and to leave it to him to arrange with the Shipping Controller, so far as possible, to make the necessary provision.

LORD CURZON observed that the assistance for General Denikin would go on for some months. It must be spread over a prolonged period, and he did not think the strain on the Ministry of Shipping would be as great at the present moment as Sir Joseph Maclay feared.

MR BONAR LAW suggested that the Secretary of State for War should arrange for somebody in the War Office to have the function of investigating the War Office shipping requirements, and of discussing them some time in advance with the Shipping Controller.

MR CHURCHILL said that Sir Sam Fay[1] was already doing that.

SIR JOSEPH MACLAY said that he assumed it was understood that we should endeavour to get Allied ships for the purpose, should it be possible.

The War Cabinet decided that—

> The Shipping Controller should confer with the Secretary of State for War, and should endeavour to do everything possible to provide the shipping necessary to carry out the War Cabinet's decision as to the transport of the material to the Black Sea for the support of General Denikin, on the understanding that the provision of supplies would be spread over a period of several months.

Winston S. Churchill to Sir John Maclay

(*War Office papers: 32/5683*)

6 March 1919 War Office
Secret

My dear Maclay,

The matter on which General Radcliffe seeks to see you is one of urgent military importance. A ship is required on March 10th to carry aeroplanes to Murmansk. These aeroplanes are to bomb the Bolshevik flotilla now icebound in the upper waters of the Dwina. Every day counts and there is not a

[1] Sam Fay, 1856–1953. Entered the railway service as a clerk. Appointed General Manager of the Great Central Railway in 1902, a post he held for twenty years. Knighted, 1912. Member of the Railway Executive Committee, and of the Ports and Transit Executive Committee, 1913–21. Director of Movements and Railways, War Office, 1917–18; Director-General, 1918–19. Member of the Army Council, 1918–19. President of the Institute of Transport, 1922–3. He published *The War Office at War* in 1937.

moment to lose. The ice on the upper waters melts before the ice at the mouth of the river. Therefore the danger to our forces will be serious in the early days of May, when the Bolshevik steamers will be able to descend the river and attack us, and before the port is open for evacuation or reinforcement.

The action proposed is the only possible defence.

I have the Prime Minister's approval of the plan and earnestly ask for your whole-hearted co-operation in a matter which affects the lives and safety of a considerable British force.

Believe me,
Yours sincerely
Winston S. Churchill

Winston S. Churchill to David Lloyd George

(*Churchill papers: 16/5*)

8 March 1919[1] War Office

My dear Prime Minister,

I send you the following notes on our conversation this morning.

(1) It is your decision and the decision of the War Cabinet that we are to evacuate Murmansk and Archangel as soon as the ice melts in the White Sea. Russians (including women and children) who have compromised themselves through working with us are to be transported, if they desire it, to a place of refuge.

If reinforcements are required to cover the extrication of our forces and the withdrawal of the aforesaid Russians, they may be taken for this purpose from the volunteers now re-engaging for service in the army. It will be made clear to these men that they are only going to extricate their comrades and not for a long occupation of Northern Russia.

Subject to the above, I am to make whatever military arrangements are necessary to carry out your policy.

(2) It is also decided by you and the War Cabinet that we are to withdraw our army from the Caucasus as quickly as possible. This will certainly take 3 or 4 months, as the detachments which have been thrown out as far as Kars to the Southward and the troops on the other side of the Caspian have also to be withdrawn, and our lines of communication from Hamadan to Enzeli have to be wound up.

Denikin will be compensated for the loss of the support of this army (a) by arms and munitions and (b) by a military mission, which may if necessary

[1] Churchill circulated copies of this letter to his Cabinet colleagues on 3 April 1919.

amount to 2,000 in all of technical assistants and instructors. This military mission is to be formed of officers and men who volunteer specially for service in Russia and not by men of the regular volunteer army ordered to proceed there. In return for this support, we should secure from Denikin undertakings not to attack the Georgians and others South of a certain line which the Foreign Office are tracing; and later instalments of arms and munitions will be dealt out to him as he conforms to this agreement. If he fails to conform to this agreement, it will be open to us to withdraw our mission. The limits of our assistance to Denikin will be clearly stated to him, and it will be open to him to accept or reject our conditions and our help.

(3) You have also decided that Colonel John Ward and the two British battalions at Omsk are to be withdrawn (less any who volunteer to stay) as soon as they can be replaced by a military mission, similar to that to Denikin, composed of men who volunteer specifically for service in Russia.

(4) On these lines and within these limits, I should be prepared to be responsible for carrying out the policy on which you and the War Cabinet have decided. It will be necessary to inform the allies of our intention, and this I presume will be done by yourself or Mr Balfour.

If, however, I have wrongly interpreted your decisions in any respect, I hope you will let me know what you really wish, in order that I may see whether it can be done.

Yours very sincerely
Winston S. Churchill

Sir Henry Wilson: diary

(*Wilson papers*)

9 March 1919 Paris

Winston & I discussed LG. Winston thinks LG is riding for a fall by not facing the problem of Russia nor the problem of what is to be done if the Boches refuse our military & economic terms when we present them. I agree with Winston.

General Bridges[1] *to Winston S. Churchill*

(*Churchill papers: 2/105*)

10 March 1919 GHQ Constantinople

My dear Winston,

I have never written you a word of congratulation on your new appointment. The congrats are rather on our side. It is a great thing for the Army to have one at the helm nowadays with youth & energy & a deep knowledge of the social problems of the country.

I am having a most interesting time here. Things are never dull. The Turk is just beginning to look round & wonder what is going to happen to him. I don't think he will give much trouble even if he is dismembered, but we are taking precautions especially on the Asiatic side.

It will interest you to know that I have talked to several Turkish officers of the GS about the Dardanelles Campaign. So far I have only heard one opinion ie that another attack by the fleet would have succeeded and was anticipated. The capital was already packing up to go to Konia (the war archives had actually gone & most of them have been lost) & there was a panic. The bulk of the officers (my informants say) would have been greatly relieved to see British Warships in the Bosphorous & glad to capitulate. At that time the Turks were very short of ammunition, mines & torpedoes.

I remember how you backed up & encouraged the Admirals on the spot & it does seem a thousand pities that you did not get your way & even fell under the shadow of public odium—though the latter is the daily portion of great men in great crises!

I had the nerve to cable you for a motor boat. Can't get one here: We all live on the Bosphorous but rather far apart—for instance Milne is 8 miles from me by water & 14 by bad road.

I hope this will find you well. Please give my respects to Mrs Churchill.

Yrs ever
Tom Bridges[2]

[1] George Tom Molesworth Bridges, 1871–1939. Entered Royal Artillery, 1892. Lieutenant-Colonel 4th Hussars, 1914. Head of British Military Mission, Belgian Field Army, 1914–16. Major-General commanding the 19th Division, 1916–17. Wounded five times. Lost a leg at Passchendaele. Head of British War Mission, USA, 1918. Head of British Mission, Allied Armies of the Orient, 1918–20. Knighted, 1919. Governor of South Australia, 1922–7. He published his memoirs, *Alarms & Excursions* in 1938 (with a Foreword by Churchill).

[2] Churchill replied to Bridges by telegram on 25 March 1919: 'I am much obliged to you for your letter. It is of historic importance to establish what the true position was. If you have time please collect written evidence from Turkish General Staff on the chances of the Fleet passing the Straits in March 1915.' (*Copy, Churchill papers: 2/105*)

Sir William Sutherland[1] *to Winston S. Churchill*

(*Churchill papers: 16/21*)

11 March 1919 10 Downing Street

Private

Dear Mr Churchill,

Regarding the projected Russian Advance from Finland on Petrograd, I hear from various quarters that this scheme may have more elements of success in it than any other in Russia at the present moment. The reason I write is to suggest that the matter may be important enough (it certainly seems so to me) to *justify the War Office sending out at once officers who can* investigate and report on the matter fully; officers who are acquainted with the conditions that prevail in Russia.

The promoters of the scheme aim at striking at the heart of Bolshevism in Petrograd from Finland; and the help they want from us is to send food (not a very large quantity) to the Baltic so as to be able to put it into Petrograd immediately they, operating from Finland, seized Petrograd. I have seen many men from Russia and Finland recently and all agree that the prospect of food getting into Petrograd in such circumstances might well be the most powerful of all High Explosives for removing Bolshevism from its principal dugouts. . . .

Yours sincerely,
William Sutherland

War Cabinet: minutes

(*Cabinet papers: 23/9*)

RETURN OF THE GUARDS REGIMENTS FROM FRANCE

13 March 1919

THE SECRETARY OF STATE FOR WAR strongly urged that sanction should be given to the proposed expenditure on the occasion of the return of the Guards, in view of their splendid record and the opportunity the occasion offered of striking a patriotic note. He deprecated the subject being treated in a niggardly spirit. Our people had fought and worked, splendidly,

[1] William Sutherland, 1880–1949. Secretary to the Cabinet Committee on Supply of Munitions, 1915. Private Secretary to Lloyd George, 1915–18; Parliamentary Secretary, 1918–20. Liberal MP for Argyllshire, 1918–24. Knighted, 1919. A Junior Lord of the Treasury, 1920–2. Chancellor of the Duchy of Lancaster, April–October 1922.

and they had suffered grievous losses; and the chance of welcoming, in a becoming manner, their men back from France, could not fail to stimulate their patriotism and to have a wholesale effect upon their spirits at a time when there was so much to depress them.[1]

Winston S. Churchill to David Lloyd George

(*Churchill papers: 16/21*)

14 March 1919 War Office

My dear Prime Minister,

You should see the enclosed. It is only typical of many pieces of information which are reaching me. All of these point to the fact that we are steadily losing strength and opportunities. The four months which have passed since the armistice was signed have been disastrous almost without relief for the anti-Bolshevik forces. This is not due to any great increase in Bolshevik strength, though there has been a certain augmentation. It is due to the lack of any policy on the part of the allies, or of any genuine or effective support put into the operations which are going on against the Bolsheviks at different points in Russia.

Prinkipo has played its part in the general discouragement and relaxation which has set in. The fact that the German troops were commanded to withdraw from the Ukraine without any provision being made to stop the Bolshevik advance, has enabled large portions of this rich territory full of new supplies of food to be over-run, and the Bolsheviks are now very near the Black Sea at Kherson. There are many signs of weakness in Kolchak's forces, and, as you have observed, many Bolshevik manifestations are taking place behind the Siberian front, in one of which the Japanese have had quite severe fighting.

I regret very much that you did not allow me to bring Marshal Foch to see you, so that he might have laid before you the not unreasonable proposals which he expounded to me.

I feel quite powerless to avert the grave developments I see approaching. Although I have at the present time no responsibility for policy, they cause me increasing anxiety. You and President Wilson have, I fear, definitely closed your minds on this subject and appear resolved to let Russian affairs take their course. You are the masters and you may, of course, be right in

[1] Following Churchill's appeal, the War Cabinet agreed to spend £3,000 in order to pay for bunting and decorations. It was pointed out that when President Wilson had visited London nearly £10,000 had been spent.

thinking that no other course is possible. It is my duty, however, to warn you of the profound misgivings with which I watch the steady degeneration of so many resources and powers which, vigorously used, might entirely have altered the course of events.

I say nothing about Germany, on which I am in whole-hearted agreement with your wise food policy. But it is vain to suppose that any real peace or revival can come to Europe while Russia is in anarchy. I apprehend that after enormous possibilities and opportunities have been lost and great potential resources have been dissipated, we shall nevertheless be drawn, in spite of all your intentions, into the clutches of the Russian problem in some way or another, and we shall then bewail the loss of much that is now slipping through our fingers unheeded. This was the fate of Mr Pitt in regard to France.

When the Bolshevik frontier in Siberia is limited only by whatever line the Japanese choose to keep for themselves, when the whole of the Caucasus and Trans-Caspia have fallen into Bolshevik power, when their armies are menacing Persia and Afghanistan and their missionaries are at the gates of India, when one after another the Border States in the West have been undermined by want and propaganda or overborne by criminal violence, not only the League of Nations but the British Empire, with which we are particularly concerned, will wake up to the fact that Russia is not a negligible factor in world politics.

Yours vy sincerely
Winston S. Churchill

Sir Henry Wilson to Winston S. Churchill
(*Churchill papers: 16/5*)

15 March 1919 Paris
Secret

. . . I saw Foch about the proposal to train Russians to send to Murmansk and Archangel in order to stiffen up those garrisons when we come away. He was entirely opposed to the idea saying that he saw no good in trying to bolster up Russians under those conditions and therefore he did not propose to help us in either collecting Russians or training them for that purpose. Our Prime Minister also spoke to me on this subject. He is very apprehensive that we may be starting another very expensive 'Denikin' and 'Kolchak' in Archangel and Murmansk, and there is certainly something to be said from that point of view.

I think that before you take action, either in sending a mission to General Yudenitch[1] or in beginning to collect up the Russian officers and men with a view to shipment to Northern Russia, that it would be well to wait for the decision of the Supreme Council as to future action in Russia. When this decision will be given I have no idea because as I have told you the subject of Russia has never been considered, and so far as I know is not yet over the horizon, but the Prime Minister is so averse from spending more money, either on a mission to Yudenitch or in training the Russians, or in, as it were, starting another 'Denikin' in Northern Russia, that I think it will be wise to pause before you do anything further in the matter. . . .

H. W. Massingham to Winston S. Churchill

(*Churchill papers: 2/105*)

16 March 1919 Reform Club
Pall Mall

Dear Mr Churchill,

Considering our long relationship I don't quite like to leave the dispute between us with the letter I wrote yesterday to Marsh. Anger & bitterness were in my mind, but I don't know that anger & bitterness are much good, & it was & is despair that is in my heart. That with your gifts you should start again this crazy game of war, when for years every country will be hanging on by its eyelids to mere existence, is more than I can understand; & though I didn't want to wound you by having to oppose you, I feel that we belong to different worlds. I suppose you think that in view of our commitments a great army is still necessary: but here we, again, touch fundamentals. A peace on these old lines I hold to be a crime against the future of mankind; & both the idea of it & the necessary material supports (of course they are necessary) I view, not with the mind of the average critic, but with a horror that I have never experienced in any previous approach to political problems. Therefore I feel that I want neither friendship or any ordinary human relationship until either (which is most probable) people like me are utterly beaten & destroyed, or until we set up our conception of State life above yours.

[1] Nikolai Nikolaevich Yudenitch, 1862–1933. Entered the Russian Army, 1879. Served as an infantry officer in the Russo-Japanese War, 1904–5, and in the punitive expedition against Armenia, 1905–6. Chief of Staff, 1913. Commanded the Russian Forces in the Caucasus, 1915 and 1917. Commanded the anti-Bolshevik North-Western Army in the attack on Petrograd, 1919. After his offensive failed, he was arrested by a fellow General, but on British insistence was released, and emigrated to Britain. He himself anglicized his name as 'Youdenitch'.

So that all I wanted to say was what perhaps I said more briefly yesterday that I cannot think of life any longer in any other way than as a conflict between forces that cannot be reconciled, in which I've made my choice, one way, which you, I cannot but conclude, have made your choice too, on the opposite side.

It occurred to me that you might think there was a suggestion of lack of personal gallantry. That, of course, never entered my head.

Yours truly,
H. W. Massingham

Winston S. Churchill to H. W. Massingham

(*Churchill papers: 2/105*)

17 March 1919 War Office

Dear Massingham,

The last paragraph of yr second letter removes from my mind the apprehensions which were aroused by reading the passage in the Nation to which Marsh referred. I am glad that this is so. I think you will see on reading the passage through again that it was capable of—shall I say—an even more unpleasant interpretation than you intended, or than you consider I have deserved.[1]

At any rate I am obliged to you for reassuring me. I do not think I am touchy about these sort of things, but there are limits which are decisive, & I am genuinely pleased to know that yr criticisms were not such as to give me any cause for *personal* complaint.

So far as policy is concerned I do not think we are so far apart as you suppose. But I am in contact with certain practical realities for meetings which I am directly responsible; & it is possible that words spoken in their special connexion may jar on one who is looking on the general picture only.

But even this general picture is terrible & melancholy beyond description.

Yours very truly
Winston S. Churchill

[1] On 15 March 1919 the *Nation* had published a criticism of British intervention in Russia. At one point the article criticized a recent remark of Churchills about the 'fine adventure' on which the volunteers in Russia were embarked. 'Adventures are to the adventurer,' the article went on, 'but the House remembers that after a very few weeks of shivering in the trenches, Mr Churchill himself preferred to shine in the Senate.'

War Cabinet:[1] *minutes*

(*Curzon papers*)

17 March 1919 10 Downing Street

MR CHURCHILL stated that he had circulated the two Memoranda in response to the desire of the General Staff, but had not put them forward as his policy. He felt that the War Cabinet decision with regard to Murmansk and Archangel, when known, would deal a considerable blow to the Russian cause generally. At the same time the Murmansk–Archangel line was so unpromising in a strategic sense that he did not think it wise to press the Russians to make special efforts to defend it, as efforts there would lead to nothing. He had just heard from the Chief of the Imperial General Staff the result of conversations he had had in Paris with our Prime Minister and with Marshal Foch. Marshal Foch was opposed to encouraging the Russians to go in at this point, and the Prime Minister similarly feared that the policy suggested in the War Office Memoranda would only lead to costly enterprises like that in which we were participating with General Denikin. General Wilson went on to suggest that before sending a Mission to the Baltic it was necessary to wait for a decision on Russian policy from the Supreme War Council; but when that would be obtained he had no idea.

MR CHURCHILL, continuing, said that the War Cabinet must face the fact that the North of Russia would be overrun by Bolsheviks, and many people would be murdered. He was increasingly distressed with the way the situation had developed since the Armistice. Everything was going wrong. The continued disheartening of the Russian forces friendly to us had led to a great falling off in their *moral*. When firing stopped, the Ukraine was occupied by the Germans. We requested them to withdraw, but we put in no Allied force there, and now that area, rich in food, was in the hands of the Bolsheviks. The Bolsheviks were taking Nicholiev and Kherson, and were advancing on the Black Sea. Odessa might soon be invested. Four months had passed in a policy of drift, and great potential resources which might have helped us were being dissipated. It was idle to think we should escape by sitting still and doing nothing. Bolshevism was not sitting still. It was advancing, and unless the tide were resisted it would roll over Siberia until it reached the Japanese, and perhaps drive Denikin into the mountains, while the border Baltic States would be attacked and submerged. No doubt when all the resources friendly to us had been scattered, and when India was

[1] Three members of the War Cabinet were present: Bonar Law (in the Chair), Lord Curzon and Austen Chamberlain. Also attending were Churchill, Walter Long (First Lord of the Admiralty), Rear-Admiral S R Fremantle (Deputy Chief of the Naval Staff) and Thomas Jones (Acting Secretary).

threatened, the Western Powers would bestir themselves and would be prepared to put forth ten times the effort that at an earlier stage would have sufficed to save the situation. He could only express the profound apprehension with which he awaited what was coming. He had been backwards and forwards to Paris in vain. He had discussed the situation with Marshal Foch, who had a definite plan for action without the use of British and French forces, or money, but only by guaranteeing loans to the smaller States.

Both THE PRIME MINISTER and PRESIDENT WILSON were against intervention.

MR LONG said that unless some large organised policy were pursued by the Allies, Russia would be reduced for a long time to anarchy and misery, and, with such a precedent, how could the Powers sign a Treaty of Peace in Paris?

MR CHAMBERLAIN said there was not the slightest chance of securing financial help from France or Italy for undertakings against Russia. If, therefore, it meant that the whole burden of resisting Russian Bolshevism was to be thrown on this country, we should break down under the strain. That was a very real danger. He thought it would be useful to learn from the proposed Committee what exactly was involved in carrying along Esthonia and Latvia. He had seen no calculation of what would be required in the way of military, naval and financial assistance. He had expressed his willingness to give them credit to cover the provision of machinery, but had made it plain that for other assistance they must turn to the United States.

MR BONAR LAW asked whether it was possible to put down with any definiteness the probable cost in ships, men and money.

ADMIRAL FREMANTLE said the answer would depend upon what troops the Bolsheviks would concentrate in any particular place. Esthonia had been able, with the help of Finnish volunteers, British arms and British ships, to clear her territory of Bolsheviks; but Latvia had been over-run. We were at present helping Latvia with the moral support of our ships, and our coal, oil and military supplies were really now being used to the advantage of the Germans.

MR CHURCHILL said we were really helping the Germans, because in this case the Germans were helping us. We were able to control the Germans, but we were not able to control the Bolsheviks.

MR CHAMBERLAIN pointed out that Marshal Foch had refused to allow further reinforcements of Germans to be landed.

MR CHURCHILL said that our representatives at Spa were being pressed by the Germans as to what exactly we wanted them to do.

LORD CURZON said he wished to obtain a decision from the Peace

Conference. He doubted whether the appalling character of the situation was fully realised in Paris.

MR CHURCHILL said it was difficult to frame estimates when there were so many uncertain counters and factors of every degree of variation in the situation. If, for instance, we decided to wage war on the Bolsheviks, then the stock of Denikin and Kolchak would immediately go up; so would that of the Esthonians and the Letts. One could not calculate the cost exactly until the Allies made up their minds whether they were out for a vigorous campaign or not.

MR BONAR LAW said that an effort must be made to distinguish our activities in the Baltic States from the larger Russian policy. We had undertaken to support the Baltic States against the menace of Bolshevism.

Winston S. Churchill to Sir Hugh Trenchard

(*Trenchard papers*)

18 March 1919

I am looking forward very much to yr coming back at the end of April. Mind you get thoroughly fit first. There is no question whatever of anyone taking yr place & I have no intention of acting upon your various offers to resign wh arise from yr high sense of duty. I am sure you have most valuable work to do for the Flying Service & we will hold the fort until you are restored.

Sir Henry Wilson to Winston S. Churchill

(*Churchill papers: 16/5*)

18 March 1919 Paris

Secret

Dear S of S

Yesterday at our meeting of the Supreme Council President Wilson arrived with the full intention of raising the whole question of a Conscript Army. The Prime Minister in a private discussion before the meeting commenced made it so clear to him that he would not tolerate such a state of affairs that the President had to drop it. The result was that we got through all the Military Terms; all the Naval except Heligoland and the Kiel Canal; and almost all the Air Terms. Heligoland was referred to you at the War Cabinet in London for an expression of opinion, and the Kiel Canal was referred to the big Commission which sits here on Inland Waterways. I do not think either of these two things will give any very great trouble.

Having disposed thus of those three subjects Foch brought up the question of the fall of Lemberg, which he said might possibly take place in the near future, and on that he asked for permission to form an Allied Staff to examine the question, on the one hand of sending Haller with his Poles from France to Poland, and on the other hand to go into the feasibility and practicability of moving Rumanian Divisions up from Rumania to help the Poles in Lemberg. This at once raised a discussion. Foch's first proposal as regards Haller was agreed to but his second proposal was negatived.

The Prime Minister said that so far as he knew Lemberg did not belong to the Poles and he did not see why Rumanian troops should be moved up to help the Poles to hold a town which was over their own frontier, nor did he consider it a wise proceeding, when the French and Greeks were being kicked out of Southern Russia, when the Bolshevists were steadily advancing towards Odessa and Bessarabia, that Rumanian troops should be moved up towards Lemberg. In short, he looked on the proposal as the first step towards forming a considerable force of mixed troops with a view to the invasion of Russia for the defeat of the Bolsheviks, and on those grounds he was opposed to it. He was backed by President Wilson with the result that I have stated, namely, that Foch's proposal for an Allied Staff to examine such an operation was negatived.

The Prime Minister's governing idea I think was the question of cost, and this idea is always present in his mind in anything that we do for North Russia. He is afraid that we may start another 'Kolchak' and 'Denikin' in Archangel and Murmansk and that this will cost enormous sums of money and give very small results, if any. It is for this reason that I think we had better just carry out proposals which you have got him to agree to—ie, our withdrawal from Archangel and Murmansk as opportunity offers, and our gradual and steady withdrawal from the line Batoum–Baku.

There is no doubt that the money difficulties are very great and if, as seems to me quite possible, we get very little in the shape of reparation or indemnities from the Boche, and if as seems more than probable, the French continue to refuse to impose any taxation on themselves, I really do not quite know where we shall find ourselves. On the other hand it is more doubtful to me whether the policy of doing nothing in Russia will not in the end be much more expensive than those steps which Foch and we have proposed to define the eastern frontiers from the Arctic Ocean to the Black Sea, and to organise all those border states into such a condition that they are able to defend themselves against Bolshevism. In short, the picture that I see is this.—Owing to our thinking that we are going to form a League of Nations and ourselves be one of the partners, we are forbidden by the terms of such a League to form alliances and I think as a result of this we will find the Boche drawing nearer both to the Russians and to the Japanese, leaving the French and the English and possibly the Italians on the other side of the picture.

As you know I not only do not believe in the League of Nations but I am quite certain in my own mind it is a sure way to eternal war. I would like to see, personally, a combination of England, France and Germany in an alliance against Russia and Japan. So long as we cling to this League of Nations idea which consists in interfering in everybody's business and in looking after the welfare of every country in the world except our own, we are absolutely forbidden from taking what appears to me the only sensible course, and that is to place England first and to build up such alliances as we think are our strongest safeguards for the future.

Tomorrow I believe we discuss Poland, that is to say the Western Frontier and the question of Dantzic. The day after I hope we shall be on to the Rhine. Clemenceau has put in another paper, which is being typed. I have not seen it. Directly I have read it I will let you know what it contains. I am going to struggle hard to get home by the end of the week.

HW

Winston S. Churchill to Lord Curzon

(*Curzon papers*)

THE SITUATION IN EGYPT

19 March 1919 War Office

. . . I do not feel convinced myself that the situation is really dangerous from a military point of view.[1] Personally I should have let the deputation *plus* the extremists come here & I tried to say so at the end of the Cabinet. But I think it would be disastrous to the future British rule in Egypt to make any political concession until absolute tranquillity and order have been restored. I am sure we have the means to do this, and, when it has been done, you will have a fair chance of making friends again.

[1] Complete autonomy for Egypt was the demand of the Nationalist Committee set up at the end of 1918. Its Chairman, Saad Zaghlul asked to come to England to put his points to the Cabinet, but his request was refused. So too was the request of two Egyptian Ministers, Rushdi Pasha and Adly Pasha, both of whom threatened to resign unless they could go to London. On 8 March 1919 Zaghlul and three of his supporters were arrested, and deported to Malta. There were immediate repercussions in Egypt: British soldiers and civilians were attacked, railway lines torn up and telegraph wires cut. For several days Cairo itself was isolated, and at Dairut station a British inspector of prisons, two officers and five soldiers were murdered in a train by a mob. The riots were suppressed by the end of March, whereupon Lord Allenby, as Special High Commissioner as well as Commander-in-Chief, urged a policy of conciliation, and the release of Zaghlul.

I hope it will not be decided to make any surrender in the face of violence without a Cabinet meeting at which I have an opportunity of expressing the military view.

Sir Henry Wilson: diary

(*Wilson papers*)

26 March 1919 London

I went to office 10 o'c & had long talk with Winston who began by being very stuffy with me for having been away so long. He is in a very critical mood about LG & I am sure is watching an opportunity to knife him. Winston thinks the Boches will not dream of signing our present terms & he thinks that we & the French ought to make an Alliance with the Boches.

Winston S. Churchill to Lord Curzon

(*Curzon papers*)

28 March 1919 War Office

My dear Curzon,

Surely the moment has come to publish the Bolshevik atrocity blue-book. We really have no right to keep Parliament in the dark any longer. Lord Hugh Cecil[1] spoke to me strongly about this last night.

I am publishing, with the assent of the Prime Minister, the accounts of conditions in Germany as collected by our officers. I send you a copy. It has been carefully edited by the Intelligence Department.

It seems to me that publication of both these documents is necessary to a proper understanding by Parliament of the situation. In the absence of a true view about the Russian situation, I find a difficulty in supplying the necessary reinforcements for Archangel and Murmansk: public opinion is not sufficiently instructed.

Please let me know your views.[2]

yours vy sincerely
Winston S. Churchill

[1] Lord Hugh Richard Heathcote Gascoyne Cecil, 1869–1956. Known as 'Linky'. Fifth son of the 3rd Marquess of Salisbury. Conservative MP, 1895–1906; 1910–1937. Provost of Eton, 1936–44. Created Baron Quickswood, 1941. In 1908 he was the 'best man' at Churchill's wedding.

[2] The Foreign Office Blue Book on Bolshevik atrocities was published on 9 April, when it was debated in the House of Commons. When, during the debate, Churchill's friend Josiah Wedgwood described the reports of atrocities as 'anonymous tittle tattle' there were widespread shouts of 'Shame!'.

Sir Henry Wilson to Winston S. Churchill

(*Churchill papers: 16/5*)

28 March 1919 Paris
Secret

Dear S of S,

. . . Yesterday afternoon Foch, Bliss and I drew up a scheme for the occupation of Budapest and Vienna and the closing of the gap between Roumania and Poland by a force of Allied troops. This was discussed by the four Prime Ministers with Foch and myself present. I was asked my opinion of the scheme and said that in view of the fact that there was no serious Bolshevist Army moving on Budapest it was very difficult to lay out formal plans for the campaign but that I thought that Foch's proposals were as good a commencement as any others that could be thought of. I however raised the question at once as to whether the occupation of certain towns and junctions in Central Europe was the proper answer to the spread of Bolshevism.

I pointed out that if military action was not the answer to Bolshevism some other plan must be adopted or it seemed probable that the different States of Europe would one by one declare themselves 'Bolshevist' and if this happened I did not see how any terms of peace could be enforced, and if on the other hand the Prime Ministers thought that military action was the right answer then we could not start off soon enough. The military having left the room the Prime Ministers debated and our Prime Minister told me last night that they came to the unanimous conclusion that military action in Budapest and Vienna was not the answer to the spread of Bolshevism but they agreed that everything should be done to continue to support both Roumania and Poland.

I will speak to the Prime Minister on the subject you telegraphed to me about this morning, viz, Foch's attack on Denikin. But I think the PM has taken it at its proper value because Thwaites explained the situation to him at the time. . . .

Winston S. Churchill to Marshal Foch

(*Churchill papers: 16/5*)

28 March 1919
Private & Personal

My dear Marshal Foch,

I am distressed to learn from General Thwaites that at a meeting with Mr Lloyd George on the [ ][1] you expressed very unfavourable

[1] Left blank in Churchill's copy.

opinions about General Denikin's army. The War Office have committed themselves definitely to the support of this army within the limits which are permitted to us. We have made a very careful study of all the conditions there and have a considerable military mission with General Denikin's headquarters and moving about in the area where his troops are operating. The facts at our disposal do not confirm the adverse views you have formed.

On the other hand, I ventured to warn you when I had the pleasure of a conversation in Paris three weeks ago, that the state of affairs on the Black Sea Littoral was going from bad to worse and that the Greek troops there under French command were rapidly deteriorating and that the local population were being alienated. Events have only too painfully proved the truth of this forecast which I made on very full and accurate information.

Thirdly, I am very generally in agreement with your views on the whole Russian problem as you explained them to me at our meeting, and I have done and will do everything that is open to me to support and further them. I am delighted to see that, carried forward by pressure of events, they have made good progress in the last fortnight. I hope, therefore, we may both continue to do our very utmost to advance along the same line of thought and action, and that you will freely interchange opinions with Sir Henry Wilson so as to secure continuous harmony. It is specially important that no rivalry should develop between us in regard to the different Russian theatres where we are endeavouring to sustain the forces of civilisation against the Bolsheviks. There are so many opponents of action in any form at the present time that those who are agreed on its importance should be especially careful to speak with a united voice.

Accept, My dear Marshal, the sureties of my highest respect, and with all good wishes,

Believe me,
Yours sincerely,
Winston S. Churchill

Winston S. Churchill to David Lloyd George: telegram
(*Churchill papers: 16/5*)

28 March 1919

I should be extremely grateful if you could release Henry Wilson as soon as possible. For the last month I have hardly seen him and all sorts of important army questions are pending here. Of course I do not pretend to compare the relative importance of his work here and in Paris, but if you can possibly spare him please think of me.

Sir Henry Wilson to Winston S. Churchill

(*Churchill papers: 16/5*)

29 March 1919 Paris

Dear Winston,

I am so sorry. I breakfasted with the PM & we discussed my return to London, but he was adamant and has wired to you. I was not able to do anything but acquiesce, I am *so* sorry.

I live in the hopes that it won't mean a long stay as LG means to get back himself next week if he can manage it.

Meanwhile as we are not taking charge of affairs, affairs are taking charge of us and no one can tell what will happen in the next few days.

I will keep you posted.

Ever
Henry Wilson

David Lloyd George to Winston S. Churchill: telephone message

(*Churchill papers: 16/5*)

29 March 1919 Paris
5.10 pm

I am very sorry to keep CIGS here, for I know how badly you need him. Vital questions are under discussion which only a man of his authority can help us to decide. We greatly missed his advice during the discussions on the Austro-Hungarian question.

Today he is urgently required in regard to Dantzig and Haller's Army. Every day we require his help. I very much regret, therefore, that I cannot see my way to let him go at present. You may depend upon my not detaining him one unnecessary hour.

Your Bill seems to have gone very well and I congratulate you on your personal success.[1]

[1] The Military Service Bill. On 28 March Frederick Guest had written to Lloyd George of how Churchill 'undoubtedly succeeded in bringing the House back to a proper appreciation of the urgency and difficulty of the position. His explanation of the impossibility of getting sufficient men by voluntary enlistment in time impressed many waverers.' (*Lloyd George papers*)

War Office to General Knox

(*Churchill papers: Narrative of Events in Siberia*)

29 March 1919 London
Very secret

1. A decision has been made that the two British battalions in Siberia shall be withdrawn as soon as, but not before, they can be replaced by a body of officers and men who volunteer specially for service in Russia.

2. These volunteers will be of such numbers as to bring up the total of your Mission to a maximum of 2,000 all ranks, inclusive of Headquarter Staff and Training Staff. . . .

3. What response there will be to the call for these volunteers is not certain, but it is probable that large numbers of officers will be forthcoming, but that it will be difficult to obtain any men. Possibly, however, each officer may be able to induce 10 or 12 men to volunteer along with them.

4. Our object is of course to continue, by means of this enlargement of your Mission, a tangible guarantee of our support to Kolchak and to provide his forces with a moral stiffening however small. Here it is impossible to form more than a general idea of the necessities of the case or what could be done, but for your consideration the following ideas are suggested:—

(*a.*) To reconstitute the Canadian Brigade as a Russian formation with Russian personnel and as many British officers and men as are actually necessary, making use of all equipment which the Canadians would leave behind.

(*b.*) To allocate parties of British officers and men to fighting units at the front for the purpose of instruction, encouragement and example. This scheme as an alternative, or if numbers are sufficient, additional to (*a*) above.

5. To enable us to go ahead with the proposal you should, as soon as possible, telegraph us your views as to the best method of employing the additional numbers, remembering that the proportion of officers will be very large to that of men. . .

April 1919

Winston S. Churchill to Georges Clemenceau
(*Churchill papers: 16/6*)

1 April 1919 War Office
Private & Secret

My dear President of the Council,

You are always so kind in letting me put my views before you that I venture to write to you in your capacity as Minister for War about the position of our troops in the Far North of Russia. I am very anxious about them. Their position may easily become in the near future one of extreme danger. You are so well acquainted with all the circumstances that I do not dwell upon them.

I thought it was very hard upon us, who have the largest number of men involved in this theatre, that Monsieur Pichon should have given the exact figures of our strength to the Chamber, and thus have let the enemy see how very weak we are, and secondly that Monsieur Abrami should have declared that not another single man would be sent by France to the aid of this small force.

I have waited all these months in the vain hope of receiving from the League of Nations, so far as that body is at present in existence, some indication of the policy we should pursue towards Russia. I have received no indication. But at Archangel and Murmansk the problem is not one of policy, but of keeping our troops alive throughout this treacherous and dangerous Spring and of extricating them, and those loyal Russians dependent on them, at the earliest possible moment. This may and probably will require reinforcements to be sent, even for the purpose of evacuation. I am therefore preparing a strong brigade of volunteers and holding ships in readiness to press through as soon as it is possible, in order either to relieve the troops who are there or to cover their evacuation and that of the compromised civil population.

I hope you will be able to have language used by your Ministers which is not inconsistent with a firm posture in the face of an aggressive enemy. In the House of Commons, where of course they are very much opposed to Russian expeditions, everyone, even the most extreme opponents of the Government like Mr Hogge, have declared that if the question arises of rescuing and extricating our troops and those of our allies in North Russia, they would support the despatch of the necessary reinforcements there. I should have thought you would meet with similar support as long as the operation were clearly defined as one of succour and extrication.

Considerable difficulties have also arisen with regard to the French troops at Archangel, who are tired out with all they have gone through and have to a large extent lost heart and discipline. It is desirable that these men should be removed as soon as the ice melts, but until it is possible to bring the rest of the force away safely, you will I know feel it an obligation to take in hand preparations to replace them with fresh trustworthy men in case an emergency should arise.

I rejoice at your restoration to good health after the vile attempt upon your life. I know how grave are the anxieties and problems which you and Lloyd George are facing together at the present time. Forgive me, therefore, if I inflict upon you participation in that smaller but still very serious set of troubles with which the British War Office is confronted; and with all good wishes,

yours very sincerely
Winston S. Churchill

PS. It is almost exactly a year ago since you took me to visit the battle at Moreuil. That was a very rainy day.

Winston S. Churchill to David Lloyd George: telephone message

(*Lloyd George papers*)

1 April 1919 War Office
Late pm

Have received a report from Maynard, Murmansk, in which he states that he has absolutely reliable information that the Finnish Legion intends to revolt and join Bolsheviks. A large number of Karelians are expected to join them and proposed day of rising is April 6th. The Finnish Legion number 1,400 and might get anything up to 2,000 Karelians to join, and movement, if successful, would cut off all troops south of Kandalaksha. You will see from the map that this revolt will cut in two our slender and heterogeneous forces in the Murmansk Sector. The Murmansk Force has been reduced to its lowest limit in order to help Archangel through this dangerous Spring and if the Murmansk troops are massacred the fact must react on the larger forces now in the Archangel region.

Maynard asks urgently for reinforcements of at least 400. Two American cruisers leave here on the 2nd carrying 200 American railway engineers and some British details. I am making preliminary arrangements for the despatch of British infantry but they cannot arrive in time if Maynard's information is correct.

I hope you will ask President Wilson urgently to authorise landing parties from the two American cruisers in case of necessity to be carried out at General Richardson's[1] discretion. Richardson is the United States Officer Commanding American Railway Troops on the cruisers. A disaster here will greatly embarrass future policy.

Sir Henry Wilson to Winston S. Churchill

(*Churchill papers: 16/6*)

2 April 1919 Paris
Secret

Dear S of S

I gave the Prime Minister your telephone message of last night re asking the President for permission to disembark the sailors from the two American cruisers at Murmansk if the situation requires it and if Richardson approves. The Prime Minister saw the President this morning who said that he had no objection but wished me to discuss it with Bliss. I have just been to see Bliss who again on his part says that he has no objection but must inform Benson[2] and get his approval, and I am waiting at the present moment for a telephone message from Bliss to say that Benson approves.

[1] Wilds Preston Richardson, 1861–1929. Born in Texas. Graduated from West Point, 1884. Instructor in tactics, West Point, 1892–7. President of the Alaska Roads Commission, 1905 (where he supervised the building of the 380-mile-long 'Richardson highway' from Valdez to Fairbanks). Brigadier-General commanding the 78th Infantry Brigade, 1918 (served on the western front, October–November 1918). Officer Commanding the United States forces at Murmansk from 14 April to 24 August 1919. Retired from the Army, 1920.

[2] William Shepherd Benson, 1855–1932. Naval cadet, 1877; Captain 1909. Commanded the battleship *Utah*, flagship of the Atlantic Fleet, 1910–13. Commandant of the Philadelphia navy yard, 1913–15. Rear-Admiral, 1915. Chief of Naval Operations, Washington, 1915–18, when he centralized naval communications and prepared plans for the improvement of navy yards. Admiral, 1916. Served on the special Mission charged with the making of peace with the Central Powers, and also as American Naval Representative in the drawing up of the naval terms of the armistice, October 1918. Naval Adviser to the American Peace Commissioners in Paris, 1919. Retired from the Navy, September 1919. Chairman of the United States Shipping Board, 1920–1. First President of the National Council of Catholic Men, 1921–5.

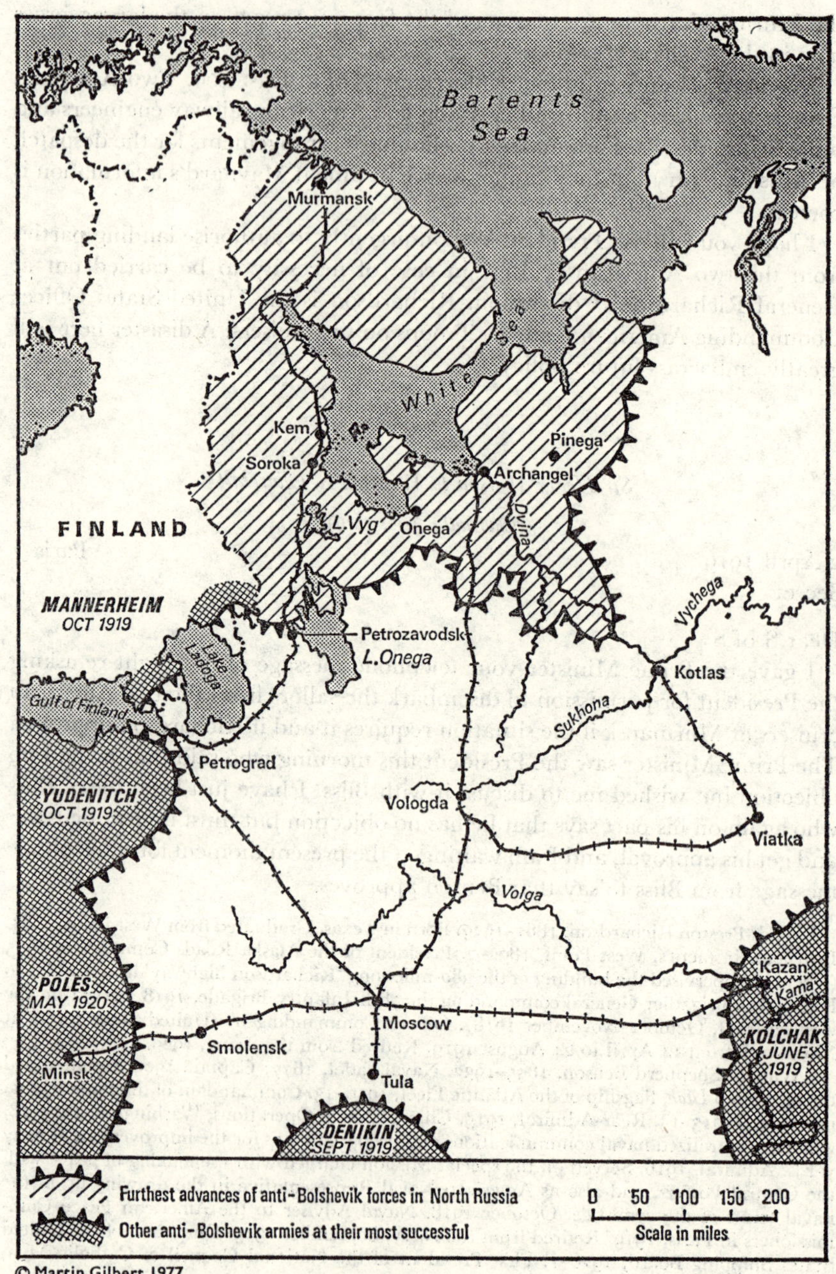

THE INTERVENTION IN NORTH RUSSIA, 1919

This morning in talking with the Prime Minister I suggested to him that in view of the unsatisfactory state of the moral of the French and the Americans we ought to let both Ironside and Maynard inform all their commands that their troops would be relieved by fresh troops as soon as the ice permitted. Bliss came to see me last night with some alarming telegrams from his people in Archangel and he was very nervous of what the Americans up there might do, hinting that it was just possible they might even join the Bolshevists. I asked him whether he thought a promise that these men would be relieved would steady them for the time being and he said he could not help thinking that it would be a very wise thing to do. The Prime Minister when I told him of these facts agreed that it was probably the best course open to us at the moment, so I have asked Radcliffe to telephone over now to Kirke to get your approval for telegrams in the above sense to be sent to both Maynard and Ironside.

Foch is off to Spa tonight. He wanted me to go with him but it is impossible for me to be away at the moment. The Boche now seem to be going to try to take charge of the situation by making offers to us as to the course we should pursue; thus we hear it likely that they will offer to transport the whole of Haller's Polish troops from France across Germany and put them into Poland, thus obviating their going via Dantzig, and, as it appears to me, incidentally challenging Paris to enforce its views as regards the passage of Polish troops from Dantzig into Poland. The Boche also seem to be going to make an offer to rebuild with their own men and their own material all the towns and villages in France which they destroyed. Both these proposals seem to me to be in the nature of an attempt to take the conduct of the future out of the hands of Paris and to put it under the roofs of Berlin.

I expect the Italian officers who are going to go out to Constantinople and on to the Caucasus to turn up here in the next couple of days, when we will show them all the information we possess as regards Milne's and the Caspian naval dispositions, and push them off with all speed to Constantinople. I am personally in a hurry to get out of the Caucasus because I am not quite clear that the Turks and the Bulgars are not going to combine and make it very difficult for us to maintain our position, either in the Caucasus or in Constantinople. It is a pity that the American Constitution is so cumbersome because if it is settled that the Americans take over Constantinople it will be a great convenience if they will do it at once, whereas, apparently, there is no possibility of such a thing because any proposal of that description has to go before Congress before it can be adopted by the President. I have asked for a ruling as to which country is responsible for enforcing Armistice or Peace Terms on the Turks, as if we are the people we ought to set to work at once to make our plans.

Bliss has just telephoned that Admiral Benson has told the 2 cruisers to land what men they can if so desired.

HW

Winston S. Churchill to David Lloyd George

(*Churchill papers: 16/6*)

2 April 1919 War Office

Personal & Secret

Your message to War Cabinet about Abrami's[1] statement is not I trust intended to veto any reinforcements wh may be necessary for the purpose of extricating our troops at Archangel & Murmansk & covering their evacuation. We are preparing a brigade for this purpose & holding ships in readiness in accordance with my letter to you when I was in Paris of wh you have a copy. It may not be necessary to send these reinforcements but if the safety of our men & their efficient withdrawal requires it at any moment I am sure you wd wish them to go and I must have them ready to go. We cannot abandon our own men and a certain number of Russians who have compromised themselves will have to be brought off too. The Admiralty got 900 volunteers in two days for North Russia. Even Hogge declared in the House that if it were a question of rescue or extrication conscripted men shd be sent if necessary. It was shameful of the French to disclose our weakness & intention to withdraw to the enemy and might easily lead to the destruction of our whole force while it is still cut off by ice.

David Lloyd George to Winston S. Churchill: telephone message

(*Churchill papers: 16/6*)

3 April 1919 Paris

I regret Abrami's statement as much as you do. The first I heard of the matter was when I read the speech in the papers next day. I do not wish any

[1] Léon Pierre Abrami, 1879–1939. Born in Constantinople, of Italian-Jewish parents. Naturalized as a Frenchman at the age of one. Studied law, political science and oriental languages in Paris. Practised as a Barrister in Paris from 1903. Private Secretary to the Minister of Marine, 1913. Elected to the Chamber of Deputies, 1914, as a left-republican. On active service in Lorraine and the Argonne, 1915–16. Senior Staff Officer on the staff of General Sarrail, Commander of the Army of the East, 1916–17. A critic of the Greek policy of the Briand Government, 1917. Appointed by Clemenceau as Under-Secretary of State for War (with special responsibility for pensions), 1917–20. Served as a Deputy until 1936. In a statement at the end of March 1919 he had declared, of the French troops in North Russia, that 'not another single man would be sent to the aid of this small force'.

interference with any arrangements you may have made for making evacuation of troops and those associated with them in Northern Russia, perfectly safe.[1]

Winston S. Churchill to David Lloyd George: telegram

(*Churchill papers: 16/6*)

3 April 1919 War Office
5 pm
Secret

Very many thanks for your message. I was sure that would be your view.

Sir Henry Wilson: diary

(*Wilson papers*)

3 April 1919 Paris

The meeting of the British Delegation was adjourned to 6 pm. Then office where I found a letter from Winston to Clemenceau which he asked me to read & send on. Winston is manoeuvring for position ag^t LG. Winston also sent wires of effusion to Ironside, Maynard, Kolchak, Franchet to keep himself in the limelight.

Sir Henry Wilson to Winston S. Churchill

(*Churchill papers: 16/6*)

3 April 1919 Paris
Secret

Dear S of S,

I got your note with the two enclosures, one of which I despatched at once after reading and the other I have sent across to the PM and hope to be able to add a line before the post goes giving his approval. I was with him all the morning, and all this afternoon he is working with the other Prime Minister.

I saw in a paper which reached me this morning that the Canadians propose to withdraw certain men from their two batteries in Archangel at once

[1] Churchill noted on this message: 'Copy to War Cabinet'.

and without relief. I would have spoken to Borden about this but he left for England this morning, and I think it would be well if you saw him and asked him to hold his hand and let these two batteries, which have done admirable work, remain on there with our troops and take part in the final operations. This of course quite apart from the fact that practically speaking they cannot be withdrawn now.

The four Prime Ministers are today discussing the boundaries of the Jugo-Slavia-Serbian people. It seems to me to be rather an academic performance and that there are other and more pressing things, but the despatch of Smuts to Budapest[1] has postponed the discussion of matters, in Central Europe, and the despatch last night of Foch to Spa has postponed the discussion of Polish affairs.

The more I see of Paris the more confirmed I am in my opinion of your wisdom in not being here.

All the afternoon I have been trying to get an answer about your wire from the PM but so far with no success.

I am telephoning to tell you.

HW

Winston S. Churchill to General Harington and General Kirke

(*Churchill papers: 16/6*)

4 April 1919 War Office

The telephone message I have received from the Prime Minister fully empowers me to take all necessary measures for the relief and rescue of our troops in North Russia.

I am ready, therefore, to receive proposals for strong action. I consider the force we are forming should be known as 'The Rescue Force', which will in every way shield it from criticism and gain it support.

I do not see why we should not call for volunteers in addition to those we have already selected. It would be interesting to see what response we got.

Let me know what happened to the Admiralty scheme for getting men. Apparently they got their 900 men almost immediately.

The terms of engagement should be for 9 months and carry with them, say,

[1] Where the Hungarian communists, led by Bela Kun, had seized power on 21 March 1919. The Allies hoped to persuade them to accept a new frontier with Rumania, whereby some 2,000 square miles of predominantly Magyar territory would either come under Rumanian rule, or be a neutral zone. Smuts reached Budapest on 4 April, but negotiations for a compromise soon broke down, and on 16 April the Rumanians moved their troops into the disputed zone.

a £30 bounty. We might quite easily find ourselves tapping a new source of re-enlisting men.

Speak to me to-day about this after you have discussed it among yourselves.

Winston S. Churchill to General Milne

(Churchill papers: 16/16)

4 April 1919 War Office

I attach the greatest importance to helping Denikin and am most anxious that there should be no friction or misunderstanding which can possibly be avoided. Is it not possible for you to travel swiftly yourself to his headquarters or some intermediate rendezvous and try to reach a thoroughly good working arrangement for our common interests. If you did this you might take General Bridges with you so that a complete accord could be reached between Denikin, yourself and Franchet D'Esperey. Denikin is very hard-pressed and requires encouragement, and I am sure that if you all get together you will be able to settle matters satisfactorily.

Now that it has been settled that the Italians shall relieve us in the Caucasus, the military operations against the Bolsheviks will soon be our sole concern. Do your utmost to help them forward within the strict limits which are assigned to us by Cabinet policy. I shall be glad to hear from you personally.

Winston S. Churchill to General Harington

(War Office papers: 32/5749)

4 April 1919 War Office

Are you sure that it is wise to give away the secret of our new gas for the sake of such a small application as would be possible in North Russia?

Winston S. Churchill: message to British troops in North Russia

(Churchill papers: 'The Campaign in North Russia')

4 April 1919 War Office

Although you are cut off from your country by the ice, you are not forgotten. Your safety and well-being, on the contrary, is one of the main anxieties of the War Office, and we are determined to do everything in our power to help you and bring you safely home. You were sent to North Russia to help draw off the Germans from attacking our armies in France, and undoubtedly you helped last year to keep large numbers of German troops away from the battlefield and so enabled a decisive victory to be won.

Whatever may be the plan of action towards Russia decided on by The League of Nations, *we intend to relieve you at the earliest possible moment*, and either bring the whole force away or replace you by fresh men. These reliefs are being prepared now, and will come through the ice to your aid at the earliest moment when the ships can break through. Meanwhile, your lives and your chance of again seeing your home and friends and your fellow-countrymen, who are looking forward to give you a hearty welcome, depend absolutely upon your discipline and dogged British fighting qualities. All eyes are upon you now, and you represent the British Army which has fought and won and which is watching you confidently and earnestly. *You will be back home in time to see this year's harvest gathered in*, if you continue to display that undaunted British spirit which has so often got us through in spite of heavy odds and great hardships.

Only a few more months of resolute and faithful service against this ferocious enemy and your task will have been discharged. Carry on like Britains fighting for dear life and dearer honour, and set an example in these difficult circumstances to the troops of every other country. Reinforcement and relief on the way. We send you this personal message with the most heartful wishes for your speedy, safe and honourable return.

Winston S. Churchill to David Lloyd George: unsent telegram

(*Churchill papers: 16/6*)

6 April 1919 War Office

Secret and Personal

On hearing from CIGS that you approved Murmansk message to troops subject to it emanating from War Office and not from me personally, message was altered accordingly and despatched before receipt of your private and personal telegram.

Necessity for message was strongly urged by General Staff and precedents exist for either form.

Danger is that the troops are becoming discouraged by their isolation amid much danger and discomfort in absence of any policy which could be explained to them. The French troops and considerable portions of the Americans are in a state of mutiny and we have had four or five unpleasant incidents ourselves.

The local Cs-in-C have of course issued repeated appeals and exhortations, and my advisers here have been pressing for a fortnight that these should be supplemented in the manner which would most effectively command their attention.

It is true that the operations in North Russia are tiny compared with the great war in Europe, but from the point of view of the 13,000 British troops, who think themselves forgotten there, they seem quite important.

I have personally no responsibility whatever for this expedition and my only endeavour is to be in a position to carry out, without disaster, the policy on which you may decide. If this should be achieved, I do not doubt their friends and fellow-countrymen will give them a hearty welcome on their return home, but message clearly does not commit you to any public action in this respect.

Sir Henry Wilson: diary

(*Wilson papers*)

8 April 1919 Paris

. . . then I went down to LG's flat after dinner to see what Bonar—who flew over this afternoon—had to say. Bonar was ultra-pessimist. Ireland was going into Revolution, Labour was ever more hostile, Eric Geddes impossible, Winston very difficult, the H of C hostile to LG and so on.

H. A. L. Fisher to his wife

(*Fisher papers*)

8 April 1919 London

I had a long talk with Winston to-day. He is very anti-Bolshevik: 'After having defeated all the tigers & lions I don't like to be beaten by baboons.'

Winston S. Churchill to David Lloyd George: unsent letter

(*Churchill papers: 16/6*)

9 April 1919 War Office
Private

My dear Prime Minister,

Many thanks for your wire received this morning.[1] A month has passed since we met—almost the longest hiatus in a political association of so many years. I have seen and understood the problems you have been up against and have felt that probably the best way I could help was to keep the position here good and solid as far as the Army was concerned and War Office business in the House of Commons.

Parliament is, I think, on the whole quite contented with the state of military business, and as for the Army, instead of about 20 mutinies a week we are now getting a solid disciplined force, in which I am glad to say nearly a month has passed without one untoward incident. Voluntary recruiting is as follows:—

Re-engagements for 2, 3 or 4 years . . . 64,000, but now I am getting scarcely 300 a day on the average, instead of 1,000.

New young boys joining for the first time 11,000; rate about 1,300 a week, which is a large increase on the ordinary pre-war intake.

Special re-engagements for one year for the Army of the Rhine, about . . . 8,000, 2,000 of whom came in in the last week.

I do not think there is any prospect of raising by voluntary means the necessary armies next year, even assuming that we only want about half as many men as we now have. It may well be that later on in the year I shall have to ask you to call out the new young boys in order that they may be trained in time to set their fathers free next year. In that event I should hope that it would be possible to say that every man who had fought in the war could come home and be discharged, leaving the clearing up to be done only by those who had escaped altogether the severities of the struggle and volunteers who had embraced a military career. No decision on this is needed for some months to come, but I mention it to you now because it is clearly approaching us.

In regard to Russia, I am proceeding in strict accordance with my letter to you of the 7th March, of which you have a copy, diverging in no way from what you then approved. I have organised one brigade, taken from the men who had already volunteered for general service, as a relief force to cover the evacuation of Murmansk and Archangel, and I am now calling for volunteers to form a second brigade, which may or may not have to go, as

[1] Not found in the Churchill papers.

circumstances dictate. We shall see what response we get in the course of a few days.

The talk about reinforcements, the call for volunteers, and our clear intention not to let our men be cast away or abandoned, will be one of the greatest preventives against the Bolsheviks picking out our North Russian force as an objective for an overwhelming attack. Lying as they do at the centre and fighting armies straggled out on an enormous circumference detached from one another, the Bolsheviks can on interior lines concentrate against any one of their enemies. Nothing will encourage them more to do this than statements like that made by Abrami that not a single man will be sent to their relief. Nothing will discourage them more than clear evidence that they will have a very warm reception if they interfere with us. I have chosen the name 'Relief Force' because it leaves it ambiguous whether it is 'relief' in the sense of rescue or 'relief' in the sense of replacement. This is necessary because once it is openly apparent that we are going to quit, the Russian population among whom our force is living and the Russian troops who have been organised to help us will be honeycombed with treachery and discouragement, knowing well that they will soon have to reckon upon the vengeance of their present enemies after being deserted by their present friends. I do not think I shall have the slightest difficulty in explaining and justifying the measures we are taking to the satisfaction of Press, Parliament and Public.

No official communiqué was issued about Archangel to the press. The Assistant Director of Operations gives them a lecture once a fortnight, and on this occasion he told them about North Russia, meaning to create an atmosphere favourable to the despatch of the relief force which we are preparing. What he said was very sensible and had it appeared textually would have done no harm. However, the press jumped to conclusions far in advance of anything justified by his words, and fortified also by the arrival of Shackleton, the Arctic explorer, who was somewhat alarmist, gave an unduly pessimistic impression, which I have corrected. However, it was a good thing that people should be woken up, because if a disaster occurred through measures being neglected, it would do irreparable harm to the Government.

Seely tells me that you inveigh against me for inspiring an article in the 'Daily Mail' advocating an attack on Petrograd. I have never done anything of the sort. My advisers are very doubtful about the Petrograd plan, and the only step I have ever taken in connection with it is to forward to you a letter from Master Sutherland, who seems to have been bitten with it.[1] Disabuse your mind I beg you, therefore, of this impression.

[1] Sir William Sutherland's letter to Churchill, sent to him from 10 Downing Street on 11 March 1919 (see page 584).

I send you herewith Haking's[1] report, which is a remarkable document to have been written by a soldier. All the soldiers are agreed that the most important military action required from the allies is to feed Germany, not only with food but with raw materials, and to raise the blockade. They think that Germany is on the verge of a complete collapse, and there is no doubt that it would from many points of view pay her to escape the consequences of the war by taking refuge in Bolshevism. Once you are a Bolshevist you are apparently immune. All past crimes are forgiven and forgotten; all past sentences are remitted and all debts are forgiven; all territory that you want to have is restored to you. You may fight anybody you like and nobody may fight against you. The mighty armies of the victorious allies are impotent against you. You boot the French into the Black Sea, or the British into the White Sea, and everybody else (except the Japanese) into the Yellow Sea. Altogether you have a splendid time and incidentally you deal with the domestic capitalist and landlord. Can one wonder that the creed should be so popular? I observe, however, that Lenin[2] is becoming very particular, and that he made careful enquiries about Bela Kun's[3] doctrinal position before giving him a 'coupon'. Therefore, I think the German Government would be mad to accept the first lot of terms with which they are presented. Even if they continue in their position until you have all agreed on the terms, it seems to me almost certain that they will reject them and disclaim further

[1] Richard Cyril Byrne Haking, 1862–1945. Entered Army, 1881. On active service in Burma, 1885–7 and South Africa, 1899–1900. Commanded the 5th Brigade, 1914; the 1st Division, 1915. Promoted Major-General for distinguished service in the field, 1915. Lieutenant-General commanding the XI Corps, 1915–18. Knighted, 1916. Commanded British Military Mission to Russia and the Baltic Provinces, 1919. Commanded the Allied Troops in the Plebiscite Area, East Prussia and Danzig, 1920. High Commissioner, League of Nations, Danzig, 1921–3. General Officer Commanding the British Troops in Egypt, 1923–7.

[2] Vladimir Ilich Ulyanov, 1870–1924. Known as 'Lenin'. Son of an inspector of schools. In 1887 his elder brother was executed for the attempted assassination of Alexander III. Joined a Marxist circle in Kazan, 1887; banished to Siberia, 1897–1900; founded the Russian Social Democratic Labour Party, 1898. Emigrated to western Europe, 1900. Leader of the Bolshevik (majority) section of his Party from 1903. In 1912 he severed relations with all other Parties and factions. With only a brief return to Russia in October 1905, he lived in exile in Europe from 1900 to 1917. Returned to Russia in April 1917. Chairman of the Council of People's Commissars (Prime Minister) from the revolution of October 1917 until his death.

[3] Bela Kun, 1886–1936. A Hungarian Jew, he worked before 1914 as a journalist on a Socialist newspaper in Budapest. Served as a Lieutenant-Commander of an ammunition supply column, 1914. Captured by the Russians on the Eastern Front and imprisoned in Russia, 1915–17. He supported the Bolsheviks in 1917; in October 1918 he returned to Hungary as leader of a revolutionary party. Prime Minister of Hungary, March–August 1919, when he instituted a communist regime. In July 1919 the Allies halted his invasion of Slovakia. He fled to Vienna in August 1919, and was interned in a lunatic asylum. Allowed by the Allies to go to Russia, 1920, he became a leading figure of the Comintern. Eventually he was imprisoned, then murdered on Stalin's orders.

responsibility. On the other hand, there is a very fair chance that they will be overthrown before the end of the present month.

Meanwhile Russia is, I think, undergoing a certain change, similar to that which passed over the French Revolution under the Directory—all civil society being destroyed, it was only by the military hierarchy that its structure could be re-constituted. It seems to me very likely that the purely military phase will soon be reached. I am told that on the Southern Front there are good Bolshevik Generals and disciplined troops and that the atrocities there have gradually diminished, while all the time the military attack becomes more formidable. On the other hand, Denikin is still alive, little though he has been helped, and his army is still a real factor. Kolchak has done very well, though apparently because the forces on his front have been greatly weakened for the sake of the Southern attack. Some of the new divisions he is raising will soon be ready to strengthen his fighting front. His right hand is gradually stretching out towards the Archangel region.

My view of the future is therefore rather inclining in the direction of a purely military Russia in one form or another coming to the aid of a Bolshevist Germany and Austria and Hungary, and thus confronting us after a few years with a situation very formidable to France and Britain, and to the United States as well unless she keeps out of it. It seems to me that Japan will certainly be drawn to act with Germany and Russia in this eventuality. Already we receive reports of her engaging German officers, both naval and military. I am assured that she had relations with Germany in October last year. Clearly this big block of the Central Empires, Russia and Japan, is the prime interest of all parties to it. So you may have two Leagues of Nations instead of one, and the beaten ones re-arming while the victorious ones are disarming.

If I put these thoughts forward in a light form, do not suppose that I am not conscious of their gravity and tragedy. The only course I have to suggest, which I now believe an enormous body of educated opinion would support, and particularly military opinion, is as follows—'Feed Germany; Fight Bolshevism; make Germany fight Bolshevism'. It may well be that it is too late for this. It may well be that even if time remained you could never get the allies to agree.

I have to make a speech on Friday at the Aldwych Club. I thought of saying that your policy had consistently been to feed Germany, to disarm Germany, and to make peace with Germany. I shall also denounce Bolshevism and urge the need of fighting it not only by arms but by far-reaching social reforms. If there is anything you would like me to say, please let me know.

I am so glad you have recovered from your chill. My house has been stricken with influenza. 3 children, 2 nurses and my wife—all down together. Alas, the poor nurse died yesterday morning, but, thank God, the others are all getting over it. It has been a great anxiety. There seems to me no doubt whatever that inoculation repeated at intervals is the right cure. I have so far survived.

Yours always
W

Winston S. Churchill to David Lloyd George

(*Churchill papers: 16/6*)

10 April 1919 War Office
Personal & Secret

I am sending you Haking's memo & a few other papers of interest. No communiqué was issued about Archangel but newspapers took an alarmist view of the forthright lecture to the Press given by the Assistant Director of Military Operations reinforced by Sir Ernest Shackleton's[1] independent statements. Bolsheviks of course are accurately informed about situation in North Russia as our forces are living among Russian population partly Bolshevik. Therefore I do not consider any harm has been done & indeed it was high time the public woke up to the dangers wh wd follow the neglect of our forces in N Russia & gave the Government the necessary support.

Declarations like Abrami's indicating that not a single man more wd be sent to their aid are very bad. General Staff are satisfied with the measures we are taking to relieve the force & so long as they are carried out I do not think you need feel unduly anxious.

Secondly the debate last night showed a practical unanimity against any negotiations with the Bolsheviks or any recognition of Lenin and Trotsky. Your own Labour group[2] has the most Anti-Bolshevik element. I do trust

[1] Ernest Henry Shackleton, 1874–1922. Served in Scott's Antarctic Expedition, 1901–4. Commanded the British Antarctic Expedition of 1914–16. Headed the British Propaganda Mission to South America, 1917–18. Major, on the staff of General Maynard at Murmansk, in charge of equipment, clothing, rations and transport of the mobile columns, 1918–19. Resigned his commission, February 1919, in order to negotiate a trade concession from the North Russian Government; his North Russian concession was rejected by the Soviets when they extended their control to Archangel. Employed by the Government to organize a London bus service in the event of a General Strike of transport workers, 1920. Commanded the British Oceanographical and Sub-Antarctic Expedition, 1921–2. He died off South Georgia Island during the expedition.

[2] The National Democratic Party, founded shortly before the 1918 election to unite Labour movement support behind Lloyd George's Government. It was supported by a

President Wilson will not be allowed to weaken our policy against them in any way. His negotiations have become widely known and are much resented. . . .[1]

Winston S. Churchill to Sir Henry Wilson

(*Churchill papers: 16/6*)

11 April 1919 War Office

Many thanks for your letter received this morning. I am very much in the dark about what is going on, and cannot help feeling that things are getting worse and worse. By the time a paper agreement is reached between the Allies, the whole situation may have got out of hand, and even after that there is the Bosche to be persuaded. I had to make a speech of some importance to-day at the Aldwych Club, in which I exposed some of those truths we have been looking at together of which the newspapers seem so largely oblivious.[2]

The volunteers are coming in well for Murmansk and Archangel. We had on the Horse Guards Parade to-day a scene which recalled the early days of the war, when a compact body of about 100 magnificent men marched from the recruiting office to the depot. The Adjutant General seems quite confident that he will get all he is asking for and more.

I hear that David Henderson[3] will soon cease to be Military Attaché in

---

number of anti-socialist Trade Unions. In the 1918 election it put up 28 candidates, all in working-class constituencies, and 15 were returned to Parliament. In 1922 all these MPs joined the National Liberal Party, but only one was re-elected. The Party was dissolved in 1923.

[1] On 22 February 1919 a young American diplomat, William Christian Bullitt, had been sent by Woodrow Wilson direct to Moscow from Paris to negotiate with the Bolsheviks. On 8 March he had begun seven days of discussion with Lenin, Chicherin and Litvinov, and in the first week of April he had brought several Soviet peace proposals to both Woodrow Wilson and Lloyd George in Paris; but, to his chagrin, these were at once rejected. In 1933 President Roosevelt sent Bullitt to Moscow as the first American Ambassador to the Soviet Union; his two years there made him a vehement critic of the Soviet regime.

[2] In his speech, Churchill dwelt on Bolshevik atrocities. 'Of all tyrannies in history,' he said, 'the Bolshevik tyranny is the worst, the most destructive, the most degrading.' The atrocities committed under Lenin and Trotsky were 'incomparably more hideous, on a larger scale, and more numerous than any for which the Kaiser is responsible'. The decision of Russia to leave the war was a betrayal of honour and an act of murder. 'Every British and French soldier, killed last year,' Churchill declared, 'was really done to death by Lenin and Trotsky, not in fair war, but by the treacherous desertion of an ally without parallel in the history of the world.'

[3] David Henderson, 1862–1921. Entered Army, 1883. Captain, 1890. Director of Military Intelligence, South Africa (under Lord Kitchener), 1900–2. Learned to fly, 1911. Advocated the formation of a Royal Flying Corps for the Army, 1912. Director-General of Military Aeronautics, 1913–18. Major-General, 1914. Appointed General Officer Commanding

Paris and that this appointment will be vacant. It seems to me that Spears is unquestionably the best man we could have in this important post. No one possesses half his brains, half his knowledge, half his connections, or half his wound-stripes. I therefore attach much importance to his being appointed. We really cannot afford to employ any but the best agents in these sort of positions.[1]

I look forward very much to seeing you when you return. Many important matters connected with the organisation of the office have been simmering and will soon be ready for action.

Edward Marsh to Charles Ogden[2]

(*Churchill papers: 1/132*)

11 April 1919 War Office

Dear Sir,

Mr Churchill was very much surprised to see in the leading article of the 9th inst the statement that he had mentioned at the General Election the figure of £50,000,000,000 as the sum wh shd be extracted from Germany. There is no truth whatever in this. Mr Churchill referred on one occasion to 'the nonsense of supposing' that 20 or 30 thousand millions cd be got from Germany, & the only estimate to which he committed himself was two thousand millions, though he said that he would have been glad to get more if possible.

Further, Mr Churchill attached three special conditions to the extraction of any indemnity from Germany, viz (1) it must not harm our trade (2) it must not force Germany into a state of Bolshevism (3) it must not create servile conditions of labour in Germany, as these wd react on our own labour standards.

Royal Flying Corps, 5 August 1914; he took his force to France, 13 August 1914. Knighted, 1914. Lieutenant-General, 1918. Vice-President of the Air Council, January 1918; resigned, April 1918, after a disagreement with the Air Minister, Lord Rothermere. Military Counsellor, British Embassy, Paris, October 1918–June 1919. Director, League of Red Cross Societies, Geneva, 1920–1. His only son was killed in a flying accident in 1918.

[1] Sir Henry Wilson, who distrusted Spears intensely, refused to support him for the post of Military Attaché in Paris. He was supported in his refusal by the Ambassador in Paris, Lord Derby. After a long, acrimonious correspondence, Churchill agreed not to insist upon Spears' appointment.

[2] Charles Ogden, 1863–1945. Entered journalism in Bradford, 1881. One of the founders of the Independent Labour Party, 1891. Joined the Liberal Party, 1900. Active in recruiting work, 1914–18. Editor of the *Yorkshire Observer*, 1918–26. Deputy Chairman of the Bradford Liberal Federation, 1928.

Mr Churchill regrets very much that such a loose & ill-informed statement shd appear in yr columns & he thinks you shd take an opportunity of correcting it.

Yours faithfully
E. Marsh

Winston S. Churchill to the Duke of Marlborough

(*Churchill papers: 1/132*)

12 April 1919 War Office

I hope you will read in the Daily Telegraph the verbatim report of my speech yesterday. It expresses the military view of the present situation and is concurred in by all my principal advisers. We cannot afford to go on maltreating the Germans while we have this Bolshevik peril on our hands.

I am afraid things are very difficult in Paris, and the time lost in sterile discussions about the League of Nations may prove irretrievable.

I do not attach too much importance to the bye-elections, because after such an idiotic swing our way at the polls, it was inevitable that there should be a violent reaction.[1]

Winston S. Churchill to General Harington, General Thwaites and General Radcliffe

(*War Office papers: 32/5378*)

16 April 1919 War Office

Pray meet together to-day and, after discussion between yourselves, present to me through the CIGS a statement marshalling the grave reasons which exist against the wholesale repatriation to Russia of Russian prisoners of war in Germany.

Whereas we could have made out of these an army of loyal men who would have been available to sustain the defence of Archangel and Murmansk or to aid General Denikin and Kolchak, we are now I presume simply sending a reinforcement of 500,000 trained men to join the armies of Lenin and Trotsky. This appears to me to be one of the capital blunders in the history of the world.

[1] On 1 March 1919 the Coalitionists had lost Leyton West to an Independent Liberal Candidate, and on 29 March they lost Hull Central, likewise to an Independent Liberal. On 16 April a third Coalition seat, Central Aberdeen and Kincardine, likewise fell to an Independent Liberal. All the Coalition losses were in previously Conservative-held seats.

Winston S. Churchill to General Briggs:[1] *telegram*

(*War Office papers: 32/5678*)

19 April 1919 War Office

1. Though the situation in South Russia is at present critical I am hopeful for the future. I should like you to know that the position at the beginning of this year in Siberia was as bad, if not worse, than it is to-day in South Russia. Almost incredible changes have taken place for the better during the past three months. Kolchak's offensive has met with outstanding success and the position of the Government has been so strengthened that the British High Commissioner has felt justified in recommending its recognition as a Provisional Government of Siberia. Moreover Kolchak feels that the presence of Allied troops, is now unnecessary on the Eastern front.

2. The reverses suffered by the enemy in the East are bound to re-act immediately on other fronts and I sincerely trust that will give Denikin the necessary breathing space to re-organise and make effective use of the stores we are supplying.

3. That Denikin has been led to expect assistance in the shape of Allied troops is greatly to be regretted, as public opinion is absolutely opposed to such a measure in this country. There are, too, other grave objections to this course. Many authorities on the Russian situation hold that the effort must be made from within if Russia is to be regenerated. It is very questionable whether Russia will ever be able to stand alone if it comes from without.

4. Financial assistance is not a question with which the War Office is empowered to deal. You can, however, readily understand the objections to sinking further large sums in addition to our already huge commitments. I trust the steps which Denikin has already taken to obtain paper money from America will relieve the situation.

5. Finally, it is most unfortunate that Denikin should be filled with the notion that the Allies favour a policy which aims at Russia's dismemberment. Denikin maintains the thesis that he is still an Ally and he must recognise the fact that the Allies are pledged to consider all claims to self determination. It does not follow by any means that the independence of all would be states claiming it is, or will be, recognised and as far as Russia is concerned it is highly probable that such claims will not be dealt with until the Russian problem is settled as a whole.

[1] Charles James Briggs, 1865–1941. Entered the Army, 1886. On active service in South Africa, 1899–1902. Lieutenant-Colonel, 1902. Brigadier-General, commanding the 1st Cavalry Brigade, 1913–14. Major-General, February 1915. Lieutenant-General, commanding the 16 Army Corps at Salonika, 1916–18. Knighted 1917. Head of the British Mission to South Russia, 1918–19.

Authority over the embryo republics in the South Caucasus is in the meantime by no means essential to Denikin in his anti-Bolshevik campaign, and it is on the latter that he should concentrate his whole efforts secure in the knowledge that such action will not in any way prejudice but will tend to strengthen Russia's case.

Winston S. Churchill to David Lloyd George

(*Churchill papers: 16/6*)

20 April 1919 War Office

My dear Prime Minister,

I am somewhat perplexed by the letter signed by the four Prime Ministers to Dr Nansen.[1] I do not understand what course you actually contemplate. The armies of Kolchak and Denikin are not short of food and, as you pointed out in your speech, the districts which they hold are some of the richest and best supplied in Russia. Therefore to give food to the rest of Russia is to put the Bolsheviks on an equality with these loyal armies and to rob the latter of one of their principal advantages.

Further, the economic pressure in Bolshevik Russia is undoubtedly a tremendous weapon leading to the breakdown and overthrow of the Bolshevik regime. If this pressure is removed, the regime will be strengthened.

Thirdly, it seems to me impossible to carry out any scheme of re-victualling of this kind without coming into close and complicated relations with the Government of Lenin and Trotsky. This will certainly increase their prestige.

Thus from every point of view it seems to me that the proposal to feed Russia 'impartially', which means in practice feeding Bolshevik Russia, as the others already have food, will not commend itself to Denikin and Kolchak. Kolchak's armies are advancing victoriously at the present time on a very wide front, and there are good hopes that this advance will continue. They will certainly not want to stop fighting in order that the Bolsheviks may be fed. I do not think they could afford to do so for a moment, because their armies, if remaining stationary during a kind of armistice, would disintegrate and Bolshevik propaganda, which is even more formidable than Bolshevik arms, would continue unabated during the truce.

[1] Fridtjof Nansen, 1861–1930. Born in Christiania, Norway. Explorer. His North Pole Expedition of 1893–96 reached the highest latitude then obtained (86° 34′ n). Professor of Zoology, Christiania. Norwegian Minister, London, 1906–8. Honorary knighthood, 1906. Professor of Oceanography, Christiania, from 1908 until his death. Organized a scheme to feed the famine-struck Russians, 1919–21. Nobel Peace Prize, 1921. Active in refugee resettlement work, 1921–30.

On the other hand, I understand your letter to say that if all parties do not stop fighting, the feeding scheme cannot go forward. What will happen then? Will you simply drop the proposal, or will you wish to put pressure on Kolchak? I cannot help fearing lest that may be the outcome and that he may be denied the munitions which he has been promised and which are indispensable to his continued success. I hope indeed that this will not be so.

Winston S. Churchill to Lord Curzon

(*Curzon papers*)

22 April 1919 War Office
Private & Secret

My dear Curzon,

I send you a copy of a letter which I have written to the Prime Minister about feeding the Bolsheviks. I must frankly confess myself utterly unable to understand how we can feed the Bolsheviks with the one hand and fight them with the other, and how we can reconcile feeding Bolshevik Russia with re-arming the armies of Denikin and Kolchak. Is it our plan to keep both sides going in order that they may continue fighting for ever?

I am very glad that you have advocated the recognition of Kolchak. The General Staff consider that the moment has come for this, but how can it be done at the same time as we are feeding Lenin and Trotsky?

Yours sincerely
Winston S. Churchill

Winston S. Churchill to Austen Chamberlain

(*Churchill papers: 16/6*)

22 April 1919 War Office

I send you herewith a copy of an official letter we are forwarding to the Treasury on the subject of continuing to pay the Russian Military Agency and Mission.

I do not think I can add anything to what is set out in the letter of the General Staff. In spite of the luke-warm and feeble support which we have given to the armies of Kolchak and Denikin and the open discouragement which the rumours of our evacuation must have conveyed to the Russian troops on the Archangel front, all these Russian forces have exhibited a continual increase of fighting strength and efficiency; and Admiral Kolchak in particular is advancing on an enormous front across the plains of Siberia, has already recovered more than 200 miles in depth of territory, and has very good prospects of reaching the line of the Volga. The weakness shown by the Bolshevik troops whenever they are grappled with becomes more and more apparent, and the strength of the loyal Russian forces is growing relatively.

At this moment to paralyse the Russian missions here for the sake of sums in the neighbourhood of £1,236 is, I think, wholly out of harmony with the interests of the country and the policy we have been definitely authorised to pursue.

If the only point in question is that the charge should be placed on Army Votes, we shall make not the slightest objection so long as the necessary funds are forthcoming from the Treasury, but I do trust that nothing will be done at this juncture which will prevent these missions from being properly sustained. It may well be that before a year is out they will be the representatives of a Government speaking in the name of a united Russia. How short-sighted it would be for us to cripple them at this moment?

I hope this matter may have your personal attention. The subordinate officials of the Treasury seem to me to hit out blindly at every item of expenditure, however necessary or however small, without any clear conception of the policy which the Government proposes to pursue. The Chief of the Imperial General Staff, with whom I have been talking about this, would be very much obliged if you would discuss the matter with him should you find it difficult to agree to our renewed request, and he will hold himself at your disposal almost any time this week.

Winston S. Churchill to Sir Henry Wilson

(*Churchill papers: 16/16*)

22 April 1919 War Office
Secret

A wire arrived the other day from Ironside about withdrawing his present troops the moment our reinforcements arrive. In my opinion it is too soon now to take decisions of this character. Before it is possible for us to withdraw, we must have completed our reinforcement of the North Russian theatre. When all our troops have arrived and are in position and we are at our maximum strength, it will be easy to disentangle the tired troops from the line first. But there may easily be one month in which both the relief force and the present force are in contact with the enemy together. Nothing will be lost if this occurs. I did not contemplate the ships being filled up with men pulled out of the line and sent back to England immediately and in proportion as each relieving detachment arrives.

The policy is that we are to go, but as between June and July I conceive we have latitude, and every day gained may enable the Russian forces we are raising to acquire strength to hold their positions, and secondly may enable Kolchak's forces to come into touch on our left Archangel flank.

It would be a great pity to sacrifice these possibilities for the sake of a few weeks one way or the other. Therefore, in my opinion we should first of all establish our position strongly by the arrival of the reinforcements, and having made the front secure should then consider how the evacuation can be carried out.

Pray let me see before it is sent any telegram to Ironside and Maynard in answer to the one to which this minute refers.

WSC

Sir Henry Wilson: diary

(*Wilson papers*)

23 April 1919

I had a mil: members meeting at 10.30 to explain all the things I want for India.[1] Army Council meeting at 3 o'c at which I proposed to prepare 9 Cav: Rgts & 20 Batt[n] here in England to be ready for India but I explained to Winston that this would not be possible, as the men were on leave, unless he made it clear to the Country that India was in danger.

Winston is not prepared to do that at present, & so all I can do is to send India such small personnel in wireless, MG etc as I can, & such armoured cars, wireless installations etc as we have got—also I arranged with AG to see Mercer[2] the Roy Marine AG to see if we could not build up a Naval

[1] Since the beginning of 1919 India had been the scene of severe internal unrest, and on 30 March M K Gandhi had declared a 'hartal', or closure of all shops. This led to clashes between police and protestors in Delhi, Lahore, Amritsar and other cities. On 10 April mobs seized control of a number of towns in the Punjab, murdering several English officials and businessmen. On 13 April nearly 400 unarmed Indians were killed when General Dyer ordered his troops to open fire at a crowd assembled in a confined space at Amritsar. These disturbances inside India encouraged the new Amir of Afghanistan, Amanullah (whose father had been murdered on 20 February) to incite the border tribes to invade British India, and he himself began, in the last two weeks of April, to mobilize his tropps in the Khyber Pass.

[2] David Mercer, 1864–1920. Entered Royal Marine Light Infantry, 1883. Brigadier-General commanding the 1st Royal Naval Brigade, 1914–16; served at Gallipoli and on the western front. Adjutant-General, Royal Marine Forces, from 1916 until his death. Major-General, 1916. Knighted, 1918. ADC to the King, 1918.

Division. The whole thing is unsatisfactory as I really have not enough troops to cope with possible difficulties. Before long we shall have to call up the 18 year old boys to set free the older soldiers.

The response for Archangel—3500 men—is good, & Winston & I discussed a good punch towards Viatka to join with Kolchak before we cleared out.

Winston S. Churchill to Lord Curzon

(*Curzon papers*)

26 April 1919 War Office
Private

My dear Curzon,

I enclose herewith a secret paper prepared by the General Staff on the evacuation of North Russia. I am asking that this shall be considered by the Cabinet either on Wednesday or Thursday next, and I am sending a copy to the Prime Minister.

You will see that, owing to Kolchak's victories, the improvement in the morale and increase in numbers of the Russian troops in North Russia, and the fact that we have at our disposal a compact body of highly disciplined volunteers, there is now a prospect, for the first time, of our getting clear from North Russia without humiliation to ourselves and disaster to all who have trusted in us.

I beg you will give this paper your most careful attention, as I propose to press for a formal Cabinet decision upon it. I earnestly hope, and confidently expect, that you will be in general agreement with the policy proposed by the General Staff.

Yours vy sincerely
Winston S. Churchill

Winston S. Churchill to Walter Long

(*Churchill papers: 16/6*)

26 April 1919 War Office

The enclosed gave me a great deal of satisfaction. It reflects great credit on Admiral Calthorpe[1] that he should have such a firm grip of the rights and

[1] Somerset Arthur Gough-Calthorpe, 1864–1937. Second son of the 7th Baron Calthorpe. Entered Royal Navy, 1878. Naval Attaché to Russia, Norway and Sweden, 1902–5. Com-

wrongs of this question. Wherever the Bolsheviks have been stood up to, as in North Russia, Siberia and on Denikin's front, they have shown much weakness, and the loyal troops have maintained their spirit. Wherever anything in the nature of a truce or parley has been arranged, Bolshevik propaganda has undermined all the troops against them and has proved far more effective than Bolshevik force. The French behaviour in South Russia and the Crimea has been from every point of view deplorable and has led to disastrous results quite gratuitously courted.

I wished to let you know how closely the War Office are in agreement with the policy announced by your Admiral.

Winston S. Churchill to David Lloyd George

(*Churchill papers: 16/6*)

26 April 1919 War Office

My dear Prime Minister,

I do hope that amid your many anxieties and preoccupations you have not lost sight of the very considerable change which has come over the military situation in Siberia.

Kolchak has been steadily making his way through innumerable difficulties and is achieving at the present time a very remarkable measure of success. It is thought that he now has a very good chance of reaching the line of the Volga in the near future, and there are possibilities that he may be able to advance further towards Moscow. At the same time his advance enables him to stretch out his right hand in the direction of the Archangel force, and communication by patrol has actually been established between them in the neighbourhood of Vyatka. The Russian forces in the Archangel area, which now number 15,000, have been fighting extremely well, and if the dangers of the next month are passed through satisfactorily in that quarter, this Russian force may well increase in numbers to 25,000 men.

It seems to me that this development would be important for you because if fostered and seconded with real goodwill it would enable you to withdraw from North Russia without either having to carry away many thousands of

---

manded the 2nd Cruiser Squadron, 1914–16. Knighted, 1916. Second Sea Lord, 1916. Admiral Commanding Coastguards and Reserves, 1917. Commander-in-Chief, Mediterranean, 1917–19 and also British High Commissioner at Constantinople, 1918–19. Commander-in-Chief, Portsmouth, 1920–3. Admiral of the Fleet, 1925.

the local inhabitants who have compromised themselves with us or leaving them to be massacred by the Bolsheviks.

The Government of Monsieur Tchaikowsky[1] which we have called into being in North Russia is the most democratic of the three Russian National Governments, and it would have been an unpleasant thing to have had to leave them in the lurch. There is, however, now a fresh chance of avoiding this and the reproach inseparable from it and at the same time carrying out your policy of evacuation.

Everything is, of course, very changeable in these Russian situations, but the changes which have taken place and appear still to be taking place in Siberia seem to offer us the prospect of escaping from our difficult position without discredit.

It seems to me, therefore, that we should do everything in our power to help and encourage Kolchak and to build up these Russian forces in North Russia which may conceivably, in the improving circumstances, be able to defend themselves when we are gone.

The advance of Kolchak's armies is the more remarkable in view of the fact that it is being conducted exclusively with Russian troops. The Czechos, who were formerly the only other troops on this front, are now employed simply on guarding the railway a long way back. The whole credit of regaining this really enormous stretch of country rests with a purely Russian army of about 100,000 men. There is, however, as you know, a Russian army of 100,000 in an advanced state of formation in Siberia, and five divisions from this army are expected to reach Admiral Kolchak during the course of the next three months. As the front has advanced Westward, districts containing large numbers of men have been recovered, and these men are already being used to fill up the divisions at the front. Apparently wherever Bolshevism has been tried it is loathed. It is only popular where it has not been felt, and Kolchak's armies have been well received by the population on their onward march.

We can, I think, claim to have given more effective support to Kolchak than any of the other great Powers, as we have supplied him with nearly 12 million pounds' worth of our surplus munitions, and by the labours of our officers and agents this great mass of stuff has been filtered along the Siberian railway. In fact, the Russian forces in which we are interested, whether in

[1] Nikolai Vasilievich Tchaikowsky, 1850–1926. Active in the first revolutionary Populist organization in St Petersburg, in the 1870s (known as the Tchaikowsky circle). In the 1880s he left Russia for the United States, where he tried to establish a religious commune. He returned to Russia during the 1905 revolution and was a leading member of the Popular Socialist Party. Strongly opposed the Bolsheviks in 1917. Head of the Provisional Government of North Russia (at Archangel), 1918–19. Went to Paris to plead the anti-Bolshevik cause at the Paris Peace Conference, 1919. He died in exile in England.

North Russia, Siberia or those of Denikin, have received from us assistance which has already been substantial and may shortly prove effective.

You will have seen papers circulated by the Foreign Office and the General Staff advocating the recognition of Admiral Kolchak's Government. This is the advice given by Eliot[1] as well as by the military men, and I most earnestly press it upon you at this juncture. Its influence on the military situation would be most favourable. It would give the greatest possible satisfaction to the overwhelming mass of your Parliamentary supporters. It would consolidate our Russian policy and strengthen your hand in many directions. It would be entirely justified on account of the solid support which we are giving in munitions and organisers.

Before such recognition is accorded, however, I think it would be a very good thing if your suggestion of trying to secure a democratic programme about Russian land from Kolchak were carried through. In this connection it is worth noticing that Monsieur Tchaikowsky, the Head of the North Russian Government, the most democratic Government in the field against the Bolsheviks, is, it is believed, about to become a member of Kolchak's Government. The moment appears, therefore, very favourable for securing from the Kolchak Government a declaration of policy in regard to (a) the land and (b) a constitutional and non-democratic regime, in return for their simultaneous recognition by the Allies, or at any rate by Great Britain.

I send you herewith a military paper which has been prepared by the General Staff, to the general policy of which I desire to obtain your approval and that of the Cabinet. If necessary Wilson and I can come over to see you on this subject, which seems to me to be of equal importance and urgency.

[1] Charles Norton Edgcumbe Eliot, 1862–1931. Boden Sanskrit Scholar, Oxford, 1883; Craven Prizeman, 1884. Entered the Diplomatic Service, as 3rd Secretary, St Petersburg, 1886–92. High Commissioner, Samoa, 1899. Knighted, 1900. British Agent, Zanzibar, 1900–4. Resigned from the Diplomatic Service, 1904. Member of the Royal Commission on Electoral Systems, 1909. Principal of the University of Hong Kong, 1912. Returned to the Diplomatic Service as High Commissioner, Siberia, 1918–19 and as Ambassador to Japan, 1919–26.

Winston S. Churchill to David Lloyd George

(*Churchill papers: 2/105*)

28 April 1919 War Office
Personal & Private

My dear PM

I have been annoyed to read this bloody paragraph in the Sunday Times[1] & in some doubt as to whether I ought not to take notice of it. What do you think. They are trying to make mischief & Northcliffe in the Despatch is on the same line. There is no bottom to the depths wh some of these writers have sunk. On the whole I think it better to ignore it; but I have asked Freddie to get the Pall Mall & Chronicle to comment on this kind of journalism.

You seem to be having exciting times in Paris & Wilson having quarrelled with Italy will have to be extra-civil to the British Empire. I suppose you foresaw that trend of events.

Don't be vexed with me about my Kolchak. There really is a good chance of his pulling the chestnuts out of the fire for all of us. The volunteering for N Russia is quite good, & almost all are men who wd not join the ordinary Army. I am reaching the modest limit we require very soon & shutting it down. 'House full'.

Yours always
W

Sir Henry Wilson to Winston S. Churchill

(*Churchill papers: 16/6*)

28 April 1919 Paris
Secret

Dear S of S

I dined with the Prime Minister last night and after dinner had a short discussion with him on the subject of your letter and the Russian paper. I have been round to see him again this morning and had a further talk but as

[1] On 27 April 1919 *The Sunday Times* published a paragraph, entitled 'The manoeuvres of Winston', which read: 'Political gossip continues to concern itself with the newest orientation of the Secretary of War. That inconstant personage is credited with the conviction that the prestige of Mr Lloyd George has been greatly impaired by the recent newspaper attacks upon him, and that any material disappointment of popular expectations of the Peace terms, notably in the matter of indemnities, may easily bring about the downfall of the Premier and the break-up of the Coalition. In that event there will be an opportunity for the "Central" Party which still remain in embryo to emerge, under such capable and determined leadership as Mr Churchill could afford them.' The article went on to refer to 'the coquettings of the War Secretary with the little group of young Tories and Liberal imperialists'.

you can readily imagine our conversations were constantly interrupted by other people and even by the intrusion of other subjects, because, as the Boches are arriving tomorrow and as it appears possible there may be a meeting on Wednesday the pressure to complete all those subjects which have to be submitted to the Boches is very great. However, as a result of my two talks with the PM I find his mind is travelling in the following order of ideas—

> He wants to know exactly what it is you mean by recognising the Government of Kolchak. He says that he cannot find in your letter a clear definition of your proposal, and he wants to know whether you think Kolchak ought to be recognised as the *de facto* Governor of Siberia, in which case he thinks we may clash both with Kolchak and with Sazonoff,[1] who claim that Kolchak represents the Government of all Russia; or
>
> Whether you wish to recognise Kolchak as the Governor of all Russia, ie European Russia and Siberia?

I told him that I thought it would be sufficient if Kolchak was recognised up to the limit of those parts of Siberia and European Russia where his writ ran, and that similarly we could recognise Tchaikowsky as the *de facto* Governor for the country in which his writ runs. I pressed strongly the view that without unnecessarily delaying our own departure from Archangel and Murmansk we ought to do all in our power to stretch out a hand to Kolchak's people so that before we went the Tchaikowsky Government and the Kolchak Government would be in immediate touch. I did not find the Prime Minister opposed to this idea although he was not as enthusiastic about it as we are. I pointed out that a paper which has been drawn up here on the Russian Situation states that from all the evidence that we possess here it would appear that the Bolsheviks are getting tired of their campaigns, both in the north and in the east, and appear to be going to concentrate their activities for the future towards the Ukraine. This is all in favour of our plan and makes our proposals all the easier.

I hope to have another talk with the PM, either this evening or tomorrow, and will let you know how the matter stands. . . .

[1] Sergei Dmitrievich Sazonoff, 1866–1927. Russian Minister of Foreign Affairs, 1910–15. Dismissed by the Tzar in November 1915 following his advocacy of Home Rule for Poland. Chief Representative Abroad of Admiral Kolchak, 1919–20. Nominated Foreign Minister of Russia by both Kolchak and Denikin, he made his headquarters in Paris. Died in exile in France.

Winston S. Churchill to Sir Henry Wilson: telegram

(*Churchill papers: 16/6*)

29 April 1919 War Office
Secret

Reference your discussions with the Prime Minister, what has been the result concerning the General Staff memorandum on policy in Russia. Mr Bonar Law thinks that till the Prime Minister's opinion has been expressed it cannot be brought before the Cabinet. On the other hand I consider it indispensable that in the near future a formal decision should be given by the Cabinet either for or against the course recommended by the General Staff. Some authority must bear the responsibility of acting or of forbidding action as such matters cannot remain indefinitely in suspense.

I hope therefore you will endeavour first of all to convince the Prime Minister of the wisdom and necessity of the course we propose, and that he will remit the matter to the Cabinet with a favourable expression of his opinion. If, however, he is not convinced, I still hope that, as I feel it is only fair that there shall be a formal definite record of the decision taken, he will allow the matter to be discussed in the Cabinet.

I trust, however, that I shall hear from you that he is quite in agreement with our proposals.

War Cabinet: minutes

(*War Office papers: 32/5384*)

29 April 1919

With reference to War Cabinet 558, Minute 1, the War Cabinet had under consideration a memorandum by the Secretary of State for War (Paper GT–7149) relating to the relaxation of the blockade of Germany.

MR BONAR LAW said that he did not think it would be advisable for the Cabinet to discuss this question at this moment, when we were on the eve of presenting the Preliminary Peace Terms to Germany. The subject had been discussed by the War Cabinet on the 17th April (War Cabinet 558, Minute 1), when Lord Robert Cecil had been present, and he thought it was unnecessary to go beyond the decision then arrived at.

THE SECRETARY OF STATE FOR WAR said that he wanted to make it quite clear that his military advisers had held the view for some time that it would be desirable to raise the blockade to some extent, as there would be less chance, if this were done, of Germany relapsing into complete anarchy;

and if Germany were allowed to do a certain amount of trading, the threat to re-impose the blockade would have greater effect than if it had never been raised.

LORD CURZON said that certain military authorities, together with the French, were against the giving up of our sole remaining offensive weapon. It had been stated that if the blockade was withdrawn it would be easy to re-impose it at any given moment. This, however, was not so in reality. In his view, the blockade should be retained until it was known whether or not the Germans would sign the Preliminary Peace Terms.

THE FIRST LORD OF THE ADMIRALTY agreed with Lord Curzon. He said that the blockade machinery had been built up after much labour, and if it were once raised it would take a considerable time to re-impose it. In his view, it would not be advisable to take any action at the present moment on the Secretary of State for War's memorandum.

The War Cabinet took note of the memorandum by the Secretary of State for War on the relaxation of the blockade of Germany (Paper GT–7149) but, in view of the fact that negotiations with the German Peace Delegates would take place during that week, came to no decision.

War Cabinet: minutes

(*Cabinet papers: 23/10*)

29 April 1919

THE SECRETARY OF STATE FOR WAR said that he hoped Mr Bonar Law, during his visit to Paris, would draw the Prime Minister's attention to the memorandum which had been prepared by the War Office (Paper GT–7117) regarding the recognition of Admiral Kolchak's Government, and, if possible, to obtain his views upon it. On the previous night a telegram had been received to the effect that Admiral Kolchak expected to be in Kotlas by the end of May or the beginning of June. If this was the case, it would greatly facilitate future operations. He thought it would be advisable, however, before Admiral Kolchak was recognised, to obtain a declaration from him regarding his democratic policy on land questions, &c. The people of this country should be reassured that we were not endeavouring to reinstate a Czarist régime.

THE SECRETARY OF STATE FOR WAR said he also hoped Mr Bonar Law would draw the Prime Minister's attention to the General Staff Paper (P–114) on the situation in North Russia. It was most important that some decision should be arrived at on the questions set forth in this memorandum.

Winston S. Churchill to Sir Henry Wilson and General Harington

(*Churchill papers: 16/6*)

30 April 1919 War Office

Pray examine the following:—

We have 6 Brigades in the Caucasus, two-thirds of which are non-retainable men. We cannot keep these men waiting about till the Italians take over. We should therefore begin at once to evacuate the Caucasus, sending home all the non-retainable men and forming the retainables into, say, two good Brigades.

In order to make up to Denikin for the loss of this indirect support in his rear, these two Brigades should be used in support of his left flank against Bolshevik attacks from the Crimea, notably on the Kertsch Peninsula.

Winston S. Churchill to Sir Henry Wilson

(*Churchill papers: 16/16*)

30 April 1919 War Office

We have only a limited quantity of equipment. We have to supply Kolchak and also Denikin. 150,000 equipments were diverted from Denikin to Roumania, and since then Denikin has declared his ability to take them. We cannot fail to fall short of our original undertaking to Denikin to supply him with up to 250,000 sets as and when he can effectively use them. Therefore the 150,000 sets to Roumania are a new drain on our resources not foreseen at the time when the Kolchak and Denikin undertakings were given. Can it be met?

The possible expansion of Kolchak's armies must also be considered. Already we are asked whether we can supply 100,000 equipments for a general mobilisation around Vyatka, should that fall into Kolchak's hands. I am strongly in favour of supplying these equipments, although it is a new demand. Then there is the expansion of the Russian forces at Archangel, which may require another 10,000 or 15,000 equipments.

It seems to me that the equipment of these Russian armies is the first charge on all our resources, and next to that comes Roumania. Until I know how far we are in a position to discharge these obligations, I find great difficulty in taking a new country on our hands. It is much better that the French should do their share and should be responsible for some one definite country in which, if there is a failure, they can be made to bear the discredit. If they can get us to go in with them in each of the three or four different theatres they do not do their share in any one of them. I am very much disinclined to extend our responsibilities.

At any rate, in the first instance MGO[1] should set out all our resources in surplus equipments. Rather than fail the Russians and the Roumanians, I would eat into the reserves we were hoping to put away for the 50 Division Army and keep only enough for, say, 40 Divisions. I should be quite prepared myself to face the inconveniences of a mixed equipment in some of these Russian armies.

MGO to see and supply the information simultaneously with this minute going to the CIGS.

Sir Henry Wilson to Winston S. Churchill

(*Churchill papers: 16/6*)

30 April 1919 Paris
Secret

Dear S of S

I got your wire this morning which you sent last night at half past five. . . . I was not able to catch the Prime Minister yesterday nor have I been able so far (7.0 pm) to see him today, but I have hopes of seeing him after dinner. On the other hand I got a message to him impressing him with the importance of this Russian problem and telling him how anxious you were about it and how important it was to get a decision from him at any rate to allow the matter to go before our Cabinet at home.

Bonar will be here this evening and he and I may be able to make a combined attack tomorrow. You can imagine the state of scramble that is going on in these last few hours before we meet the Boches, particularly when the position is complicated by the absence of the Italians. There was a question this afternoon as to whether the Austrians and Hungarians are to send representatives to receive their Terms or to be allowed to come to Paris but it was decided that in view of the absence of the Italians such a proceeding would not be possible.

I forgot to say that the Prime Minister saw Tchaikowsky yesterday and enquired from him what manner of Government he and Kolchak were proposing to set up in Russia—whether it would be a form of Czardom or a more democratic institution. I understand that Tchaikowsky has promised to obtain some information from Kolchak and then to lay the matter before the Prime Minister.

[1] Lieutenant-General Sir William Furse (see page 17, note 3).

May 1919

Sir Henry Wilson: diary
(Wilson papers)

1 May 1919 Paris

Bonar & I discussed Russia & I was able to persuade him that there was a good military chance of joining Archangel to Kolchak.

Then Bonar & I dined alone with LG. We had a long talk about Russia. After great struggles LG agreed to my proposals to let Ironside join Gaida[1] at Kotlas. Could not get any decision about feeding Petrograd if the Finns take it next week.

Winston S. Churchill to David Lloyd George
(Churchill papers: 16/7)

1 May 1919 War Office
Personal & Secret

My dear Prime Minister,

Austen Chamberlain yesterday mentioned to the House the figure of 110 millions as being the total he contemplated spending on the three Forces in the first normal year. Without in any way pre-judging such a matter, I should like to point out to you that a large reduction in naval expenditure is essential to any satisfactory solution of the combined problem.

The responsibilities of the Army will have been increased by the war. The whole East is unsettled by the disintegration of Turkey, and we shall have large additions of territory in Palestine and Mesopotamia to maintain. Our pre-war army was not primarily designed to participate in European conflicts. An Expeditionary Force of six divisions was organised out of the ordinary garrisons of the United Kingdom and of the linked battalions maintained on the Cardwell system to supply our garrisons abroad. This Expeditionary Force would have been needed whether there had been any European problem or not, because it is the only reserve which can proceed

[1] The Czechoslovak anti-Bolshevik General (see page 638, note 2).

to the support of any part of the British Empire in which war breaks out. It was only incidentally that this force became available to intervene in Europe, and I do not think that it can be argued that it was larger than either the requirements of maintaining order at home or of Imperial defence imposed upon us.

I do not contemplate any important increase in our pre-war military forces, except such increase as may be necessary to garrison the new territories annexed by us or, of course, any increase arising out of treaty obligations which you may make with France. Even this latter I hope to meet by a proper organisation of the 14 pre-war Territorial Divisions, which will now for the first time be composed of trained men and supplied with good war material. But although our little pre-war army may, subject to certain modifications and expansions, remain substantially the model for post-war necessities, it will undoubtedly cost a great deal more. First, because everything costs more and money is worth less. Secondly, because the officers and men have received large increases of pay which I do not imagine for a moment will ever be given up: indeed, if the voluntary system is to be adhered to we may have to contemplate a further advance. Thirdly, because although our numbers will not be increased, the complexity and scientific character of the service has been greatly enhanced. On the other hand we have such a good supply of weapons and munitions that for the first two years there should be some considerable relief from this source.

I have been addressing my mind to the problem as a whole and I do not think it is impossible to find a satisfactory solution. But this depends entirely upon a saving from the Navy which should to a large extent counterbalance some of the increases I have mentioned as inevitable. I do not see why there should not be a great saving from the Navy, at any rate until some entirely new competition develops. For this purpose it is absolutely vital to persuade President Wilson not to start building new big ships. If he wants to increase the American Navy, let him take some of the best German ships and fit them up. We could afford to give these ships to the United States Navy to a reasonable extent without adding at all to our own battleship and battle-cruiser strength. It would be a mark of great confidence and trust, and would do more to lay naval competition to rest than anything else. On the other hand, if he starts building vessels of a superior type, we cannot fall behind equality, and though we might wait for a year or two to see how things went on, we should soon have to start designing superior craft to match the Americans. Therefore it is really vital that he should understand that a mere increase in the size of the American Navy would not light up anew the fires of competition, but that novel departures in the direction of greater power, speed, armament, etc, would after a few years revive that competition in the most painful and embarrassing form. The old ships are quite good enough to maintain the balance of sea power throughout the world, unless better ones are built which make them obsolete. It would be criminal to start this again, and I am sure that with the great hold you must now have over President Wilson and the great measure of his confidence which you have won for yourself and for this country during these negotiations, you should be able to arrive at a good agreement on this point. What spectacle could be more foolish than for Britain and America to begin by sinking all these fine German ships and then starting to waste material and money on building new ones? It is fit for a madhouse.

If you are able to arrive at a satisfactory arrangement on these lines, there ought to be no need for naval new construction, except of a minor character, for many years to come. The Dockyards are choked with war vessels, and I cannot conceive that any new construction is required. In the year before the war my New Construction Vote was over 20 millions, which at present day prices is considerably over 30 millions. It is from this source alone that in the present circumstances a saving can be made which will enable us to reconcile Imperial defence and national economy.

Again, the Air Service is a newcomer. She is most expensive. All the arts and sciences are involved. Only the most skilful mechanics and highest paid craftsmen are of any use: only the best materials will serve. I do not think, however, that the Air Service should be a net addition to the two older Services. It must be made to discharge a portion of the work hitherto done by the Army in the garrisoning of our Eastern possessions. It must also be made to take the place of naval expenditure on cruisers built or maintained in commission and on the arrangements for watching and patrolling the coasts. Here is the second field in which, as I see the problem, a compensatory saving can be made. But both these two depend upon the Navy, which is our absolute master. Look at the way in which through the last two years of the war, while the German Fleet as we know was unfit to come out of harbour, they were trenching on our limited resources and adding to their own overwhelming accumulation of strength. You must remember how repeatedly I pointed this out.

If you wish to bring your expenditure on defence within reasonable limits, it is imperative that the Admiralty should be willing to make a really great contribution towards solving the problem, and all your authority will be necessary for that.

At the present moment we have new proposals for increasing the pay of the Navy as the result of the Jerram[1] Committee. These proposals com-

[1] Thomas Henry Martyn Jerram, 1858–1933. Entered the Royal Navy, 1871. Commander-in-Chief, China Station, 1913–15. Knighted, 1914. Vice-Admiral commanding the 2nd

promise the whole field of Army and Air Force expenditure, and will probably lead to the spending of three or four pounds on the Army and Air Force for every one for which the benefit is urged for the Navy. The matter has been carried to such a point, without any consultation with the War Office or the Air Ministry, by a purely naval committee, that we are now presented with a fait accompli and invited to accept it or face an outbreak in the Fleet. I am really very much inclined to think that these proposals require reconsideration. It is possible that the same results might be attained in a different way, ie without upsetting the Army and the Air Force scales. I feel also that we are in a much stronger position than we were three or four months ago with regard to the fighting services. Prices are falling and the labour market is congested, and although, as you know, I have always been an advocate of increasing the sailors' pay, I do not think we ought to be rushed into partial proposals without fully examining their consequential re-actions.

Another point of the highest practical importance is this, and I am sure you will permit me to write frankly but in the greatest secrecy to you about it. Wemyss is a very good First Sea Lord and I think, although I did not agree with it at the time, that your choice has been very largely justified. At the same time he is in a weak position in his own profession and far overshadowed by Beatty.[1] Beatty is very anxious to become First Sea Lord and was I believed encouraged by Eric Geddes to believe that his appointment was imminent. At any rate, it seems to me that sooner or later Beatty will have to replace Wemyss, and in a reasonable time I think this would be the right thing to do. On the other hand you must remember that once Beatty is enthroned he will be in a position to champion the particularist interest of the Admiralty to an extent which it would be quite impossible for Wemyss to do. It is therefore extremely important that no change should take place at the present time, that the main finance of the three services should be discussed and adjusted, and that then any newcomer should be invited to come in on the basis that he accepts in principle the decisions arrived at.[2]

Battle Squadron, Grand Fleet, 1915; led the battle line at the battle of Jutland, 1916. Admiral, 1917. Appointed President of the Committee set up to examine naval pay scales, September 1918; the rates he proposed were much reduced by the Treasury. President of the permanent naval Welfare Committee, 1919. President of the Naval Prize Tribunal, 1925.

[1] David Beatty, 1871–1936. Entered Navy, 1884. Rear-Admiral, 1910. Churchill's Naval Secretary, 1912. Commander of the Battle Cruiser Squadron, 1913–16. Knighted, 1914. Vice-Admiral, 1915. Commander-in-Chief of the Grand Fleet, 1916–19. First Sea Lord, 1919–27. Created Earl, 1919. Admiral of the Fleet, 1919. Order of Merit, 1919.

[2] Beatty replaced Wemyss as First Sea Lord on 1 November 1919, and remained First Sea Lord until 1927. Wemyss, who was specially promoted Admiral and raised to the peerage as Baron Wester Wemyss, received no further naval or political appointment.

You will not mind me putting these matters to you I am sure, because although they travel outside my sphere they affect all the problems with which I have myself to deal.

Winston S. Churchill to Lord Curzon

(*Churchill papers: 2/105*)

1 May 1919 War Office
Private

My dear Curzon

I send you herewith a private note I have had from Henry Wilson which deals with matters in which we are jointly interested. Will you kindly send it back after you have read it?

Will you also let me know how you think the question asked by the Prime Minister at 'A' should be answered? Is it not possible to recognise Kolchak as 'The Russian Government' without defining its actual territorial scope either as against the Bolsheviks or as between united Russia and the Allies? The French expression that Kolchak's Government represents 'La Principe Russe' is a very convenient one. In harmony with this, could we not perhaps recognise the Omsk Government as the 'Russian National Government' as opposed to the International conceptions of Lenin and Trotsky? It seems to me important that we should have a clear idea of what we mean.

Yours vy sincerely
Winston S. Churchill

Lord Curzon to Winston S. Churchill

(*Churchill papers: 2/105*)

2 May 1919 1 Carlton House Terrace

My dear Churchill,

In response to a call from the PM, we yesterday sent over to Paris from the FO a series of hastily compiled memoranda on the various embryo states or Govts in Russia. With reference to Kolchak we answered your question of anticipation.

We did not think that anything so wide or compromising as the Russian Govt or the Rn National Govt would be advisable. We contented ourselves with the more modern formula of 'The Provisional Government of Siberia'.

There is as you know great suspicion of Kolchak's imperialistic indiscretions in many Russian quarters, and any too ambitious designation wd be quite as likely to bring about his downfall as to give him help.

Yours sincerely
Curzon

Sir Henry Wilson to Winston S. Churchill: telegram

(*Churchill papers: 16/7*)

2 May 1919 Paris
Secret and Personal

Last night Bonar Law and I dined with Prime Minister and we had a long discussion on Russia and on your telegram No 77557 which reached me just before dinner and which I gave to Prime Minister. We, ie, Bonar Law and I, obtained no decision about the subject of your telegram and your proposal to have a squadron and some foodships in a handy (? groups omitted). Prime Minister returned to your letter which I brought over last Sunday and said he had never found out what you meant by recognising Kolchak. You will remember I wrote to you last Monday on the subject and asked you to let me know.

My own opinion is that we should ascertain from Kolchak how he would view an occupation of Petrograd by a mixture of Mannerheim[1] and Yudenitch before we commit ourselves to approving and possibly supporting such an operation.

As regards Gaida's[2] move on Viatka and Kotlas. Prime Minister would not

[1] Carl Gustav Emil Mannerheim, 1867–1951. Member of a distinguished Finnish noble family. Served for thirty years as an officer in the Imperial Russian Army, 1887–1917. Served as a Lieutenant-Colonel in the Russo-Japanese War, 1904–5. Major-General, 1911. Commanded the 12th Russian Cavalry Division, 1915–16. Commanded a joint Rumanian and Russian Army Group in the Carpathians, 1916–17. Returned to Helsinki after Finland proclaimed its independence from Russia, 1917. Commander-in-Chief of the Finnish Army 1918. Fought against the Russians, and against the Red Finns, 1918. Entered Helsinki at the head of 16,000 men, May 1918. Regent of Finland, 1919. Recalled as Commander-in-Chief during the Russo-Finnish War, 1939–40. President of Finland, 1944.

[2] Rudolph Gaida, 1892–1949. Born in Moravia (then a part of Austria-Hungary). Trained as a pharmacist in Bohemia. Conscripted into the army medical corps, July 1914. Deserted to a Montenegrin regiment, pretending to be an officer, 1915. Captured by the Russians, 1917. In May 1918, with the rank of Captain, he served in the Czechoslovak Corps, and favoured fighting the Bolsheviks. Colonel commanding the Czech forces in Central Siberia, July–October 1918. Supported Admiral Kolchak's seizure of power at Omsk, November 1918. Promoted Major-General by Kolchak, November 1918. Commanded Kolchak's Northern Army, June–July 1919, with the rank of Lieutenant-General. Dismissed by Kolchak, July 1919. Attempted unsuccessfully to seize power at Vladivostock, November

go further than to say that if Gaida reaches Viatka and establishes himself there firmly and if he moves up the railway to Kotlas there would be no objection to Ironside having everything prepared for a blow up the Dwina on Kotlas but that Cabinet would have to be consulted before such a move were actually carried out.

Bonar Law, who returns home probably on Sunday, was present during the whole of these conversations and will be able to fill in many details.

This evening I hope to see Tchaikowsky and will communicate to you the result of my interview.

Winston S. Churchill to Sir Henry Wilson: telegram

(*Churchill papers: 16/7*)

3 May 1919
Secret

I should personally have been prepared to advise recognition of Kolchak's Government as the Russian National Government, thus distinguishing it from the Inter-National Government or Soviet Government.

However, I consulted Curzon on the point and he tells me he has already advised the Prime Minister to recognize it in the more moderate form of the Provisional Government of Siberia.

War Office to General Ironside

(*Churchill papers: 'Campaign in North Russia'*)

4 May 1919 London

You are authorized to make all preparations, with the resources at your disposal, to strike a heavy blow against the Bolsheviks in the direction of Kotlas, if a favourable opportunity should occur for effecting a junction with Gaida about that point. Before such a move is actually carried out, however, Cabinet approval will have to be obtained.

1919. Returned to Czechoslovakia, 1920. Chief of the Czech General Staff, 1926. Cashiered for trying to take part in a fascist putsch. Imprisoned for 'banditry', 1931. Headed the Czech Fascist organization, 1939–45. Arrested as a collaborator, 1945, but then amnestied. Re-arrested, 1948, tried by a 'People's Tribunal', and shot.

Winston S. Churchill to Sir Henry Wilson: telegram

(*Churchill papers: 16/7*)

5 May 1919 War Office
Secret

The right thing to do would be to recognize Omsk as the National Provisional Government of all Russia. If you cannot obtain approval for this, the next best would be to recognize them as National Provisional Government of Siberia. The important thing is to recognize them at the earliest possible moment. Now is the time to help them. More than a fortnight has already passed since War Office and Foreign Office papers were written and we are still paralysed. I am sending you a copy of the telegram I am sending to Prime Minister.

Winston S. Churchill to David Lloyd George: telegram

(*Churchill papers: 16/7*)

5 May 1919 War Office

CIGS tells me that you have several times asked what exactly I mean as to recognizing Kolchak. I consider that the Omsk Government should at once be recognized as the National Provisional Government of all Russia. Please see Lindley's[1] telegram No 281 which shows that this is what has been done by Tchaikowsky's North Russian Provisional Government.[2] The word National draws a clear distinction from the International character of the Bolshevik Government. If however you prefer National Provisional Government of Siberia that would be better than nothing. Nearly a fortnight has passed since the Foreign Office and War Office brought this question before you and I earnestly hope you will be able either to give a decision yourself or to allow

[1] Francis Oswald Lindley, 1872–1950. 4th son of Baron Lindley. Entered Diplomatic Service, 1897. 3rd Secretary at Vienna, 1899. 2nd Secretary, Cairo, 1904–6. Counsellor of Embassy, Petrograd, 1915–17. Commissioner in Russia, 1918; Consul-General, Russia, 1919; High Commissioner Vienna, 1919–20. Minister to Athens, 1922–3; to Oslo, 1923–9. Knighted, 1926. He published his memoirs, *A Diplomat off Duty*, in 1928. Ambassador to Portugal, 1929–31; to Japan, 1931–4. Member of the Home Office Advisory Committee on Interned Aliens, 1939–45.

[2] Lindley's telegram (no 281) read: 'Provisional Government have informed diplomatic representatives that they decided on 30 April officially to recognize Omsk Government as national Provisional Government of all Russia. Pending establishment of direct contact with Siberian Government and receipt from them (?of) detailed instructions Provisional Government will carry on as hitherto.' Copies were sent by the Foreign Office to both Churchill and Sir Henry Wilson.

the matter to be discussed in Cabinet subject to any guidance you may wish to give them. If Kolchak continues to advance successfully there is a good chance of securing at no distant date a civilized Government for a united Russia more friendly to Britain than to any other power.

Further the overthrow of Bolshevism in Russia is indispensable to anything in the nature of a lasting peace and will cut off from Germany that refuge in Bolshevism which she may seek in her despair. I need scarcely say how extremely advantageous the recognition of Kolchak's Government would be among the political forces in the House of Commons on which you are relying.

Winston S. Churchill to Sir Henry Wilson: telegram

(*Churchill papers: 16/7*)

5 May 1919
Secret and Personal

Are we not getting off the main line? There are two distinct cases. First, that the Finns go for Petrograd whether we like it or not. In this case surely the more Yudenitch co-operates and the quicker a British or Allied squadron arrives in Petrograd, the better Kolchak and Denikin will be pleased, because the enterprise will cease to be a purely Finnish show. The second case is whether we should encourage Mannerheim and Yudenitch jointly to make this move. I agree with you that we have not the information at our disposal at the present time to justify any such action on our part. We have no means of knowing whether the operation is feasible, and certainly we should commit a grave imprudence to mix up ourselves with what may possibly be a hopeless failure. When Gough has got out there and has reported fully, we shall be in a position to make up our minds. Therefore the only question open is the first, on which I hope we are agreed.

Please see also telegram No 804, Mr Balfour 3rd May, paragraph 2 (b). Baron Makino seems to me to have been entirely on the right line. His information is that General Yudenitch is acting in co-operation with Admiral Kolchak. This is also vehemently asserted by the Clem Edwards[1] group, who are by no means ill-informed. I am therefore sorry to see that Hardinge[2]

[1] Allen Clement Edwards, 1869–1938. Barrister, 1899. Liberal MP, 1906–18. National Democratic Party MP, 1918–1922. Chairman of the National Democratic Party (see page 614, note 2). Subsequently Labour editor of *The Sun*, and Special Commissioner for the *Daily News*.

[2] Charles Hardinge, 1858–1944. Entered Foreign Office, 1880. Knighted, 1904. Ambassador at Petrograd, 1904–6. Permanent Under-Secretary of State for Foreign Affairs, 1906–10. Created Baron Hardinge of Penshurst, 1910. Viceroy of India, 1910–16. Reappointed Permanent Under-Secretary of State for Foreign Affairs, 1916–20. Ambassador to Paris, 1920–2. His elder son, Lieutenant Edward Charles Hardinge, died of wounds received in action, December 1914.

opposed any attempt being made to secure from Finland a free hand for Yudenitch. On my first assumption, viz that the Finns are going for Petrograd on their own, surely at the very least our policy should be to urge them to let Yudenitch have a free hand to co-operate.

I telegraphed to you also to-day about the recognition of Kolchak. What we recognise him as is a small matter. The vital thing is recognition. Recognition is taking sides formally, and once committed to this, wider forms of recognition must follow.

I have sent a telegram to Knox asking him to find out what Kolchak really wishes about Yudenitch and the Finns.

I have offered the mission to Gough, who I think will accept.

War Cabinet: minutes

(*Cabinet papers: 23/10*)

6 May 1919

The War Cabinet had before them a Memorandum by the Secretary of State for War regarding the provision of Russian officers for service in North Russia and Siberia (Paper GT–7165).

The Memorandum stated that, since the signing of the armistice, it had become increasingly evident that an indefinite continuance of the occupation of parts of North Russia by Allied troops was neither desirable nor feasible, and that an early opportunity for withdrawal must be sought. It was therefore incumbent on the British Government to provide for those Russians who had remained loyal to, and had fought for, the Allied cause in those regions. The formation of an efficient Russian national force was urged as one of the first necessary steps to the attainment of this object, and it was stated to be essential to secure Russian officers from some source and despatch them without delay to Archangel. For this purpose the General Staff had calculated that it would be necessary to provide a body of 675 officers for the Archangel area, besides 25 for the Murmansk theatre—making a total for North Russia of 700. It was also considered necessary to despatch 500 Russian officers to Vladivostock. In order to carry out this scheme, the Memorandum asked for authority—

(a) To provide these Russian officers with free transport to the United Kingdom from the country where they were now living, and from the United Kingdom to Archangel or Vladivostock.

(b) To feed them during the period from their departure from the United Kingdom until their arrival in Russia.
(c) To outfit them completely with British uniforms and equipment.
(d) To enable them to provide themselves with other articles, and to meet small current expenses.

It was stated that, although an accurate estimate of the cost of the scheme could not be given, 100*l* per officer, or 120,000*l* for the 1,200 officers, would be required in the first instance.

THE SECRETARY OF STATE FOR WAR said that the scheme outlined in his Memorandum was all part of the process of evacuating our troops from Russia, and making the Russians fend for themselves. There were now 15,000 Russian troops in North Russia, and this number would probably be increased soon to 25,000; in fact, he had been asked to provide equipment later on for as many as 100,000 Russians in that part of the world. Affairs in North Russia were at the moment satisfactory; Admiral Kolchak was moving rapidly, and proposed to go to Archangel himself very soon; he expected his right wing to get to Kotlas by the 15th June, and there was no doubt that this purely Russian army was really rolling forward, and would add to its ranks in the districts through which it proposed to advance. Five new Russian divisions had been formed in Siberia, and were now being brought into action. The victories of these troops were being won with British weapons and uniforms.

With regard to Archangel, MR CHURCHILL thought the situation was satisfactory, and the gunboats were now being used. Plans were being made for handing over to Admiral Kolchak the whole of our obligations in North Russia. The Prime Minister had discussed the situation with the Chief of the Imperial General Staff, and had authorised certain plans and preparations to be made, but no action would be undertaken without a Cabinet decision. The reports from General Maynard were satisfactory; the Finns had made a successful push at Petrozavodsk, and had succeeded in cutting the railway behind the Bolshevists in front of General Maynard. With regard to Generals Mannerheim and Yudenitch, it was very uncertain what their movements and intentions were. The War Office, however, were sending out a mission to investigate the position. The only unsatisfactory news was from Esthonia and the other Baltic provinces.

In conclusion, MR CHURCHILL said the Cabinet would therefore see the importance of carrying out the scheme of sending Russian officers to North Russia. It was quite possible that the Bolshevik régime would crumple up, and we should get a civilised Russia friendly to us above all other Powers if events continued to proceed on satisfactory lines. He therefore wanted to obtain for Russia every officer that was available. The Russians were now fighting bravely, and all the help we could give them now would facilitate the eventual evacuation of our forces from Russia and the establishment of friendly relations when peace came.

THE CHANCELLOR OF THE EXCHEQUER stated that the situation had changed since his predecessor in office had considered it unwise to provide the financial help required, as requested by the General Staff in December, and he raised no objection to the scheme as outlined by the Secretary of State for War.

LORD CURZON said that he understood that the Murmansk expedition commenced as an Allied expedition, and had never ceased to be one. He therefore thought that, although the British had done all the fighting, the expenses should be borne by our Allies as well as by ourselves.

THE CHANCELLOR OF THE EXCHEQUER said that this was the case, and the outlay should be charged to the joint account of the Allies, although the British Government would have to provide the funds in the first instance, and it was unlikely that they would ever recover anything from France or United States of America.

The War Cabinet decided that—

> The Treasury should provide the necessary funds to transport, feed, and equip the 1,200 Russian officers whom the Secretary of State for War proposed to recruit and send to North Russia.

David Lloyd George to Winston S. Churchill: telegram

(*Churchill papers: 16/7*)

6 May 1919 Paris

Secret

Surely question of recognition of Kolchak's Government is a matter for the whole of the Allies acting together. We have all been very hard pressed with the completion of German Treaty and the Italian discussion and it was impossible to suspend these urgent discussions because War Office a fortnight ago came to certain novel conclusions about Kolchak's Government. We intend to review the whole Russian situation as soon as peace terms have been presented to German delegates and Italian crisis is disposed of. Meanwhile I have had a long interview with Tchaikowsky and Paderewski[1] upon

[1] Ignacy Jan Paderewski, 1860–1941. Pianist and Composer. A leading propagandist for Polish independence, 1914–17, based at Veney in Switzerland. Organized, in the United States, a Polish army to fight in France, 1917. Representative of the Polish National Committee

the position in Russia and regret that neither of them take your views as to Kolchak and Denikin and their entourage: on the contrary they are genuinely alarmed lest their success should result in the triumph of reaction. Whatever steps are taken by us we must have guarantees on this subject. Otherwise if our efforts simply ended in establishing a reactionary Military Regime in Russia British Democracy would never forgive us.

I can conceive no greater peril either to Democracy in Europe or to British interests in the East. Both Paderewski and Tchaikowsky especially warned me against Denikin's right hand man, a certain General Lukomski.[1] They described him as not only reactionary but strongly pro-German. When we finally review the situation all these considerations must be taken into account. As this review will probably take place next week I think it extremely desirable that you should be here and whatever happens we must act in concert with our Allies. Separate action will result in serious misunderstandings and the British Cabinet ought not to act alone. I am afraid that it will be difficult for Lord Curzon to leave the Foreign Office otherwise it might be helpful for him to be here *as well.*

Winston S. Churchill to David Lloyd George: telegram

(*Churchill papers: 16/7*)

7 May 1919 War Office
Personal & Secret

By all means let us take united Allied action if there is any chance of it. I agree absolutely with you about exacting guarantees to secure the democratic future of Russia and the land for the peasants. I feel convinced that now is the time and that if the opportunity is lost Kolchak may either become too weak to be of any use or too strong to require our advice. It seems to me we have a tremendous chance of securing the future of Russia as a civilized democratic state friendly above all to us and that an event of this kind is

---

in the United States, 1917–18. Disembarked at Danzig from a British cruiser, 24 December 1918. Prime Minister of Poland, and also Foreign Minister, January–Novemeber 1919. One of the two Polish signatories of the Versailles Treaty, June 1919. Polish Representative at the League of Nations, Geneva, 1920–1. An opponent of Pilsudski's regime, he lived in Switzerland, and on his estate in California, 1921–39. Chairman, Polish National Council (in exile), 1939–41. He died in New York.

[1] A. S. Lukomsky. A Tsarist General Staff Officer, he was a keen supporter of Korniloff's attempt to overthrow the Provisional Government in 1917. After the October revolution he escaped from house arrest (together with Denikin) at Bykhov, and went south to the Kuban to join the Volunteer Army. One of the most active and successful generals of that army, in 1920 he went into exile, when he wrote an account of his civil war career.

indespensable to the completion of the main work in which you are engaged. Such a policy whole-heartedly carried through would secure overwhelming approval here. I have to go to Dundee 14th and 15th on a long standing engagement when Haig receives the freedom but can be in Paris night of Friday 16th. Shall I arrange accordingly.

Winston S. Churchill to A. J. Balfour: telegram

(*Churchill papers: 16/7*)

8 May 1919 War Office
Personal and Secret

I do not often trouble you with my anxieties but I am profoundly shocked by the action which is being taken to repatriate Russian war prisoners from Germany to Russia. What choice have the great mass of these men got but to join the Bolshevik armies or starve or be put to death. It is no use saying that if they like to refuse to leave Germany they can stay where they are. The temptation to go home is overwhelming and when they are received by the Bolshevik commissaries they will be at their mercy. Such instance of a state deliberately presenting its enemies with a reinforcement of 500,000 trained men is without parallel. I implore you to see whether you cannot do something to arrest or at any rate delay such a disaster. The Army Council and Cabinet here were unanimous. Still the thing is going on.

General Spears to Winston S. Churchill

(*Churchill papers: 16/36*)

8 May 1919 Mission Militaire Britannique
Secret Paris

Dear Secretary of State,

The advance of Kolchak, the recognition of his Government by that of Archangel and the Prince Regent of Serbia,[1] would seem to justify the optimistic attitude of the Russian Committee the members of which do not

[1] Alexander Karadjordjevic, 1888–1934. Crown Prince of Serbia. Appointed Prince-Regent, 1914. On 1 December 1918 he assumed the Regency of the new Yugoslav State (known officially as the Kingdom of the Serbs, Croats and Slovenes). Survived an attempted assassination, June 1921. King of Yugoslavia, August 1921. Abolished the Constitution, and dissolved the political parties, January 1929. Shot dead, by a Macedonian assassin at Marseilles (while on a state visit to France), October 1934. The French Foreign Minister, Barthou, was assassinated at the same time.

hesitate to state that Russia 'will have lots of friends when Kolchak gets to Nizhni-Novgorod'.

In the meanwhile there is no doubt that practically all Russians, non-Bolsheviks as well as Bolsheviks have become profoundly anti-Entente. It is realised by them that the French are pursuing a suicidal policy in Russia and of all the Allies we are perhaps the least unpopular. It is obvious that some one will have to 'rediscover Russia' and help her to work out at least her economic salvation. The Russians would perhaps still be ready to accept this form of control from us—certainly not from the French or Americans: but if we wait too long they will accept it from the Germans who will *have* to look East in the future.

It is worth remembering that the shortest road from Berlin to Petrograd and Great Russia lies not through Warsaw but through Kovno. Lithuania constitutes the highroad between Germany and Russia, and the Germans have seized the opportunity during the war to pave it to their liking.

Of all the Baltic provinces, Lithuania is the only one which would seem to have any real chance of remaining independent of a reconstituted Russia.

The Germans have for the moment gained the day in Latvia and have the de facto Lithuanian Government—which is more anti-Polish than anything else—if not in their pay at any rate largely in their power.

It is here in the Baltic Province, and at the other extremity of Russia—the Caucasus—that we can constitute a controlling factor in the reorganisation of Russia. The control of the Caucasus, moreover, need not be wholly unremunerative to us. Between these points any action we might show signs of taking would probably tend to be resented by the French, who are the more susceptible in regard to their policy in the Ukraine as it becomes more and more apparent that they have none.

Yours sincerely
E. L. Spears[1]

Winston S. Churchill to Sir George Ritchie

(*Churchill papers: 5/21*)

9 May 1919 War Office

My dear Ritchie,

Many thanks for your letter of the 6th instant. You are always quite right to tell me exactly what our friends in Dundee are thinking, but I must say

[1] On 11 May Churchill sent this letter to Sir Henry Wilson with the covering note: 'This is a vy good specimen of the admirable reports & sagacious outlook of General Spears. I do not find this grasp of the true situation in many others who are so readily accepted as fit to fill quasi-military positions. It is a gt criticism of a department that it prefers blunt tools.'

that I think the complaints which are made are unreasonable and unfair. In my long experience of Government, I have never in my life been confronted with so many extraordinary difficulties, and I have no doubt that what I am facing here finds their counterpart in every other Government Department.

When I look back on all that has been achieved since the Armistice, it seems to me that extraordinary progress has been made, far more than I ever dared to hope. Nearly 3 million men have been demobilised from the Army and the Air Force; all the munition works have been closed down or opened up with peace-time products; the bulk of our shipping has been liberated; an enormous mass of Dominion troops have been sent home; order has been maintained; discipline has been restored to the Army; labour troubles have been tidied over; and the general stability of British society, which might well have reeled under the sudden change from war to peace, has been greatly consolidated.

At the same time agreement on the Peace Terms has been secured among all the Allies, which fulfil the most ardent expectations of sensible men, whether as regards the terms to be imposed upon the enemy or the advantages to be reaped by our own country, and these Terms have been secured not only without a quarrel with the United States but in particularly close sympathy and agreement with them.

It seems to me that the By-Elections and the sort of querulous dissatisfaction which they represent in the country are themselves a justification for taking the General Election when we did. It is perfectly clear that had that been postponed until the present time, the Coalition Government would have been broken up and a fierce Parliamentary faction fight resumed between the great parties, with the certainty that no Government could have been brought into existence strong enough to deal with the enormous problems and many perils of the situation.

Least of all do I think there is good ground for complaint from Liberals in regard to the Budget, which lays its only increases of taxation on alcoholic liquors and death duties. I regard, and have always regarded, the giving of a preference to the Dominions on existing duties as a very small matter so long as there is no question of the protective or preferential taxation of food. Anyhow, the electors were most clearly informed before the poll that it was the intention of the Government, if returned, to give such a preference.

I am bound to return to London by the night train on Thursday night, as I have to travel immediately to Paris, where I am due on Friday. I could have a private meeting from 6 to 7.15 or earlier, on Thursday, with our Liberal friends, if that would be convenient. In that event will you arrange about the East Coast train, or shall I?

Winston S. Churchill: departmental minute

(*Churchill papers: 16/16*)

12 May 1919 War Office

I do not understand this squeamishness about the use of gas. We have definitely adopted the position at the Peace Conference of arguing in favour of the retention of gas as a permanent method of warfare. It is sheer affectation to lacerate a man with the poisonous fragment of a bursting shell and to boggle at making his eyes water by means of lachrymatory gas.

I am strongly in favour of using poisoned gas against uncivilised tribes. The moral effect should be so good that the loss of life should be reduced to a minimum. It is not necessary to use only the most deadly gasses: gasses can be used which cause great inconvenience and would spread a lively terror and yet would leave no serious permanent effects on most of those affected.

Winston S. Churchill to Sir Charles Harington

(*War Office papers: 32/5687*)

12 May 1919 War Office

Every endeavour should be made to raise these missions at once to 2,000 each. We must act up to the full limit of the authority which has been granted to us.

I do not consider that the stores and equipments, either for Kolchak or Denikin, are necessarily limited by the amounts which have been agreed upon. If more can be used, every effort should be made to provide them and to secure the necessary authority.

I hope General Holman[1] is asking for everything he requires and will go out with the feeling that his mission is being well provided for.

WSC

[1] Herbert Campbell Holman, 1869–1949. Entered Army, 1889. On active service in Burma, 1891 (wounded). Served in China as an interpreter, 1900. Attaché with the Russian Forces in Manchuria, 1905. Lieutenant-Colonel, 1914. Served on the western front, 1914–19. Brigadier-General, in charge of Q services, 4th Army, 1918. Major-General, 1919. Chief of the Military Mission to South Russia, 1919–20. Knighted, 1920. Deputy Quartermaster General, India, 1921–2. Lieutenant-General commanding the 4th Indian Division, 1924–7. From 1940 to 1944 he served as a Private in the Home Guard. On 25 July 1919 Churchill described him to the War Cabinet as 'a very efficient officer with wide experience in and a good knowledge of the Russian language'. (*Cabinet papers: 23/11*)

Winston S. Churchill to General Denikin

(*Churchill papers: 16/7*)

[12] May 1919

We are sending you from the British War Office General Holman to be the Head of the Mission which His Majesty's Government have authorised me to maintain at your Headquarters.

General Holman has been in charge of all the Q services of General Rawlinson's 4th Army during the whole of the great operations which terminated victoriously on the 11th November last. He is, therefore, a technical authority of the highest order in all such matters. In addition he has the qualification of speaking Russian well and of being a great admirer and friend of the Russian people. He comes out to help you and to aid you in every way in your task of warring down the Bolshevik tyranny. He will be in direct communication with me and with the Chief of the Imperial General Staff. I hope you will regard him as a friend and comrade and treat him with every confidence, and will not hesitate to send messages through him to me or to the Chief of the Imperial General Staff. Agreeably with the policy of His Majesty's Government, we shall do our utmost to assist you in every respect.

General Holman is the bearer to you of the Insignia of the Knight Commandership of the Order of the Bath which the King has graciously conferred upon you. He bears with him also a number of other British decorations which should be awarded to Russian officers under your command whom you and General Holman may decide have specially merited recognition.

Winston S. Churchill to Austen Chamberlain

(*Austen Chamberlain papers*)

13 May 1919 War Office

My dear Chancellor of the Exchequer,

I am afraid that my objections to the proposal which we discussed this morning have not been in any way removed. It seems to me that Ministers ought to deal with Ministers, and that the proposals of great Government Departments ought to be submitted in the name of their responsible Heads to the Chancellor of the Exchequer or to other Cabinet colleagues affected. I cannot think that it is proper or in accordance with the principles upon which Government in this country has been carried on in time of peace, that a Secretary of State should be forced to submit the schemes and policy of his Department to the criticisms of a Committee which has neither Parliamentary nor Ministerial authority, but is composed of subordinates from various Departments including his own.

Therefore I must formally demur to becoming a party to such a procedure. The relations between the Head of a great spending Department and the Chancellor of the Exchequer are of a very special character, and I recognise fully how much the success of your work depends on my loyal endeavours to keep expenditure within the narrowest possible limits. I recognise also the very broad-minded and helpful spirit in which you have hitherto met War Office demands, and I sympathise keenly with you in the embarrassments in which you were placed by the circumstances in which the Jerram Committee Report came into being.

If I take objection to these new proposals, it is because I wish to preserve unimpaired the proper constitutional relationship which should exist between a Secretary of State and the Chancellor of the Exchequer, and not at all because I wish to deprive you of any means of scrutinising estimates or co-ordinating expenditure between one Department and another. But I conceive that I have a right to deal with the Chancellor of the Exchequer direct in all matters involving the relations of the War Office and the Treasury. This does not at all mean that it is necessary for you or me to deal with the details of expenditure and of elaborate schemes of pay and allowances by personal conference. The demands on your time and on mine render such a course impossible. Still, I accept full responsibility for every proposal which I put before you, and I consider that I am entitled to receive from the Treasury a reply invested with an equal authority.

I cannot see why the existing arrangements are not capable of being made to meet your needs and wishes. Why do you not set up the identical Committee which you propose under your own authority as a definite part of the Treasury machinery for examining estimates, for examining and co-ordinating rates of pay between the fighting services. I would nominate with pleasure a representative of this office to attend and explain the War Office point of view and give any information that you might require. The Committee would simply be a departmental process of the Treasury to advise you in regard to particular proposals from the spending Departments. There is no limit to the investigations which the Chancellor of the Exchequer may pursue into the financial administration of other Departments of State, and it is the duty of every Minister to facilitate to the utmost his enquiries. But what is vital is that the Chancellor of the Exchequer should himself take direct responsibility for dealing with the Heads of other Departments, and should cover with his position and authority whatever administrative processes he calls into being within the limits of his own Department.

Bonar Law, when he held your office, adopted a method which proved extremely convenient and might well now serve as a precedent. He appointed the Colwyn[1] Committee, by which many questions of great complexity were settled, to which I gladly sent my representatives from the Ministry of Munitions, and which I was perfectly willing to attend informally myself in order to facilitate their investigations.

But when all is said and done, the official answer to the considered proposals of the War Office or the Admiralty should be given in the name and upon the personal responsibility of the Chancellor of the Exchequer. If differences exist between us, then is the moment when they should come before the Cabinet, when the responsible Ministers can meet together and come to a definite decision upon the broad points of policy which are outstanding. Surely this is the right way to do things, and surely it is the obvious business of the Treasury to set up the necessary co-ordinating machinery within its own domestic compass. In this way the power of the Treasury would be augmented and not diminished. On the other hand, Ministerial responsibility would not be weakened by the Heads of Departments having to plead before irresponsible and subordinate tribunals.

I should hope that with your long experience of public Government you would see how easy it is to secure all you wish in the most efficient manner while at the same time safeguarding the form and traditions of Cabinet Government.

I am sending a copy of this letter to Mr Bonar Law and the Prime Minister.

yours vy sincerely
Winston S. Churchill

General Spears to Winston S. Churchill

(*Churchill papers: 16/36*)

15 May 1919 Paris

The CIGS told me you had written him that you were in favour of my being made Military Attaché here, many thanks for doing this; he himself did not appear to have made up his mind one way or another: he made some objections which did not appear very convincing, namely, that I had seen more of the political than the military side of war (I think I have seen more

[1] Frederick Henry Smith, 1859–1946. India rubber and cotton manufacturer. Knighted, 1912. A director of several railway and colliery companies. High Sheriff of Carnarvonshire, 1917–18. Created Baron Colwyn, 1917. Chairman of the Government Contracts Committee, the Royal Commission on Income Tax, the Bank Amalgamation Committee, the Flax Control Committee and the Admiralty Committee on Dockyards. Vice-Chairman, Post Office Advisory Council.

fighting and done more staff work than most), and his other reason was that I might possibly resign soon and my experience as Military Attaché be lost to the Army! Now my chief reason for asking for the appointment is that you should go on benefiting by the experience I have already gained.

I saw Derby after seeing HW. He told me he was not prepared to favour my appointment. There seemed to be no point in discussing the matter with him to any length; his last words were 'LONDON will decide'.

I understand perfectly Derby's point of view; he said a month ago that he wanted me as Military Attaché but that the War Office would not hear of it. Now he says I don't get on with the French.

Your letter to the CIGS proves the contrary of the first, and my work the contrary of the second.

The fact is that the better I get on with the French, and the more work I do for you, the less Derby likes it.

I can't help thinking that in spite of this opposition it would be worth while maintaining me in PARIS where I have made a position for myself not only with the French but also with the small nationalities that are bound to foregather here for some time to come.

In any case, I am at your entire disposal for any work you may wish to give me here or anywhere else.

Winston S. Churchill to General Harington and General Radcliffe

(*War Office papers: 32/5222*)

17 May 1919

Paragraph (1) of DMO's minute does not take into consideration the possibility which is now within reach of supplying aeroplane stations direct from the air. A small number of machines each capable of carrying a five-ton load could quite easily and rapidly establish landing grounds, repair shops and petrol dumps at a distance of 100 miles from any road or railhead, and in a roadless country the cost of transportation by air would compare favourably with that by road. There would be no difficulty at the present time in making supply aeroplanes, any one of which could make three or four journeys in a day.

It is just because these possibilities are not studied in the light of the present and future developments that a limited view is taken. For instance, an aeroplane could quite easily carry 15 or 20 men a distance of 100 miles in an hour and a half, and thus it should be possible to set up quite easily and rapidly in a roadless and broken country a series of posts and keep them well supplied from the air with all that they require. It is this aspect of the question which requires to be studied at the present time by the Air Ministry and the General Staff.[1]

Sir Henry Wilson: diary

(*Wilson papers*)

17 May 1919 Paris

Winston arrived at 2 am this morning. I had an hour with him at 9 am. He is in good form.

A wire from Viceroy of India [Lord Chelmsford] asking permission to occupy Jellalabad at once.

We had an informal meeting at mid-day of Winston, Milner, Montagu, Bikanir[2] & Self.

We all thought we would like some more information before deciding. Then we had a Cabinet at 3 o'c & LG agreed to the above so Montagu wired to Viceroy & I to Monro[3] asking for information.

At 4.30 Derby & I had a long talk with Winston about Spears. Derby & I both refused to agree to Spears as Mil: Attaché vice David Henderson. Winston very mulish.

Sir Robert Borden to Winston S. Churchill

(*Lloyd George papers*)

18 May 1919 Claridge's Hotel, London

Dear Mr Churchill,

Beyond question it is imperative that the Canadian Forces now at Archangel should be withdrawn without delay. The demobilization of the

[1] The first use of troop-carrying aeroplanes during a military campaign took place on 21 February 1923, when 2 companies of Indian troops and 2 British officers were flown from Baghdad to Kirkuk, in nine aeroplanes, in order to go into action against a Kurdish rebellion. The journey, which would have taken a week overland, took less than two hours by air.

[2] Narendra Shiromani Maharaja Sri Ganga Singbji Bahadur, 1880–1943. Succeeded as Maharaja of Bikanir at the age of seven. Assumed full ruling powers at the age of 18. On active service in China, 1901, commanding the Bikanir Camel Corps. Knighted, 1904. Major-General, 1917. One of the three Indian representatives at the Imperial War Cabinet, and Paris Peace Conference, 1919. Led the Indian delegation to the League of Nations Assembly, 1930. Member of the Indian States Delegation, London Round Table Conference, 1930–1 and 1931. Promoted General, 1937.

[3] Charles Carmichael Munro, 1860–1929. Lieutenant-General, in charge of the Gallipoli evacuation, 1915–16. Knighted, 1915. Commander-in-Chief, India, 1916–20. Governor of Gibraltar, 1923–8.

Canadian Corps and the withdrawal of Canadian Troops from Siberia render any further continuance of our forces at Archangel absolutely impracticable. On the 10th of March the War Office suggested that Canadian Troops could not be withdrawn until the port of Archangel should be opened for navigation. The period thus indicated has now arrived. However, on 30th April a letter from the War Office indicates that it is not proposed to withdraw them until late summer or Autumn. Many of these troops were sent in the first instance for instructional purposes. Doubtless they have not objected to the active service which has been substituted for the original purpose. Recently, there has been unfortunate evidence of keen resentment on their part at the continued delay. A few weeks ago a very capable Canadian Officer who had just arrived from Archangel emphasized the very trying effects of long continued service in that region and told me that not only the Canadians but all the forces at Archangel and Murmansk who have been there more than six or eight months should be relieved as soon as conditions of navigation permit.

However, I have no right to speak for the others; but I do insist that the Canadians shall be withdrawn immediately.

Sir Robert Borden to David Lloyd George

(Lloyd George papers)

18 May 1919 Claridge's Hotel, London

Dear Mr Lloyd George,

As the accompanying letter to Mr Churchill involves a question of policy I am sending a copy to you. It will be most unfortunate if the War Office persists in its apparent determination to extend the period of service for the Canadians at Archangel.

I must insist that they shall be withdrawn without the slightest unnecessary delay.

Winston S. Churchill to Sir Robert Borden: telegram

(Churchill papers: 16/7)

20 May 1919

Your letter of 18th May. I trust I am right in interpreting your letter in the sense that the Canadians from Archangel and Murmansk are to be withdrawn at the earliest moment compatible with the safety of their British comrades on this front. The operations which are now proceeding have reached a critical and hopeful phase which may enable us to extricate ourselves from our responsibilities without dishonour before the Summer is over. I earnestly hope that the Canadian detachments will not abandon their British comrades until at least adequate arrangements have been made to replace them.

Winston S. Churchill to David Lloyd George

(*Lloyd George papers*)

20 May 1919

I have read the memoranda by General Smuts and Mr Barnes on the subject of the Peace negotiations with the Germans. In my opinion it is of profound importance to reach a settlement with the present German Government, and to reach it as speedily as possible. Although no doubt the allied armies can advance rapidly into Germany, we shall only find ourselves involved in greater difficulties with every step of our forward movement. Large masses of the German population will come upon our hands and we shall have to feed them and make them work. We shall be involved in an infinite series of political and social questions of the most painful complexity, and the rigorous enforcement of the renewed blockade would aggravate these difficulties.

(2) Our military strength is dwindling every day, not only through demobilisation but through the growing impatience of all ranks of the army to return home. The formidable pre-occupations which are arising in the East, where British interests are so pre-eminently engaged, must be taken into consideration before a policy which commits us to a long occupation of Germany in force is resorted to.

(3) The newspapers and public opinion at home, so far as it is vocal, claims the enforcement of the most extreme terms upon the vanquished enemy.

At the same time, however, all classes demand the rapid demobilisation of the army, the release of innumerable categories of soldiers, and the removal of restrictions of all kinds and of all precautions inseparable from a state of war. The same crowd that is now so vociferous for ruthless terms of peace will spin round to-morrow against the Government if a military breakdown occurs through the dwindling forces which are at our disposal. It is one thing to keep a compact force for a long time in comfortable billets around Cologne in a well-administered and adequately rationed district. It is quite another to spread these young troops we have over large areas of Germany holding down starving populations, living in houses with famished women and children, and firing on miners and working people maddened by despair. Disaster of the most terrible kind lies on that road, and I solemnly warn the Government of the peril of proceeding along it. A situation might soon be reached from which the British moral sentiment would recoil.

I consider that we shall commit a political error of the first order if we are drawn into the heart of Germany in these conditions. We may easily be caught, as Napoleon was in Spain, and gripped in a position from which there is no retreat and where our strength will steadily be consumed. Meanwhile, what is going to happen in India, in Egypt, and the Middle East, and in Turkey?

(4) I wish to place on record my opinion that the military forces at our disposal are not adequate in numbers, and still less in morale, for the prolonged execution of the kind of policy that is now coming into view. You cannot carve up and distribute at pleasure the populations of three or four enormous Empires with a few hundred thousand war-weary conscripts and 150,000 slowly organising volunteers. Our strength is ebbing every day, and although the excitement of a swift advance on Berlin might pull all ranks together for the moment, all the difficulties which I now envisage will recur with greatly increased force the moment the forward movement ceases.

(5) On every ground, therefore, I strongly urge settling up with the Germans now. Now is the time, and it may be the only time, to reap the fruits of victory. 'Agree with thine adversary whilst thou art in the way with him.' Everything shows that the present German Government is sincerely desirous of making a beaten peace and preserving an orderly community which will carry out its agreement. It seems to me quite natural that they should put forward a series of counter propositions, and we ought to take these up seriatim with patience and goodwill and endeavour to split the outstanding differences. In this way we shall get a genuine German acceptance of a defeated peace and not be drawn into new dangers measureless in their character.

(6) The British Empire is in a very fine position at the present moment, and we now require a peace which will fix and recognise that position. Let us beware lest in following too far Latin ambitions and hatreds we do not create a new situation in which our advantages will largely have disappeared. Settle now while we have the power, or lose perhaps for ever the power of settlement on the basis of a military victory.

WSC

Sir Henry Wilson: diary

(*Wilson papers*)

21 May, 1919 Paris

Winston sent me up at 8 am a note about occupation of more German territory showing the danger of it & how slender are our resources.

Then at 10.30 I went down to see Winston. I found him with Spears! Winston asked Spears if he ever got any of his information by underhand means! Spears said he never did. When Spears had left Winston told me he had seen Derby who would not fight the thing out, but he had also seen Clemenceau who was very much opposed to the appointment. Of course it is a most amazing obsession of Winston's.

Winston S. Churchill to David Lloyd George

(*Churchill papers: 16/7*)

21 May 1919

The following is my suggested answer to Mr Bonar Law about Russia:—

Our policy In Russia has been repeatedly explained to Parliament. Russia must work out her own salvation. It is only by Russian manhood that this can be achieved. We have no intention, and we never had any intention, of sending British or allied armies into Russia to enforce any particular solution of their internal affairs. We are, however, bound in honour to assist those Russian forces which were called into the field largely at our instigation and in the allied interest during the period of the war with Germany. We are doing so by munitions and supplies and technical assistants attached to Military Missions. At Omsk, the centre of Admiral Kolchak's Government, we have two British battalions with Colonel John Ward, MP, and some small detachments of French and Italian troops. These men are not fighting, but their presence gives a certain moral support to the Omsk Government. The Czechos, the Japanese, and the Americans are keeping the Siberian Railway in working order and are preventing it from being destroyed by roving bands. This they will continue to do. We British have an army of about 30,000 men in the Caucasus which it has been decided to withdraw at the earliest possible moment: the process of evacuation has already begun and in three or four months it should be complete. In North Russia we are engaged in extricating our troops from the positions in which they had been placed during the war with Germany and where they were cut off by the ice of the Winter. For this purpose a relief force of volunteers has been despatched and is now landing. This relief force will cover the withdrawal of the conscript troops who are now there: they are themselves only recruited on a twelve months' engagement, and it is intended to withdraw them at an early date when there is good reason to believe that the local Russian forces, which are rapidly increasing in strength, will be able to look after themselves. The evacuation of the tired conscript troops has already begun.

It does not seem necessary to explain what is happening on the Western Front of Russia from the Baltic to the Black Sea. There can be no dispute about our duty to help these little or new States—Esthonia, Latvia, Lithuania, Poland and Roumania—to make headway against the invasions of the Bolshevik armies by which they have been threatened. No British troops, however, are engaged along the whole of this front and the assistance which is being given to these small new States to protect themselves from being over-run is part of the definite policy undertaken in concert by the Allied Powers.

Finally, there is no use concealing the fact that we are helping the anti-Bolshevik forces in Russia against the Bolsheviks, and that with our help their position is rapidly improving. This makes it all the more necessary at the present time to secure from these anti-Bolshevik Governments which have themselves all accepted the supreme authority of Admiral Kolchak's Government, definite guarantees that their victory will not be used to re-establish a reactionary Czarist regime. We do not intend a Red Terror to be succeeded by a White one. We are therefore seeking guarantees from Admiral Kolchak's Government which will secure the summoning of a constituent assembly based on a wide democratic franchise, which assembly will decide the future Government of Russia and secondly will secure an agrarian policy of a genuinely democratic kind. Failing these guarantees we should hold ourselves free to re-consider the whole position.

Winston S. Churchill to David Lloyd George

(*Churchill papers: 16/7*)

21 May 1919

I have read the two papers you gave me this morning from Lord Hardinge and M Vandervelde.[1] In principle I think there is no difference between any of us.

[1] Emile Vandervelde, 1866–1938. Joined the Belgian Labour Party in 1886, and soon became its leader. Entered Parliament, 1894. Joined the Government as Minister of State on the outbreak of war in August 1914. Minister of Civil and Military Administration, 1916–18. Minister of Justice, 1918–21. In the immediate aftermath of war he used his influence to obtain the inclusion of labour clauses (especially those relating to the 8-hour day) in the Versailles Treaty. Active in the reform of the prison system. Minister for Foreign Affairs, 1925–7; he negotiated and signed the Locarno Pact on behalf of Belgium. Minister of Public Health, 1936–7.

This is clearly the moment to secure from Admiral Kolchak's Government, in return for formal recognition and active support, effective guarantees for (a) a constituent assembly on a democratic franchise to decide the future form of Russian Government, (b) a bold agrarian policy, (c) the acceptance of the independence of Poland and of the autonomous existence of Finland, and (d) the acceptance of the fact that the provisional arrangements which the allies have made in regard to Esthonia, Livonia, Latvia, Lithuania, Georgia, and Azerbaijan shall be dealt with only in accordance with the agreements reached between the new Russia and the League of Nations.

In return for a satisfactory agreement of this kind with the Kolchak Government, I consider that the allies should together recognise that Government as 'The National Provisional Government of Russia', thus distinguishing it from the International Soviet Government of Russia. The Bolsheviks, whose aims are international and world-wide, have no right to the use of the word 'National' in any circumstances. The use of the word 'Provisional' safeguards the allies from any inconveniences that might result from having to admit representatives of the Kolchak Government to allied conferences at the present time. That must be reserved until after a constituent assembly has conferred power upon a new Russian administration. On the other hand, M Sazonoff and other accredited representatives of the Kolchak Government and, indeed, of the Russia that was our ally in the first two years of the war—should be treated with proper consideration and not treated simply as a pack of worthless emigrants. In a very little while the wheel of fortune may place these men—some of whom are experienced statesmen with whom we have worked for many years—in positions of authority, and it is only prudent to preserve civil and considerate relations with them.

Once definite guarantees for the democratic government of Russia have been obtained, I would suggest that a Minister or other important officer should be definitely charged by the Council of Heads of Governments with the duty of reporting to them on the Russian situation in its entirety, and of offering guidance in their name to the representatives of the National Provisional Government of Russia, as well as with the general concerting of all the measures which it would be proper for us to take to assist them after recognition.

Mr Vandervelde's first condition of the constituent assembly is fully met, and I see no reason why the Russians should not be approached to find out what kind of guarantees they are able to give for its effectual execution. I do not, however, think that it would be fair to expect the Kolchak Government to carry out elections at the present time. They are struggling for life under conditions of war and internal discord of the most extraordinary kind. Even great nations like France and Britain, engaged unitedly in a quarrel which excited every patriotic and moral instinct, found it impossible to hold elections during the period of the war, and it is putting too much upon a struggling administration to insist upon such a condition at the present time. As it is, Kolchak has been blamed for his *coup d'état* of November last, but it is probable that unless he had taken this step he never could have 'got a move on' and re-established and organised the structure of a disciplined army. It is to be observed that he has recently received the formal support of the Socialists of Siberia as well as of Monsieur Sazonoff.

Lord Hardinge's paper contains a proposal that both parties in Russia should be invited to cease fighting. We have tried this already twice and have been rebuffed from all quarters. There can be no question of Kolchak's Government ceasing fighting at the present time. If their armies stopped fighting they would disintegrate, and Bolshevik propaganda is more dangerous in a truce than when actual fighting is taking place. The Bolsheviks on the other hand will not cease fighting either. It is probable that they still think they have a chance of victory. At any rate they know that there is so much country to be covered that their span of existence must at any rate be prolonged for several months. Further, they must have hopes that Germany and Austria will collapse into Bolshevism in the same way as Hungary has done, and that although they are losing on their Eastern Front by Kolchak's advance, they may move forward into new regions with their propaganda and their political system among the defeated States of Central Europe.

It would be quite inconsistent with the policy which we have already announced to Parliament, and which we have been steadily carrying out for the last four months, to threaten Kolchak with a stoppage of supplies unless he agreed to stop fighting. I should personally have great difficulty in agreeing to this, in view of the statements which I have made with full authority on behalf of the Government. I cannot understand how Lord Hardinge could put such a proposal forward at this time of the day. It betrays most complete want of comprehension of the issues which are at stake in Russia. You might as well ask fire and water to cease their conflict.

Winston S. Churchill: departmental minute
(War Office papers: 32/5185)

22 May 1919 War Office

The objections of the India Office to the use of gas against natives are unreasonable. Gas is a more merciful weapon than high explosive shell, and compels an enemy to accept a decision with less loss of life than any other agency of war. The moral effect is also very great.

There can be no conceivable reason why it should not be resorted to. We have definitely taken the position of maintaining gas as a weapon in future warfare, and it is only ignorance on the part of the Indian military authorities which interposes any obstacle. Having regard to the fact that they are retaining all our men, even those who are most entitled to demobilisation, we cannot in any circumstances acquiesce in the non-utilisation of any weapons which are available to procure a speedy termination of the disorder which prevails on the frontier.

If it is fair war for an Afghan to shoot down a British soldier behind a rock and cut him in pieces as he lies wounded on the ground, why is it not fair for a British artilleryman to fire a shell which makes the said native sneeze? It is really too silly.

CIGS concurs.

Sir Henry Wilson: diary

(*Wilson papers*)

26 May 1919 Paris

I telephoned this morning to P de B to find out if he had been consulted by the India Office about their approval to India for an advance on Jellalabad & he said he had *not*.

I brought this to Winston's notice this morning & he told me he had already written to LG pointing out that war with Afghanistan had been begun without the Cabinet having been brought in. . . .

I saw Winston before dinner, he had had a bad day at his flying practice & so was very quiet—said his nerve was going & so forth—threw out, suddenly, a suggestion for Charlie Grant[1] to be MA, never mentioned Spears, passed all the Honours & Rewards papers & altogether was very amiable.

[1] Charles John Cecil Grant, 1877–1950. Entered Coldstream Guards, 1897. Brigade Major, France, 1914–15. Brigadier-General commanding the 1st Infantry Brigade, 1917–18. Brigadier-General, General Staff, 1918–19. Commanded the 3rd Battalion, Coldstream Guards, 1919–21. Colonel on the Staff, Egypt, 1921–5. Commanded London District, 1932–4; Scottish Command, 1937–40. Knighted, 1934. In 1903 he married Lady Sybil Primrose, elder daughter of the 5th Earl of Rosebery.

The Five[1] *to Admiral Kolchak: telegram*

(*Churchill papers: 5/29*)

26 May 1919 Paris

The Allied and Associated Powers feel that the time has come when it is necessary for them once more to make clear the policy they propose to pursue in regard to Russia.

It has always been a cardinal axiom of the Allied and Associated Powers to avoid interference in the internal affairs of Russia. Their original intervention was made for the sole purpose of assisting those elements in Russia which wanted to continue the struggle against German autocracy and to free their country from German rule, and in order to rescue the Czecho-Slovaks from the danger of annihilation at the hands of the Bolshevik forces. Since the signature of the Armistice on November 11th, 1918, they have kept forces in various parts of Russia. Munitions and supplies have been sent to assist those associated with them at a very considerable cost. No sooner, however, did the Peace Conference assemble than they endeavoured to bring peace and order to Russia by inviting representatives of all the warring Governments within Russia to meet them in the hope that they might be able to arrange a permanent solution of Russian problems. This proposal and a later offer to relieve the distress among the suffering millions of Russia broke down through the refusal of the Soviet Government to accept the fundamental condition of suspending hostilities while negotiations or the work of relief was proceeding. Some of the Allied and Associated Governments are now being pressed to withdraw their troops and to incur no further expense in Russia on the ground that continued intervention shows no prospect of producing an early settlement. They are prepared, however, to continue their assistance on the lines laid down below, provided they are satisfied that it will really help the Russian people to liberty, self-government, and peace.

The Allied and Associated Governments now wish to declare formally that the object of their policy is to restore peace within Russia by enabling the Russian people to resume control of their own affairs through the instrumentality of a freely elected Constituent Assembly and to restore peace along its frontiers by arranging for the settlement of disputes in regard to the boundaries of the Russian state and its relations with its neighbours through the peaceful arbitration of the League of Nations.

They are convinced by their experiences of the last twelve months that it is not possible to attain these ends by dealings with the Soviet Government

[1] The five senior allied leaders at the Paris Peace Conference: Clemenceau (France), Lloyd George (Great Britain), Orlando (Italy), Woodrow Wilson (USA) and Saionji (Japan).

of Moscow. They are therefore disposed to assist the Government of Admiral Kolchak and his Associates with munitions, supplies and food, to establish themselves as the government of all Russia, provided they receive from them definite guarantees that their policy has the same objects in view as that of the Allied and Associated Powers. With this object they would ask Admiral Kolchak and his Associates whether they will agree to the following as the conditions upon which they accept continued assistance from the Allied and Associated Powers.

In the first place, that, as soon as they reach Moscow they will summon a Constituent Assembly elected by a free, secret and democratic franchise as the Supreme Legislature for Russia to which the Government of Russia must be responsible, or if at that time order is not sufficiently restored they will summon the Constituent Assembly elected in 1917 to sit until such time as new elections are possible.[1]

Secondly, that throughout the areas which they at present control they will permit free elections in the normal course for all local and legally constituted assemblies such as municipalities, Zemtsvos, etc.

Thirdly, that they will countenance no attempt to revive the special privileges of any class or order in Russia. The Allied and Associated Powers have noted with satisfaction the solemn declaration made by Admiral Kolchak and his associates that they have no intention of restoring the former land system. They feel that the principles to be followed in the solution of this and other internal questions must be left to the free decision of the Russian Constituent Assembly; but they wish to be assured that those whom they are prepared to assist stand for the civil and religious liberty of all Russian citizens and will make no attempt to reintroduce the regime which the revolution has destroyed.

Fourthly, that the independence of Finland and Poland be recognised, and that in the event of the frontiers and other relations between Russia and these countries not being settled by agreement, they will be referred to the arbitration of the League of Nations.

Fifthly, that if a solution of the relations between Esthonia, Latvia, Lithuania and the Caucasian and Transcaspian territories and Russia is not speedily reached by agreement the settlement will be made in consultation and co-operation with the League of Nations, and that until such settlement is made the Government of Russia agrees to recognise these territories as

[1] In rejecting the Allied demand to recall the Constituent Assembly of 1917, Kolchak's emissary in London, Monsieur Nabokoff, informed Curzon on 5 June: 'The Peace Delegates in Paris had probably forgotten, if they were ever aware of it, that Lenin and Trotsky and other notorious Bolsheviks had been members of that Assembly.' Was it proposed, Nabokoff asked, 'that Admiral Kolchak should summon them and assure their safety'?

autonomous and to confirm the relations which may exist between their *de facto* Governments and the Allied and Associated Governments.

Sixthly, that as soon as a Government for Russia has been constituted on a democratic basis, Russia should join the League of Nations and co-operate with the other members in the limitation of armaments and of military organisation throughout the world.

Finally, that they abide by the declaration made by Admiral Kolchak on November 27th, 1918, in regard to Russia's national debts.

The Allied and Associated Powers will be glad to learn as soon as possible whether the Government of Admiral Kolchak and his associates are prepared to accept these conditions, and also whether in the event of acceptance they will undertake to form a single Government and army command as soon as the military situation makes it possible.

G. Clemenceau
D. Lloyd George
V. E. Orlando[1]
Woodrow Wilson
Saionji[2]

Lord Derby to Sir Henry Wilson

(*Derby papers*)

28 May 1919 Paris

I feel therefore that with your very different views on the subject Winston's wishes will not now prevail, especially as AJB is equally against Spears. It was rather amusing yesterday. Winston handed a cutting from French's article on the subject of Spears to LG. Neither of them had their glasses so I had to read it to the PM, which naturally I did without any comment whatever. I must say French does slobber people. He attributes every virtue to Spears and there is only one which he really possesses and that is bravery.

[1] Vittorio Emanuele Orlando, 1860–1952. Born at Palermo, Sicily. Elected a Deputy in the Italian Parliament, 1898. Minister of Education, 1903–5; of Justice, 1907–9 and 1914–16; of the Interior, 1916–17. Prime Minister of Italy, October 1917–June 1919. President of the Chamber, December 1919. A supporter of Mussolini in 1922, he opposed the Fascist Party at the Palermo municipal election of August 1925, and retired from Parliament.

[2] Kimmochi Saionji, 1849–1940. Studied law in France, 1879–80. Founded the Meiji Law School, Tokyo. Started the newspaper *Tōyō Jiyū Shimbun* to popularize European democratic ideals. Minister to Austria-Hungary, 1885. Vice-President of the House of Peers, 1888. Minister of Education, 1894. Twice Prime Minister of Japan, in 1906, when he nationalized the railways, and 1911–12. Headed the Japanese delegation to the Paris Peace Conference, 1919. Created Prince, 1920, and retired from public life.

He undoubtedly is brave but to say that he is tactful and popular with both French and English Staffs seems to me the absolute limit of inaccuracy.

I think if the PM does not send to you to talk to you about Spears the best thing would be for you to ask to see him. We really must get the matter settled and Winston's proposal that the Mission should go on and that I should be left here without a Military Attaché at all seems to me a monstrous and insulting proposal which I very much resent.[1]

War Cabinet: minutes

(*Cabinet papers: 23/10*)

29 May 1919

2. With reference to War Cabinet 502, Minute 5 and Appendix, the War Cabinet had under consideration a Memorandum by the Secretary of State for War on the Railway Situation in South Russia (GT–7348). The Memorandum pointed out that the condition of the railways in the area controlled by General Denikin was very unsatisfactory; their capacity had dropped to 20 per cent. as compared with pre-war days, and the quantity of stores on hand was barely sufficient for four months. This state of affairs was seriously affecting the military situation. The minimum value of the material required was £500,000 for actual railway stores and a further £500,000 for equipment, clothing, and medical stores for the railway staffs, and certain lorries. The question had been taken up with the Supreme Economic Council in Paris, but the Council had refused assistance, as the area was not one for which it had made itself responsible.

THE DEPUTY DIRECTOR OF MILITARY OPERATIONS [General Kirke] said that the general staff regarded the whole success of future operations in South Russia as hingeing upon the re-establishment of railway communication. General Denikin had at present only 240 locomotives out of 800 which could be used. It was, however, not locomotives that were required, but material for their repair. The efficiency of the Russian railway employés was much affected by the fact that they had no proper clothes or boots, and General Briggs, the British Staff Officer attached to General Denikin, was pressing for the immediate supply of the articles enumerated in

[1] On 9 June 1919 Ian Malcolm wrote to Lord Curzon from Paris: 'The truth is that there is a great fight going on between Winston and the Ambassador as to the merits of General Spiers, whom Winston is anxious to nominate, but with whom Derby has declared that he will have nothing to do. And, from all we can hear, Clemenceau and Foch agree with the Ambassador; but of course AJB has not heard this first hand from them. We are also told that Henry Wilson dislikes the suggested appointment.' (*Curzon papers*)

the War Office Memorandum. General Kirke pointed out that until the railway service was effectively reorganised it was impossible for General Denikin to distribute and make proper use of the great quantities of military stores which we had supplied to him. Moreover, the political situation in the Caucasus would be greatly influenced by the success or failure of General Denikin, and this affected the possibility of withdrawing our troops.

THE CHANCELLOR OF THE EXCHEQUER [Austen Chamberlain] said that £12,500,000 sterling had already been placed at the disposal of the Supreme Economic Council in Paris for relief purposes in Russia. In the case now before the Cabinet the familiar procedure had been adopted, that is to say, that the Supreme Economic Council had been approached in the first instance and, as assistance was not forthcoming in that quarter, application had been made to the War Cabinet. The whole burden of fighting the Bolshevists in Russia was now being borne by Great Britain alone, and the situation was becoming intolerable. The million pounds now asked for might be no great matter, but it must be remembered that it was required in order to distribute millions of pounds of stores which had been sent out to General Denikin. He understood that a certain amount of railway material would be shortly taken away from Salonika, in which case he enquired whether it could not be diverted to South Russia. If, as he understood, we were exceedingly short of railway material in this country, we would hardly be justified in supplying General Denikin. It was not so much the actual cost of the material required but the fact that this material was urgently needed for our own railways in order to set our trade going once more. He suggested, as another alternative, that the Minister of Munitions should be consulted as to the possibility of supplying General Denikin's requirements from stores which had been returned from France and elsewhere.

THE PRESIDENT OF THE BOARD OF TRADE[1] pointed out that there was a very grave shortage of iron and steel at present for our own rolling stock. Already our export trade was being held up to a serious extent on this account, and he thought it would be short-sighted policy for us to provide material for South Russia at the expense of essential services in this country. He felt it his duty to impress upon the War Cabinet the fact that the transport situation in Great Britain gave cause for profound anxiety.

SIR GRAEME THOMPSON,[2] in reply to an enquiry, said that the Ministry of Shipping might be able to provide the necessary tonnage, but he

[1] On 26 May 1919 Sir Auckland Geddes (Conservative) had succeeded Sir Albert Stanley (Liberal) as President of the Board of Trade. Geddes held the post until March 1920.

[2] Graeme Thomson, 1875–1933. Entered Admiralty, 1900. Director of Transports, 1914–17. Director of Shipping at the Admiralty and Ministry of Shipping, 1917–19. Knighted, 1919. Colonial Secretary of Ceylon, 1919–22. Governor of British Guiana, 1922–5. Governor of Nigeria, 1925–31. Governor of Ceylon, 1931–3.

would like to be informed as to what the requirements would amount to in bulk. He noticed that among the things particularly asked for were lorries, which were especially bulky articles, and he hoped that these could be supplied from countries nearer to South Russia than Great Britain.

MR BONAR LAW thought that the War Office should explain in greater detail exactly what they wanted, shewing where they thought they could get it, and what it would all amount to in bulk. This might be done by that Department in consultation with the Board of Trade and the Ministry of Munitions.

The War Cabinet decided:—

(1.) That the War Office should prepare detailed estimates of these requirements, indicating possible sources of supply, and stating exact amount of tonnage that would be needed.

(2.) To sanction the required expenditure if the President of the Board of Trade, after consultation with the Ministry of Munitions, was satisfied that the said requirements could be met without any sacrifice of the essential interests of this country.

General Denikin to Winston S. Churchill

(*Churchill papers: 16/7*)

30 May 1919 Ekaterinodar

My dear Mr Churchill,

General Holman has handed me your esteemed letter, and it is with feelings of the deepest satisfaction I learn that His Majesty's Government have chosen such an eminent General as their representative at my Headquarters.

It is unnecessary to add that General Holman will receive our most attentive and cordial support, worthy of the high mission with which he is entrusted and of his qualifications. I am quite sure that the most sincere and friendly relations will be established between him, myself and my subordinates.

I beg you at the same time to submit to His Majesty King George the expression of my deep gratitude for the high award he has been graciously pleased to bestow upon me, and which I am more than proud to receive. I also beg you to express to His Majesty in my own name and in the name of those of my officers who have been honoured by decorations, the feelings of devotions to His Majesty with which we are animated.

Every facility will be given to General Holman to keep you informed of all events on the front of the Armed Forces of Southern Russia, and I am convinced that the British nation with that high sense of justice peculiar to their race, will appreciate the spirit of self-sacrifice with which the Volunteer Army is fighting the Bolsheviks whose evil designs are directed alike against all civilized nations and the progress of the world in general.

With God's help the operations on our front are developing successfully, and we all are animated with a spirit of steadfast faith in the ultimate triumph of righteousness of our cause.

With a feeling of deep regret I am parting with General Briggs, who during his short stay with us has won our sympathy and has rendered precious services to our work. General Briggs is perfectly acquainted with the situation of Southern Russia and I would be greatly obliged to you if you would hear an account of our work directly from him. I would be happy to renew one day, if it were given to me, my collaboration with him, which has lasted such a short time. I acknowledge and am deeply grateful for, the generous support given to us by Britain in supplying my armies with war material and in sending us specialists, and the success of our struggle against the common enemy must in a great degree be attributed to this help. The generous assistance given by the British nation in these times of stress will never be forgotten by Russian patriots and will establish a bond of still firmer friendship and mutual sympathy between Great Britain and regenerated great Russia.

Please accept the assurance of my deep respect and believe me to be,

Yours sincerely
A Denikin

Sir Samual Hoare[1] *to Winston S. Churchill*

(*Churchill papers: 16/7*)

31 May 1919 — 18 Cadogan Gardens
Private & Personal

Dear Churchill,

You must allow me to write these two or three lines of most sincere congratualtions and gratitude for all that you have done in the matter of

[1] Samuel John Gurney Hoare, 1880–1959. Conservative MP for Chelsea, 1910–44. Succeeded his father as 2nd Baronet, 1915. Lieutenant-Colonel, British Military Mission to Russia, 1916–17 and to Italy, 1917–18. Deputy High Commissioner, League of Nations, for care of Russian refugees, 1921. Secretary of State for Air, October 1922–January 1924 and 1924–9. Secretary of State for India, 1931–5; for Foreign Affairs, 1935. First Lord of the Admiralty, 1936–7; Home Secretary, 1937–9; Lord Privy Seal, 1939–40; Secretary of State for Air, April–May 1940. Ambassador to Spain, 1940–4. Created Viscount Templewood, 1944. Among several books of memoirs, he described his Russian experiences in *The Fourth Seal* (1930).

Russia. For the last six months I have been convinced that the whole future of Europe, and indeed of the world, depends upon a Russian settlement and the destruction of Bolshevism. If I may say so, you alone of the Allied Ministers have consistently held and expressed the same view. Whilst however there was little that I or the group of Members with whom I work could accomplish, you fortunately were in a position to carry your convictions into effect. The result is not only a great personal triumph for yourself but also a long step taken towards a permanent peace. The Russians, and indeed to judge from the article in the 'Temps' of May 27, the French also, declare with truth and justice that the great change for the better in Paris has been due to you. Let me therefore say what is in the mind of many members who hold my views that we are all most grateful to you.

The only hitch that I think is possible in the negotiations between the Allied Delegates and Kolchak is in connection with the Baltic Nationalities. You better than anyone will realise that from the military point of view the new Russia must have guarantees from Finland as to a frontier that is only a few miles distant from Petrograd, and from the naval point of view it is necessary to the existence of Russia to retain outlets upon the Baltic. I have told Sazonoff and other representative Russians that I cannot conceive how either the Allied Delegates or the League of Nations could ever fail to recognise Russia's necessity in these two vital respects.

Please do not trouble to answer this letter.

Yours sincerely,
Samuel Hoare

Sir Henry Wilson: diary

(*Wilson papers*)

31 May 1919 Paris

Then I dined with LG who asked all the Cabinet just come from London. There were LG, AJB, FE, Winston, Barnes, Austen, Fisher, Montagu, Bob Cecil.

For 3 hours after dinner we discussed the peace Terms & the Boch answer and it was amazing what unanimity there was in criticizing *all* the Peace terms. No one was satisfied either with the military occupations, nor the frontiers, nor the cession of territories nor with reparations. All agreed they were much too severe. This will put LG in a very difficult position.

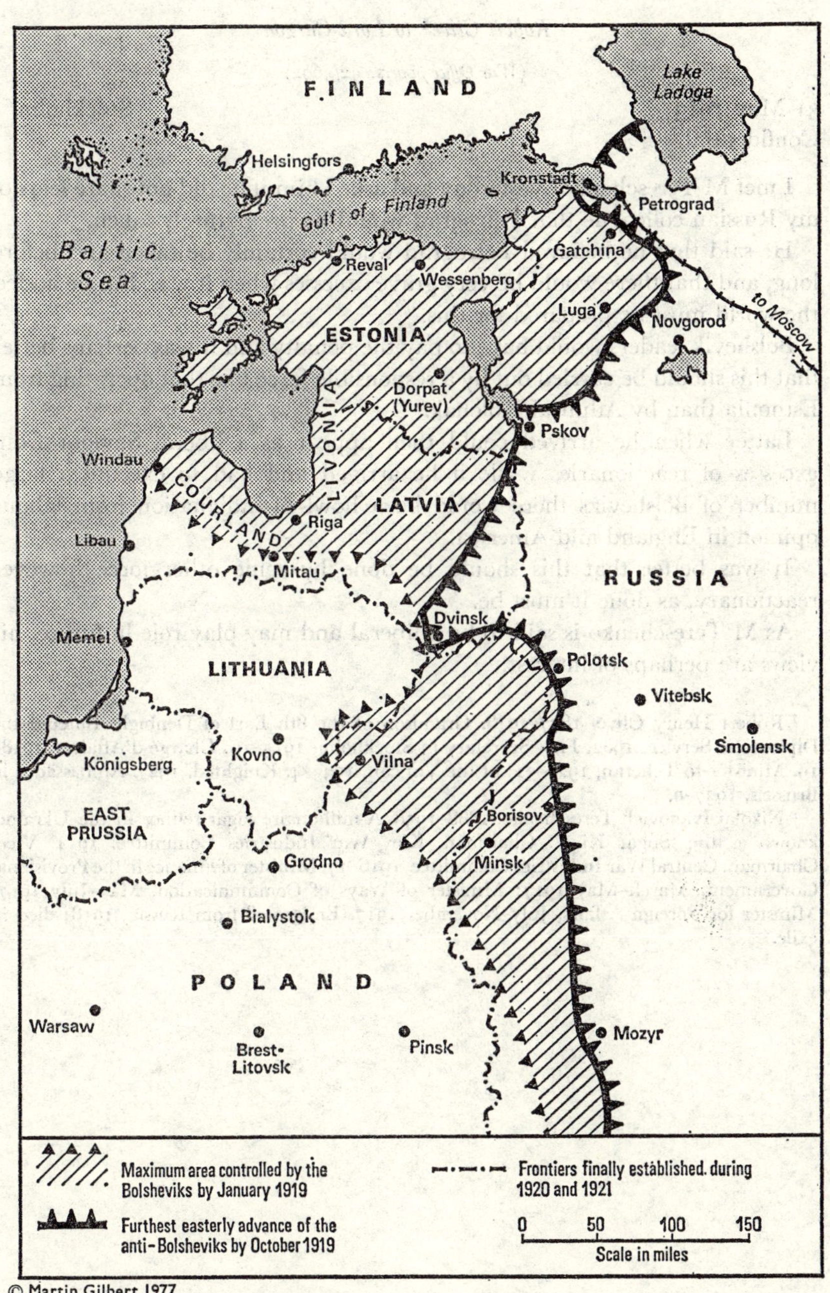

THE BALTIC, 1919–1920

Robert Clive[1] to Lord Curzon

(*War Office papers: 32/5692*)

31 May 1919 Stockholm
Confidential

I met M Tereschenko[2] yesterday and asked him if he did not share fears of my Russian colleague that Petrograd would be prematurely taken.

He said that he believed Petrograd would certainly be taken and before long, and that there would be very grave excesses when it was. But he added the world must be prepared for this.

Bolshevik leaders would have to pay the penalty and it was perhaps better that this should be carried out by a responsible force like that operating from Esthonia than by Admiral Kolchak.

Latter when he arrived could then appear as a liberal Saviour from excesses of reactionaries while if he arrived and had to execute a large number of Bolsheviks there would be a howl of indignation from labour opinion in England and America.

It was better that this should be done by some other force however reactionary, as done it must be.

As M Tereschenko is said to be a liberal and may play role in future, his views are perhaps of interest.

[1] Robert Henry Clive, 1877–1948. Grandson of the 8th Earl of Denbigh. Entered the Diplomatic Service, 1902. First Secretary in Stockholm, 1915–19; Chargé d'Affaires, 1918–19. Minister to Teheran, 1926–31; at the Vatican, 1933–4. Knighted, 1927. Ambassador in Brussels, 1937–9.

[2] Nikolai Ivanovich Tereschenko, 1888–1958. A millionaire sugar refiner in the Ukraine, known as the 'Sugar King'. Chairman, Kiev War Industries Committee, 1914. Vice-Chairman, Central War Industries Committee, 1916–17. Minister of Finance in the Provisional Government, March–May 1917; Minister of Ways of Communication, May–July 1917; Minister for Foreign Affairs, July–November 1917. Emigrated from Russia, 1918; died in exile.

June 1919

Winston S. Churchill to General Harington

(*War Office papers: 32/5692*)

2 June 1919 War Office

We cannot acquiesce in A.[1] Any force wh we support even indirectly must proceed according to the recognised laws & customs of war & be guided by human considerations. Let me have a draft of a telegram to General Gough on these lines.

This message will do us harm in our own councils if it is left unchallenged & unexplained.

Wholesale executions are unpardonable in policy as well as on moral grounds.

WSC

War Cabinet: minutes

(*Cabinet papers: 23/10*)

4 June 1919

The War Cabinet considered what replies should be given in the House of Commons to the following questions:—

(1.) Whether Field-Marshal Lord French has published various confidential documents which he learned of in his official capacity, including his original instructions from Field-Marshal Lord Kitchener and a Memorandum which he addressed to the War Cabinet; and, if so, what action it was proposed to take.

(2.) Whether the report by Lord Kitchener, on the supply of shrapnel and high explosive shells in September and October 1914, can be issued as a Parliamentary Paper.

[1] The statement by Tereschenko that when Petrograd was captured by the anti-Bolsheviks 'grave excesses' would be committed (see previous document, and see also Churchill to General Gough, 6 June 1919, quoted on page 677).

THE SECRETARY OF STATE FOR WAR said that, in his opinion, the Government should reply to all such questions to the effect that, in view of the partial disclosures in various quarters, the Government proposed to table a Blue Book containing all the relevant documents bearing on the question of the supply of ammunition to the armies in the field in the early part of the war. He would go further, and announce that the Government, after the signing of peace, would publish a series of Parliamentary Papers which would give the story of the great episodes of the war to the public in an authentic form. The various documents would be edited as the public interest demanded, but the Government would take responsibility for giving a fair, full, and representative account of the events that had taken place. Mr Churchill added that one of the main advantages of such a course would be that historians would have authentic documents on which to base their narratives. He had talked this matter over with the Prime Minister, who had approved the suggestion, and had said that he would very much like to have published an authentic account of the munitions crisis.

THE FIRST LORD said that he had discussed the matter with his Naval Advisers, who were all of the opinion that any attempt to publish all the papers connected with the War would inevitably strike a serious blow at Staff work and administration. It was impossible to call upon men to defend every decision taken at a moment's notice and in the heat of conflict. The Admiralty were, however, preparing a record of the events of the War, although they could not agree to the publication of the secret documents.

The War Cabinet decided that—

(*a.*) The Secretary of State for War should reply to the Question concerning the publication by Lord French of confidential documents on the following lines:—

> 'I have now had the articles referred to examined in the War Office. The publication of certain of these documents was unauthorised. On the other hand, had permission been sought it is probable that it would have been accorded, as publication of none of these documents is in any way detrimental to the public interest. The whole subject is now in the region of public controversy, and I do not contemplate any special action in regard to it.'

(*b.*) He should reply to the Question regarding the publication of Lord Kitchener's report on shells, in the sense that the Government were not prepared to publish any documents giving a partial or one-sided view of the events of the War.

(*c.*) He should add that the Government had under consideration the question of the more general publication, at a later stage, of official documents bearing on the events of the War.

Winston S. Churchill to General Spears
(*Churchill papers: 16/37*)

4 June 1919 War Office
Secret

You should read the enclosed letter, seal it up and give it personally yourself to M Sazonoff. You are at liberty to use any arguments you like to M Sazonoff in accordance with the sense of this letter but without committing me directly. You should make a point of keeping in touch with him and becoming a channel through which he can communicate readily with me.

Secondly, M Sazonoff and the Russian group have apparently got it into their heads that Philip Kerr is hostile to loyal Russia and favours the Bolsheviks. This is quite untrue. Mr Philip Kerr has been most helpful and useful, especially lately. It is a pity that criticisms of him which must have originated from Russian sources in Paris should have appeared in a leading article in the 'Morning Post'. The Prime Minister's attention was drawn to this and he was not at all pleased. Thus difficulties are made at a time when everything counts. If M Sazonoff likes at any time to communicate with me through you or through Sir Samuel Hoare, he can do so quite readily and freely.

Thirdly, Sir Samuel Hoare, MP, is coming to Paris on Thursday. You should get in touch with him and let him put you into relations with the Russian group in so far as that is necessary.

I should like you to report to me fully and constantly on these Russians in Paris, always using great discretion not to commit me in any way. If they put Kolchak off accepting the Allies' conditions they will have rendered the worst possible service to themselves.

General Spears to Winston S. Churchill
(*Churchill papers: 16/37*)

5 June 1919 Paris
Personal & Secret

Dear Secretary of State,

1. I saw Mr Sazonoff (whom I knew before) to-day and gave him Sir Samuel Hoare's letter which he read before me.

Mr Sazonoff assured me that Hoare's fears that the Russian Delegation in

PARIS had advised Kolchak to refuse the Allied terms was absolutely unfounded. He assured me that the contrary was the case and to prove this he shewed me a long wire he has sent to Kolchak urging upon him the acceptance of the Allied terms. The only reservation contained in this wire was concerning the meeting of the Constituent Assembly of '17, which is considered by the Russians as quite unacceptable, the original one having been convened by the Bolsheviks.

Admiral Kolchak is asked by Mr Sazonoff to recognise all national minorities insofar as these interests do not clash with those of the country as a whole. Sazonoff, in explaining this clause verbally to me, said that as regards the BALTIC Provinces, for instance, they could use their own language and have their own universities, elect their own governors, and in short, do everything that does not threaten national unity in the broadest sense.

As regards FINLAND, the above mentioned wire simply states that in all probability the Russian Constituent Assembly would have no objections to the frontiers with the freely recognised state of FINLAND being laid down by the League of Nations.

In conversation, however, Mr Sazonoff pointed out that RUSSIA could not allow the Treaty with FINLAND to give the Germans a possibility of gaining a footing in the Gulf of Finland.

Mr Sazonoff asked me to assure you in the strongest possible terms that he fully realised the importance of Admiral Kolchak accepting the Allied terms with but the smallest exceptions. He could not understand where Sir Samuel Hoare had got his ideas from.

2. As regards Mr Philip Kerr, it is very evident that Mr Sazonoff like the remainder of the Russians I have seen here, looks upon Mr Lloyd George and Mr Kerr as unfavourable to the RUSSIA he represents. He however gave me his word that neither he nor any of the other representative Russians have said anything whatsoever that could have inspired the 'Morning Post' article. No English journalists have been seen by the Russians in PARIS, and when in LONDON, Mr Sazonoff saw and approved an article on RUSSIA prepared by the 'Morning Post' correspondent after an interview given by him but he states that this interview could not form a pretext for the article complained of. He has asked me to do everything in my power to dispel the impression created by this article, and I am accordingly going to tell Miss Stevenson that, having met some of the Russians here, they expressed to me their deep regret at the 'Morning Post' article, for which they entirely disclaimed all responsibility.

I did everything in my power to point out to Mr Sazonoff that Mr Philip Kerr had been most helpful and useful as regards RUSSIA lately, but I will have to keep on at this question as Sazonoff has got it into his head that the least favourable of the clauses regarding RUSSIA submitted to Admiral Kolchak were inserted at Philip Kerr's instigation; this he says he has got on excellent authority.

3. Mr Sazonoff asked me to tell you that you were the most popular Englishman in RUSSIA to-day, and that it was fully recognised by all Russians what you had done for their country. He told me that he had wished to see you in LONDON but had not done so for fear of embarrassing you.

4. Mr Sazonoff, with whom I am on excellent personal terms, has promised to keep me au courant of the situation and to use me as his channel of communication with you. You may rest assured that I will not commit you in any way.

Yours sincerely,
E. L. Spears

Winston S. Churchill to General Gough: telegram

(*War Office papers: 32/5692*)

6 June 1919 War Office
Secret

Tereschenko the ex Minister Foreign Aflairs Kerenski[1] Government who is now in Stockholm has expressed view that grave excesses will take place when Petrograd is taken and that the world must be prepared for this. He stated Bolshevik leaders would have to pay penalty and that it was preferable this should be carried out by a force like that operating from Esthonia and not by Kolchak. Tereschenko holds no official position so far as is known and does not speak for Kolchak movement but his words emphasize what is in reality grave danger. Excesses by anti-Bolsheviks if they are victorious will alienate sympathies British nation and render continuance of support most difficult. This should be represented tactfully but strongly to Yudenitch, and other leading Russians with whom you come in contact. You should press for fair public trial of all culprits and stringent orders against terrorism and indiscriminate shooting. In view of prominent part taken by Jews in Red terror and regime there is special danger of Jew pogroms and this danger must be combated strongly.

[1] Alexander Feodorovich Kerensky, 1881–1970. A Labour member of the Russian Duma, 1912. Minister of Justice in the Provisional Government, February 1917; Minister of War and the Navy, May 1917. Urged the continuing prosecution of the war, and sought to raise army morale, May–July 1917. Prime Minister, July–October 1917, and Supreme Commander-in-Chief, September–October 1917. Fled from Petrograd, October 1917. In exile in France, 1918–40 and then in the United States.

Winston S. Churchill to General Spears

(*Churchill papers: 16/37*)

8 June 1919 War Office

. . . Are you in touch with Kerensky. I hear he is in Paris and is making mischief for the Kolchak–Sazonoff group. He is said to be declaring that Kolchak is not democratic, and that he (Kerensky) will not work with him. He is now quoted boldly against Kolchak and our policy of supporting him by the extremists in the House of Commons. This is probably only due to the fact that he has been left out. It seems to me most important that all Russians should concentrate and that no one should be driven away through injured vanity. I am only going on hearsay, but it seems to me probable enough. You should talk to Sazonoff discreetly, and if you think it practicable see if you can establish some sort of a relationship between them. Really all Russians ought to unite at the present time to give their country national expression.

Report fully as soon as you can.

Winston S. Churchill to Sir Henry Wilson

(*Churchill papers: 16/8*)

8 June 1919 War Office

The enclosed has doubtless reached you from other sources by now.[1] If you consider that the plan proposed is sound in a military sense, will you please bring it before the Prime Minister as soon as possible and ask him to sanction it.

You should represent to him that it is not a matter of policy but a purely military operation within the limits of the policy which has already been pursued. Unless he wishes it, therefore, it does not require to be brought specially before the Cabinet, though I am quite ready to do so with his authority.

If you have any difficulty in obtaining the Prime Minister's assent, please let me know at once and I will come over myself on Thursday or Friday, as I attach the greatest importance to a speedy settlement of this business. I hope, however, to receive a telegram from you on Tuesday, or Wednesday at the

[1] General Ironside's proposal to advance with two Brigades from Archangel towards Kotlas, and to try to link up with Kolchak's anti-Bolshevik forces in Siberia. Churchill was opposed to any press publicity for this scheme (see his note to General Harington on 10 June, quoted on page 679).

latest, saying that it is allright. I am sure that if you go to breakfast and have Kisch[1] in attendance with his maps, you will obtain a favourable result.

Sir Henry Wilson: diary

(*Wilson papers*)

10 June 1919 Paris

A letter from Winston wants to know if LG agrees to Ironside's proposals for going to Kotlas.

I lunched with LG & afterwards explained Ironside's proposals to him & to Bonar on the map & he made no objection. His mind was full of Fiume[2] & terms for the Boches & against the Roumanians, & anger against Winston for giving Gough a GCMG!

Winston S. Churchill to General Harington

(*Churchill papers: 16/16*)

10 June 1919 War Office

This is very disquieting. I have lately been carefully dwelling on the process of evacuation in public in order to conceal any impending movement. I cannot understand how General Ironside could have allowed himself to use language of this kind in an untrustworthy quarter.

Apart altogether from the military disadvantages, political difficulties will be caused here if it is thought that an offensive operation is impending. I have been considering what course we should actually adopt when the

[1] Frederick Hermann Kisch, 1888–1943. Entered the Royal Engineers, 1907. Captain, 1914. On active service in France, 1914–15 and Mesopotamia, 1916–17, when he was wounded three times. Lieutenant-Colonel, General Staff, War Office, 1917–19. A Member of the British delegation to the Paris Peace Conference, 1919. Retired from the Army, 1922, and emigrated to Palestine. Chairman of the Palestine Zionist Executive, 1923–31. He published *Palestine Diary* in 1938. Rejoined the Royal Engineers, 1939. Brigadier, 1942. Killed in action, by a mine, in North Africa, 7 April 1943.

[2] On the eastern Adriatic coast, the only port of Hungary before 1914. Promised to Croatia by the Treaty of London, 1915. Demanded by Italy, 1918. Seized by Croat troops, 23 October 1918. Claimed by Italy throughout the summer of 1919, when Italian ships entered the harbour, but were later replaced by American naval forces, pending a decision on the future of Fiume by the Peace Conference. On 12 September 1919, before any decision was reached, the port was occupied by the Italian poet and soldier-of-fortune, Gabriele D'Annunzio, and the Italians remained in control until 1945, when Fiume was transferred to Yugoslavia.

operation starts. Should we, for instance, allow daily progress to be chronicled or should we shut off all news for ten days or so until definite results have been obtained? I favour the latter. I think Ironside should get his correspondents together on the eve of the advance, take them into his confidence, and then shut off all references of any kind to his forward movement.

Pray let me know to-morrow what you think.

War Office to General Knox: telegram

(*Churchill papers: 'Narrative of Events in Siberia'*)

10 June 1919 London

It is suggested that a portion of the Czecho-Slovak troops might be employed again on the front, in view of the reserves which are now taking place on the Siberian front, and which may postpone for a considerable period the junction with the Archangel forces.

It might be possible to use one or two brigades of these Czecho-Slovak troops in conjunction with the Anglo-Russian Brigade on the right flank of the army. It is possible that they might welcome the prospect of cutting their way through to Archangel, and their eventual repatriation by this route, as this would be shorter and quicker than *via* Vladivostok. If a start was made with a small force, others might be induced to follow their example. You might suggest it to Kolchak if you consider that such a course is possible and desirable. If he approves it would be necessary for the Japanese to take the place of the Czechs. . . .

Sir Henry Wilson to Winston S. Churchill: telegram

(*Churchill papers: 16/8*)

10 June 1919 Paris

I have received your letter regarding Ironside's proposals and have explained the whole situation to Prime Minister who raises no objection I cross tonight and hope to see you tomorrow afternoon.

Lord Curzon to Winston S. Churchill

(*Churchill papers: 16/8*)

10 June 1919 1 Carlton House Terrace

My dear Churchill,

I am afraid that I could not approve of the suggested telegram to General Milne on the double ground that it is inconsistent with the policy which we have hitherto pursued & are still pursuing, & that it would be unwise in itself.

I know of no ground for believing that officers in the Caucasus are unduly favouring the Republic at the expense of Denikin. Rather is it the other way about.

As regards Georgia I do not know if you are aware that Balfour definitely recognised its independence & pledged our support to its cause at the Peace Conference.

Further at the very moment when you propose to telegraph to Milne telling him & his officers not to show too much sympathy with the Republicans, *your own office* is telegraphing a strong warning to Denikin not to overstep a given line separating him from the Republicans on pain of the severe displeasure of HMG.

Should General Milne therefore receive your proposed instructions I think he would find no small difficulty in deciding on which leg he was expected to stand.

Finally I submit that the only way in which to secure Denikin's success is to keep the Caucasus quiet behind him. This can only be done by recognising the 'Separatist interests of the Republics'.

They cordially dislike & distrust Denikin & would sooner become Bolsheviks than accept his dispensation. The worst thing that could happen to Denikin would therefore be in my judgement that the Republics should be snubbed, for it is on Denikin that they would take it out.

I hope therefore that you will not send the proposed draft but will allow our policy to proceed on its present difficult but not irrational lines.

Yours ever
Curzon

Winston S. Churchill to General Harington

(*Churchill papers: 16/16*)

10 June 1919 War Office

Very Urgent

I understood that it had been satisfactorily arranged that the date for evacuation was provisionally postponed to July 15th, in order that the success or failure of General Denikin's operations against Astrakhan could be definitely decided. Has this been done.

I do not understand why these telegrams are being sent off as late as the 7th instant in apparent ignorance of the fact that July 1st is no longer the date. Are you in touch with the Admiralty, and are you making sure that no premature action in regard to withdrawal will be taken on their part. It is some days ago since I gave you Lord Curzon's letter, and I understood that you were going to speak to CIGS on the telephone.

Please report to me to-morrow (Wednesday) what the position is.

Secondly. Has General Holman arrived at General Denikin's headquarters? We have not heard anything from him yet.

Thirdly. It is astonishing that we have not heard from General Knox any clear military account of the extent and character of the defeat sustained by Kolchak's Southern Wing. We often get from Knox long telegrams on obscure matters of Siberian politics, but here a great operation has taken place profoundly modifying the whole situation and we are told nothing which enables an opinion to be formed. We are not, for instance, even told what losses there have been in men and guns on the Russian side. Unless you have received this information without my seeing the telegram, pray telegraph and ask for a specific report.

Winston S. Churchill: notes for Colonel Ludlow Hewitt[1]

(*Churchill papers: 16/1*)

10 June 1919

(1) The first thing to aim at is to make a thoroughly efficient RAF which will last year after year in a good condition and be a credit to the country.

[1] Edgar Rainey Ludlow-Hewitt, 1886–1973. 2nd Lieutenant, Royal Irish Rifles, 1905. Transferred to the Royal Flying Corps, 1914. Major, 1915. Commanded the 10th Brigade, Royal Air Force, 1918. Awarded the DSO and the MC. Chief Staff Officer, Royal Air Force Headquarters, France, 1918–19. Group Captain, 1919. Private Secretary to the Secretary of State for Air, 1919–21. Commandant, Royal Air Force Staff College, 1926–30. Air Officer. Commanding, Iraq, 1930–2. Knighted, 1933. Director of Operations and Intelligence, Air Ministry, 1933–5. Commanded RAF India, 1935–7. Commander-in-Chief Bomber Command, 1937–40. Inspector-General of the RAF, 1940–5.

All questions connected with the indirect effects of the education and training of the RAF on the general population are secondary to the particular task in which we are interested. This does not mean that vicious methods should be adopted which injure national life, but it does distinctly mean that our primary task is one limited in its character which must not be merged in general aims.

(2) Framework is very important for the RAF and must be solid. CAS spoke to me some time ago about his wish to introduce something like the regimental system of the Army into the RAF, thus preserving the identities of the more famous squadrons. With this I am heartily in accord. We must create definite units of a permanent character possessing their own *esprit de corps* with good strictly managed messes, the officers of which know each other, and where there is a strong public opinion on questions of behaviour. A ceaseless fluctuation of individuals cannot be allowed: the presumption of every officer should be that he will be working with the same lot of fellows at any rate for several years to come. Units when formed should every few years move from station to station and from home to foreign service according to a roster. Officers would have choice of units and be able to exchange from units or obtain transfers, but broadly speaking they should be kept together as far as possible. This does not, of course, conflict with the idea of a general list but it is a general list modified in practice by the needs of keeping units together as much as possible.

(3) The first essential is a good college filled by competitive examination, preferably from the public schools. The training should, I think, be for two years, and four principal features should be—

(i) The discipline and bearing of an officer and a gentleman.
(ii) War studies: not only air war but war as a whole.
(iii) Technical instruction in mechanics of the kind given at Dartmouth with special reference to aviation needs.
(iv) A certain amount of flying instruction to be regarded as a privilege in the first year, and only obligatory in the second year. During the first year cadets would begin to specialise either on the technical or the flying side. All must be technical and all must fly, but the emphasis will be different according to aptitudes. The Navy, with its specialisation on gunnery, torpedo and salt-horse categories, will furnish many illustrations. We must aim at having some of the very best practical engineers and technicians trained in our own hands and offer them good permanent careers. As there will only be one Air College it must really in a way play the part both of Woolwich and Sandhurst.

(4) I presume you are setting on foot good schools of mechanics. These

must be caught early. Although the trade unions have played a very valuable part in national life, it would never do for the RAF to become *wholly* dependent upon their craftsmen. Here, again, the Navy affords much valuable experience on their training establishments on the 'Fisgard', etc, for producing the boy artificer, which is an indispensable element in a force so largely dependent upon mechanics. We should aim at a minimum of training at least one-third and preferably one-half directly ourselves, giving them a really first-rate education from an early age on, and these boys ought to serve on a long engagement so that we can get the benefit of their skill when we have trained them. Again they must have a definite career opened out to them.

I should be glad if you would let me know in writing how your schemes are shaping, especially with some reference to the numbers involved and the size of the educational establishments contemplated.

Winston S. Churchill to Lord Curzon

(*Curzon papers*)

11 June 1919 War Office

My dear Curzon,

I think you underrate the extent to wh the original instructions given to our officers have become obsolete in view of our impending abandonment of this whole theatre. We shd have actually cleared out on Sunday next, but for the interests of Denikin's operations. Our present date is July 15: after wh the Italians or chaos or both!

Let me have my telegram back. I certainly meet soldiers who seem to be toiling to build up 'strong independent Republics'; & who think we have a policy in that direction for wh we are going to make exertions & sacrifices. Surely they shd be undeceived.

Yours vy sincerely

W

War Cabinet:[1] *minutes*

(*Curzon papers*)

SITUATION IN NORTH RUSSIA

11 June 1919 — Lord Curzon's room
am — Foreign Office

LORD CURZON said that he had summoned the Cabinet that evening at the request of the Secretary of State for War, who had just returned with the Chief of the Imperial General Staff from Paris. Our Commander in North Russia proposed to conduct certain operations in North Russia at an early date, with a view to relieving the situation there. He understood that the plan of these operations had been submitted to the Prime Minister in Paris, and that the latter had accorded them his sanction, subject to their receiving the approval of the War Cabinet.

THE SECRETARY OF STATE FOR WAR explained that General Ironside, commanding in North Russia, had now completed his plans, which the Chief of the Imperial General Staff would presently outline to the War Cabinet. These plans had been carefully examined by the General Staff, in concert with the Admiralty, and had been approved. On the previous day the Chief of the Imperial General Staff had put them before the Prime Minister and Mr Bonar Law, who had provisionally sanctioned them, subject to the Cabinet's approval. In the ordinary course it would not have been necessary for him to refer the matter to the Prime Minister and the Cabinet; it was, however, desirable in this case, as for the first time we proposed to depart from our present defensive policy and embark upon definite aggressive action against the Bolsheviks.

THE CHIEF OF THE IMPERIAL GENERAL STAFF then read to the War Cabinet telegram No 78771, dated June 10, 1919, to General Knox, summarising General Ironside's intentions, and he explained the situation with the aid of a map. General Ironside proposed to advance with one British and one Russian Brigade against Kotlas, which he expected to be able to take within fifteen days from the commencement of the operation. Simultaneously, a Russian force would move down the Vologda railway to Plesetskaya. Should it appear feasible to effect a junction with General Gaida after the capture of Kotlas, General Ironside intended to take part of

[1] The only member of the War Cabinet present was Lord Curzon. Also attending were Lord Milner (Secretary of State for the Colonies), Churchill, Sir Henry Wilson, H A L Fisher (President of the Board of Education), Edwin Montagu (Secretary of State for India), Walter Long (First Lord of the Admiralty), Sir Auckland Geddes (President of the Board of Trade) and Admiral Wemyss (First Sea Lord and Chief of the Naval Staff).

his force thirty miles South of Kotlas to block the Suchena, while another portion of his command would clear the Wichegda area and get into touch with the right flank of the Siberians. Should it not appear practicable to join up with Gaida, his intention was to hold Kotlas as long as possible and to clear the Wichegda area, sending all craft down the river to Archangel, thus denying Kotlas to the Bolshevists as a base before the winter. His preparations would be sufficiently advanced to enable him to commence operations in two or three weeks' time, but before advancing he stipulated that Admiral Kolchak should keep his right flank where it was at present, near Glasovo. While General Ironside was advancing towards Kotlas, Admiral Kolchak would co-operate by moving in the direction of Viatka. If once these two could join hands, our communications would be assured and General Ironside would be able once more to base himself on Archangel. The *moral* of our two Brigades, which were composed of picked men only, was excellent, and the Slovak troops who would be taking part in the operations were also in very good heart.

THE SECRETARY OF STATE FOR WAR observed that the plan of operations precluded any possibility of General Ironside's troops being cut off.

THE CHIEF OF THE IMPERIAL GENERAL STAFF, continuing, said that the worst that could happen would be (a) that the enemy would not face us and that we should merely strike a blow in the air; and (b) that Gaida should fail to make headway from the South and link up with us. In any case it could always be open to us to withdraw. Unfortunately, the enemy had only to evaporate in order to spoil the *coup*. Our object was two-fold; (i) to hit the enemy hard, and (ii) to join up with the friendly forces in the South. If once we could establish connection, we would hand over control of the operations to Admiral Kolchak, and proceed ourselves to withdraw from North Russia. The whole intention of these operations was to facilitate that withdrawal. If, however, we attempted to clear out without striking a blow first and establishing touch with the troops in the South, we would have the whole pack of Bolsheviks at our heels and would be risking a possible disaster. As the Secretary of State for War had said, our troops ran no danger of being cut off. General Ironside had been ordered, whatever happened, to effect the withdrawal of our troops from North Russia before the winter. In reply to a question, General Wilson said that the port closed in October or November, according as winter set in early or late.

THE FIRST LORD OF THE ADMIRALTY informed the War Cabinet that it must be clearly understood that owing to the ice, the end of November is the latest date upon which our ships must be withdrawn. He enquired whether the War Office were prepared to feed the people on the river.

THE CHIEF OF THE IMPERIAL GENERAL STAFF replied that the War Office were prepared to do this.

THE FIRST SEA LORD said that arrangements had been made for our Naval forces in that theatre to co-operate in the contemplated operations. As, however, they would have to advance along the river in boats, they would have to proceed cautiously owing to mines, and might take longer than fifteen days to reach their objective. The Naval ratings who would take part in the expedition were not conscripts, but ordinary long-service men, and absolutely to be trusted. Our Naval policy in North Russia was simply to support the Army. Unfortunately, our Monitors would not form part of the Naval force, which would consist of 10 gun-boats and 6 motor-boats. We were, in addition, sending a number of barges and heavy guns. In reply to a question, Admiral Wemyss said that the third week in October was the latest safe date for our men to clear out of North Russia.

THE SECRETARY OF STATE FOR INDIA stated that Parliament had been informed that all the troops we had sent and were sending to North Russia were despatched with the sole purpose of enabling us to withdraw in safety the men we already had there. Was this move a part of that operation?

THE CHIEF OF THE IMPERIAL STAFF replied that the operations under discussion were in no sense inconsistent with, and were indeed intended to facilitate, the promised withdrawal from Archangel and the North of Russia before the ice set in.

LORD CURZON also enquired whether the projected expedition was inconsistent with any pledges that we had given in either House. The contemplated operations presented a new situation. This was the first time that we were taking the offensive against the Bolsheviks.

THE CHIEF OF THE IMPERIAL GENERAL STAFF said that the men taking part in these operations were not 'driven conscripts', but were, on the contrary, tremendously keen about the whole expedition. In reply to a question, he said that Admiral Kolchak had known all along that we intended to carry out some such operations as those now contemplated, but this was the first time that they had been put forward in any detailed form. Admiral Kolchak's own forward movement would be all right if he secured command of the river. We were maintaining a powerful Mission with Admiral Kolchak, who was fully aware that, whatever happened and whatever pressure he might exert later, we did not intend to remain in North Russia another winter. The area in which the operations were to take place could supply us with ample food, especially if we managed to link up with the South.

THE SECRETARY OF STATE FOR WAR, in reply to Lord Curzon and the Secretary of State for India, said that, in a recent speech in the

House of Commons, he had fully explained our policy. That speech had met with a very satisfactory reception. He himself did not think that there was anything in the operations now projected which was inconsistent, or could not easily be reconciled, with what he had stated in Parliament. He foresaw no difficulty in justifying to Parliament the present plans, which were simply designed to secure our withdrawal from North Russia, more especially if, as he saw no reason to doubt, they were successful. The repatriation of the Czecho-Slovaks would be much facilitated by the proposed operations. They would be told that it was up to them to fight their way home through Kotlas, etc before the coming November. He thought that, as they professed a great contempt for the Bolsheviks, they might be induced to make the effort. General Denikin had gained, a week or two back, a great victory over the 10th Bolshevik Army, who had been repulsed with heavy losses, no less than 15,000 prisoners being taken. General Denikin was now advancing with powerful forces. If he could take Astrakhan and Tzaritzin, he could consolidate his position and dominate the Caspian. Mr Churchill said that the recognition of Admiral Kolchak would be considerably to our advantage, as by this action we might induce both the Americans and the Japanese to play a larger part in that theatre of war.

The War Cabinet decided—

To approve the proposed operations.

Sir Henry Wilson: diary

(*Wilson papers*)

11 June 1919 Havre

Cabinet at 6.30. Curzon, Long, Montagu, Fisher, Winston & Milner. I explained our proposals for Ironside's attacks on Kotlas & joining hands with Kolchak via Kotlas & Viatka. They all agreed to my proposals.

War Cabinet: minutes

(*Cabinet papers: 23/10*)

11 June 1919
pm

With reference to War Cabinet 567, Minute 3, THE SECRETARY OF STATE FOR WAR said that he wished to refer to a Memorandum by himself which he had recently circulated to the War Cabinet, entitled 'The Expansion of General Knox's Mission in Siberia' (Paper GT–7415). The idea was to form a Slavo-British unit with British officers and non-commissioned officers, and the proposal had been approved on the 14th May by himself as a Departmental matter. On the same day the Chancellor of the Exchequer had drawn the attention of the War Cabinet to a telegram from Mr Hodgson,[1] in which the latter referred to the proposal, and Mr Chamberlain had pointed out that this step committed us to a more definite support of Kolchak's Government than we had hitherto afforded. Lord Curzon had agreed that this was closely related to the question of recognition of Kolchak, and also the Cabinet had decided to refer the proposal to the Foreign Office, the War Office, and the British representatives in Paris; and that, pending receipt of the latter's views, sanction should not be given.

His own opinion, in which Mr Balfour, with whom he had discussed the matter in Paris, had concurred, was that details of how the increased personnel of the Mission should be employed was a purely Departmental matter. On the 23rd May, General Knox had telegraphed making further proposals on the same lines, and Mr Churchill said that he had approved this and had given direction that steps should be taken to give effect.

When talking over the matter with Mr Balfour he had demurred at having to refer the matter again to the Cabinet, as no new principle was created, and the question was quite within his own scope and was also in accordance with his policy. Mr Balfour had agreed that, in the circumstances, further reference to the War Cabinet seemed unnecessary. In reply to a question, Mr Churchill said that he had had no opportunity of discussing the matter with the Prime Minister but only with Mr Balfour.

The War Cabinet took note of the statement of the Secretary of State for War.

Lord Curzon to Winston S. Churchill

(*Churchill papers: 16/8*)

11 June 1919 1 Carlton House Terrace, S.W.1

My dear Churchill,

In view of our decision this afternoon I am rather concerned at WO telegram from Brit Minister at Vladivostock this evening, no 3195 June 5.

[1] Robert MacLeod Hodgson, 1874–1956. Vice-Consul, Marseille, 1901–6; Vladivostok, 1906–11. Consul, Vladivostok, 1911–19. Acting British High Commissioner in Siberia, 1919–21. British Agent to the Soviet Government, 1921–4. Chargé d'Affaires, Moscow, 1924–7. Knighted, 1925. Minister to Albania, 1928–36. British Agent in Nationalist Spain, 1937–9; Chargé d'Affaires, Burgos, 1939. Foreign Office Adviser to the Censorship, 1942–4.

I agree that Gaida on whom you relied for the advance to meet our forces, is in a serious position & that the Siberians any more postpone all idea of renewal & its advance for the present. In these circumstances are you not apprehensive of a fiasco?

Yours sincerely
Curzon

Winston S. Churchill to Sir Henry Wilson

(*Churchill papers: 16/8*)

12 June 1919 War Office

Last week I asked Sir Samuel Hoare, MP, to speak to Monsieur Sazonoff in Paris about the extreme folly of the Paris Russians tempting Kolchak to boggle over our recognition conditions. I did this in consequence of Hoare's influence with the Paris Russians and personal friendship with Sazonoff, and also because I could see that the Prime Minister was vexed at the mischief which he believed the Russians were creating.

I wrote to Spears and told him to get in touch with Hoare in Paris and to transmit to me any telegrams which Hoare might wish to send me. Spears and Hoare discharged their mission quite successfully. Satisfactory assurances were received from Sazonoff, and Hoare sent me a telegram to this effect. This telegram was transmitted by Spears acting upon my direct request. As soon as I received it I sent it on to you for your information.

I now learn that the DMI, purporting to act on your instructions, censured Spears for having forwarded the telegram to me. I therefore write at once to tell you that the responsibility for the telegram being sent is solely my own, that Spears' action in forwarding it is covered by my authority. In these circumstances I cannot acquiesce in the censure which has been inflicted upon Spears by the DMI and I would ask you to instruct General Thwaites that this censure shd be withdrawn.

I am sure you wd want to treat me in this matter w the same consideration wh I always desire to show to you.

Winston S. Churchill to the Editor of 'The Times'

(*Printed in 'The Times': 13 June 1919*)

12 June 1919

Sir,

Observing reports in various newspapers that prayers are about to be offered up for rain in order that the present serious drought may be terminated, I venture to suggest that great care should be taken in framing the appeal.

On the last occasion when this extreme step was resorted to, the Duke of Rutland[1] took the leading part with so much well-meaning enthusiasm that the resulting downpour was not only sufficient for all immediate needs, but was considerably in excess of what was actually required, with the consequence that the agricultural community had no sooner been delivered from the drought than they were clamouring for a special interposition to relieve them from the deluge.

Profiting by this experience, we ought surely on this occasion to be extremely careful to state exactly what we want in precise terms, so as to obviate the possibility of any misunderstanding and to economize so far as possible the need for these special appeals. After so many days of drought, it certainly does not seem unreasonable to ask for a change in the weather, and faith in a favourable response may well be fortified by actuarial probabilities.

While therefore welcoming the suggestion that His Grace should once again come forward, I cannot help feeling that the Board of Agriculture should first of all be consulted. They should draw up a schedule of the exact amount of rainfall required in the interests of this year's harvest in different parts of the country. This schedule could be placarded in the various places of worship at the time the appeal is made. It would no doubt be necessary to read out the whole schedule during the service, so long as it was made clear at the time that this is what we have in our minds, and what we actually want at the present serious juncture.

I feel that this would be a much more businesslike manner of dealing with the emergency than mere vague appeals for rain. But after all, even this scheme, though greatly preferable to the haphazard methods previously employed, is in itself only a partial makeshift. What we really require to pray for is the general amelioration of the British climate. What is the use of having these piecemeal interpositions—now asking for sunshine, and now for rain? Would it not be far better to ascertain by scientific investigation, conducted under the auspices of a Royal Commission, what is the proportion of sunshine and rain best suited to the ripening of the British crops? It would no doubt be necessary that other interests besides agriculture should be represented, but there must be certain broad general reforms in the British weather upon which an overwhelming consensus of opinon could be found. The proper proportion of rain to sunshine during each period of the year; the

[1] Lord Henry John Brinsley Manners, 1852–1925. Principal Private Secretary to the Prime Minister (Lord Salisbury) 1885–8. Conservative MP, 1888–95. Succeeded his father as 8th Duke of Rutland, 1906. Knight of the Garter, 1918. His residences were Belvoir Castle, Grantham, Haddon Hall, Derby, and 5 Audley Square, London.

relegation of the rain largely to the hours of darkness; the apportionment of rain and sunshine as between different months, with proper references not only to crops but to holidays; all these could receive due consideration. A really scientific basis of climate reform would be achieved.

These reforms when duly embodied in an official volume, could be made the object of the sustained appeals of the nation over many years, and embodied in general prayers of a permanent and not of an exceptional character. We should not then be forced from time to time to have recourse to such appeals at particular periods, which since they are unrelated to any general plan, must run the risk of deranging the whole economy of nature, and involve the interruption and deflection of universal processes, causing reactions of the utmost complexity in many directions which it is impossible for us with our knowledge to foresee.

I urge you, Sir, to lend the weight of your powerful organ to the systematization of our appeals for the reform of the British climate.

Yours very sincerely
'Scorpio'

Winston S. Churchill to Lord Curzon

(*Curzon papers*)

12 June 1919
Private

My dear Curzon,

The news from the Siberian front is disappointing but not necessarily final. There is no question of any move on our part before the 1st of July, and it would be possible to stop the operations up to the very last moment, when the whole situation must be re-surveyed in the light of the existing facts. The military authorities are inclined to consider the seizure of the enemy's flotilla, which is to be done at the first stroke, as an essential step in a well conducted evacuation. In any case, however, there is no need to take a final decision now. . . .

I have, of course, had many talks with Derby on the subject of the Paris appointment. There can be no question in my opinion that General Spears is incomparably the best, most skilful, and most instructed agent that we could employ in Paris as Military Attaché in this critical and difficult time. This is also the view of the Prime Minister, who knows Spears and who, like myself, follows with great attention his admirable work. A very great storm of intrigue has raged to prevent this appointment, and it would no doubt suit the French to have some social simpleton appointed to this post instead of a man possessing the formidable knowledge and aptitudes of Spears.

It would be a great injustice to pass over this officer, who, apart from his special aptitudes, has been four times wounded, and I am very reluctant to do so. In fact as at present advised I do not feel able to make any other nomination to the Foreign Office.

There really is not work enough at the present time for a separate Military Attaché of high rank and a Military Mission at the French War Office. The social duties of the Chancery are being carried out at present by the Assistant Military Attachés, and I am deriving all my information from the same source as the General Staff, viz from General Spears' Mission. I am inclined to think therefore that in all the circumstances it will be better to leave the post of Military Attaché in Paris unfilled until the general winding up of war matters renders the continuance of a special mission unnecessary. The Air Attaché[1] is also available for the social duties, as his air work is very light indeed.

I hope therefore that you will agree with me in thinking that it is best to allow a little time to pass before raising the question, which must undoubtedly bring about a considerable conflict of opinion. In a few months the problem may have solved itself.

Yours sincerely
Winston SC

Winston S. Churchill to David Lloyd George

(*Churchill papers: 16/8*)

13 June 1919 War Office

It would be a great advantage if the Czecho troops who are now in Siberia guarding the railway could once again be induced to take part in the actual fighting. The need of strengthening the Northern part of Kolchak's front is serious, and I do not see at the present time what resource other than the Czechos is available.

The supreme desire of the Czechos in Siberia must naturally be to go home. Our original plan was that they should go home via Vologda and Archangel, and to facilitate this movement was one of the reasons which originally led to the expedition to North Russia. It is thought that an offer should now

[1] Norman Roderick Alexander David Leslie, 1889–1937. Succeeded his father as 8th Baronet, 1905. Entered Army 1908. Major, 1916. Royal Flying Corps, 1916–18. Air Attaché, Paris, 1919. Assistant Secretary (Air), Committee of Imperial Defence, 1924.

be made to the Czechos in Siberia to repatriate them all, or as many of them as care to go, via Archangel before the Winter ice closes in in November of this year, provided that they for their part will cut their way through as a definite part of the operations which are contemplated to secure the junction between Kolchak's right wing and the Archangel force. The Czechos who volunteer for this service would therefore be available to strengthen the Northern front and to aid the operation of effecting the junction during July, August, September and part of October. They would reach their homes before Christmas.

If you approve in principle of this policy, it seems desirable that it should be initiated from Paris by the Council of Five, that the leaders of the Czecho-Slovak Republic should be negotiated with, and that if they agree should transmit the offer to the Siberian Czechos. In the meanwhile, during these negotiations, Kolchak will be simultaneously consulted.

It would also be necessary that the section of the Siberian Railway now guarded by such of the Czechos as volunteer or are persuaded to undertake this service should be taken over by the Japanese or the Americans.

In view of the acceptance by Kolchak of the allied conditions and the notes issued yesterday by the Council of Five endorsing his acceptance, the moment seems opportune for this. The Chief of the Imperial General Staff agrees with me in thinking this plan useful, hopeful and necessary. He will himself bring it before you, and I would ask you to consider whether you will not raise it at the earliest convenient opportunity at the Council of Five. It would, in my opinion, form a definite part of our policy to evacuate non-Russian troops from Russia while at the same time raising the strength of the anti-Bolshevik Russian forces to a point where they become self-supporting.

(2) I send you attached a report by General Janin[1] on the defeat of Kolchak's Southern Army. This is the first clear and comprehensive military account which has reached us, and I am bound to say that it compares very favourably with the sloppy, piecemeal and amateurish productions which we are receiving from Knox. The latter is a good energetic man, but appears to me to be lacking both in military knowledge and mental force. I am therefore considering the selection of a more adequate officer.

[1] Pierre Thiébaut Charles Maurice Janin, 1862–1946. Born in Paris. Entered the French Army, 1882. Lieutenant-Colonel, 1907. Liaison officer to the Russian Staff College, 1910. Général de Brigade, 1915. On active service in North-East France, 1915–16. Head of the French Military Mission to Russia, 1916. Général de Division, 1916. Head of the Franco-Czechoslovak Mission in Siberia, 1918. Commander of the Czech Army in Siberia, 1918–19. Commander in Chief of all the Allied forces in Siberia, August 1918–19. Returned to Paris, May 1920. Commanded the French 8th Army Corps, 1921–4.

Winston S. Churchill to Sir Henry Wilson

(*Churchill papers: 16/16*)

13 June 1919 War Office
Very Secret

On other papers I have commented on the poor quality of the reports and messages we receive from General Knox. The telegram from General Janin dated the 30th of May throws into painful contrast the military quality of the information with which Knox has supplied us. Here is a terse and comprehensive staff paper drafted in admirable military form and presenting a clear impression of the situation as a whole. Surely there are officers in our service capable of similar work. We should have at this most important centre an officer of the highest attainments in whose judgment we have the utmost confidence, and not merely a good energetic man who is clearly out of his depth.

I have been wondering whether we could spare Macdonogh for this extremely important service. Maxse[1] is another man who would be adequate. There is no doubt that we require a figure of a certain size at this centre. Already Gough is making a considerable difference in the theatre where he is working clamping things together and keeping us well-informed. The paramount importance of these Russian matters requires us to employ officers of proved capacity possessing unimpeachable military credentials.

Pray let me know if you have any alternative suggestions to make and generally what you think.[2]

Sir Samuel Hoare to Winston S. Churchill: telegram

(*Churchill papers: 16/8*)

13 June 1919 Prague
Personal

A. Situation is most critical.

B. I am convinced if Bela Kun not crushed Vienna will go Bolshevist,

[1] Frederick Ivor Maxse, 1862–1958. Brother of Leo Maxse (editor of the *National Review*) and of Violet Maxse (wife of Lord Milner). Entered Army, 1882. Brigade-Major at the battle of Omdurman, 1898. Transport Officer, South Africa, 1899–1902 and Commander of the Pretoria Police after the city's capture. Major-General, commanding the 1st Guards Brigade on the western front, 1914. Commanded the 18th Division at the Battle of the Somme, 1915. Lieutenant-General commanding the XVIII Corps at Passchendaele, 1917. Knighted, 1917. Inspector-General of Training in France, 1918. General Officer Commanding Northern Command (United Kingdom), 1919–23. General, 1923. Retired, 1926, and devoted himself, successfully, to commercial fruit growing.

[2] Neither Macdonogh nor Maxse were sent to Russia, and General Knox remained the senior British officer in Siberia until the collapse of the anti-Bolshevik armies.

Silesian coal fields lost and Junction be eventually effected between the Magyar and Russian Bolshevist.

C. Prestige of Entene already much shaken will be irrevocably destroyed in any case State go to pieces.

D. On no account should any negotiations be entered into with Kun.

General Gough to Winston S. Churchill

(*Churchill papers: 16/8*)

14 June 1919 Helsingfors

My dear Winston,

I find a post is going to England in a few minutes, so I will take advantage of it to write you a line to thank you very much for your nice wire about my Grand Cross. I am glad of it for the sake of my men in the 5th Army, as it will help to restore their reputation to a position to which their great fight entitles them. I am sure both the Army & myself owe this act of recognition principally to your good offices, so please accept my best thanks for the same & remember that I will be grateful!

I have not time to write you fully on all the many questions that crop up out here, most conflicting & complex as they are, but our official wires etc, keep you informed I hope.

Tallents,[1] who has just arrived as FO representative, is not much of a man. He lacks force, & experience & is very much in the hands of French, or Germans, whichever are nearest him at the moment. He means well however.

In Finland, Mannerheim is dying to attack Petrograd & is being backed by Yudenitch, so perhaps Russian objections may be discounted. But on the other hand, Mannerheim's own position in Finland is not too firm & he is certainly risking it by any such action. The Whites in power are not progressive & hold down the Specialists etc, pretty tight, and they only represent about 50% of the country. They have no dealings with the opposition parties

[1] Stephen George Tallents, 1884–1958. Entered the Board of Trade, 1909. Served with the Irish Guards, 1914–15 (wounded). Worked in the Ministry of Munitions, 1915–16. Member of the Food Council, 1918. Chief British Delegate for the Relief and Supply of Poland, 1919. British Commissioner for the Baltic Provinces, 1919–20. Private Secretary to the Lord Lieutenant of Ireland (Viscount Fitz-Alan), 1921–2. Imperial Secretary, Northern Ireland, 1922–6. Secretary, Empire Marketing Board, 1926–33. Knighted, 1932. Public Relations Officer, GPO, 1933–5. Controller of Public Relations, BBC, 1935–40. Principal Assistant Secretary, Ministry of Town and Country Planning, 1943–6.

& it is considered a dreadful thing for any of us to even meet them, so we have to tread warily. . . .

On the South side, the principle & great danger is the Germans. I think our only chance there now is to take up a very firm resolute attitude towards them & insist on their evacuating the country as soon as possible. I have already taken on myself, based on the latest instructions wired out by you, to order the Germans to commence by withdrawing half their forces at once. As they have I believe some 70,000 this will still leave 35,000, which should be ample to deal with Bolsheviks, now somewhat on the down grade in these parts. It would be a great help if you would support this demand by some energetic orders issued via Spa. The Germans here—(S of Gulf) are intriguing with everyone, against everyone! With Russians, with local people etc. I think we ought to firmly insist on maintenance of local Governments, & probably anyhow for the present, of total exclusion from these Governments of the German Baltic Barons. They are in reality nothing but German Agents. It is in handling them that I think Tallents has shown most weakness & lack of political sense.

No more now. I hope all goes well with you.

Yrs ever
H. Gough

Winston S. Churchill to General Spears

(*Churchill papers: 16/37*)

15 June 1919 War Office

Your letter of the 10th June.

(1) Take no further action about Kerensky.

(2) Seek an opportunity of talking to Philip Kerr and telling him of the steps I have taken through you to dispel the unfavourable impressions which the Paris Russians had formed of his influence. I do not believe he had any long conversation with Kerensky. If it is proved that he did not see Kerensky on the subject, you should disabuse Sazonoff's mind accordingly.

(3) I consider Kolchak's answer very good and well-conceived, and in view of the fact that the allies have accepted it as satisfactory, there is nothing more to be said.

(4) I will ask CIGS what he thinks about our transmitting Sazonoff's despatches instead of the French.

(5) We are arranging for a W/T installation to connect Denikin and Kolchak, and much progress has been made.

(6) I should like you to get in touch with the Savinkoff[1] group and let me know more about them.

Sir Henry Wilson to Winston S. Churchill

(*Churchill papers: 16/8*)

16 June 1919 Paris
Secret & Personal

Dear S of S

I have now had two talks with the Prime Minister about your proposal to get the Czechos, who are now in Siberia, to fight their way out to Viatka and Archangel, and I think he will do all he can to further this scheme. I will, however, jog his memory day by day and will lose no opportunity of pressing your proposal.

This morning at and after breakfast the Prime Minister and Lindley, who as you know is back from Archangel, and myself had a long talk about Northern Russia. The Prime Minister is rather frightened and very much averse from getting in any way much mixed up by a too forward advance from Archangel, and the paragraph which particularly caught his eye was Ironside's proposal (Telegram E1426 dated June 6th. Ironmay) under certain eventualities to go 30 miles south of Kotlas. Lindley gave Ironside the highest character as a man of sober sense and good judgment and this had considerable weight with the Prime Minister, but he asked me to send a wire to Ironside making two points quite clear; first, that under no circumstances whatever was he to get himself so embroiled that it would be necessary to send an expedition to pull him out, because no expedition would be sent; and secondly, under no circumstances whatever was he to run any chance of not being able to withdraw the whole of his force from Archangel before the ice set in. I pointed out to him that in Ironside's telegram both these questions had already been answered, and I made him read this telegram again, but

[1] Boris Viktorovitch Savinkoff, 1877–1925. Russian nihilist. Exiled to Siberia as a student, for revolutionary activity. Escaped to Switzerland. Returned to Russia, 1905; and took part in the assassination of Archduke Serge. Condemned to death. Escaped to Switzerland for a second time. He described his revolutionary work in a novel, *The Pale Horse*, published in 1909. Political commissar for the Provisional Government, charged with restoring discipline on the eastern front, July–August 1917. Deputy Minister of War in the Provisional Government, August 1917. An opponent of Bolshevism, he joined General Alexeiev's forces on the Don, November 1917. Accredited Agent in Paris, first of Alexeiev, then of Kolchak and finally of Denikin, 1918–20. Organized an anti-Bolshevik army in Poland, 1920. Returned to the Soviet Union voluntarily, 1924. Tried, condemned to death, and given a commuted sentence of ten years in prison, 1924. Died in prison, possibly by suicide, 1925.

he still expressed so strong a desire for me to send a telegram to Ironside that of course I at once agreed I would do so. I enclose you a copy of what I propose to send and I am sending it off to the DMO to despatch from the War Office after you and he have seen it. . . .

This morning after discussing Archangel the Prime Minister and I had a long talk about the Italian occupation of the Caucasus and our attitude generally speaking towards the Italians. I told him that I personally was much in favour of keeping friendly with the Italians and of helping them in small ways to any of their legitimate or possibly even illegitimate aspirations. His own mind was travelling in the same order of ideas and he sent for Sonnino to have a quiet talk with him after I had left. . . .

War Cabinet:[1] *minutes*

(*Curzon papers*)

18 June 1919 10 Downing Street

(1) LORD CURZON explained that, at a Meeting of the War Cabinet held on June 11 (War Cabinet 578 A), the Secretary of State for War had put forward proposals for an advance by our North Russian detachments which had already been considered and approved by the Prime Minister, and after a discussion the War Cabinet had concurred in these proposals. Almost immediately afterwards, telegrams had been received recording the serious setback which had been suffered by Admiral Kolchak, and subsequent telegrams received from that area since then were far from reassuring. He was so much disturbed at the possibility of our undertaking a venture which would prove unsuccessful that he had written to the Secretary of State for War enquiring whether these reverses to Admiral Kolchak's army in any way affected the plans that had been made. Mr Churchill had replied that he recognised the gravity of the situation in which we were now placed, and he had promised that, before orders were given for an advance by General Ironside's troops, the Cabinet would have an opportunity to review their former decision in the light of subsequent events. He had spoken to the

[1] Present at this meeting were Bonar Law (in the Chair), Lord Curzon and Austen Chamberlain (all members of the War Cabinet), together with Lord Milner, Churchill, Sir Auckland Geddes, Walter Long, H A L Fisher, Major-General Radcliffe and Rear-Admiral J A Fergusson (Deputy Chief of the Naval Staff). Later that day Thomas Jones circulated a typescript of the Minutes with the covering note: 'It is requested that this copy may be returned as soon as possible. Owing to the secret nature of these Minutes it is not proposed to print them at present.' (*Curzon Papers*). The minutes were never printed, but Curzon kept his copy among his private papers.

Chancellor of the Exchequer and the Secretary of State for the Colonies, and they had both agreed that it was desirable for the Cabinet to re-consider this question. He felt that, before the actual order for advance was given, the Cabinet should go into the matter carefully once more.

THE SECRETARY OF STATE FOR WAR read out a telegram which had been despatched to General Ironside by the Chief of the Imperial General Staff, emphasising the Prime Minister's wishes that under no circumstances were the British troops to become so embroiled in the South as to necessitate a relief column being sent out from England, as no such troops could or would be sent; and, secondly, the absolute necessity of ensuring that the operations were so timed as to allow for the British forces being embarked and safely got away from Archangel before the ice set in. Mr Churchill pointed out that the position at Archangel was not wholly dependent on the operations of General Gaida. The proposed advance of the Archangel forces was a part of the plan for withdrawing our troops from that district. The military experts believed that the real trouble on the Kolchak front was now coming to an end, as the distances the enemy had moved from their base would begin to operate against them. He must confess, however, that the position was not quite a happy one. On the other hand, the success of General Denikin in the South was remarkable. He had gained considerably more ground than Admiral Kolchak had lost, and was being joined by the forces of a large insurrectionary movement headed by the General of the 8th Bolshevist Army. He had taken 20,000 prisoners, a number of guns, and considerable booty. The military authorities thought that he could not progress much further without attracting to his front Bolshevist troops which were now operating against Admiral Kolchak; and, if this happened, the situation as regards the latter would be considerably relieved. By the date of our operations it was possible that the situation would have improved. In any case, he had no doubt, that the military experts would be able to make a case for our advance, even though the plan of joining hands with Admiral Kolchak was no longer feasible. He was prepared to promise the War Cabinet that, before our troops moved, they would have an opportunity of reviewing the situation and of revising their former decision. The Chief of the Imperial General Staff would be coming over from France on the following Thursday, and would be able to give them his views on the matter.

MR BONAR LAW stated that when the Chief of the Imperial General Staff had gone into this question with the Prime Minister and himself in Paris, the only doubt in his own mind was as to whether there was any great advantage in the plan if the possibility of joining up with Admiral Kolchak were to be ruled out. General Wilson had told him at that time that he was pressing Admiral Kolchak, through General Knox, to give up his plans for an advance on Moscow, and to concentrate all his energies on effecting a junction with the Archangel troops.

LORD CURZON said it was true that General Denikin had won considerable victories in South Russia. On the other hand, the reverses suffered by Admiral Kolchak were very severe. A telegram received on the previous day stated that Admiral Kolchak had been defeated by forces which were numerically inferior to his own, and inferior by at least 10,000 men. He (Lord Curzon) was in favour of a forward policy, but he was not prepared to give his assent to a population that might launch our men on an expedition into Central Russia which was doomed to failure. He was afraid that Admiral Kolchak would still be 100 or 200 miles removed from us, and our troops might be driven to evacuate the territory we had covered, with the additional stigma of failure. He did not wish our plans to be so far advanced that our Commander-in-Chief in North Russia could say that his preparations for an advance were all ready, that he was not dependent on Admiral Kolchak, and that he was going forward on his own account. Lord Curzon added that he had no desire to depart from the policy which had been decided upon by the War Cabinet, but he feared that this policy had much less chance of reaching a successful issue than it had a fortnight previously.

THE DIRECTOR OF MILITARY OPERATIONS said it had always been the view of the Chief of the Imperial General Staff that, in order to make a safe evacuation of Archangel, it was first necessary for us to strike an effective blow on that front, and that was the main object of the attack proposed by General Ironside. It would be so much the better if, as a result of our attack, we formed a junction with Admiral Kolchak. In any case whether the latter was possible or not, our attack could only have the effect of improving the situation and facilitating our withdrawal, and we should be able to leave the North Russian Government in a position which would enable it effectively to protect its territory. There appeared to be every reason, both military and political, for carrying out the attack.

MR BONAR LAW repeated his statement that, when the Chief of the Imperial General Staff had spoken to the Prime Minister and himself on the matter, the impression left on their minds was that the operation should not be undertaken unless there was a possibility of joining up with Admiral Kolchak.

THE SECRETARY OF STATE FOR WAR suggested that he should allow all preparations for the operation to go forward, but that, before orders were given for an actual advance to be made, the War Cabinet should review the situation in the light of the position at that time.

THE CHANCELLOR OF THE EXCHEQUER enquired whether that would be sufficient. The situation caused him grave concern. General

Ironside had been informed that his proposed operations were approved by the War Cabinet, and he was making all preparations for going on with them. He (Mr Chamberlain) thought that some warning should be given to General Ironside that the defeat of Admiral Kolchak had altered the situation and might mean a reconsideration of the plan of operations. Would it not be preferable to do this now, rather than leave General Ironside without any warning that the Government might go back on their decision, and suddenly at the eleventh hour veto his plans? If it was absolutely necessary for a safe withdrawal that our forces should first advance, he would offer no objection; but when it became a question of prestige, that was a political consideration, and in his opinion our prestige would gain in no degree by advancing into Central Russia and then immediately withdrawing our troops.

THE DIRECTOR OF MILITARY OPERATIONS pointed out that the advance would not be undertaken by British troops alone. General Ironside had 23,000 Russians who would co-operate with us, who would help in the advance and do their share of the fighting, and who would be left in the occupied territory when we retired.

THE SECRETARY OF STATE FOR WAR said he was prepared to give the War Cabinet a guarantee that the operations would be stopped in a fortnight's time before a man had been moved, if the War Cabinet desired it, after further consideration of the situation.

THE DIRECTOR OF MILITARY OPERATIONS, replying to Mr Bonar Law as to the advisability of obtaining General Ironside's views, explained that the War Office had already done so, and General Ironside had expressed the opinion that the capture of Kotlas would be invaluable from the point of view of future operations, particularly having regard to our coming evacuation.

LORD CURZON referred to a telegram from Mr Hodgson, at Omsk, describing the situation on Admiral Kolchak's front, which, he said, gave a blacker view of the situation than even the military telegrams. In this telegram (No 534, of June 11) it was stated that the situation on that front was still bad, the Western Army still largely in a demoralised state, and that failure on the front had caused the latent discontent against General Headquarters at Omsk to break out. Certain changes in the Commands had been made, and, while they should be beneficial it would be some time before the army, which had been seriously shaken by recent events, would be able to renew the offensive. Lord Curzon added that the telegram also stated that Ufa was being bombarded by the Bolsheviks, and he understood that the latter had since captured the town.

THE SECRETARY OF STATE FOR WAR said that he had read a telegram on the previous day from General Janin, in which it was pointed out that a great many of the reserves of the Northern Siberian Army had been thrown in to defend the Western front of that Army, and, consequently, these reserves had been dissipated. On the other hand, the distances between the Northern and the Western fronts were considerable. In the region in which operations were now taking place, the Bolshevist thrust had turned up towards the Perm area, which was at least 200 miles from Admiral Kolchak's right wing. Consequently he did not at all exclude the possibility of Admiral Kolchak being able to co-operate with our troops at Archangel, but, of course, the Cabinet must know what the situation was before they gave final orders for an advance. If it became certain that Admiral Kolchak would be unable to give any help, an entirely new situation would be created, which the War Cabinet would have to review; and it would then be for the military authorities to justify that advance from the point of view of our successful evacuation of the Archangel district.

LORD CURZON suggested that General Ironside should be informed that the situation would have to be reviewed in the light of the latest information that the War Cabinet had concerning Admiral Kolchak.

MR BONAR LAW enquired whether it would upset General Ironside's plans if he were informed that the War Cabinet had approved of his venture in the hope that he would be able to effect a junction with Admiral Kolchak, and, since the latter possibility seemed now to be so far removed, the whole position would have to be reviewed by the War Cabinet once more.

THE DIRECTOR OF MILITARY OPERATIONS said he did not think it would upset General Ironside's plans, as he was already authorised to make all preparations for the advance. It would, however, be rather unsettling to him not to know whether the advance would actually be made.

The War Cabinet decided—

> To discuss this matter again on June 27, in the light of the situation on the various fronts on that date, and to ask the Chief of the Imperial General Staff to be present on that occasion. In the meantime, while General Ironside should go forward with his plans for the operations as previously agreed upon by the War Cabinet, he should not undertake a definite advance until the War Cabinet had finally decided upon the course of action.

War Office to General Ironside

(Churchill papers: 'Campaign in North Russia')

18 June 1919 London

Your proposed operations have been approved and that approval stands. Cabinet approval was, however, obtained as part of an operation to join hands with Kolchak.

The defeats which Kolchak's armies sustained in the centre and south may preclude the effective junction which we had in view. In these circumstances, with the Secretary of State's concurrence, the Cabinet have decided to review on 27th June the entire situation in the light of all information available then. After hearing the military advice they will then decide—

(*a.*) Whether there is sufficient prospect of obtaining a real junction with Kolchak to justify the operation as originally presented to them, or

(*b.*) Whether your operation should proceed independently as an indispensable part of the process of evacuation in spite of the fact that no effective junction with Kolchak can be hoped for.

Therefore, you should not begin your movement without informing us beforehand and receiving our confirmatory wire. Meanwhile, on the assumption that sanction will be given you should continue preparations and you are invited to telegraph your views on (*a*) and (*b*) so that on 27th June they may be laid before the Cabinet.

Winston S. Churchill to Lord Curzon

(Foreign Office papers: 371/3941)

ANGLO-SOVIET NEGOTIATIONS ON BRITISH PRISONERS OF WAR

19 June 1919

I am asked to express an opinion on these papers.

I greatly regret that it shd be necessary to correspond & negotiate in these terms with the Bolshevik Government, especially by wireless en clair. It shows them to the public as extorting all the usages of civilised diplomacy from the British Government.

I shd have thought the proper course was to draw up lists of prominent members of the Bolshevik Government and notify them that they are held personally responsible for the treatment of our prisoners & will be persued without hope of pardon wherever they may be as long as they live if they do not insure their proper treatment.[1]

General Ironside to Winston S. Churchill: telegram

(*War Office papers: 32/5693*)

19 June 1919 Archangel

Preparations for advance on KOTLAS are nearing completion. Mine sweeping commences tomorrow under air and flotilla bombardment. *Enemy behaviour under bombardment should show their value and give indications of what his front line battalions intend to do.* As regards (a) you can judge better of Kolchak's operations than I can but in any case two points should be borne in mind.

1. Russians are easily affected by success and if there were any wavering our *arrival at KOTLAS might just give that extra moral required.*

2. That in any case I should be able to pull in Kolchak's right wing from the direction of Yarensk on the Witchegda and make a large reinforcement to the Russian force detailed from our forces to move just south of KOTLAS by arming the badly armed and unarmed. As regards (B) I would put forward following points. *In order to be certain of an orderly evacuation it should be carried out as a peace operation. To ensure this I must disengage myself on all my fronts and render an offensive by the Bolsheviks during a reasonable period an impossibility.* I must therefore take an offensive on the important points of my front and these offensives must be carried out against definite objective the gaining of which will:

(1) disengage my forces and enable me to embark in peace.

(2) Place the Russians in a position to maintain themselves even though they do not join up with Kolchak.

Roughly these objectives are three in number and I wire them with a short resumé of reasons.

(1) Capture of Plesetskaya on the Vologda railway so as to destroy enemy's base and capture the junction of roads leading from railway line towards Onega on the West and Tarasevo and Shenkursk on the east and so prevent an enemy winter campaign.

(2) Clearing of the Pinega area so that whole of northern region shall be clear of Bolsheviks.

(3) Advance on Kotlas for the object of destroying all workshops depots

[1] On 24 June Lord Curzon replied: 'The main thing is to get our people out and there is no use our standing on our dignity if we are to succeed.' (*Foreign Office papers; 371/3941*)

wharves capturing all enemy boats and rendering the place useless as a base during this summer or winter. Also to bring in the right wing of Siberians and arm them and to clean up the Witchegda area. These 3 objectives gained, the evacuation before November 10th should be effected as a peace operation leaving behind the mission of strength to be decided later. I am employing troops so that brunt of work falls upon Russians who will be fighting practically unsided in objectives 1 and 2 and in objectives 3 I am employing the Russians and SB Legion to move to the south of Kotlas if that is necessary and the Volunteer Brigade under Jackson[1] to clean up Witchegda area, while the regular brigade under Grogan[2] will return as occasion offers at base to take the place of conscripts being demobilised by September 1st and perhaps to supply small detachments for Pinega.

In no case do I think that any advance less than to Kotlas will have any effect of disengaging our forces and it does offer possible chance of bringing on Kolchak. *I have no intention of allowing British forces to get into such a position that they would require relief or that they could not withdraw.* I do not think that it would be advisable to continue an advance against Kotlas if the enemy really puts up a stubborn resistance.

Winston S. Churchill to Bonar Law, Lord Curzon and Austen Chamberlain

(*War Office papers: 32/5693*)

20 June 1919 War Office

You shd glance at this.[3] The military view has always favoured this operation even if isolated. There is no change of view.

[1] Lionel Warren de Vere Sadleir-Jackson, 1876–1932. Entered Army, 1898. On active service in South Africa, 1900. Major, 1915. Brigadier-General commanding the 54th Infantry Brigade in France, October 1917–November 1918. Brigadier-General commanding the Volunteer Brigade, Archangel, 1919; during the Kotlas operation his Brigade was in action on the Dwina river. Inspector-General of Levies, Iraq, 1921–3. Co-author of *Hints on Polo Co-ordination*.

[2] George William St George Grogan, 1875–1962. Entered Army, 1896. Employed with the Egyptian Army, 1902–7. Lieutenant-Colonel, 1915. Commanded the 23rd Infantry Brigade on the western front; awarded the Victoria Cross, 1918. Brigadier-General commanding the 1st Brigade, Russian Relief Force, 1919; his brigade was in action on the Pinega river, August 1919. Gentleman-at-Arms, HM Bodyguard, 1933–45. Colonel, Worcestershire Regiment, 1938–45.

[3] General Ironside's telegram of June 19, printed above. Churchill had underlined the passages printed here in italics.

Austen Chamberlain to Winston S. Churchill, Lord Curzon, and Bonar Law

(War Office papers: 32/5693)

20 June 1919 Treasury

I quite agree that the marked passages fairly bear the interpretation placed upon them. But it will be observed that in para 13 (i) two objects are enjoined in one sentence. General Ironside is to strike as effective a blow as possible at the hostile forces (1) to facilitate withdrawal of the British forces thereafter.

As to this, & in so far as the blow is necessary for this, no question arises.

(2) 'under such conditions as will enable the NR Army to keep the field & maintain the stability of the Archangel Gov!'

This is a quite distinct object, desirable in itself, but as I conceive incapable of realisation unless (a) the Archangel Gov! has real inherent strength (b) the Russian forces at its disposal when set on their legs can stand alone, & (c) Kolchak can effect a link up with them & exert such pressure that they cannot be effectively threatened.

I am doubtful whether any of these conditions (a) (b) or (c) do exist in fact; & I am afraid that, under colour of facilitating withdrawal, Gen Ironside should be induced or encouraged to undertake operations, not needed for withdrawal but intended to enable the Russian Army to keep the field, & the Archangel Gov! to be maintained, only to find in the end that our sacrifices have been in vain, that the Russian Army left alone has not fought & that the Archangel Gov! has been overthrown or fallen on its own inherent weakness.

Winston S. Churchill to General Harington

(War Office papers: 32/5693)

21 June 1919 War Office

I understand that the General Staff consider that the advance will not involve serious fighting by the British troops; & that the Russian troops will be strong enough to hold Kotlas after it has been taken while the British withdraw: & that the destruction of the Kotlas base, flotilla etc will protect Archangel from any speedy attack.

Sir Henry Wilson: diary

(*Wilson papers*)

21 June 1919 Paris

Winston flew over & I saw him just before dinner. He agrees with me. The news of Kolchak is bad; he is now retiring from Glazov in front of Viatka. This looks as though Ironside would not join hands.

General Spears to Winston S. Churchill

(*Churchill papers: 16/37*)

21 June 1919 Paris
Personal & Secret

Dear Secretary of State,

I saw Philip Kerr this morning. He told me that he has not seen Kerensky since he (Kerensky) came to ENGLAND for the first time. I am going to so inform all the Russians. I spoke to him on the line mentioned in paragraph 2 of your Memorandum of the 15th.

Kerr spoke to me at some length about the Russians here, and he told me the Prime Minister was determined not in any way to be mixed up with what could be described as the 'emigré' element, which includes Sazonoff. I spoke to him also about Savinkoff and he agreed with me that the latter did not come under the heading of 'emigré'.

Yours sincerely,
E. L. Spears

Sir Henry Wilson: diary

(*Wilson papers*)

22 June 1919 Paris

I sat on Winston's bed for an hour at 8.30 & discussed matters.

He again offered me a Peerage & a Grant or a Field Marshal. I told him I had already been amply rewarded but he said both PM & he were determined I should be given one or other. So of course I accepted the Field Marshal.

7 pm. I found the Boch answer had just come in & the Frocks were sitting. LG wanted me to dine so I came back & changed, & Winston & I went

over. Also Montagu & Hankey & Lady Hankey to dinner & AJB came in later.

As Winston & I arrived the Frocks meeting was breaking up & LG came out & handed us the Frocks answer to the Boch reply which we had not seen. The Frocks replied that they had already given full thought & would change nothing. Then we had dinner & at 9 pm the other 3 Frocks collected up in LG's room and confirmed their before dinner opinion & sent their wire.

At dinner I asked LG if my cousin [President Wilson] would stand fast & agree to advance at 7.1 pm Monday even if the Boches ask for a further extension because I don't believe he will, however LG swore he would. This is all like Aug: 1914. So exciting.

Winston S. Churchill to Austen Chamberlain

(*Churchill papers: 16/8*)

22 June 1919 Paris

In all the clearing up that remains to be done after the war, the armoured car will play a vital part. Instead of large forces of infantry, cavalry and heavy artillery maintained as garrisons, we require in many places smaller forces with machine guns in armoured cars which are very mobile and which can move into streets and villages and push out across the deserts in suitable country and support civil and police administration. There is no other way of holding and administering the very large regions we have in our charge except by an undue expenditure of troops organised on the old lines. Everyone is crying out for armoured cars—India, Egypt, Mesopotamia, Denikin, Ireland, the Army of the Rhine—and I am sure that in the next few years great reliances will be placed upon this means of maintaining order which can so often operate without loss of life.

On the other hand the Treasury is resisting even the armouring of 100 lorries which are most urgently required, and their opposition has already resulted in a delay of some weeks.

The Master General of Ordnance[1] tells me that you wish to see me on the subject. I write this letter to explain the situation to you and to point out how we are being hampered by the delay. If reductions in troops are to be effected in India, Egypt, etc, it can only be by armoured cars and aeroplanes in definite combination.

If after reading this letter you think it is of any use our discussing the

[1] Lieutenant-General Sir William Furse (see page 17, note 2).

matter further, I shall be delighted to do so; but if not you will perhaps wish that a Cabinet decision should be obtained.

Winston S. Churchill to David Lloyd George

(*Churchill papers: 16/8*)

23 June 1919 War Office

Following on our conversation, I send you the final list of high military honours which I would recommend.

For SIR DOUGLAS HAIG:	An Earldom & £100,000.
For General PLUMER,[1] ,, ALLENBY, ,, BYNG, ,, RAWLINSON	Baronies with £30,000.
For General PLUMER, ,, ALLENBY, ,, SIR H. WILSON	Promotion to Field Marshal.

I consider that the great responsibilities borne by Sir Henry Wilson as Chief of the Imperial General Staff, not only as the supreme military adviser of the Government but as the executive officer responsible for the distribution of forces between the various theatres, constitute an ample case for a Field-Marshal's baton, although he has not held a great command in the field. Sir William Nicholson,[2] who had never commanded in war, was made a Field-Marshal, and there is no comparison between the claims. During the present war the responsibilities of the Chief of the Imperial General Staff have been superior and the conditions very similar to those of a Commander-in-Chief in the field: they are certainly far superior to those of Army Commanders. I therefore have no hesitation in making the recommendation. I have already obtained from the Treasury the necessary sanction to enable the extra batons to be bestowed.

[1] Herbert Charles Onslow Plumer, 1857–1932. Entered the Army, 1876. On active service in the Sudan, 1884 and in South Africa, 1899–1902. Brigadier-General, 1902. Major-General, 1903. Knighted, 1906. Lieutenant-General, 1908. Commanded the II Corps in France, 1914–15; the Second Army, 1915–17. Commanded the Franco-British Forces in Italy, 1917–18. Resumed Command of the Second Army, March 1918. Commanded the British Army of Occupation in Germany, 1918–19. Created Baron, appointed Field-Marshal, and granted £30,000 by Parliament, 1919. Governor of Malta, 1919–24. High Commissioner to Palestine, 1925–8. Created Viscount, 1929.

[2] William Gustavus Nicholson, 1845–1918. Served in the Afghan War, 1878, in Egypt, 1882, Burmah, 1886 and the Tirah (as Chief of Staff), 1897. Director of Transport, South Africa, 1900. Major-General, 1900. Chief of the General Staff, 1908–12. Created Field-Marshal and Baron, 1912.

I further propose that Generals HORNE,[1] MILNE and BIRDWOOD should be created Baronets and receive grants of £10,000.

I consider that it is necessary that one high honour should be bestowed upon the Air Service, and I know of no one whose services, character and presentation can compare with TRENCHARD. I therefore propose that he should be created a Baronet and should receive a grant of £10,000.

You will remember that when a Viscounty was conferred upon Sir John French, no grant accompanied it owing to the war being still in progress. I am strongly of opinion that a grant of £50,000 should be made to this officer, who bore the brunt in the immortal battles of the beginning of the war and for the first 16 months of its duration.

There remains the case of SIR WILLIAM ROBERTSON, who was Chief of the Imperial General Staff for more than two years. His position in the Army is a very solid one and I am of opinion that if he is wholly excluded from the list of high rewards he will be thought to have been 'victimised', and that the resulting controversy will be detrimental to our general interests, both military and political. The fact that Sir Henry Wilson will be promoted Field-Marshal over his head will emphasise the slight. I therefore recommend that Sir William Robertson should be given a Baronetcy and a grant of £10,000. This is putting him in the lowest category of these high honours, but at the same time it is not entirely excluding him from them. No one needs the £10,000 so much as he does, and he has risen from the ranks—this is also a point to be borne in mind in estimating his position in the Army.

You will observe that General GOUGH is wholly excluded from this list of high honours, although he was for a very long period in command of an Army and although military opinion acquits him of blame for the disaster to the 5th Army. But I entirely agree with you that Gough's fighting and personal qualities are not accompanied by the mental equipment necessary for the discharge of a command so extensive as that of an Army, and that he never ought to have been appointed to any command above a Corps. I am therefore of opinion that the GCMG which he has already received must be considered acquittance in full.

It is not my duty to make recommendations about HANKEY, but I am most strongly of opinion that his brilliant services deserve exceptional

[1] Henry Sinclair Horne, 1861–1929. Lieutenant, Royal Artillery, 1880. Served in the South African War, 1899–1902. Brigadier-General, 1912. Brigadier-General, Royal Artillery, 1st Army Corps, France, August 1914. Major-General, October 1914. Commanded the 2nd Division, 1st Corps, at Loos, September 1915. Sent to Egypt to devise a scheme of defence for the Suez Canal, December 1915. Lieutenant-General, January 1916. Commanded the 1st Army in France, 1917–18. Knighted, 1918. Created Baron, 1919. General Officer Commanding, Eastern Command, England, 1919–23. His *Diaries of the South African War* were privately printed in 1900. He refused several offers of Colonial Governorships after 1919.

recognition; and since you have talked the matter over with me I would suggest to you that he should be made a Privy Councillor and receive a grant of £20,000, but that this should be announced in a separate part of the list to the military honours.[1]

You will see that I have somewhat reduced the scale of the high rewards, and by introducing Baronetcies with £10,000 grants in lieu of Peerages in certain cases have reduced the expense to the public. The total cost of military honours (excluding Hankey but including Robertson) will be £320,000.

I have given long and careful consideration to these proposals and have discussed them at various times with several people on whose judgment I rely. . . .

I hope you will let me know your views on these proposals as soon as possible in order that I may make the formal submissions. It would be very appropriate if these announcements were made as part of the Peace Celebrations.

Sir Henry Wilson to Winston S. Churchill

(*War Office papers: 32/5693*)

26 June 1919

Since the Chancellor of the Exchequer's Minute was written we have received General Ironside's cable dated 19th June, which, I think, puts the case very clearly, and in conjunction with his previous wire of 6th June, answers all objections.

Although from every point of view, as I have previously pointed out, the junction of the Archangel forces with Kolchak's right wing is desirable, the necessity for General Ironside's operation in no way depends on this junction being effected; in fact the contrary is the case. For if the Bolshevik forces are relieved from all anxiety on Kolchak's front, they will be free to mass against Ironside and will thus be enabled to harass his withdrawal, and render the latter not only a difficult but a hazardous operation.

Quite apart from any question of stabilising the Archangel Government or even the maintenance of British and Allied prestige, it is essential in order to ensure that the withdrawal of British troops is carried out in safety that this withdrawal should be preceded by offensive operations. General Ironside states very clearly what the object and scope of these operations should be,

[1] Hankey was not made a Privy Councillor until 1939, but he did receive a cash grant, of £25,000. Churchill's other suggestions were accepted.

viz, to disengage his front and render an offensive by the Bolsheviks during a reasonable period an impossibility, in order to ensure that the evacuation of British troops can be carried out practically under peace conditions. The capture of Kotlas will, it is confidently anticipated, realise this condition by rendering possible the destruction of all workshops, depots, wharves and river craft, by which alone the enemy could follow us up down the Dwina. No advance short of Kotlas would effect this object. Moreover, as General Ironside has pointed out in his telegram of June 4th, there will be no danger of our troops being cut off as with the flotilla now available our line of retirement from Kotlas is assured, and there will be ample time to carry out the operations and embark before the port closes in the third week of October.

The preliminary operation recently carried out at Troitska with a view to removing the enemy's mines, and which General Ironside had previously intimated would afford a valuable indication of the enemy's fighting value, has given most encouraging results, and if our success is followed up there is every reason to hope that the Bolshevik forces will become very rapidly disorganised.

In view of the above considerations I would strongly urge that General Ironside be immediately authorised to proceed with his operations which I have no hesitation in saying are not only desirable, but essential to the safe and orderly withdrawal of the British forces in North Russia.

General Spears to Winston S. Churchill

(*Churchill papers: 16/37*)

26 June 1919 Paris
Personal & Secret

Dear Secretary of State,

I had a very long talk yesterday with M Savinkoff. I will not repeat what he said re the operations against PETROGRAD as he told me you had discussed this subject with him and were in complete accord. He, however, expressed the following views which he had meant to express to you had he had time.

RUSSIA cannot stand alone. It is therefore conceivable that a combination of RUSSIA, GERMANY and JAPAN might be created. Were he in power, he (Savinkoff) might be in favour of this idea were it not that RUSSIA would not be the dominant factor in such a combination, but would merely provide man-power and the natural resources for the other two.

In Savinkoff's opinion, any monarchist restoration in RUSSIA is bound to lean for support on GERMANY. A monarchy could only maintain itself by the promise of restoring the lost non-Russian territories and of obtaining possession of CONSTANTINOPLE. Any monarchy in RUSSIA must therefore be prepared to reconquer POLAND and FINLAND at the point of the sword. This would be impossible without the aid and assistance of the Germans who have every interest in combining with RUSSIA to crush POLAND.

Savinkoff thinks that if the Poles and Roumanians succeed in obtaining a common frontier line, and if the former are allowed to keep EASTERN GALICIA (he expressedly excepts the district of LEMBERG) and thus interpose a barrier between the Czechs and the Russians, RUSSIA pushed to the East will be bound to ally herself with GERMANY.

Speaking as a republican, Savinkoff expressed himself as apprehensive of the future régime in RUSSIA. He is not at all sure that his Party will carry the day. He points out that although Kolchak's Government is a Social-Democrat one, and is comparatively strong, Denikin's Government is frankly reactionary. Denikin, who is much more a soldier than a politician, is surrounded with avowed monarchists, and has recently admitted to his Cabinet Krivoshein a notorious reactionary and pro-German, who held ministerial rank under the Empire. Savinkoff pointed out that although any public pronouncement of our policy towards Russian internal affairs would be most unfortunate, the British representatives with Kolchak and Denikin can exercise a very great deal of influence, and he specially laid stress on the fact that Generals Knox and Briggs should be requested to oppose, to the best of their ability, all monarchist tendencies which may exist in the entourages of Kolchak and Denikin. (Savinkoff stated that Sazonoff was appointed Minister of Foreign Affairs of the Denikin Government at the suggestion of Lieutenant Ehrlich, a French representative.) Savinkoff seemed impressed with the tact and ability of General Knox.

Savinkoff is convinced that Bolshevism is on the wane, and he pointed out that 70% of the commerce done in RUSSIA to-day is done by private persons, that is to say, in defiance of the Bolshevik authorities, who summarily shoot anybody found trading on his own account. Of course very few are, in practice, shot, and those who are not detected are amassing considerable fortunes. A new bourgeoisie is thus being created to replace the old one stamped out by the Bolsheviks.

According to Savinkoff, the first General to reach MOSCOW will be the master of RUSSIA. If this General is a monarchist, it will be relatively easy to 'rig' the Constituent so that it votes monarchist—appeals could be made to national feeling and a monarchy would be presented as the only means by which RUSSIA could regain her old pride of place.

It is pretty evident that Savinkoff thinks that the Russian monarchists have already designated their candidate for the throne, but he was naturally averse from pursuing this subject.

He thinks that it is important that the Kerensky–Avksentiev[1] group should be kept quiet, and although he admits that it is impossible to win them over at the present time, he says that they can be kept from attacking Kolchak's Government. Savinkoff has exactly the same feeling about Kerensky's value as Sazonoff, and neither of them will have anything to do with him.

Yours sincerely,
E. L. Spears

Sir Henry Wilson: diary

(*Wilson papers*)

27 June 1919

Cabinet meeting at which I persuaded Cabinet to allow Ironside to go to Kotlas.

War Cabinet: minutes

(*Curzon papers*)

NORTH RUSSIA

27 June 1919 10 Downing Street

THE SECRETARY OF STATE FOR WAR said that the growth of the Russian Army in this area during the last five months appeared to him to be remarkable. The Russian forces co-operating with us now amounted to some 22,000 men whose fighting value as compared with the best European troops might not be very great. He had reason to believe, however, that the material was quite good. In addition to the two picked British Brigades and the purely Russian units there was the Slavo-British Brigade composed of Russians with

[1] Nikolai D Avksentiev. A leading Social Revolutionary before 1914. Deported to Siberia, 1905. In exile in Germany, 1905–14. From 1915 to 1917 he published in Switzerland a pro-Entente newspaper, *Priziv.* Returned to Russia in the spring of 1917. Representative of the Peasants in the Provisional Government, July 1917. Minister of the Interior in Kerensky's Government, August–October 1917. Fled to Siberia, November 1917. Chairman of the Omsk Directorate, 1918. Arrested, with other Social Revolutionary leaders, by Admiral Kolchak, at midnight on 17 November 1918, in Omsk (after which Kolchak declared himself 'Supreme Ruler of Russia').

a considerable portion of British officers. There was therefore in North Russia what was rapidly developing into a very useful and self-sufficient Russian force. The War Cabinet had recently given him permission to collect and train some 1200 Russian Officers in England who would be sent out to North Russia as soon as their training was sufficiently advanced. We had, therefore, reason to hope that when we withdrew in October we would leave behind us at Archangel an established Russian Government supported by an army which should be quite capable of defending itself from such attacks as might be expected in so out-of-the-way place. It was, however, unlikely that Bolshevists would concentrate against Archangel in any considerable force. Their attention would be mainly directed between Kolchak and Denikin and the operations which were taking place around Petrograd. He thought it was reasonable therefore, taking into consideration both the military and political aspects of the problem, that when we retired the Russian Government would be able to offer adequate protection to the 15,000 friendly inhabitants referred to by Lord Curzon; in other words that, on withdrawing, we should leave matters in such a posture that no discredit would attach to us. In reply to a question by Lord Curzon Mr Churchill said, that the Tchaikowsky Government at Archangel was the most democratic of all the three separate Governments that we were supporting. This Government was at present dependent upon us and would no doubt be very much upset at our going, but they knew that our decision to withdraw was irrevocable. The Bolshevist Government itself, however, was far from stable and its forces not in any way reliable. The wars, in fact, that were taking place in different parts of Russia were on both sides wars of the weak.

Proceeding, MR CHURCHILL said that as to our future policy he thought it would be a great mistake for us to break our political necks for Russia by maintaining indefinitely a kind of equipoise warfare. He was in full agreement with the Prime Minister that next year our policy generally would require reconsideration. He himself did not believe in an early collapse of the Bolshevists power; but he did hope that the Anti-Bolshevist armies would be self-supporting in 1920. His aim was successfully to disentangle and withdraw our troops from North Russia and to wind up affairs there in such a way that when we went no dishonour could attach to us. Our policy, however, could only be successful, in his view, if our military Advisers were allowed to carry out their carefully made plans for the withdrawal of our troops. He thought that the Chief of the Imperial General Staff had been rightly cautious in his statement and had guarded himself at every point. General Wilson had complete faith in Ironside, who was confident that he could not be cut off, that the proposed operation would be successful, and that he would not have difficulty in withdrawing at any time.

General Ironside's plans had the full approval of the General Staff who strongly recommended they should be adopted.

LORD CURZON referred to certain regrettable incidents which had recently taken place at Murmansk and asked whether the War Office had any reason to apprehend similar trouble at Archangel.

THE CHIEF OF THE IMPERIAL GENERAL STAFF said, that the War Office saw no reason to fear anything of this kind. Our troops at Murmansk were thoroughly tired, and disheartened at not having been demobilised; General Ironside's on the other hand contained two picked Brigades composed of men who were all volunteers and in excellent heart.

THE PRESIDENT OF THE BOARD OF EDUCATION [H A L Fisher] said, that when the present project was first submitted to the War Cabinet, one of the leading arguments in its favour was that, if successful, it would enable Admiral Kolchak to base himself upon Archangel and it would secure for us a safe and honourable retreat from that port. He understood that the river Dwina was the only line of advance and retreat in that area. He inquired, therefore, whether we could not completely secure our position and our withdrawal by mining the river.

THE CHIEF OF THE IMPERIAL GENERAL STAFF said, there was a great deal to be said for that point of view; but if Mr Fisher's suggestion were adopted it would mean that we must relinquish all possibility of joining up with General Gaida, and Archangel and the Tchaikowsky Government would be placed in a very unhappy position.

THE SECRETARY OF STATE FOR WAR pointed out that in order to secure command of the river we must first capture the enemy's steamers; and to do this, a forward move was necessary. Moreover, if this operation were successful it was quite possible that the numbers of the Russian forces with General Ironside might swell from 22,000 to 33,000 or even more before the ice sets in. It was incumbent upon us to give the Archangel Government the best possible chance of maintaining itself through the Winter. He did not think that we could possibly slink out of the country and leave nothing between that Government and the Bolshevist forces but a few mines in the river. Our credit, which to-day stood very high throughout Russia was at stake. All the civilised forces in that country realised that we alone (with the doubtful exception of the Japanese), had really befriended and assisted them; and if we turned round now and cleared off our reputation would suffer irretrievably.

THE SECRETARY OF STATE FOR WAR said he was quite prepared to defend our policy in Parliament. The evacuation of our troops in every part of Russia from Archangel to the Caucasus was proceeding day by day and the line he would take in the House of Commons was that we were in fact withdrawing our troops and that the present operation was only designed to cover the safe and complete evacuation of our forces in the north.

THE PERMANENT SECRETARY TO THE MINISTRY OF LABOUR[1] warned the War Cabinet that there was bound to be trouble if early in September at or about the Meeting of the Trade Union Congress a casualty list were published of British soldiers killed in Russia while fighting to suppress a Soviet Government.

LORD CURZON agreed with the Secretary of State for War that, if necessary, a very strong case could be made in Parliament in defence of the policy of the Government.

THE PERMANENT SECRETARY TO THE MINISTRY OF LABOUR regretted the fact that at the present time there was no Labour Member of standing, of the calibre for example of Mr A Henderson and Mr Ramsay Macdonald,[2] who could take the responsibility of replying to the Government case in the House.

THE CHIEF OF THE IMPERIAL GENERAL STAFF suggested that what was necessary was careful and well-constructed propaganda to state the true facts and explain the Government policy to the working men of the country.

THE FIRST LORD OF THE ADMIRALTY agreed that this was very desirable and said that he thought it was unfortunate that little or no action so far had been taken to justify to the country the policy of the Government.

THE SECRETARY OF STATE FOR WAR said that if he thought that the proposed operations in North Russia were likely to culminate in a really big battle with heavy casualties, he would take a different line. He himself, however, doubted whether the Bolsheviks would offer any really serious resistance. In another part of Russia General Maynard with indifferent troops and an armoured train or two, and with the aid of plenty of bluff, had on more than one occasion defeated the Bolsheviks with hardly a casualty at all. All experience went to show that the Bolsheviks had never been able to screw up enough courage to offer any prolonged resistance. General Denikin again and again had defeated them with odds against him of 10 to 1.

[1] David James Shackleton, 1863–1938. Worked in a cotton mill, 1880–1900. Secretary, Ramsbottom Weavers' Association, 1893–4; Darwen Weavers' Association, 1894–1907. Labour MP, 1902–10. President of the Trade Union Congress, 1904–10. Chairman of the National Labour Party, 1905. A leading advocate of votes for women, 1910. Senior Labour Adviser (to Churchill) at the Home Office, 1910–11. National Health Insurance Commissioner, 1911–16. Knighted, 1917. Permanent Secretary, Ministry of Labour, 1917–21. Chief Labour Adviser to the Government, 1921–5.

[2] James Ramsay MacDonald, 1866–1937. Labour MP, 1906–18, 1922–9 and 1929–31. Leader of the Labour Party, 1911–14. Prime Minister and Secretary of State for Foreign Affairs, January to November 1924. Prime Minister, 1929–35. National Labour MP, 1931–5. Lord President of the Council, 1935–7.

His own feeling was that the Bolsheviks in the present instance would not put up much of a fight.

THE CHIEF OF THE IMPERIAL GENERAL STAFF pointed out to the War Cabinet that the alternative to the proposed operations—that is to say, any attempt to withdraw without first striking a blow—was much more dangerous.

THE CHANCELLOR OF THE EXCHEQUER said that this argument had convinced him that the War Cabinet should sanction the operation.

LORD CURZON thought that the propaganda suggested by General Wilson might be making too much of what was, after all, a comparatively insignificant movement.

THE CHIEF OF THE IMPERIAL GENERAL STAFF said the propaganda he had in mind was designed to explain our whole policy in every part of Russia, and not this particular item in it.

THE CHANCELLOR OF THE EXCHEQUER thought that much valuable propaganda might be conducted through the medium of the Sunday newspapers.

THE SECRETARY OF STATE FOR WAR said that there would be no difficulty at all in defending the Government policy, which was, to withdraw our troops from all theatres of war in Russia.

The War Cabinet decided—

> To sanction General Ironside's proposed operations, on the conditions laid down.[1]

General Spears to Winston S. Churchill

(*Churchill papers: 16/37*)

27 June 1919 Paris
Secret

Dear Secretary of State,

I saw SAZONOFF to-day. I must say I do not understand his attitude as regards PETROGRAD. He is very anxious to see the place taken, but is not prepared to pay the requisite price. He does not see the urgency of the matter, nor is he prepared to make the necessary concessions or promises to the Finns. It seems possible, for instance, that the Finns would accept a statement to the effect that a claim would be submitted to the Constituent Assembly with the

[1] That same day the War Office telegraphed to Ironside: 'After consideration of all provisions and arguments contained in your telegram of 19 June, and opinion expressed in your telegram of 6 June . . . you are authorized to carry out advance as proposed.'

favourable recommendation of the present Russian Committee. (This is SAVINKOFF's opinion, but I fear that SAZONOFF will not even go as far as this at present.)

Sir Henry Wilson: diary

(*Wilson papers*)

30 June 1919

Office all morning. Saw Winston, but not much gossip except good news from Denikin who has taken Kharkof.

Kolchak is going to take Perm, but Denikin has taken Kharkof. Also the Finns won't go to Petrograd; they have begun to ask for guns, maxims, clothing etc! No business doing!